Religion, Families, and Health

Religion, Families, and Health

Population-Based Research in the United States

EDITED BY

CHRISTOPHER G. ELLISON

ROBERT A. HUMMER

RUTGERS UNIVERSITY PRESS

NEW BRUNSWICK, NEW JERSEY, AND LONDON

LIBRARY OF CONGRESS CATALOGING-IN-PUBLICATION DATA

Religion, families, and health : population-based research in the United States /
edited by Christopher G. Ellison and Robert A. Hummer.
    p.   cm.
Includes bibliographical references and index.
ISBN 978-0-8135-4718-3 (hardcover : alk. paper)
ISBN 978-0-8135-4719-0 (pbk. : alk. paper)
    1. United States—Religion.   2. Medicine—United States.   3. Family—United States.
I. Ellison, Christopher G., 1960–   II. Hummer, Robert A.
BL2525.R4633 2010
306.60973—dc22   2009020402

A British Cataloging-in-Publication record for this book is available
from the British Library.

Visit our Web site: http://rutgerspress.rutgers.edu

Manufactured in the United States of America

CONTENTS

PART TWO
Religion and Health Outcomes

PART THREE
Looking Ahead

ACKNOWLEDGMENTS

We wish to express our appreciation to a number of individuals and entities for providing us with the support and resources that were needed to complete this volume. In particular, Richard Lariviere, former Dean of the College of Liberal Arts at the University of Texas at Austin, provided the initial funding and support for the conference that stimulated this volume; we gratefully acknowledge his enthusiastic support. Jenny Trinitapoli, now an assistant professor of sociology at the Pennsylvania State University, and Mary De La Garza of the Population Research Center at the University of Texas at Austin were instrumental in helping make that conference a success. In addition, our colleagues Norval Glenn, John Mirowsky, and Bob Woodberry provided very useful comments on a number of presentations at the conference.

We gratefully acknowledge an infrastructure grant from the Eunice Kennedy Shriver National Institute of Child Health and Human Development (grant number 5 R24 HD042849) to the Population Research Center (PRC) at the University of Texas at Austin. Throughout the project, the administrative and computing staff at the PRC provided us with assistance in numerous ways in seeing this project through to completion. Research grants from the National Science Foundation (grant number 0243189, PI Robert Hummer) and the National Institute of Aging (5 R01 AG18432–02, PI Christopher Ellison) also provided important financial resources that helped us get this project off the ground. We also thank the University of Texas at Austin Subvention Grant Program, which is funded by a generous gift from the University Co-operative Society, for providing us with a grant to help keep this volume as affordable as possible.

We are also grateful to the staff at Rutgers University Press for their help, patience, and encouragement as we produced this volume. The two anonymous peer reviewers of the volume also provided us with very useful comments on an initial draft.

The large number of chapters and chapter authors involved in this volume made it both a very challenging endeavor for us as well as one that will hopefully result in an extremely useful product for readers. We thank all of the chapter authors and co-authors for their outstanding contributions, and for their patience as we worked to bring this project to fruition.

Finally, we thank our respective spouses, Sharon Sandomirsky and Dawn Hummer, for their tremendous support and encouragement of our work.

Christopher G. Ellison
Robert A. Hummer

Religion, Families, and Health

1

Introduction

CHRISTOPHER G. ELLISON AND ROBERT A. HUMMER

Founded in part by immigrants searching for religious freedom, the United States remains a religious country by most conventional indicators (Sherkat and Ellison 1999). This social fact runs counter to the expectations of generations of social scientists, and is not fundamentally altered by the steady declines in weekly religious attendance that occurred during the latter half of the twentieth century (Presser and Chaves 2007), or by the modest growth of the "no religion" category in surveys of American adults (Hout and Fischer 2002; Sherkat, Chapter 20 of this volume). Indeed, recent data indicate that patterns of religious attendance have remained stable since approximately 1990 (Presser and Chaves 2007), and that many core Judeo-Christian religious beliefs retain widespread support among American adults. For example, roughly 60 percent of Americans claim to believe in God "without any doubts," while only 10 percent unequivocally reject belief in God. Although less than one-third of Americans believe that the Bible is the literal Word of God, nearly four in five adults agree that this scripture is divinely inspired. Belief in an afterlife (of whatever sort) has increased steadily since the 1970s among Protestants, Catholics, and Jews, to approximately 80 percent of U.S. adults in 2006 (Hout and Greeley 1999; Davis, Smith, and Marsden 2006). Other survey data confirm that majorities of Americans continue to endorse Christian-influenced views about heaven and hell.

Beyond individual beliefs, organized religion also remains a vibrant institutional force in the contemporary United States. According to recent estimates, more than one-half of American adults claim to belong to a local religious congregation, and a much larger figure—nearly 85 percent—report a religious preference; that is, they identify with, or express an affinity for, an established religious community. General Social Survey (GSS) data indicate that 25–28 percent of U.S. adults identify themselves as Catholic, and a similar (or perhaps even slightly larger) percentage identify with Baptist or other conservative Protestant faiths (Davis, Smith, and Marsden 2006). Among the long list of such groups are other fundamentalist churches (e.g., Churches of Christ, independent Bible churches), evangelical churches (e.g., Evangelical Free Church, Christian Reformed Church), or charismatic churches (e.g., Assemblies of God, Pentecostal or Holiness), as well as many nondenominational conservative congregations. Overall, America's once-dominant Protestant majority is slipping (Smith and Kim 2005), and a wealth of data reveal that over the past half century conservative Protestant churches have made major gains in numbers and religious market share, while mainline Protestant bodies (e.g., United Methodist, Episcopal, Presbyterian Church USA) have been steadily losing members (Finke 2005). Further, several thousand religious groups are represented in the United States, and nontrivial numbers of Americans also identify with nontraditional Christian groups (e.g., Latter Day Saints or Mormon, Jehovah's Witness) and various non-Christian traditions (e.g., Judaism, Islam, Buddhism) (Sherkat and Ellison 1999; Sherkat, Chapter 20 of this volume). Not only do most Americans report an allegiance to some form of organized religion, many persons also donate significant amounts of time and money to religious communities. Indeed, American households are estimated to contribute tens of billions of dollars each year to religious organizations (U.S. Bureau of the Census 2005, table 570), although recent research has underscored the limits of this generosity (Smith, Emerson, and Snell 2008).

Although U.S. religious attendance figures have declined over the past several decades, rates of individual religious participation in the United States remain high compared to those in many other nations. Most high-quality survey data indicate that around 30 percent of Americans claim to attend religious services once a week or more (Davis, Smith, and Marsden 2006; Hout and Greeley 1998; Smith 1998). Despite persuasive evidence that survey data on attendance reflects overreporting, even the most critical estimates suggest that 20–25 percent of Americans attend some type of religious services during any given week (Hadaway et al. 1993; Hadaway, Marler, and Chaves 1998; Presser and Stinson 1998). Around 30 percent of U.S. adults report not attending services at all during the past year (Davis, Smith, and Marsden 2006). Private devotional activities also appear quite common among the American public; for example, nearly 60 percent of adults indicate that they pray at least once a day, while only around 10 percent say they never pray. Self-reported figures for other types of devotional pursuits, such as reading the Bible (or other religious scriptures or texts), or watching or listening to religious programs, also remain relatively high (Sherkat and Ellison 1999).

Given the preceding figures, it should be of little or no surprise that religious beliefs, affiliations, and behaviors have the potential to exhibit profound influences on American family life, health patterns, and more. Indeed, if the time and money that U.S. individuals spend being involved with religious organizations and partaking in private religious activity did not have such impacts, it would be, quite frankly, astonishing. However, what may be of greater surprise is that the scientific community—and perhaps particularly scholars in demography and sociology—has not always shared the view that religious factors have important impacts on family life and health outcomes in the United States. Although earlier generations of social demographers examined religious differentials in a host of demographic outcomes (ranging from fertility and related behavior to socioeconomic attainment), most of that work centered on variations within the non-Hispanic white population and especially on either Catholic–Protestant differences and/or on differences among various European American religious-ethnic groups (Featherman 1971; Ryder and Westoff 1971; Westoff, Potter, and Sagi 1964). These groups included substantial numbers of first- and second-generation individuals and, as they assimilated culturally and structurally, interest in this line of research diminished and then largely disappeared (e.g., Stryker [1981] was the last major example of this line of published research for over ten years).

In sociology, a host of factors influenced the marginalization of the social scientific study of religion for several decades. These factors included, first, the close association of the sociology of religion with Parsonian structural-functionalism, which was increasingly falling out of favor in the discipline in the 1960s through the 1980s. Second, and perhaps more important, the close association between religion and social conservatism and the institutional status quo increasingly served to marginalize this subfield of sociology as more and more sociologists identified with liberal social perspectives and were advocating social change (Hadden 1987).

However, several developments sparked a resurgence of interest in social scientific studies of religion in the late 1980s and into the 1990s and 2000s. First, and contrary to the expectations of many social scientists, there was recognition of the stubborn persistence and vitality of organized religion in the United States (Cadge and Ecklund 2007; Eck 1997; Finke 2005; Smith 2002). Second, there was visible growth of interest in personal spirituality as well. This is illustrated both by some of the data on prayer and beliefs in God and the afterlife, as mentioned earlier, as well as the expansion of public interest in noninstitutionalized forms of spirituality, such as the growth of New Age spirituality, the increasing proportion of Americans who identify as spiritual but not religious, and the tremendous popularity of books on spirituality, meaning, and purpose (Hadaway and Marler 2002; Roof 2000; Shahabi et al. 2002; Wuthnow 1998; Zinnbauer, Pargament, and Scott 1999). Third, increased population diversity in the United States—particularly influenced by changes in U.S. immigration laws in the 1960s—also led to increased religious diversity in the country. Indeed, U.S. growth in non-Western world religions—such as Islam, Hinduism, and Buddhism—has fueled growing interest in the sociology of religion on the implications of these changes (Smith 2002; Wuthnow 2005). Such increasing diversity has the potential to continue to spark major research interest in this area of study for decades to come, as we discuss in Chapter 21 of this volume.

Finally, the resurgence of religious actors in the political arena and in public life more broadly—with the Religious Right the most obvious example—brought with it great interest among sociologists, in particular, and social scientists more generally in understanding the causes and consequences of this movement. Taken together, these developments helped to foster a new generation of well-trained, theoretically and empirically minded scholars for whom the significance of religion was quite evident, and also elicited attention from older and more established scholars who had not previously focused on the role of religion in American life.

Through the 1980s and even into the 1990s, for example, the idea that religious involvement might have an impact on mental and physical health outcomes was met with great skepticism in both the social and medical sciences. Around that time, scholars like Ellen Idler and Jeffrey Levin were particularly influential in developing the religion-health area with excellent reviews of the literature and the development of theoretical models to guide the study of religion and health (e.g., Idler 1987; Levin and Vanderpool 1987, 1989). Rigorous empirical work in the area was slower to develop, but with the gradual inclusion of rudimentary religion items on population-based health surveys, this also began to change throughout the 1990s and into the 2000s (Chatters 2000; Ellison and Levin 1998; Koenig, McCullough, and Larson 2001). The interest of private foundations (most notably the John Templeton Foundation) and government agencies (most notably the National Institute on Aging and the National Center for Complementary and Alternative Medicine) has also led to significantly increasing funding opportunities for researchers interested in religion and health. Most recently, interest in the role of religion and health at the population level has been fueled by innovative and high-quality research being undertaken in several fields, including demography, sociology, gerontology, and public health. Recent high-quality empirical articles on the links between religion and population health outcomes have appeared in some of the best journals in those disciplines, and have been featured in leading news magazines, newspapers, and other major media outlets throughout the country. To be sure, this particular area of research has remained quite controversial, both because of the outstanding empirical questions yet to be tackled and because of differences in the interpretation of empirical findings by researchers, physicians, and the media. Indeed, critiques of the designs and interpretations of a number of these studies, spearheaded by Richard Sloan and colleagues, have appeared in some of the leading medical journals in the world (Sloan, Bagiella, and Powell 1999; Sloan et al. 2000). Taken together, however, the increased visibility of the religion–health area and the improving quality of research designs has convinced many observers of the viability of religious influences on mental and physical health outcomes, mortality risk, psychosocial adjustment to illness, and related outcomes, as well as the continued need for research that better documents and explains these relationships.

Since the early 1960s, major changes in American family life (e.g., increased female labor force participation, increased average age at marriage, increased divorce rate, declines in fertility, increased cohabitation of unmarried partners, the legalization of abortion, and more) have elicited serious research into the causes and consequences of such changes, as well as heated debates regarding policy responses. Not only have these changes fueled the social and political agendas of the Religious Right, but they have also spurred funding agencies (such as the National Institute of Child Health and Human Development) to devote significant resources toward research in the area. However, in somewhat of a contrast to the religion–health area previously described, there has been less sustained academic interest in the linkages between religion and family life outcomes in the United States in recent years, particularly among scholars in family studies. According to a recent analysis of articles appearing in the major journals published by the National Council on Family Relations (i.e., *Journal of Marriage and Family*, *Journal of Family Issues*, *Family Relations*) during the period from 1980 to 2008, only 1.5 percent of those articles focused on religion, and only approximately 11 percent included any kind of religion variable at all (Ellison and Storch 2009). Given the long-standing interdependent relationship between the social institutions of religion and family, this relative lack of attention to religion by family scholars in the United States seems like a major oversight. Nevertheless, during the 1980s, 1990s, and 2000s, some social scientists did investigate relationships between religion and fertility and child rearing, cohabitation and marriage, and other crucial topics (Christiano 2000; Edgell 2006; Wilcox 2004). Despite the relative absence of such research from family studies outlets, key contributions did appear in the *American Sociological Review*, the *American Journal of Sociology*, *Demography*, and other leading journals during this period (e.g., Thornton, Axinn, and Hill 1992; Ellison and Sherkat 1993; Lehrer and Chiswick 1993; Pearce and Axinn 1998; Wilcox 1998). As a number of chapters in this volume emphasize and empirically demonstrate, it is important that religion be given even more serious consideration in this area of study if researchers and policymakers wish to better understand American family life.

Aims of the Volume

It is clear that religion continues to be a major social institution in the United States. While the scientific community has recently experienced resurgence in the idea that there are potentially important empirical linkages between religion and family life and religion and health outcomes in the United States, this area of work is still in its early stages of development, is scattered across multiple journals and disciplines, and is of uneven quality. To date, there has been no published monograph that has featured both reviews of the literature and new empirical findings that defines this area for the present and sets the agenda for further work in this area for the twenty-first century. We aim here to fill that substantial void. Thus, the central goal of the volume is to bring together some of the leading social scientists in the country to examine the multifaceted role of religion in shaping important family life and health outcomes in the United States. Moreover, we pay particular attention to diversity within American religion and within the American public by focusing a number of chapters on a set of religio-ethnic minority subpopulations, including African Americans, Jews, Muslims, Catholics, Mormons, and new immigrants to the United States. Further, we conclude the volume by looking ahead, with chapters that outline the changing religious demography of the U.S. population and the key gaps in current research that we have identified and hope to spur in the future study of this area. Some of the individual chapters are written by the most well-known scholars in the sociology of religion and social demography, respectively. Others are written by younger, very productive scholars in this area, some of whom are doing the most creative and thought-provoking work on the relationship between religion and family life and religion and health outcomes in the United States. Overall, the chapters provide a theoretically rich, methodologically rigorous, and exciting glimpse into this fascinating area of scientific inquiry.

Organization of the Volume

The remainder of this volume is split into three parts. The first part focuses on religion and family life outcomes. Here, the volume examines associations between religion variables and outcomes like nonmarital and marital fertility, the ways in which we raise our children, adolescent sexual behavior, ties between generations, gender ideologies, family-related attitudes, and the accumulation of assets during early adulthood. Religion and health linkages are considered in the second part of the volume. This particular area of study has received considerable attention in the last decade and the chapters included here build on this momentum to provide new insights into the mechanisms by which religion is influencing adult health and mortality outcomes in the United States. Throughout the chapters on family life and health outcomes, a number of them specifically examine religious and ethnic minority subpopulations. While no single volume could possibly examine all of the religious and ethnic subgroups that would encompass this area, chapters in this volume specifically focus on religion–family or religion–health linkages among African Americans, Muslim and Christian Arab Americans, Jews, Catholics, Mormons, and new immigrants, respectively. We return to this key issue of population diversity in the concluding chapter of the volume, and suggest that this is one of the most promising themes for future research on religious influences in the United States. Finally, Part Three of the volume looks to the future, with specific chapters focusing on the changing religious demography of the United States and on major research issues for the field to consider as we look ahead to the coming decades in this fascinating area of study.

Part One: Religion and Family Life Outcomes

Lisa Pearce begins the first part in Chapter 2 by assessing the influence of the religious affiliation in which one is raised, as well as the frequency of religious attendance, on the risk of timing of both premarital and marital childbearing for a sample of young men and women in the United States. The relationship between religious involvement and fertility behavior received considerable attention in social demography in the 1950s and 1960s, largely due to a focus on Catholic–Protestant differences in fertility at the time. Pearce effectively brings new attention to this area by empirically showing that both the religious denomination in which one is raised as well as the frequency of religious attendance during adolescence and young adulthood is related to the timing of premaritally and maritally conceived first births, even net of a range of other social and demographic factors.

Duane Alwin and Jacob Felson consider how variations in religion shape the way that the parental role is enacted and influences child development in Chapter 3. Within the parenting literature, extraordinarily little research has been devoted to the topic of religious influences. At the same time, Alwin and Felson argue that the religious doctrines to which parents subscribe, as well as the intensity with which they participate, have an important impact on parental orientations to children. Not only are such differential parenting approaches in and of themselves interesting, they also have consequences for children. Thus, Alwin and Felson conclude by stressing that much additional research attention needs to be devoted to better understanding the influences that religion has on the lives of children, particularly through the ways that the parental role is practiced.

In Chapter 4, Mark Regnerus turns to the examination of the linkage between religion and U.S. adolescent sexuality and behavior. Research on religion and adolescent sexual behavior is still considered nascent by leading experts in the field. Building on a conceptual model of religious influences on adolescent sexual behavior, Regnerus estimates the effects of multiple dimensions of religion on sexual behaviors among two large, nationally representative studies of American adolescents, taking care to especially investigate race differences in the relationship between religion and sexual behaviors. This chapter continues an important line of work he is spearheading (e.g., Regnerus 2007) that is carefully examining adolescent health and behavior and finding clear impacts of religious beliefs and practices in the lives of adolescents.

Valarie King analyzes the influence of religion on ties between the generations in Chapter 5. Few studies have empirically examined whether and how religion influences the type and quality of involvement between generations. A recent and growing body of research, however, suggests that religious involvement may foster more frequent and positive ties between family members. King's chapter reviews the growing literature in this area and offers a new analysis that expands our understanding of the linkages between religion and intergenerational ties among fathers. The analysis shows that there are indeed closer ties between religious fathers and their adult offspring compared to less religious fathers and their offspring.

In Chapter 6, John Bartkowski and Xiaohe Xu examine gender traditionalism among Conservative Protestants. There has been concern in some circles regarding the gendered division of labor and gender-related attitudes in the growing number of Conservative Protestant households in the United States. Bartkowski and Xu closely analyze these associations using a nationally representative data set. Interestingly, they find that religious denominational affiliation of any sort tends to be associated with more traditional attitudes about gender compared to persons who express no religious affiliation, although Conservative Protestants tend to express the most traditional views. However, such affiliation differences are brought about by both differing levels of religious attendance and differing religious beliefs across denominations. They conclude that religious influences on gender ideology come about because of a combination of an individual's degree of integration within a religious community and the internalization of theological views within that particular community.

Amy Burdette and Teresa Sullivan analyze family attitudes of young Catholics forty years after Vatican Two in Chapter 7. Compared with other major American denominations, Catholics in the United States are younger, on average, and more ethnically diverse—patterns that are largely fueled by continuing waves of immigrants from Latin America. Young Catholics, defined as those aged thirty and younger, have all been born since the dramatic changes of the Second Vatican Council (1962–1965). Of the many changes and issues that young Catholics have experienced has been the continuing conflicts over the Church's conservative code of personal behavior accompanied by the well-publicized scandals over clerical abuse of children. This chapter, then, uses thirty years of data from the GSS to analyze family-related attitudes among young Catholics. They find substantial trends for Catholics in a number of family-related attitudes—such as those regarding family size, abortion, extramarital sexual behavior, premarital sexual behavior, homosexuality, and more—that are not always consistent with Church teachings.

Linda Waite and Alisa Lewin examine religious intermarriage and conversion in Chapter 8. A vast majority of American adults marry at some time in their lives. Perhaps most interestingly, this chapter shows that nearly one-half of all higher-order (e.g., second, third, etc.) U.S. marriages include spouses from different religious denominations. Among first marriages, this figure is lower (28 percent), but still quite common and increasing across birth cohorts. Waite and Lewin also show that a higher percentage of individuals switch religions for first marriages compared with higher-order marriages. Religious conversion behavior is particularly influenced by childhood religion among first marriages, but less so among higher-order marriages. Notably, religious conversion behavior among marital partners is decreasing. Thus, Waite and Lewin help draw out the complex ways in which religion affects adult marital behavior and differentially so according to whether marriages are first or higher order. They also discuss the possible consequences that increasing levels of marital religious heterogamy and decreasing levels of religious conversion may or may not have for U.S. couples.

In an interesting and newly developing strand of literature in the social scientific study of religion, Lisa Keister examines the relationship between childhood religion and early adult asset accumulation in Chapter 9. Wealth inequality has become increasingly severe in recent years in the United States, but the processes that generate wealth inequality are still unclear. Childhood religion is one factor that likely shapes adult wealth ownership in critical ways. Yet the role of religion has received almost no attention by scholars studying wealth. Keister argues, however, that childhood religious upbringing is likely to affect wealth ownership directly because it shapes values and priorities, contributes to the set of competencies from which action is constructed, and may provide important social contacts. Keister finds very distinctive patterns between childhood religious denominational affiliation and young adult wealth ownership and portfolio mix, even net of controls for inheritance levels, parental-level and individual-level education and income, and more. Such patterns are all the more intriguing given the young ages of the adults under study, the oldest of which were only in their early forties.

Chapter 10, by Evelyn Lehrer, analyzes the effects of religious affiliation and participation as determinants of women's educational attainment and wages. This chapter builds on earlier studies by employing a large-scale national survey to ascertain whether the relationships found in earlier and smaller studies hold. Further, few studies in this area have focused specifically on women. Like Lisa Keister's findings in Chapter 9, Lehrer also shows distinctive differences between religious denominational groups, as well as differences by levels of religious involvement within denominational groupings, in both women's educational attainment and adult wages. Also similar to Keister, Lehrer suggests that childhood religious influences on socioeconomic attainment may work by both shaping children's attitudes toward higher education and by the social capital that is enhanced through religious networks.

Jen'nan Ghazal Read's chapter on the relationship between religion, family, and women's employment among Muslim and Christian Arab Americans closes out this part. Indeed, as Bartkowski and Xu highlight in Chapter 6, religious influences on family and gender roles are at the center of numerous debates about the role of religion in contemporary American life. The accepted wisdom is that the tenets of major religious traditions restrict women's achievements in the public sphere by prioritizing their obligations to the home and family.

Recent studies on Judeo-Christian groups are beginning to challenge this view, finding that the relationships between family, religion, and women's economic activity are more complicated than previously believed. To a lesser but growing extent, research is also contesting homogeneous images of U.S. Muslim women that depict them as universally oppressed by a patriarchal religious culture. Read's chapter uses data from a national sample of Arab American women to extend our understanding of the religion-family-work connection among a growing ethno-religious population. Most important, she finds that Muslim versus Christian affiliation is much less important for women's labor force participation compared to the degree of religious involvement within those particular traditions. Further, for women without children, there is no inverse relationship between religiosity and labor force participation among Arab Americans.

Part Two: Religion and Health Outcomes

Part Two of the volume focuses on one of the most hotly debated and vibrant areas of the scientific study of religion in the United States: the relationship between religion variables and health and mortality outcomes. Neal Krause, a leading figure in this area of study, begins this part in Chapter 12 by analyzing the relationship between religious meaning and the avoidance of, and coping with, mental health problems among U.S. adults. He develops a conceptual framework that links religious meaning and other dimensions of religion to depression at different points in the life cycle and then systematically uses data from a nationwide sample of older adults to test his ideas. Together with evidence that Krause pulls in from earlier work, he concludes that there is convincing evidence that religion can play a role in helping people to either avoid or better deal with mental health problems.

In Chapter 13, Marc Musick and Meredith Worthen lay out a set of sophisticated frameworks for studying the linkage between religion and physical health. They argue that the study of religion and its effects on physical health is not new; indeed, over one hundred years ago Emile Durkheim based one of his most famous works, *Suicide* ([1897] 1951), on the topic. But, during the ensuing century, the study of religion and health largely went by the wayside. The revival of the topic in the mid-to-late 1980s eventually led to research in the 1990s that showed that, contrary to the arguments of Freud, Ellis, and others, religious involvement actually seemed to have overall beneficial effects for mental and physical health outcomes at the population level. Their chapter then provides a new empirical study of religion and physical health in the United States and finds support for both the religious causation and social selection frameworks.

Few topics in this area of study have received more attention than the relationship between religious involvement and adult mortality. In Chapter 14, Robert Hummer and colleagues build on previous work by examining the relationship between religious attendance and mortality risk among a specific age range of adults: individuals aged fifty-one to sixty-one at baseline in 1992 and statistically followed for survival status for eight years. This age range is important to study for at least three reasons:

1. Deaths in this age range are clearly premature in the context of current U.S. life expectancy and are largely preventable.
2. A large subset of the studies of religious involvement and health and mortality outcomes to date has focused on the elderly only.
3. One prominent study (Musick, House, and Williams 2004) has pointed to a stronger relationship between religious attendance and mortality risk among younger adults (less than sixty) than among older adults (sixty and above).

This chapter finds sizable differences in mortality risk over this time period by religious attendance, consistent with Musick, House, and Williams (2004), and also shows that these differences do not vary across sociodemographic groups of the population.

In a companion chapter also focused on mortality, Richard Rogers and colleagues examine in fine detail the relationship between religious involvement and cause-specific adult mortality in Chapter 15. Despite the growing literature on religion and U.S. adult mortality, little research has examined the relationship between religious involvement and specific causes of death at the national level, although cause of death analyses may provide insight into the mechanisms that link religious involvement and mortality risk. They find that the religion–mortality association varies both across causes and, within causes, by gender. Similar to the findings of Hummer and colleagues in Chapter 14 of this volume, Rogers and colleagues also find the strongest association between religious involvement and mortality among middle-aged, and not older, adults, whereas a great deal of prior literature in this area has focused on the elderly. They conclude with a balanced assessment of what these findings might mean with regard to future research and to the health care setting.

Although a solid set of empirical studies have linked religion with a number of health and mortality outcomes, this research has focused mainly on non-Hispanic whites. Until recently, few studies explored these relationships within minority populations, and even fewer examined race/ethnic differences in the health implications of religious involvement. Fortunately, this pattern of neglect has begun to change during the past decade, and in Chapter 16, Christopher Ellison and colleagues address this topic among African Americans. Specifically, their contribution: (a) identifies distinctive health-relevant features of African American religious institutions, values, and practices; (b) summarizes the evidence regarding salutary religious effects on mental and physical health, including mortality risk, among African Americans; (c) reviews the available work on black–white comparisons of religious effects; (d) discusses a number of potential explanations for salutary health consequences of African American religious involvement, particularly those suggested by the life stress paradigm within medical sociology; and (e) notes several major gaps in this literature. They conclude by highlighting promising directions for future research at the intersection of race, religion, and health.

In Chapter 17, Isaac Eberstein and Kathleen Heyman examine health differences among Jewish Americans. Jewish identification is conceptualized in terms of three distinct dimensions—subjective identification, organizational affiliation, and behavior—that help to more fully tap into the voluntary and often symbolic notions of identity. Data from the National Jewish Population Survey of 2000 to 2001 are used to indicate denominational identification, synagogue membership, and frequency of service attendance or other ritual observance. Eberstein and Heyman find strong evidence that Jews with a greater degree of distinctive Jewish identity report more favorable health than Jews with a less distinctive identity. They conclude by discussing possible reasons for this association between degree of Jewish identity and health that may also be germane to differences within and across Christian denominations.

Tim Heaton focuses on the relationship between religion, sexual behavior, and reproductive health among Mormons in Chapter 18. He explores the possibility that religious constraints on types of family formation may reduce the risk of certain reproductive health problems. The focus is on members of the LDS Church (Mormons) because the Church teaches that sex should be restricted to marital partners. Although the emphasis on nonmarital chastity is not unique to Mormons, the LDS doctrine linking conformity with prospects of continued marital relationships after death is highly distinctive. Using data from the National Survey of Family Growth, Heaton finds substantial religious group differences in sexual behavior and reproductive health that are consistent with his expectations, and that cannot be accounted for by a number of control variables.

Helen Rose Ebaugh closes out this part in Chapter 19 by discussing how new immigrants in the United States are faring with respect to health behavior and access to health care. Profound market share changes in religion are occurring in the United States as a result of the increasing numbers and diversity of post-1965 immigrants (Finke 2005). This chapter first discusses the most recent immigration trends to the United States and their implication for religious diversity, and second, how immigrant religious communities are operating to influence the health care access and health behavior of their members. With such profound change occurring within the U.S. religious landscape due to the recent high levels of immigration, it is clear that this will continue to be an area of substantial research concern in the coming decades.

Part Three: Looking Ahead

In Chapter 20, Darren Sherkat expertly analyzes the religious demography of the United States. Until recently, little systematic information was known about American religious demography. Religious diversity by denomination, race, nativity, and region—combined with a lack of census data on religious affiliation, participation, and belief—prevented the development of a systematic demography of American religion. Over the course of the twentieth century, scholarship on American religious demography was invigorated by the accumulation of cross-sectional surveys that enabled inferences about the dynamics of affiliation, participation, and some aspects of religious belief. Sherkat provides a great service to the field by analyzing religious demography based on data from 1972 to 2002. If two concepts can capture the complex patterns that he lays out, they are "change" and "diversity." Such change and diversity can, and hopefully will, lead to an even more vibrant scientific study of religion in future decades. At the same time, Sherkat effectively warns us that, absent census-based measures of religion, population-based religion data are difficult to come by. Even the staple of information in this area, the GSS, lacks some key items of religion and is not large enough on a year-to-year basis to accurately draw inferences among religious and ethnic subgroups.

Chapter 21, our concluding chapter, highlights themes that will be of critical importance in moving the social scientific study of religion forward in the twenty-first century. Included among these themes are: (a) the need to better conceptualize and measure religion in population-level research; (b) the need to better address and understand subgroup, and particularly racial/ethnic, variations in the relationship between religion and various family life and health outcomes; (c) the need to better understand the degree to which the relationships between religion and various family life and health outcomes are causal, bidirectional, or spurious; and (d) the continued push for high-quality data at the population level that will allow for the more advanced understanding of religious influences on family life and health among the U.S. population. Indeed, it may be that the last of these items is most crucial in further developing our base of knowledge in this exciting area of scientific inquiry.

Conclusion

Our aspirations for the volume are twofold: (a) to enhance current understanding of these complex relationships, and (b) to stimulate greater interest, and innovative new research, in this exciting area of scientific inquiry. Although no volume of this breadth and scope can claim to be exhaustive, this project has brought together leading researchers from multiple academic disciplines, including sociology, demography, public health, economics, and religious studies. As such, the book is intended as a contribution that bridges what is often a chasm between the social scientific study of religion, on the one hand, and population studies and demography on the other. Taken together, the chapters in this volume are important examples of, and strong additions to, a resurgent strand of high-quality work on contemporary links between religion, family life, and health outcomes in the United States.

REFERENCES

Cadge, W., and E. Ecklund. 2007. "Immigration and Religion." *Annual Review of Sociology* 33:359–379.

Chatters, L. 2000. "Religion and Health: Public Health Research and Practice." *Annual Review of Public Health* 21:335–367.

Christiano, K. J. 2000. "Religion and the Family in Modern American Culture." In *Family, Religion, and Social Change in Diverse Societies*, ed. S. K. Houseknecht and J. G. Pankhurst, 43–78. New York: Oxford University Press.

Davis, J., T. Smith, and P. Marsden. 2006. "The General Social Surveys: Cumulative Codebook, 1972–2006." Chicago: National Opinion Research Center. Machine-readable data file (MRDF) distributed by the Interuniversity Consortium for Political and Social Research (ICPSR), Ann Arbor, MI.

Durkheim, E. [1897] 1951. *Suicide: A Study in Sociology*. New York: Free Press.

Eck, D. 1997. *A New Religious America*. San Francisco: Harper Books.

Edgell, P. A. 2006. *Religion and Family: Understanding the Transformation of Linked Institutions*. Princeton, NJ: Princeton University Press.

Ellison, C. G., and J. Levin. 1998. "The Religion-Health Connection: Evidence, Theory, and Future Directions." *Health Education and Behavior* 25:700–720.

Ellison, C. G., and D. Sherkat 1993. "Conservative Protestantism and Support for Corporal Punishment." *American Sociological Review* 58:131–144.

Ellison, C. G., and J. E. Storch. 2009. "Why is Religion Virtually Absent from the Family Studies Journals?" Paper presented at the annual meeting of the Association for the Sociology of Religion, San Francisco, August 8–10.

Featherman, D. 1971. "The Socioeconomic Achievement of White Religio-Ethnic Subgroups: Social and Psychological Explanations." *American Sociological Review* 36:207–227.

Finke, R. 2005. "Religious Involvement in America: Trends and Explanations." In *Handbook of Religion and Social Institutions*, ed. H. Ebaugh, 335–352. Springer Press.

Hadaway, C. K., and P. L. Marler. 2002. "Being Religious or Being Spiritual in America: A Zero Sum Proposition?" *Journal for the Scientific Study of Religion* 41 (2): 289–300.

Hadaway, C. K., P. L. Marler, and M. Chaves. 1993. "What the Polls Don't Show: A Closer Look at U.S. Church Attendance." *American Sociological Review* 58: 741–752.

Hadaway, C. K., P. L. Marler, and M. Chaves. 1998. "Reply: Over-Reporting Church Attendance in America: Evidence that Demands the Same Verdict." *American Sociological Review* 63 (1): 122–130.

Hadden, J. 1987. "Toward Desacralizing Secularization Theory." *Social Forces* 65 (3): 587–611.

Hout, M., and C. Fischer. 2002. "Why More Americans Have No Religious Preference: Politics and Generations." *American Sociological Review* 67 (2): 165–190.

Hout, M., and A. Greeley. 1998. "Comment: What Church Officials' Reports Don't Show: Another Look at Church Attendance Data." *American Sociological Review* 63 (1): 113–119.

———. 1999. "Americans' Increasing Belief in Life After Death: Religious Competition and Acculturation." *American Sociological Review* 64:813–835.

Idler, E. 1987. "Religious Involvement and the Health of the Elderly: Some Hypotheses and an Initial Test." *Social Forces* 66:226–238.

Koenig, H., M. McCullough, and D. Larson. 2001. *Handbook of Religion and Health*. New York: Oxford University Press.

Lehrer, E., and C. Chiswick. 1993. "Religion as a Determinant of Marital Stability." *Demography* 30:385–403.

Levin, J., and H. Vanderpool. 1987. "Is Frequent Religious Attendance Really Conducive to Better Health? Toward an Epidemiology of Religion." *Social Science and Medicine* 24:589–600.

————. 1989. "Is Religion Therapeutically Significant for Hypertension?" *Social Science and Medicine* 29:69–78.

Musick, M., J. House, and D. Williams. 2004. "Attendance at Religious Services and Mortality in a National Sample." *Journal of Health and Social Behavior* 45 (2): 198–213.

Pearce, L., and W. Axinn 1998. "The Impact of Family Religious Life on the Quality of Parent–Child Relationships." *American Sociological Review* 63:810–828.

Presser, S., and M. Chaves. 2007. "Is Religious Service Attendance Declining?" *Journal for the Scientific Study of Religion* 46: 417–423.

Regnerus, M. D. 2007. *Forbidden Fruit: Sex and Religion in the Lives of American Teenagers.* Oxford: Oxford University Press.

Roof, W. C. 2000. *Spiritual Marketplace: Baby Boomers and the Remaking of American Religion.* Princeton, NJ: Princeton University Press.

Ryder, N., and C. Westoff. 1971. *Reproduction in the United States: 1965.* Princeton, NJ: Princeton University Press.

Shahabi, L., L. H. Powell, M. A. Musick, K. I. Pargament, C. E. Thoresen, D. Williams, L. Underwood, and M. A. Ory. 2002. "Correlates of Self-Perceptions of Spirituality in American Adults." *Annals of Behavioral Medicine* 24 (1): 59–68.

Sherkat, D., and C. G. Ellison. 1999. "Recent Developments and Current Controversies in the Sociology of Religion." *Annual Review of Sociology* 25:363–394.

Sloan, R., E. Bagiella, and T. Powell. 1999. "Religion, Spirituality, and Medicine." *Lancet* 353:664–667.

Sloan, R., E. Bagiella, L. VandeCreek, and P. Poulos. 2000. "Should Physicians Prescribe Religious Activities?" *New England Journal of Medicine* 342:1913–1916.

Smith, C., M. O. Emerson, and P. Snell. 2008. *Passing the Plate: Why American Christians Don't Give Away More Money.* New York: Oxford University Press.

Smith, T. 1998. "A Review of Church Attendance Measures." *American Sociological Review* 63 (1): 131–136.

————. 2002. "Religious Diversity in America: The Emergence of Muslims, Buddhists, Hindus, and Others." *Journal for the Scientific Study of Religion* 41:577–585.

Smith, T., and S. Kim. 2005. "The Vanishing Protestant Majority." *Journal for the Scientific Study of Religion* 44:211–223.

Stryker, R. 1981. "Religio-Ethnic Effects on Attainments in the Early Career." *American Sociological Review* 46 (2): 212–231.

Thornton, A., W. Axinn, and D. Hill. 1992. "Reciprocal Effects of Religiosity, Cohabitation, and Marriage." *American Journal of Sociology* 98:628–651.

U.S. Bureau of the Census. 2005. *Statistical Abstract of the United States: 2006.* 125th ed. Washington, DC: Bernan Press.

Westoff, C., R. Potter, and P. Sagi. 1964. "Some Selected Findings of the Princeton Fertility Study, 1963." *Demography* 1:130–135.

Wilcox, W. 1998. "Conservative Protestant Childrearing: Authoritarian or Authoritative?" *American Sociological Review* 63:795–809.

————. 2004. *Soft Patriarchs, New Men: How Christianity Shapes Fathers and Husbands.* Chicago: University of Chicago Press.

Wuthnow, R. 1998. *After Heaven: Spirituality in America Since the 1950s.* Berkeley: University of California Press.

————. 2005. *America and the Challenges of Religious Diversity.* Princeton, NJ: Princeton University Press.

Zinnbauer, B. J., K. I. Pargament, and A. B. Scott. 1999. "The Emerging Meanings of Religiousness and Spirituality: Problems and Prospects." *Journal of Personality* 67 (6): 889–919.

PART ONE

Religion and Family
Life Outcomes

2

▶ ▶ ▶ ▶ ▶ ▶ ▶ ▶ ▶ ▶ ▶ ▶ ▶ ▶ ◀ ◀ ◀ ◀ ◀ ◀ ◀ ◀ ◀ ◀ ◀ ◀ ◀ ◀

Religion and the Timing of First Births in the United States

LISA D. PEARCE

Religion is an ideational force capable of helping to shape humans' reproductive strategies and actions through a variety of mechanisms, only some of which have been extensively explored by social scientists. Understanding religion's connections to fertility behavior requires a comprehensive approach to conceptualizing both religious influences and fertility processes, one that recognizes their dynamic and reciprocal nature. This chapter outlines previous research on the links between religion and fertility, draws out the major theoretical contributions of this literature, and reveals ways in which new conceptualizations of religious influence suggest further theoretical and methodological advances in the study of religion and fertility. Based on two of these specific suggestions, original analyses are performed to assess the influence of the religious affiliation in which one is raised and religious practice on the risk or timing of both premarital and marital childbearing for a sample of young men and women in the United States. The findings increase our understanding of how religious affiliation and practice early in the life course shape subsequent fertility outcomes.

Linking Religion and Fertility

Beginning with demographic transition theory, a number of explanations for fertility recognize the role of religion. Although demographic transition theory and its many refinements are often criticized for a lack of attention to cultural and ideational processes, the role of religion has been pervasive. Notestein (1945) discusses how religious doctrine can encourage high fertility and writes that the power of values and customs could limit the influence of economic development on fertility. Elaborating classic transition theory, Lesthaeghe (1983; Lesthaeghe and Surkyn 1988; Lesthaeghe and Wilson 1986) argues that secularization, or the loss of religious authority over realms of life such as family formation, along with increasing individualism, were both key factors in European fertility transitions.

Also, adaptations of the microeconomic theories of fertility, such as Easterlin's framework (1975, 1978; Easterlin and Crimmins 1985), leave room for religion as a force that might increase the demand for children or perhaps increase the "psychic costs" of fertility limitation. All of these are examples of how religion has been conceptualized within major theories of fertility transitions. Highlighted in the following are the ways in which religion's role has been measured and analyzed using survey data.

Religious Group Differences

The majority of research that attempts to understand connections between religion and fertility at the micro-level focuses on religious group differences in fertility behavior. For example, from the mid-1940s through the late 1960s, researchers found that Catholics desired, expected, and had more children than Protestants in the United States (Freedman, Whelpton, and Campbell 1959; Ryder and Westoff 1971; Westoff, Potter, and Sagi 1964; Whelpton, Campbell, and Patterson 1966). Since the 1970s, Catholic–Protestant differences in fertility have converged and now non-Hispanic white Catholics have fewer children than non-Hispanic white Protestants (Mosher and Hendershot 1984; Mosher, Johnson, and Horn 1986; Mosher, Williams, and Johnson 1992; Westoff and Jones 1979). One exception to this pattern of results is that Williams and Zimmer (1990) found higher Catholic marital fertility among the general population of the Providence, Rhode Island, metropolitan area in 1967 and 1980. They hypothesized that the high concentration of Catholics in this region reinforces high fertility norms.

Within Protestantism, studies show substantial variation in fertility across affiliations (DeJong and Ford 1965; Marcum 1981). Also, several studies have highlighted the distinctively higher fertility of Mormons compared to other religious groups in the United States (Heaton and Goodman 1985; Spicer and Gustavus 1974; Thornton 1979; Westoff and Potvin 1967).

In contexts outside the United States, other religio-ethnic differences in fertility have been noted. Chamie (1981) found that Lebanese Muslims and Christians differ from each other in their fertility behavior, fertility preferences, and contraceptive knowledge. Knodel, Chamrathrithirong, and Debavalya (1987) found higher fertility among Thai Muslims compared to Thai Buddhists. Others find differences between the fertility preferences and behaviors of Hindus, Christians, and Muslims in India (Dharmalingam and Morgan 2004; Johnson 1993; Mishra 2004; Morgan et al. 2002). These many examples of how fertility differs across religious groups suggest some connection between religion and fertility. Next, I outline some of the explanations offered for these differences.

Theorizing Links between Religion and Fertility

Three different, but not mutually exclusive, hypotheses have been offered for the many examples of religious group differentials in fertility. First, Goldscheider (1971) argues that there are *particularized theologies* that support certain types of demographic behavior. Among certain religious groups, explicit theological canon about family size and contraception may affect what adherents deem as possible and preferable. The often cited example is that of Catholic doctrine prohibiting most forms of contraception and all uses of abortion (Noonan 1986). Goldscheider (1971) also writes that religion shapes general value orientations or worldviews that could influence demographic behavior. For example, religions that encourage early marriage, a patriarchal home environment in which women have little say in reproductive decisions, son preference, or an overall fatalistic outlook in life, also indirectly promote higher fertility. In general then, those who belong to an affiliation or religio-ethnic group in which particularized theologies or general value orientations encourage larger families, will desire and have more children than those affiliated with religio-ethnic groups whose ideologies are less pro-natalist.

A second explanation often offered for religio-ethnic fertility differentials is the *characteristics* proposition. This explanation focuses on nonreligious characteristics that differentiate religio-ethnic groups and that are also related to fertility (Chamie 1981; Goldscheider 1971). The social, demographic, and economic attributes of religio-ethnic groups often partly explain how a group's reproductive behavior differs from others. For example, explanations for why Jewish fertility is lower than Catholic or Protestant fertility in the United States center on features of the Jewish population, such as higher rates of urban residence, higher educational attainment, and higher occupational prestige (Freedman, Whelpton, and Smit 1961; Goldscheider and Uhlenberg 1969; Thomlinson 1965). As another example, Jeffery and Jeffery (1997) posit that two primary reasons why Muslim fertility is higher than that of other religio-ethnic groups in India are that Muslims tend to live in more rural settings and have less access to educational and economic opportunities.

A third explanation often offered for religio-ethnic fertility differentials is the *minority status hypothesis*. This proposition holds that members of some minority groups (religious or otherwise) may have fewer children than non-minorities when they desire acculturation, have similar socioeconomic characteristics as nonminorities, and when they are not influenced by pro-natalist religious theologies (Goldscheider 1971; Goldscheider and Uhlenberg 1969). The minority status hypothesis encourages investigations of religious identity and fertility to consider the larger social context and interactions between religious and socioeconomic factors.

Operationalizing Links between Religion and Fertility

All three of the explanations for religio-ethnic fertility differentials may operate simultaneously and must be considered in any investigation of the relationship between religion and fertility outcomes. The most common way in which these ideas are tested is to ascertain respondents' religious affiliation or identification and assign dummy variables delineating the major religious groups to be compared. Baseline models include the dummy variables and basic controls, and then subsequent models include variables measuring socioeconomic characteristics to see if this results in the effects of religious affiliation being minimized or even disappearing. After controlling for all socioeconomic measures available, if statistically significant differences between various affiliations or religio-ethnic groups remain, there is usually said to be evidence for a particular theologies effect and sometimes a mention of the possibility of a minority status effect. This type of approach is limited, because residual statistically significant differences might also stem from other nonreligious unmeasured characteristics. In addition, little is learned as to exactly how membership in certain religious groups relates to differential fertility or how other dimensions of religion such as practice or salience help explain religion's impact on fertility.

Although the bulk of theories and empirical analyses regarding relationships between religion and fertility focus on group differences, increasingly studies are recognizing the multidimensional nature of religion and finding links between the religious practice or salience of individuals and their fertility behavior. Positive associations between religiosity and fertility have been found in Catholic, Protestant, Mormon, and Jewish samples (Goldscheider 1967; Heaton 1986; Ryder and Westoff 1971; Bouvier and Rao 1975; Westoff and Ryder 1977). Further, after controlling for affiliation differences, those who attend religious services have been found to desire and have more children (Mosher et al. 1986; Mosher, Williams, and Johnson 1992; Pearce 2002a). Another recent study shows that private and public worship are both positively correlated with ideal family size in Nepal (Pearce 2002b, 2006).

Another improvement in recent studies on religion and fertility is the recognition of the role of other family members' religious characteristics in influencing individual-level fertility outcomes. This is a part of a broad advancement within studies of religious influence in general, where researchers are realizing that the influence of one's own religious identity is modified by the religious identity of those around him/her. Stark and colleagues (Stark 1996; Stark, Kent, and Doyle 1982) found that the effects of individual-level religiosity are more strongly related to delinquency in community contexts where the individual teen's religion is the majority religious group and religious practice is relatively high. Studies of other family outcomes suggest that the family-level context of religiosity is important (Ellison, Bartkowski, and Anderson 1999; Pearce and Axinn 1998), and evidence that the family religious context holds importance for fertility comes from two studies by Pearce (2002a, 2006). First, for young adults in the United States, having had a Catholic mother and/or a mother who attended religious services frequently while her child/ren grew up, results in young adults being less approving of voluntary childlessness and more desirous of larger families of their own than those with non-Catholic or less religiously active mothers during childhood (Pearce 2002a). Also, in Nepal, Pearce (2006) finds that ideal family size among young adults is associated with family members performing worship rituals in the home and visiting temples. This specific evidence about intergenerational religious dynamics and fertility attitudes suggests we should more fully explore the role of parental, spousal, peer, and community religious dynamics for a wide range of fertility outcomes.

Future Directions for Exploring the Links between Religion and Fertility

Clearly, progress has been made in measuring and assessing the relationships between multiple dimensions of religion and fertility outcomes. Further advancement will require a new level of dedication from those creating surveys to design, test, and incorporate reliable measures of multiple dimensions of religion, including various forms of practice, the strength of certain beliefs, and the level of salience with which religion operates in individuals' lives.

Another way in which religious influences can be better understood is if we continue to improve on ways of analyzing the influences of religious contexts. For example, further work is needed to identify key dimensions of community-, family-, and peer-level religious influences. This will also require creativity on the part of those designing studies. In a quest to enhance what we can reliably say about national-level patterns in the relationship between religion and family outcomes, social scientists have become narrowly focused on fielding national-level probability samples of individuals, which makes it incredibly difficult to collect much information on the religious lives of relevant others in these individuals' lives. What few data sources that do exist for measuring community-level (e.g., data from the Churches and Church Membership in the United States, 1980 study published by the Glenmary Research Center), family-level (e.g., Intergenerational Panel Study of Mothers and Children and the National Study of Youth and Religion), and school-level (e.g., The National Longitudinal Study of Adolescent Health) effects should be used to more fully explore these contextual influences.

Another weakness of survey data analyses exploring the relationship between religion and fertility is that measures of religion rarely precede the fertility attitude or behavior being studied. This is problematic, because studies have shown that individuals' religious affiliation and practice can change after births and when children reach school age (Marcum 1981; Stolzenberg, Blair-Loy, and Waite 1995). Some surveys obtain retrospective reports of religious affiliation or practice to gain leverage on the causal processes in operation. However, these retrospective reports are likely to be biased, and a preferable approach would be to ask questions about religious affiliation, beliefs, practices, and salience over time to be able to relate them to fertility attitudes and behavior as they unfold over the life course. For the most part, this problem will be best addressed with future data collection improvements. However, one data set that can be used to preliminarily test relationships between religion measured at one point in time and subsequent fertility behavior is the National Longitudinal Survey of Youth of 1979 (NLSY79). In the following, I test hypotheses about the relationship between the religious tradition in which one was raised and recent religious service attendance on subsequent fertility timing.

Most existing research on religion and fertility behavior uses "children ever born" as the dependent variable (e.g., Heaton 1986; Knodel et al. 1999; Mosher, Williams, and Johnson 1992). This analytic strategy is limited because fertility is a process and using a measure of children ever born truncates family size for those that may go on to have more children. Sometimes this limitation is addressed by focusing on cohorts of women over age forty-five, so the assumption can be made that their family size is complete. However, because the timing of fertility changes from cohort to cohort, what is learned about women at the end of their reproductive years may not reflect the processes that younger cohorts are currently experiencing. One analytic strategy that can say something about the process of fertility for all adults is the use of event history modeling (Teachman 1982). Through such models, the timing of births can be assessed for all individuals in a study. An example of this technique can be found in an article by Heckert and Teachman (1985). They find that those who are more religious have second births at a faster rate than those who are less religious, and that religiosity is more strongly related to a faster pace of second births for women who have received a sectarian education and those who are Catholic. Using a similar strategy, I now discuss how two dimensions of religion might be related to the timing of first births in the United States and test these hypotheses with data from the NLSY79 panel study.

Examining the Impact of Religion on
First Birth Timing in the United States

Given the extensive research literature suggesting that religious affiliation and religious service attendance are related to family size in the United States, this analysis investigates whether or not religious affiliation and religious service attendance are related to the timing of first births: both premaritally and maritally conceived. In thinking about the connection between religion and fertility over the life course, an obvious starting point is to consider the role of the specific religious tradition in which an individual was raised. Religious affiliation in adulthood is strongly correlated with that in childhood (King and Elder 1999), and regardless of whether religious beliefs and practices carry into adulthood, religious socialization may shape family attitudes and behaviors for years to come.

Religious groups vary both in their specific and general ideology related to premarital and marital births. For example, virtually all Judeo-Christian religions prefer birth within marriage. Marriage is held up as an ideal and thought of as the best institution for bearing and rearing children. These kinds of messages should make those raised in any religious tradition less likely to have a premarital birth than those raised in no religious tradition. Beyond that, certain religions are more adamant than others in encouraging marriage and discouraging sexual activity before marriage. Among the major denominations in the United States,

Jews and mainline Protestants seem least focused on encouraging marriage and discouraging premarital sex while Catholics and Evangelical Protestants seem to be more pro-marriage and opposed to premarital sex (Pearce and Thornton 2006). On the other hand, young adulthood is a period dense with transitions, and perceived role conflict often leads to strategies meant for efficient timing of all transitions (Rindfuss 1991). Research shows that being enrolled in school delays marriage and fertility (Teachman and Polonko 1988; Thornton, Axinn, and Teachman 1995). Based on the logic of the characteristics hypothesis, the general Catholic emphasis on education may counteract any pro-natalist influence and the high educational attainment of Jews and mainline Protestants may also delay their first births compared to other religious groups.

Another dimension of religion thought to be related to fertility is religious service attendance. Attendance signals a commitment to religion, a social institution that typically discourages premarital sex (and premarital birth) and encourages marriage (Pearce 2002). Attendance also involves a social linkage to others who share similar values (Goodman and Heaton 1986). Within religious institutions in the United States, marriage and childbearing within marriage are idealized and promoted through religious life cycle rituals and organizational structures that promote family formation and involvement (Pearce 2002a; Pearce and Axinn 1998). Based on this, I hypothesize that religious service attendance will reduce the risk of a premarital birth and speed up the timing of marital births.

To summarize, the hypotheses being tested here are as follows:

1. Those raised with no particular religious affiliation will be the most at risk of a premaritally conceived birth, and those raised as either Catholic or Evangelical Protestant will face the least risk, with those raised in other religious affiliations falling in between.
2. Controlling for religious affiliation, the more often a never married person attends religious services, the less risk he/she has of having a child.
3. Once married, those raised with no particular religious affiliation will wait the longest to have a first birth, and those raised as either Catholic or Evangelical Protestant will have a first child more quickly, with those raised in other religious denominations falling in between.
4. Controlling for religious affiliation, the more often a married person attends religious services, the more quickly he/she will have his/her first child.

Data and Methods

I use data from the first nineteen waves of the NLSY79. Beginning in 1979, a national probability sample of 12,686 youth ages fourteen to twenty-two were interviewed yearly until 1994 and then biannually from 1996 onward. In 2000, the final year of data used in these analyses, the study had a retention rate of

80.6 percent (NLYS79 User's Guide 2001). The NLSY79 contains rich prospective data on fertility, marriage, cohabitation, schooling, and work behaviors, as well as a handful of items on religious affiliation and religious service attendance asked at multiple points in the panel study. I use the marital and fertility information to construct the dependent variables for analyses. I use the other prospective data and a variety of baseline measures from the 1979 survey about family background and sociodemographic characteristics as independent variables. The key advantage to using these data to study religion and fertility is the longitudinal nature of the data, thus allowing fertility timing to be modeled using measures of religious affiliation and religious service attendance that precede fertility timing.

Two dimensions of religion are measured: religious affiliation and public religious attendance. Religious affiliation is measuring by asking respondents, "In what religion were you raised?" If the respondent said, "Protestant" or "Christian," a probe was used to try and identify a specific denomination. Based on the answers to these questions, responses were coded into one of seven categories (Catholic, mainline Protestant, Evangelical Protestant, African American Protestant, other Protestant, other religion, and no religion) based on the coding scheme described by Steensland and colleagues (2000). Once the categories were delineated, dummy variables were created for membership in each category.

To measure the frequency of religious service attendance in 1979 and 1982, respondents were asked, "In the past year, about how often have you attended religious services—more than once a week, about once a week, two or three times a month, about once a month, several times or less during the year, or not at all?" The coding of these responses ranges from $1 =$ "not at all" to $6 =$ "more than once a week." Because the units of analysis for these analyses are person-year observations, frequency of religious service attendance is a time-varying measure. For those person-year observations that take place after 1979, but before 1982, the measure of religious service attendance that is used is from 1979. For those person-year observations that take place after 1982, the measure of religious service attendance in 1982 is used. In both cases, the measure of frequency of religious service attendance comes before the risk period, but this strategy allows for the most recent report of religious service attendance to be used.

According to the characteristics hypothesis, there are certain sociodemographic characteristics that may explain a relationship between religion and fertility; thus, I include controls for a variety of these factors. Background sociodemographic characteristics include gender, race/ethnicity, mother's education, and whether the individual lived with two biological parents at age fourteen. All of these characteristics were measured in 1979. Descriptions of how these variables are coded, and their distribution among the person-year observations for each analysis, are provided in Table 2.1. In all models, I also include a set of dummy variables for ages fifteen to forty-one and leave out the dummy variable for age fourteen for comparison purposes. This controls for the passage of time in these processes; these coefficients are not presented in the tables to save space.

Other factors that may serve as mechanisms of religious influence include educational attainment and whether or not an individual is enrolled in school, employed, cohabiting, or married. These variables are all coded as time-varying and are measured at each interview (the beginning of each person-year period of observations). Thus, for example, I estimate the effect of whether or not a person is enrolled in school at time t on whether or not a person has a birth between t and $t + 1$.

I employ discrete-time event history models to estimate the relationship between religious affiliation in childhood and recent frequency of religious service attendance on timing of first births (Allison 1984; Petersen 1986, 1991). The unit of analysis is the person-year of exposure to first childbirth. Thus, the data contain multiple observations for each respondent; the number of observations corresponds to the number of years the individual is at risk for a first birth. For each year before the year of the pregnancy that resulted in the first birth, the dependent variable is coded 0 and the year in which the pregnancy leading to the first birth occurred is coded 1. For respondents who did not experience a first birth before the final interview in 2000, the dependent variable is coded 0 for all person-years.

I use logistic regression to estimate the discrete-time hazard models. Although sample size is increased substantially by using person-years of exposure to risk as the unit of analyses, Petersen (1986, 1991) and Allison (1984) show that the use of discrete-time methods does not deflate the standard errors, and thus provides appropriate tests of statistical significance. In addition, because the probability of becoming pregnant within each one-year interval is relatively small, the estimates obtained via discrete-time methods approximate those that would be obtained through continuous-time methods. Furthermore, discrete-time methods using person-years of exposure are appropriate because the data about first birth timing are precise to the year. Because the data collection began in 1979, the hazard models begin in that year. The respondents who had a first birth prior to 1979 are excluded from these analyses.

The additive effects on log-odds ratios are presented in Tables 2.2 and 2.3. The effect of each coefficient can be interpreted as the additive effect on the yearly log-odds of having a first birth for each one-unit change in the independent variable. Thus, a negative coefficient indicates decreased yearly log-odds (or a later first birth), a positive coefficient indicates increased yearly log-odds (or an earlier first birth), and a zero indicates no effect. Because so few births occur per year, the yearly log odds (exp{log-odds}) of a first birth are very similar to the yearly first birth rate. Therefore, although coefficients represent the additive effects on the log-odds of a first birth, in the following discussion, I

TABLE 2.1

Descriptive Statistics for Variables in Event History Analysis of Transitions to First Marital and First Premarital Births: NLSY79 Data from 1979–2000

Variable	Description	Person-Year Observations for First Premarital Birth Analyses		Person-Year Observations for First Marital Birth Analyses	
		Mean	SD	Mean	SD
Premarital birth	Premarital birth transition between t & t+1	.04	.20		
Marital birth	Marital birth transition between t & t+1			.04	.20
Raised Catholic	Raised in Catholic tradition	.37	.48	.35	.48
Raised mainline Protestant	Raised in a mainline Protestant tradition	.21	.41	.19	.39
Raised Evangelical Protestant	Raised in an Evangelical Protestant tradition	.17	.38	.17	.38
Raised African American Protestant	Raised in an African American Protestant tradition	.13	.34	.16	.37
Raised other Protestant	Raised in a Protestant tradition other than those listed above	.05	.21	.05	.21
Raised other religion	Raised in a religion other than those listed above	.04	.21	.04	.19
Raised no religion	Raised in no religious tradition	.03	.20	.04	.20

Variable		Mean	SD	Mean	SD
Frequency of religious service attendance	Frequency of religious service attendance from most recent survey, 1979 or 1982 (ranges from 1 = not at all, to 6 = more than once a week)	3.11	1.68	2.97	1.67
Gender	Self-identified gender (0 = male; 1 = female)	.44	.50	.46	.50
Age	Age in years at t	21.29	4.28	24.30	5.56
Race/Ethnicity					
White	Self-identified as non-Hispanic white	.46	.50	.41	.49
Black	Self-identified as non-Hispanic black	.20	.40	.25	.43
Latino	Self-identified as Hispanic	.14	.34	.14	.35
Other	Self-identified as other race	.21	.40	.19	.39
Mother's education	Mother's years of schooling	11.23	3.20	11.00	3.19
Two bio parents at age 14	Lived with two biological parents at age 14 (0 = no; 1 = yes)	.72	.45	.68	.46
Accumulated years of education	Years of school completed at t	12.14	2.46	12.30	2.40
Currently enrolled in school	Enrolled in school at t (0 = no; 1 = yes)	.39	.49	.24	.43
Currently employed	Employed at t (0 = no; 1 = yes)	.78	.41	.83	.34
Currently cohabiting	Cohabiting with romantic partner at t	.05	.22		
Currently married	Married at t (0 = no; 1 = yes)			.59	.49
N		58,483		133,966	

sometimes express the coefficients in terms of multiplicative (exponentiated) effects on the first birth rate for ease of interpretation.

To examine how religion is related to the timing of both premaritally and maritally conceived first births, I estimate separate hazard models using a competing risks framework. For premaritally conceived first births, marriage is the competing risk; therefore, respondents who married without a premaritally conceived first birth are no longer considered at risk, once they have married. For maritally conceived first births, a premarital first birth is the competing risk; therefore, respondents who conceived a first birth before marriage are no longer considered at risk of a marital first birth.

In the analyses of premarital childbearing, only first births that occur either before marriage or fewer than nine months after marriage are considered to be premarital births. In the analyses of marital childbearing, respondents are considered to be at risk of a marital first birth starting from the beginning of the study in 1979, but only first births that occur at least nine months after marriage are considered marital births. As indicated in Table 2.1, individuals had a first birth in 4 percent of the person-year observation intervals. Similarly, individuals had a marital birth in 4 percent of the person-year observation intervals.

Results

Risk of Premaritally Conceived First Birth

Table 2.2 displays analyses that explore the relationship between the religion in which a respondent was raised, the frequency with which an individual attends religious services, and the risk of a premaritally conceived birth. The first model includes only those variables measured in 1979. The three following models add time-varying measures of education, employment, and union experience. In all four models, those raised Catholic or Evangelical Protestant are more likely to have a premaritally conceived birth than those raised mainline Protestant. In other analyses not shown here, they are also significantly more likely to have a premaritally conceived first birth than those raised in African American Protestant, other Protestant, or other religious traditions. In fact, those raised Catholic or Evangelical Protestant are just as likely as those raised with no religion to have a premaritally conceived first birth. These results run counter to my hypothesis that those raised Catholic or Evangelical Protestant would be the least likely to have a premaritally conceived child. Perhaps those raised Catholic or Evangelical Protestant are less likely to abort mistimed pregnancies than those raised with another or no religious affiliation; therefore, they have higher premaritally conceived birthrates. Also, those raised in Catholic or Evangelical Protestant homes probably received more abstinence-only sex education, and thereby less education about contraceptive methods, making them less likely to use contraception when sexual intercourse occurs (Regnerus 2005). These

TABLE 2.2

Logistic Regression Analysis of Transition to First Premarital Birth, Treating Marriage as a Competing Risk: NLSY79 Data from 1979–2000

	Hazard of First Premarital Birth			
	(1)	(2)	(3)	(4)
Raised Catholic[a]	.28+	.24+	.23+	.23+
Raised Evangelical Protestant[a]	.42+	.26+	.25+	.26+
Raised African American Protestant[a]	.07	-.01	-.02	-.02
Raised other Protestant[a]	.20	.13	.14	.14
Raised other religion[a]	-.05	-.06	-.05	-.05
Raised no religion[a]	.46***	.28*	.27*	.27*
Frequency of religious service attendance	-.07***	-.03*	-.03*	-.03
Gender	.11**	.21***	.20***	.18***
Race/Ethnicity[b]				
Black	.91***	.90***	.92***	.94***
Latino	.25**	.20*	.21*	.23*
Other	.15*	.12	.13	.13
Mother's education	-.06***	-.03***	-.03***	-.04***
Two bio parents at age 14	-.36***	-.29***	-.29***	-.27***
Accumulated years of education		-.11***	-.12***	-.11***
Currently enrolled in school		-.40***	-.38***	-.37***
Currently employed			.16**	.15*
Currently cohabiting				.72***
Chi-square value	668.389	618.90	615.17	671.37
Degrees of freedom	40	42	43	44
Number of person-years	54,004	50,880	50,245	50,239

Notes: All chi-square values are significant at .001. Models also include dummy variables representing each age from fourteen to forty-one (not shown).

a. Reference group is "Raised in mainline Protestant tradition."

b. Reference group is white.

*p < .05, **p < .01, ***p < .001 (one-tailed tests), +p < .05 (two-tailed tests) possible explanations should be explored further in order to fully understand the relationship between religious affiliation in childhood and later life fertility and family formation outcomes.

Another consistent result across all the models is the statistically significant negative effect of religious service attendance. In the first model, each unit increase in religious service attendance corresponds to a 6 percent decrease in the risk of a premaritally conceived birth. Thus, independent of the religious tradition in which one is raised, those who attend more frequently are less likely to have a premaritally conceived first birth. This effect shrinks in half when controls are added for educational attainment and whether an individual is currently enrolled in school. This suggests that high attendees' educational achievement partially explains their lower rate of premaritally conceived births. Perhaps religious service attendance signals a stronger conformance to a conventional life involving high levels of education and the delaying of births until after marriage. The addition of a control for being currently employed does not alter the coefficient for religious service attendance, nor does it add much to the fit of the model. However, in the fourth model, when a control is added for whether or not the individual is presently cohabiting, the coefficient for religious service attendance becomes statistically insignificant. This suggests that part of the reason religiously active individuals are less likely to have a premaritally conceived first birth is that they are less likely to be in cohabiting unions, where many premarital conceptions occur. All in all, this evidence suggests that religious service attendance is correlated with high educational achievement and low cohabitation rates, which help explain why those who attend more frequently are at less risk for a premaritally conceived first birth.

Timing of Maritally Conceived First Births

Table 2.3 displays the results that examine religious affiliation in childhood, religious service attendance, and the timing of maritally conceived first births. Fewer differences by religion in which a person was raised are apparent in these models. In the first model, the coefficient for being raised Catholic is negative and statistically significant. Converted to an odds ratio, this means that the rate of marital first birth timing is 6 percent lower for Catholics than mainline Protestants. However, this difference disappears after controls for education are included in the model. This suggests that delayed childbearing among Catholics may be partly a result of their higher educational attainment. Across the models, there is a consistent negative relationship between being raised in some indeterminate or "other" Protestant affiliation (as compared to being raised mainline Protestant) and the timing of a first marital birth. This result is difficult to interpret, because the composition (and therefore the experiences and ideological leanings) of this small group of respondents is difficult to ascertain. Respondents fall into this category if they either could not remember the name

TABLE 2.3

Logistic Regression Analysis of Transition to First Marital Birth, Treating Premarital Birth as a Competing Risk: NLSY79 Data from 1979–2000

	Hazard of First Marital Birth			
	(1)	*(2)*	*(3)*	*(4)*
Raised Catholic[a]	-.08*	-.08	-.08	-.06
Raised Evangelical Protestant[a]	.01	.03	.04	.00
Raised African American Protestant[a]	.06	.02	.02	.03
Raised other Protestant[a]	-.17+	-.18+	-.18+	-.23+
Raised other religion[a]	-.09	-.10	-.09	-.06
Raised no religion[a]	-.11	-.04	-.03	-.06
Frequency of religious service attendance	.06***	.06***	.06***	.06***
Gender	.20***	.19***	.20***	.15***
Race/Ethnicity[b]				
Black	-.41***	-.41***	-.40***	-.41***
Latino	.00	-.06	-.06	-.07
Other	.01	.01	-.09	.01
Mother's education	-.01**	-.02**	-.02*	-.02*
Two bio parents at age 14	.04	.05	.04	.08*
Accumulated years of education		.09***	.09***	.12***
Currently enrolled in school		-.92***	-.90***	-.76***
Currently employed			.18***	.27***
Currently married				1.42***
Chi-square value	750.06	984.11	963.01	2111.35
Degrees of freedom	40	42	43	44
Number of person-years	122,183	111,875	110,981	110,981

Notes: All chi-square values are significant at .001. Models also include dummy variables representing each age from fourteen to forty-one (not shown here).

a. Reference group is "Raised in mainline Protestant tradition."

b. Reference group is white.

*p < .05, **p < .01, ***p < .001 (one-tailed tests), +p < .05 (two-tailed tests) of their Protestant affiliation at the time of the survey, or if they gave names of denominations or nondenominational organizations that were unclassifiable. Assuming that many of the frequent attendees that fall into this group may belong to more conservative groups (e.g., charismatic, independent, or storefront-type churches), I conducted analyses where I moved all weekly or more frequent attendees (as of 1979) into the Evangelical Protestant group, and the significant negative coefficients for "other Protestant" remained across the models. Those results are not presented here.

A stronger and more consistent pattern is exhibited when the measure of religious service attendance is considered. In all four models, attendance is positive and significantly associated with marital fertility. This suggests that, even after controlling for a wide set of sociodemographic characteristics, individuals in each level of religious service attendance have marital first births at about a 6 percent faster rate than those in the category below them.

Discussion and Conclusion

Increasing attention is being paid to connections between religion and fertility as demographers further explore cultural explanations for fertility behaviors (McQuillan 2004). Taking what we already know about religion's influence, future work should focus on better operationalizing the multiple dimensions of religious influence, the religious contexts in which individuals' live, and the dynamic and reciprocal nature of religion and fertility processes across the life course.

The empirical results presented here demonstrate that religious affiliation in childhood and more proximate religious participation are related to the rate of premaritally and maritally conceived first births. There are stronger and more surprising relationships between the religious affiliation one is raised in and the risk of a premaritally conceived birth than for first marital birth timing. This could result both from premaritally conceived births being more proximate to childhood religious exposure and from there being more variance between religious groups in the messages sent regarding premarital sex and birth and less variance in the messages about birth timing within marriage. Overall, it seems that those raised in mainline Protestant, African American Protestant, or other (non-Christian) religions are least at risk of a premaritally conceived birth. Those raised as Catholic, Evangelical Protestant, or in no religious group are more likely to have a premaritally conceived child. In the results section, I discussed possible reasons for these findings. Further exploration of the relationship between religious affiliation and pregnancy, pregnancy resolution, and marital timing will shed more light on these processes.

In addition, more work is needed to understand exactly what messages religious institutions and parents are sending youth, how salient the messages are to youth, whether and how the messages vary by religious affiliation, and whether any variance is related to differential use of contraception, risk of mistimed conceptions, or pregnancy resolution. This relates back to my call in the first half of this chapter for researchers to more thoroughly explore why religio-ethnic differences in fertility behavior exist, especially the ideological mechanisms that may be at play. As in the analyses presented here, researchers have typically been more apt to provide evidence for ways in which socioeconomic characteristics explain religio-ethnic differences, and only hypothesize about how any remaining differences may be indicative of ideological mechanisms. Often, as is the case in this chapter, the inability to explore ideological explanations is a result of there being no measurement of the theorized mechanisms in the data we use. A solution to this problem would be increased inclusion of the values, norms, and attitudes expected to vary by religious affiliation and to explain religio-ethnic differences in fertility behavior. These include, but are not limited to, attitudes toward premarital sex, contraceptive use, ideal age for marriage and first births, and ideas about men's and women's roles in marriage and family life, and educational and career realms.

The relationship between religious service attendance and first birth timing, both premarital and marital, is consistent and persistent. Controlling for religious affiliation and other standard demographic and socioeconomic variables, the more often an unmarried person attends religious services, the less likely he/she is to have a child, and the more often a married person attends services, the more quickly he/she will have a first child. As discussed in the beginning of this chapter, although there may be some variance in the strength with which discouragement against having sex or encouragement to marry and have children (in that order) is conveyed, almost every religious group is supportive of marital childbearing; thus, increased participation in religious institutions will discourage premarital sex (and thus premaritally conceived first births) and encourage fertility within marriage. In the results presented here, higher educational attainment and less nonmarital cohabitation among frequent attendees is partly responsible for this group's lower risk of premaritally conceived births, but again, we need to know more about other mechanisms. Is it the case that these frequent attendees are less likely to have sex before marriage, or if they do, do they have sex less often, have fewer partners, or have different contraceptive use patterns than less frequent attendees? There may also be family-level mechanisms at play. Studies have shown that when mothers and fathers are frequent attendees at religious services, especially when the family attends religious services together, parent–child relationships are more close and affectionate (Pearce and Axinn 1998; Regnerus and Burdette 2006; Wilcox 2004). These close relationships may be protective against early and risky sexual behavior.

Questions also remain regarding exactly how religious service attendance is related to a higher rate of marital first births. What is it about frequent attendance that is associated with earlier first births? Are there class or other non-religious characteristics not well measured here that could shed more light on this relationship, or are there messages being sent from religious organizations about the value of parenting that speed the transition to first birth? Perhaps there are organizational features of religious institutions that ease childcare burdens, making earlier first births more feasible. Exploring these possible mechanisms will enhance our understanding of the relationship between religion and fertility and family formation.

The results presented here shed new light on the religion and fertility nexus by demonstrating relationships between religious affiliation in childhood, more proximate religious service attendance, and premaritally and maritally conceived births. However, as outlined earlier in this chapter, there are other advances the field is poised to make with other existing data sources and with new data collection efforts. First, there are other dimensions of religiosity to study. Here, the focus was on affiliation and religious service attendance, but we should also explore how the salience of religion in a person's life may be related to the timing of first and other premaritally and maritally conceived births, independent of religious affiliation or attendance at religious services. Adherence to specific beliefs, like whether or not premarital sex is viewed as a sin, may also help us understand the theological dimensions of religious influence. Second, studies of religion's influence on fertility behavior, like the results presented here, tend to focus on individual-level religious characteristics, but individuals' religious lives involve interaction with others who have their own religious beliefs and practices, so it may be insightful to find ways to examine the influence of parents, partners, peers, and/or religious leaders or co-congregants' religious characteristics and beliefs. As we continue to improve our conceptualization, measurement, and analysis of religion and fertility processes, we will learn even more about the ways in which these two aspects of life are related, further broadening our grasp of connections between the institutions of religion and family in general.

REFERENCES

Allison, P. D. 1984. *Event History Analysis.* Beverly Hills, CA: Sage Publications.

Bouvier, L. F., and S. L. Rao. 1975. *Socioreligious Factors in Fertility Decline.* Cambridge, MA: Ballinger.

Chamie, J. 1981. *Religion and Fertility: Arab Christian-Muslim Differences.* Cambridge: Cambridge University Press.

De Jong, G. F., and T. R. Ford. 1965. "Religious Fundamentalism, Socioeconomic Status, and Fertility Attitudes in the Southern Appalachians." *Demography* 2: 540–548.

Dharmalingam, A., and S. P. Morgan. 2004. "Pervasive Muslim-Hindu Fertility Differences in India." *Demography* 41 (3): 529–545.

Easterlin, R. A. 1975. "An Economic Framework for Fertility Analysis." *Studies in Family Planning* 6:54–63.

———. 1978. "The Economics and Sociology of Fertility: A Synthesis." In *Historical Studies of Changing Fertility,* ed. C. Tilly, 57–133. Princeton, NJ: Princeton University Press.

Easterlin, R. A., and E. Crimmins. 1985. *The Fertility Revolution: A Supply-Demand Analysis.* Chicago: University of Chicago Press.

Ellison, C. G., J. P. Bartkowski, and K. L. Anderson. 1999. "Are There Religious Variations in Domestic Violence?" *Journal of Family Issues* 20 (1): 87–113.

Freedman, R., P. K. Whelpton, and A.A. Campbell. 1959. *Family Planning Sterility, and Population Growth.* New York: McGraw-Hill.

Freedman, R., P. K. Whelpton, and J. W. Smit. 1961. "Socioeconomic Factors in Religious Differentials in Fertility." *American Sociological Review* 26: 608–614.

Goldscheider, C. 1971. *Population, Modernization, and Social Structure.* Boston: Little Brown.

Goldscheider, C. 1967. "Fertility of the Jews." *Demography* 4: 196–209.

Goldscheider, C., and P. R. Uhlenberg. 1969. "Minority Group Status and Fertility." *American Journal of Sociology* 74:361–372.

Goodman, K., and T. B. Heaton. 1986. "LDS Church Members in the U.S. and Canada." *AMCAP Journal* 12: 88–107.

Heaton, T. B. 1986. "How Does Religion Influence Fertility? The Case of Mormons." *Journal for the Scientific Study of Religion* 25(2): 248–58.

Heaton, T. B., and K. L. Goodman. 1985. "Religion and Family Formation." *Review of Religious Research* 26: 343–359.

Heckert, A., and J. Teachman. 1985. "Religious Factors in the Timing of Second Births." *Journal of Marriage and the Family* 47: 361–367.

Jeffery, R., and P. Jeffery. 1997. *Population, Gender, and Politics: Demographic Change in Rural North India.* Cambridge: Cambridge University Press.

Johnson, N. E. 1993. "Hindu and Christian Fertility in India: A Test of Three Hypotheses." *Social Biology* 40 (1/2): 87–105.

King, V., and G. H. Elder, Jr. 1999. "Are Religious Grandparents More Involved Grandparents?" *Journal of Gerontology: Social Sciences* 54B: S317-S328.

Knodel, J., A. Chamrathrithirong, and N. Debavalya. 1987. *Thailand's Reproductive Revolution.* Madison, WI: University of Wisconsin Press.

Knodel, J., R. S. Gray, P. Sriwatcharin, and S. Peracca. "Religion and Reproduction: Muslims in Buddhist Thailand." *Population Studies* 53(2): 149–164.

Lesthaeghe, R. 1983. "A Century of Demographic and Cultural Change in Western Europe: An Exploration of Underlying Dimensions." *Population and Development Review* 9 (3): 411–436.

Lesthaeghe, R., and J. Surkyn. 1988. "Cultural Dynamics and Economic Theories of Fertility Change." *Population and Development Review* 14 (1): 1–45.

Lesthaeghe, R., and C. Wilson. 1986. "Modes of Production, Secularization, and the Pace of the Fertility Decline in Western Europe, 1870–1930." In *The Decline of Fertility in Europe,* ed. A. J. Coale and S. C. Watkins, 261–292. Princeton, NJ: Princeton University Press.

Marcum, J. 1981. "Explaining Fertility Differences among U.S. Protestants." *Social Forces* 60:532–543.

McQuillan, K. 1999. *Culture, Religion and Demographic Behaviour: Catholics and Lutherans in Alsace, 1750–1870.* Montreal: McGill-Queen's University Press.

McQuillan, K. 2004. "When Does Religion Influence Fertility?" *Population and Development Review* 30: 25–56.

Mishra, V. 2004. "Muslim/Non-Muslim Differentials in Fertility and Family Planning in India." Working Paper, East-West Center, Honolulu, HI.

Mosher W. D.; Hendershot G. E. 1984. "Religion and Fertility: A Replication. *Demography* 21 (2): 185–91.

Mosher, W. D., D. P. Johnson, and M. Horn. 1986. "Religion and Fertility in the United States: The Importance of Marriage Patterns and Hispanic Origin." *Demography* 23(3): 367–379.

Mosher, W. D., L. B. Williams, and D. P. Johnson. 1992. "Religion and Fertility in the United States: New Patterns." *Demography* 29 (2): 199–214.

Morgan, S. P., S. Stash, H. L. Smith, and K. O. Mason. 2002. "Muslim and Non-Muslim Differences in Female Autonomy and Fertility: Evidence from Four Asian Countries." *Population and Development Review* 28 (3): 515–537.

NLSY79 User's Guide. 2001. Prepared for the U.S. Department of Labor by the Center for Human Resource Research, The Ohio State University, Columbus OH.

Noonan, J. T., Jr. 1986. *Contraception: A History of its Treatment by the Catholic Theologians and Canonists.* Cambridge, MA: Belknap Press of Harvard University.

Notestein, Frank W. 1945. "Population—The Long View." In *Food for the World*, ed. T. W. Schultz, 36–69. Chicago: University of Chicago Press.

Pearce, L. D. 2006. "Religion's Role in Shaping Family Size Preferences." Working Paper, Carolina Population Center, University of North Carolina at Chapel Hill.

———. 2002a. "The Influence of Early Life Course Religious Exposure on Young Adults' Dispositions toward Childbearing." *Journal for the Scientific Study of Religion* 41 (2): 325–340.

———. 2002b. "Integrating Survey and Ethnographic Methods for Systematic Anomalous Case Analysis." *Sociological Methodology* 32 (1): 103–132.

Pearce, L. D., and W. G. Axinn. 1998. "The Impact of Family Religious Life on the Quality of Parent-Child Relationships." *American Sociological Review* 63:810–828.

Pearce, L. D., and A. Thornton. 2006. "Religious Identities and Family Ideologies." Working Paper, Carolina Population Center, University of North Carolina at Chapel Hill.

Petersen, T. 1986. "Estimating Fully–Parametric Hazard Rate Models with Time–Dependent Covariates. Use of Maximum Likelihood." *Sociological Methods and Research* 14(3): 219–246.

Petersen, T. 1991. "The Statistical Analysis of Event Histories." *Sociological Methods and Research* 19(3): 270–323.

Regnerus, M. D. 2005. "Talking about Sex: Religion and Patterns of Parent–Child Communication about Sex and Contraception." *The Sociological Quarterly* 46:79–105.

Regnerus, M. D., and A. Burdette. 2006. "Religious Change and Adolescent Family Dynamics." *The Sociological Quarterly* 47:175–194.

Rindfuss, R. R. 1991. "The Young Adult Years: Diversity, Structural Change, and Fertility." *Demography* 28(4): 493–512.

Ryder, N., and C. Westoff. 1971. *Reproduction in the United States: 1965.* Princeton, NJ: Princeton University Press.

Spicer, J. C., and S. O. Gustavus, S.O. 1974. "Mormon Fertility Through Half a Century: Another Test of the Americanization Hypothesis." *Social Biology* 21(1): 70–76.

Stark, R. 1996. "Religion as Context: Hellfire and Delinquency One More Time." *Sociology of Religion* 57 (2): 163–173.

Stark, R., L. Kent, and D. Doyle. 1982. "Religion and Delinquency: The Ecology of a Lost Relationship." *Journal of Research in Crime and Delinquency* 19:4–24.

Steensland, B., J. Park, M. D. Regnerus, L. Robinson, W. B. Wilcox, and R. Woodberry. 2000. "The Measure of American Religion: Toward Improving the State of the Art." *Social Forces* 79:291–318.

Stolzenberg, R. M., M. Blair-Loy, and L. J. Waite. 1995. "Religious Participation in Early Adulthood: Age and Family Life Cycle Effects on Church Membership." *American Sociological Review* 60:84–103.

Teachman, J. 1982. "Methodological Issues in the Analysis of Family Formation and Dissolution." *Journal of Marriage and the Family* 44:1037–1053.

Teachman, J., and K. Polonko. 1988. "Marriage, Parenthood and the College Enrollment of Men and Women." *Social Forces* 67: 512–523.

Thomlinson, R. 1965. *Population Dynamics*. New York, NY: Random House.

Thornton, A. 1979. "Fertility and Income, Consumption Aspirations, and Child Quality Standards." *Demography* 16(2): 157–75.

Thornton, A., W. G. Axinn, and J. Teachman. 1995. "The Influence of Educational Experiences on Marriage and Cohabitation in Early Adulthood." *American Sociological Review* 60: 762–774.

Westoff, C., and E. F. Jones. 1979. "Patterns of Aggregate and Individual Changes in Contraceptive Practice: United States, 1965–1975." *Vital and Health Statistics*, Series 3(17): 1–23.

Westoff, C., R. Potter, and P. Sagi. 1964. "Some Selected Findings of the Princeton Fertility Study, 1963." *Demography* 1:130–135.

Westoff, C. F., and R. H. Potvin. 1966. "Higher Education, Religion, and Women's Family-size Orientations." *American Sociological Review* 31(4): 489–496.

Westoff, C. F., and N. B. Ryder. 1977. *The Contraceptive Revolution*. Princeton: Princeton University Press.

Whelpton, P., A. Campbell, and J. Patterson. 1966. *Fertility and Family Planning in the United States*. Princeton, NJ: Princeton University Press.

Wilcox, W. B. 2004. *Soft Patriarchs, New Men: How Christianity Shapes Fathers and Husbands*. Chicago: University of Chicago Press.

Williams, L. B. and B. G. Zimmer. 1990. "The Changing Influence of Religion on U.S. Fertility: Evidence from Rhode Island." *Demography* 27(3): 475–481.

3

Religion and Child Rearing

DUANE F. ALWIN AND JACOB L. FELSON

Train up a child in the way he should go: and when he is old, he will not depart from it. (Proverbs 22:6)

Parenthood is both a biological and social status. Viewed within a biological life cycle framework, parenthood can be seen as a natural outcome of reproduction and regeneration. Viewed from a social and cultural perspective, the situation of parenthood conveys certain rights, responsibilities, obligations, and associated expectations regarding the care and nurture of children. While the biological role of parenthood has important consequences for children—particularly in the transmission of genetic information and predispositions that may have developmental consequences—our focus here is on parenthood as a social and cultural phenomenon. The objective of this review is to consider how variations in religion—religious identities, beliefs, and behavior—shape how the parental role is enacted and the possible consequences for child development.

Despite its ubiquity, parenting as a focus of research has never received a great deal of attention. It is now becoming an established subfield that crosses several disciplinary traditions; however, within the literature on parenting relatively little research has been devoted to the topic of religion and child rearing practices. For example, a recent *Handbook of Parenting* (Bornstein 2002) containing over eighty review chapters (some 2,300 pages in all) written mostly by developmental psychologists paid virtually no attention to religion. An even more recent *Handbook of Father Involvement* (Tamis-LeMonda and Cabrera 2002) containing some twenty-two chapters specifically devoted to various aspects of the role of fathers in childhood mentioned religion only once! There is clearly a need for defining the relevance of religion to the study of variation in child rearing practices.

For lack of a better term we refer to the outcomes of interest as parental orientations—a very broad term that includes the totality of attitudes, values, beliefs, and behaviors that parents bring to settings in which they interact with their child or children. Parenting continues long after the childhood years

(Zarit and Eggebeen 2002); however, in this chapter, we restrict our attention primarily to parental orientations to dependent children. Although we restrict the focus in this way, the coverage otherwise is quite broad. What parents want for their children, and what they believe is the best approach to achieving their goals through their parenting practices, will depend not only upon a host of parental and child characteristics but upon a number of historical, economic, demographic, cultural, ecological, and structural variables that shape child rearing approaches.

While we recognize there may be some universal consequences that derive from the parent–child relationship, there is widespread recognition that the meaning of parenthood is quite diverse even within the same historical period and in the same society. The rights and obligations of parenthood depend on a host of parental and child characteristics. For example, what it means to be a mother versus what it means to be a father are generally quite different things in virtually all cultural and subcultural settings, and the ways in which parents interpret their role depends upon the religious doctrines to which they subscribe and the teachings about child rearing conveyed by their faith communities. The guiding hypothesis upon which the material presented here is based is that the manner in which the parental role is enacted is strongly related to their exposure to religious teachings and belief systems, as reflected in religious identities, beliefs, and behavior.

It is important to place the topic of religion and parental orientations in a historical perspective, both because it is clear that contemporary religious differences in child rearing orientations have their origins in religious traditions and because secular changes in society potentially have an impact on doctrinal differences that in turn affect orientations to children. The chapter is organized around three main themes: (a) historical patterning to religious themes regarding child rearing, (b) the persistence of religious differentiation in contemporary child rearing orientations, and (c) the evidence that religious differences in parenting have measurable consequences for child development. Before turning to these topics, we first clarify how the literature on this topic conceptualizes the phenomenon of child rearing.

Patterns of Child Rearing

As mentioned in the preceding introduction, the term "child rearing" is quite broad and the literature on this topic includes a lot of different kinds of things, including value orientations, parenting styles, and quite specific kinds of parenting practices, such as the use of corporal punishment. One of the key concepts employed in the recent literature on religion and child rearing is the concept of "parental values," and we therefore devote some time to a clarification of this concept and why it is important. Social psychologists define values as central to other cognitive phenomena, and it is important for present purposes to clarify the relationship of values to other "ideational" or "subjective" phenomena. Values are defined as essential "standards" that govern behavioral choices, and thus, parental values are those standards that help shape behavior with respect to children. As we noted earlier, as a general phenomenon "beliefs" are cognitive representations of "what is." Values are a subclass of beliefs: assertions about what is "good" or "desirable."

Another phenomenon often confused with beliefs and values, which is not covered in the present development but that deserves some mention, is the concept of attitude, specifically attitudes toward child rearing (see Holden and Buck 2002). Attitudes are predispositions to respond or behave in particular ways toward social objects along a positive or negative dimension (e.g., approval versus disapproval, approach versus avoidance, satisfaction versus dissatisfaction) and are thought to have emotional, cognitive, and behavioral dimensions, all of which are "evaluative" in nature. Such evaluations are often easily manipulated and are subject to situational factors. Some social psychologists have concluded that there is little evidence that stable, underlying attitudes can be said to exist (see review by Alwin 1994). While the attitude concept is an important one in its own right, in part because it is often easier to measure than other aspects of cognitive functioning, it is often viewed as epiphenomenal because it is derived from things more basic, namely values and beliefs. Also, note that while attitudes are conceived of with respect to specific objects and situations, values can be thought of as "abstract ideals, positive or negative, not tied to any specific attitude object or situation, representing a person's beliefs about ideal modes of conduct and ideal terminal goals" (Rokeach 1970, 124). Elsewhere we develop the argument for considering beliefs, values, and preferences—and not attitudes—in the understanding of childbearing and child rearing (see Alwin 2001, 2005, 2006).

Values for Obedience versus Autonomy in Children

Social historians have pointed to differences in conceptions and treatment of children over time, resulting from cultural changes, as well as the evolution of technology, demography, and social organization (e.g., Coleman 1990; Zelizer 1985). A principal contrast of interest here, which is in line with several scholarly treatments of parental values, is the contrast between autonomy versus obedience, or put simply, the contrast between "thinking for oneself" versus "obeying" adult authority. This contrast has been written about widely. Regardless of the particular language used, it is remarkable that a number of scholars over the years have all pinpointed the same dimensions of relevance in describing the nature of values underlying parent–child relations (e.g., Duvall 1946; Kohn 1969; Lynd and Lynd 1929; Miller and Swanson 1958; Schaefer 1987).

Such contrasts in values are central to the dimensions along which substantial social change has occurred in American society, although the two concepts of "autonomy" and "obedience" should probably not just be viewed in terms of their contrast, but separately, especially to the extent they are changing independently (see Ellison and Sherkat 1993b). In any event, this contrast is definitely linked to the central dimension of historical social development in Western industrialized societies, which have increasingly required the exercise of independent thought and action (Stone 1977; LeVine and White 1986, 1987). In addition, this set of distinctions is also developmentally relevant, since it is normally believed that children progress from a relatively "obedient" to a relatively "autonomous" state as they mature cognitively, emotionally, and socially (see Piaget 1932). This is particularly interesting, as mentioned earlier, to the extent that "developmental" trajectories and "historical" trajectories interact to produce different requirements of children at different historical periods.

Parenting Styles

Values and other beliefs are linked to behavior and intentions, although these relationships are often ambiguous. It is one thing to conceptualize dimensions of what parents desire in their children. It is quite another to connect such values to actual parenting and parental approaches to raising their children. How do parents achieve the end-states manifest in their preferences for particular child qualities? Parents clearly differ in the manner by which they go about achieving what they value, and it is difficult to sort out the nature of the causal dynamics linking values and behavior. Indeed, the classic statement of the inherent implausibility of any causal interpretation was made by Kohn (1969, 146), who noted that the punishment of children by spanking illustrates how difficult it is to link a particular mode of child rearing to any particular parental value orientation. Parents may spank children regardless of whether they value autonomy or obedience—it is the reason behind the punishment that gives clues as to the nature of the parental value, not the behavior itself.

On the other hand, some would argue that punitiveness, as a child rearing approach, is an embodiment of certain values for obedience. How is behavior linked to values, if it is not a reflection of underlying values, or if they are not reflections of the same underlying phenomenon? It is useful in this regard to consider the approach taken by Diana Baumrind (1989, 1991a, 1991b), who defines certain pure types of parental behavior in a fourfold classification based on the dimensions of parental demandingness and parental responsiveness. Baumrind contrasts parental behavior that is "authoritarian" (behavior that is demanding and directive, but not responsive, stressing obedience and respect for authority) with that which is "authoritative" (behavior that is both demanding and responsive, assertive, but not intrusive or restrictive). According to Baumrind (1989, 1991a, 1991b), this classification describes how parents reconcile their approach to the joint needs of children for nurturance and limit-setting. The definitions of the four types are as follows (see Baumrind 1991a):

Authoritarian—Parents who are demanding and directive, but not responsive. They are obedience and status oriented, expecting their orders to be obeyed without explanation. They provide an orderly environment and a clear set of regulations, monitoring their children's activities carefully.

Authoritative—Parents who are both demanding and responsive. They impart clear standards for their children's conduct. They are assertive, but not intrusive or restrictive. Their disciplinary methods are supportive rather than punitive. They want their children to be assertive as well as socially responsible, and self-regulated as well as cooperative.

Permissive—Nondirective parents who are more responsive than they are demanding. They are lenient, do not require mature behavior, allow considerable self-regulation, and avoid confrontation.

Rejecting-neglecting—Disengaged parents who are neither demanding nor responsive. They do not structure and monitor their children's behavior, and are not supportive. They may be actively rejecting or neglect their child rearing responsibilities altogether.

Although this scheme is intended to have broad applicability to the description of parents' behavior, Baumrind (1991a, 62) indicates that the "operational definitions of these four prototypes—authoritative, authoritarian, permissive, and rejecting-neglecting—differ somewhat depending on social context, developmental period, and method of assessment, but share certain essential features." There is a literature, primarily in human development, that has developed on the basis of Baumrind's work and argues that what is critical in child development with respect to parenting behavior involves the contrast in the behavior of parents who are authoritative versus authoritarian in their approach to children. According to this literature, the former are more likely to instill autonomy, as an aspect of competence, in children, the overall conclusion of which is that the success of authoritative parents can be measured in higher degrees of self-esteem and competence, and lower levels of juvenile delinquency and drug use, for example. An "authoritative upbringing" in contrast to an "authoritarian upbringing" consistently generates adolescent competence and deters problem behavior in both boys and girls at all developmental stages.

Elsewhere, Alwin (2001, 122–127) has shown how these various dimensions are related to parental values for autonomy versus obedience. Results show that high levels of autonomy and low levels of obedience are associated with the combination of low demandingness and low nurturance. Generally speaking, parents who score high on the measure of demandingness tend to prefer autonomy over obedience, but there is an interaction with the parental warmth dimension. This is particularly true for the trait "thinks for self" where there is a clear ordering of parenting styles. Those parents who are neither demanding nor supportive are the ones who emphasize "thinks for self" the most, followed by those who are high on nurturance and low on demandingness. The reverse pattern is true for measures of parental valuation of obedience. Those parents who are high on demandingness clearly prefer obedience in their children.

These results lend themselves to more than one interpretation. Are parental child rearing behaviors embodiments of parental values? Or are parental values merely a reflection of behavioral norms? There is certainly support for both such interpretations at a theoretical level, but there is no real empirical basis for ruling one or the other out. The important thing to take from this research is that there are predictable relationships among measures of parental behavior, as indicated by our operationalization of Baumrind's parenting styles, and parental values, as measured by Lenski's measure of parental values for autonomy versus obedience. We return to a discussion of these issues in a later section of the chapter, focusing on the linkage between religion and parenting, seeking to discover if there is any overall effect of religion on child developmental outcomes.

Historical Perspectives

There has been quite a lot written in recent years about changes in the European and American family going back over the past three or four centuries. While many of the family's institutional functions have remained the same over such lengthy spans of time—e.g., the family has continued to be the primary agent for the care and nurture of children—the nature of parent–child relationships have experienced some significant changes (Vinovskis 1987; French 2002). One needs to exact a certain degree of care in approaching the historical literature on the nature of the family and parent–child interactions, as historians often lack a direct empirical portal into the past. History is always written from the point of view of the present and of the writer. There is often a tendency to perceive different periods of time in terms of an evolution of stages, whereas in fact the temporal continuities and discontinuities may not be driven by any such evolutionary mechanisms (Thornton 2001). We nonetheless find a great deal of value in what historians of the family have to say about historical contrasts in parental practices because it alerts us to the potential for change in the environments in which children and parents interact and some of the explanations for change in the child rearing orientations of some religious groups.

One does not have to look very far into the past to see some changes in parental orientations to children. The recognition of this fact should help signify that the potential for change in parental practices over long spans of time can be great. Wrigley (1989) performed a content analysis of child rearing manuals published in the United States over the twentieth century and found that the professional advice of child experts has changed from a preoccupation with such things as nutrition and toilet-training toward a greater emphasis on the need for cognitive development. These results are complemented by Alwin's (1996) use of several different sources of survey data over the twentieth century that show significant changes have occurred in Western countries in the values they emphasize in raising their children. There is a fairly clear pattern of increasing preferences for an emphasis that stresses the autonomy of children and a decline in the valuation of obedience. Over the periods and settings studied, parental orientations to children changed from a concentration on fitting children into society to one of providing for children in a way that would enhance their development (see Alwin 1984, 1988, 1989, 1996, 2006).

Looking back even further, the historical literature has suggested that there have been major changes in the role of parents in the socialization of children from medieval times onward. In one of the most cited works on the history of childhood, Ariès (1962) argued that during the medieval period the boundaries between the household and the rest of society were relatively less rigidly defined than they are in their modern Western counterparts and this had major implications for the parental responsibility in the socialization of children. Relationships within the nuclear family were not necessarily closer than those outside and there was greater reliance on neighbors, relatives and friends in the monitoring of children's behavior (see also Stone 1977; Vinovskis 1987). This may have been a consequence as much as anything else of smaller, more closely spaced living quarters.

Parenting practices depend (among other things) upon beliefs about the nature of children, and not only has the perception of the nature of childhood itself undergone dramatic change over long periods of history, this is an area where religious groups may differ dramatically in their beliefs. Ariès (1962) argued that in the Middle Ages, due in part to high rates of infant mortality, mothers were indifferent to their infants and did not display a great deal of grief if they died. He argued additionally that the discipline of children was often harsh and that this lack of affection for children continued until the sixteenth and seventeenth centuries. In the eighteenth and nineteenth centuries, according to Ariès (1962), there emerged the development of the idea of the individuality of children, the acceptance of their inherent worth, and the emergence of an awareness of the innocence and purity of childhood. Not everyone agrees with the Ariès's (1962) thesis. Indeed, his claims sparked a debate among historians and others on this issue, encouraging further empirical examination of ideas about childhood (see Heywood 2001). For example, Pollock's (1983) examination of diaries among the educated classes of England across the sixteenth through the nineteenth centuries casts considerable doubt on the assumption of maternal indifference to children during that period. And others (e.g., Shorter 1975) have argued that the harsh treatment of children persisted into the eighteenth and nineteenth centuries among all social classes in Western Europe.

On the other hand, Lesthaeghe (1995) points to the Enlightenment near the end of the eighteenth century, which he refers to as one of the most important ideational legacies of Western history, as redefining the position of the individual relative to society, legitimizing the principle of individual freedom of choice. Twentieth-century changes, which he refers to as the "second demographic transition," have continued to produce greater emphasis on individualism, and other changes in the family (e.g., the legitimation of nonmarital cohabitation, rising ages of first marriage, voluntary childlessness, sexual freedom, rises in divorce, and the demand for abortion) can be seen as part of the larger picture of social change in the direction of religious secularization and the rise of individualism. What is central to Lesthaeghe's (1995) conceptualization is that educational institutions are of major importance, especially given that educational elites are on the vanguard of social change, and that the long-term trends toward individualism and away from institutional control are due to "generational" differences, or more precisely to processes of cohort socialization in young adulthood (Alwin and McCammon 2003). His research shows that for a number of indicators, including measures of values regarding parental emphasis on the autonomy and obedience of children, there is some tangible evidence of cohort differences. Compared to earlier-born cohorts (born in 1936 or before), the later-born cohorts (born after 1936) showed much greater preference for an emphasis on the imagination and independence of children and lesser preference for social conformity and obedience to traditional institutional authority. Lesthaeghe's (1995) results pertain more generally to cohort differences in values across several domains of social life experiences, including marriage, the family, work, religion, and sociopolitical orientations. He argues that these intercohort differences in value orientations reflect historically specific sets of conditions, resulting in a permanent ideational or cultural imprinting that generates a momentum of its own. Thus, with each new generation there are potentially different value orientations, absorbed from the historical milieu during youthful socialization, which tend to persist over time (see Alwin 1989, 1996b, 2006).

We have argued that it is important to place the topic of religion and parental orientations in American society in a historical perspective, both because it is clear that contemporary religious differences in child rearing orientations have their origins in religious traditions, and because secular changes in society potentially have an impact on doctrinal differences that in turn affect orientations to children. Nowhere is this clearer than in historian Philip Greven's (1973, 1977) treatment of the differences in patterns of child rearing among Protestant religious traditions. Greven (1977, 17) begins with the assumption, unlike many other historians, that "there never was a single consistent set of beliefs or one mode of piety characteristic of Protestants anywhere at any time." He argues that the "distinctive expressions of temperament" found in the public writings of religious men and women are "sufficiently distinctive as to be visible and significant factors in the historical experiences of people" in the Anglo-American societies.

Greven's argument stresses the continuities in methods of child rearing over long periods of time that are linked to what he calls particular types of "religious temperaments." He identifies three modes of religious thought: (a) Evangelical, (b) Moderate, and (c) Genteel Protestants, which he argues were characterized by distinctive "modes of child rearing" and orientations to children. He links the Evangelical Protestants to authoritarian modes of child rearing, Moderate Protestants to authoritative modes of childrearing, and the Genteel Protestants to affectionate modes of child rearing. He argues these divergences in approaches to child rearing can be found in American Protestantism throughout the seventeenth, eighteenth, and nineteenth centuries. These enduring themes, he argues, transcend time and space, and even denominations, and reflect clear differences among religious groups. His linkage of these patterns of religious thought to three distinctive modes of child rearing—authoritarian, authoritative, and affectionate—correspond nicely to some of those articulated by Baumrind (1989, 1991a, 1991b), about which more will be said later, but what is particularly interesting in the present context is his explicit attempt to relate these parenting styles to types of religious orientation.

Contemporary Differences among Religious Groups

It is not at all surprising that we can identify these various modes of child rearing in historical materials connected with religious groups over past centuries. Greven's (1973, 1977) exhaustive examination of letters and diaries expressing how men and women of past centuries reared their children, how they chose to feed, to clothe, to discipline, and to educate their children, provides a unique portal into the past, and provides a framework for understanding recent research on religion and child rearing. The question for our present discussion is whether and to what extent these connections between religious views and child rearing are present in contemporary society. Here we consider the research literature that has developed over the past forty to fifty years on the topic of religion and child rearing; however, we must abandon the methods of the historian for the methods of social science. Using survey data, we focus on the persistence of religious differentiation in child rearing orientations.

Parental Child Rearing Beliefs and Values

We have noted at several points in this discussion that the term "child rearing" is quite broad and refers to several distinct phenomena. The literature on this topic includes the study of child rearing beliefs, value orientations, parenting styles, and quite specific kinds of parenting practices, such as the use of corporal punishment. One of the key concepts employed in the recent literature on religion and child rearing is the concept of values. Contemporary interest in parental values originated in the work of Gerhard Lenski (1961) on the "religious factor," which advanced a claim for Protestant–Catholic differences in a range of areas of life. Focusing specifically on the family, Lenski argued that the religious views of American Catholics and their traditional orientation to defining family relationships fostered greater dependence on the kinship system, greater adherence to religious institutions, and a greater reliance on institutionalized doctrine than was true for American Protestants. Lenski theorized that the different value orientations of Catholics and Protestants manifested themselves in a variety of economic and family contexts, and his research devoted considerable attention to these differences in several aspects of family life, including kinship relationships, orientations to child rearing, and fertility behavior.

With regard to child rearing, Lenski's research suggested that Catholics were more traditional than Protestants in their orientations to children and held values that put more emphasis on obedience to authority than on personal autonomy or self-direction. Catholics were reportedly more likely than Protestants to use physical punishment, less likely to encourage a future orientation in their children, and more likely to exact obedience from them. Using data from a probability sample of the Detroit metropolitan area in 1958, Lenski (1961) examined some of these issues empirically, and one of the central findings of his original research, which received considerable attention later on, involved his analysis of patterns of parental values for autonomy (thinking for oneself) versus conformity (or obedience to adult authority). He examined a measure of this contrast in values across categories defined by social class and religio-ethnic differences, and concluded that in virtually every category of socioeconomic position, Catholics had the least preference for autonomy relative to obedience.

Lenski (1971) later suggested that these differences may have converged in the years following the second Vatican Council, and Alwin (1984, 1986) verified this using comparable data from the Detroit metropolitan area, involving probability samples in 1971 and 1983. Alwin's (1986) conclusion was that few if any differences remained between Protestants and Catholics in a range of measures of values and orientations to children and the family. He raised the possibility that religious identities (denominations)—particularly Catholic versus Protestant differences—might no longer matter for adult values for children, and that "although there has been a gradual convergence of values among American Protestants and Catholics in the aggregate, there are other dimensions of importance arising from the religious context" (Alwin 1986, 435–436). He noted the claim in the literature up to that time that Protestants with "more fundamentalist orientations are more distinctive in values and religious practices" and examined differences among Protestant groups. He reported that "fundamentalists prefer less autonomy and greater obedience," but these differences were not statistically significant (see Alwin 1986, 435). A reanalysis of these data using improved measures of fundamentalist and nonfundamentalist Protestantism shows that these differences among fundamentalists and nonfundamentalists are in fact significant (Alwin and Felson 2004).

Beginning in 1986, the General Social Survey (GSS) (see Davis and Smith 2003) included the Lenski (1961) measures of parental values and this set of measures has been included in twelve successive GSS studies from 1986 to 2002.

Using the 1988 GSS data, Ellison and Sherkat (1993b) found that conservative Protestants are significantly different from nonconservative Protestants in placing a greater emphasis on desiring obedience in children. They found, however, that conservative Protestants were no less enthusiastic than others about intellectual autonomy in children. Their analysis revealed that the valuation conservative Protestants placed on obedience was related to three theological positions—Biblical literalism, belief in human nature as sinful, and punitive attitudes toward sinners.

One of the novel findings in Alwin's (1986) research was that "generic religiosity" may be increasingly important, and more so than denominational identity differences per se. Specifically, Alwin (1986: 435–436) found that "religious participation," i.e., church attendance, was related to parental values. He reported that "parents who participate in church activities more frequently, regardless of denomination, (were) significantly more likely to value obedience in their children relative to other qualities . . . (and that) the magnitude of the relationship was considerable stronger than the relationships (between) parental values and (denomination)." Alwin (1986: 436) concluded that "there is greater variation within major denominational categories than between them and that attitudes and values are linked to other important dimensions of religious behavior," particularly church attendance.

In a recent replication of Alwin's (1986) analysis of his 1983 Detroit data, along with parallel analyses of Lenski's 1958 Detroit data, and two additional Detroit studies, a 1971 survey conducted by Duncan, Schuman, and Duncan (1973) and a 1988 survey conducted by Alwin (n.d.), we examined these issues (Alwin and Felson 2004). These results provide support for several conclusions: (a) the distinctiveness of Catholics from white nonfundamentalist Protestants is apparent only in the 1958 survey—where Catholics are less likely to prefer think over obey—which is consistent with Lenski's (1961) results, and never thereafter, as shown by Alwin (1986) previously for the 1971 and 1983 surveys; (b) in the 1971, 1983, and 1988 surveys, members of fundamentalist Protestant groups reveal a persistently greater preference for obedience relative to autonomy in children, findings consistent with Alwin (1986) and Ellison and Sherkat (1993b); (c) black Protestants, regardless of whether they are fundamentalist or nonfundamentalist, show consistently greater preferences for obedience relative to autonomy in children in all surveys from 1971 onward, a result that is consistent with Alwin's (1984, 1986) previous analysis of the 1971 and 1983 data; and (d) higher frequency of church attendance leads to a greater preference for obedience relative to autonomy across all years, at a level that appears to be systematically increasing with time.

Parental Behavior and Parenting Styles

As noted earlier, it is not readily apparent how parental values and other beliefs about children are linked to behavior and intentions and in some instances the relationships can be ambiguous. It is one thing to conceptualize dimensions of what parents desire in their children and it is another to connect such values to actual parenting and parental approaches to raising their children. In the earlier discussion we suggested that there may be a great deal to be gained through attention to the approach taken by Diana Baumrind (1989, 1991a, 1991b), who contrasted parental behavior that is "authoritarian" (behavior that is demanding and directive, but not responsive, stressing obedience and respect for authority) with that which is "authoritative" (behavior that is both demanding and responsive, assertive, but not intrusive or restrictive). Both of these parenting styles stress high degrees of parental demandingness and control but differ in their extent of punitiveness. Virtually no attention has focused on contrasts between Baumrind's other ideal types—the "permissive" or the so-called "rejecting/neglecting" parental styles.

A growing body of literature has focused on the distinctive child rearing beliefs and behavior of conservative Protestants. In a study of popular advice manuals for parents, Bartkowski and Ellison (1995) compared the recommendations of mainstream child rearing experts with those advanced by their conservative Protestant counterparts. Their analysis suggests that fundamentalist and evangelical authors are distinctive in four main areas: (a) their long-term parenting goals—emphasizing "authority training" that prepares them for righteousness and salvation, rather than simply "healthy" personalities and social competence; (b) the structure of parent–child relations—presenting a strong preference for hierarchical (rather than egalitarian) parent–child relations; (c) the definition of parental roles—expressing a marked preference for well-defined, gendered parental roles; and (d) strategies of child discipline and punishment that emphasize the use of corporal punishment (Bartkowski and Ellison 1995).

As we also noted earlier, the distinction between "authoritarian" versus "authoritative" parenting was also stressed in Greven's (1977) historical analysis of the differences among Protestant groups in colonial America. Interestingly, this contrast has been the focus of a considerable amount of research on the disciplinary practices of conservative Protestants over the past several years, and there is increasing support for the view that conservative Protestants are disproportionately more likely to endorse and use corporal punishment in child rearing (Bartkowski 1995; Bartkowski and Ellison 1995; Ellison and Bartkowski 1995; Ellison and Sherkat 1993a; Ellison, Bartkowski, and Segal 1996a, 1996b; Gershoff, Miller, and Holden 1999). The use of physical punishment in child rearing is a controversial matter, as severe forms of such punishment can be considered abusive and can have harmful effects (Miller 1990; Greven 1990; Daro and Gelles 1992; Straus 1994; Ellison 1996).

Research on this topic was stimulated in part by Ellison and Sherkat's (1993a) analysis of data in the GSS on approval of child discipline using "a good hard spanking" (Davis and Smith 2003). They argued that the approval of corporal punishment would be disproportionately higher among conservative Protestants, reflecting their greater adherence to the doctrine of Biblical literalism, the conviction that human nature and the nature of children was inherently sinful, and the belief that sin demands punishment. Using GSS data from 1988, Ellison and Sherkat (1993a) found weak but significant relationships among their variables of interest. However, due to the questionable causal assumptions involved in their analyses, and due to the attitudinal nature of their data, they called for more research on religious differences in the practice of physical discipline (Ellison and Sherkat 1993a, 141).

Several analyses of data from the National Survey of Families and Households (NSFH) followed their call. Using the 1987–1988 NSFH data on parents, Ellison, Bartkowski, and Segal (1996a, 1996b) found that persons with conservative Protestant denominational identities reported to have engaged in more physical punishment than parents with less conservative denominational identities. They examined the extent to which these effects could be explained with reference to conservative scriptural beliefs (i.e., "The Bible is God's word and everything happened or will happen exactly as it says"), and authority-minded parental values. Generally, they were able to account for the conservative and nonconservative Protestant differences in the use of corporal punishment by controlling for these factors.

Bartkowski and Wilcox (2000) studied the extent to which parents yell at their children as a key indicator of an authoritarian style of parenting. They reviewed two kinds of evidence on this issue. First, they examined parenting advice from conservative Protestant elites, who advocate physical punishment of children, but who discourage yelling at children. Second, they examined data from the NSFH, finding that parents of preschool and school-age children who have conservative Protestant denominational identities are significantly less likely than others to report yelling at their children. Using a measure of theological conservatism (based on respondents' beliefs about the inerrancy of the Bible and a belief that the Bible provides answers to human problems), they partially accounted for the distinctiveness of the conservative Protestants' reported absence of parental yelling.

Two categories in Baumrind's taxonomy of parenting types—authoritarian and authoritative—both included parents who were demanding and directive, but where the authoritarian approach was punitive in nature, the authoritative was high in responsiveness. In order to test the hypothesis that conservative Protestants are distinctive in this additional aspect of authoritative parenting, Wilcox (1998) examined data from the NSFH. He argued that while conservative Protestant child rearing is characterized by strict discipline, this approach is also accompanied by an "unusually warm and expressive style of parent–child interaction" (Wilcox 1998, 796). He found that respondents who identify with conservative Protestant denominations are more likely to praise and hug their children than parents with nonconservative Protestant denominational identities. He also found that the core religious ideology of conservative Protestant churches (measured using a composite of "The Bible is God's word and everything happened or will happen exactly as it says" and "The Bible is the answer to all important human problems") is a more important predictor of parental responsiveness and accounts for some of the effect of denominational identity. On this basis Wilcox (1998) suggested that the "portrait that has recently emerged of a strict parenting style among conservative Protestants should be modified." While Wilcox acknowledged that "conservative Protestant parents are more likely to rely on corporal punishment," he points out that "they are (also) more likely than other parents to practice warm and expressive emotion work with their children" (Wilcox 1998, 807). He argues, therefore, that rather than being authoritarian or authoritative, conservative Protestant parenting lies somewhere in between. These results are reinforced by Bartkowski and Xu's (2000) findings that conservative Protestant fathers combine a strict approach to discipline with a parenting style in nondisciplinary situations that is nurturing and responsive.

The results reviewed here provide a mixed picture of the relationship between religion and child rearing behavior. On the one hand, research on physical punishment (e.g., Bartkowski and Ellison 1995; Ellison, Bartkowski, and Segal 1996a, 1996b; Ellison and Bartkowski 1995) not only reinforces findings from Greven's (1977) historical analysis about the parenting styles of persons with conservative religious orientations, but also suggests that some aspects of a punitive orientation thought to be a part of an authoritarian parenting style, e.g., parental yelling, are not found to be more prevalent among conservative Protestants (Bartkowski and Wilcox 2000). Moreover, some nurturing aspects of parenting styles, namely parental responsiveness, are found to be more prevalent in these groups (Wilcox 1998; Bartkowski and Xu 2000; Bartkowski and Ellison 2009). Although critics, such as Greven (1990), worry that conservative Protestant ideologies legitimate authoritarian and abusive child rearing practices, such concerns may be exaggerated. Ellison (1996) argues, for example, that religious child rearing manuals offer careful advice on how to administer mild-to-moderate corporal punishment.

Implications for Child Development

This section of the chapter focuses on the consequences of religion for child outcomes linked to development. By child outcomes we refer to any differences in well-being, personality, values, preferences, interests, skills, accomplishments, ways of behaving, and the like. There are three broad categories of possible ways that differences among families—or "between-family" differences—can produce individual differences in child outcomes. These explanations are: (a) families can differ in the opportunities for development of particular outcomes; (b) families can differ in genetic endowments that contribute to the development of particular outcomes; or (c) families can differ in the way in which they nurture or socialize their children. These three explanations do not address the possibility that there are "within-family" differences in parenting practices that contribute to child outcomes, an important topic but one that will be ignored in this review. The problem with sorting out these various explanations is that the key explanatory factors highlighted by each category are correlated with one another. If genetic differences between families have educational and socioeconomic consequences for children, then they are likely to be related, for example, to the factors that shape differential opportunity structures. Parental socialization practices are linked to family differences in opportunities for their children and may not be adding anything independent to the explanation of individual differences in developmental outcomes; their role may be primarily one of mediating the effects of other (genetic and environmental) differences among families.

Explanation of family differences by theories of socialization propose that differences in child outcomes stem not from family differences in opportunities afforded by favorable environments or genes, but from differences in parenting practices. The question for this review is to ask whether the literature suggests an overall effect of religious differentiation in socialization practices that may have a differential impact on developmental outcomes. Baumrind's (1991a, 91) study of adolescent outcomes indicates that more than any other type, "the success of authoritative parents in protecting their adolescents from problem drug use and in generating competence should be emphasized." She suggests that "authoritative upbringing" consistently generates adolescent competence and deters problem behavior in both boys and girls at all developmental stages. Other researchers have reinforced this conclusion (see. e.g., Darling and Steinberg 1993; Steinberg et al. 1995; Steinberg and Silk 2002).

The preceding review indicates that conservative Protestant parents stress authoritative parenting, along with corporal punishment, to a greater extent than other religious groups. To the extent that Baumrind's results can be generalized to this group, these results support the idea that there may be a salutary effect of a conservative Protestant upbringing. In addition, there is a literature that suggests that attendance at religious services and other activities sponsored by religious organizations is linked to better health and less risk-taking (see review by Regnerus and Smith 2005), but whether these activities result from parental behaviors, or any particular type of parenting, is not answered by this research (e.g., Bartkowski, Xu, and Levin 2008). Positive involvement of parents with children in such activities may have predictably salutary effects on child outcomes. For example, Wilcox (2002), using data from the NSFH, found that religion is related to father involvement in several areas of family activity: one-on-one engagement, dinner with one's family, and volunteering for youth-related activities. He argues these effects can be accounted for by the specific attention that religious institutions devote to family life.

At the same time, the use of physical punishment in child rearing is a controversial matter, as severe forms of such punishment can be considered abusive and can have harmful effects (e.g., Bugental, Martorell, and Barraza 2003; Strassberg et al. 1994). Corporal punishment may be highly stressful for children, especially at younger ages, and increasingly the results of research on neurobiological processes suggests that stressful experiences in childhood can have negative long-term consequences for healthy development (Bremner and Narayan 1998; Cicchetti and Rogosch 2001a, 2001b; Glaser 2000; Sapolsky 1996). The question is, of course, whether the forms of physical punishment referred to earlier induce stressful experiences.

Recent unpublished research by Ellison, Musick, and Holden (1999) addresses these issues in outlining a series of arguments suggesting that religion, and specifically a conservative Protestant background, may moderate the effects of spanking on children's well-being. Because parental use of corporal punishment is viewed as an indication of parental engagement, and because there are often concrete guidelines intended to buffer any potentially negative effects (e.g., parental anger and loss of control), it is likely that corporal punishment is practiced differently, and interpreted differently, within conservative Protestant faith communities. Using panel data from the NSFH, Ellison, Musick, and Holden (1999) found that there are no significant long-term effects of parental use of corporal punishment on measures of emotional problems or aggressive behavior for children from conservative Protestant backgrounds. These analyses support the conclusion that religion buffers the link between corporal punishment and negative child outcomes.

Discussion and Conclusion

Although there are clear secular shifts in the direction of granting greater individual freedom and autonomy to children, there also seems to be plenty of support for the idea that some religious groups depart from this overall trend and that religious differentiation is related to child rearing approaches. These patterns are largely consistent with expectations based in the historical literature, particularly the writings of Philip Greven (1973, 1977), who identified more conservative approaches to piety with orientations to children that emphasize adherence to the dictates of authority and corporal forms of punishment. In looking over the contemporary American religious landscape, it is apparent that adherents to conservative Protestantism place more emphasis on obedience than on autonomy in children. They also place a great deal of faith in physical punishment in achieving their parenting objectives. At the same time, some aspects of punitiveness, e.g., parental yelling, often thought to be a part of an authoritarian parenting style, are not found to be more prevalent among conservative Protestants, and relevant studies have found significantly higher levels of certain nurturing aspects of parenting styles among conservatives.

These practices square with evidence from conservative Protestant child rearing manuals that rather than legitimizing authoritarian and abusive parenting styles emphasize the use of mild-to-moderate corporal punishment (see Bartkowski and Ellison 2009).

This would be primarily of sheer academic interest if there were no discernable consequences of subgroup child rearing practices for the children themselves. Except in the case of severely abusive forms of punishment, we do not yet know enough to draw firm conclusions about the consequences of physical discipline on children's development. However, there is enough tangible evidence of the possible relationship between physical punishment and stress-induced neurobiological outcomes to support further inquiry into the effects of such child rearing practices on child development. Measurement to date of the potentially harmful consequences of physical punishment rests on self-reports, and has not employed relevant biomarker techniques (e.g., Schwartz et al. 1998). The emergence of conservative religious doctrine as a powerful institutional force in contemporary life (Smith et al. 1998; Sherkat and Ellison 1999; Woodberry and Smith 1998), along with its distinctive emphasis on the physical punishment of children, offers new opportunities for the development of research strategies that are commensurate with the challenges involved in measuring the consequences of religion for the lives of children.

NOTE

The authors gratefully acknowledge the McCourtney endowment, College of the Liberal Arts, Pennsylvania State University, in the support of this research, and the suggestions of Chris Ellison and John Bartkowski on previous drafts of this chapter.

REFERENCES

Alwin, D. F. 1984. "Trends in Parental Socialization Values: Detroit, 1958 to 1983." *American Journal of Sociology* 90:359–382.

———. 1986. "Religion and Parental Child rearing Orientations: Evidence of a Catholic–Protestant Convergence." *American Journal of Sociology* 92:412–440.

———. 1988. "From Obedience to Autonomy: Changes in Traits Desired in Children." *Public Opinion Quarterly* 52:33–52.

———. 1989. "Cohort Replacement and Parental Socialization Values." *Journal of Marriage and the Family* 52:347–360.

———. 1994. "Aging, Personality and Social Change: The Stability of Individual Differences over the Adult Life Span." In *Life Span Development and Behavior, Volume 12D*, ed. L. Featherman, R. M. Lerner, and M. Perlmutter, 135–185. Hillsdale, NJ: Lawrence Erlbaum Associates.

———. 1996a. "From Childbearing to Childrearing: The Link between Declines in Fertility and Changes in the Socialization of Children." *Population and Development Review* 22:S176–S196.

———. 1996b. "Parental Socialization in Historical Perspective." In *The Parental Experience at Midlife*, ed. C. Ryff and M. M. Seltzer, 105–167. Chicago: University of Chicago Press.

———. 2001. "Parental Values, Beliefs, and Behavior: A Review and Promulga for Research into the New Century." In *Children at the Millennium: Where Have We Come From, Where Are We Going?* ed. S. J. Hofferth and T. J. Owens, 97–139. New York: JAI Press.

———. 2005. "Attitudes, Beliefs and Childbearing." In *The New Population Problem: Why Families in Developed Countries are Shrinking and What It Means*, ed. A. Booth and A. C. Crouter, 115–126. Mahwah, NJ: Lawrence Erlbaum Associates.

———. 2006. "The Disciplined Self: Transformations of Child Rearing in American Society Over the Twentieth Century." Unpublished manuscript. Population Research Institute, Pennsylvania State University.

———. n.d. "Religion in Detroit, 1958 to 1988." Unpublished paper. Survey Research Center, University of Michigan, Ann Arbor, MI, 48106.

Alwin, D. F., and J. L. Felson. 2004. "The Religious Factor Revisited: Religious Identities, Behavior and Parental Values for Children." Paper presented at the ninety-ninth annual meetings of the American Sociological Association, San Francisco.

Alwin, D. F., and R. J. McCammon. 2003. "Generations, Cohorts and Social Change." In *Handbook of the Life Course*, ed. J. T. Mortimer and M. Shanahan, 2–49. New York: Kluwer Academic/Plenum Publishers.

Ariès, P. 1962. *Centuries of Childhood: A Social History of Family Life*. New York: Knopf.

Bartkowski, J. P. 1995. "Spare the Rod . . . or Spare the Child? Divergent Perspectives on Conservative Protestant Child Discipline." *Review of Religious Research* 37:97–116.

Bartkowski, J. P., and C. G. Ellison. 1995. "Divergent Perspectives on Childrearing in Popular Manuals: Conservative Protestants vs. the Mainstream Experts." *Sociology of Religion* 56:21–34.

———. 2009. "Conservative Protestants on Children and Parenting." In *Children and Childhood in American Religions*, ed. B. Miller-McLemore and D. Browning, 42–55. New Brunswick, NJ: Rutgers University Press.

Bartkowski, J. P., and W. B. Wilcox. 2000. "Conservative Protestant Child Discipline: The Case of Parental Yelling." *Social Forces* 79:265–290.

Bartkowski, J. P., and X. Xu. 2000. "Distant Patriarchs or Expressive Dads? The Discourse and Practice of Fathering in Conservative Protestants Families." *Sociological Quarterly* 41:865–885.

Bartkowski, J. P., X. Xu, and M. L. Levin. 2008. "The Impact of Religion on Child Development: Evidence from the Early Childhood Longitudinal Study." *Social Science Research* 37: 18–36.

Baumrind, D. 1989. "Rearing Competent Children." In *Child Development Today and Tomorrow*, ed. W. Damon, 349–378. San Francisco: Jossey-Bass.

———. 1991a. "The Influence of Parenting Style on Adolescent Competence and Substance Use." *Journal of Early Adolescence* 11:56–95.

———. 1991b. "Parenting Styles and Adolescent Development." In *Encyclopedia of Adolescence*, ed. R. M. Lerner, A. C. Peterson and J. Brooks-Gunn, 758–772. New York: Garland.

Bornstein, M. H. 2002. *Handbook of Parenting, Volumes 1–5*. Mahwah, NJ: Lawrence Erlbaum.

Bremner, J. D., and M. Narayan. 1998. "The Effects of Stress on Memory and the Hippocampus Throughout the Life Cycle: Implications for Child Development and Aging." *Development and Psychopathology* 10:871–885.

Bugental, D. B., G. A. Martorell, and V. Barraza. 2003. "The Hormonal Costs of Subtle Forms of Infant Maltreatment." *Hormones and Behavior* 43:237–244.

Cicchetti, D., and F. A. Rogosch. 2001a. "Diverse Patterns of Neuroendocrine Activity in Maltreated Children." *Development and Psychopathology* 13:677–693.

———. 2001b. "The Impact of Child Maltreatment and Psychopathology on Neuroendocrine Functioning." *Development and Psychopathology* 13:783–804.

Coleman, J. S. 1990. *Foundations of Social Theory*. Cambridge, MA: Belknap Press of the Harvard University Press.

Darling, N., and L. Steinberg. 1993. "Parenting Style as Context: An Integrative Model." *Psychological Bulletin* 113:487–496.

Daro, D., and R. J. Gelles. 1992. "Public Attitudes and Behaviors with Respect to Child Abuse Prevention." *Journal of Interpersonal Violence* 7:517–531.

Davis, J. A., and T. W. Smith. 2003. *General Social Surveys, 1972–2002: Cumulative Codebook*. Chicago: National Data for the Social Sciences at the National Opinion Research Center.

Duncan, O. D., H. Schuman, and B. Duncan. 1973. *Social Change in a Metropolitan Community*. New York: Russell Sage Foundation.

Duvall, E. M. 1946. "Conceptions of Parenthood." *American Journal of Sociology* 57: 193–203.

Ellison, C. G. 1996. "Conservative Protestantism and the Corporal Punishment of Children: Clarifying the Issues." *Journal for the Scientific Study of Religion* 35:1–16.

Ellison, C. G., J. P. Bartkowski, and M. L. Segal. 1996a. "Conservative Protestantism and the Parental Use of Corporal Punishment." *Social Forces* 74:1003–1028.

———. 1996b. "Do Conservative Protestant Parents Spank More Often? Further Evidence from the National Survey of Families and Households." *Social Science Quarterly* 77:663–673.

Ellison, C. G., M. A. Musick, and G. W. Holden. 1999. "The Effects of Corporal Punishment on Children: Are They Less Harmful for Conservative Protestants?" Paper presented at the annual meeting of the Society for the Scientific Study of Religion, Boston, MA.

Ellison, C. G., and D. E. Sherkat. 1993a. "Conservative Protestantism and Support for Corporal Punishment." *American Sociological Review* 58:131–144.

———. 1993b. "Obedience and Autonomy: Religion and Parental Values Reconsidered." *Journal for the Scientific Study of Religion* 32:313–329.

French, V. 2002. "History of Parenting: The Ancient Mediterranean World." In *Handbook of Parenting: Biology and Ecology of Parenting*, 2nd ed., vol. 2, ed. M. H. Bornstein, 345–376. Mahwah, NJ: Lawrence Erlbaum.

Gershoff, E. T., P. C. Miller, and George W. Holden. 1999. "Parenting Influences from the Pulpit: Religious Affiliation as a Determinant of Parental Corporal Punishment." *Journal of Family Psychology* 13:307–320.

Glaser, D. 2000. "Child Abuse and Neglect and the Brain—A Review." *Journal of Child Psychology and Psychiatry* 41:97–116.

Greven, P. J., Jr. 1973. *Child Rearing Concepts, 1628–1861: Historical Sources*. Itasca, IL: F. E. Peacock.

———. 1977. *The Protestant Temperament: Patterns of Child Rearing, Religious Experience, and the Self in Early America*. New York: New American Library.

———. 1990. *Spare the Child: The Religious Roots of Punishment and the Psychological Impact of Physical Abuse*. New York: Knopf.

Heywood, C. 2001. *A History of Childhood: Children and Childhood in the West from Medieval to Modern Times*. Cambridge, UK: Polity Press.

Holden, G. W., and M. J. Buck. 2002. "Parental Attitudes toward Childrearing." In *Handbook of Parenting*, 2nd ed., vol. 3, ed. M. H. Bornstein, 537–562. Mahwah, NJ: Lawrence Erlbaum.

Kohn, M. L. 1969. *Class and Conformity: A Study in Values*. Homewood, IL: Dorsey Press.

Lenski, G. 1961. *The Religious Factor: A Sociological Study of Religion's Impact on Politics, Economics and Family Life*. Garden City, NY: Doubleday.

———. 1971. "The Religious Factor in Detroit Revisited." *American Sociological Review* 36:48–50.

Lesthaeghe, R. 1995. "The Second Demographic Transition in Western Countries: An Interpretation." In *Gender and Family Change in Industrialized Countries*, ed. K. O. Mason and A. M. Jensen, 17–62. Oxford: Clarendon Press.

LeVine, R. A., and M. White. 1986. *Human Conditions: The Cultural Basis for Educational Development*. London: Routledge and Kegan Paul.

———. 1987. "Parenthood in Social Transformation." In *Parenting across the Life Span: Biosocial Dimensions*, ed. J. B. Lancaster, J. Altmann, A. S. Rossi, and L. R. Sherrod, 271–293. New York: Aldine de Gruyter.

Lynd, R. S., and H. M. Lynd. 1929. *Middletown: A Study in Contemporary American Culture*. New York: Harcourt-Brace.

Miller, A. 1990. *For Your Own Good: Hidden Cruelty in Child Rearing and the Roots of Violence*. New York: Farrar, Straus and Giroux.

Miller, D. R., and G. E. Swanson. 1958. *The Changing American Parent*. New York: John Wiley.

Piaget, J. 1932. *The Moral Judgment of the Child*. New York: The Free Press.

Pollock, L. A. 1983. *Forgotten Children: Parent–Child Relations from 1500 to 1900*. Cambridge: Cambridge University Press.

Regnerus, M. D., and C. Smith. 2005. "Selection Effects in Studies of Religious Influence." *Review of Religious Research* 47:23–50.

Rokeach, M. 1970. *Beliefs, Attitudes and Values*. San Francisco: Jossey-Bass.

Sapolsky, R. M. 1996. "Why Stress Is Bad for Your Brain." *Science* 273:749–750.

Schaefer, E. 1987. "Parental Modernity and Child Academic Competence: Toward a Theory of Individual and Societal Development." *Early Child Development and Care* 27:373–389.

Schwartz, E. B., D. A. Granger, E. J. Susman, M. R. Gunnar, and B. Laird. 1998. "Assessing Salivary Cortisol in Studies of Child Development." *Child Development* 69:1503–1513.

Sherkat, D. E., and C. G. Ellison. 1999. "Recent Developments and Current Controversies in the Sociology of Religion." *Annual Review of Sociology* 25:363–394.

Shorter, E. 1975. *The Making of the Modern Family*. New York: Basic Books.

Smith, C., with M. Emerson, S. Gallagher, P. Kennedy, and D. Sikkink. 1998. *American Evangelicalism: Embattled and Thriving*. Chicago: University of Chicago Press.

Steinberg, L., N. E. Darling, and A. C. Fletcher. 1995. "Authoritative Parenting and Adolescent Adjustment: An Ecological Journey." In *Examining Lives in Context: Perspectives on the Ecology of Human Development*, ed. P. Moen, G. H. Elder, Jr., and K. Lüscher, 423–466. Washington, DC: American Psychological Association.

Steinberg, L., and J. S. Silk. 2002. "Parenting Adolescents." In *Handbook of Parenting*, 2nd ed., ed. M. H. Bornstein, 103–133. Mahwah, NJ: Lawrence Erlbaum.

Stone, L. 1977. *The Family, Sex and Marriage in England, 1500–1800*. New York: Oxford University Press.

Strassberg, Z., K. A. Dodge, G. S. Pettit, and J. E. Bates. 1994. "Spanking in the Home and Children's Subsequent Aggression toward Kindergarten Peers." *Development and Psychopathology* 6:445–461.

Straus, M. 1994. *Beating the Devil Out of Them: Corporal Punishment in American Families and Its Effects on Children*. Boston: Lexington Books.

Tamis-LeMonda, C. S., and N. Cabrera, eds. 2002. *Handbook of Father Involvement: Multidisciplinary Perspectives*. Mahwah, NJ: Lawrence Erlbaum Associates.

Thornton, A. 2001. "The Developmental Paradigm, Reading History Sideways, and Family Change." *Demography* 38:449–465.

Vinovskis, M. A. 1987. "Historical Perspectives on the Development of the Family and Parent–Child Interactions." In *Parenting across the Life Span—Biosocial Dimensions*, ed. J. B. Lancaster, J. Altmann, A. S. Rossi, and L. Sherrod, 295–314. New York: Aldine de Gruyter.

Wilcox, W. B. 1998. "Conservative Protestant Parenting: Authoritarian or Authoritative?" *American Sociological Review* 63:796–809.

———. 2002. "Religion, Convention, and Paternal Involvement." *Journal of Marriage and the Family* 64:780–792.

Woodberry, R. D., and C. S. Smith. 1998. "Fundamentalism et al.: Conservative Protestants in America." *Annual Review of Sociology* 24:25–56.

Wrigley, J. 1989. "Do Young Children Need Intellectual Stimulation? Experts' Advice to Parents, 1900–1985." *History of Education Quarterly* 29:41–75.

Zarit, S. H., and D. J. Eggebeen. 2002. "Parent–Child Relationships in Adulthood and Later Years." In *Handbook of Parenting*, 2nd ed., vol. 1, ed. M. H. Bornstein, 135–161. Mahwah, NJ: Lawrence Erlbaum.

Zelizer, V. A. 1985. *Pricing the Priceless Child: The Changing Social Value of Children*. New York: Basic Books.

4

▶ ▷ ▶ ▷ ▶ ▷ ▶ ▷ ▶ ▷ ▶ ▷ ▶ ▷ ◁ ◀ ◁ ◀ ◁ ◀ ◁ ◀ ◁ ◀ ◁ ◀ ◁ ◀

Religion and Adolescent
Sexual Behavior

MARK D. REGNERUS

In the United States, about 80 percent of young people experience sexual intercourse at some point during their teenage years (Singh and Darroch 1999). One important but poorly understood pathway that shapes sexual practice is religion and spirituality. There are numerous ways in which religion could affect adolescent sexuality and its practice, including contraceptive decisions, nonmarital sexual activities, and use of pornography. Religion can also influence sexual choices indirectly through its effects on friendship choices and dating patterns (Wallace and Williams 1997). Yet how religion in fact contributes to sexual values and behaviors is not well documented. Research on religion and adolescent sexual behavior is still considered "nascent . . . despite the fact that researchers have been conducting studies on the topic for at least four decades" (Whitehead, Wilcox, and Rostosky 2001, 46). This chapter takes a solid step in the direction of making the association of religion and adolescent sexuality clearer, drawing upon data from the National Longitudinal Study of Adolescent Health (Add Health) and the National Study of Youth and Religion (NSYR). I first highlight a number of the key recent studies in the field of religion and adolescent sexual behavior and then outline a conceptual framework by which religious influences on adolescent sexual behavior are typically understood. Finally, I address three research questions:

1. What are current levels of various sexual behaviors (e.g., virginity loss, oral sex, pornography use)?
2. Do these vary by religion—that is, religious affiliation, identity, and behaviors?
3. How does race/ethnicity moderate the association between religion and sexual behavior?

Research on Religion and Adolescent Sexual Behavior

Most studies of first sex find that more frequent attendance at religious services and greater religious salience tend to delay the timing of adolescents' first
experience of sexual intercourse (Brewster et al. 1998; Jones, Darroch, and Singh
2005; Ku, Sonenstein, and Pleck 1993; Lammers et al. 2000; Meier 2003). A number of studies examining denominational differences in timing of first sex have
found more diverse results than in studies of religiosity per se. Several investigators conclude that adolescents from evangelical, fundamentalist, or sectarian
(such as Mormon or Jehovah's Witness) backgrounds are more likely to delay
sex than other youth, especially compared to those from mainline Protestant
or nonreligious backgrounds (Miller and Olson 1988; Beck, Cole, and Hammond
1991). Catholics may be the most likely to remain virgins until marriage (Casper
1990), but some researchers dispute this conclusion (Thornton and Camburn
1989; Beck, Cole, and Hammond 1991), granting Jewish adolescents the distinction instead. A common problem in these studies, however, is that effects of
religious affiliation are often estimated and reported without controls for other
religion variables. Estimates of denominational differences in adolescent sex
often change with the addition of such controls.

There has also been a significant amount of talk recently about youth
preferring oral sex in order to maintain a "technical" virginity and to avoid
pregnancy and some types of sexually transmitted diseases (STDs) (Lewin 1997;
Remez 2000; Schuster, Bell, and Kanouse 1996). Scholars know much less about
this practice than they do about vaginal intercourse, but data are emerging. The
2002 National Survey of Family Growth reports that 40 percent of adolescent
boys age fifteen to seventeen have received oral sex and 28 percent have given it.
Among fifteen- to seventeen-year-old girls, 38 percent have received and 30 percent have given oral sex. Additionally, about 10 percent of girls and 13 percent
of boys age fifteen to seventeen have experienced heterosexual oral sex but not
vaginal intercourse (Mosher, Chandra, and Jones 2005). Yet no published study
of adolescents has focused on religious variations in experience of oral sex.

Finally, data on religion's influence on pornography use is limited as well,
although a strong connection between religiosity and the condemnation of
pornography has been noted (Sherkat and Ellison 1997). Religious organizations, sometimes in alliance with feminists, have commonly crusaded against
pornography. A descriptive study of Internet sex chat-room participants finds
that half of them report no religious affiliation and that religion holds no influence in their lives (Wysocki 2001). A recent study of the 2000 General Social
Survey (GSS) finds that the strongest predictors of Internet pornography use
(at least once a month) are weak ties to religion and the absence of a happy
marriage (Stack, Wasserman, and Kern 2004). Religion, the authors conclude,
works as a social control mechanism in helping prevent adult men from perus-
ing pornography.

Race, Religion, and Adolescent Sex

One of the more compelling issues in the area of adolescent sexual behavior is the intersection of religion, race, and sex. That is, we know that African American youth are, on average, more religiously devout than white youth (Johnston, Bachman, and O'Malley 1999). We also know that in spite of their higher religiosity, African American youth—especially males—also display consistently earlier transitions to sexual activity, a finding reported in many studies (e.g., Bearman and Brückner 2001; Marsiglio and Mott 1986). Over twenty years of research suggests that the association between religiousness and sexual behavior is weaker among African American adolescents than among whites (Benson, Donahue, and Erickson 1989). Overall, religion's influence on sex appears strongest (most protective) among white adolescent girls (Bearman and Brückner 2001; Benson, Donahue, and Erickson 1989). Among African American adolescent girls, religiosity is occasionally protective against sexual practice (McCree et al. 2003; Steinman and Zimmerman 2004). But evidence linking religion and sex among African American boys is slim. In fact, most recent studies note no effect of religiosity on patterns of sexual behavior among them (Bearman and Brückner 2001; Billy, Brewster, and Grady 1994; Cvetkovich and Grote 1980; Day 1992; Ku, Sonenstein, and Pleck 1993). And at least two studies find that more religious African American adolescent boys are in fact among the most likely to have had sex (Ku et al. 1998; Rostosky, Regnerus, and Wright 2003).

Indeed, the research literature on religion and adolescent sex is characterized by several critical limitations: work in this area has often been based on small or localized samples, cross-sectional data, antiquated measures of affiliation, and limited religious measures in general. Additionally, there are outcomes such as oral sex and Internet pornography use whose relationship with religion has never been systematically studied among adolescents. This chapter breaks considerable new ground in its investigation of the relationship between religion and sexual behavior, as I focus on racial/ethnic differences, understudied behaviors (e.g., oral sex), and a variety of religious sources of influence on both sexual attitudes and behavior.

Data and Measures

Data

Two sources of data are used: the first two waves of the Add Health study (1994 and 1995) and the first wave of the NSYR. Add Health is a current, large, nationally representative, longitudinal data source focusing on adolescents and young adults. The data include information on the important contexts in an adolescent's life: parents, schools, communities, friends, and romantic partners. Over-samples of Cubans, Puerto Ricans, Chinese, and high socioeconomic status blacks allow for the study of linkages between religion and sexual behaviors, motivations, and attitudes separately for African Americans, Latinos, Asian Americans, and non-Hispanic whites. The NSYR fielded a nationally random survey of thirteen- to seventeen-year-olds and their parents from 2002 to 2003. The survey also over-sampled households of ethnic and religious minorities, for a total of over 3,300 completed cases. Whereas Add Health specialized in measuring adolescent health outcomes and behaviors, the NSYR is strong in particularly religious behaviors, beliefs, and identities.

Measures

SEXUAL BEHAVIORS. A key strength of Add Health is its inclusion of an extensive range of questions about adolescent sexuality. I primarily assess virginity status at both waves of data collection. The NSYR also includes this variable (although question wording varies slightly) and I evaluate it cross-sectionally. Key variables such as oral sex and pornography use are only available in the NSYR. Pledging to abstain from sexual intercourse until marriage is also a salient factor in sexual decision-making, and measures of attitudes about pledging (NSYR) and actually pledging abstinence (Add Health) are each utilized here. Bearman and Brückner (2001) find that pledging effectively delays initiation of intercourse (an average of eighteen months) in schools where some students, but not too few or too many, take the pledge. The NSYR also includes a question about the merits of waiting until marriage to have sex. Finally, I construct a measure tapping the "sexual climate" in Add Health schools. This measure consists of each school's percent of respondents who report no longer being virgins (at Wave I).

RELIGION. Add Health's religion measures can be grouped into three different classes: religious involvement (public religiosity), salience of religious faith (private religiosity), and religious affiliation and identity. These measures were administered to the adolescent respondent at both waves, and to the respondent's parent at Wave I. Religious involvement is measured in two ways: the frequency of religious service attendance (parent and child), and the frequency of involvement in religious activities such as a youth group or choir (child). (Religious service attendance is the most commonly used indicator of religious involvement in most studies of adolescent behavior.) Salience of religious faith is measured by asking how important religion is to the respondent (parent and child). Four possible answers are available to them: not important, fairly unimportant, fairly important, or very important. While both Add Health and the NSYR include a measure of religious affiliation, the latter offers far more detailed categories than the former. Consistent with previous research (e.g., Roof and McKinney 1987; Steensland et al. 2000), I begin by recoding these denominations into several categories (conservative Protestant, mainline Protestant, Catholic, Jewish, Hindu, Muslim, etc.) as their representation in the samples permits. Additionally, the NSYR includes a number of unique religion and spirituality questions that I employ here, including to what degree respondents identify with the phrase "spiritual but not religious."

SELECTION EFFECTS AND CONTROLS. Observational data are limited in their ability to determine without doubt the direction of cause and effect between religion and the outcomes under consideration. In an effort to pursue statistical rigor, therefore, I include measures of potential "selection effects" where possible, primarily by the use of factors that may account for variance in both religion and sexual behavior outcomes. These include—besides age, race, region, and gender—measures of interest in risk-taking and an index of "strategic-ness" or "plan-fulness." The first is a single item measure indicating the respondent's proclivity for risk-taking. It consists of the level of agreement (1–5) with the statement: "You like to take risks." The second variable is a five-item index of "plan-fulness," the proclivity to strategize one's decisions; does the respondent usually go with a "gut feeling" or a thoughtful weighing of consequences?

Some scholars suggest that asking about religiosity on surveys may invoke above-average social desirability bias (Hadaway, Marler, and Chaves 1993). Evidence for this is stronger with private religiosity than with such measures as attendance (Batson, Naifeh, and Pate 1978; Trimble 1997). With this in mind, I include a summed index measure of social desirability constructed from three dichotomous variables, derived loosely from the Marlowe-Crowne Social Desirability Scale (Crowne and Marlowe 1980). Finally, in various models I include a number of other control variables in keeping with the conceptual model outlined previously. These include: a measure of the respondent parent's perception of the child's friends (as more or less of a positive influence upon them), a three-item index of parent–child relationship quality, average parent education, family structure variables, race/ethnicity variables, gender, age, a measure (or a series of measures) of the adolescent's moral decision-making criteria, dating habits, thoughts about cohabiting, and the parent's assessment of the rebelliousness of the adolescent.

Results

Bivariate Results

Table 4.1 displays the percentage of adolescents who have had sexual intercourse, have had oral sex, and had viewed Internet pornography across categories of several religion variables. The frequency of both sexual intercourse and oral sex appears slightly lower in the NSYR (just over 20 percent for each outcome) than in other data sets, due in part to the filter questions used prior to survey queries about these two behaviors. All three outcomes, however, clearly vary across religion measures. Intercourse measures range from a peak among nonattenders (27 percent) to a trough among youth who attend more than once a week (11.5 percent). The variation in oral sex is comparable, although a look at how each varies by affiliation indicates that the two are far from equated by most respondents. Black Protestant youth report the highest percentage of nonvirgins (28 percent) but the next-to-lowest percentage of oral sexual experience (12.7 percent). Jewish and mainline Protestant youth report being more likely to have had oral sex than intercourse. Only nonreligious youth display elevated levels of both experiences, and Mormons display low frequencies for both. Evangelical Protestant adolescents appear middle-of-the-pack on both counts.

Adolescents who see themselves as distinctly "spiritual but not religious" report slightly higher rates of all three behaviors than do youth who do not so identify. The moral decision-making variables indicate the most extensive variance of all in Table 4.1: the 12 percent of youth who would do what would "help them get ahead" report frequencies of intercourse and oral sex that each top 30 percent, while the 27 percent of youth who would do what would "make them happy" report comparably high numbers. The highest category in Table 4.1 for having had sexual intercourse is youth who do what would "help them get ahead," at 33 percent. For oral sex, the highest prevalence is among youth who think religion is not important at all—32 percent.

Only about 6 percent of youth report regular (at least monthly) use of Internet pornography, and this figure too varies by religion: whereas 11 percent of youth who never attend services report regular use, only about 3 percent of adolescents who attend more than once a week report comparably. Religion's salience for daily life sorted youth on this count even more extensively: 16 percent of youth who consider religion not important at all report regular internet pornography use, compared to only 2.4 percent of youth who find religion extremely important. Jewish and nonreligious youth report the highest rates of pornography use (17 and 13 percent, respectively). Since Internet pornography usage first implies access to the Internet, the numbers displayed in Table 4.1 comprise the percentage of the overall NSYR sample (about 80 percent) who indicate such access.

Table 4.2 displays percentage distributions from the NSYR, but this time split by race (only black/white, due to small sample size for other groups). What is most evident here is the relatively linear effect of religiosity on both types of sex among white youth, but a fairly random association with religiosity among African American adolescents. For the latter, only the highest religiosity categories—the "more than once a week" attenders and those who feel religion is "extremely important"—display consistently lower levels of each type of behavior. Other levels of religiosity appear randomly related to both behaviors. For white youth, on the other hand, the relationship appears more obvious, peaking among the least religious and indicating fairly low levels among the most religious.

TABLE 4.1

Percent of NSYR Respondents Who Report Having Had Sexual Intercourse, Having Had Oral Sex, and Average at Least Monthly Internet Pornography Use across Categories of Religion Variables

	Sex	Oral Sex	Monthly + Web Porn
Religious Attendance			
Never	27.0	27.7	10.6
Few times a year	25.2	26.4	11.8
Many times a year	22.2	17.3	7.2
Once a month	27.2	25.6	8.4
2–3 times a month	23.5	21.4	8.5
Once a week	16.3	18.1	4.9
More than once a week	11.5	11.7	3.3
Importance of Religion in Shaping Daily Life			
Not important at all	28.0	32.2	15.7
Not very important	24.5	31.4	12.6
Somewhat important	23.6	23.4	8.7
Very important	19.5	17.6	5.6
Extremely important	14.1	12.3	2.4
Thinks of Self as "Spiritual but not Religious"			
Very true	27.6	28.3	10.2
Somewhat true	21.7	21.6	8.6
Not true at all	18.8	18.8	6.1
How R Decides Between Right and Wrong			
Do what makes me happy	29.4	31.3	10.9
Do what helps me get ahead	32.7	30.2	13.6
Follow adult's/parent's advice	15.7	15.3	5.3
Do what God or Scripture says	11.2	11.2	3.8
Religious Affiliation			
Mainline Protestant	14.9	24.1	6.5
Roman Catholic	17.3	17.6	8.2
Evangelical Protestant	19.3	21.2	4.3
Black Protestant	27.5	12.7	7.4
Jewish	19.0	28.0	17.4
Latter-day Saint (Mormon)	15.5	10.6	4.4
Not religious	27.3	28.1	13.3
Other religion	21.4	22.3	6.9

TABLE 4.2

**Percent of NSYR Respondents Who Report Having Had
Sexual Intercourse and Oral Sex, by Race/Ethnicity**

	Have Had Sexual Intercourse		Have Had Oral Sex	
	White	African American	White	African American
Church Attendance				
Never	29.6	30.2	34.2	14.0
Few times a year	22.4	38.4	28.3	19.7
Many times a year	21.3	20.0	24.8	9.5
Once a month	26.1	28.6	26.3	17.9
2–3 times a month	21.6	30.6	27.8	9.5
Once a week	14.7	35.1	20.6	20.0
More than once a week	11.3	18.1	13.4	11.2
Importance of Religion in Shaping Daily Life				
Not important at all	31.2	26.7	39.5	20.0
Not very important	22.7	30.4	31.8	21.7
Somewhat important	23.1	36.7	27.2	19.6
Very important	18.4	25.0	21.8	12.7
Extremely important	11.4	23.7	13.7	9.1

Table 4.3 uses Add Health data to display percentage distributions for sexual intercourse and its variation by race/ethnicity and abstinence pledging. The sample employed here includes only those youth who indicate at Wave I that they have not yet had sexual intercourse. Keep in mind that this sample of virgins in Add Health, then, is not random but rather includes youth who are more likely to have delayed sex to begin with. Here the relationship between religiosity and reporting intercourse at Wave II is slightly more linear for African American youth than it was in the NSYR data but again not nearly as linear as among white adolescents. The gap in reporting vaginal sexual experience between the most and least religious is six to seven percentage points for African Americans, compared to fourteen to sixteen percentage points among white youth. On the other hand, Asian youth—who are least likely to adhere

TABLE 4.3

Percent of Add Health Respondents Who Report Having Had First Sex at Wave II, Split by Race/Ethnicity and Wave I Pledging Status (Sample of Wave I Virgins Only)

	Experienced First Sex			
	White	African American	Hispanic	Asian American
Church Attendance				
Never	26.6	31.9	27.8	7.4
Less than once a month	22.7	28.6	24.1	19.8
Less than weekly	18.9	26.6	24.5	14.4
Weekly or more	12.9	24.3	20.4	12.9
Importance of Religion				
Not important at all	29.7	30.7	30.2	9.0
Fairly unimportant	22.8	29.2	32.2	8.1
Fairly important	19.1	29.3	27.0	14.5
Very important	13.8	24.7	17.5	13.2

	Experienced First Sex	
	Pledged at Wave I	Did Not Pledge at Wave I
Church Attendance		
Never	21.2	26.1
Less than once a month	17.3	24.1
Less than weekly	16.5	21.7
Weekly or more	12.6	17.7
Importance of Religion		
Not important at all	22.6	28.2
Fairly unimportant	21.9	23.3
Fairly important	17.8	21.7
Very important	12.7	18.5

to Christian religious traditions—display no clear relationship between religiosity and sexual behavior. If anything, Asian American youth reporting the lowest religiosity are also least likely to report having experienced intercourse between Waves I and II.

The combination of religiosity and pledging abstinence appears to make for a consistent (though hardly large) four to six percentage point (lower) difference in sexual experience between study waves than does religiosity without pledging abstinence. Pledging is thus helpful but not necessary for a religiosity effect to appear, since its influence on sexual experience appears linear in both columns. Overall, Table 4.3 indicates that the category of youth most likely to have lost their virginity between study waves are Hispanic adolescents who consider religion fairly unimportant and African Americans who never attend religious services. On the other hand, the youth least likely to have had sex between study waves—apart from several categories of Asian American youth—are the most religious youth (those that frequently attend services, or consider religion very important) who have also pledged abstinence from sex until marriage.

Multivariate Results

Table 4.4 commences our consideration of more rigorous statistical tests of religious effects. It displays odds ratios from ordered logistic regression estimates predicting sexual motivations (from Add Health Wave I). These motivations tend to precede sexual decision-making. Clearly, very strong religious effects are at work here. Controlling for virginity status, youth who are higher in either type of religiosity tend to anticipate (or experience) greater sex-related guilt and think that their having sex would upset their mother. To a lesser extent, youth high in personal religiosity are significantly less likely to think that having sex would make their friends respect them. Religious group differences emerge as well: Evangelical Protestant adolescents (together with Mormons and those of other religions) are most likely to anticipate sexual guilt and think that sex would upset their mother. Black Protestants are more likely than Evangelical Protestants (prior to additional controls) to say that their friends would respect them more if they were to have sex. The religious effects largely survive the inclusion of a variety of control variables, too, suggesting that their effect on sexual motivations is robust and direct (and quite likely indirect as well). Quite clearly, religious adolescents—and especially religiously conservative ones—tend to anticipate (or experience) greater sexual guilt and perceive their family (and to a lesser extent, their friends) to be opposed to sexual involvement.

Table 4.5 uses data from the NSYR to display odds ratios from a pair of regression estimates on experiencing sexual intercourse, experiencing oral sex, and frequency of internet pornography use. Again, this sample includes all respondent youth and gives no attention to the timing of the behaviors. Sexual intercourse or oral sex could have occurred several years prior to the survey, while for others they may have been more recent. Several notable religious affiliation and identity distinctions in sexual experience emerge. Youth claiming to be "spiritual but not religious" are more likely to report having had oral sex, while black Protestants are more likely than Evangelical Protestants (the reference category) to report intercourse but less likely to report oral sex. As in Table 4.1, Jewish adolescents are less likely than Evangelical Protestants to report having had sex but more likely to view pornography, net of controls. Evangelical Protestants seem to exhibit a greater likelihood of experiencing intercourse and oral sex than do youth from several religious traditions (including mainline Protestantism and Catholicism). In other words, Evangelicalism, net of religiosity at least, seems to be associated with earlier sexual activity. Evangelical Protestants also appear among the least likely to report pornography use. All other affiliations are either equivalent or more likely than Evangelical Protestants to report more frequent pornography use.

Religious attendance and salience are strong predictors of the three measures before the inclusion of controls, indicating a robust, yet largely indirect, effect of religiosity on most types of sexual activity. The weakest effect is that of attendance—the key indicator of public religiosity—on pornography use (although religion's importance for daily life matters considerably here). For every unit increase in religion's importance, the odds that youth report intercourse or oral sex diminish by about 15 and 23 percent, respectively. For unit increases in attendance, the same figures are 14 and 9 percent, respectively. I should note that youth who claim to be "not religious"—while appearing here to be less likely than Evangelicals to have intercourse or oral sex—nevertheless tend to follow the elevated sexual patterns noted in Table 4.1. Controlling for two types of religiosity in Table 4.5, however, tends to mask this effect. A more accurate picture of their sexual activity would be to note the religiosity effects: as attendance or salience decreases toward complete irreligiosity, the likelihood increases of reporting intercourse or oral sex.

In more rigorous regression models (those with controls in Table 4.5), I add several value and relationship measures that considerably reduce the influence of the religion measures—indicating again the likelihood that most of the religious effects are channeled through other variables (like adolescent sexual values and parent–child relations). Intuitively, dating habits influence opportunities for sexual involvement. And peer influence, preferences for/against sexual abstinence, and moral inclinations are simply much more proximate to adolescents' actual sexual decision-making than are religiosity and religious affiliations. Alternate modeling procedures (such as structural path modeling with longitudinal data) would further clarify the pathways by which religion affects sexual behavior.

Table 4.6 displays predictors of Wave II sexual intercourse experience of Add Health respondents, drawing upon two distinct samples—those adolescents who claim virginity at Wave I, and all respondents (regardless of Wave

TABLE 4.4

Odds Ratios from Ordered Logistic Regression Estimates of Sexual Motivations on Respondent Characteristics and Behaviors, Add Health Wave I

Effect	Experienced or Anticipates Sexual Guilt		Having Sex Would Upset Mother		Friends Would Respect You More if You Had Sex	
Reported having had sex at Wave I	0.276***	0.249***	0.373***	0.437***	1.673***	1.533***
Religious service attendance	1.256***	1.283***	1.358***	1.313***	0.957	0.968
Importance of religion	1.291***	1.364***	1.282***	1.262***	0.842***	0.890*
Black Protestant	0.655**	0.543***	0.543***	0.577*	1.548**	1.002
Catholic	0.617***	0.588***	0.709**	0.751*	1.225+	1.271*
Mainline Protestant	0.738**	0.721**	0.719**	0.713**	1.023	1.029
Latter-day Saint (Mormon)	1.332	1.228	1.349	1.478	1.060	0.957
Jewish	0.422***	0.458***	0.360***	0.294***	1.258	1.467
Other religion	1.038	0.986	0.852	0.885	0.913	0.845
No religion	1.264	1.334+	1.116	1.125	0.813+	0.863
School percent nonvirgins	0.569+	0.618	0.446**	0.504**	1.984*	2.187**
Age		0.981		0.811***		0.977
Intact biological family		1.249***		1.662***		0.898+

Female		2.000***		2.154***		0.255***
Lives in South		1.088		1.079		1.133
African American		0.806		0.952		1.744**
Hispanic		0.777*		0.758**		1.064
Asian American		1.458*		1.468*		1.238
Mother's education		0.934		1.126		1.095
Self-image		0.980+		1.029**		0.965**
Family satisfaction		1.032*		0.959**		0.986
Number of recent romantic partners		0.897**		0.977		1.096**
Plan-ful or strategic personality		1.048***		1.026*		0.970*
Not averse to risks		0.994		0.995		1.062+
Social desirability index		1.168		1.147		1.184
Model Fit Statistics						
-2 Log Likelihood	21277.5	20839.4	18155.4	17530.8	20402.3	19420.7
Pseudo R-square	0.073	0.092	0.059	0.091	0.015	0.063
N	7,016	7,016	6,820	6,820	7,025	7,025

+p < .10 *p < .05 **p < .01 ***p < .001 (two-tailed tests)

TABLE 4.5

Odds Ratios from Logistic Regression Estimates of Experiencing Intercourse and Oral Sex, and Ordered Logistic Estimates of Internet Pornography Use, NSYR

Effect	Experienced Intercourse	Experienced Oral Sex	Frequency of Internet Porn Use
"Spiritual but not religious"	1.126	1.010	1.116
Mainline Protestant	0.636*	0.736	1.329
Black Protestant	1.470*	0.439*	2.249+
Catholic	0.673**	0.399***	1.532*
Latter-day Saint (Mormon)	0.772	0.337*	0.930
Jewish	0.598+	0.595	2.836**
Not religious	0.715+	0.553*	1.029
Other religion	0.834	0.540	2.373+
Religious service attendance	0.865***	1.003	0.976
Importance of religion in daily life	0.855**	1.036	0.925

Effect	Experienced Intercourse	Experienced Oral Sex	Frequency of Internet Porn Use
"Spiritual but not religious"	0.930	1.185*	1.090
Mainline Protestant	0.444***	1.007	1.418+
Black Protestant	0.895	0.442***	1.279
Catholic	0.423***	0.591***	1.381+
Latter-day Saint (Mormon)	0.984	0.419+	1.315
Jewish	0.417*	0.887	2.005*
Not religious	0.465**	0.694+	0.987
Other religion	0.517+	0.769	2.068*
Religious service attendance	0.941+	0.907***	0.926*
Importance of religion in daily life	1.083	0.773***	0.749***
Parents perceive R's friends as positive	0.707***	0.823**	0.726***

Parents' education (average)		0.913**		0.972		1.083*
Age		2.290***		1.844***		1.322***
Female		0.866		0.624***		0.056***
Quality of parent–child relations		0.913*		0.897**		0.858***
R does what "makes him/her happy"		1.353*		1.433**		1.133
Proponent of abstinence until marriage		0.214***		0.214***		0.585***
Is currently in a dating relationship		3.193***		2.391***		1.467**
Would consider cohabiting in the future		1.239		1.544**		1.486*
Parent respondent considers R rebellious		1.259***		1.267***		0.948
Model Fit Statistics						
-2 Log Likelihood	2984.6	2021.5	2979.0	2194.1	2731.9	2203.5
Pseudo R-square	0.033	0.345	0.045	0.297	0.031	0.219
N	3,029	3,029	3,022	3,022	2,454	2,454

Note: Models also include control variables for different race/ethnic groups and other family structures (coefficients not shown).

+p < .10 *p < .05 **p < .01 ***p < .001 (two-tailed tests)

TABLE 4.6

Odds Ratios from Logistic Regression Estimates of Experiencing First Sex on Respondent Characteristics and Behaviors, Add Health Data

Effect	Wave I Virgin-Only Sample			Full Sample		
	Experienced Sexual Intercourse, Wave II			Experienced Sexual Intercourse, Wave II		
Adolescent's religious service attendance	0.865*		0.908			
Adolescent's importance of religion		0.817*	0.820*			
Parent's religious service attendance				0.831***		0.845***
Parent's self-rated importance of religion					1.012	1.059
Black Protestant			2.620*			2.070**
Catholic			1.053			0.957
Mainline Protestant			0.875			0.853
Latter-day Saint (Mormon)			0.824			0.386*
Jewish			0.226***			0.458*
Other religion			1.278			0.926
No religion			1.146			1.401*
Age	1.309***	1.283***	1.290***	1.510***	1.526***	1.497***
Biologically intact family	0.587***	0.656***	0.712**	0.489***	0.526***	0.546***

Female	1.098	1.147	1.473**	1.070	1.068	0.982
African American	1.393*	1.411*	0.699	1.603***	1.817***	1.115
Hispanic	0.824	0.955	0.883	1.079	1.144	1.201
Asian American	0.705	0.777	0.834	0.618*	0.660*	0.725
Mother's education	0.644**	0.693**	0.631**	0.644***	0.684***	0.641***
Plan-ful or strategic personality	0.952*	0.957*	0.970	0.940***	0.941***	0.942***
Not averse to risks	1.106*	1.099+	1.048	1.208***	1.206***	1.157***
Social desirability index	1.184	1.170	1.282+	1.126	1.108	1.152
School percent nonvirgins	4.009**	4.009**	3.670*	10.117***	9.187***	8.478***
Number of recent romantic partners			1.765***			1.797***
Sex would make R feel guilty			0.684***			
Having sex would upset R's mother			0.968			
Friends would respect R more if R had sex			1.218**			
Model Fit Statistics						
-2 Log Likelihood	4224.8	4168.5	3849.4	12642.1	12561.0	11801.7
Pseudo R-square	0.041	0.054	0.126	0.171	0.177	0.227
N	3,794	3,794	3,794	10,575	10,575	10,575

Note: Model also includes control variables for level of autonomy, family satisfaction, self-image, and Southern residence (coefficients not shown).

+p < .10 *p < .05 **p < .01 ***p < .001 (two-tailed tests)

TABLE 4.7

Reverse Causation: Odds Ratios from Ordered Logistic Regression of Wave II Attendance and Importance of Religion on Having Experienced Sexual Intercourse between Study Waves (Wave I Virgin-Only Sample)

Effect	Attendance	Importance
Had sex, Wave II	0.922 (.08)	0.774** (.07)
Model Fit Statistics		
-2 Log Likelihood	14492.9	13181.1
Pseudo R-square	0.235	0.237
N	6,929	6,928

Note: Models include but do not display estimated coefficients from lagged dependent variable, demographic covariates, social desirability, personality traits, etc.

+p < .10 *p < .05 **p < .01 ***p < .001

I virginity status). The first three models in Table 4.6 analyze only those who report virginity at Wave I. As noted earlier, this is not a random sample, since virginity is not randomly distributed in a population of adolescents. However, evaluating the effects of current religiosity on what may be past behavior (i.e., losing virginity several years prior to being surveyed) is methodologically suspect and could well confuse the direction of influence. The second trio of models evaluates all Add Health respondents but examines the effects of parental, not adolescent, religiosity. Not only might substituting parental religious attendance and salience for an adolescent's be acceptable in general (especially during early adolescence and as a measure of general family religiosity), but it is also more time-stable, less prone to being affected by their children's actions, and perhaps more statistically sound (since it lacks the time-order problem that adolescent religiosity entails).

The first model of Table 4.6 assesses the baseline effects of demographic, personality, and the social desirability index factors on the likelihood of Wave I virgins reporting having had sex at Wave II. Age, family structure, race (African American), mother's education, strategic personality, and proclivity to risk-taking all affect sexual behavior in intuitive directions. With the addition of religion measures and school sexual climate in the second model, most of these variables remain unaffected in their relationship to the outcome. Among virgins, both church attendance and religious salience affect subsequent sexual intercourse: for each unit increase in religious salience, the odds of reporting intercourse a year later diminish by about 18 percent (and 14 percent for a unit increase in attendance). Notably, the inclusion of religious affiliations, dating habits, and sexual attitudes (in the third model) does not diminish the protective effects of religious salience, although it does reduce the effect of attendance. Black Protestants report significantly higher odds—and Jewish youth, considerably lower odds—of reporting first sex when compared with Evangelical Protestant youth. No other religious affiliation stands out from Evangelical Protestants in the Add Health virgin sample, net of other variables. Finally, dating habits clearly affect the sexual behavior of this sample, as do two of the three sexual attitudes: anticipated guilt and anticipated respect of friends.

The second trio of models in Table 4.6 reports estimated coefficients from logistic regression models on the odds of first sexual intercourse using the full sample of adolescents. Here the primary logic is to examine the effect of parental religiosity (for reasons stated earlier) on first sex, as well as to compare side by side the differences in effects when using the different sample criteria. In contrast to that of adolescents, parental attendance appears to matter a great deal in predicting the sexual behavior of youth. On the other hand, parental religious salience matters not in the least here. Adolescents whose parents are active in their congregations are considerably less likely to report having had sex at Wave II. Jewish and Mormon youth are each significantly less apt than Evangelical Protestant youth to report having had sexual intercourse at Wave II. On the other hand, black Protestants and those without a religious affiliation are more likely than Evangelical Protestants to report sexual experience, even when controlling for African American race.

Additionally, the preference for risk-taking and having a strategic orientation are much more robustly related here to sexual experience than they are in the virgin-only sample, indicating that these may be distinctly related to early sexual behavior. I did not include sexual attitudes in the full sample models, due primarily to the likelihood that they would be confounded by Wave I virginity status (which is not evaluated here). As in the virgin-only sample, these associations with first sexual intercourse behavior hold even while accounting for the sexual climate of the adolescent's school—an influential measure of the percentage of classmates who report having had sex.

Finally, Table 4.7 considers the possibility of reverse causation. Might first sexual intercourse experience elicit a subsequent decline in religiosity, so that researchers have the order of influence reversed? Since the most common religious moral codes discourage or forbid premarital sexual activity, the expression of such activity may lead adolescents to avoid religious involvement rather than suffer cognitive dissonance—a perceived gap between one's personal religious ideals and one's sexual choices. Controlling for Wave I attendance, the effect of having reported first sex (at Wave II) does not appear to affect Wave II attendance in a sample of virgins. This would suggest that sexual activity is not particularly effective in reducing adolescents' patterns of public religiosity. On the other hand, it does appear to alter their private religiosity. Having had first sex between study waves appears to diminish adolescents' reports of religious salience, net of their Wave I report of the same. In other words, youth who have had sexual intercourse tend to consider themselves slightly less religious than those who have not. This makes considerable sense, since cognitive dissonance would likely most affect internal or private religiosity. Still, these numbers are not as large as might be expected if sexual behavior shapes religiosity, rather than the other way around. Adolescents' religious attendance patterns are unaffected by sexual intercourse experience, and their assessment of personal religiosity appears only modestly diminished by sexual experience. Several studies suggest that the association between religiosity and sexual behavior is not bidirectional (Hardy and Raffaelli 2003; Meier 2003). While all researchers' conclusions are sensitive to the religiosity measures they employ, this analysis reveals modest evidence that the association is bidirectional, with private religiosity but not public religiosity influenced by sexual behavior.

Discussion and Conclusions

What can be said with confidence about the influence of religion on adolescent sexual behavior? First, it is evident that African American youth—especially boys—are among the earliest to experience sexual intercourse, and religion does not appear to play a significant role in delaying this. African American youth— including religious ones—appear to display less restrictive sexual motivations and practices than those of devoutly religious white youth. The exception is oral sex: African American youth, religious or not, are considerably more likely to avoid oral sex. Several possible explanations for the lack of association between religion and sex among African American youth have been tendered: African American congregations may be less judgmental (Furstenberg et al. 1987; Lincoln and Mamiya 1990; Smith 1994); their congregations and families may be overextended and thus less able to provide social control over adolescent sexuality (Amey, Albrecht, and Miller 1996).

Other key advances of this study include one of the first analyses of religion and its association with oral sex and Internet pornography use among adolescents. While pornography can only be loosely termed a sexual behavior (perhaps more appropriately a "sex-related" behavior), its inclusion has shed some light on other findings about religion and sex. To begin, it appears that Internet pornography use is not as extensive among American adolescent boys as some believe. (On the other hand, serious underreporting due to social desirability bias would be no surprise here.) Additionally, it is evident that Jewish youth (and to a lesser extent, mainline Protestant youth) are fairly effective in delaying first intercourse and appear to be replacing intercourse with oral sex and (at least among Jewish adolescent boys) pornography. Both mainline Protestant and Jewish youth also tend to be from relatively high socioeconomic backgrounds, and these forms of sexual behavior are inherently less risky and less threatening to long-term economic life chances. African

American youth, who tend to suffer inordinately from lower average socioeconomic status, appear much more drawn to intercourse than to either oral sex or pornography.

Another finding that stands out is that the influence of adolescent religiosity on sexual behaviors tends to be indirect rather than direct. While in the models, religious salience appears protective, when sexual attitudes, moral decision-making criteria, penchant for risk-taking, and abstinence pledges are added, the direct influence of adolescent religiosity often disappears. This is not unexpected and is actually quite helpful in identifying the sources by which religion shapes the sexual decision-making process. Just because a particular youth values religion or attends church would not likely, at least conceptually, directly alter her or his behavior choices. Instead, elevated religiosity typically leads to exposure to supportive friends, family, and religious teachings that—given an existing religious commitment—would more effectively "stick" with adolescents and shape their actions. At the same time, personal religiosity appears to take a hit (in Table 4.7) when youth experience first sex; the new status appears to contribute to a decline in religious salience but not attendance. In analysis of the full Add Health sample, parental attendance is quite strong in its association with adolescent first sex, suggesting that the household religious atmosphere and family religious involvement provide a context in which sex is more easily delayed.

It has been thought that Evangelical Protestants are the most conservative American religious tradition with respect to sexual attitudes and behaviors. My analyses support this claim only in part. While Evangelical Protestants tend to hold very conservative attitudes about sex (as evident in Table 4.4), they are not the religious group least apt to report having had sex (see Tables 4.5 and 4.6). In the full sample, Mormons, Jews, and mainline Protestant youth all appear less likely to report first sex, controlling for religiosity and other variables (which, again, may channel indirect effects).

My attempt to account for risk-averse and strategic orientations—primarily in response to criticisms about religiosity's endogenous status—is enlightening in its own right. Strategically oriented adolescents hold more conservative sexual attitudes, regardless of religiosity, and they appear to significantly delay first intercourse in both the full and virgin-only samples, even after controlling for sexual attitudes. In the full sample, youth not averse to risks are more likely to report first sex (by Wave II).

At times my analysis may seem atheoretical, but that would be a hasty conclusion. There is simply not a considerable amount of helpful theorizing upon which to draw in this field. General social control theories and differential association theories have been applied to studies of adolescent sex, typically borrowed from delinquency studies. In essence, they suggest that by either cognitive or actual opportunity restriction, religion helps adolescents to avoid some action they might otherwise have pursued (e.g., sexual activity). This suggestion, of course, presumes that adolescents of both sexes and all ages want to engage in sexual behavior, and this is not the case.

What are the key issues looming on the horizon in this field? One particularly urgent need is to better assess, in as sensitive a manner as possible, the very early sexual behavior of a minority of adolescents, especially African American youth. If in fact one-quarter of African American males experience intercourse by age thirteen, then much remains to be learned about the context and setting for such experiences (Centers for Disease Control and Prevention 2002).

Change in the American religious landscape should also be addressed. Since this study and numerous others have linked sexual behavior with religiosity, it is conceivable that if the religious landscape changes—especially in terms of diminishing religiosity—a concordant change may be evident in adolescent sexual behavior. Most forms of adolescent religiosity, though, have not changed notably (by growth or decline) in thirty years (Smith et al. 2002). On the other hand, change in the popularity of certain sexual behaviors may lead to a heightening or diminishing religious effect.

There has been speculation that high school students who considered themselves virgins were nonetheless sexually active in ways that put them at risk for STDs (Brückner and Bearman 2005). Performing oral sex may be a strategy used to maintain "technical" virginity and avoid pregnancy. The extent to which highly religious adolescents use this strategy to avoid the perceived negative emotional consequences of violating their religious values is worth examining in future studies.

Subsequent waves of data collection for the NSYR will enable a more thorough, longitudinal look at several of these outcomes. Retrospective data collected from adolescents concerning exact timing of first sex can be error-prone. Additional study waves—with less time between them—and an earlier study commencement are ways (albeit expensive ones) to minimize recall error. Finally, a mixed methods approach in which survey data analyses are informed by conversations with adolescents is optimal here, given the sensitive nature of the topic.

NOTES

This research uses data from Add Health, a program project designed by J. Richard Udry, Peter S. Bearman, and Kathleen Mullan Harris, and funded by a grant (P01-HD31921) from the National Institute of Child Health and Human Development, with cooperative funding from seventeen other agencies. Special acknowledgment is due Ronald R. Rindfuss and Barbara Entwisle for assistance in the original design. Persons interested in obtaining data files from Add Health should contact Add Health, Carolina Population Center, 123 W. Franklin Street, Chapel Hill, NC 27516–2524 (www.cpc.unc.edu/addhealth/contract.html). The author was supported by a research grant from the National Institute of Child Health and Human Development (R03-HD048899–01) and a grant from the Lilly Endowment (#2001 0966–000) for the NSYR (Christian Smith, PI). Data access was funded in part by a grant from the National Institute of

Child Health and Human Development under grant R01 HD40428–02 to the Population Research Center, University of Texas at Austin (Chandra Muller, PI). Opinions reflect those of the author and not necessarily those of the granting agencies.

REFERENCES

Amey, C. H., S. L. Albrecht, and M. K. Miller. 1996. "Racial Differences in Adolescent Drug Use: The Impact of Religion." *Substance Use and Misuse* 31:1311–1332.

Batson, C. D., S. J. Naifeh, and S. Pate. 1978. "Social Desirability, Religious Orientation, and Racial Prejudice." *Journal for the Scientific Study of Religion* 17:31–41.

Bearman, P. S., and H. Brückner. 2001. "Promising the Future: Virginity Pledges and the Transition to First Intercourse." *American Journal of Sociology* 106:859–912.

Beck, S. H., B. S. Cole, and J. A. Hammond. 1991. "Religious Heritage and Premarital Sex: Evidence from a National Sample of Young Age." *Journal for the Scientific Study of Religion* 30:173–180.

Benson, P. L., M. J. Donahue, and J. A. Erickson. 1989. "Adolescence and Religion: A Review of the Literature from 1970 to 1986." In *Research in the Social Scientific Study of Religion*, ed. M. L. Lynn and D. O. Moberg, 153–181. Greenwich, CT: JAI Press, Inc.

Billy, J. O., K. L. Brewster, and W. R. Grady. 1994. "Contextual Effects on Sexual Behavior of Adolescent Women." *Journal of Marriage and the Family* 56:387–404.

Brewster, K. L., E. C. Cooksey, D. K. Guilkey, and R. R. Rindfuss. 1998. "The Changing Impact of Religion on the Sexual and Contraceptive Behavior of Adolescent Women in the United States." *Journal of Marriage and the Family* 60:493–504.

Brückner, H., and P. S. Bearman. 2005. "After the Promise: The STD Consequences of Adolescent Virginity Pledges." *Journal of Adolescent Health* 36:271–278.

Casper, Lynne M. 1990. "Does Family Interaction Prevent Adolescent Pregnancy?" *Family Planning Perspectives* 22:109–114.

Centers for Disease Control and Prevention. 2002. "Youth Risk Behavior Surveillance—United States, 2001." http://www.cdc.gov/mmwr/PDF/SS/SS5104.pdf (accessed January 26, 2004).

Crowne, D. P., and D. Marlowe. 1980. *The Approval Motive: Studies in Evaluative Dependence*. Westport, Connecticut: Greenwood.

Cvetkovich, G., and B. Grote. 1980. "Psychosocial Development and the Social Problem of Teenage Illegitimacy." In *Adolescent Pregnancy and Childbearing: Findings from Research*, ed. C. S. Chilman, 15–41. Washington, DC: U.S. Department of Health and Human Services.

Day, R. D. 1992. "The Transition to First Intercourse among Racially and Culturally Diverse Youth." *Journal of Marriage and the Family* 54:749–762.

Furstenberg, F. F., Jr., P. S. Morgan, K. A. Moore, and J. L. Peterson. 1987. "Race and Adolescent Sexual Behavior." *American Sociological Review* 52:511–518.

Hadaway, C. K., P. L. Marler, and M. Chaves. 1993. "What the Polls Don't Show: A Closer Look at U.S. Church Attendance." *American Sociological Review* 58:741–752.

Hardy, S. A., and M. Raffaelli. 2003. "Adolescent Religiosity and Sexuality: An Investigation of Reciprocal Influences." *Journal of Adolescence* 26:731–739.

Johnston, L. D., J. G. Bachman, and P. M. O'Malley. 1999. *Monitoring the Future: Questionnaire Responses from the Nation's High School Seniors*. Ann Arbor, MI: Institute for Social Research.

Jones, R. K., J. E. Darroch, and S. Singh. 2005. "Religious Differentials in the Sexual and Reproductive Behaviors of Young Women in the United States." *Journal of Adolescent Health* 36:279–288.

Ku, L., F. L. Sonenstein, L. D. Lindberg, C. H. Bradner, S. Boggess, and J. H. Pleck. 1998. "Understanding Changes in Sexual Activity among Young Metropolitan Men: 1979–1995." *Family Planning Perspectives* 30:256–262.

Ku, L., F. L. Sonenstein, and J. H. Pleck. 1993. "Factors Influencing First Intercourse for Teenage Men." *Public Health Reports* 108:660–684.

Lammers, C., M. Ireland, M. Resnick, and R. Blum. 2000. "Influences on Adolescents' Decision to Postpone Onset of Sexual Intercourse: A Survival Analysis of Virginity among Youths Ages 13 to 18 Years." *Journal of Adolescent Health* 26:42–48.

Lewin, T. 1997. "Teen-Agers Alter Sexual Practices, Thinking Risks Will Be Avoided." *New York Times*, April 5, 8.

Lincoln, C. E., and L. H. Mamiya. 1990. *The Black Church in the African American Experience*. Durham, NC: Duke University Press.

Marsiglio, W., and F. L. Mott. 1986. "The Impact of Sex Education on Sexual Activity, Contraceptive Use and Premarital Pregnancy among American Teenagers." *Family Planning Perspectives* 18: 151–154 and 157–162.

McCree, D. H., G. M. Wingood, R. DiClemente, S. Davies, and K. F. Harrington. 2003. "Religiosity and Risky Sexual Behavior in African-American Adolescent Females." *Journal of Adolescent Health* 33:2–8.

Meier, A. M. 2003. "Adolescents' Transition to First Intercourse, Religiosity, and Attitudes about Sex." *Social Forces* 81:1031–1052.

Miller, B. C., and T. D. Olson. 1988. "Sexual Attitudes and Behavior of High School Students in Relation to Background and Contextual Factors." *Journal of Sex Research* 24:194–200.

Mosher, W. D., A. Chandra, and J. Jones. 2005. "Sexual Behavior and Selected Health Measures: Men and Women 15–44 Years of Age, United States, 2002." *Advance Data from Vital Health Statistics*, 362: 1–56. Hyattsville, MD: National Center for Health Statistics.

Remez, L. 2000. "Oral Sex among Adolescents: Is It Sex or Is It Abstinence?" *Family Planning Perspectives* 32:298–304.

Roof, W. C., and W. McKinney. 1987. *American Mainline Religion*. New Brunswick, NJ: Rutgers University Press.

Rostosky, S. S., M. D. Regnerus, and M. L. C. Wright. 2003. "Coital Debut: The Role of Religiosity and Sex Attitudes in the Add Health Survey." *Journal of Sex Research* 40:358–367.

Schuster, M. A., R. M. Bell, and D. E. Kanouse. 1996. "The Sexual Practices of Adolescent Virgins: Genital Sexual Activities of High School Students Who Have Never Had Vaginal Intercourse." *American Journal of Public Health* 85:1570–1576.

Sherkat, D. E., and C. G. Ellison. 1997. "The Cognitive Structure of a Moral Crusade: Conservative Protestant Opposition to Pornography." *Social Forces* 75:957–980.

Singh, S., and J. E. Darroch. 1999. "Trends in Sexual Activity among Adolescent American Women: 1982–1995." *Family Planning Perspectives* 31:211–219.

Smith, C., M. L. Denton, R. Faris, and M. D. Regnerus. 2002. "Mapping American Adolescent Religious Participation." *Journal for the Scientific Study of Religion* 41:597–612.

Smith, T. W. 1994. "Attitudes toward Sexual Permissiveness: Trends, Correlates, and Behavioral Connections." In *Sexuality across the Life Course*, ed. A. S. Rossi, 63–97. Chicago: University of Chicago Press.

Stack, S., I. Wasserman, and R. Kern. 2004. "Adult Social Bonds and Use of Internet Pornography." *Social Science Quarterly* 85:75–88.

Steensland, B., J. Park, M. D. Regnerus, L. Robinson, W. B. Wilcox, and R. Woodberry. 2000. "The Measure of American Religion: toward Improving the State of the Art." *Social Forces* 79:291–318.

Steinman, K. J., and M. A. Zimmerman. 2004. "Religious Activity and Risk Behavior among African American Adolescents: Concurrent and Developmental Effects." *American Journal of Community Psychology* 33:151–161.

Thornton, A., and D. Camburn. 1989. "Religious Participation and Adolescent Sexual Behavior and Attitudes." *Journal of Marriage and the Family* 51:641–653.

Trimble, D. E. 1997. "The Religious Orientation Scale: Review and Meta-Analysis of Social Desirability Effects." *Educational and Psychological Measurement* 57:970–986.

Wallace, J. M. and D. R. Williams. 1997. "Religion and Adolescent Health-Compromising Behavior." In *Health Risks and Developmental Transitions During Adolescence*, ed. J. Schulenberg, J. L. Maggs, and K. Hurrelmann, 444–468. New York: Cambridge University Press.

Whitehead, B. D., B. L. Wilcox, and S. S. Rostosky. 2001. *Keeping the Faith: The Role of Religion and Faith Communities in Preventing Teen Pregnancy*. Washington, DC: National Campaign to Prevent Teen Pregnancy.

Wysocki, D. K. 2001. "Let Your Fingers Do the Talking: Sex on an Adult Chat Line." In *Readings in Deviant Behavior*, ed. A. Thio and T. Calhoun, 258–263. Boston: Allyn and Bacon.

5

▶ ▶▶ ▶▶ ▶ ▶▶ ▶▶ ▶▶ ▶▶ ▶▶ ▶▶ ▶▶ ▶▶ ▶ ◀ ◀◀ ◀◀ ◀◀ ◀ ◀◀ ◀◀ ◀ ◀◀ ◀◀ ◀ ◀◀ ◀

The Influence of Religion on Ties between the Generations

VALARIE KING

Although prior research has examined the influence of religion on a variety of family behaviors and attitudes (e.g., marital quality, divorce, parenting practices; Mahoney et al. 2001), fewer studies have empirically examined whether and how religion influences the type and quality of involvement between the generations. A recent and growing body of research, however, suggests that religion may foster more frequent and positive ties between family members. An understanding of what motivates and fosters strong ties between the generations is crucial given the importance of strong affective ties and involved parenting (Borkowski, Ramey, and Bristol-Power 2002; Pleck 1997) and grandparenting (King, Elder, and Conger 2000; Tomlin 1998) for child well-being. In addition to the positive benefits children receive, parents (Arendell 2000; Palkovitz 2002) and grandparents (Tomlin 1998) benefit from engagement in their role, deriving meaning, enjoyment, and companionship from relationships with children and grandchildren.

In this chapter I review the growing literature and offer a new analysis that expands our understanding of the linkages between religion and intergenerational family ties. I focus on studies, particularly those nationally representative or large in scope, that consider the linkages between dimensions of religiousness (e.g., church attendance, importance of religion) and interpersonal intergenerational relationships (e.g., quality, level of involvement) between mothers and children, between fathers and children, and between grandparents and grandchildren.

My analysis uses national data from fathers and their adult offspring to examine the relationship between a father's religiousness and the quality of father–child ties. I focus on father–child ties because less is currently known about the role that religion plays in fostering father–child relationships compared with mother–child relationships. In addition, understanding what motivates fathers to become involved in their children's lives is crucial at a time when fathers are increasingly being called upon to take a more active role with their children given the positive benefits that father involvement can have for child well-being (King 2003).

Why Might Religious Parents and Grandparents Be More Involved with, and Foster Closer Ties to, Children and Grandchildren?

Scholars have suggested several reasons why religious parents and grandparents might be more involved with their children and grandchildren than their less religious peers. Religious teachings and values emphasize and support the centrality of family life, the importance of positive family relationships (including spending time with children), and a focus on the concerns and needs of others over the self (Abbott, Berry, and Meredith 1990; Ellison 1992; Pearce and Axinn 1998; Wuthnow 1991). Religious institutions promote pro-family messages through sermons, scriptural stories, church publications, and other church teachings. They are reinforced by private religious activities such as Bible reading. Thus religious individuals are involved in a culture that shapes their values and behaviors by emphasizing the importance of family relationships and a commitment to others that encourages them to be actively involved in the lives of their children and grandchildren (Wilcox 2002). Relatedly, religious individuals may sanctify family roles or relationships, infusing them with religious or spiritual meaning that leads to placing a high priority on fostering close and involved relationships with children (Mahoney et al. 2001, 2003).

Religious institutions also sponsor and support activities that bring family members together (Abbott, Berry, and Meredith 1990; Ellison 1992; Pearce and Axinn 1998). Church services and related religious activities provide opportunities for family members to interact and share experiences with one another, potentially enhancing the quality and closeness of their relationships. In addition, individuals who participate in religious activities are surrounded by like-minded coreligionists and may seek out friends who share similar beliefs, which can also reinforce pro-family teachings and family-oriented activities.

In addition to these more direct influences, the effect of religiousness on family ties may be mediated through other mechanisms. For example, King (2003) reports that marital quality is an important mechanism linking religious fathers to their children. Religious fathers have higher quality marriages, which in turn helps foster their involvement with children.

Religious individuals may also be more involved with children for reasons that have little to do with their religiousness. Therefore, it is important to control for factors that might select individuals into religion or that may account for a spurious relationship between religiousness and ties to children. For example, if religious involvement identifies people who are predisposed to all types of social interaction and civic participation then it may be this characteristic that propels fathers to be active with children, not their religiousness; King (2003) and Wilcox (2002) provide evidence dispelling this notion.

Religion and Ties between Mothers and Children

Compelling evidence for a positive link between a mother's religiousness and the quality of mother–child relations is reported in a study by Pearce and Axinn (1998). The study is based on the Intergenerational Panel Study of Mothers and Children, a probability sample representing white families with a first, second, or fourth child born in 1961 in the Detroit metropolitan area. Although limited geographically, the researchers capitalize on longitudinal data collected at several points between 1962 and 1985 from over eight hundred families. An important advantage of this study is that they have reports on the quality of the mother–child relationship from both the mother and the child. Relying on reports only from mothers regarding their religiosity and the quality of the mother–child relationship could bias results due to shared method variance.

Pearce and Axinn found that the mother's view of the importance of religion in 1980 positively predicted both the mother's perception of the quality of the mother–child relationship in 1985 (when the child was twenty-three years old) as well as the child's perception of relationship quality. The mother's religiosity was, however, an even more highly significant predictor of the mother's report of relationship quality than the child's report of relationship quality. Mother's church attendance in 1961 and increases in church attendance between 1961 and 1980 also predicted the mother's, but not the child's, perception of relationship quality. Once the importance of religion was included in the model, however, church attendance and increases in church attendance no longer remained significant predictors of mother reports of relationship quality. The mother's religious denomination had no effect on either mother or child reports of relationship quality.

Two recent national studies of adolescents also provide evidence for the link between parental religiosity and mother–child (and father–child) ties. Using the National Longitudinal Survey of Youth (NLSY97), Smith and Kim (2003) examined three dimensions of family religious involvement as reported by the adolescent's parent: how often the family did something religious together, parental church attendance, and parental prayer. In the majority of cases, the parent report came from the mother, so the measures of parental church attendance and prayer largely reflect the mother's religiousness. Each dimension of religious involvement was significantly associated with at least several measures of mother–child and father–child ties as reported by the adolescent. For example, youth in religiously involved families were more likely than youth in less religious families to report that they admire their mother, aspire to be like her, enjoy time with her, and receive help, praise, and support from their mother. Similar findings are reported for the father–child relationship.

Using the National Longitudinal Study of Adolescent Health, Regnerus and Burdette (2006) also report that parental religiosity as indexed by its importance is positively related to adolescent reports of mother–child and father–child relationship quality. Parental church attendance was also a positive but less influential predictor of relationship quality, whereas conservative Protestant affiliation had no influence. Similar to Smith and Kim's study, the parent report largely came from mothers (80 percent) and so is a stronger test of the role of the mother's religiousness than the father's religiousness on parent–child ties.

Religion and Ties between Fathers and Children

Researchers have only recently begun to directly explore the issue of whether religion affects the nature of the father–child relationship. Three studies based on the National Survey of Families and Households provide somewhat limited evidence that religiousness influences father involvement. Wilcox (2002) found that a father's church attendance was significantly related to his involvement in youth-related activities, although his participation in these activities was not necessarily with his own child. However, church attendance was not significantly related to a father having dinner with his children, and it was negatively related to the father's involvement in one-on-one activities with his children.

Bartkowski and Xu (2000) found that a father's church attendance was positively related to paternal supervision, father–child interaction, and affective parenting (giving praise and hugs), although controls reduced the latter two relationships to nonsignificance and marginal significance (p < .10), respectively. Cooksey and Craig (1998) also examined the influence of church attendance but focused on nonresident fathers and the frequency of their contact with children, both face-to-face and by phone or letter. They reported no influence of father's church attendance on either type of contact.

The preceding studies also considered a father's denominational affiliation, but only a few limited differences in father–child ties were found. Furthermore, many of these differences were reduced to nonsignificance after controls for church attendance were factored in.

Recent evidence suggests that the influence of religion on father–child ties may be underestimated in these studies because they rely on church attendance as the measure of religiousness. King (2003) explored multiple indicators of a father's religiousness using national data from the National Survey of Midlife Development in the United States. In terms of predictive significance, religiosity as indexed by its personal importance, having a religious preference, and believing religious instruction is important for children were most salient, whereas seeking religious comfort, identification with a particular religious group, and church attendance were less so. Religious fathers reported better quality relationships with children, had greater expectations for positive relationships in the future, reported a greater amount of thought and effort going into relationships with children, felt a greater degree of obligation to maintain regular contact with adult children, and were more likely to provide emotional support and unpaid assistance to children and grandchildren. Many of these significant associations held up even after controls were considered, and the positive influence of the father's religiousness applied to both married and divorced fathers.

One important limitation that all of these studies on father's religion share, however, is that all of the information is obtained only from the fathers, creating potential bias due to shared method variance that could lead to inflating the magnitude of the observed correlations (and increasing the risk of type I errors) between father's religiousness and father–child ties.

Religion and Ties between Grandparents and Grandchildren

To my knowledge, only two studies have considered the issue of whether religion affects the nature of the grandparent–grandchild relationship, and they reach opposite conclusions. Both studies rely solely on grandparent reports. Using data based on the National Study of Children, Cherlin and Furstenberg (1986) found no relationship between the grandparent's frequency of church attendance and the frequency of grandparent–grandchild exchange or grandparent engagement in parent-like behaviors with adolescent grandchildren.

King and Elder (1999), however, consider a much broader set of measures of grandparenting and of religiousness and conclude that religious grandparents are more likely to be involved with their grandchildren in multiple ways. Using data from two related longitudinal studies of rural families in Iowa (the Iowa Youth and Families Project and the Iowa Single Parent Project), they consider fourteen measures of grandparent–grandchild ties including relationship quality (e.g., closeness, conflict), interaction (e.g., contact, shared activities), and the educative role of grandparents (e.g., mentoring, discussing the grandchild's future and personal problems). Four dimensions of religiousness were examined including attendance at church services, public religious participation (e.g., teaching Sunday School, attending a religion class), private devotion (e.g., praying, reading the Bible), and religious orientation (e.g., importance of religion, seeking spiritual comfort). They found that each of the grandparenting measures was significantly predicted by at least one of the dimensions of religiousness, and usually by two or more. Few differences in grandparenting were reported by religious denomination, however.

The Influence of Religion on Father's Ties to Adult Children: A New Analysis

The current analysis examines the influence of a father's religiousness on the quality of the relationship between fathers and their adult children. Although prior research on the influence of a father's religiousness on father–child relationship quality suggests a positive link between the two, this is the first study to use separate reporters. Fathers report on their religiosity whereas their children report on the quality of the father–child relationship. It is also the first study of father's religiousness to capitalize on longitudinal data spanning a major portion of the life course of fathers and their children, allowing for a measure of the father's religiousness over most of the offspring's childhood and young adulthood, as well as a major portion of the father's adulthood. Individual religiosity can change throughout the life course as individual circumstances change (Pearce and Axinn 1998; Stolzenberg, Blair-Loy, and Waite 1995).

This analysis considers three factors not accounted for in prior research that might explain the positive association between a father's religiousness and the quality of ties to children: (a) involved fathering during adolescence, (b) the child's behavior while growing up, and (c) the adult child's religiousness. A final mediating factor considered in this study that has been shown to be important in prior research (King 2003) is the quality of the father's marriage.

One mechanism through which a father's religiousness may influence relationship quality with adult children is by fostering the involvement of fathers in their children's lives as they are growing up. To the extent that religious fathers do more with their children as they are growing up, they may set the stage for enjoying higher quality relationships after children leave home and enter adulthood.

A child's behavior is also likely to influence the ease with which fathers get along with their children. Fathers may find it difficult to establish close bonds to children when offspring exhibit problematic behaviors while growing up, with lasting negative implications for their future relationship. Perhaps religious fathers have children who are easier to raise, paving the way for closer relationships to develop. Certainly a number of studies suggest that greater parental or child religiousness is associated with youth exhibiting fewer behavior problems, less delinquency, less drug and alcohol use, and greater prosocial traits (Mahoney et al. 2001; Regnerus, Smith, and Fritsch 2003).

The strong link between parent and child religiousness is well documented in the literature (King, Elder, and Conger 2000; Myers 1996). To what extent does the positive effect of a father's religiousness on father–child ties reflect the higher level of religiousness among their offspring? Does the child's religiousness have an independent effect on the father–child relationship or is the father's religiousness most consequential?

King (2003) found that marital quality explained part, although not all, of the association between a father's religiosity and his positive ties to his children (see also Regnerus and Burdette 2006). Religious fathers reported higher quality marriages than less religious fathers and men who reported being in good marriages were significantly more involved with their children and they reported higher quality father–child ties. It is unknown whether the influence of the parental marriage will be as notable in this study given that the focus is on father–child relationships in adulthood when most of the offspring have left home, sometimes many years ago. The quality of the father's marriage may be more salient when parents and children are all living together and are more interdependent.

Data and Methods

Data

A seventeen-year longitudinal study, Marital Instability over the Life Course (Booth et al. 1998), was used to examine the questions advanced here. A national sample of 2,033 married persons (not couples) age fifty-five and under were interviewed by telephone in 1980. Husbands or wives were selected for an interview using a second random procedure. When compared with U.S. Census data, the sample was representative with respect to a variety of variables, including age, race, household size, housing tenure, presence of children, and region of the country. The sample was contacted again in 1983, 1988, 1992, and 1997, with reinterview rates of 78 percent, 84 percent, 89 percent, and 90 percent, respectively.

A sample of offspring was included as part of the 1992 and 1997 waves of data. To be eligible, offspring had to be nineteen years of age or older at the time of the interview and had to have resided in the parental household in 1980. Eighty-seven percent of the parents provided names and telephone numbers of children and interviews were obtained with 88 percent of these individuals for an overall completion rate of 77 percent. In households where there was more than one eligible child, a random procedure was used to select the child for inclusion in the study. Overall, 471 offspring in 1992 and an additional 220 who had reached the age of nineteen by 1997 were interviewed. Reinterviews were conducted in 1997 with 426 of the offspring first interviewed in 1992.

The present analysis relies on the subset of male main respondents and their interviewed offspring (n = 243). The few stepfather respondents were deleted. Offspring data from 1997 is used in the analyses except for the eleven offspring who were interviewed only in 1992; their data are all taken from the 1992 interview.[1]

Measurement

QUALITY OF THE FATHER-ADULT CHILD RELATIONSHIP. Six items from the offspring interview were averaged to form a scale (mean = 2.54, standard deviation = .51, Cronbach's Alpha = .90) tapping the quality of their current relationship with their fathers: how well the father understands them, how much they trust their father, how much respect, how much fairness, and how much affection they receive from their father (1 = very little, 2 = some, 3 = a great deal), and a final question on overall closeness (1 = not very, 2 = somewhat, 3 = very).

FATHER RELIGIOUSNESS. A father's religiousness is based on a question regarding how much religious beliefs influence his daily life (1 = not at all, 2 = a little, 3 = some, 4 = quite a bit, 5 = very much) averaged across the four time points in which it was asked: 1980, 1988, 1992, and 1997 (mean = 3.63, standard deviation = 1.12).[2]

FATHER INVOLVEMENT. Father involvement is the average of three items (mean = 1.95, standard deviation = .55, Cronbach's Alpha = .72) asked of offspring at their first interview (1992 or 1997) regarding how involved their father was with them when they were a teenager: how often the father helped them with schoolwork, helped with personal problems, and how often they had talks together (1 = never, 3 = often).

DIFFICULT CHILD. Difficult child is the average of ten items (mean = 1.32, standard deviation = .33, Cronbach's Alpha = .83) based on father reports in 1997 regarding behavioral problems their offspring might have exhibited while growing up: (a) trouble getting along with other children, (b) bullied or was cruel or mean to others, (c) cheated or told lies, (d) was disobedient at home, (e) had a strong temper and lost it easily, (f) was restless or overly active and could not sit still, (g) was stubborn or irritable, (h) argued too much, (i) destroyed own or other's things, and (j) disobeyed at school (1 = not true, 3 = often true; based on Achenbach and Edelbrock 1981). Missing values (n = 29) were coded to the mean score and a dummy variable indicating the missing cases was also created (1 = missing, 0 = not missing) and included in the regression models.

Both this measure of child difficulties and the previous measure of father involvement are based on retrospective reports and as such are subject to recall error. At least several, and in some cases many, years have passed since the offspring was a child or teenager. Some adults may have difficulty accurately remembering events from their childhood or from their children's early years. In addition, the recall of past events may be reinterpreted in light of present circumstances. For example, offspring who currently have high-quality relationships with their fathers may "remember" the father as being more involved than perhaps he really was, overstating the association between past and current events. Similarly, fathers who enjoy high-quality relationships with their adult children may be more likely than fathers with lower quality relationships to "forget" some of the behavioral problems their children exhibited while growing up. Despite these concerns, Shaw and colleagues (2004) argue that there is mounting evidence that bias in recalling experiences from childhood is not as great as some fear.

OFFSPRING RELIGIOUSNESS. Offspring religiousness is based on a single item in 1997 regarding how much (1 = not at all, 5 = very much) religious beliefs influence their daily life (mean = 3.14, standard deviation = 1.35).

FATHER'S MARITAL QUALITY. Several scales assessing different dimensions of marital quality are available (Johnson et al. 1986). Each scale was averaged over the five time points that the fathers were interviewed (1980, 1983, 1988, 1992, and 1997), creating indicators of marital quality over a substantial portion of the father's and offspring's life course. These indicators were only created for fathers who remained in intact marriages (n = 204). Marital happiness is an eleven-item scale tapping the father's happiness with different aspects of his marriage, such as the amount of love and affection received, with the spouse as someone to do things with, and with their sexual relationship (mean = 28.55, standard deviation = 3.45). Marital instability is a twenty-seven-item logged scale (mean = .22, standard deviation = .25) tapping thoughts or behaviors regarding divorce, such as thinking about divorce or talking to someone about it. Marital disagreements is a four-item scale tapping the frequency of a range of conflicts from mild disagreements over the division of household chores to whether individuals get so mad they slap, kick, shove, or hit the spouse (mean = 3.61, standard deviation = 1.81). Marital problems is a thirteen-item scale assessing whether either spouses personal traits and behaviors (such as jealousy, moodiness, drinking, or drug use) create a problem in the marriage (mean = 2.15, standard deviation = 1.91). Finally, marital interaction assesses how often fathers engage in five different joint activities with their spouse, including visiting friends, going out, and eating the main meal together (mean = 15.37, standard deviation = 2.04).

BACKGROUND CONTROLS. A number of background characteristics known to be associated with father–child ties that might otherwise confound any relationship between religion and father–child relationship quality were controlled for (King 2003; Wilcox 2002). Father's education is the number of years of education in 1980 (M = 14.21, SD = 2.48). Father's race is dichotomized into white (= 1; 94 percent) and nonwhite (= 0). Offspring characteristics include age (in years; M = 27.7, SD = 5.6), gender (1 = male, 51 percent; 0 = female), and marital status (1 = married, 50 percent; 0 = not married). Distance is the number of miles that the offspring reports living away from his or her father in 1997 (M = 309, SD = 897); this number is divided by one thousand in the regression models. Missing values (n = 20) were coded to the mean and a dummy variable indicating the missing cases (1 = missing, 0 = not missing) was created and included in the regression models. Parental divorce is a dichotomous variable based on offspring reports indicating whether their parents ever divorced (1 = yes, 16 percent; 0 = no).

Results

Do Religious Fathers Have Higher Quality Relationships with Their Adult Children?

As the bivariate model (Model 1) in Table 5.1 reveals, a father's religiousness is significantly associated with offspring reports of higher quality father–child relationships in adulthood.[3] Controlling for father and offspring background

TABLE 5.1

Quality of the Father–Adult Child Relationship Predicted by Father's Religiousness
(Unstandardized Regression Coefficients)

	Model 1	Model 2	Model 3	Model 4	Model 5	Model 6
Father religiousness	.08 **	.08 **	.06 *	.08 **	.07 *	.06 *
Father education		-.01	-.01	-.00	-.00	-.01
White father		-.08	-.09	-.10	-.07	-.10
Offspring age		-.00	.01	-.00	-.00	.01
Male offspring		.01	.01	.01	.02	.01
Offspring married		-.03	-.02	-.05	-.04	-.04
Distance		.04	.03	.04	.05	.03
Parents divorced		-.43 ***	-.29 ***	-.44 ***	-.42 ***	-.29 ***
Father involvement			.43 ***			.42 ***
Difficult child				-.18 +		-.11
Offspring religiousness					.03	.01
R²	.03	.14	.33	.15	.14	.34

N = 243

+p < .10 *p < .05 **p < .01 ***p < .001

characteristics (Model 2) has no influence on the effect of the father's religiousness, although parental divorce is itself a strongly significant predictor of lower quality father–child relationships.[4]

The level of father involvement during the teen years is both a positive significant predictor of high-quality father–child relationships in adulthood and a partial mediator of the father's religiousness (Model 3). The coefficient for father's religiousness is reduced somewhat although it is still significant. The negative influence of parental divorce is also somewhat reduced when father involvement is added to the model because divorced fathers are less likely to be involved with their teenage children than married fathers.

Father reports of their child as difficult to raise are only marginally negatively associated (p < .10) with offspring reports of current father–child relationship quality (Model 4). It does not, however, mediate or help explain the effect of a father's religiousness.[5]

Not surprisingly, preliminary analyses revealed that offspring religiousness is significantly correlated with father's religiousness (r = .39, p < .001). Although offspring religiousness is also correlated with offspring reports of the father–child relationship (r = .15, p < .05), it is no longer a significant predictor in the multivariate model (Model 5).[6] The father's religiousness, on the other hand, remains significant and is only slightly reduced in magnitude.[7] The final multivariate model (Model 6) including all predictors yields similar findings.

In sum, religious fathers have higher quality relationships with their adult offspring. Since the adult child is the one reporting on the relationship, we can rule out the possibility that this is due to religious fathers being less likely to acknowledge lower quality relationships or to shared method variance that can result when both reports are obtained from only one person. Further, it does not appear that religious fathers have higher quality relationships with children because their children were easier to raise. The child's religiosity is a less important predictor of relationship quality than the father's level of religiousness, and it does not play much of a mediating role. Offspring reports of having had more involved fathers during the teen years significantly predicts father–child relationship quality in adulthood and partially explains (although only modestly) the positive link between father's religiousness and father–child relationship quality.

Table 5.2 considers the role of the parental marriage for those families in which the parents remained married throughout the course of the study. Bivariate models indicate that various dimensions of marital quality are associated with higher quality father–child relationships in adulthood. Marital happiness positively predicts, and marital instability and marital problems negatively predict, father–child relationship quality. Marital disagreements and marital interaction are of marginal significance (p < .10). Model 1 replicates the findings of the final multivariate model (Model 6) in Table 5.1 on the reduced sample of continuously married fathers. Models 2 through 6 consider the effect of adding

TABLE 5.2

Quality of the Father–Adult Child Relationship Predicted by Father's Religiousness in Intact Families (Unstandardized Regression Coefficients)

	Model B	Model 1	Model 2	Model 3	Model 4	Model 5	Model 6
Father religiousness	.08 **	.06 *	.05 *	.05 *	.06 *	.05 *	.05 *
Father's education		-.002	-.001	.001	.001	-.001	-.002
White father		-.11	-.12	-.14	-.10	-.13	-.12
Offspring age		.01	.01	.01	.01	.01	.01
Male offspring		.01	.01	.003	.01	.02	.01
Offspring married		-.07	-.07	-.07	-.08	-.07	-.07
Distance		.03	.03	.03	.03	.03	.03
Father involvement		.40 ***	.40 ***	.39 ***	.40 ***	.40 ***	.39 ***
Difficult child		-.11	-.10	-.10	-.09	-.08	-.12
Offspring religiousness		.03	.03	.03	.03	.03	.03
Marital happiness	.02 *		.01				
Marital instability	-.26 *			-.18 +			
Marital disagreements	-.03 +				-.03 +		
Marital problems	-.03 *					-.03 *	
Marital interaction	.02 +						.01
R^2		.35	.35	.36	.36	.37	.35

N = 204

Note: Model B = bivariate coefficients.

+p < .10 *p < .05 **p < .01 ***p < .001

each dimension of marital quality separately to the multivariate model (these dimensions are considered separately because they are highly correlated, many at around .6). The direct effect of marital quality on the father–child relationship is reduced in the multivariate models. Only marital problems remain a significant predictor (at p < .05). Furthermore, the marital quality measures have little effect on the link between father's religiousness and father–child relationship quality.

Thus, although religious fathers report significantly higher levels of marital quality (father's religiousness is significantly correlated with every indicator except marital disagreements), this does not explain why they are able to establish better relationships to their children in adulthood. It appears that the role of marital quality in promoting father–child relationships (and in explaining at least part of the influence of father's religiosity on father–child ties) may be most salient when children are younger and still in the household (King 2003).

What Difference Does a Father's Religiousness Really Make?

Consistent with prior research, the influence of a father's religiousness on the quality of the father–child relationship is modest and should not be overstated (King 2003). Only 3 percent of the variance in relationship quality is explained by religiousness alone. Nevertheless, there appears to be something about religiousness that directly enhances men's ties to children. Table 5.3 illustrates the magnitude of these differences by comparing men at different levels of religiousness on each of the items that make up the relationship quality scale (focusing on the percentage who answer "a great deal," the highest score on the three-point response category). At one extreme are the "most" religious fathers, forty men with the highest possible score of a five on the religiousness scale, which means they said that religious beliefs very much influence their daily life in every year that they were questioned about it. At the other extreme are the "least" religious fathers, twenty-seven men who received a score of two or less on the religiousness scale (where 2 = a little and 1 = not at all). The remaining fathers fell between these two extremes and were defined as "less" or "more" religious according to whether they scored below (n = 84) or above (n = 92) the mean religiousness score of 3.6.

In general, the percentage of offspring who score their fathers in the top category of each relationship quality item increases as the level of the father's religiousness increases. Differences are most dramatic when comparing the two extreme groups of fathers. For example, 65 percent of offspring with the most religious fathers report that their father understands them a great deal compared to only 33 percent of offspring with the least religious fathers. Similarly, offspring with the most religious fathers are more likely to trust their fathers (90 percent versus 67 percent), and they report receiving more respect (88 percent versus 44 percent), fairness (88 percent versus 67 percent), and affection (50 percent versus 33 percent). Finally, 65 percent of offspring with the most

TABLE 5.3

Differences in Father–Adult Child Relationships by Levels of Father's Religiousness (In Percentages)

	Least religious fathers (n = 27)	Less religious fathers (n = 84)	More religious fathers (n = 92)	Most religious fathers (n = 40)
Father understands child	33	50	49	65
Child trusts father	67	83	85	90
Child receives respect	44	73	77	88
Child receives fairness	67	70	74	88
Child receives affection	33	46	49	50
Child and father very close	30	42	51	65

Note: Percentages correspond to those who report "a great deal" versus "very little" or "some" (closeness item compares "very close" to "somewhat" or "not very" close). Least religious fathers are defined as scoring 2 or less on religiousness and most religious fathers are defined as scoring 5 on religiousness. The remaining fathers were defined as less or more religious according to whether they scored below or above the mean religiousness score of 3.6.

religious fathers report being very close to them compared to only 30 percent of offspring with the least religious fathers.

Other Indicators of Religiousness

The single-item measure of father religiousness used in this study, which taps how much religious beliefs influence daily life, was the only religious indicator available across the four time points from 1980 to 1997. Previous research indicates that indicators of the importance or perceived influence of religion in an individual's life are particularly salient factors affecting parent–child ties (King 2003; Regnerus and Burdette 2006). Several other indicators of father religiousness were available in the data set, although only across three time points, from 1988 to 1997 (they were not available in 1980): frequency of church attendance, participation in a church social activity, prayer, watching or listening to religious broadcasts, and reading the Bible or other religious material. In additional analyses, I explored whether these other measures were as predictive of father–child relationship quality as the perceived influence of religious beliefs by comparing standardized coefficients for each of these measures as predictors of relationship quality in a bivariate (equivalent to Model 1 in Table 5.1) and multivariate (equivalent to Model 6 in Table 5.1) model. A new measure of the perceived influence of religious beliefs that only used responses from the same three time points as the other religious indicators was created to ensure that any differences that emerged would not be due to having measures at different time points.

Church attendance predicted relationship quality almost as strongly as the perceived influence of beliefs. Participation in church social activities had the strongest bivariate relationship with relationship quality, but was similar in magnitude to church attendance after controls. Thus, all three of these religious indicators were fairly similar in predictive strength. Not surprisingly, these indicators were highly intercorrelated (from .72 to .77). On the other hand, the frequency of prayer and reading the Bible were only marginally related (p < .10) to relationship quality in the bivariate models, and no longer significant in the multivariate model, despite being highly correlated with the aforementioned religiousness indicators (from .65 to .81). The frequency of watching or listening to religious broadcasts was unrelated to relationship quality in both the bivariate and multivariate model (it was also less strongly correlated with the other religious indicators, from .34 to .59 with an average correlation of .46). Overall, it appears that indicators of private religious practices are less predictive of quality ties between fathers and adult children than measures of public religious participation or the influence of religious beliefs.

A Note about Denomination

Prior research on fathers also finds that measures of religiosity that tap its importance to the individual (like the one used in this study) are more significant predictors of the father–child relationship than is denominational affiliation[8] (King 2003). Results from this study are consistent with prior research, although only broad denominational difference could be considered (for example, it was not possible to compare within Protestant subgroups such as between conservative/fundamentalist Protestants and mainline Protestants). I found no differences in the quality of the father–child relationship between fathers who identified as Protestant (59 percent), Catholic (26 percent), other (9 percent), or no affiliation (6 percent). Potential interactions between father's religiousness and denomination were also explored but were not significant.

Does It Matter Whether We Use Father or
Child Reports of the Father–Child Relationship?

By using offspring reports of the father–child relationship, the results from this study provide evidence that the positive influence of a father's religiousness is not simply a result of religious fathers being more likely to believe that they should report more positive relationships or being less willing to see or acknowledge problems in their relationships with children. At the same time, however, I found evidence that the association between father's religiousness and the quality of the father–child relationship is stronger when father reports are used for both measures.

Although fathers were not asked all of the items that the offspring were regarding the father–child relationship, they were asked the single item regarding how close they were overall to their adult child in 1997. The correlation between the father's religiousness and his report of closeness is .24 (p < .001) compared with the correlation of .18 (p < .01) between the father's religiousness and the relationship quality scale based on offspring reports.[9] If only the single closeness item is used, the correlation between father's religiousness and offspring reports of closeness is .14 (p < .05).

Further, I found that father's religiosity was positively correlated with a measure of social desirability[10] (r = .19, p < .01), suggesting that religious fathers may have a greater tendency to describe themselves (and their relationships with others) in more favorable terms than less religious fathers (social desirability scores were significantly correlated with four of the five marital quality indicators at p < .001, and marginally correlated with father, but not child, reports of father–child closeness at p < .10). Thus, research that relies on information from only a parent is likely to find a somewhat stronger relationship between parental religiosity and parent–child ties.

Discussion and Conclusions

Religious fathers have higher quality relationships with their adult offspring. By using offspring reports of the relationship, we can rule out the possibility that this is an artifact of shared method variance or to misreporting biases among religious fathers. Further, the higher quality relationships that religious fathers have with their adult offspring do not appear to result from them having children who were easier to raise. The child's religiosity is a less important predictor of relationship quality than the father's level of religiousness, and it does not play much of a mediating role. Although religious fathers report significantly higher levels of marital quality, this also does not explain why they are able to establish better relationships to their children in adulthood. It appears that the role of marital quality in promoting father–child relationships may be most salient when children are younger and still in the household.

Offspring reports of having had more involved fathers during the teen years significantly predict father–child relationship quality in adulthood and partially explain (although only modestly) the positive link between father's religiousness and father–child relationship quality. Thus, religious fathers set the stage for enjoying higher quality relationships after children enter adulthood in part by being more actively engaged with their children while they are growing up.

The last few years have witnessed a growing literature devoted to under-standing the linkages between religion and intergenerational relationships. Efforts have been aided by the availability of data sets that contain information on both religiousness and intergenerational ties. Research to date suggests that religion can enhance ties across the generations, between parents and children, and between grandparents and grandchildren.

The importance or perceived influence of religion in an individual's life seems to be a particularly salient factor affecting family ties (King 2003). Denominational affiliation, on the other hand, is not strongly linked to relation-ship quality or involvement between the generations. Prior research, however, does find denominational affiliation (particularly conservative Protestantism and conservative theological beliefs) to be important for other aspects of family relationships, such as parenting practices and beliefs (e.g., Ellison, Bartkowski, and Segal 1996; Wilcox 1998). The foregoing suggests that different aspects of religiousness may be more influential in some domains of intergenerational relationships than others. Researchers are only beginning to unravel some of these complexities, a task made difficult by the often limited number of reli-giousness indicators in many data sets that also have measures of family ties (which may also be limited).

Research also reveals that it can matter whether information is obtained from more than one source. Studies based on two reporters suggest that single-source reports can potentially overestimate the link between religion and family ties, and future research would benefit from multiple-source reporters. Future research would also benefit from considering parent–child relationships at different stages of the life course. For example, what is the role of religion in relations between adult children and aging parents in terms of coresidence, providing care to parents, and other types of supportive exchanges?

Further, we know nothing about how religion influences family ties beyond the parent–child and grandparent–grandchild relationships. For example, does it influence the way that aunts or uncles relate to their nieces or nephews? It is not surprising that research has focused on the primary tie between parents and children, but a consideration of the role of religiousness beyond the confines of the nuclear family could help illuminate the extent to which religiousness is a pervasive influence on an individual's orientation to others.

Perhaps the most significant gap in our current knowledge is an understand-ing of why and how religion fosters positive intergenerational ties. Research is needed to shed light on what it is about religion that enhances family ties, such as the relative importance of religious teachings and beliefs, religious activities and opportunities for family interaction, and participation in religious net-works. Although research is beginning to point to potentially important mediat-ing factors that tie religion to positive family relationships, the processes behind them are still unclear. For example, marital quality appears to play an important mediating role between parental religiousness and parent–child ties, at least for younger children and adolescents, yet the processes through which this occurs need further exploration. Understanding the linkages between religiousness and family ties is vitally important given the significance of both religion and family relationships in many people's lives, and the benefits to well-being that can accrue from positive engagement with each of them.

NOTES

This research was supported by funding from the National Institute of Child Health and Human Development (NICHD) to Valarie King (R01 HD43384), principal investigator, and from core funding to the Population Research Institute (R24 HD41025), The Pennsylvania State University.

1. With respect to long-term panel attrition, a search was made for variables in 1980 that predicted whether an offspring interview was successfully obtained in 1992 or 1997. In 1980, 1,436 respondents lived in households with a child two years of age or older and interviews were later obtained with offspring in 691 (48 percent) of these households. Interviews were less likely to be obtained when parents were male, young, poorly educated, nonwhite, and living in rented accommodations. Heckman's (1979) widely used method was relied on to examine the extent of attrition bias. Based on a regression equation estimating the probability that each case (that is, a parent–child dyad) would yield a completed offspring interview (as mentioned earlier, significant predictors included parent's education, age, race, gender, education, and housing status), a variable referred to as *lambda* was created and included as a control in the analyses (not shown). It was not significant in any of the models and its inclusion had little effect on the estimates reported here, indicating that attrition bias was not a problem.

2. For the eleven offspring who were interviewed only in 1992, father's religiousness is the average across 1980, 1988, and 1992. An additional eleven fathers had missing information at just one time point so the average of the other three waves was used. Correlations of the religiousness item between waves ranged from .71 to .77.

3. The influence of the father's religiousness was similar for daughters and sons. An interaction term between the father's religiousness and offspring gender in these models was not significant.

4. I also tested whether the influence of father's religiousness differed by whether fathers were divorced or not (by adding an interaction term to the models); it did not, a finding consistent with King (2003).

5. Father reports of their children as difficult to raise were significantly associated ($p < .01$) with father reports of current father–child closeness (to be discussed shortly), although it did not mediate the effect of father religiousness on his report of the father–child relationship either.

6. Some research suggests that dissimilarity in parent–child levels of religiousness is an additional factor that can influence parent–child relationship quality (Pearce and Axinn 1998; Regnerus and Burdette 2006). I found little evidence that parent–child dissimilarity in religiousness (using 1997 reports from fathers and children) affected relationship quality. The limited size of my sample, however, precluded a thorough investigation of this issue.

7. A test for an interaction between the father's religiousness and the offspring's religiousness failed to reach significance.

8. Lack of differences by denomination is also reported in research on mother–child (Pearce and Axinn 1998; Regnerus and Burdette 2006) and grandparent–grandchild ties (King and Elder 1999).

9. Although the father's religiousness was a somewhat stronger predictor of the father's report of closeness than offspring reports of relationship quality, other predictors in the models behaved fairly similarly regardless of whose report of the father–child relationship was used. Although significant for both offspring and father reports, parental divorce and father involvement in the teenage years were even stronger predictors of offspring reports of the current relationship. As noted earlier, the major difference was that offspring behavior problems had a significantly more negative influence on father reports of closeness than on offspring reports of relationship quality (but this did not mediate the influence of father's religiousness on closeness).

10. Social desirability is the tendency of describing the self in favorable terms in order to earn the approval of others, and is measured in this study with four items adapted from the Marlowe-Crowne Social Desirability Scale (Crowne and Marlowe 1964).

REFERENCES

Abbott, D. A., M. Berry, and W. H. Meredith. 1990. "Religious Belief and Practice: A Potential Asset in Helping Families." *Family Relations* 39:443–448.

Achenbach, T. M., and C. S. Edelbrock. 1981. "Behavioral Problems and Competencies Reported by Parents of Normal and Disturbed Children Aged Four through Sixteen." *Monographs of the Society for Research in Child Development* 46: 1–88.

Arendell, T. 2000. "Conceiving and Investigating Motherhood: The Decade's Scholarship." *Journal of Marriage and Family* 62:1192–1207.

Bartkowski, J. P., and X. Xu. 2000. "Distinctive Patriarchs or Expressive Dads: The Discourse and Practice of Fathering in Conservative Protestant Families." *Sociological Quarterly* 41:465–486.

Booth, A., P. Amato, D. R. Johnson, and J. N. Edwards. 1998. *Marital Instability over the Life Course: Methodology Report for the Fifth Wave.* Lincoln: University of Nebraska Bureau of Sociological Research.

Borkowski, J. D., S. L. Ramey, and M. Bristol-Power. 2002. *Parenting and the Child's World: Influences on Academic, Intellectual, and Social-Emotional Development.* Mahwah, NJ: Lawrence Erlbaum.

Cherlin, A. J. and F. F. Furstenberg, Jr. 1986. *The New American Grandparent: A Place in the Family, A Life Apart.* New York: Basic Books.

Cooksey, E. C., and P. H. Craig. 1998. "Parenting from a Distance: The Effects of Paternal Characteristics on Contact between Nonresidential Fathers and their Children." *Demography* 35:187–200.

Crowne, D. P., and D. Marlowe. 1964. *The Approval Motive: Studies in Evaluative Dependence.* New York: John Wiley and Sons.

Ellison, C. G. 1992. "Are Religious People Nice People? Evidence from the National Survey of Black Americans." *Social Forces* 71:411–430.

Ellison, C. G., J. P. Bartkowski, and M. L. Segal. 1996. "Conservative Protestantism and the Parental Use of Corporal Punishment." *Social Forces* 74:1003–1028.

Heckman, J. 1979. "Sample Selection Bias as a Specification Error." *Econometrica* 47: 153–61.

Johnson, D., L. White, J. Edwards, and A. Booth. 1986. "Dimensions of Marital Quality: Toward Methodological and Conceptual Refinement." *Journal of Family Issues* 7:31–49.

King, V. 2003. "The Influence of Religion on Fathers' Relationships with Their Children." *Journal of Marriage and Family* 65:382–395.

King, V., and G. H. Elder, Jr. 1999. "Are Religious Grandparents More Involved Grandparents?" *Journal of Gerontology: Social Sciences* 54B:S317–S328.

King, V., G. H. Elder, Jr., and R. D. Conger. 2000. "Church, Family, and Friends." In *Children of the Land: Adversity and Success in Rural America*, ed. G. H. Elder, Jr., and R. D. Conger, 151–163. Chicago: University of Chicago Press.

Mahoney, A., K. I. Pargament, A. Murray-Swank, and N. Murray-Swank. 2003. "Religion and the Sanctification of Family Relationships." *Review of Religious Research* 44:220–236.

Mahoney, A., K. I. Pargament, N. Tarakeshwar, and A. B. Swank. 2001. "Religion in the Home in the 1980s and 1990s: A Meta-Analytic Review and Conceptual Analysis of Links between Religion, Marriage and Parenting." *Journal of Family Psychology* 15:559–596.

Myers, S. M. 1996. "An Interactive Model of Religiosity Inheritance: The Importance of Family Context." *American Sociological Review* 61:858–866.

Palkovitz, R. 2002. *Involved Fathering and Men's Adult Development*. Mahwah, NJ: Lawrence Erlbaum.

Pearce, L. D., and W. G. Axinn. 1998. "The Impact of Family Religious Life on the Quality of Mother-Child Relations." *American Sociological Review* 63:810–828.

Pleck, J. H. 1997. "Paternal Involvement: Levels, Sources, and Consequences." In *The Role of the Father in Child Development*, 3rd ed., ed. M. E. Lamb, 66–103. New York: John Wiley and Sons.

Regnerus, M. D., and A. Burdette. 2006. "Religious Change and Adolescent Family Dynamics." *Sociological Quarterly* 47:175–194.

Regnerus, M. D., C. Smith, and M. Fritsch. 2003. *Religion in the Lives of American Adolescents: A Review of the Literature: A Research Report of the National Study of Youth and Religion. Number Three*. Chapel Hill: University of North Carolina.

Shaw, B. A., N. Krause, L. M. Chatters, C. M. Connell, and B. Ingersoll-Dayton. 2004. "Emotional Support from Parents Early in Life, Aging, and Health." *Psychology and Aging* 19:4–12.

Smith, C., and P. Kim. 2003. *Family Religious Involvement and the Quality of Family Relationships for Early Adolescents: A Research Report of the National Study of Youth and Religion. Number Four*. Chapel Hill: University of North Carolina.

Stolzenberg, R. M., M. Blair-Loy, and L. J. Waite. 1995. "Religious Participation in Early Adulthood: Age and Family Life Cycle Effects on Church Membership." *American Sociological Review* 60:84–103.

Tomlin, A. M. 1998. "Grandparents' Influences on Grandchildren." In *Handbook on Grandparenthood*, ed. M. E. Szinovacz, 159–179. Westport, CT: Greenwood Press.

Wilcox, W. B. 1998. "Conservative Protestant Childrearing: Authoritarian or Authoritative?" *American Sociological Review* 63:796–809.

———. 2002. "Religion, Convention, and Paternal Involvement." *Journal of Marriage and Family* 64:780–792.

Wuthnow, R. 1991. *Acts of Compassion: Caring for Others and Helping Ourselves*. Princeton, NJ: Princeton University Press.

6

Religion and Family Values Reconsidered

Gender Traditionalism among Conservative Protestants

JOHN P. BARTKOWSKI AND XIAOHE XU

The resurgence of conservative Protestantism during the past several decades, and its adherents' vigorous defense of traditional family values, has given rise to a body of scholarship on the gender attitudes of those within this religious subculture. Early research demonstrated that conservative Protestants have much more traditional attitudes concerning wifely domesticity, a patriarchal family structure, and marriage as a lifelong commitment (e.g., Gay, Ellison, and Powers 1996; Grasmick, Wilcox, and Bird 1990; Hertel and Hughes 1987; Huber and Spitze 1983; Roof and McKinney 1987; Wilson and Musick 1996; see Peek, Lowe, and Williams 1991 for a review of early research). Subsequent studies have demonstrated that conservative Protestant women are more likely to limit their labor force opportunities in favor of domestic and child-care commitments (Lehrer 1995; Sherkat 2000), and perform considerably more housework than non-Evangelical wives even if they are employed outside the home (Ellison and Bartkowski 2002). In this sense, conservative Protestants seem to be the key source of religious advocacy for traditional gender relations in America's culture war over the family (Hunter 1991; see also Bendroth 1999).

Yet, countervailing evidence has revealed that gender dynamics within conservative Protestant homes may not be so different from those observed in other American families. Qualitative scholarship has underscored the negotiated—rather than overtly patriarchal—character of spousal relationships in conservative Protestant families (e.g., Bartkowski 2001, 2004, 2007; Gallagher 2003; Gallagher and Smith 1999). And survey-based research has highlighted considerable attitudinal diversity within this religious subculture and progressive family practices that include egalitarian decision-making and greater paternal involvement (Bartkowski and Xu 2000; Denton 2004; Gallagher 2004; Gay, Ellison, and Powers 1996; Peek, Lowe, and Williams 1991; Wilcox 2004; Wilcox and Jelen 1991).[1] This body of scholarship suggests that conservative Protestant men and women are accommodating to mainstream American views on gender and family, or at least exhibit a more conciliatory stance toward gender egalitarianism than was initially thought.

Divergent viewpoints about gender and family are manifested among conservative Protestants not only at the grass roots of domestic life, but also among its leading spokespersons (Bartkowski 2001; Smith 2000). Not long ago, the Southern Baptist Convention alarmed feminists and progressive-minded Americans by championing a wife's "submission" to her husband's domestic authority. Yet, at the same time, elite conservative Protestant accommodation to gender egalitarianism has been evidenced by the rise of groups such as Christians for Biblical Equality, which blends theological orthodoxy (scriptural inerrancy) with an advocacy of progressive gender ideas, and the Promise Keepers, which largely jettisoned the language of patriarchy favored by old-guard evangelicals for softer, more conciliatory terms such as male servant-leadership in the home and marital partnerships (Bartkowski 2001, 2004).

Study Foci and Contributions

Given these competing scholarly perspectives and contradictory cultural patterns, a number of important questions emerge. First, do conservative Protestants exhibit distinctively traditional attitudes about gender and family? The answer to this question may not be as straightforward as it would first seem. As noted earlier, there is recent evidence that conservative Protestants may be more accommodating to gender egalitarianism than was initially suspected. Yet, gender is not a unidimensional social phenomenon. Conservative Protestant accommodation may be evidenced more greatly in some battlefronts in the "gender wars" than in others. For instance, conservative Protestants may join other Americans in accepting women's paid labor force participation, but still distinguish themselves by viewing child care as the divinely ordained responsibilities of mothers. Thus, traditional notions of womanhood may be more closely tied to maternalism (a mother's specific charge to care for children) than domesticity (a wife's broader responsibility for homemaking). Our study utilizes two different measures of gender traditionalism to determine if conservative Protestant orientations toward contemporary gender norms vary by the type of domestic role conventionally assigned to women (mother versus homemaker).

In attempting to determine if conservative Protestants are more inclined toward gender traditionalism, it is also important to acknowledge that previous research is characterized by methodological shortcomings. In much prior research on religion and gender traditionalism, the mediating effects of different religious variables have been largely overlooked. While it is important to consider the independent effects of different dimensions of religiosity (e.g., denominational affiliation, theological conservatism, and worship service attendance) on gender traditionalism, care needs to be exercised in parsing out the relationship between various forms of religiosity. It is possible that the effects of conservative Protestant affiliation on gender traditionalism are, in fact, a product of religious conservatives' churchgoing habits or their distinctive convictions about the inerrancy of the Bible. The approach we employ here analyzes the independent effects of denominational affiliation on gender traditionalism, and the possible mediating influences of biblical inerrancy and worship service attendance. The empirical importance of this approach is underscored by, first, prior research that demonstrates that evangelicalism is a religious movement that cuts across religious denominations, and second, the tendency for some persons to claim a denominational affiliation even though they are not actively practicing their faith (nominal affiliation) (see Ellison and Bartkowski 2002). Consequently, it is important to determine more precisely the combined effects of various religious factors on gender traditionalism.

Second, no previous study of which we are aware has examined how conservative Protestant support for gender traditionalism might change over the course of a person's adult life. According to the life course stability perspective outlined in previous work (Alwin 1994), persons who enter a relationship with more traditional views about gender would be expected to remain more committed to gender traditionalism throughout that relationship. However, the life course stability perspective has not been explored with reference to the relationship between religion and gender. And, of course, any longitudinal examination of possible ideological changes in gender traditionalism must avoid treating religion as a static entity by accounting for circumstances in which religious switching or changes in religiosity have occurred, and exploring the possible effects of such changes on gender ideologies.

It is against this backdrop that the current study is undertaken. In what follows, we analyze data from two waves of the National Survey of Families and Households (NSFH-1, NSFH-2) to explore several new dimensions of the relationship between conservative Protestantism and gender traditionalism. We begin with a brief description of the data and measures used in this study. Thereafter, we seek to address the questions raised earlier. Our investigation proceeds in two analytical phases. In phase one of our study, we use cross-sectional data from NSFH-1 to explore the effects of religious mediators of the relationship between denominational affiliation and traditionalist gender ideologies. These analyses are conducted with a multidimensional measure of religion that accounts for denominational affiliation (conservative Protestant, Moderate Protestant, liberal Protestant, Catholic, and unaffiliated persons), theological beliefs (biblical inerrancy), worship service attendance, and a series of statistical controls (relationship type[2] as well as respondents' race, class, gender, employment status, and birth cohort). Regression models are run to determine both the independent and combined effects of various religious factors on two measures of gender traditionalism—maternalist ideology and separate spheres ideology.

In phase two, we analyze data from both NSFH waves to determine the extent to which conservative Protestant commitments to gender traditionalism are marked by stability or change five years after the initial wave of data was collected. While this time span is less than ideal to measure life course change, it provides insight into the stability or, alternatively, the variability of ideological support for gender traditionalism among respondents. We again apply statistical controls and account for the role that changes in religious affiliation and personal religiosity might exert on gender ideologies over time. We also explore mediating effects of biblical inerrancy and worship service attendance on the relationship between denominational affiliation and gender traditionalism.

Data, Measures, and Methods

Data

This study utilizes data from two waves of the NSFH. The NSFH is a national probability sample, with data collection overseen by sociologists at the University of Wisconsin. The NSFH-1 features a rich repository of survey data collected from 13,017 adult respondents (Sweet, Bumpass, and Call 1988), with over-samples of African American, Latino, and cohabiting respondents, among other special populations. The follow-up wave of data, the NSFH-2, was collected between 1992 and 1994 (Sweet and Bumpass 1996). These data are suitable for this study because they provide a wide range of measures on religion, including denominational affiliation, theological beliefs, and worship service attendance. The NSFH also features several measures of gender traditionalism, two of which are utilized in this study, and a series of measures that are enlisted as controls. The measures used in this study are featured in both waves of the NSFH, thereby eliminating problems that would emerge from data collected at only one point in time.

Measures

DEPENDENT VARIABLES. There are two dependent variables used in this study, both of which gauge gender traditionalism. The first dependent variable, maternalist ideology, is based on the item, "It is all right for mothers to work full-time when their youngest child is under age five." In wave one of the NSFH, responses to this item range on a seven-point Likert scale from strongly disagree = 1 to strongly agree = 7. In wave two, responses range on a five-point Likert scale from strongly disagree = 1 to strongly agree = 5. For both waves, responses to this item were reverse-coded so that higher scores reflect greater gender traditionalism. This variable measures a commitment to maternalist ideology, namely, beliefs about a woman's prioritization of motherhood while children are young.

The second dependent variable, separate spheres ideology, is based on the item, "It is much better for everyone if the man earns the main living and the woman takes care of the home and family." Response categories on this item range from strongly disagree = 1 to strongly agree = 5 in both waves of the NSFH. This item measures a commitment to separate spheres for husbands (provider role) and wives (homemaker role).

These measures tap different dimensions of gender traditionalism and, it would seem, different levels of commitment to a traditionalist gender ideology. They are analyzed as separate dependent variables for face validity reasons. The maternalist ideology measure can be viewed as a less stringent measure of traditionalism. Maternalist ideology presumes more flexibility with respect to women's employment, implying that women's employment is acceptable if they do not have preschool-age children and that part-time employment for women may be acceptable when children are young. Conversely, the separate spheres ideology is less forgiving. This measure suggests support for a more global, long-standing commitment to home and family on the part of women. Based on this item, regardless of whether or not women have young children, everyone is seen as benefiting from wifely domesticity.

INDEPENDENT VARIABLES. Several religion variables are included in this study. First, denominational affiliation was coded using the Smith (1990) coding scheme, with the following categories: conservative Protestant, Moderate Protestant, liberal Protestant, Catholic, and unaffiliated (no religion). Other religious groups were excluded because of inadequate case numbers. In all tables, denominational affiliation is dummy-coded with unaffiliated as the reference category. In phase two of our study, we also explore the influence of denominational switching on gender traditionalism, dummy-coded to distinguish "stayers" (retain same denominational affiliation) from "switchers" (changed denominational affiliation), with switching as the reference category. Biblical inerrancy is our second religion variable, and is an index measure (alpha = .85) composed of two items:

1. "The Bible is God's word and everything happened or will happen exactly as it says."
2. "The Bible is the answer to all important human problems."

Responses range from strongly disagree = 1 to strongly agree = 5. The third and final religion measure gauges attendance at religious worship services, ranging from 1 = never attends to 7 = attends more than once per week. This measure generally corresponds with the religious attendance scale from the General Social Survey.

CONTROL VARIABLES. Though the coefficients for covariates are not shown in tables to conserve space, we include statistical controls for a wide range of factors that previous research suggests may be important. All control variables that are subject to change over time were measured at waves one and two. (Thus, the respondent's race, gender, and birth cohort were measured at wave one only.) We control for the type of intimate relationship reported by the respondent, with dummy-coded variables that include previously married (divorced, separated, or widowed), cohabiting, and currently married. Race was dummy-coded, and includes white, black, and Hispanic, with white as the reference category. Respondents of other races were excluded from the analyses because of inadequate case numbers. Birth cohort was measured so that respondents were placed into the following categories based on their year of birth: pre-1945 cohort, 1945–1959 cohort, and 1960–1971 cohort, with the first of these serving as the reference category. Education was measured as a continuous variable by determining the years of formal education reported by the respondent. Finally, employment status was ascertained, distinguishing those employed full-time, employed part-time, and others (unemployed, retired), with the last of these serving as the reference category in all tables.

Methods

Phase one of the study uses ordered logistic regression to analyze wave one of the NSFH. This technique explores the cross-sectional (static) effects of religion on gender traditionalism. In phase two, ordered logit conditional change models are used to estimate the longitudinal (dynamic) effects of religion on gender traditionalism with the lagged dependent variables (gender traditionalism at time one) controlled (Finkel 1995).

A listwise deletion procedure was used to generate four subsamples for analysis in this study:

- cross-sectional sample using the maternalist ideology measure (i.e., inappropriateness of employment for mothers of preschool children) as the dependent variable (n = 11,368)
- cross-sectional sample featuring the separate spheres ideology measure (i.e., support for husband-provider and wife-homemaker) as the dependent variable (n = 11,449)
- panel sample using the maternalist ideology measure as the dependent variable (n = 8,146)
- panel sample using the separate spheres ideology measure (n = 8,258)

We used nested model regression to generate findings, reporting odds ratios and significance levels.

Results

Descriptive statistics for all variables used in the study from both waves of NSFH data are featured in Table 6.1. Number of cases and proportions (percentages) are displayed for all categorical variables. For continuous variables, means and standard deviations are featured.

TABLE 6.1

Sample Characteristics

| | Maternalist Ideology | | | | Separate Spheres Ideology | | | |
| | Cross-sectional NSFH-1 | | Panel NSFH 1–2 | | Cross-sectional NSFH-1 | | Panel NSFH 1–2 | |
	n	%	n	%	n	%	n	%
Maternalist ideology (wave 1[a])	3.56	1.86	3.60	1.84	—	—	—	—
Maternalist ideology (wave 2[a])	—	—	3.06	1.04	—	—	—	—
Separate spheres (wave 1[a])	—	—	—	—	2.62	1.23	2.70	1.23
Separate spheres (wave 2[a])	—	—	—	—	—	—	2.87	1.25
Male (wave 1)	4,552	40.04	—	—	4,588	40.07	—	—
Female (wave 1) (reference)	6,816	59.96	—	—	6,861	59.93	—	—
Male (wave 2)	—	—	3,161	38.80	—	—	3,205	38.81
Female (wave 2) (reference)	—	—	4,985	61.20	—	—	3,205	38.81
Currently married (wave 1)	6,018	52.94	—	—	6,059	52.92	—	—
Previously married (wave 1)	3,253	28.62	—	—	3,287	28.71	—	—
Cohabiting respondent (wave 1)	2,097	18.45	—	—	2,103	18.37	—	—
Currently married (wave 2)	—	—	4,722	57.97	—	—	4,778	57.86
Previously married (wave 2)	—	—	2,425	29.77	—	—	2,468	29.89
Cohabiting respondent (wave 2)	—	—	999	12.26	—	—	1,012	12.25

White (reference)	8,464	74.45	6,285	77.15	8,513	74.36	6,352	76.92
Black	2,050	18.03	1,349	16.56	2,074	18.12	1,384	16.76
Hispanic	854	7.51	512	6.29	862	7.53	522	6.32
Birth cohort (before 45 reference)	4,678	41.15	3,042	37.34	4,736	41.37	3,114	37.71
Birth cohort (45–59)	4,381	38.54	3,370	41.37	4,395	38.39	3,396	41.12
Birth cohort (60–71)	2,309	20.31	1,734	21.29	2,318	20.25	1,748	21.17
Respondent's education (wave 1[a])	12.24	2.98	—	—	12.23	2.99	—	—
Respondent's education (wave 2[a])	—	—	12.74	2.90	—	—	12.73	2.91
Unemployed (wave 1) (reference)	4,551	40.03	—	—	4,593	40.12	—	—
Employed full-time (wave 1)	4,898	43.09	—	—	4,928	43.04	—	—
Employed part-time (wave 1)	1,919	16.88	—	—	1,928	16.84	—	—
Unemployed (wave 2)	—	—	3,084	37.86	—	—	3,143	38.06
Full-time (wave 2)	—	—	3,665	44.99	—	—	3,703	44.84
Part-time (wave 2)	—	—	1,397	17.15	—	—	1,412	17.10
Religious none (wave 1) (reference)	900	12.84	—	—	903	7.89	—	—
Catholic (wave 1)	2,869	25.24	—	—	2,888	25.22	—	—
Liberal Protestant (wave 1)	1,055	9.28	—	—	1,062	9.28	—	—
Moderate Protestant (wave 1)	2,634	23.17	—	—	2,657	23.21	—	—
Conservative Protestant (wave 1)	3,910	34.39	—	—	3,939	34.40	—	—
Religious none (wave 2) (reference)	—	—	742	9.11	—	—	750	9.08

(continued)

Table 6.1. Sample Characteristics *(continued)*

	Maternalist Ideology				Separate Spheres Ideology			
	Cross-sectional NSFH-1		Panel NSFH 1–2		Cross-sectional NSFH-1		Panel NSFH 1–2	
	n	%	n	%	n	%	n	%
Catholic (wave 2)	—	—	1,954	23.99	—	—	1,981	23.99
Liberal Protestant (wave 2)	—	—	842	10.34	—	—	853	10.33
Moderate Protestant (wave 2)	—	—	1,625	19.95	—	—	1,652	20.00
Conservative Protestant (wave 2)	—	—	2,983	36.62	—	—	3,022	36.59
Stayer (no switching)	—	—	6,598	81.00	—	—	6,687	80.98
Mover (switching, reference)	—	—	1,548	19.00	—	—	1,571	19.02
Biblical inerrancy (wave 1[a])	3.51	1.13	3.47	1.13	3.51	1.13	3.47	1.13
Biblical inerrancy (wave 2[a])	—	—	3.46	1.13	—	—	3.46	1.13
Attendance (wave 1[a])	5.99	3.88	6.09	3.87	5.99	3.88	6.10	3.87
Attendance (wave 2[a])	—	—	5.75	3.88	—	—	5.76	3.88
N	11,368		8,146		11,449		8,258	

a. Means and Standard Deviations.

Recall that our analytical strategy requires that we first run cross-sectional analyses, which are displayed in Table 6.2. In the table, we feature the results of nested regressions models, structured as follows. Model 1 estimates the effects of denominational affiliation and control variables on the dependent variable in question (maternalist ideology in Table 6.2a, separate spheres ideology in Table 6.2b). In Models 2 and 3, we enter additional religious variables (one per model). This strategy is employed because it estimates the independent effects of denominational affiliation while exploring the mediating influences of biblical inerrancy (Model 2) and worship service attendance (Model 3). In Tables 6.2a and 6.2b, Model 4 is the full model, estimating the effects of all study variables on the dependent variable.

Table 6.2a presents the estimated effects of variables on maternalist ideology, that is, the belief that mothers with preschool-age children should not be employed full-time. We find that denominational affiliation (of any sort), biblical inerrancy, and worship service attendance all predict higher levels of maternalist ideology. Models 2–4 indicate that biblical inerrancy and worship service attendance mediate the relationship between denominational affiliation and maternalist ideology. Thus, there is an indirect relationship between denominational affiliation and maternalist ideology through biblical inerrancy and worship service attendance. In the full model, conservative Protestant affiliation (along with other Protestant groups) drops to insignificance while Catholic affiliation remains significant. In this model, biblical inerrancy and worship service attendance persist as robust predictors of a maternalist ideology, net of all of other factors and statistical controls.

Tables 6.2b displays the estimated effects of independent variables on our second gender traditionalism measure, namely, separate spheres ideology (husband-provider, wife-homemaker). Religion variables exhibit a similar influence on the separate spheres ideology dependent variable, such that denominational affiliation of any sort predicts more traditional views about separate spheres. In addition, these denominational effects are largely mediated by biblical inerrancy and worship service attendance, such that the predictive power of denominational affiliation is significantly reduced in Models 2–4. However, as revealed in Model 4, these mediating effects do not eliminate the influence of denominational affiliation for conservative Protestants. This finding is somewhat different from that found in Model 4 of Table 6.2a, where the Catholic denominational affiliation was the only significant affiliation that survived. Overall, these disparate findings suggest that it is important to distinguish between different types of gender traditionalism. Conservative Protestant affiliation is more strongly predictive of separate spheres ideology while Catholic affiliation is more robustly predictive of a maternalist ideology.

Having run cross-sectional analyses in phase one of our study, we now turn to phase two of the investigation. Phase two entails longitudinal analysis of NSFH-1 and NSFH-2 panel data (see Finkel 1995 for panel data analysis

TABLE 6.2

Odds Coefficients of Ordered Logit Cross-Sectional Regression of Gender Traditionalism (NSFH-1)[a]

Variables	Model 1	Model 2	Model 3	Model 4
A. Maternalist Ideology				
Catholic	1.408***	1.254***	1.194*	1.153*
Liberal Protestant	1.301***	1.186*	1.160†	1.121
Moderate Protestant	1.243***	1.049	1.092	0.994
Conservative Protestant	1.545***	1.203**	1.298***	1.122
Biblical inerrancy		1.205***		1.172***
Attendance			1.038***	1.023***
Model Chi-square	829***	941***	888***	960***
Df	14	15	15	16
N	11,368	11,368	11,368	11,368

B. *Separate Spheres Ideology*

Catholic	1.686***	1.257***	1.222**	1.114
Liberal Protestant	1.474***	1.158†	1.189*	1.072
Moderate Protestant	1.667***	1.075	1.304***	0.997
Conservative Protestant	2.461***	1.290***	1.770***	1.172*
Biblical inerrancy		1.664***		1.600***
Attendance			1.076***	1.033***
Model Chi-square	2,350***	3,125***	2,573***	3,164***
Df	14	15	15	16
N	11,449	11,449	11,449	11,449

Note: All variables are NSFH wave 1 measures.

a. Covariates such as gender, marital status, race/ethnicity, birth cohort, educational attainment, and employment status are included in all models.

†p < 1.0; *p < .05; **p < .01; ***p < .001

TABLE 6.3

Odds Coefficients of Ordered Logit Conditional Change Regression of Gender Traditionalism (NSFH 1–2)[a]

Variables	Model 1	Model 2	Model 3	Model 4
A. *Maternalist Ideology*				
Catholic (wave 2)	1.259**	1.065	0.991	0.953
Liberal Protestant (wave 2)	1.278**	1.122	1.097	1.049
Moderate Protestant (wave 2)	1.130	0.887	0.934	0.830*
Conservative Protestant (wave 2)	1.540***	1.046	1.188*	0.968
Stayer (switching is reference)	0.934	0.944	0.905†	0.925
Biblical inerrancy (wave 1)		1.071**		1.044
Biblical inerrancy (wave 2)		1.232***		1.190***
Attendance (wave 1)			1.029***	1.017*
Attendance (wave 2)			1.035***	1.023**
Model Chi-square	1,543***	1,676***	1,636***	1,706***
Df	16	18	18	20
N	8,146	8,146	8,146	8,146

B. Separate Spheres Ideology

Catholic (wave 2)	1.456***	1.138	1.179†	1.089
Liberal Protestant (wave 2)	1.386***	1.141	1.207*	1.111
Moderate Protestant (wave 2)	1.400***	0.982	1.184*	0.956
Conservative Protestant (wave 2)	1.889***	1.067	1.506***	1.035
Stayer (switching is reference)	0.966	0.995	0.942	0.987
Biblical inerrancy (wave 1)		0.973		0.963
Biblical inerrancy (wave 2)		1.566***		1.547***
Attendance (wave 1)			1.023***	1.008
Attendance (wave 2)			1.034***	1.008
Model Chi-square	2,785***	3,166***	2,863***	3,170***
Df	16	18	18	20
N	8,258	8,258	8,258	8,258

a. Covariates such as gender, marital status, race/ethnicity, birth cohort, educational attainment, and employment status are included in all models.

† p < 1.0; * p < .05; ** p < .01; *** p < .001

considerations). The logic of the nested regression models employed in this phase of the analysis is identical to those used in phase one of the study. Moreover, the first dependent variable analyzed in this phase of the study is again maternalist ideology. The second dependent variable is again separate spheres ideology. Both of these variables are derived from wave two measures. Because this portion of the study is longitudinal, we control for gender traditionalism from the first wave of the NSFH. Consequently, measures used as dependent variables in our cross-sectional analyses become independent variables in phase two (longitudinal analyses). Similarly, we control for biblical inerrancy and worship service attendance from wave one. These measures now become lagged independent variables to examine the enduring effects of religion on gender traditionalism. In phase two of the study, we also introduce denominational switching measures. (Thus, measures of denominational stability serve as a type of lagged independent variable.)

Table 6.3 features findings derived from longitudinal data analyses. In the table, we feature the results of nested regressions models, structured as follows. Model 1 again estimates the effects of denominational affiliation and control variables on the dependent variable in question (maternalist ideology in Table 6.3a, separate spheres ideology in Table 6.3b). In Models 2 and 3, we enter biblical inerrancy and worship service attendance, respectively. In Tables 6.3a and 6.3b, Model 4 is again the full model, estimating the effects of all study variables on the dependent variable.

In Table 6.3a, enduring effects are observed because the lagged variables from time one (biblical inerrancy and attendance from NSFH-1) are statistically significant predictors of maternalist ideology at time two. Stable effects are evidenced through the statistical significance of biblical inerrancy and worship service attendance at time two. Models 2–4 reveal the existence of mediating effects, because the persistent significance of biblical inerrancy and worship service attendance eliminates statistical significance for the vast majority of denominational affiliation variables.

Turning finally to the longitudinal effects of religious factors on separate spheres ideology (husband-provider, wife-homemaker) in Table 6.3b, a number of religious effects are observed. Like the findings for the maternalist ideology measure, significant effects of denominational affiliation on separate spheres ideology are initially observed (Model 1 of Table 6.3b). However, these effects are reduced to insignificance (mediated) when biblical inerrancy is entered into the regression models (Model 2). Mediating effects are also observed, but are less pronounced, when worship service attendance is entered into the models (Model 3). Together, biblical inerrancy and worship service attendance completely eliminate statistically significant effects of denominational affiliation (Model 4).

In summary, religious factors exert considerable influence on traditionalist gender ideologies, both in terms of maternalism (views of the inappropriateness of employment for mothers with preschool-age children) and separate spheres ideology (belief in a husband-provider, wife-homemaker ideal). Denominational differences that are initially observed typically are significantly reduced or eliminated when biblical inerrancy and worship service attendance are entered into models. However, the nature of religious effects varies across dimensions of gender ideology. Longitudinal analyses reveal that the effects of religion are more enduring and stable for a maternalist ideology than for a separate spheres ideology.

Discussion and Conclusions

This study has explored the influence of religious factors on two dimensions of gender traditionalism, namely, maternalist ideology (views about the inappropriateness of maternal employment when children are preschool age) and separate spheres ideology (attitudes toward a husband-provider, wife-homemaker family ideal). This study is distinguished from prior scholarship in various ways, most importantly by, first, examining religious factors' effects on two different measures of gender traditionalism (maternalist ideology and separate sphere ideology), and second, conducting both cross-sectional and longitudinal analyses to determine if the effects of religious factors on gender traditionalism were stable (observed cross-sectionally) and/or enduring (observed longitudinally).

Several key findings emerged from this study. Where maternalist ideology is concerned, results of the cross-sectional analyses of NSFH-1 data reveal conservative Protestants and Catholics to be the denominational families that are most committed to the view that a mother's employment harms young children. This finding is in line with previous scholarship. However, for conservative Protestants (and other Protestant groups), these effects are mediated by biblical inerrancy and worship service attendance. Thus, denominational affiliation has an indirect effect on maternalist ideology, with direct effects manifested by biblical inerrancy and worship service attendance. To identify biblical inerrancy and worship service attendance as strong and direct predictors of maternalist ideology is not to say that conservative Protestant affiliation is irrelevant. Denominational affiliation indeed matters. However, in the real world, it seems that the ideological commitment to maternalism evinced by conservative Protestants is bolstered considerably by their inerrantist scriptural views and their churchgoing habits.

These conclusions are lent further credence by longitudinal findings that surface from analyses conducted with two waves of NSFH data. Using panel data from NSFH-1 and NSFH-2, we find both stable and enduring effects of biblical literalism and worship service attendance on maternalist ideology. Therefore, the influence of biblical literalism and worship service attendance is powerful in shaping gender ideology both at a particular point in time (cross-sectionally) and over a long period of time (longitudinally).

Cross-sectional analyses of the separate spheres ideology indicator yielded some similar findings and a few distinctive patterns. For all respondents claiming a denominational affiliation, strong independent effects are observed on attitudes toward husband-providership and wifely domesticity (separate spheres ideology). Once again, conservative Protestants are most strongly in favor of a separate spheres arrangement in the home. However, these effects are once again largely mediated by biblical inerrancy and worship service attendance. So, conservative Protestant affiliation is a key predictor of an attitudinal commitment to separate spheres, but this commitment is routed largely through orthodox theological convictions and frequent churchgoing.

Analyses of the longitudinal effects of religion on separate spheres ideology, however, revealed that biblical inerrancy alone mediates the effect of denominational affiliation. Thus, theological conservatism is the only religious factor that exhibits stable effects on separate spheres ideology, which is to say that biblical inerrancy at time two predicts support for separate spheres at time two. Biblical inerrancy, however, does not exhibit enduring effects on separate spheres ideology; thus, biblical inerrancy at time one has no effect on separate spheres ideology at time two. This finding contrasts with that for maternalist ideology, in which enduring (long-term) effects of biblical inerrancy were observed.

Why does the drawing of such distinctions between the stable and enduring effects of particular religious factors on various sorts of gender traditionalism matter? Does the drawing of such distinctions merely amount to sociological hairsplitting? In a word, no. A careful identification of such patterns is important because it demonstrates that specific religious mechanisms are responsible for sustaining an attitudinal commitment to particular forms of gender traditionalism over time. Mapping the linkages between religion and gender traditionalism longitudinally thus requires a commitment to methodological precision and an appreciation for conceptual complexity (for both religion and gender traditionalism) that has been sorely lacking in most prior scholarship. Thus, beyond highlighting the general conservative Protestant penchant for gender traditionalism, this study demonstrates that both religiosity and gender traditionalism must be conceptualized in ways that are complex enough to map precisely what religious mechanisms yield significant effects on particular forms of gender traditionalism. The now axiomatic principle that not all dimensions of religiosity are equal in their influence should be complemented by an appreciation for the variegated forms in which gender traditionalism may be manifested (mother versus homemaker roles, father versus breadwinner roles).

In summary, this study has revealed that a wide range of religious factors exert a strong influence on gender traditionalism. In general, denominational affiliation of any sort tends to produce more traditional attitudes about gender, and conservative Protestants are the most inclined toward traditional family values of any religious group. Yet, these effects are clearly mediated by other religious factors—namely, biblical inerrancy and worship service attendance—which seem to be the most powerful religious forces shaping gender ideologies. This conclusion is consistent with previous research that has suggested that conservative Protestantism is not restricted to particular denominations, but rather is a religious movement that creates a cognitive framework in which attitudes about social and cultural issues, especially those related to gender, are evaluated in light of biblical prescriptions (Ellison and Bartkowski 2002; Sherkat and Ellison 1997). This is not to say that organized religion has an ineffectual influence on gender traditionalism. Worship service attendance is also a key mediator of the relationship between denominational affiliation and traditional gender ideologies. Thus, the most profound influence on gender ideologies is exhibited by a combination of one's integration within religious networks and internalization of theological views (Bartkowski and Xu 2007). Moreover, the influence of these religious factors on gender traditionalism is generally persistent over time, lending credence to the life course stability hypothesis.

Future research is needed to extend the conclusions drawn in this study, particularly given that only five years had elapsed between the two waves of data analyzed here. Consequently, analyses of additional longitudinal data, perhaps those stretching over a greater expanse of time, are in order. Another promising avenue for future research would entail conducting gender-specific analyses in which the effects of religious variables are estimated separately for men and women. Prior research suggests that the mediating effects of biblical inerrancy on the relationship between denominational affiliation and gender traditionalism would be stronger for women than for men (Peek, Lowe, and Williams 1991).[3] More generally, the role of mediators such as biblical inerrancy, worship service attendance, and other religious factors (e.g., salience, self-acclaimed conservative Protestant religious identities such as Evangelical, fundamentalist, and Pentecostal) deserve more sustained attention using additional data sources, and further research is needed to explore the possible interaction effects of these religious factors on gender traditionalism. Until such research is conducted, this study has demonstrated that a wide range of religious factors exerts robust and sustained effects on attitudes toward gender. In attempting to explain the continued bases of support for gender traditionalism and conservative family values in contemporary American society, researchers neglect religious influences at their own peril.

NOTES

The authors gratefully acknowledge the support of the Criss Fund at Mississippi State University for a research award that supported this study.

1. Qualitative researchers have also documented a wide range of viewpoints within the conservative Protestant universe concerning gender and family issues (Bartkowski 2001; Smith 2000).

2. Regrettably, previous research has either entirely overlooked the potential confounding influence of the intimate relationships in which respondents are situated, or has

reduced it to a dichotomous marital status measure (currently married, currently unmarried) (e.g., Peek, Lowe, and Williams 1991). Yet, given the dramatic rise of cohabitation and divorce in the United States (Xu, Hudspeth, and Bartkowski 2006), research is needed to determine if the influence of conservative Protestant affiliation on gender traditionalism is mediated by relationship type (e.g., currently married, divorced, widowed, cohabiting). The cultural primacy of marriage as a sacred institution within this religious subculture might be a key influence on conservative Protestants' commitment to gender traditionalism (Wilson and Musick 1996; Xu, Hudspeth, and Bartkowski 2005), requiring that researchers carefully control for relationship type. This issue is also vitally important because it is possible that marriage, as a conventional social institution, creates a more traditional ethos in a relationship irrespective of religious differences, thus perhaps trumping religious variations in gender traditionalism.

3. Recent research has called attention to the gender gap in biblical inerrancy within conservative Protestant denominations, such that women within this faith tradition are significantly more inclined to view the Bible as the actual word of God than are their male counterparts (Hoffmann and Bartkowski 2004). The gender gap in biblical inerrancy is much more muted in liberal religious groups. The gender difference in biblical inerrancy among conservative Protestants is thought to stem from conservative religious men's opportunities to express their religious commitment through formal organizational means, given the pervasiveness of male-only congregational leadership in conservative religious denominations. Barred from exercising formal religious authority in such denominations, women's religiosity is expressed in a more subjective form.

REFERENCES

Alwin, D. F. 1994. "Aging, Personality, and Social Change: The Stability of Individual Differences over the Adult Life Span." In *Life-Span Development and Behavior*, ed. D. Featherman, R. Lerner, and M. Perlmutter, 135–185. Mahwah, NJ: Lawrence Erlbaum Associates.

Bartkowski, J. P. 2001. *Remaking the Godly Marriage: Gender Negotiation in Evangelical Families*. New Brunswick, NJ: Rutgers University Press.

———. 2004. *The Promise Keepers: Servants, Soldiers, and Godly Men*. New Brunswick, NJ: Rutgers University Press.

———. 2007. "Connections and Contradictions: Exploring the Complex Linkages between Faith and Family." In *Everyday Religion: Observing Modern Religious Lives*, ed. N. T. Ammerman, 153–166. New York: Oxford University Press.

Bartkowski, J. P., and X. Xu. 2000. "Distant Patriarchs or Expressive Dads? The Discourse and Practice of Fathering in Conservative Protestant Families." *Sociological Quarterly* 41:465–485.

———. 2007. "Religion, Social Capital, and Teen Drug Use: A Preliminary Investigation." *American Journal of Preventive Medicine* 32 (6S): S182–S194.

Bendroth, M. L. 1999. "Fundamentalism and the Family: Gender, Culture, and the American Pro-Family Movement." *Journal of Women's History* 10:35–54.

Denton, M. L. 2004. "Gender and Marital Decision Making: Negotiating Religious Ideology and Practice." *Social Forces* 82:1151–1180.

Ellison, C. G., and J. P. Bartkowski. 2002. "Conservative Protestantism and the Division of Household Labor among Married Couples." *Journal of Family Issues* 23:950–985.

Finkel, S. E. 1995. *Causal Analysis with Panel Data*. Thousand Oaks, CA: Sage Publications.

Gallagher, S. K. 2003. *Evangelical Identity and Gendered Family Life.* New Brunswick, NJ: Rutgers University Press.

———. 2004. "Where Are the Antifeminist Evangelicals? Evangelical Identity, Subcultural Location, and Attitudes toward Feminism." *Gender and Society* 18:451–472.

Gallagher, S. K., and C. Smith. 1999. "Symbolic Traditionalism and Pragmatic Egalitarianism." *Gender and Society* 13:211–233.

Gay, D. A., C. G. Ellison, and D. A. Powers. 1996. "In Search of Denominational Subcultures: Religious Affiliation and 'Pro-Family' Issues Revisited." *Review of Religious Research* 38:3–17.

Grasmick, H. G., L. P. Wilcox, and S. R. Bird. 1990. "The Effects of Religious Fundamentalism and Religiosity on Preference for Traditional Family Norms." *Sociological Inquiry* 60:352–369.

Hertel, B. R., and M. Hughes. 1987. "Religious Affiliation, Attendance, and Support for 'Pro-Family' Issues in the United States." *Social Forces* 65:858–882.

Hoffmann, J. P., and J. P. Bartkowski. 2004. "Sex, Religious Tradition, and Biblical Literalism." Paper presented at the annual meetings of the Society for the Scientific Study of Religion, Kansas City, MO.

Huber, J., and G. Spitze. 1983. *Sex Stratification: Children, Housework, and Jobs.* New York: Academic Press.

Hunter, J. D. 1991. *Culture Wars.* New York: Basic.

Lehrer, E. L. 1995. "The Effects of Religion on the Labor Supply of Married Women." *Social Science Research* 24:281–301.

Peek, C. W., G. D. Lowe, and S. Williams. 1991. "Gender and God's Word: Another Look at Religious Fundamentalism and Sexism." *Social Forces* 69:1205–1221.

Roof, W. C., and W. McKinney. 1987. *American Mainline Religion.* New Brunswick, NJ: Rutgers University Press.

Sherkat, D. E. 2000. "'That They Be Keepers of the Home': The Effect of Conservative Religion on Early and Late Transitions into Housewifery." *Review of Religious Research* 41:344–358.

Sherkat, D. E., and C. G. Ellison. 1997. "The Cognitive Structure of a Moral Crusade: Conservative Protestantism and Opposition to Pornography." *Social Forces* 75:957–982.

Smith, C. 2000. *Christian America? What Evangelicals Really Want.* Berkeley: University of California Press.

Smith, T. 1990. "Classifying Protestant Denominations." *Review of Religious Research* 31:225–245.

Sweet, J. A., and L. L. Bumpass. 1996. "The National Survey of Families and Households—Waves 1 and 2: Data Description and Documentation." Unpublished manuscript, Center for Demography and Ecology, University of Wisconsin, Madison.

Sweet, J. A., L. L. Bumpass, and V. Call. 1988. "The Design and Content of the National Survey of Families and Households." NSFH Working Paper, number one, Center for Demography and Ecology, University of Wisconsin, Madison.

Wilcox, C., and T. G. Jelen. 1991. "The Effects of Employment and Religion on Women's Feminist Attitudes." *International Journal for the Psychology of Religion* 1:161–171.

Wilcox, W. B. 2004. *Soft Patriarchs, New Men: How Christianity Shapes Fathers and Husbands.* Chicago: University of Chicago Press.

Wilson, J., and M. Musick. 1996. "Religion and Marital Dependency." *Journal for the Scientific Study of Religion* 35:30–40.

Xu, X., C. D. Hudspeth, and J. P. Bartkowski. 2005. "The Timing of First Marriage: Are There Religious Variations?" *Journal of Family Issues* 26:584–618.

———. 2006. "The Role of Cohabitation in Remarriage." *Journal of Marriage and Family* 68:261–274.

7

From Generation to Generation

Religious Involvement and Attitudes toward Family and Pro-Family Outcomes among U.S. Catholics

AMY M. BURDETTE AND TERESA A. SULLIVAN

Catholicism is the most common religious affiliation in the United States, accounting for 27 percent of the U.S. population (Froehle and Gautier 2000). Recent estimates suggest that this religious group will continue to grow, largely due to the immigration of Asian and Hispanic Catholics (Davidson 2005). This large and diverse religious body has experienced a great deal of change over the last forty years. Far from being a monolithic body of believers, American Catholics have experienced and will continue to experience changes that affect their attitudes toward family life. While changes in society at large over this time period have influenced Catholics along with other religious groups, there is reason to believe that Catholics have been particularly impacted because of dynamics within the denomination. However, it is uncertain whether all generations of Catholics have been impacted in the same way by these changes. It is also unclear whether these changes are due to differences in religious commitment.

Although scholars have noted important generational variations among U.S. Catholics, few (if any) studies have examined generational specific trends in family and pro-family issues. Because this religious affiliation accounts for such a large and diverse segment of society, changes within this religious body drive trends in attitudes toward fertility, sexuality, gender roles and other social issues in society at large. Therefore, this chapter investigates the following research questions: Are Catholics liberalizing in relation to family and pro-family issues? If so, are these trends consistent across generations of Catholics? Are these trends explained by sociodemographic differences among generations, or by differences in level of religious commitment?

The remainder of this chapter proceeds as follows. We begin by discussing endogenous, exogenous, and compositional sources of changes within the Church, as well as previous research on Catholicism and family-related issues. We then explore the aforementioned research questions, employing data from the 1974–2004 General Social Surveys (GSS) (Davis, Smith, and Marsden 2004).

All data analyses are limited to non-Hispanic white Catholics. Although other racial and ethnic groups are certainly important to family life among Catholics, the GSS simply does not contain sufficient numbers of nonwhite Catholics (particularly Latinos) to support accurate investigation. And the limitation of the GSS to English-speaking respondents excludes monolingual Spanish speakers, many of whom are Catholic. Following the presentation of results, we discuss the implications of our findings, note the limitations of our study, and identify promising directions for future research.

Theoretical Background

Sources of Change within the Catholic Church

The Second Vatican Council, held between 1962 and 1965, was a major event in the life of the Catholic Church. For U.S. Catholics, it marked a change to liturgies held in English with new music, new architecture, new icons, and new rituals. Despite language about mere "updating" of Church teachings, there was also an expectation that sweeping changes were pending in Church doctrine and discipline. Numerous scholars have noted the dramatic impact of Vatican II, moving the Catholic Church from a strong tradition of uniformity to greater acceptance of national, regional, and individual variations in practice (e.g., D'Antonio 1985; McNamara 1992; Pogorelc and Davidson 2000; D'Antonio et al. 2001).

In the immediate post–Vatican II years, there was a ferment of ideas and proposals, but there was also a quick and determined reaction. One such issue that took on great symbolic significance occurred in 1968, when Pope Paul VI disagreed with his own expert panel and reaffirmed a ban on artificial birth control. Countless scholars have noted the incredible impact of the so-called "birth control encyclical" on the already declining religious authority of the Catholic Church (Greeley 1989; D'Antonio et al. 2001). D'Antonio (1985) argues that this action did more damage to the formal teaching authority of the Pope than any other action in that century.

The year 1979 marked another key event in recent Catholic Church history. For the first time in centuries, a non-Italian occupied the throne of Peter. Karol Wojtyla, styled as Pope John Paul II, began his reign to great but conflicting expectations—some expecting continued change, others longing for stern stability. Young American Catholics coming of age at that time were also assimilating the effects of the civil rights revolution, the Vietnam protests, and the feminist movement. Pope John Paul's lengthy reign of twenty-five years marked a renewed role of the papacy in geopolitics but also led to a consistent reinforcement of the traditional teachings on sexuality, reinforced by a philosophical joining of these issues to what the Pope called "the seamless garment" of issues related to biological human life.

Possibly as a result of these and other changes, there has been a notable decline in Catholic Mass attendance over the last fifty years. Evidence suggests that the rate of decline in attendance has been steeper for Catholics than for Protestants (Greeley 1989), and has occurred among all age-groups younger than sixty-five (Sander 2000). Although much of this decline occurred following the changes that took place in the Church during the 1960s, very few people actually left the Church during this time period. Instead, many Catholics who disagreed with the teachings of the Church simply reduced their frequency of attendance (Hout and Greeley 1987). Further, some scholars have argued that the core elements of Catholic identity (e.g., sacraments, belief in life after death) have not changed over time (Hoge 1999, 2002). This may indicate that generational differences in belief do not parallel the declines in ritual participation (e.g., Kennedy 1988).

A related set of controversies about the nature of Catholic leadership is also relevant. The limitation of Catholic priesthood to celibate males has been questioned by some American Catholics, particularly as they see women and married men leading congregations in other denominations throughout the United States. Although the Catholic population continues to grow, the number of priests has continued to shrink dramatically relative to the Catholic population (Schoenherr and Yang 1992). While 35 percent of Catholic laity is between eighteen and thirty-four years of age, only 5 percent of priests are in this age-group (Davidson 2005, 104). As a result of these two figures, young Catholics may have a difficult time finding a priest their own age, especially one who has the time to provide counsel. Thus, young Catholics may feel further alienated from the Church. In addition, the current Catholic immigrants to the United States have generally not brought a large number of priests with them, in sharp contrast to the large Catholic immigration streams of the nineteenth and early twentieth centuries.

The issues of leadership and sexual teaching have intersected in the recent scandal over sexual contact between priests and young people and subsequent cover-ups by the Church hierarchy. A recent study by the John Jay College of Criminal Justice (2004) shows that between 1950 and 2002, 4,392 priests were accused of at least one credible incident of immoral sexual conduct with a young person. Parishioners see this as one of the most important problems facing the Church, and many believe that some bishops have not done enough to stop abuse by priests, although opinions on the scandals vary by generation (Davidson and Hoge 2004).

Compositional changes in the Catholic population may also have an impact on family-related issues, as well as Catholicism more generally. As noted, the Catholic Church continues to grow as the result of immigration. Current estimates indicate that approximately 71 percent of Catholics are white, 22 percent are Hispanic, 3 percent are African American, 3 percent are Asian, and 1 percent is Native American. Catholics are the largest religious group among new immigrants, making up 42 percent of this population (Davidson 2005). Additionally, while the number of children born to non-Hispanic Catholics is somewhat below the national average, this is not the case for foreign-born Hispanic women (Froehle and Gautier 2000).

Two additional sociodemographic changes among Catholics could potentially influence family life: increases in their overall socioeconomic status and shifts in their regional concentrations. Historical data indicate that Catholics have made great gains in income and education. For most of the eighteenth and nineteenth century, Catholics (mainly European immigrants) had limited educational backgrounds and held low-wage jobs (D'Antonio et al. 2001). Many contemporary Catholics are firmly planted in the nation's upper-middle class (Greeley 1989); the current wave of Catholic immigrants, however, has a relatively low level of education (Davidson 2005). Related to immigration, there have been notable shifts in regional concentrations of Catholics. Specifically, the Catholic population appears to be declining in the Northeastern United States while increasing in the Southwest and Southeast (Davidson 2005). This increase in Southern residence, particularly those spending their formative years in this area, is of particular interest due to the generally conservative attitudes held by members of this region. Because Church infrastructure has traditionally been linked to population concentration, Catholic services are in short supply in the South and Southwest, while parishes, schools, and other Catholic institutions are often being closed in the Northeast. Thus, the most rapidly growing segment of the Catholic population is also located in geographic areas that have traditionally had few Catholic institutions.[1]

It is also important to remember that changes within the Catholic Church have not occurred in isolation. Many of these trends within the Church mirror the shifts in society at large. The 1960s and 1970s were a time of great liberalization in many attitudes related to family issues, particularly sexuality. This was followed by a conservative rebound in the 1980s and early 1990s. Since that time there is some evidence of liberalization with regard to family and pro-family outcomes (e.g., Loftus 2001; Thornton and Young-DeMarco 2001). Evidence from a study of Catholic college students finds a dramatic liberal shift in attitudes from 1961 to 1971—the period when the Baby Boom was first entering college—followed by a conservative turn from 1971 to 1982 (Moberg and Hoge 1986).[2] This parallels trends in society at large during this time period (Smith 1990; Davis 1992).

Catholicism and Family Issues

Scholars have long noted the relationship between Catholic religious affiliation and family-related outcomes, particularly fertility. Traditionally, the Catholic Church has taught that procreation is a primary purpose of marriage, and that periodic abstinence is the only acceptable means of birth control for married couples (D'Antonio and Cavanaugh 1983; D'Antonio 1985). One of the most important findings on religion and marital fertility has been that, at least among older cohorts, the fertility of Catholics has been higher than that of non-Catholics (Westoff 1979; Westoff and Jones 1979; Mosher, Johnson, and Horn 1986).

These studies also indicate a convergence between Catholics and non-Catholics by the mid-1970s for non-Hispanic white women (Sander 1995). Although current non-Hispanic Catholic fertility is now similar to or lower than that of non-Catholics (Mosher, Williams, and Johnson 1992; Froehle and Gautier 2000), some evidence suggests that Catholic women still have a preference for larger than average families (Pearce 2002).[3] Much of this unrealized fertility appears to be due to delayed marriage patterns among Catholics (Mosher, Williams, and Johnson 1992). However, few scholars have examined current trends in ideal family size among Catholics.

In addition to what could be termed direct family outcomes or behaviors, researchers have investigated a number of social and political attitudes related to family life. These topics (e.g., abortion, sexuality, and gender roles), which scholars have labeled "pro-family issues," have received great attention from media and Church leadership alike (D'Antonio et al. 2001, 75). In general, Catholics tend to report moderate attitudes on most "pro-family" issues, falling between conservative Protestants and nonaffiliates on the conservative–liberal continuum (Roof and McKinney 1987; Hoffman and Miller 1997). While Catholics report the most conservative views on abortion among the various religious affiliations, they report more tolerant attitudes toward premarital sexual behavior than members of some other religious groups (e.g., Southern Baptists, Presbyterians). Catholics also exhibit slightly greater than average homogeneity on gender role ideology, but somewhat more internal diversity than the norm in their attitudes toward abortion and homosexuality (Gay, Ellison, and Powers 1996).

Religious variations in abortion attitudes have perhaps received the most attention with regard to trends in "pro-family" issues (e.g., Sullins 1999; Evans 2002; Hoffman and Johnson 2005). While the Catholic Church has taken a strong, uncompromising pro-life position on abortion, evidence suggests that even highly committed Catholic laity have become more permissive in their attitudes. It also appears that younger generations of Catholics are the driving force behind the liberalization in abortion attitudes (Sullins 1999). Further, Catholics appear to be internally polarizing on this issue over time. Some scholars argue that this polarization is due to the incredibly diverse nature of the Church, which has been kept together in one religious body by a strong hierarchal structure (Evans 2002).

Religious-based differences in attitudes related to human sexuality (e.g., premarital sex, homosexuality, extramarital sex) have received somewhat less attention in the literature. In general, evidence suggests that Americans have become more liberal in their attitudes toward premarital sex and homosexuality, but not extramarital sex (Loftus 2001; Thornton and Young-DeMarco 2001). There is also some evidence that suggests that Catholics in particular are becoming more liberal in their attitudes toward premarital sex than other religious affiliations (Hoffman and Miller 1997; Bolzendahl and Brooks 2005). However, the recent sexual abuse scandal within the Church could threaten this liberalizing trend, given that some Catholics blame the inappropriate sexual behavior with minors on homosexual priests, and, as a consequence, want to exclude gay men from the ministry (Davidson 2005, 92).

Like some issues related to sexuality, evidence suggests that Americans have become increasingly liberal over the last thirty years in their attitudes toward the role of women in society (Thornton, Alwin, and Camburn 1983; Brewster and Padavic 2000; Thornton and Young-DeMarco 2001). Some research points to Catholics as being important contributors to the changes observed in society as a whole (Alwin et al. 2004). Despite the generally liberal attitudes held by Catholics toward gender roles, the Church itself remains conservative in its view of the place of women in society. Because of their exclusion from the priesthood, women continue to be marginalized in many of the Church's decision-making processes, despite the fact that a number of parishes are headed by women administrators (D'Antonio et al. 2001). Further, the majority of lay ministers, an important resource for dealing with the priest shortage, are married women (Davidson 2005).

This chapter makes several contributions to the existing literature on Catholics and family related issues. First, through limiting our analysis to Catholics, we are able to examine Catholic-specific generational trends. By employing theoretically relevant generational categories—pre–Vatican II (birth cohort of 1901–1943), Vatican II (birth cohort of 1944–1960) and post–Vatican II (birth cohort of 1961–1984)—we are able to study variations in attitudes toward family-related issues. These generational distinctions are based on the timing of key shifts within the Church. The pre–Vatican II generation spent their formative years within the traditional Catholic Church, whereas the Vatican II generation grew up in a time of dramatic change within both the Catholic Church and the United States. For the post–Vatican II generation, religious training occurred during the 1970s or later, a time when catechetical styles were dramatically different from the rote-learning methods used until the late 1960s (Froehle and Gautier 2000).

Second, although previous research has noted generational variations in family issues (e.g., Hoge 1999; D'Antonio et al. 2001; Davidson 2005), few studies have included controls for important sociodemographic variables related to family outcomes. Our research investigates whether these generational variations in family and pro-family issues are accounted for by generational variations in education, income, region of residence, and other important variables. Finally, scholars have noted important generational variations in level of religious involvement among Catholics (D'Antonio et al. 2001). We therefore investigate whether these generational trends are explained by variations in religious participation.

Data and Methods

Data

To chart attitudes toward family and pro-family issues across generations and overtime, we analyze data from the 1974–2004 GSS, conducted by the Chicago-based National Opinion Research Center (Davis, Smith, and Marsden 2004). The annual GSS is based on a national probability sample of noninstitutionalized United States residents' eighteen years of age and older. Between 1972 and 1993, the GSS was conducted annually (except for 1979, 1981, and 1992, when no surveys were fielded). Beginning in 1994, the GSS has been conducted in even-numbered years only, but has involved larger samples than in the pre-1994 years. Since 1987, the GSS has used a split-ballot design in data collection to maximize the number of items included in each year. As a result of this design, however, many items (except for a group of "core" questions that are included on all surveys) have been asked of only a randomly selected subset of GSS respondents. Although this split-ballot design reduces the available N for our analyses, the fact that these ballots are randomly assigned minimizes the potential for sample bias. As noted earlier, all analyses are limited to non-Hispanic white Catholics (N = 9,257 for the total sample of Catholics).

Measures

INDEPENDENT VARIABLE: YEAR OF SURVEY. The year that the survey was completed is the key variable under investigation for all Catholics and within each generation. Examining the year of the survey allows for the investigation of general trends in Catholicism over time, as well as generation specific trends.

DEPENDENT VARIABLES: FAMILY AND PRO-FAMILY ATTITUDES. Attitudes concerning ideal family size are tapped via responses to the following item: "What do you think is the ideal number of children for a family to have?" Although the original response categories ranged from 0 (none) to 7 (seven or more) this item was recoded to range from 0 (none) to 4 (four or more), due to the distribution of this variable.[4]

"Pro-family" (or traditional) attitudes are tapped using items measuring attitudes toward abortion, premarital sex, homosexuality, extramarital sex, and gender roles. There is well-developed Catholic doctrine proscribing abortion, sexual intercourse outside marriage, and sexual activity between people of the same sex. With respect to gender roles, there is less clarity, and recent popes have made a point of supporting women's economic and social roles. Motherhood is always praised as a high calling for married women. On the other hand, the restriction of the priesthood to celibate men is consistent with traditional views of gender roles.

Abortion attitudes are measured using a scale consisting of seven dichotomous items. Respondents were asked if a pregnant women should be able to obtain a legal abortion in the following circumstances: if there is a strong chance of serious defect in the baby, if she is married and does not want any more children, if the woman's own health is seriously endangered by the pregnancy, if the family cannot afford any more children, if the pregnancy is the result of rape, if she is not married, or if she wants an abortion for any reason. The higher the score, the more restrictive the view toward abortion. The theoretical range of the scale is 0 to 7. The alpha level for the scale is 0.89 with a mean of 2.98 and a standard deviation of 2.45.

Attitudes toward premarital sex are tapped using the question "If a man and woman have sexual relations before marriage, do you think it is (1) always wrong, (2) almost always wrong, (3) wrong only sometimes, or (4) not wrong at all?" Attitudes toward homosexuality were measured using the question, "What about sexual relations between two adults of the same sex—do you think it is (1) always wrong, (2) almost always wrong, (3) wrong only sometimes, or (4) not wrong at all?" Finally, attitudes toward extramarital sexual behavior were measured using the question, "What is your opinion about a married person having sexual relations with someone other than the marriage partner—is it (1) always wrong, (2) almost always wrong, (3) wrong only sometimes, or (4) not wrong at all?" These items, used to investigate attitudes toward sexuality, were recoded so that higher scores indicate more conservative responses.

Attitudes toward gender roles were measured using a scale including four items. Respondents were asked about their (dis)agreement with the following statements: "A working mother can establish just as warm and secure a relationship with her children as a mother who does not work," "A preschool child is likely to suffer if his or her mother works," "It is much better for everyone involved if the man is the achiever outside the home and the woman takes care of the home and family," and "It is more important for a wife to help her husband's career than to have one herself." Response categories range from (1) strongly agree to (4) strongly disagree, and the scale has a theoretical range from 1 to 13. These items were recoded so that larger numbers indicate more conservative responses. The alpha level for the overall scale is 0.79 with a mean of 6.13 and a standard deviation of 2.63.

INDEPENDENT VARIABLES: RELIGIOUS INVOLVEMENT AND SOCIODEMO-GRAPHIC CONTROLS. Religious involvement is tapped using two items: frequency of church attendance and strength of affiliation. Respondents were asked to indicate how often they attend religious services. Response categories for this item range from (0) never to (8) more than once a week. Self-rated strength of affiliation measures responses to the following question: "Would you call yourself a strong <insert religious affiliation> or a not very strong <insert religious affiliation>?" Response categories for this item have been dummy-coded such that the category of interest indicates a strong (in this case, Catholic) religious affiliation.

Numerous background factors have been associated with attitudes toward family issues as well as generational changes within Catholicism. In accordance with prior research, subsequent multivariate analyses include controls for sex (1 = female), age (in years), education (in years), household income (standardized, imputing the mean for missing data for each year for the total GSS sample), full-time employment (1 = employed full-time), marital status (1 = currently married), whether the respondent has even been divorced (1 = ever divorced), region of residence (1 = Southern resident), rural residence (1 = rural resident), and number of children (actual number).

Analytic Procedures

Our analytic strategy proceeds in three general steps. First, we provide descriptive statistics in Table 7.1 for variables measuring religious involvement and background factors. Second, Table 7.2 provides means to demonstrate differences in attitudes toward family and pro-family issues by generation. Third, in Tables 7.3 to 7.5, we provide appropriate ordinary least squares and ordered logistic regression estimates to formally evaluate the net effects of trends in predictor variables for all Catholics and separately by generation. More specifically, in Model 1 of Tables 7.3 through 7.5 we evaluate whether there is a trend in the dependent variable for Catholics in general and within each generation. In Model 2 of Tables 7.3 to 7.5 we explore whether or not this trend is explained by variations in sociodemographic characteristics. Finally, we investigate whether each trend is accounted for by variations in religious involvement.

Results

Descriptive statistics for the background and religious involvement variables used in our analyses are displayed in Table 7.1. The average GSS Catholic is about forty-five years of age, female (56 percent), has slightly more than a high school education (12.75 total years completed), and is employed full-time (53 percent). Most respondents are currently married (57 percent), and few have ever been divorced (9 percent). Further, few live in rural areas (15 percent) or are Southerners (18 percent). Respondents on average have around two children (1.94). On average, non-Hispanic white GSS Catholic respondents report attending religious services slightly more than once per month (4.35). Although the majority of these respondents do not consider themselves strongly attached to their religious affiliation, a significant minority considers themselves to be strong Catholics (39 percent).

Table 7.1 also reveals several notable generational differences in background and religion items. Both the Vatican II generation and the post–Vatican II generation are significantly more educated and more likely to be employed full-time than the pre–Vatican II generation. The pre–Vatican II and Vatican II generations are more likely to currently be married or to have experienced a divorced

TABLE 7.1

Mean Levels of Religious Involvement and Control Variables[a]

	All Catholics (n = 9,257)	Pre–Vatican II Generation (n = 3,910)	Vatican II Generation (n = 3,476)	Post–Vatican II Generation (n = 1,871)
Female	.56	.57	.56	.54
Age	44.70	60.17	36.35	27.87
	(17.24)	(13.03)	(9.42)	(6.14)
Years of Education	12.75	11.71	13.48	13.56
	(3.01)	(3.24)	(2.67)	(2.42)
Household Income	.14	.03	.29	.07
	(.87)	(.91)	(.80)	(.85)
Employed Full-Time	.53	.34	.66	.69
Currently Married	.57	.61	.61	.41
Ever Been Divorced	.09	.10	.10	.04
Rural Resident	.15	.17	.14	.13
Southern Resident	.18	.17	.19	.22
Number of Children	1.94	2.81	1.58	.82
	(1.84)	(2.03)	(1.42)	(1.14)
Church Attendance	4.35	4.97	4.07	3.55
	(2.54)	(2.59)	(2.44)	(2.27)
Strong Catholic Affiliation	.39	.49	.34	.27

a. Standard deviations are included in parentheses where appropriate.

compared to the post–Vatican II generation. Members of the pre–Vatican II generation are slightly more likely to live in a rural area than the other two cohorts, while members of the post–Vatican II generation are more visible in the South. With regard to religious differences, the pre–Vatican II cohort appears to attend church more frequently and to hold stronger ties to the Catholic Church, compared with the other two cohorts. Conversely, the post–Vatican II generation reports attending church less frequently than the other two cohorts, and are less likely to hold a strong Catholic affiliation.

Table 7.2 shows unadjusted mean comparisons of all of the family and pro-family variables by generation. There are a number of significant generational differences in attitudes toward these issues. The pre–Vatican II generation appears to be the most distinct in their attitudes toward family-related issues;

TABLE 7.2

Unadjusted Mean Comparisons of Dependent Variables by Generation[a]

	All Catholics (N = 9,257)	Pre–Vatican II Generation (N = 3,910)	Vatican II Generation (N = 3,476)	Post–Vatican II Generation (N = 1,871)
Ideal Number of Children	1.66	1.83[xxx]	1.62***	1.37***[xxx]
Abortion Attitudes Scale[b]	4.02	3.46[xxx]	2.63***	2.67***
Attitudes toward Premarital Sex	2.08	2.60[xxx]	1.73***	1.62***[xx]
Attitudes toward Extramarital Sex	3.64	3.70[xxx]	3.54***	3.71[xxx]
Attitudes toward Homosexuality	3.13	3.50[xxx]	2.92***	2.69***[xxx]
Scale of Gender Role Attitudes	6.16	7.46[xxx]	5.45***	5.08***[xx]

a. Asterisks (*) indicate differences from the pre–Vatican II Generation, Xs (ˣ) indicate differences from the Vatican II generation.

b. Higher values indicate more conservative attitudes for all attitude items.

*p < .05 **p < .01 ***p<.001 [x]p < .05 [xx]p < .01 [xxx]p<.001

indeed, they are significantly more traditional, on average, than the Vatican II and post–Vatican II generations in every outcome except attitudes toward marital infidelity. Although the Vatican II generation holds more traditional attitudes than the subsequent generation toward ideal family size, premarital sex, homosexuality, and gender roles, the post–Vatican II generation holds more conservative views toward extramarital sexual behavior. Interestingly, there are no significant differences between the Vatican II generation and the post–Vatican II generation with regard to abortion attitudes.

Ideal Number of Children

Model 1 of Table 7.3 tests whether there are significant trends in attitudes toward the ideal number of children a family should have among Catholics in general and within each generation. Evidence suggests that ideal family size has grown smaller over the past thirty years. This trend exists for all three generations. Model 2 of Table 7.3 includes the sociodemographic controls shown in Table 7.1. Although the inclusion of these controls reduces the trend for the Vatican II generation, a significant trend remains for all generations. The final model,

TABLE 7.3

Unstandardized OLS Coefficients Predicting Ideal Number of Children and Abortion Attitudes by Generation

	Ideal Number of Children				Abortion Attitudes Scale			
	All Catholics (N = 8,856)	Pre–Vatican II Generation (N = 3,687)	Vatican II Generation (N = 3,349)	Post–Vatican II Generation (N = 1,820)	All Catholics (N = 5,040)	Pre–Vatican II Generation (N = 2,073)	Vatican II Generation (N = 2,002)	Post–Vatican II Generation (N = 963)
I. Unadjusted Model								
Year	-.058***	-.064***	-.053***	-.055***	-.010	.000	.010	.019
Adjusted R^2	.081	.087	.070	.026	.000	.000	.000	.000
II. Demographics[a]								
Year	-.056***	-.065***	-.034***	-.052***	-.006	-.015	.011	.039
Adjusted R^2	.086	.094	.076	.026	.058	.042	.045	.020
III. Religion Variables[b]								
Year	-.055***	-.064***	-.034***	-.051***	.013*	.000	.033*	.058**
Adjusted R^2	.087	.097	.076	.026	.206	.216	.189	.136

Note: GSS (1974–2004)

a. Adds controls for gender, age, years of education, income, full-time employment, whether R is currently married, ever been divorced, rural resident, Southern resident, and number of children.

b. Adds controls for church attendance and strength of affiliation.

*p < .05; **p < .01; ***p<.001

Model 3, includes our measures of religious involvement. Neither frequency of church attendance, nor strength of affiliation, appears to diminish the observed trend for Catholics as a whole or for any of the generations.

Abortion Attitudes

Turning to our analysis of abortion attitudes, our initial model suggests that attitudes toward abortion have been generally stable among Catholics.[5] Specifically, there is no zero-order trend in attitudes for either the total sample or for any individual generation, until both sociodemographic and religious variations are taken into account. Once religion variables are controlled, a trend toward more conservative abortion attitudes emerges for the total sample, as well as for the Vatican II and post–Vatican II generations. This pattern of suppression suggests that the conservative trend in abortion attitudes would be stronger if not for declines in religious involvement over the study period. There appears to be little change over time in abortion attitudes among pre–Vatican II generation Catholics.

Premarital Sex

Table 7.4 presents results of our analysis of attitudes toward premarital sex and extramarital sex for the total sample, as well as separate analysis for each generation. Model 1 of Table 7.4 shows a significant liberalizing trend in attitudes toward premarital sex among Catholics as a whole, as well as for the post–Vatican II generation. In this initial model, there does not appear to be a liberalizing trend for either the pre–Vatican II or Vatican II generations; however, once adjustments are made for sociodemographic variables, there is a significant liberalizing trend for all three generations, as well as for the total Catholic sample. With the inclusion of variables measuring religious involvement in Model 3, this liberalizing trend becomes insignificant for the Vatican II generation, and is reduced for the post–Vatican II generation.

Extramarital Sex

In contrast to the liberalizing trends found for most other pro-family outcomes, it appears that Catholics are becoming more conservative in their attitudes toward extramarital sex. Based on findings from Model 1, it appears that this conservative trend exists for Catholics in general and within each generation. Nevertheless, in Model 2, with the addition of sociodemographic controls, this trend disappears for pre–Vatican II Catholics, but not for the other two generations. The addition of religion variables in Model 3 does little to modify the findings from Model 2.

Homosexuality

Model 1 of Table 7.5 shows a liberalizing trend in attitudes toward homosexuality among Catholics as a whole, as well as within each generation. With the

TABLE 7.4

Odds Ratios for Ordered Logistic Regression of Attitudes toward Premarital Sex and Extramarital Sex by Generation

	Attitudes toward Premarital Sex				Attitudes toward Extramarital Sex			
	All Catholics (N = 5,688)	Pre–Vatican II Generation (N = 2,465)	Vatican II Generation (N = 2,190)	Post–Vatican II Generation (N = 1,033)	All Catholics (N = 5,667)	Pre–Vatican II Generation (N = 2,484)	Vatican II Generation (N = 2,121)	Post–Vatican II Generation (N = 1,062)
I. Unadjusted Model								
Year	.967***	.995	1.002	.959**	1.034***	1.020**	1.050***	1.083***
Model Chi-Square	89.60	.70	.08	7.68	51.71	6.91	46.19	19.10
II. Demographics[a]								
Year	.959***	.955***	.975*	.954*	1.048***	.998	1.065***	1.145***
Model Chi-Square	1169.61	290.69	108.42	46.54	306.08	163.00	133.19	53.90
III. Religion Variables[b]								
Year	.967***	.960***	.981	.962*	1.059***	1.008	1.075***	1.156***
Model Chi-Square	1707.16	479.80	360.81	122.50	491.63	243.36	216.17	65.89

Note: GSS (1974–2004)

a. Adds controls for gender, age, years of education, income, full-time employment, whether R is currently married, ever been divorced, rural resident, Southern resident, and number of children.

b. Adds controls for church attendance and strength of affiliation.

*p < .05; **p < .01; ***p<.001

TABLE 7.5

Regression Analyses for Attitudes toward Homosexuality and Gender Roles[a]

	Attitudes toward Homosexuality				Gender Role Attitudes			
	All Catholics (N = 5,415)	Pre–Vatican II Generation (N = 2,370)	Vatican II Generation (N = 2,030)	Post–Vatican II Generation (N = 1,015)	All Catholics (N = 3,185)	Pre–Vatican II Generation (N = 1,249)	Vatican II Generation (N = 1,237)	Post–Vatican II Generation (N = 699)
I. Unadjusted								
Year	.955***	.980**	.986*	.911***	-.144***	-.127***	-.064***	-.043
Model Chi-Square/ Adjusted R²	122.27	7.54	4.68	38.55	.070	.068	.014	.00
II. Demographics[b]								
Year	.959***	.947***	1.009	.882***	-.119***	-.148***	-.067**	-.036
Model Chi-Square/ Adjusted R²	810.38	197.53	185.32	129.83	.272	.211	.098	.077
III. Religion Variables[c]								
Year	.965***	.955***	1.015	.885***	-.114***	-.143***	-.065**	-.033
Model Chi-Square/ Adjusted R²	1014.03	257.28	280.42	170.93	.283	.219	.112	.082

Note: GSS (1974–2004)

a. Attitudes toward homosexuality are measured using ordered logistic regression analysis. Gender role attitudes are measured using OLS regression.

b. Includes controls for gender, age, years of education, income, full-time employment, whether R is currently married, ever been divorced, rural resident, Southern resident, and number of children.

c. In addition to the sociodemographic controls, include controls for church attendance and strength of affiliation.

*p < .05; **p < .01; ***p < .001.

addition of sociodemographic controls in Model 2, the same liberalizing trends exist for Catholics in general, as well as the pre–Vatican II and post–Vatican II generations. However, the effect of year becomes insignificant for Vatican II generation Catholics with controls for sociodemographic characteristics. In the final model, Model 3, the same general trends found in Models 1 and 2 persist despite controls for frequency of church attendance and strength of religious affiliation.

Gender Roles

Table 7.5 also shows trends in attitudes toward gender roles. There appears to be a liberalizing trend in attitudes toward gender roles for Catholics as a whole, as well as for pre–Vatican II and Vatican II Catholics. Model 2 includes sociodemographic controls such as age, gender, years of education, and rural residence. The inclusion of these sociodemographic controls does little to change the effect of year on attitudes toward gender roles. Model 3 includes controls for religious involvement. Like the sociodemographic controls, including measures for frequency of church attendance and strength of Catholic affiliation does little to alter the liberalizing trend in attitudes toward gender roles among Catholics in general, or pre–Vatican II and Vatican II Catholics.

Ancillary Analysis

In addition to our main effects models, we also ran a series of ancillary models to determine whether trends described here were specific to, or stronger among, various subgroups of the Catholic population—i.e., whether the effect of year varied by gender, education, or Southern residence on each of our outcomes. Table 7.6 displays the significant interaction effects for the total sample of Catholics as well as by generation. For the total sample of Catholics, it appears that the effect of year on both attitudes toward gender roles and extramarital sexual behavior varies as a function of education. Specifically, while Catholics are liberalizing in their attitudes toward gender roles over time, more educated Catholics are liberalizing at a slower rate than less educated Catholics. Furthermore, while Catholics are becoming more conservative in their attitudes toward extramarital sex over time, this process has been slower for those with lower levels of education. Conversely, those with higher levels of education are becoming more conservative in their attitudes toward extramarital sex at a faster rate compared to their less educated counterparts.

Although there is a decrease over time in ideal family size among all pre–Vatican II Catholics, this decrease is greater for men than for women. Once again, it is important to remember that women initially preferred smaller families, so this effect could be viewed as a "catching up" effect by men, leading toward gender convergence in attitudes. Similarly, while there is a liberalizing trend in gender role attitudes among this generation, this trend is more pronounced for Southerners than non-Southerners. However, initial gender role attitudes were

TABLE 7.6

Significant Interaction Effects of Year by Gender, Education, and Region on Family and Pro-Family Issues

Dependent Variable/Sample	Year Effect	Gender Effect	Education Effect	Region Effect	Interaction Term
Gender Role Attitudes/Total Sample	-.763***		-.564***		.187**
Extramarital Sex Attitudes/Total Sample	.384***		-.307***		.089*
Ideal Number of Children/Pre–Vatican II	-.074***	-.214*			.018*
Gender Role Attitudes/Pre–Vatican II	-.132***			1.299*	-.0689*
Gender Role Attitudes/Vatican II	-.061**		-1.003***		.035*
Ideal Number of Children/Vatican II	-.030***	.020		.316*	-.018*
Ideal Number of Children/Post–Vatican II	-.108*				-.176**
Premarital Sex Attitudes/Post–Vatican II	-.232**			.304	.380*

Note: Interaction models include controls for all covariates included in the full model. All components of interaction terms are zero-centered, as recommended by Aiken and West (1991).

*p < .05   **p < .01   ***p < .001

much more conservative among Southern residents, compared to those from other regions of the country.

There are also several notable interaction effects among Vatican II generation Catholics. Like the overall sample, Vatican II Catholics are liberalizing in their attitudes toward gender roles over time. As in the total sample, however, more educated Vatican II Catholics are liberalizing at a slower rate than less educated Vatican II Catholics. Additionally, although there is a decrease in ideal family size among Vatican II generation Catholics, this decrease is greater for Southern residents compared to other regions of the country.

Finally, while there is a general decrease in ideal family size among post–Vatican II generation Catholics, this decrease is greater for women than men—the opposite of the trend among pre–Vatican II Catholics. Additionally, although there is a decrease in conservative attitudes toward premarital sex among post–Vatican generation Catholics as a whole, this decrease did not occur among post–Vatican II Southern residents. In other words, while post–Vatican II Catholics are liberalizing in their attitudes toward premarital sex, post–Vatican II Southern Catholics remain relatively conservative in their attitudes compared to residents of other regions of the country.

Discussion and Conclusions

In this chapter, we examined trends in attitudes toward family and pro-family issues among non-Hispanic white U.S. Catholics. While previous research has noted both generational variations in attitudes among Catholics (e.g., Hoge 1999; D'Antonio et al. 2001; Davidson 2005), as well as liberalizing trends regarding social attitudes (Hoffman and Miller 1997; Sullins 1999; Bolzendahl and Brooks 2005), few studies (if any) have investigated generational specific trends in family and pro-family issues. We employed data from the 1974–2004 GSS, a national probability sample of noninstitutionalized, English-speaking U.S. residents eighteen years of age and older. In addition to examining trends for non-Hispanic white Catholics as a whole, we also investigated generation specific trends among Catholics who became adults before Vatican II (born 1901–1943), those who became adults during the Vatican II years (born 1944–1960), and those who reached adulthood after Vatican II (born 1961–1984). We also examined the extent to which these trends where explained by sociodemographic and religious variations.

Our results show several significant trends in attitudes toward family-related issues. With regard to ideal family size (our sole measure of direct family outcomes), it appears that there is a clear trend favoring smaller families. Further, there appears to be a general liberalizing trend among non-Hispanic white Catholics with regard to most pro-family issues. The two exceptions to this overall liberalization involve attitudes toward extramarital sexual behavior and abortion. Catholics have actually become more conservative over time in their attitudes toward marital infidelity. Unlike previous research (e.g., Sullins 1999), our results show a conservative trend in abortion attitudes among Vatican II and post–Vatican II Catholics, once individual-level variation in religious involvement is controlled. However, declines in religious involvement among these two generations have suppressed this conservative turn in attitudes toward abortion.

Our results also show that significant generational variations exist for all of our family-related issues. While the post–Vatican II generation generally appears to hold the most liberal views, our results also show that significant change has occurred among the older generations as well. In other words, overall changes among Catholics in attitudes toward premarital sex, homosexuality, and gender roles are not solely occurring as the result of cohort replacement, but are due in part to changing attitudes among older Catholics. The results also suggest that current liberalizing trends within the Catholic Church are not explained by changes in sociodemographic characteristics, or by changes in level of religious commitment. This general lack of mediation suggests that scholars may have exaggerated the impact of declining religious involvement within the Catholic Church on social attitudes, at least with regard to family and pro-family issues.

What do these changes in family and pro-family attitudes mean for the future of the Catholic Church? These generally liberalizing trends may not be good news for the Church, particularly regarding young, female Catholics. While laity may be moving in a more liberal direction, Church leadership appears to remain conservative on issues related to marriage and family. In fact, some evidence suggests that young priests are the most conservative on ecclesiastical issues, such as ordaining women, and on moral issues, such as birth control (Hoge 1998). This, coupled with the priest shortage, may lead to increased feelings of alienation among young people within the Church. Further, some evidence suggests that young women feel more alienated within the Church than young men, due in part to the Church's refusal to ordain women (Davidson 2005). One possible outcome is that Catholic women will continue to play lay leadership roles within the Church and gain more general acceptance, while sheer numbers alone may diminish the everyday leadership offered by priests.

Like all data sets, the GSS has its shortcomings. In this case, the dearth of Latino respondents prevents us from gaining an accurate view of Catholic trends in attitudes toward family and pro-family issues. Given the importance of Hispanic Catholics to the future of the Church, future data collection and analyses are needed to gauge the family-related attitudes and values of this crucial and growing segment of the U.S. Catholic population. Additionally, future studies should incorporate more sophisticated methods for examining trends within the Church. In this study, we have chosen to provide an overview of trends related to family and pro-family issues within the Catholic Church, rather than an in-depth study of any one outcome. Future research should focus on these generational trends in a more exhaustive manner. For example, future studies may examine the pace or rate at which change has occurred within specific generations.

Despite these limitations, our study provides valuable information on Catholic trends in attitudes toward family and pro-family issues. Our results demonstrate that there are significant, generally liberalizing trends within the Catholic Church regarding these outcomes. Our results also suggest that there are important generational variations in attitudes. Further, these findings lend credence to the argument that overall changes among Catholics in family-related attitudes are driven in at least in part by changes in attitudes among older generations, and not simply by cohort replacement.

NOTES

1. Catholics settling in the South and Southwest may find few Catholic institutions, but religious institutions in general are quite abundant in these regions. Both in the South and in the Southwest there are large, well-funded institutions affiliated with various Protestant groups, and Evangelicals are especially strong in this region.

2. For a variety of reasons, the Catholic Baby Boom was especially large. Young Catholics were a relatively larger proportion of their denomination than young members were in other denominations. In part, this was due to residually higher fertility among Catholics and in part to timing issues, including delayed childbearing from World War II. The mean number of siblings reported for Catholics ranged from over five for Hispanics to over three for majority whites—significantly larger than those reported for the general population in the GSS or the OCG–II (Fee et al. 1981).

3. In a national survey of Baby Boom Catholics, their mean ideal number of children was similar to that reported by other Americans, typically in the range of 2.4 to 2.6 (Fee et al. 1981, 191). But the Catholic respondents have more outliers who report a desire for large families.

4. Like Pearce (2002) we chose to use ordinary least squares regression, rather than other statistical methods, because the response categories approximate an interval level measure.

5. We also analyzed generational differences in attitudes toward elective abortions (i.e., abortion because the mother is poor, wants no more children, or is single) and duress abortions (i.e., abortion because the pregnancy is the result of rape, the child has a severe birth defect, or the mother's life is in danger) independently. Although there were some slight variations, attitudes toward both types of abortion have generally followed the same trend. Therefore, we have included only one measure of abortion attitudes.

REFERENCES

Aiken, L., and S. G. West. 1991. *Multiple Regression: Testing and Interpreting Interactions.* Newbury Park, CA: Sage Publications.

Alwin, D., P. Tufis, J. Felson, and E. Walker. 2004. "Religious Identities and Secular Change in Beliefs about Sex-Roles in American Society: 1977–2002." Paper presented at the 2004 meetings of the American Sociological Association, San Francisco, CA.

Bolzendahl, C., and C. Brooks. 2005. "Polarization, Secularization, or Differences as Usual?: The Denominational Cleavage in U.S. Social Attitudes since the 1970s." *Sociological Quarterly* 46:47–78.

Brewster, K. L., and I. Padavic. 2000. "Change in Gender-Ideology, 1977–1996: The Contributions of Intracohort Change and Population Turnover." *Journal of Marriage and Family* 62:477–487.

D'Antonio, W. V. 1985. "The American Catholic Family: Signs of Cohesion and Polarization." *Journal of Marriage and the Family* 47:395–405.

D'Antonio, W. V., and M. J. Cavanaugh. 1983. "Roman Catholicism and the Family." In *Families and Religions: Conflict and Change in Modern Society*, ed. W. V. D'Antonio and J. Aldous, 81–108. Beverly Hills, CA: Sage.

D'Antonio, W. V., J. D. Davidson, D. R. Hoge, and K. Meyer. 2001. *American Catholics: Gender, Generation and Commitment*. Walnut Creek, CA: Altamira Press.

Davidson, J. D. 2005. *Catholicism in Motion: The Church in American Society*. Liguori, MO: Liguori/Triumph.

Davidson, J. D., and D. R. Hoge. 2004. "Catholics after the Scandal." *Commonwealth* (November 19): 13–19.

Davis, J. A. 1992. "Changeable Weather in a Cooling Climate atop a Liberal Plateau." *Public Opinion Quarterly* 56:261–306.

Davis, J. A., T. W. Smith, and P. V. Marsden. 2004. "General Social Surveys: Cumulative Codebook, 1972–2004." Chicago: National Opinion Research Center. Machine-readable data file (MRDF) by Interuniversity Consortium for Political and Social Research (ICPSR), Ann Arbor, MI, and Roper Center, Storrs, CT.

Evans, J. H. 2002. "Polarization in Abortion Attitudes in U.S. Religious Traditions, 1972–1998." *Sociological Forum* 17:397–422.

Fee, J. L., A. M. Greeley, W. C. McCready, and T. A. Sullivan. 1981. *Young Catholics: In the United States and Canada*. New York: William H. Sadlier.

Froehle, B. T., and M. L. Gautier. 2000. *Catholicism USA*. Maryknoll, NY: Orbis Books.

Gay, D. A., C. G. Ellison, and D. A. Powers. 1996. "In Search of Denominational Subcultures: Religious Affiliation and 'Pro-Family' Issues Revisited." *Review of Religious Research* 38:3–17.

Greeley, A. M. 1989. *Religious Change in America*. Cambridge, MA: Harvard University Press.

Hoffman, J. P., and S. M. Johnson. 2005. "Attitudes toward Abortion among Religious Traditions in the United States: Change or Continuity" *Sociology of Religion* 66:161–182

Hoffman, J. P., and A. S. Miller. 1997. "Social and Political Attitudes among Religious Groups: Convergence and Divergence over Time." *Journal for the Scientific Study of Religion* 36:52–70.

Hoge, D. R. 1998. "Get Ready for the Post-Boomer Catholics." *America* 178:8–10.

———. 1999. "Catholic Generational Differences: Can We Learn Anything by Identifying the Specific Issues of Generational Agreement and Disagreement?" *America* (October): 14–20.

———. 2002. "Core and Periphery in American Catholic Identity." *Journal of Contemporary Religion* 17:293–302

Hout, M., and A. M. Greeley. 1987. "The Center Doesn't Hold: Church Attendance in the United States, 1940–1984." *American Sociological Review* 52:325–345.

John Jay College of Criminal Justice. 2004. *The Nature and Scope of the Problem of Sexual Abuse of Minors by Catholic Priests and Deacons in the United States 1950–2002*. Washington, DC: United States Conference of Catholic Bishops.

Kennedy, E. 1988. *Tomorrow's Catholics Yesterday's Church: The Two Cultures of American Catholicism*. New York: Harper and Row.

Loftus, J. 2001. "America's Liberalization in Attitudes toward Homosexuality, 1973 to 1998." *American Sociological Review* 66:762–782.

McNamara, P. H. 1992. *Conscience First, Tradition Second: A Study of Young Catholics.* Albany: State University of New York Press.

Moberg, D. O., and D. R. Hoge. 1986. "Catholic College Students' Religious and Moral Attitudes, 1961 to 1982: Effects of the Sixties and Seventies." *Review of Religious Research* 28:104–117.

Mosher, W. D., D. P. Johnson, and M. C. Horn. 1986. "Religion and Fertility in the United States: The Importance of Marriage Patterns and Hispanic Origin." *Demography* 23:367–379.

Mosher, W. D., L. Williams, and D. P. Johnson. 1992. "Religion and Fertility in the United States: New Patterns." *Demography* 29:199–214.

Pearce, L. D. 2002. "The Influence of Early Life Course Religious Exposure on Young Adults' Dispositions toward Childbearing." *Journal for the Scientific Study of Religion* 41:325–340.

Pogorelc, A. J., and J. D. Davidson. 2000. "American Catholics: One Church, Two Cultures?" *Review of Religious Research* 42:146–158.

Roof, W., and W. McKinney. 1987. *American Mainline Religion.* New Brunswick, NJ: Rutgers University Press.

Sander, W. 1995. *The Catholic Family: Marriage, Children and Human Capital.* Boulder, CO: Westview Press.

———. 2000. "The Allocation of Time to Religion." Unpublished paper, Department of Economics, DePaul University, Chicago.

Schoenherr, R., and L. Yang. 1992. *Full Pews, Empty Altars: The Demographics of the Priest Shortage in U.S. Catholicism.* New Brunswick, NJ: Rutgers University Press.

Smith, T. W. 1990. "Liberal and Conservative Trends in the United States since World War II." *Public Opinion Quarterly* 54:479–507.

Sullins, D. P. 1999. "Catholic/Protestant Trends on Abortion: Convergence and Polarity." *Journal for the Scientific Study of Religion* 38:354–369.

Thornton, A., D. F. Alwin, and D. Camburn. 1983. "Causes and Consequences of Sex-Role Attitudes and Attitude Change." *American Sociological Review* 48:211–227.

Thornton, A., and L. Young-DeMarco. 2001. "Four Decades of Trends in Attitudes toward Family Issues in the United States: 1960s through the 1990s." *Journal of Marriage and Family* 63:1009–1037.

Westoff, C. F. 1979. "The Blending of Catholic Reproductive Behavior." In *The Religious Dimension: New Directions in Quantitative Research*, ed. R. Wuthnow, 231–241. New York: Academic Press.

Westoff, C. F., and E. F. Jones. 1979. "The End of 'Catholic' Fertility." *Demography* 16:209–217.

8

Religious Intermarriage and Conversion in the United States

Patterns and Changes over Time

LINDA J. WAITE AND ALISA C. LEWIN

The United States is a religious nation. The vast majority of Americans, when asked, profess a belief in God and affirm that religion is at least "fairly important" in their lives (Myers 2000, 285); about three-fifths of the population reports membership in a religious organization and 45 percent state that they attend religious services at least monthly (Sherkat and Ellison 1999). Almost all established religions encourage marriage and parenthood, and provide both guidance and support in these key tasks of adulthood. So it is no surprise that married adults and parents of school-age children are more likely to belong to and participate in religious organizations than are those who are not married. Indeed, a good deal of religious practice and religious observance takes place within the family or jointly with family members. Parents may take their children to church, say grace at meals, or prayers at bedtime. Spouses may attend services together or pray together at home (Schmidt 2005).

In this study we use the National Survey of Families and Households (NSFH) to explore the social and demographic characteristics associated with religious intermarriage, homogamy, and conversion.[1] We examine changes across marriage cohorts in the chances of in-marriage, intermarriage and conversion, and explore changes over time in the impact of religious denomination on marital homogamy.

Background

Lehrer and Chiswick (1993) argue that religion is a complementary trait within marriages, so that religious denomination and religiosity affect many activities in which spouses engage and many choices that they make. Religion may affect how people spend their time and with whom, how they spend their money, whether they have children and how many, how those children are raised and educated, and even where the family lives. So, spouses who agree on the role that religion will play in their lives, and who share a religious affiliation will, according to Lehrer and Chiswick, have a much more efficient household and one with less conflict than spouses who differ in their religion and religiosity. Lehrer and Chiswick find that marriages in which one partner converted to create a religiously homogamous union were at least as stable as unions where both partners had the same religion before marriage, suggesting that marital stability is affected more by compatibility during marriage than similarity in religious upbringing.

Clearly, marrying someone of the same religion depends on the importance of in-marriage in one's religion, and the penalties of out-marriage. Lehrer and Chiswick (1993) argue that religions differ in their level of exclusivity or inclusivity, which they call "exclusivist" and "ecumenical." Ecumenical religious groups require very little specialized training, education, or commitment to join them and place little emphasis on group boundaries. These include Unitarian and mainline Protestant Christian denominations. At the other extreme, exclusivist religion groups draw membership boundaries sharply and patrol these carefully. Exclusivist groups may prohibit out-marriage and require substantial knowledge and commitment of converts. These groups also differ in the importance of religious faith and religious practice in family life. Lehrer and Chiswick (1993) use the exclusivist–ecumenical distinction to divide Protestant religious groups into two categories: Ecumenical Protestant (corresponding to mainline denominations) and Exclusivist Protestant (corresponding to Evangelical denominations). Religious in-marriage is, we expect, more likely for those raised in Evangelical Protestant denominations than for those raised in ecumenical denominations.

It is less clear how being raised in an Ecumenical versus Exclusivist Protestant religion will affect conversion in connection with marriage. Ecumenical religious groups welcome outsiders, offering a relatively quick and easy conversion process. At the same time, these groups are more tolerant of religious differences and intermarriage, reducing pressures for conversion and lowering the costs of intermarriage.

Those who state when asked that they were raised in no religion constitute a distinct category. This group probably consists of those raised in families that are ethically and morally atheist or agnostic, and those raised in families in which any specific religion was absent, possibly because the parents had themselves intermarried. These people might be more likely to intermarry, since they have few religious beliefs to conflict with those of a potential spouse. If they object to religious practice, however, they may be unappealing mates to those who desire this in their family. One might guess that those raised with no religion would be more likely than others to convert, offering a blank slate, so to speak, on which religious values and practices could be written at marriage.

At the same time that members of various religious groups face differing costs and benefits of in-marriage versus intermarriage, they also face different opportunities to do so. All else equal, members of large religious groups, and those that are widely dispersed, are more likely to marry someone of the same religious background even if they place no importance on doing so, just because of the distribution of characteristics of available mates.

A sizable body of research points to the decline of religious homogamy. Kalmijn (1991) shows that intermarriage between people with a Protestant background and a Catholic background increased dramatically between the 1920s and the 1980s. At the same time, mate choice became more homogeneous on education, especially among those with the highest levels of schooling. Waite and Friedman (1997) show, as for other religious groups, substantial increases in the likelihood of intermarriage among Jews between the 1920s and 1980.

As we argued earlier, the broad Protestant–Catholic distinction hides a great deal of variation in characteristics of religious groups that we expect to affect the chances of in-marriage and intermarriage. We hypothesize that intermarriage increased more quickly among those raised in Ecumenical Protestant denominations than among those raised in Evangelical denominations, because of the much greater importance of religious belief and practice to family life in the latter.

Demographers and economists have argued that early age at marriage is indicative of a truncated search for a partner, and an inferior match, factors that are later associated with marital dissolution. In this study we examine the relationship between age at marriage and religious homogamy. Perhaps earlier marriages are more affected by parental preferences than marriages at later ages, and thus are more religiously homogamous. Religious institutions provide educational and social services that families utilize in different stages of their lives, yet these services tend to target "conventional" families. Churches may provide social activities for single men and women, with the explicit intent of serving as marriage markets. These activities may be geared to specific, conventional age-groups, and may exclude older never married, previously married, and single-parent members, who then conduct their search for partners in religiously mixed environments.

This study of religion and marriage is innovative in a number of ways. First, while most studies of religious homogamy focus only on intermarriage, we also examine conversion in connection with marriage. Second, while most studies focus on first marriages, we compare first marriages with higher-order marriages. Third, we distinguish religious groups much more finely than most previous studies, which tend to either use a crude Protestant–Catholic distinction (Kalmijn 1991) or focus on only one religious group (Waite and Friedman 1997).

Data, Measures, and Methods

Data

We use the first wave of the NSFH carried out in 1987–1988.[2] This data set is appropriate for the study of religious intermarriage for two main reasons. First, it has detailed information on religion and conversion of both spouses, and second, it has this information for all first marriages, not just marriages at time of survey, so our results are not biased towards surviving marriages. Information on spouses was collected from the spouse in current marriages, and was reported by the respondent if the marriage had ended (by death or divorce) or if the spouse was not present.[3]

In our analyses, we distinguish between first marriages and higher-order marriages. We consider a marriage to be a first marriage if it is the first marriage for both the respondent and the spouse, and as a higher-order marriage if either the respondent or the spouse had been previously married.[4]

The sample includes all respondents who were ever married at wave one. We excluded Asians and Native Americans due to small sample size. We also excluded people married outside the United States because the availability of coreligionists differs by country, and the mechanisms of assortative mating by religion are culturally specific and may differ by country.

Variables

Table 8.1 shows the operational definitions and the percentage distributions of variables in the analyses. The dependent variable has three categories, distinguishing whether the spouses had the same religion (religious homogamy), whether they had different religions (religious intermarriage), and whether one spouse converted for the marriage (conversion). The independent variables include respondent's religion in childhood, age at marriage, education at marriage, year of marriage, race, and gender.[5]

We distinguish between six religious categories, based on the classification developed by Lehrer and Chiswick (1993). The categories are as follows: no religion, Catholic, Jewish, mainline Protestant (Episcopalians, Methodists, Presbyterians, Lutherans, and Unitarians), conservative Protestants (Baptists, Jehovah's Witnesses, Seventh-Day Adventists, Christian Scientists, and other fundamentalists), and Mormons. Other religions were excluded from the analyses.

We divided age at marriage into three categories, by frequency, separately for men and women. For women, age at first marriage has three categories: before age eighteen, between ages eighteen and twenty-one (which is the reference category in the regression models), and after age twenty-one. For men, the three categories of age at first marriage were defined as follows: before age twenty-one, between ages twenty-one and twenty-four (reference category), and after age twenty-four. The distribution of age at higher-order marriages is wider than age at first marriage, and is reflected in the definitions of the categories. For women in higher-order marriages the categories are: before age twenty-three, between twenty-three and thirty-one (reference category in regression models), and after age thirty-one. For men the categories are before age twenty-seven, between age twenty-seven and thirty-five, and after age thirty-five.

Education at time of marriage was coded in years and collapsed into four categories. We rounded the number of years to correspond with degree or

TABLE 8.1

Operational Definition and Percentage Distribution of Variables in the Analyses, by Marriage Parity

Variable name	Variable definition	First Marriages		Higher-Order Marriages	
		Men	Women	Men	Women
Dependent Variable					
Intermarriage	0 = religious homogamy (reference category)				
	1 = religious intermarriage	28%		47%	
	2 = religious conversion for marriage	16		9	
Independent Variables					
Respondent's religion	Set of six binary variables:				
	No religion	4%		4%	
	Catholic	25		23	
	Jewish	2		2	
	Mainline Protestant (reference category)	33		34	
	Conservative Protestants	34		35	
	Mormons	2		2	
Respondent's age at marriage[a]	Three categories as defined by distribution, separately for men and women, in first and higher-order marriages:				
	"Early" (reference category),	44%	35%	35%	34%
	"Normative"	29	35	33	34
	"Late"	27	30	32	32

Respondent's race		
Set of three binary variables:		
White (reference category in regressions)	80%	82%
African American	15	13
Hispanic	5	4
Respondent's education at marriage		
Set of four binary variables, by years of schooling and diploma earned:		
< 12 years, less than high school diploma	32%	26%
12 years, high school (reference category)	41	41
13–15, some college	16	18
16 + ,college degree	11	14
Marriage cohort		
Set of five binary variables by year of marriage:		
before 1950	25%	9%
1950–1959	14	8
1960–1969	19	13
1970–1979 (reference category)	25	26
1980–1988.	18	49
Respondent gender		
0 = male	40%	42%
1 = female	60	58
N	7,324	2,291

a. Respondent's age at marriage is defined by distribution, separately for men and women, in first and higher-order marriages as follows: First marriage, women: early—before age eighteen; normative—ages eighteen to twenty-one; late—after age twenty-one. First marriage, men: early—before age twenty-one; normative—ages twenty-one to twenty-four; late—after age twenty-four. Higher-order marriages women: early—before age twenty-three; normative—ages twenty-three to thirty-one; late—after age thirty-one. Higher-order marriages men: early—before age twenty-seven; normative—ages twenty-seven to thirty-five; late—after age thirty-five.

diploma at time of marriage as follows: less than high school (less than twelve years of education and no diploma), high school (twelve years or diploma), tertiary (twelve to fifteen years no degree), and academic (at least sixteen years of education or academic degree).

We distinguish between five marriage cohorts in our analyses, by year of marriage, as follows: before 1950, 1950–1960, 1960–1970, 1970–1980 (reference category in regressions), 1980–1988.

We distinguish between three racial and ethnic groups: non-Hispanic whites, African Americans, and Hispanics. Finally, we include a dummy variable for gender.

Methods

The analysis has two stages. The first is primarily descriptive. We compare means and percentage distributions of characteristics of marriages by religious homogamy, intermarriage, and religious conversion, separately for first and higher-order marriages. Then, we conduct multivariate analyses examining the odds of religious homogamy, intermarriage, and conversion. We calculate multinomial regressions predicting the odds of religious intermarriage and conversion for marriage versus religious homogamy, for first and higher-order marriages.[6]

Results

Table 8.1 shows the percentage distribution of the variables in the analyses, by marriage order. The most striking finding is that religious intermarriage is more prevalent in higher-order marriages than in first marriages. Almost half (47 percent) of all higher-order marriages involve spouses from different religious categories, compared to less than a third of all first marriages (28 percent). Less than one-fifth (16 percent) of all first marriages involve a conversion of one spouse, compared to 9 percent of higher-order marriages.

The religious composition of first and higher-order marriages is about the same, suggesting that members of all religious categories enter higher-order marriages at about the same rate. About one-third of all respondents are mainline Protestants, another third are conservative Protestants, and a quarter of the respondents are Catholics. Four percent of respondents claim to have been raised with no religion, 2 percent are Jewish, and 2 percent are Mormons.

The racial composition of first and higher-order marriages differs slightly, suggesting that whites are somewhat more likely than African Americans and Hispanics to remarry. The great majority of respondents are white (80 percent of first marriages, 82 percent of higher-order marriages), followed by African Americans (15 percent of respondents in first marriages, 13 percent of respondents in higher-order marriages), and a small minority of respondents are Hispanic (5 percent of first marriages, 4 percent of higher-order marriages).

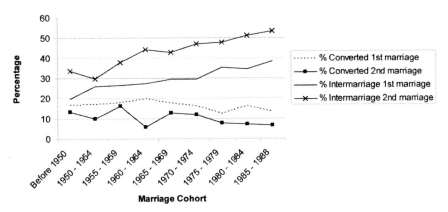

FIGURE 8.1 Intermarriage and conversion by marriage order and marriage cohort.

The mean age at marriage (not shown) is substantially higher in higher-order marriages (thirty-one years) than in first marriages (twenty-one years). The corresponding standard deviation (not shown) is larger in higher-order marriages (eleven years), compared to first marriages (four years), suggesting that there is wider variation in the timing of higher-order marriages compared to first marriages. Though respondents have slightly higher education in higher-order marriages compared to first marriages, the difference is small. This may reflect respondents' overall tendency to time their first marriage after completing their education, and not to increase their education substantially after marriage.

The incidence of first and higher-order marriages differs by marriage cohort, reflecting the rise in divorce and remarriage since 1950. While only 18 percent of first marriages occurred in the most recent period (1980–1988), almost half of the higher-order marriages occurred in this period. While one-quarter of first marriages took place before 1950, only 9 percent of higher-order marriages took place in this earliest period under investigation.

Figure 8.1 shows trends in intermarriage and conversion, for first and higher-order marriages. We see an increase in the percentage of religious inter-marriages, with time, and a slight decrease in marriages that involve a religious conversion. The figure also depicts two important differences between first and higher-order marriages. First, intermarriage is more common in higher-order marriages than in first marriages in all periods under investigation. Second, conversion for marriage is more common in first marriages than in higher-order marriages in all marriage cohorts.

First Marriages

Table 8.2 shows regression coefficients predicting the odds of intermarriage or conversion versus marrying a coreligionist in first and in higher-order marriages. The findings show that the religion in which people were raised is important in

TABLE 8.2

Multinomial Logistic Regression Coefficients Predicting the Log Odds of Intermarriage and Conversion in First Marriages

	First Marriages		Higher-Order Marriages	
	Intermarriage vs. Religious Homogamy	Conversion vs. Religious Homogamy	Intermarriage vs. Religious Homogamy	Conversion vs. Religious Homogamy
Respondent's Religion Raised				
No Religion	0.536**	-0.492*	0.723**	-0.877
Catholic	-0.479**	-0.610**	0.225	-0.020
Jewish	-0.898**	-1.848**	-0.250	-1.299
Conservative Protestant	-0.482**	-0.612**	-0.107	-0.607**
Mormon	-0.918**	-1.391**	-0.284	-0.747
Respondent's Age at Marriage[a]				
"Normative"	-0.199**	0.064	0.132	0.232
"Late"	-0.072	-0.052	0.245*	0.193
Respondent's Race/Ethnicity				
Black	-.191*	-0.572**	0.057	-0.028
Hispanic	-0.705**	-1.180**	-0.581*	-0.310

	(1)	(2)	(3)	(4)
Year of Marriage				
Before 1950	-0.747**	0.013	-0.498**	0.201
1950—1960	-0.301**	0.190	-0.528**	0.123
1960—1970	-0.126	0.258*	-0.171	-0.018
1980—1988	0.182*	0.085	0.101	-0.339
Respondent's Education				
< 12 Years	-0.022	-0.433**	0.044	-0.114
13—15 Years (Some College)	-0.144	0.140	-0.044	-0.158
16 + Years (College Degree)	-0.023	0.166	0.197	0.434
Respondent Female	0.196**	0.146*	0.288**	0.246
Constant	-0.321	-0.948	-0.516	-1.762
-2 Log Likelihood	3863.527		1950.206	
N	7258		2268	

Note: Reference category for religion is mainline Protestant. Reference category for race/ethnicity is white. Reference category for year of marriage is 1970–1980. Reference category for education is twelve years of schooling (high school).

a. Reference category for age at marriage is youngest age category. Respondent's age at marriage is defined separately by sex and marriage parity as follows: First marriage, women: early—before age eighteen; normative—ages eighteen to twenty-one; late—after age twenty-one. First marriage, men: early—before age twenty-one; normative—ages twenty-one to twenty-four; late—after age twenty-four. Higher-order marriages women: early—before age twenty-three; normative—ages twenty-three to thirty-one; late—after age thirty-one. Higher-order marriages men: early—before age twenty-seven; normative—ages twenty-seven to thirty-five; late—after age thirty-five.

* p < 0.05 ** p < 0.01

predicting the odds of intermarriage and conversion in first marriages. People who were raised with no religion have higher odds of intermarriage than people who were raised as mainline Protestants (the omitted category). Members of all other religions (Catholics, Jews, conservative Protestants, and Mormons) have lower odds of intermarriage in first marriages than do mainline Protestants, and these results are all statistically significant at the .01 level. Members of all religions, including those with no religion, have lower odds than mainline Protestants of converting for marriage.

Age at marriage predicts intermarriage, but does not predict conversion in first marriages. People who marry later have lower odds of intermarriage than people marrying at the youngest ages. This may suggest a truncated search for a partner (for example, an unplanned pregnancy or a similar occurrence; see Becker, Landes, and Michael 1977; Lehrer 1998). The effect is only significant for those marrying at a middle age compared to those marrying at the youngest age.

The effect of race is statistically significant in predicting both intermarriage and conversion in first marriages. Blacks and Hispanics have lower odds of either intermarriage or conversion than do whites. These differences may follow from the relationship between race/ethnicity, religion, and marital homogamy by race/ethnicity. Hispanics are predominantly Catholic and blacks conservative Protestant. These religions have lower odds of conversion and intermarriage than mainline Protestants, who are mostly white. Blacks are especially unlikely to marry someone of another race or ethnicity, with Hispanics substantially more likely (Qian 1997). Thus, religious homogamy may follow, especially for blacks, from racial homogamy. We speculate that for Hispanics, a shared religious upbringing makes ethnic out-marriage with a coreligionist more likely than a marriage that is heterogamous on both ethnicity and religion.

A period effect is also evident for intermarriage, but not for conversion. Marriages that occurred in earlier years have lower odds of intermarriage than marriages that took place in 1970–1979 (the omitted category), and most recent marriages (1980–1988) have higher odds of intermarriage. Interactions (not shown) between religion and year of marriage suggest that the increase in intermarriage is similar for all religious groups, though it happened faster for people with no religion, and more slowly for conservative Protestants than for mainline Protestants (the omitted category).

This suggests that a shift has taken place toward marriages that start out as religiously heterogamous and remain that way. Conversion is no less common, but in-marriage has fallen and intermarriage has increased. Clearly, some of those who in earlier cohorts would have converted to make their marriages homogamous on this dimension, or to make their spouse or in-laws happy, no longer feel the need to do so.

Education at the time of marriage has no effect on intermarriage, although it may affect religious intermarriage through its effect on age at marriage. People who had not completed high school before marriage have lower odds of converting for marriage than those with a high school diploma. We suspect that this results from the relationship between education and religious affiliation. People with no religious affiliation and conservative Protestants are overrepresented in the "less than high school" category, and they also have lower odds of converting than mainline Protestants.

Finally, and surprisingly, women have higher odds of intermarrying and converting for marriage than men, net of all the variables in the equations.[7] This gender difference probably results from differential reporting of the same events by men and women.

Second Marriages

The last two columns of Table 8.2 show multinomial logistic regression coefficients predicting the odds of intermarriage or conversion versus marrying a coreligionist in higher-order marriages. The results for higher-order marriages differ substantially from the results for first marriages. With the exception of people raised with no religion, who have higher odds of intermarriage in second marriages than mainline Protestants, the effect of religion is not statistically significant. Conservative Protestants have lower odds of converting than mainline Protestants; all other effects of religion are not statistically significant.

Age at second marriage does increase the odds of intermarriage; those marrying at the oldest ages have higher odds of intermarriage than those marrying at younger ages. This suggests a marriage market effect, with a shortage of religiously compatible mates among the limited pool available to those previously married. But there is no effect of age at marriage on odds of conversion. We also suspect that those who remarry at older ages more often expect this marriage to be childless than do those who are younger. Since many of the issues raised by religious differences within a marriage center on children, pressures to in-marry or convert may be much reduced among those remarrying at older ages.

In second and later marriages Hispanics have lower odds of intermarriage than whites, but there is no difference between racial groups in the odds of conversion in second marriages. There is a period effect on odds of intermarriage (but not conversion) in second marriages. Marriages before 1959 have lower odds of being intermarriages than marriages that were contracted between 1970 and 1979.

Education has no effect on intermarriage or conversion at second marriage. One explanation could be that education may be a good predictor of remarriage, and this selection may offset any effect there may be on the match. Education had little effect in first marriages too, perhaps because other variables are related to the effect of education—for example, age at marriage, religion, and race are all related to education. There is a gender effect, and women have higher odds than men of intermarrying, but not of converting, in second marriages.

Discussion and Conclusions

A long tradition of research demonstrates that being married positively affects physical health (Lillard, Brien, and Waite 1995; Goldman, Korenman, and Weinstein 1995; Umberson 1992). Married adults show better health outcomes than the unmarried across a variety of acute and chronic conditions, including colds, cancer, heart attacks, and surgery (Cohen et al. 1997; Gordon and Rosenthal 1995). Married persons are also less likely to die in any given period than the unmarried (Lillard, Brien, and Waite 1995; Ross, Mirowsky, and Goldsteen 1990). Married men and women also appear to have better mental health than their unmarried counterparts (Horwitz, White, and Howell-White 1996; Marks and Lambert 1998; Mirowsky and Ross 2003; Umberson et al. 1996; Waite and Hughes 1999). However, remarriage seems to enhance mental health less than first marriages (Barrett 2000; Marks and Lambert 1998; Williams 2003).

Waite and Lehrer (2003) point out the similarity between the protective impact of marriage on health and that of religious participation. Both being married and participating in religious activities are linked empirically to positive outcomes, including physical and mental health, economic outcomes, and the processes of raising children. Both seem to operate—at least in part—by increasing social integration and through regulation of health behaviors.

Marriages in which spouses share the same religious beliefs show higher levels of intergenerational transmission of religiosity than marriages in which spouses differ in their religious affiliation (Myers 1996). Of course, individuals to whom religious participation is relatively unimportant are almost certainly more likely to marry someone with a different religion than are individuals to whom religion is important. So out-marriages almost certainly select those with little or weak attachment to religious affiliation and practice. At the same time, the religious participation of spouses depends in part on the behavior and values of their wife or, less often, husband (Wilson, Simpson, and Jackson 1987). So those who marry someone of the same religion are more likely to engage in religious activities, regardless of their initial level of commitment and attachment, because it is more likely that their spouse will want to participate and will solicit and encourage their involvement. Similarity of religious affiliation lowers the cost to the spouse of this involvement (Azzi and Ehrenberg 1975). Parents become more involved in religious organizations when their children reach the appropriate age for religious education (Stolzenberg, Blair-Loy, and Waite 1995), and this process is facilitated if parents share the same religion.

Marriages in which the spouses share the same religion are less likely to end in divorce than those in which they do not (Lehrer and Chiswick 1993). This is the case both for homogamous marriages in which both spouses were raised in the same religion and for marriages in which one spouse converted at marriage. Sharing the same religion during the marriage seems to matter, rather than previous religion. A number of scholars argue that shared religious values and practices increase the quality and efficiency of a marital match, reduce the chances of conflict over religious values and practice and the lifestyle decisions that follow from these, and improve parenting (Lehrer and Chiswick 1993; Curtis and Ellison 2002).

To the extent that religious participation provides health and economic benefits to individuals and families, and to the extent to which spouses in homogamous marriages are more likely to participate in religious activities, the substantial declines in religious homogamy that our results show may raise some issues. First, declines in religious homogamy of marriages may underlie şome of the high levels of marital instability facing families. Second, declines in the religious homogamy of marriages may reduce the health and economic benefits of marriage, at least for heterogamous marriages. Third, declines in religious homogamy may introduce conflict in marriages (Curtis and Ellison 2002) and especially in issues of parenting, which may negatively affect quality of parenting.

These consequences of declines in religious homogamy of marriages in the United States may follow only to the extent that the relationships between religious participation, health, economic well-being, and parenting have not weakened, which they may have done. In fact, increases in religious out-marriage and declines in conversion among those who marry someone who affiliates with a different major religious group suggest that boundaries between religious groups have fallen, at least to some extent. Since marriage represents the most intimate voluntary social contract possible between individual adults, increases in intermarriage point to a substantial weakening of the social boundaries between major religious groups in the United States. But, as of yet, we know little about the implications of this change for the health, well-being, and family life of the individuals involved, religious organizations, or society as a whole.

NOTES

This chapter was supported by the Alfred P. Sloan Center on Parents, Children, and Work at the University of Chicago.

1. In a fairly dated study, Newport (1979) found that between 25 percent and 32 percent of Americans switch religions, and about 40 percent of these switches are related to marriage.

2. The survey was designed by Bumpass and Sweet, Center for Demography and Ecology, University of Wisconsin; the fieldwork was carried out by the Institute for Survey Research, Temple University.

3. We use only the first wave of the NSFH because following waves do not include a question on conversion.

4. This is different from other studies that look at marriage parity of respondent only (e.g., Lehrer and Chiswick 1993).

5. We use a different measure of religion depending on whether religion is a dependent or independent variable. As an independent variable, we use respondent's religion

raised, because this indicates an openness to intermarriage and conversion. But our dependent variable sets out to measure the match between the spouses. There is no information in NSFH on religion raised for current spouse. Therefore, in our dependent variable that measures religious match, we use religion at time of survey for respondents and current spouses. For first spouses in marriages that terminated before the time of survey we use religion at time of marriage. We argue that our measure is appropriate for this investigation because we directly account for conversion for marriage. But we acknowledge that this measure assumes that people do not change their religion after marriage, or, if they do, they change together. Cases of marriages that were religiously homogamous at time of marriage and one spouse switched religion later were coded as religious intermarriages.

6. The data were not weighted for these analyses.

7. This gender difference is reduced, but not eliminated entirely, when using the same categories of age at marriage for men and women.

REFERENCES

Azzi, C., and R. Ehrenberg. 1975. "Household Allocation of Time and Church Attendance." *Journal of Political Economy* 83 (1): 27–56.

Barrett, A. E. 2000. "Marital Trajectories and Mental Health." *Journal of Health and Social Behavior* 41:451–464.

Becker, G. S, E. M. Landes, and R. T. Michael. 1977. "An Economic Analysis of Marital Instability." *Journal of Political Economy* 85 (6): 1141–1187.

Cohen, S., W. J. Doyle, D. P. Skoner, B. S. Rabin, and J. M. Gwaltney, Jr. 1997. "Social Ties and Susceptibility to the Common Cold." *Journal of the American Medical Association* 227 (24): 1940–1944.

Curtis, K. T., and C. G. Ellison. 2002. "Religious Heterogamy and Marital Conflict: Findings from the National Survey of Families and Households." *Journal of Family Issues* 23 (4): 551–576.

Goldman, N., S. Korenman, and R. Weinstein. 1995. "Marital Status and Health among the Elderly." *Social Science and Medicine* 40 (12): 1717–1730.

Gordon, H. S., and G. E. Rosenthal. 1995. "Impact of Marital Status on Hospital Outcomes: Evidence from an Academic Medical Center." *Archives of Internal Medicine* 155:2465–2471.

Horwitz, A. V., H. R. White, and S. Howell-White. 1996. "Becoming Married and Mental Health: A Longitudinal Study of a Cohort of Young Adults." *Journal of Marriage and the Family* 58:895–907.

Kalmijn, M. 1991. "Shifting Boundaries: Trends in Religious and Educational Homogamy." *American Sociological Review* 56:786–800.

Lehrer, E. L. 1998. "Religious Intermarriage in the United States: Determinants and Trends." *Social Science Research* 27:245–263.

Lehrer, E., and C. Chiswick. 1993. "Religion as a Determinant of Marital Stability." *Demography* 30:385–404.

Lillard, L. A., M. J. Brien, and L. J. Waite. 1995. "Pre-Marital Cohabitation and Subsequent Marital Dissolution: Is It Self-Selection?" *Demography* 32:437–458.

Marks, N. F., and J. D. Lambert. 1998. "Marital Status Continuity and Change among Young and Midlife Adults: Longitudinal Effects on Psychological Well-Being." *Journal of Family Issues* 19:652–686.

Mirowsky, J., and C. E. Ross. 2003. *Social Causes of Psychological Distress*. New York: Aldine De Gruyter.

Myers, David G. 2000. *The American Paradox: Spiritual Hunger in an Age of Plenty*. New Haven, CT: Yale University Press.

Myers, S. M. 1996."An Interactive Model of Religiosity Inheritance: The Importance of Family Context." *American Sociological Review* 61:858–866.

Newport, F. 1979. "The Religious Switcher in the United States." *American Sociological Review* 44:528–552.

Qian, Z. 1997. "Breaking the Racial Barriers: Variations in Interracial Marriage between 1980 and 1990." *Demography* 34:263–277.

Ross, C. E., J. Mirowsky, and K. Goldsteen. 1990. "The Impact of the Family on Health: Decade in Review." *Journal of Marriage and the Family* 52:1059–1078.

Schmidt, J. 2005. "Religiosity, Emotional Well-Being and Family Processes in Working Families." In *Being Together, Working Apart: Dual-Career Families and the Work-Life Balance*, ed. B. W. Schneider and L. J. Waite, 303–324. Cambridge: Cambridge University Press.

Sherkat, D. E., and C. G. Ellison. 1999. "Recent Developments and Current Controversies in the Sociology of Religion." *Annual Review of Sociology* 25:363–394.

Stolzenberg, R. M., M. Blair-Loy, and L. J. Waite. 1995. "Religious Participation over the Life Course: Age and Family Life Cycle Effects on Church Membership." *American Sociological Review* 60:84–103.

Umberson, D. 1992. "Gender, Marital Status and the Social Control of Health Behavior." *Social Science and Medicine* 34 (8): 907–917.

Umberson, D., M. D. Chen, J. S. House, K. Hopkins, and E. Slaten.1996. "The Effect of Social Relationships on Psychological Well-Being: Are Men and Women Really So Different?" *American Sociological Review* 61:837–857.

Waite, L. J., and J. S. Friedman. 1997. "The Impact of Religious Upbringing and Marriage Markets on Jewish Intermarriage." *Contemporary Jewry* 18:1–23.

Waite, L. J., and M. E. Hughes. 1999. "At Risk on the Cusp of Old Age: Living Arrangements and Functional Status among Black, White, and Hispanic Adults." *Journal of Gerontology: Social Sciences* 54B (3): S136–S144.

Waite, L. J., and E. Lehrer. 2003. "Religion and Marriage: A Comparative Analysis of the Ties that Bind." *Population and Development Review* 29:255–276.

Williams, K. 2003. "Has the Future of Marriage Arrived? A Contemporary Examination of Gender, Marriage, and Psychological Well-Being." *Journal of Health and Social Behavior* 44:470–487.

Wilson, J., I. H. Simpson, and D. K. Jackson. 1987. "Church Activism among Farm Couples." *Journal of Marriage and the Family* 49:875–892.

9

Childhood Religious Denomination and Early Adult Asset Accumulation

LISA A. KEISTER

Wealth inequality has become increasingly severe in recent years. Basic characteristics of the distribution of wealth are well established, but the processes that generate this inequality are unclear. Wealth, or net worth, is the value of a person's assets less their debts. Between the 1960s and the 1990s, total household wealth in 2000 dollars grew from $8 trillion to nearly $24 trillion (Keister 2000). Between 1989 and 1998, median household net worth increased more than 20 percent, and the number of billionaires in the Forbes 400 rose from 85 to 267 (Kennickell 2000). During that time, the proportion of wealth owned by the top 1 percent of families increased from about 33 percent to more than 38 percent, while the share owned by those in the lower 90 percent declined from 33 to 30 percent of the total (Wolff 1998). The implications of this severe and growing inequality are apparent when the advantages of wealth ownership are considered. Wealth provides current use value (as in the ownership of a home), generates more wealth when it is invested, provides a buffer during financial emergencies, and can be passed to future generations. Moreover, wealth may increase political influence, educational and occupational opportunities, and social advantages for both current and future generations. Although wealth ownership is clearly concentrated, the processes that generate this inequality are only vaguely understood.

Childhood religious denomination is one factor that may shape adult wealth, but the role of religion has received almost no research attention. A rich tradition of research demonstrates clear religious differences in child rearing, marital stability, divorce, and fertility (Alwin 1986; Ellison, Bartkowsi, and Segal 1996; Lehrer 1996b; Sherkat and Ellison 1999), earnings, education, and female employment rates (Darnell and Sherkat 1997; Lehrer 1999; Wuthnow and Scott 1997), and even mortality and quality of life (Hummer et al. 1999; Pearce and Axinn 1998). Extending this research to wealth ownership suggests that religion may shape wealth through its effect on these other social and economic processes (Keister 2003). Religion may affect asset ownership *indirectly* because it shapes the processes that determine family wealth. It may also affect wealth ownership *directly* because it shapes values and priorities, contributes to the set of competencies from which action is constructed, and provides social contacts. Although researchers have begun to identify a strong relationship between childhood religion and adult wealth (Keister 2003), the nature of this relationship remains unclear.

In this chapter, I explore the role that childhood religion plays in shaping adult wealth. I use the 2000 wave of the National Longitudinal Survey of Youth (NLSY79), which includes updated wealth information that has not been incorporated into previous research on religion and wealth. I explore the effect of religious background on the components of wealth (e.g., homeownership, stock ownership, business ownership) in more depth than has been done previously. I also investigate the role that inheritance and other intergenerational transfers play in mediating the relationship between religion and wealth. I focus on wealth accumulation in young adulthood because it is during this time that people establish the savings and investment patterns that continue throughout their lives and because saving behavior during the early working years creates the financial basis for later wealth ownership.

Childhood Religious Denomination and Wealth

Religion is part of a complex set of factors that shape wealth accumulation. The process begins in childhood with interactions, experiences, and events that do not all appear to be related to adult wealth ownership. It then extends through adolescence and early adulthood. Over the life course, multiple interacting processes and events shape the trajectory that an individual follows. Figure 9.1 outlines a set of factors that are likely to be important and highlights the position of childhood religion in the model. The figure suggests that religious upbringing affects adult wealth indirectly by shaping inheritance and educational attainment, which in turn affect other adult outcomes. While the model does not depict a direct relationship between religion and adult wealth, it is likely that religious upbringing does affect wealth ownership directly. That is, religion shapes values and priorities, contributes to the set of competencies from which action is constructed, and may provide important social contacts that all affect adult wealth. I discuss these processes in more detail later.

Religious denomination shapes adult wealth indirectly through its effect on education—and the outcomes of education such as fertility—that shape asset accumulation. Variations in fertility across faiths and even denominations within a single faith, for example, are important determinants of family resources and ultimately children's life attainment. People who are raised in religions where fertility is relatively low may accumulate more wealth over their

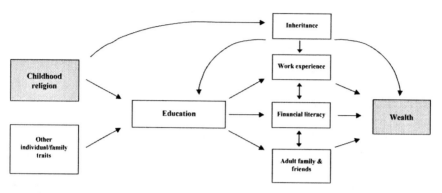

FIGURE 9.1 Childhood religion and adult wealth.

lives. Similarly, religious differences in attitudes toward educational attainment, and returns to education, are important determinants of wealth ownership. Thus, those from religious backgrounds that encourage educational advancement are likely to have an advantage in wealth accumulation over those who are affiliated with a religion that either does not incorporate ideas about education or that is either skeptical of or overtly hostile toward secular education. Similar arguments can be made about the relationship between religion and other family practices such as parental work behavior, union formation, and other critical determinants of wealth accumulation. These are certainly important determinants of economic behavior, and because of these differences, there are likely to be important differences in wealth ownership across people from different religious backgrounds.

Religion can also shape action directly both by defining the end values toward which behavior is oriented and by providing a tool kit that people draw on to construct "strategies of action." Religious affiliation and participation in religious ceremonies expose people to rituals, symbols, beliefs, and expectations that identify worthwhile objectives. Swidler (1986) proposed that religious habits and practices transmitted by parents or during religious services during youth shape the set of competencies from which strategies of action are constructed. Similarly, exposure to religious ideals and views in adulthood may define the repertoire of capacities from which actions are formulated. From this perspective, strategies organize life and make particular choices and habits both sensible and useful. A similar frame is Bourdieu's notion that cultural patterns provide a structure against which individuals formulate and implement strategies or habits (Bourdieu 1977). The ideas are quite similar and both imply the same outcome for wealth accumulation. That is, people draw on the tools they learn from religion to develop consistent strategies for dealing with problems and for making decisions such as savings, investment, and consumption decisions. In terms of wealth accumulation, for example, the frequent recourse to prayer and trust in God among conservative Protestants may reduce their inclination to invest.

In addition to shaping strategies, childhood religious denomination may affect wealth accumulation directly by providing social contacts that provide information, assistance, and referrals to those who can provide these important things. Like intergenerational influences in other domains, savings behavior reflects parental asset ownership and the asset ownership of others to whom people are exposed during childhood (Chiteji and Stafford 2000). Knowledge about the importance of saving, the avenues available for saving, and saving strategies is at least partly gained through exposure to the savings behavior of others. Wealth accumulation depends on having information about a number of financial instruments and their features. Because information barriers make it largely impossible for people to gather this information individually, information from social contacts is often used instead. Social contacts may also provide direct assistance in the form of capital transfers such as capital for starting a business, making an initial financial investment, or making a down payment on a home. The information that contacts have will vary by religion and their ability to assist more directly will vary as well.

These processes are likely to vary in important ways across religious groups. In the following sections, I explore how Jews, conservative Protestants, mainline Protestants, and Roman Catholics may accumulate wealth differently.

Jews

A host of unique demographic traits lead to high levels of attainment for Jews that are likely to increase wealth accumulation indirectly (Chiswick 1986; Chiswick 1993; DellaPergola 1980; Wuthnow 1999). Jewish families have a history of developing human capital and investing less in physical capital (Brenner and Kiefer 1981). Moreover, both fertility rates and rates of female employment when children are young are relatively low in Jewish families (Chiswick 1986; DellaPergola 1980). As a result, there tend to be high levels of investment in child quality, high educational attainment, and relatively high returns to educational investments among Jews (Chiswick 1988; Lehrer 1999). Because fertility rates are low, the dilution of material resources that are transferred in the form of inheritance is low and strains on resources in the adult family are minimal. High rates of homogamy among Jews also suggests that the influence of these demographic traits is likely to be enhanced by marriage to a person with a similar propensity for attainment (Kalmijn 1991; Thornton 1985). High levels of attainment suggest that wealth accumulation among Jews is likely to exceed that of other groups.

There may also be a direct effect of Judaism on wealth. While there is certainly tremendous variation, accumulation and occupational success are often seen as indicators of success in Jewish families (Stryker 1981). The encouragement of this-worldly pursuits, including actual accumulation of wealth and other activities that lead to wealth accumulation such as high-income careers and investing, are common (Bonder 2001). Jewish families are more likely to invest in financial assets that are high risk and have high returns (Keister 2003), increasing overall wealth. Opportunities to build relevant social capital are also relatively high in Jewish families. Social connections developed through schools and universities can provide information about investment strategies, actual investment opportunities, and access to capital for investing (Sherkat and Ellison 1999). Because Judaism is also an ethnicity, the Jewish cultural repertoire is likely to be more salient than the repertoires established in other faiths, and the direct Jewish effect on wealth accumulation is likely to be even stronger than it might otherwise be.

For these reasons, I expect that those raised Jewish accumulate more wealth as adults than those who were not Jewish. Jews may inherit more wealth because of the intergenerational transmission of both wealth and the behaviors that increase wealth accumulation. Yet, the direct effect of Judaism on wealth suggests that Jews will accumulate more wealth even at similar levels of inheritance than non-Jews. Similarly, while educational attainment, fertility, female employment patterns, and other demographic differences will increase wealth accumulation for Jews, there will be a direct effect of Jewish religious affiliation reflecting the importance of the cultural repertoire that is transferred intergenerationally in Jewish families.

Conservative Protestants

In contrast to Jewish families, wealth accumulation among conservative Protestants is likely to be relatively low. Americans have recently become more accepting of egalitarian gender roles, divorce, smaller families, childlessness, and other nontraditional family behaviors. Conservative Protestants have also become more accepting of these behaviors, but change in this group has been less pronounced and slower than among nonconservatives. As a result, conservative Protestants have become relatively more traditional than others (Lehrer 1999; Smith 1998; Wilcox 1998). Traditional attitudes have translated into relatively high fertility rates that are likely to decrease wealth accumulation by diluting both material and nonmaterial resources during childhood, reducing inheritance, and making saving more difficult in adulthood (Lehrer 1999; Thornton 1985). Similar to Jewish families, female employment when children are young is also low among conservative Protestants (Thornton 1985). While this suggests that there is potential for greater investments in children in conservative Protestant families, the effect is likely offset by relatively high fertility rates (Lehrer 1999).

Reduced achievement among conservative Protestants is evident in low levels of educational attainment in these families. In addition to high fertility, resistance against formal education and the scientific method resulting from literal Bible interpretation reduce educational advancement (Lehrer 1999).

Because the aim of science is the pursuit of truth rather than the blind acceptance of God's word, secular education contests the beliefs of conservative Protestants (Darnell and Sherkat 1997). Parental expectations for educational attainment are thus low among conservative Protestants; children in these families are relatively more likely to be schooled at home and parents are less likely to save for education (Darnell and Sherkat 1997; Lehrer 1999). Moreover, while conservative Protestant mothers and Jewish mothers both exit the labor force to take care of their young children, the typical level of education of a conservative Protestant mother is much lower than that of a Jewish mother. As a result, the stay-at-home mother who is a conservative Protestant is likely to have less effect on her children's educational development. For each of these reasons, children from conservative Protestant families achieve lower levels of education and the rate of return to education is lower for individuals raised in conservative Protestant families. Because education is an important predictor of wealth accumulation, this is likely to reduce wealth accumulation.

While indirect factors are important, there is also likely to be a direct effect of conservative Protestant culture on the accumulation of wealth. The strategies of action that become part of the repertoire of conservative Protestants, however, are unlikely to include skills that facilitate asset accumulation. Traditional gender role attitudes and corresponding family division of labor reduces female employment out of the home, which, in turn, reduces saving and contributes to the creation of patterns that do not include high savings (Sherkat and Ellison 1999). When saving is not common, strategies for investing naturally do not develop and social capital that might provide either information or financial backing is not present. Literal Bible interpretation can also lead to the conclusion that wealth accumulation should be avoided, and a steadfast devotion to tithing exacerbates this. Conservative Protestants "are not averse to worldly pursuits. However, they are admonished to avoid choices that might endanger their souls" (Darnell and Sherkat 1997: 314). Few American religions discourage hard work, saving, or investment. Yet religious groups also seldom promote the idea that God favors the rich over the poor (Wuthnow and Scott 1997), and conservative Protestant religious doctrine includes more messages of this sort than other doctrine. Like Jews, conservative Protestants are unlikely to marry people of other religions and thus unlikely to expand their repertoire of skills and strategies by marrying someone with a different tool kit (Kalmijn 1991; Thornton 1985). The result in the case of conservative Protestants, however, is that they are likely to accumulate less wealth, not more. As these patterns cumulate across generations, they may result in lower rates of inheritance and lower overall wealth, even where there is an inheritance.

Mainline Protestants and Catholics

Mainline Protestants and Roman Catholics were at one time distinct from each other in the United States. That distinctiveness, however, has diminished in recent years in such areas as fertility (Lehrer 1996a; Westoff and Jones 1979). Convergence has also been documented in educational attainment (Lehrer 1999; Sherkat and Ellison 1999), female labor force participation, time alloca- tion (Lehrer 1996b), union formation (Lehrer 1998; Sander 1995; Sherkat and Ellison 1999), and separation and divorce (Lehrer and Chiswick 1993). Mainline Protestants and Catholics also account for the bulk of the U.S. population, suggesting that they are unlikely to have accumulation patterns that appear distinct. However, because the convergence of these two groups is relatively recent, there is likely to be some residual effect of the distinctiveness of prior generations. In particular, those who were raised as mainline Protestants may inherit more wealth on average because their parents were part of a religious group that was relatively more affluent than it is today. Catholics may have started off relatively disadvantaged, but they appear to be relatively upwardly mobile (Keister 2003). As a result, there may be very little effect of a Catholic upbringing on adult wealth.

Data, Measures, and Methods

Data

I used the NLSY79 cohort to test these ideas. The NLSY is a nationally representa- tive longitudinal survey that was administered nineteen times between 1979 and 2000 by the Bureau of Labor Statistics (BLS). The initial NLSY sample included 12,686 individuals age fourteen to twenty-two in 1979 (i.e., born between 1957 and 1964). Nearly ten thousand of the respondents were interviewed through 2000. An extensive battery of wealth questions was added to the NLSY in 1985 when the youngest respondents were twenty years old. I used data from 1985 through 2000 to estimate pooled cross-section time series models of wealth ownership. I also drew on earlier surveys to gather information about the respondents' family backgrounds. Wealth questions were not asked in 1991, and the BLS began conducting the NLSY every other year starting in 1994. Thus, I used wealth data for 6,111 respondents at eleven time points (1985–1990, 1992, 1993, 1995, 1996, 1998, and 2000), with sample sizes varying slightly across tables because of missing data.

The NLSY is ideal for answering questions about family background and adult wealth because it combines broad longitudinal coverage of a large sample with detailed information about wealth holdings, family background, life tran- sitions, and adult status. In each survey year beginning in 1985, respondents reported whether they owned a comprehensive list of assets and debts and the value of each asset or debt if they owned it. Other sources of survey data on wealth ownership provide more wealthy individuals. The Survey of Consumer Finances (SCF), for example, is a panel data set that over-samples high-income households to more accurately estimate wealth distribution (Kennickell, Starr- McCluer, and Sunden 1997; Wolff 1995). Because the NLSY does not over-sample wealthy households, it may underestimate wealth concentration (Juster and Kuester 1991; Juster, Smith, and Stafford 1999).

Measures and Methods

I used four dependent variables in the analyses. First, I modeled value of total net worth in the respondent's adult family. Net worth is the value of total assets less the value of total liabilities. The financial assets included stocks and bonds; cash accounts such as checking accounts; trust accounts; Individual Retirement Accounts; 401K plans; and Certificates of Deposit. The real assets included the primary residence or home; a business, farm, or investment real estate; a car; and other possessions. The debts included mortgages on the primary residence; debt on businesses, farms, or investment real estate; debt on automobiles; and other debt. I used the CPI to adjust all asset and debt values to 2000 dollars. Second, in order to explore the degree to which the relationship between religion and wealth accumulation reflects the religious practices and wealth of prior generations, I modeled the likelihood that the respondent ever received an inheritance. This dichotomous indicator includes inheritances received both during the 1985–1998 period when the NLSY asked specific questions about wealth and inheritances received prior to 1985. Modeling the value of the inheritances produced similar results. Third, I modeled the likelihood that the respondent received a trust account, owned a home, or owned stocks and bonds.

I included a series of dichotomous variables, coded from reports in the 2000 data wave, to indicate religious affiliation in childhood. In the regression models, I included measures that the person was Jewish, Baptist, or another type of conservative Protestant. The omitted category is all other religious affiliations. I based my classification of Protestants as closely as possible on categories used by Lehrer (1999), Lehrer and Chiswick (1993), and Steensland and colleagues (2000). In some descriptive statistics, I also distinguish mainline Protestants by denomination. Measures for those who were raised Roman Catholics and mainline Protestant were not significantly different from zero. I did not include these measures in the final regression models because people raised as Roman Catholic and mainline Protestant comprise the bulk of the population. I did not include measures for more underrepresented religious groups (e.g., Muslims, separate indicators for Orthodox Jews, those raised with no religious affiliation) because of small samples sizes.

I experimented with a very wide range of classifications of denominations, including categorizing those who are evangelical as conservative regardless of the standard classification and including relatively small sects and relatively distinct sects of conservative Protestants in their own categories and in various combinations of categories. Across a multitude of specifications, the results did not change in a substantive way. The models were extremely robust to changes in the way I grouped religions. Including separate indicators for various groups that might seem unique did not change the results. For example, including separate indicators for Mormon, Hindu, Buddhist, Christian Science, and Unitarian did not change the results. Also, some of my descriptive results suggest that Episcopalians are unique among mainline Protestants, but including separate indicators for Episcopalians did not change the results. The measures I use are from reports in the 2000 survey. I also experimented with using earlier data, from 1980, to report religious affiliation. Using data from the earlier year also did not change the substance of the results because there was a tremendous amount of consistently between reported religious upbringing in the two data waves. Finally, including measures of adult religious affiliation does not change the substance of the findings because the correlation between childhood and adult religion is relatively high for all religious groups.

I controlled for various individual and family attributes that are related to wealth ownership, including financial resources. Parents' net family income (logged) controls for the family's resources. I also included a dummy variable indicating that the respondent had not provided information about family income in 1978 to control for patterns that might be common to those with missing values on this key variable (Sandefur and Wells 1999). I included measures of parents' education, race, and gender. Previous literature suggests that resources are diluted in large families, and each additional sibling diminishes adult attainment (Downey 1995). I used the total number of siblings the respondent ever had, reported in 2000, to indicate family size in childhood. Because family disruption may also reduce the time parents have available to nurture children (Mechanic and Hansell 1989), I included two dummy variables giving a snapshot of the respondent's family structure at age fourteen. I used dummy variables to indicate whether the respondent's parents worked full-time (more than thirty-five hours per week) to control for whether nonmaterial parental resources were diluted because both parents were absent.

I included a series of education dummy variables indicating whether the respondent had completed high school, some college, a bachelors degree, or an advanced degree. The omitted category for education is respondents who had not completed high school. To capture the level of nonwealth financial resources available in the respondent's household, I controlled for income from entrepreneurship, the number of weeks the respondent worked in temporary positions, and total household income (logged). I indicated age in number of years in the current year and also included an age-squared term to control for changes in religiosity with age (Stolzenberg, Blair-Loy, and Waite 1995). I included dummy variables indicating marital status in the current year. I included a continuous variable indicating the number of children born to the respondent for those who had children.

I included a dummy variable indicating whether the person ever received a trust account or inherited. I included a value for the estimated family wealth in 1979. I calculated this variable using other family measures in 1979 including income, family structure, parents' education, other parent traits, and other individual traits. This variable has an expected positive effect on wealth and allows interpretation of the final regression model in terms of change in wealth since childhood. Controlling for wealth in 1985—in order to explore change since early adulthood—produced comparable results. I controlled for foreign birth and the number of weeks the respondent's spouse worked. Finally, I included four dummy variables indicating region of residence to capture variations in economic conditions and opportunities. A single indicator of urban residence captures urban–rural differences in wealth ownership. This variable uses census data to indicate whether the county of residence had a central core city and adjacent, closely settled area with a total combined population of fifty thousand or more. Because controls for residence in New York City and other specific locations, housing price variations, and regional indicators did not affect the results, I did not include them in the final models.

I used pooled cross-section time series analyses to model wealth ownership. Thus, the unit of analysis in all models was the person-year between 1985 and 2000, and both independent and dependent variables can change in each year. I used Estimated Generalized Least Squares (EGLS) regression to model net assets because the error terms were both heteroskedastic and correlated over time. I used logistic regression to model the likelihood the respondent received an inheritance, a trust, owned a home, or owned stock or bonds.

Results

Descriptive statistics suggest that there are indeed very large differences in adult wealth by childhood religion. Table 9.1 provides details regarding wealth position in 2000 by childhood religion. I include estimates for those who were raised Baptist, the largest conservative Protestant group represented in the data. I also include several mainline Protestant denominations, Roman Catholic, and Jewish. I do not include more detailed classifications because of space considerations but also because additional detail provides no new information. The estimates in Table 9.1 demonstrate that there are very important differences in the percentage of people who are rich as adults given their religious upbringing. About 3 percent of the full sample is a millionaire in 2000. However, only 1 percent of those who were Baptists during childhood are this wealthy. Similarly, only 2 percent of those raised Roman Catholic or Lutheran are millionaires. For the Roman Catholics and Lutherans, getting rich more typically means having a slightly smaller fortune. For both groups, 6 to 9 percent have net worth in the next two wealth groups shown (greater than $300,000 but less than $1 million). A slightly larger group of those raised Methodist or Presbyterian are millionaires, perhaps because of the residual effects of the wealth of prior generations. The most striking difference again is in the percentage of those raised Jewish who are millionaires. A full 18 percent of Jewish youth owned more than $1 million in net worth in 2000.

TABLE 9.1

Adult Wealth Ownership by Childhood Religious Affiliation

		Percent with net worth					
Childhood religion	*% sample total*	*> $1 Million*	*$500K– 999,999*	*$300K– 499,999*	*< $300K*	*Zero or negative*	*Median net worth (thousands)*
All	100%	3%	4%	6%	87%	15%	$58
Protestant							
Conservative							
Baptist	24	1	2	4	93	21	26
Other	11	1	2	5	92	17	62
Mainline							
Lutheran	8	2	6	6	86	11	83
Methodist	7	4	3	5	88	11	80
Presbyterian	3	4	9	9	78	11	101
Episcopalian	2	12	11	7	70	7	120
Catholic	32	2	6	8	84	10	79
Jewish	2	18	15	12	55	3	221
Other	6	2	3	4	91	19	34
None	5	3	2	5	90	18	40

Source: NLSY79 Cohort.

Notes: N = 4,963. All wealth estimates are for the year 2000.

Portfolio Behavior

One reason that total adult wealth varies across groups is that the components of total wealth vary. That is, families may own different types of assets—whether through saving, investment, or inheritance—that affect how much wealth they own overall. An important component of the portfolios of most Americans is the home. The home is a real (or tangible) asset that has use value as well as value as an investment. The home also generally provides long-term growth in assets that can be tapped in times of financial crisis. Table 9.2 shows that homeownership is spread rather evenly across the population, although there are some notable differences by religious background. This table includes estimates of the percentage of respondents who owned five assets, including the home, in 2000. For those who were raised mainline Protestants and Roman Catholics, these estimates suggest that Lutherans and Presbyterians are most likely

TABLE 9.2

Adult Portfolio and Childhood Religious Affiliation

| | % sample total | Home | Percent owning | | | |
			Stocks and bonds	Checking and savings	Trust account	Business
All	100%	68%	26%	77%	5%	11%
Conservative						
Baptist	24	60	16	66	3	8
Other	11	67	25	78	4	10
Mainline						
Lutheran	8	78	30	90	5	16
Methodist	7	75	31	82	6	12
Presbyterian	3	80	35	85	4	7
Episcopalian	2	68	38	86	10	6
Catholic	32	70	30	81	5	10
Jewish	2	83	62	88	15	18
Other	6	63	24	70	6	13
None	5	64	26	72	6	11

Source: NLSY79 Cohort.

Notes: N = 4,963. Wealth ownership estimates are for the year 2000.

to be homeowners. By contrast, only 60 percent of those raised Baptist were homeowners. Again, those who were raised Jewish tend to have higher rates of homeownership than other families. As Table 9.2 shows, more than 80 percent of those raised Jewish were homeowners in 2000.

Financial assets are also an important part of a wealth portfolio, and stocks and bonds are the financial instruments that a family that owns any financial assets is likely to own. While stocks and bonds can take a variety of forms, such as individual equities and mutual funds, I combine all stock and bond ownership in a single category in Table 9.2 because basic patterns tend to be the same for different types of stocks, bonds, and mutual funds. This table shows that about 26 percent of all respondents own some type of stocks or bonds. Of those raised as Baptists, only 16 percent owned any stocks or bonds in 2000, while more than 60 percent of those raised Jewish owned these financial assets. Between these two extremes were the mainline Protestant and Roman Catholics. In each of these groups, approximately one-third of respondents owned stocks and bonds.

Financial assets have historically increased in value over long periods, and own-ers of financial assets such as stocks tend to get rich must faster than those who do not own these assets. As stock values increase, in particular, those who own stocks tend to see very large increases in the value of their overall portfolios (Keister 1997). As a result, those who do not own stocks fall farther behind.

To what extent can differences in adult wealth for these groups be explained by differences in intergenerational transfers of wealth? Receiving a trust account is an important indicator of the effect of direct intergenerational transfers of financial resources. Table 9.2 also includes the percentage of NLSY respondents who ever received a trust account to begin to answer this question. The table shows that 5 percent of all respondents had received a trust account. It is inter-esting to note that 3 percent of those who were raised as Baptists inherited. While this is lower than the overall average, it is not significantly lower, suggest-ing that it is not intergenerational transfers alone that account for differences in adult wealth by religious upbringing. In contrast, 15 percent of those raised Jewish received trust accounts.

The final column in Table 9.2 shows the percentage of respondents who owned any business assets in 2000. This includes both businesses owned entirely by the respondent and investments in businesses owned primarily by others. The variable as I use it here does confound entrepreneurial behavior with a specific type of investment behavior, but the patterns are the same when I disaggregate the variable. For the entire sample, the mean percentage of respondents who owned a business was 11 percent. However, 18 percent of those raised Jewish owned business assets. By contrast, for those raised as Baptists, only 8 percent owned any business assets as adults. These patterns suggest that portfolio behavior clearly varies across these groups in ways that affect their overall wealth. These patterns also suggest that portfolio behavior is likely to tell only part of the story.

Multivariate Analyses

Multivariate analyses corroborate the patterns that emerged in the descriptive data: people raised in conservative Protestant families tend to accumulate less wealth and to be less upwardly mobile than other families, while people raised in Jewish families accumulated more wealth and are more upwardly mobile. The first model shown in Table 9.3 includes measures of childhood religion but does not control for education in order to demonstrate the base effect of religion. I also did not include inheritance measures in this model to demonstrate the relationship between religion in childhood without considering the role that assets acquired from prior generations have on adult wealth. As my conceptual model predicts, the relationship between being raised in a Jewish family and adult net worth is significantly greater than zero. In fact, the coefficient estimate for Jewish religious affiliation in childhood is more than seven times greater than its standard error. The second model pictured in Table 9.3 also controls for the respondent's educational attainment. The effect of education on wealth accumulation is quite strong and increases with the level of education achieved. Adding education controls to the model does decrease the effect of the religion indicators somewhat (confirmed with Cox tests), but the strong positive effect of being raised in a Jewish family remains. In subsequent models, I add other adult traits and inheritance indicators to the model, and the relative size, direction, and significance of the religion indicators remains.

The estimates shown in Table 9.3 provide evidence that: (a) being raised Jewish increases adult wealth accumulation and mobility, even controlling for financial resources, family background, and other important individual and family predictors of wealth; (b) being raised Jewish increases adult wealth and mobility at least partly because of its effect on educational attainment; and (c) there is a direct effect of being raised Jewish on adult wealth and wealth mobility that remains after controlling for a host of other predictors of wealth.

The results presented in Table 9.3 also provide support for my proposal that being raised in a conservative Protestant family decreases adult wealth and wealth mobility. The first model in the table shows that there is a strong, significant, and negative effect of the two indicators of being raised in a conservative Protestant denomination, before controlling for education. The second model demonstrates that the effect remains after controlling for education. Together these analyses provide support for claims that: (a) being raised conservative Protestant decreases adult wealth accumulation and mobility, even controlling for financial resources, family background, and other important individual and family predictors of wealth; (b) being raised conservative Protestant decreases adult wealth and mobility at least partly because of its effect on educational attainment; and (c) there is a direct effect of being raised conservative Protestant on adult wealth and wealth mobility that remains after controlling for a host of other predictors of wealth.

To what extent does inheritance account for these patterns? Table 9.4 includes coefficient estimates from logistic regression models predicting: (a) the likelihood the respondent ever received an inheritance; and (b) the likelihood that the respondent ever received a trust account, both as a function of childhood religious affiliation and all control variables. Consistent with my conceptual model, those who were raised in Jewish families were significantly more likely to ever receive an inheritance. Likewise, affiliation with a conservative Protestant faith in childhood was negatively associated with receiving an inheritance. Similarly, there is a positive relationship between being raised Jewish and receiving a trust account. The negative relationship between being raised in non-Baptist conservative Protestant churches is still present in models of receiving a trust, but the effect of being raised Baptist is not present in this model. The relationship between being raised Baptist and receiving a trust account was present in preliminary models, but adding parents' educational attainment to the models eliminated the significant effect. This underscores

TABLE 9.3

Religion and Total Adult Assets, 1985–2000, EGLS Parameter Estimates

	Childhood religion	Add education	Add adult traits	Add wealth measures
Family religion in childhood				
Jewish	138.52***	124.08***	111.86***	189.02***
Baptist	-8.79**	-12.33**	-9.51*	-7.84*
Other Protestant	-6.65**	-12.09**	-10.41*	-17.95*
Parents' financial resources				
Family income (log)	-1.05*	1.05*	1.00	0.90
Family income not reported	-7.40	-7.55	6.45	5.44
Father's education				
High school	16.34***	12.42***	11.53**	10.65
Some college	19.60***	10.25	8.78	12.13
College degree	35.20***	21.18***	17.91**	10.63
Advanced degree	48.38***	32.38***	31.92***	12.22
Mother's education				
High school	12.96***	6.48**	3.56	4.21
Some college	28.07***	16.15**	11.63	10.12
College degree	50.09***	33.94***	32.41***	16.58
Advanced degree	22.81	4.51	5.20	-12.30
Black	-41.44***	-38.85***	-26.18***	-25.55***
Hispanic family Age 14	-32.71***	-31.88***	-29.14***	-24.98**
Number of siblings	-2.62***	-2.53***	-2.52***	-2.82*
Stepparent family	-16.22***	-12.50**	-6.04	-6.24
Single-parent family	-8.79	-8.14	1.57	-6.39
Father worked full-time	9.13	8.45	8.83	6.15
Mother worked full-time	-2.16	-2.31	-6.51	-1.98
Respondent's education				
High school	—	17.85***	2.56	-3.75
Some college	—	34.11***	10.53*	-1.37
College degree	—	57.58***	28.46***	21.44**
Advanced degree	—	74.57***	40.51***	35.68**

(continued)

Table 9.3. Religion and Total Adult Assests, 1985–2000, EGIS Parameter Estimates *(continued)*

	Childhood religion	Add education	Add adult traits	Add wealth measures
Adult resources				
Entrepreneurial income	—	—	56.22***	61.17***
Family income	—	—	0.00***	0.00***
Intergenerational transfers				
Received a trust fund	—	—	—	334.76***
Ever inherited	—	—	—	20.62***
Estimated 1979 wealth	—	—	—	2.21***
Adjusted R²	.08	.10	.13	.15

Notes: Sample size is 6,110 after those with missing data are deleted. Sample across twelve years is 73,330 (person-years). Also controlled, but not displayed, are gender, age, marital status, adult family size, temporary work indicator, immigrant status, weeks worked by spouse, urban residence, and region of residence.

$* \ p < .10 \ ** \ p < .05 \ *** \ p < .01$

the fact that measures of intergenerational transfers are strongly related to measures of parents' achievement, and it is difficult to disentangle the effects of these influences.

What other factors might account for the relationship between religion and wealth ownership? Asset allocation, or portfolio behavior, is certainly an important contributing factor. Asset allocation refers to decisions about how to save or invest money. The simplest distinctions in asset allocation are between real assets and financial assets, and decisions within each of these categories vary in the degree to which they are risky, with riskier assets typically creating higher returns. Table 9.4 also includes logistic regression coefficient estimates for models predicting: (a) the likelihood of homeownership; and (b) the likelihood of owning stocks and bonds.

Lower homeownership rates for conservative Protestants likely contributes to the relatively small portfolios that people raised in these faiths amass, but how does lower homeownership affect the portfolios of Jews? Part of the answer is that when Jewish families do own homes, they tend to be in urban areas and thus more valuable.

However, an even more important explanation is the propensity of Jews to invest in financial assets. In contrast to the effects of childhood religion on adult homeownership, the findings presented in Table 9.4 show that those

TABLE 9.4

Religion and Wealth Components, 1985–2000:
Logistic Regression Parameter Estimates

	Ever inherited	Received a trust account	Own a home	Own stocks
Family religion in childhood				
Jewish	0.53***	0.34**	-0.41***	0.22**
Baptist	-0.27***	-0.07	-0.02***	-0.31***
Conservative Protestant	-0.08***	-0.18**	-0.10***	-0.10**
Parents' financial resources				
Family income (log)	0.01***	0.02***	0.00	0.01
Family income not reported	-0.05	-0.09	-0.04	0.02
Father's education				
High school	0.20***	0.08	0.01	0.11***
Some college	0.16***	0.05	0.20***	0.27***
College degree	0.36***	0.09	0.03	0.37***
Advanced degree	0.78***	0.32***	0.19***	0.37***
Mother's education				
High school	0.07**	0.07	0.12***	0.34***
Some college	0.20***	0.40***	0.17***	0.35***
College degree	0.39***	0.74***	0.05	0.52***
Advanced degree	0.04	0.92***	0.21***	0.36***
Black	-0.69***	-0.51***	-0.98***	-0.26***
Hispanic family at Age 14	-0.78***	-0.13	-0.46***	-0.38***
Number of siblings	-0.05***	-0.08***	-0.03***	-0.04***
Stepparent family	0.21***	0.05	-0.12***	-0.07
Single-parent family	-0.14***	-0.19***	-0.12***	-0.04
Father worked full-time	0.05	0.10	0.20***	0.22***
Mother worked full-time	-0.01	0.22***	-0.02	-0.03
Respondent's education				
High school	0.68***	0.46***	0.29***	0.16***
Some college	1.10***	0.58***	0.34***	0.46***
College degree	1.43***	0.61***	0.40***	1.03***

(continued)

Table 9.4. Religion and Wealth Components, 1985–2000: Logistic Regression
Parameter Estimates (continued)

	Ever inherited	Received a trust account	Own a home	Own stocks
Entrepreneurial income	0.34***	0.46***	0.33***	0.03
Family income	0.01***	0.01***	0.01***	0.01***
N	6,110	6,198	6,008	6,112
-2 log likelihood	61,727***	14,647***	75,017***	41,572***

Notes: Also controlled, but not displayed, are gender, age, marital status, adult family size, temporary work indicator, immigrant status, weeks worked by spouse, urban residence, and region of residence.

* p < .10 ** p < .05 *** p < .01

raised Jewish are much more likely than others to own stocks or bonds, while conservative Protestants are less likely to be owners of stocks or bonds. Moreover, the paths people take during their financial lives can also impact adult wealth in critical ways. For instance, saving early in life can disproportionately affect adult wealth because of compounding. Naturally, early saving in high-return financial instruments can have an even more noticeable impact. An important part of the financial repertoire that children learn, and that can be associated with the family's religious preferences, is a propensity to begin saving early or to save in particular ways. There is evidence that those raised as Jewish begin to invest in financial assets early in life and to stay invested in these assets more heavily than average throughout the life, even controlling for other individual and family factors that shape wealth ownership (Keister 2003). It is this pattern of financial wealth ownership, and the ability of financial assets to increase the value of total wealth, that accounts for the increase in overall wealth for Jews even in the presence of lower homeownership rates. These results also imply that the repertoire of skills and decision-making abilities learned in childhood may very well set a course of action that ultimately translates into higher levels of wealth.

Discussion and Conclusion

In this chapter, I argued that religion is an important determinant of wealth ownership, and I identified important patterns in the relationship between religion and wealth that isolate the mechanisms underlying these relationships. I argued that religious affiliation in childhood can shape action indirectly by altering fertility and marriage behavior, educational attainment, work behavior, and other behaviors and processes that influence wealth ownership. I also argued, however, that religion is an important element of culture. As such, religion directly affects wealth accumulation by defining the goals people identify as important, by creating a repertoire of skills and knowledge that people draw on when making decisions, and by determining the nature of people's social contacts. When they are exposed to religious ceremonies, rituals, and values, people develop a set of competencies and habits that they draw on in making decisions about consumption, saving, and investment. Affiliation with a religious group also creates social capital that may improve understanding of saving and investing and may actually provide investment opportunities.

I identified distinct patterns in the relationship between religious affiliation and wealth ownership. Those who were raised Jewish owned considerably more wealth than others. I showed that those who were raised Jewish are more likely to receive an inheritance, and I demonstrated that Jews own more high-risk, high-return financial assets than others and that Jews are relatively less likely to own a house. Both findings are consistent with the argument that, for historic reasons, Jews have a preference for human capital and other types of capital that are transportable rather than fixed. I also found evidence of a negative relationship between affiliation with a conservative Protestant church and wealth ownership. In direct contrast to Jews, conservative Protestants owned less overall wealth and fewer financial assets. I focused on those who were raised as Baptist, but the results are the same for other conservative Protestants.

By focusing on the relationship between religion and wealth, I do not intend to reduce the complex process of wealth accumulation or wealth inequality to a single set of inputs. In the full conceptual model I proposed in the beginning of the chapter, I suggest that wealth accumulation and mobility are the result of various interacting process, including family structure, marital behavior, and union separation and aggregate processes such as demographic trends, market fluctuations, and policy shifts. The results that I present in this chapter, however, highlight an important part of the picture. Understanding that religion is related in critical ways to wealth accumulation, net of its indirect effects on other demographic behaviors, casts light on the importance of family processes that shape the way people behave and, in this case, the way they accumulate assets.

Future research should explore the role of religious involvement in shaping adult wealth. It will also be important to consider these patterns as respondents age and with other data sets. Additional research might also investigate the role that debt plays in this process. Debt is clearly an important part of family finances (Sullivan, Warren, and Westbrook 1989, 2000), and this chapter does not begin to address religious variations in indebtedness. Future research should consider analyzing race/ethnic groups and gender groups separately. While there are certain to be important differences across demographic groups, further exploration of such patterns was beyond the scope of this chapter. Finally, additional research should explore the role that interactions between religion and other factors play in shaping wealth ownership. Ethnicity and immigration, for example, are likely to interact with religion in ways that are meaningful for understanding wealth (Ebaugh 2000; Yang and Ebaugh 2001).

NOTE

I am grateful for a grant from the National Institutes on Health, National Institute on Aging for the funds that supported this research.

REFERENCES

Alwin, D. 1986. "Religion and Parental Childbearing Orientations: Evidence for a Catholic–Protestant Convergence." *American Journal of Sociology* 92:412–420.

Bonder, R. N. 2001. *The Kabbalah of Money: Jewish Insights on Giving, Owning, and Receiving.* New York: Shambhala.

Bourdieu, P. 1977. *Outline of a Theory of Practice.* Cambridge: Cambridge University Press.

Brenner, R., and N. M. Kiefer. 1981. "The Economics of Diaspora: Discrimination and Occupational Structure." *Economic Development and Cultural Change* 29:517–533.

Chiswick, B. R. 1986. "Labor Supply and Investment in Child Quality: A Study of Jewish and Non-Jewish Women." *Review of Economics and Statistics* 68:700–703.

———. 1988. "Differences in Education and Earnings across Racial and Ethnic Groups: Tastes, Discrimination, and Investments in Child Quality." *Quarterly Journal of Economics* 103:571–597.

———. 1993. "The Skills and Economic Status of American Jewry: Trends over the Last Half-Century." *Journal of Labor Economics* 11:229–242.

Chiteji, N. S., and F. Stafford. 2000. "Asset Ownership across Generations." Working Paper, Jerome Levy Institute, New York.

Darnell, A., and D. E. Sherkat. 1997. "The Impact of Protestant Fundamentalism on Educational Attainment." *American Sociological Review* 62:306–315.

DellaPergola, S. 1980. "Patterns of American Jewish Fertility." *Demography* 17:261–273.

Downey, D. B. 1995. "When Bigger is Not Better: Family Size, Parental Resources, and Children's Educational Performance." *American Sociological Review* 60:746–761.

Ebaugh, H. R. 2000. "Structural Adaptation in Immigrant Congregations." *Sociology of Religion* 61:135–153.

Ellison, C. G., J. P. Bartkowsi, and M. L. Segal. 1996. "Conservative Protestantism and the Parental Use of Corporal Punishment." *Social Forces* 74:1003–1028.

Hummer, R. A., R. G. Rogers, C. B. Nam, and C. G. Ellison. 1999. "Religious Involvement and U.S. Adult Mortality." *Demography* 36:273–285.

Juster, T. F., and K. A. Kuester. 1991. "Differences in the Measurement of Wealth, Wealth Inequality and Wealth Composition Obtained from Alternative U.S. Wealth Surveys." *Review of Income and Wealth* 37:33–62.

Juster, T. F., J. P. Smith, and F. Stafford. 1999. "The Measurement and Structure of Household Wealth." *Labour Economics* 6:253–275.

Kalmijn, M. 1991. "Shifting Boundaries: Trends in Religious and Educational Homogamy." *American Sociological Review* 56:786–800.

Keister, L. 1997. "Who Wins When the Stock Market Booms?" Working Paper, Cornell University Department of Sociology, Ithaca, NY.

———. 2000. *Wealth in America.* New York: Cambridge University Press.

———. 2003. "Religion and Wealth: The Role of Religious Affiliation and Participation in Early Adult Asset Accumulation." *Social Forces* 82:173–205.

Kennickell, A. B. 2000. "An Examination of Changes in the Distribution of Wealth from 1989–1998: Evidence from the Survey of Consumer Finances." Working Paper, Federal Reserve Board.

Kennickell, A. B., M. Starr-McCluer, and A. E. Sunden. 1997. "Family Finances in the United States: Recent Evidence from the Survey of Consumer Finances." *Federal Reserve Bulletin* (January): 1–24.

Lehrer, E. L. 1996a. "Religion as a Determinant of Fertility." *Journal of Population Economics* 9:173–196.

———. 1996b. "The Role of the Husband's Religion on the Economic and Demographic Behavior of Families." *Journal for the Scientific Study of Religion* 35:145–155.

———. 1998. "Religious Intermarriage in the United States: Determinants and Trends." *Social Science Research* 27:245–263.

———. 1999. "Religion as a Determinant of Educational Attainment: An Economic Perspective." *Social Science Research* 28:358–379.

Lehrer, E. L., and C. U. Chiswick. 1993. "Religion as a Determinant of Marital Stability." *Demography* 30:385–404.

Mechanic, D., and S. Hansell. 1989. "Divorce, Family Conflict, and Adolescents' Well-Being." *Journal of Health and Social Behavior* 30:105–116.

Pearce, L. D., and W. G. Axinn. 1998. "The Impact of Religious Life on the Quality of Mother-Child Relations." *American Sociological Review* 63:810–828.

Sandefur, G. D., and T. Wells. 1999. "Does Family Structure Really Influence Educational Attainment?" *Social Science Research* 28:331–357.

Sander, W. 1995. *The Catholic Family: Marriage, Children, and Human Capital.* Boulder, CO: Westview Press.

Sherkat, D. E., and C. G. Ellison. 1999. "Recent Developments and Current Controversies in the Sociology of Religion." *Annual Review of Sociology* 25:363–394.

Smith, C. 1998. *American Evangelicalism: Embattled and Thriving.* Chicago: University of Chicago Press.

Steensland, B., J. Z. Park, M. D. Regnerus, L. D. Robinson, W. B. Wilcox, and R. D. Woodberry. 2000. "The Measure of American Religion: Toward Improving the State of the Art." *Social Forces* 79:291–318.

Stolzenberg, R. M., M. Blair-Loy, and L. J. Waite. 1995. "Religious Participation in Early Adulthood: Age and Family Life Cycle Effects on Church Membership." *American Sociological Review* 60:84–103.

Stryker, R. 1981. "Religio-Ethnic Effects Upon Attainments in the Early Career." *American Sociological Review* 46: 212–231.

Sullivan, T. A., E. Warren, and J. L. Westbrook. 1989. *As We Forgive our Debtors: Bankruptcy and Consumer Credit in America.* New York: Oxford University Press.

———. 2000. *The Fragile Middle Class: Americans in Debt.* New Haven, CT: Yale University Press.

Swidler, A. 1986. "Culture in Action: Symbols and Strategies." *American Sociological Review* 51:273–286.

Thornton, A. 1985. "Changing Attitudes towards Separation and Divorce: Causes and Consequences." *American Journal of Sociology* 90:856–872.

Westoff, C. F., and E. F. Jones. 1979. "The End of 'Catholic' Fertility." *Demography* 16:209–218.

Wilcox, B. W. 1998. "Conservative Protestant Childrearing: Authoritarian or Authoritative?" *American Sociological Review* 63:796–809.

Wolff, E. N. 1995. "The Rich Get Increasingly Richer: Latest Data on Household Wealth during the 1980s." In *Research in Politics and Society*, vol. 5, ed. R. E. Ratcliff, M. L. Oliver, and T. M. Shapiro, 33–68. Greenwich, CT: JAI Press.

————. 1998. "Recent Trends in the Size Distribution of Household Wealth." *Journal of Economic Perspectives* 12:131–150.

Wuthnow, R. 1999. *Growing up Religious: Christians and Jews and their Journeys of Faith.* Boston: Beacon Press.

Wuthnow, R., and T. L. Scott. 1997. "Protestants and Economic Behavior." In *New Directions in American Religious History*, ed. H. S. Sout and D. G. Hart, 260–295. New York: Oxford University Press.

Yang, F., and H. R. Ebaugh. 2001. "Religion and Ethnicity: The Impact of Majority/Minority Status in the Home and Host Countries." *Journal for the Social Scientific Study of Religion* 40:367–378.

10

Religious Affiliation and Participation
as Determinants of Women's
Educational Attainment and Wages

EVELYN LEHRER

Recent years have witnessed a renewed interest in the relationship between religious affiliation and education. Analyses of data on non-Hispanic whites from the 1987–1988 National Survey of Families and Households (NSFH) reveal that for both men and women, mainline Protestants and Catholics are at the center of the educational distribution; the mean years of schooling are about one year lower for conservative Protestants, and about two years higher for Jews (Lehrer 1999). Other research confirms that the level of schooling is relatively high for Jews (Chiswick 1983, 1988) and relatively low for conservative Protestants (Darnell and Sherkat 1997; Sherkat and Darnell 1999; Glass 1999). Other groups, including Mormons and the unaffiliated, have not been studied in most of these analyses.

There is also growing interest in the question of how educational outcomes may be affected by another dimension of religion, namely, religiosity. Religiosity encompasses such dimensions as commitment to the religion, the strength of religious beliefs, and participation in religious activities individually or as part of a congregation. Studies that have examined the linkage between religiosity and education suggest a positive association. Freeman (1986) finds a positive effect of churchgoing on school attendance in a sample of inner-city black youth. Regnerus (2000) finds that participation in religious activities is related to better test scores and heightened educational expectations among tenth-grade public school students. Muller and Ellison (2001) report positive effects of various measures of religious involvement on the students' locus of control (a measure of self-concept), educational expectations, time spent on homework, advanced mathematics credits earned, and the probability of obtaining a high school diploma.

The present study employs data from a large national survey addressed to women, the 1995 National Survey of Family Growth (NSFG). Most of our knowledge with regard to the religious affiliation–education linkage is based on data

186

collected in the 1980s and before. The 1995 NSFG provides an opportunity to ascertain whether the relationships found earlier for the main religious groups have continued to hold in more recent years. In addition, the sample size is large enough to allow inclusion of relatively small groups in the analysis, including Mormons, Jews, and the unaffiliated. The survey contains information on frequency of attendance to religious services at age fourteen, making it possible to also study how religious participation during the formative years is related to subsequent decisions regarding investments in schooling. This relationship has been examined for the case of conservative Protestants (Lehrer 2004b); the present study extends this analysis to the other main religious groups in the United States.

The evidence accumulated thus far on the effects of religious affiliation and participation on education suggests that these variables should exert similar influences on subsequent economic well-being as an adult. Consistent with this hypothesis, Keister (2003) finds that patterns of wealth accumulation by religious affiliation closely mirror the differences by education described earlier: Jews are at the upper end of the distribution, with very high levels of wealth accumulation; conservative Protestants have relatively low levels, and mainline Protestants and Catholics are at the center of the distribution; the author also documents a positive association between religious participation and wealth. Evidence on the effects of religious affiliation on other indicators of economic well-being, such as hourly wages or earnings, is very limited, with the notable exception of analyses that find a large positive influence associated with a Jewish upbringing (Chiswick 1992, 1993). Moreover, there has been no work to date on how religious participation may affect performance in the labor market. The present study seeks to close these gaps in our knowledge, for the case of women.

Analytical Framework

The Effects of Religious Affiliation and Participation on Education

Recent research has interpreted patterns of religious differences by education within the framework of a human capital model: religious affiliation is viewed as reflecting distinctive features of the home environment that can affect the supply and/or demand for funds for investments in schooling (Chiswick 1988; Lehrer 1999). On the demand side, religious affiliation can affect the returns from investments in education: among religious groups characterized by larger benefits from schooling, the incentives to pursue education are stronger and thus a higher level of attainment is expected, all else being equal. On the supply side, religious affiliation can affect parents' willingness and ability to supply funds for such investments: a higher level of education is expected for religious groups in which the parents have a greater willingness and ability to supply funds for investments in schooling, all else being equal. Using mainline

Protestants as the reference category for all comparisons, this framework is used in the following to organize various ideas suggested in earlier studies and to develop hypotheses regarding the effects of religious affiliation and participation on educational attainment.[1] The arguments for conservative Protestants, Catholics, and Jews are presented briefly, as these groups have been analyzed extensively elsewhere (Chiswick 1988; Darnell and Sherkat 1997; Sherkat and Darnell 1999; Lehrer 1999, 2004b).

CONSERVATIVE PROTESTANTS. Darnell and Sherkat (1997) and Sherkat and Darnell (1999) have suggested several reasons to expect a low level of schooling for this group. On the supply side, conservative Protestant parents often have concerns that secular schooling may adversely affect their children; such concerns may influence their willingness to supply funds for investments in secular schooling. On the demand side, a conservative Protestant upbringing may imply lower levels of certain types of home investments in child quality that affect the productivity of formal schooling; in addition, it has an adverse impact on the probability of taking college preparatory courses during high school, and hence on the ability to benefit from subsequent investments in a college education.

CATHOLICS. A large body of research shows that in recent decades there has been a convergence between Catholics and mainline Protestants in most aspects of economic and demographic behavior (Lehrer 2004a). Consistent with this transformation, there is some evidence that non-Hispanic Catholics and mainline Protestants do not differ significantly in terms of educational attainment (Lehrer 1999). It is expected that this pattern will also be observed in the more recent data.[2]

JEWS. Chiswick (1988) presents arguments for expecting a high level of educational attainment among Jews. On the supply side, historically Jews have placed a high priority on making investments in the human capital of their children, as they are more portable than investments in physical capital. Empirically, demand side forces have been found to be dominant: sibsize tends to be small in Jewish families and a large amount of resources, especially maternal time, are invested in each child during the early, formative years; these investments increase the productivity of subsequent investments in formal schooling.

MORMONS. As Albrecht and Heaton (1984) note, the Mormon Church has emphasized the importance of education from its very beginning. Theoretically, this high priority placed by the Mormon religion on schooling is a supply-side force that should lead to a high level of educational attainment. On the demand side, however, the Mormon theology is strongly pro-natalist. The early entry into motherhood and extended length of the child rearing period that are associated with high fertility imply a relatively low level of lifetime involvement in labor market activity for women, with correspondingly low expected market returns from schooling. Thus, Mormon women have fewer incentives than their mainline Protestant counterparts to make investments in secular education, and their schooling level is expected to be relatively low. The net effect is thus ambiguous a priori; empirical studies to date have produced conflicting results (Albrecht and Heaton 1984; Keysar and Kosmin 1995).

THE UNAFFILIATED AND THE ROLE OF RELIGIOUS PARTICIPATION. Theoretically, the effect on education of growing up with no affiliation can best be understood following Glenn (1987), thinking of the "no religion" category as an extreme point on the religiosity scale: children who grew up unaffiliated had no involvement in religious activities during childhood, at least not in an institutional context.[3]

A growing body of literature shows that some religious involvement may be associated with benefits for youth in a wide range of areas (Waite and Lehrer 2003; Smith 2003). Several studies show that the positive outcomes associated with religious involvement also include better performance in education, the area that is the focus of this chapter (Freeman 1986; Regnerus 2000; Muller and Ellison 2001). These studies have noted that by contributing to the development of social capital, religion can play a helpful role in the socialization of youth. Religious congregations often sponsor family activities, stimulating the cultivation of closer parent–child relations; they also bring children together with grandparents and other supportive adults (parents of peers, Sunday School teachers) in an environment of trust. This broad base of social ties can be a rich source of positive role models, confidants, and useful information. In addition, most religions encourage healthy behaviors and discourage conduct that is self-destructive, and participation in religious activities can promote emotional well-being (Levin 1994; Regnerus 2003). In these and other ways (see Smith 2003), involvement in religious activities can lead to better mental health, more constructive behaviors, and greater access to valuable resources, all of which are conducive to better schooling outcomes.

The arguments presented earlier suggest that if one compares children who grow up with no religious affiliation to their counterparts with an affiliation, the latter should have a higher level of educational attainment for demand-side reasons: such children may have lower psychological costs of attending school and their time spent on human capital investments is likely to be more productive. Empirically, the few studies on the religion–education relationship that have included the unaffiliated have found that this group indeed has relatively poor outcomes (Glass 1999; Keysar and Kosmin 1995).

In terms of the continuous religiosity variable, a higher level of religious involvement is expected to have a positive impact on educational attainment for the same demand-side reasons. However, the effects may well be of different magnitudes across religious groups. For the case of conservative Protestants, there are reasons to believe that religiosity could actually be a negative force, as the adverse effects on educational attainment associated with the conservative Protestant theology should be more pronounced among those who are more religious. Recent research, however, suggests that the beneficial effects associated with religious involvement may well outweigh this influence, as youth raised in observant conservative Protestant homes tend to benefit from interactions with fathers who have high levels of emotional and practical engagement with their families (Wilcox 2004).

The Effects of Religious Affiliation and Participation on Wages

Religious affiliation during childhood is expected to influence wages through its impact on years of schooling completed, discussed earlier, and also through its effects on employment and labor market experience (Lehrer 1995; Sherkat 2000). Additional effects may be expected. Relatively high levels of wealth accumulation among Jewish families are likely to be associated with attendance to educational institutions of higher quality, which would lead to higher wages. Furthermore, Keister (2003, 180) suggests that in their investments, Jews may benefit from a cultural repertoire transmitted across generations that encourages this-worldly pursuits. In addition, as she notes, "Social connections developed through schools and universities can provide information about investment strategies, actual investment opportunities, and access to capital for investing. Family contacts and contacts in the local Jewish community can also provide information, access to investments, and support that make investment feasible." This social capital may also be of help in the labor market, and if so, affiliation with the Jewish faith would have a positive impact on wages even after controls for education and experience. The tendency for Jews to reside in large metropolitan areas where wages are high is another factor.

At the same time, Ellison and Bartkowski's (2002) analysis implies a possible negative effect for the case of conservative Protestant women, beyond the channel operating through a lower level of schooling and labor market experience. The authors find that in conservative Protestant families, there is greater asymmetry in the intrahousehold division of labor and wives spend more time on household work. To the extent that heavier responsibilities for work in the home decrease the level of energy left for market work, the result may be lower productivity on the job and lower wages.[4] For these effects that operate through mechanisms other than investments in schooling, religious affiliation as an adult should be more relevant than affiliation during childhood.

As for religiosity, involvement in religious activities during childhood is expected to influence wages through its impact on educational attainment. During the adult years, religious participation may reinforce some of the other effects on wages identified earlier, such as those operating through the intrafamily division of labor.

Data and Methods

The analysis uses data from Cycle 5 of the NSFG, conducted in 1995 (see Kelly et al. 1997 for a description of the methodology). The questionnaires were addressed to a nationally representative sample of 10,847 civilian, noninstitutionalized women ages fifteen to forty-four of all marital statuses living in the United States. The interviews included questions on socioeconomic and family background variables, as well as information on religion, educational attainment, employment, marriage, and fertility.

The sample is restricted in three ways. First, since patterns of investments in human capital differ markedly by race and ethnicity, it is not possible to pool all groups; only non-Hispanic white respondents born in the United States are included in the analysis due to sample size limitations. Second, the sample is limited to women who were born before 1969 (ages twenty-seven and older in 1995) as respondents with later birth dates were in age categories where the schooling process is often not yet complete. Third, the sample is restricted to individuals who were raised in one of the following faiths: Roman Catholic, mainline Protestant (Presbyterian, Episcopalian, Methodist, Lutheran, Protestant with no specific denominational affiliation),[5] conservative Protestant (Baptists and smaller denominations associated with Pentecostal and various fundamentalist movements, including Assembly of God, Church of Christ, and Holiness),[6] Jewish, Mormon, and no religion. After also deleting cases with missing information for the key variables, the resulting sample size is 4,181.

The religiosity variable is based on the respondents' frequency of attendance to religious services at age fourteen. This is a measure, albeit imperfect, of the young women's involvement with religion at that age. Unfortunately, the survey does not contain information on other dimensions of religiosity at that time, nor does it contain any questions on the parents' religiosity. The working assumption used here is that at age fourteen, the child's behavior in the religious arena closely mirrors that of her parents.[7] Religious participation is operationalized as a dichotomous variable. Individuals who attended religious services one to three times per month or more frequently are classified in the high-religiosity category; others are placed in the low-religiosity group. The 1995 NSFG also includes information on religious affiliation at the time of the interview, and on frequency of attendance to religious services five years prior to the survey. These variables are used as measures of adult affiliation and participation in the wage analyses.[8]

Table 10.1 presents definitions and means for the two childhood religion variables described earlier: the affiliation in which the respondent was raised and her religious participation at age fourteen. The adult religion variables are defined in a parallel way. The variables used as controls in the regressions are defined in Table 10.2. The education models include the parents' average

TABLE 10.1

Definitions and Means of Childhood Religious
Affiliation and Participation

	Definition	Mean[a]
Religious Affiliation	= 1 if respondent (R) was raised in the affiliation shown	
(Mainline Protestant)		(0.30)
Conservative Protestant		0.23
Catholic		0.35
Jewish		0.02
Mormon		0.03
No Religion		0.06
High Religiosity	= 1 if R attended religious services one to three times per month or more frequently at age fourteen	0.75
Religious Affiliation/ Religiosity (for largest groups only)[b]	= 1 if R had the religious affiliation and participation indicated	
Mainline Protestant—low		0.07
(Mainline Protestant—high)		(0.23)
Conservative Protestant—low		0.05
Conservative Protestant—high		0.18
Catholic—high		0.30
Catholic—low		0.05

Note: n = 4,181.

a. The reference categories and mean values are noted in parentheses for variables with more than two categories.

b. The means of these variables, plus the means for Jewish, Mormon, and No Religion, add to 1.

years of schooling, dummy variables for family structure at age sixteen, whether the mother was eighteen years of age or younger at the time of her first birth, the size of the family of origin, and region of residence at birth. It would have been desirable to control also for the rural–urban nature of the area where the respondent grew up; unfortunately this information is not available. The controls for the wage regressions are the years of schooling completed by the respondent, years of full-time and part-time work experience, and region of residence and rural/urban location at the time of the survey.

Results

Effects on Educational Attainment

Table 10.3 reports regressions with years of regular schooling completed as the dependent variable. Consistent with results based on data from the 1980s (Lehrer 1999), the zero-order regression reveals that mainline Protestants and Catholics are at the center of the distribution; Jews have a higher level of education by a margin of about 2.3 years, and conservative Protestants have a lower level by a margin of about 1.2 years. The results also show that Mormons and the unaffiliated complete about six-tenths of a year less than the reference group.

All of the religion coefficients decrease in size when controls for family background variables (excluding parental education) are added in the next column, with the exception of the Catholic coefficient. Examination of means for the background variables separately by religious affiliation reveals that this is due to the larger sibling size among Catholic respondents, a reflection of the high fertility pattern that used to characterize the Catholic population (Jones and Westoff 1979). Though significant, the Catholic coefficient in this second column is small in magnitude.

A control for parental education is added in the last column. Two effects remain sizable in this specification. Net of other factors, conservative Protestants attain half a year less of schooling than mainline Protestants, and Jews complete about a year and a half more. A modest negative gap of a third of a year is observed for Mormons, along with a small positive gap for Catholics; the coefficient on the no religion variable is negative but not significant at conventional levels.

The "true" effect of religious affiliation on education, net of other factors, can be thought of as being bracketed by the estimates in columns two and three. Parental education is the best proxy for socioeconomic status in these data, and the positive coefficient on this variable in part captures an income effect that should be controlled for. At the same time, however, the education differentials by religion in the respondents' generation are mirrored by corresponding differences in their parents' generation, which are due in part to the influence of religion.

Turning to the coefficients on the other background variables, a nonintact family, a larger number of siblings, and having a mother who entered parenthood early all affect schooling negatively. The geographical area variables do not attain significance. The coefficients on these control factors provide a way to assess the relative importance of religious affiliation. For example, compared to the reference category, the coefficient on the Mormon variable in the last specification implies an influence on years of schooling completed similar in magnitude to that of having lost a parent; the coefficient on the conservative Protestant variable is similar to that of having a mother who entered parenthood at age eighteen or before.

TABLE 10.2

Definitions and Means of Control Variables

	Definition	*Mean*[a]
Controls in Education Regressions		
Parental education	= 1 if the average years of schooling completed by R's father (or father figure) and mother (or mother figure) is in category indicated[b]	
< 12		0.37
(12)		(0.26)
13–15		0.25
≥ 16		0.12
Nonintact family	= 1 if R did not live with both biological or adoptive parents at age sixteen for the reason indicated	
Death	Death of one of the parents	0.07
Separation or divorce	Parents' separation or divorce	0.19
Never married	R never lived with both natural (or adoptive) parents	0.04
(Intact family)		(0.70)
Mother eighteen years old or younger at first birth	= 1 if R's mother (or mother figure) had her first child at age eighteen or earlier	0.10
Number of siblings	Number of children born to R's mother (or mother figure)	3.95
Region at birth	= 1 if R was born in the region indicated	
Northeast		0.24
Midwest		0.33
West		0.17
(South)		(0.26)
Controls in Wage Regressions		
Years of schooling	Number of years of regular schooling completed by R	13.37
Years of full-time experience	Number of years of full-time work in the labor market	11.69
Years of part-time experience	Number of years of part-time work in the labor market	2.71

(continued)

Table 10.2. Definitions and Means of Control Variables *(continued)*

	Definition	*Mean*[a]
Region of residence	= 1 if R currently lives in the region indicated	
Northeast		0.20
Midwest		0.30
West		0.20
(South)		(0.30)
Rural Area	= 1 if R currently lives in a rural area	0.18

Notes: n = 4,181 for education regressions; n = 2,844 for wage regressions.

a. The reference categories are noted in parentheses for variables with more than two categories.

b. If the respondent was raised by some other "mother figure," such as a stepmother or grandmother, the information for this individual was used; the same was done in the case of the father. If education was missing for the father or mother, the value for the other parent was used.

Table 10.4 examines the effects of religious participation on educational attainment for the case of mainline Protestants, conservative Protestants, and Catholics. Sample size limitations precluded the possibility of examining these relationships for Jews and Mormons. The zero-order effects shown in the first column reveal a significantly positive influence associated with religious involvement for each of the three groups studied. The difference in years of schooling completed between the high and low-religiosity group is one year for conservative Protestants and the same is true for Catholics. The difference is smaller for mainline Protestants: about four-tenths of a year. All of these differences remain significant in the next two models. The mainline Protestant effect falls to three-tenths of a year; the influences for Catholics and conservative Protestants both remain sizable: between seven- and nine-tenths of a year. These results lend support to the hypothesis that children who grow up in homes where there is more religious involvement do better in terms of educational attainment. Empirically, the margin is found to be substantial in the case of Catholics and conservative Protestants, and modest in the case of mainline Protestants.

These estimates must be qualified as possibly subject to biases. If religious attendance is correlated with unobserved factors associated with generally good behaviors and outcomes, the present results would overstate the positive causal effect of religiosity on educational attainment. This would be the case, for example, if the more observant parents who encourage their children to attend

TABLE 10.3

The Role of Religious Affiliation on Educational
Attainment: OLS Regressions

	Zero-order effects	Controlling for background variables (except parental education)	Controlling for all background variables
Religion Variables			
Mainline Protestant	—	—	—
Conservative Protestant	-1.168 **	-0.911 **	-0.509 **
Catholic	0.067	0.147 *	0.193 **
Jewish	2.280 **	2.056 **	1.540 **
Mormon	-0.611 **	-0.511 **	-0.330 *
No religion	-0.583 **	-0.319 **	-0.199 #
Control Variables			
Parental education			
Under 12			-0.663 **
13–15			0.942 **
≥ 16			2.171 **
Nonintact family			
Death		-0.391 **	-0.302 **
Separation or divorce		-0.751 **	-0.669 **
Never married		-1.040 **	-0.871 **
Mother eighteen years old or younger at first birth		-1.082 **	-0.567 **
Number of siblings		-0.126 **	-0.091 **
Region at birth			
Northeast		-0.057	0.020
West		0.180 *	-0.076
Midwest		-0.123	-0.052
Constant	13.547 **	14.288 **	13.717 **
Adjusted R^2	0.065	0.126	0.263

Notes: Dependent variable: years of schooling completed. Unstandardized coefficients are reported. n = 4,181.

** $p < 0.05$; * $p < 0.10$; # $p < 0.15$

TABLE 10.4

The Role of Religiosity on Educational Attainment: OLS Regressions[a]

	Zero-order effects	Controlling for background variables (except parental education)	Controlling for all background variables
Mainline Protestant—high	—	—	—
Mainline Protestant—low	-0.432 **	-0.318 **	-0.280 **
Conservative Protestant—high	-1.057**	-0.797 **	-0.403 **
Conservative Protestant—low	-2.049 **	-1.682 **	-1.229 **
Catholic—high	0.120	0.210 **	0.231 **
Catholic—low	-0.880 **	-0.656 **	-0.425 **
Jewish	2.176 **	1.978 **	1.478 **
Mormon	-0.715 **	-0.600 **	-0.409 **
No religion	-0.688 **	-0.423 **	-0.291 **
Adjusted R^2	0.082	0.138	0.274

Notes: Dependent variable: years of schooling completed. Unstandardized coefficients are reported. n = 4,181.

a. The significance tests reflect comparisons against the reference category: high-religiosity mainline Protestants. Pairwise comparisons between low- and high-religiosity conservative Protestants, and between low- and high-religiosity Catholics reveal differences that are significant at the 5 percent level in all models. The background variables included in the column two and three models are the same as those in Table 10.3; along with the constant, they are omitted for the sake of brevity.

** $p < 0.05$; * $p < 0.10$; # $p < 0.15$

religious services are also supportive of activities that are conducive to success in the secular arena (cf. Freeman 1986).

An argument can also be made, however, for biases operating in the opposite direction. Although this issue has not yet been studied systematically, there is some evidence that religious participation may be especially valuable for individuals who are more vulnerable for reasons that might include poor health, challenging family circumstances, and adverse economic conditions (Hummer et al. 2002). To the extent that such individuals are aware of this and respond by embracing religiosity as a coping mechanism, the more religious homes would disproportionately have unobserved characteristics that affect educational outcomes adversely. If so, the estimated coefficients would understate the true

TABLE 10.5

The Role of Religious Affiliation on Wages: OLS Regressions

	Childhood Affiliation		Adult Affiliation	
	Zero-order effects	Controlling for other determinants of wages	Zero-order effects	Controlling for other determinants of wages
Religion Variables				
Mainline Protestant	—	—	—	—
Conservative Protestant	-0.153 **	-0.028	-0.206 **	-0.071 **
Catholic	0.065 **	0.010	0.038	0.002
Jewish	0.580 **	0.327 **	0.593 **	0.334 **
Mormon	-0.301 **	-0.249 **	-0.228 **	-0.190 **
No religion	-0.074	0.001	-0.107 **	-0.068 *
Control Variables				
Years of schooling		0.104 **		0.104 **
Years of full-time Experience		0.033 **		0.034 **
Years of part-time Experience		0.017 **		0.012 **
Region of residence				
Northeast		0.080 **		0.076 **
Midwest		-0.040		-0.045
West		0.080 **		0.081 **
Rural area		-0.130 **		-0.104 **
Constant	2.367	0.448 **	2.391 **	0.465 **
Lambda		0.196 **		0.212 **
Adjusted R^2	0.034	0.232	0.036	0.231
N	2,844	2,844	2,778	2,778

Notes: Dependent variable: natural log of wage. Unstandardized coefficients are reported.

** $p < 0.05$; * $p < 0.10$; # $p < 0.15$

impact of religiosity on educational attainment. A priori, it is unclear which biases are dominant.

Effects on Wages

Table 10.5 presents regressions with the log of the wage rate as the dependent variable.[9] These results are based on the subsample of respondents who were employed as of the survey date.[10] Two measures of religion are used: the affiliation in which the respondent was raised and her affiliation at the time of the interview.

Focusing first on the zero-order regressions, the results show that mainline Protestants are at the center of the wage distribution in both the childhood religion and adult religion specifications. A Catholic advantage of 7 percent can be observed with the childhood religion measure, but the effect is insignificant with the adult religion measure.[11] The opposite holds for the no-religion variable: the model with current affiliation suggests a disadvantage of about 10 percent, but the effect is insignificant in the model with childhood religion. Both specifications show a wage disadvantage for conservative Protestants and Mormons—of about 14–19 percent and 20–26 percent, respectively—and a very large advantage of 79–81 percent for Jewish women.

The models that include other determinants of wages provide estimates of the influence that remains after controlling for years of schooling, experience, and place of residence. The Catholic effect is insignificant with both religion measures. Being unaffiliated is associated with an adverse impact of about 7 percent in the specification based on adult affiliation; the effect is insignificant in the specification based on childhood affiliation. The Jewish effect falls from 79 to 81 percent in the zero-order regressions to about 39–40 percent in the regressions with controls, implying that a substantial part of the wage advantage of Jewish women is accounted for by their educational attainment and related labor market characteristics; the remainder reflects the effects of other factors not measured in these data, such as helpful social capital in the labor market, higher quality of schooling, and residence in high-wage metropolitan areas such as New York City. The Mormon effect also falls, from 20–26 percent to 17–22 percent. In this case, a relatively small fraction of the effect is due to the influence through educational attainment and experience in the labor market. Future analyses might extend the work by Ellison and Bartkowski (2002) and explore whether Mormon families, like their conservative Protestant counterparts, are characterized by substantial asymmetry in the intrahousehold division of labor.

In the models with controls, an interesting difference between the results for childhood and adult religion emerges for the case of conservative Protestants: while the effect is insignificant in the specification based on childhood religion, a significant disadvantage of about 7 percent is observed in the model that uses adult affiliation. This pattern is consistent with adult religion being most relevant for the negative effect on wages due to conservative Protestant women's greater involvement in household tasks.

Overall, the results, offered tentatively, suggest that religious affiliation is an important determinant of female wages, with some of the effects being very large. Additional research is needed to provide confirmation for these findings, based on data sets containing more precise wage information along with more complete information on key determinants of wages such as place of residence.

TABLE 10.6

The Role of Religiosity on Wages: OLS Regressions[a]

	Childhood Affiliation and Participation		Adult Affiliation and Participation	
	Zero-order effects	Controlling for other determinants of wages	Zero-order effects	Controlling for other determinants of wages
Mainline Protestant—high	—	—	—	—
Mainline Protestant—low	-0.005	0.034	0.060 #	0.030
Conservative Protestant—high	-0.139 **	-0.030	-0.143 **	-0.071 *
Conservative Protestant—low	-0.211 **	0.022	-0.175 **	-0.033
Catholic—high	0.082 **	0.013	0.072 *	-0.219
Catholic—low	-0.032	0.050	0.103 **	0.058 #
Jewish	0.579 **	0.334 **	0.642**	0.348 **
Mormon	-0.302 **	-0.239 **	-0.178 **	-0.173 **
No religion	-0.075	0.010	-0.035	-0.052
Adjusted R^2	0.033	0.232	0.034	0.232
N	2,844	2,844	2,778	2,778

Notes: Dependent Variable: natural log of wage. Unstandardized coefficients are reported.

a. The significance tests reflect comparisons against the omitted category: high-religiosity mainline Protestants. Pairwise comparisons between the low- and high-religiosity categories for each group reveal differences that are insignificant at the 0.10 level in all cases, with one exception: the difference between high- and low-religiosity Catholics in the first model. The coefficients on the constant, lambda, and the control variables are omitted for the sake of brevity.

** $p < 0.05$; * $p < 0.10$; # $p < 0.15$

In marked contrast to the affiliation results, the regressions reported in Table 10.6 show that religious participation is generally not an important determinant of wages for conservative Protestants, mainline Protestants, and Catholics. The earlier analyses showed that for mainline Protestants, the effect of religious participation on educational attainment is only modest in size; it is thus not surprising that there is no discernible effect on performance in the labor market later in life, as measured by wages. The impact of religious participation on the educational attainment of Catholics was found to be sizable, and a significant effect is observed on wages in the model of column one: Catholics who attended services frequently during adolescence have a wage advantage compared to their coreligionists who grew up with less religious observance. However, this influence disappears when education and other background variables are held constant. The two models that use adult religion show no significant Catholic effect.

There are opposing forces in the case of conservative Protestants. On the one hand, religious participation during childhood was shown above to have a sizable positive influence on years of schooling; it may also have a beneficial effect on other dimensions of educational attainment that were not measured here, such as academic performance. On the other hand, the more traditional behaviors regarding the intrafamily division of labor and the corresponding negative repercussions for female wages are expected to be more pronounced among conservative Protestants who are more observant. Coupled with the positive correlations between childhood and adult religion (both affiliation and participation), these countervailing forces probably account for the observed zero net effect of participation on wages for conservative Protestants in all specifications.

Conclusion and Discussion

This chapter examined the role of religious affiliation and participation on the educational attainment and wages of women in the United States, using data on respondents ages twenty-seven to forty-four from the 1995 NSFG. The empirical results confirm earlier findings suggesting that *ceteris paribus*, mainline Protestants and Catholics are at the center of the educational distribution, conservative Protestants attain less schooling, and Jews attain more. In addition, the results suggest that being raised as a Mormon or with no religious affiliation has negative influences on schooling. A human capital model helps interpret these findings as resulting from demand- and supply-side forces associated with membership in various religious groups.

Religious participation during childhood was hypothesized to have a positive impact on educational attainment due to demand-side effects: the beneficial impact of religious involvement on children's ability to be productively engaged in schooling endeavors. Results for Catholics, conservative Protestants, and mainline Protestants lend support to this hypothesis and indicate that the positive influences are especially pronounced for the first two groups.

The effects of religious affiliation on wages largely mirror its influences on educational attainment, consistent with the major influence that investments in schooling have on wages. The results also suggest that religious affiliation exerts additional effects beyond its impact through differences in years of schooling and related differences in labor market experience. The high wages of Jews may in part reflect a higher level of schooling quality, social capital that is helpful in the labor market, and a tendency to reside in large metropolitan areas. The relatively low wages of conservative Protestants may be due in part to asymmetry in the intrahousehold division of labor and a similar explanation may partly account for the low wages of Mormon women. While the results of this study suggest that religious affiliation is an important determinant of wages, within-group variation in religious participation was found to have little or no effect.

The present analyses raise new questions for future research. Additional investigation is needed to explore possible explanations for the finding that the beneficial effects of religious participation are higher for Catholic and conservative Protestant youth than for their mainline Protestant counterparts. Smith (2003) notes that the quality and quantity of constructive influences provided to youth vary across religious organizations, and research along these lines may provide some answers. Other work suggests it would also be useful to explore the role of theological conservatism (Ellison, Bartkowski, and Segal 1996; Wilcox 1998), which is unfortunately not measured in the 1995 NSFG. In addition, it would be desirable to replicate these analyses using data sets with much richer information on the home environment, so that problems of selectivity bias may be addressed and more accurate estimates of the causal effect of religious participation on educational attainment and wages can be produced.

The patterns of wage differentials by religion for men are likely to be different from those documented here for women, and this is a question worth pursuing in further work. In addition, due to data limitations, the present study focused only on non-Hispanic whites. A recent comparative analysis of religious differentials in the high school dropout rate for non-Hispanic whites, African Americans, and Hispanics reveals that the patterns are not uniform across racial and ethnic groups (Lehrer 2005). For example, differences in the probability of obtaining a high school diploma by the extent of religious involvement at age fourteen are especially pronounced among Hispanics. Similar differences by race and ethnicity may well also be present for the outcomes that were the focus of the present study. Our understanding of the complex effects of religious affiliation and participation on education and wages will improve as future research explores these various questions.

NOTES

I am indebted to Barry Chiswick, Christopher Ellison, and Robert Hummer for helpful comments and suggestions on earlier drafts of this chapter. I also benefited from discussions with participants at the conference on "Religion, Health, and Families in the United States" (University of Austin, Texas, April 23–24, 2004) and at the session on "Religion and Religiosity: Trends and Patterns" at the annual meetings of the Population Association of America (Philadelphia, March 31–April 2, 2005). Zhenxiang Zhao provided skillful research assistance.

1. An attractive feature of this theoretical framework is that it yields predictions regarding religious differentials in the rate of return from schooling investments, thus making it possible to ascertain in each case whether demand- or supply-side forces are dominant (Chiswick 1988; Lehrer 1999). This aspect of the model is not pursued in the present chapter because the rate-of-return calculations require separate analyses for various religious affiliation/religiosity groups and many of the subsamples in the 1995 NSFG are too small for this purpose.

2. See Sander (1995, 2001) for a discussion of related research on the effects of Catholic schools on educational attainment.

3. It is possible to believe in the supernatural and have personal religious and spiritual experiences outside of the institutional context; see Stark and Bainbridge (1985).

4. Becker (1985) has argued that women with heavier child-care and household responsibilities may seek jobs that are more convenient, require less energy, and pay lower wages.

5. One of the religious codes in the 1995 NSFG is "Protestant with no specific denominational affiliation." As Steensland and colleagues (2000) note, such individuals constitute a heterogeneous group that includes Protestants with no denomination along with nondenominational Protestants. Based on an analysis of patterns of religious participation in the non-Hispanic white sample, respondents in this category were included with mainline Protestants.

6. The 1995 NSFG includes all Baptists in one category. In his research on the classification of Protestants into fundamentalist, moderate, and liberal, Smith (1990) distinguishes between seven different Baptist denominations, classifying six of them as fundamentalist and one as moderate. This limitation of the data implies that the respondents classified in the present chapter as conservative Protestants include a small number of "moderate" religious groups.

7. While parents are likely to have considerable influence on their offspring's religious participation in early adolescence, important divergences often occur as children go through the high school years. Whether or not such differences develop has been found to be a major factor in parents' willingness to provide financial support for investments in schooling (Sherkat and Darnell 1999).

8. Although the 1995 NSFG also includes information on participation in religious services at the time of the survey, this variable was not used because it is more likely to be affected by problems of endogenicity: individuals with high wages may choose to participate less in religious activities because of their high value of time.

9. Respondents were asked about the form of compensation in their current employment (weekly, monthly, or yearly). This study used the best available estimate of the wage rate, namely, the amount earned over the relevant interval divided by the number of hours worked during the period.

10. The full sample was used to estimate a probit labor force participation equation to correct for selectivity biases. The probit equation includes all of the determinants of wages plus variables for the number of children in the household, the presence of a child under age six, marital status, and the husband's earnings if married (these results are available from the author). The inverse of Mill's ratio is shown in the table as "Lambda."

II. In a semilogarithmic regression, the percentage effect associated with c, the coefficient on a dummy variable, is 100 (exp(c)—1). See Halvorsen and Palmquist (1980).

REFERENCES

Albrecht, S. L., and T. B. Heaton. 1984. "Secularization, Higher Education, and Religiosity." *Review of Religious Research* 26 (1): 43–58.

Becker, G. S. 1985. "Human Capital, Effort, and the Sexual Division of Labor." *Journal of Labor Economics* 3 (1): S33–S58.

Chiswick, B. R. 1983. "The Earnings and Human Capital of American Jews." *Journal of Human Resources* 8:313–336.

———. 1988. "Differences in Education and Earnings across Racial and Ethnic Groups: Tastes, Discrimination, and Investments in Child Quality." *Quarterly Journal of Economics* 103 (3): 571–597.

———. 1992. "The Postwar Economy of American Jews." *Studies in Contemporary Jewry* 8:85–101.

———. 1993. "The Skills and Economic Status of American Jewry: Trends over the Last Half-Century." *Journal of Labor Economics* 11 (1): 229–242.

Darnell, A., and D. E. Sherkat. 1997. "The Impact of Protestant Fundamentalism on Educational Attainment." *American Sociological Review* 62:306–315.

Ellison, C. G., and J. P. Bartkowski. 2002. "Conservative Protestantism and the Division of Household Labor among Married Couples." *Journal of Family Issues* 23 (8): 950–985.

Ellison, C. G., J. P. Bartkowski, and M. L. Segal. 1996. "Conservative Protestantism and Support for Corporal Punishment." *Social Forces* 74:1003–1029.

Freeman, R. B. 1986. "Who Escapes? The Relation of Churchgoing and Other Background Factors to the Socioeconomic Performance of Black Male Youths from Inner-City Tracts." In *The Black Youth Employment Crisis*, ed. Richard B. Freeman and Harry J. Holzer, 353–376. Chicago and London: University of Chicago Press.

Glass, J. 1999. "Growing Up Fundamentalist: Effects on Women's Early Life Course Transitions and Adult Attainment." Paper presented at the annual meetings of the Population Association of America.

Glenn, N. D. 1987. "The Trend in 'No Religion' Respondents to U.S. National Surveys, Late 1950s to Early 1980s." *Public Opinion Quarterly* 51 (3): 293–314.

Halvorsen, R., and R. Palmquist. 1980. "The Interpretation of Dummy Variables in Semilogarithmic Equations." *American Economic Review* 70 (3): 474–475.

Hummer, R. A., Y. C. Padilla, S. Echevarria, and E. Kim. 2002. "Does Parental Religious Involvement Affect the Birth Outcomes and Health Status of Young Children?" Paper presented at the annual meetings of the Population Association of America, Atlanta, May 9–11.

Jones, E., and C. F. Westoff. 1979. "The 'End' of Catholic Fertility." *Demography* 16 (2): 209–218.

Kelly, J. E., W. D. Mosher, A. P. Duffer, and S. H. Kinsey. 1997. "Plan and Operation of the 1995 National Survey of Family Growth." *Vital and Health Statistics: Series I*(36): 1–98. Hyattsville, MD: National Center for Health Statistics.

Keister, L. A. 2003. "Religion and Wealth: The Role of Religious Affiliation and Participation in Early Adult Asset Accumulation." *Social Forces* 82 (1): 175–207.

Keysar, A. A., and B. A. Kosmin. 1995. "The Impact of Religious Identification on Differences in Educational Attainment among American Women in 1990." *Journal for the Scientific Study of Religion* 34 (1): 49–62.

Lehrer, E. L. 1995. "The Effects of Religion on the Labor Supply of Married Women." *Social Science Research* 24: 281–301.

———. 1999. "Religion as a Determinant of Educational Attainment: An Economic Perspective." *Social Science Research* 28:358–379.

———. 2004a. "Religion as a Determinant of Economic and Demographic Behavior in the United States." *Population and Development Review* 30 (4): 707–726.

———. 2004b. "Religiosity as a Determinant of Educational Attainment: The Case of Conservative Protestant Women in the United States." *Review of Economics of the Household* 2 (2): 203–219.

———. 2005. "Religious Affiliation and Participation as Determinants of High-School Completion." Paper presented at the annual meeting of the Association for the Study of Religion, Economics and Culture, Rochester, NY, November 4–6.

Levin, J. S. 1994. "Religion and Health: Is There an Association, Is It Valid, and Is It Causal?" *Social Science and Medicine* 38 (11): 1475–1482.

Muller, C., and C. G. Ellison. 2001. "Religious Involvement, Social Capital, and Adolescents' Academic Progress: Evidence from the National Education Longitudinal Study of 1988." *Sociological Focus* 34 (2): 155–183.

Regnerus, M. D. 2000. "Shaping Schooling Success: Religious Socialization and Educational Outcomes in Metropolitan Public Schools." *Journal for the Scientific Study of Religion* 39:363–370.

———. 2003. "Religion and Positive Adolescent Outcomes: A Review of Research and Theory." *Review of Religious Research* 44 (4): 394–413.

Sander, W. 1995. *The Catholic Family: Marriage, Children, and Human Capital*. Boulder, CO: Westview Press.

———. 2001. "The Effects of Catholic Schools on Religiosity, Education, and Competition." Occasional Paper No. 32, National Center for the Study of Privatization in Education, Teachers College, Columbia University.

Sherkat, D. E. 2000. "That They Be Keepers of the Home: The Effect of Conservative Religion on Early and Late Transition into Housewifery." *Review of Religious Research* 41 (3): 344–358.

Sherkat, D. E., and A. Darnell. 1999. "The Effects of Parents' Fundamentalism on Children's Educational Attainment: Examining Differences by Gender and Children's Fundamentalism." *Journal for the Scientific Study of Religion* 38 (1): 23–35.

Smith, C. 2003. "Theorizing Religious Effects among American Adolescents." *Journal for the Scientific Study of Religion* 42 (1): 17–30.

Smith, T. W. 1987. "Classifying Protestant Denominations." 1990. Review of Religious Research 31: 225–245.

Stark, R., and W. S. Bainbridge. 1985. *The Future of Religion: Secularization, Revival, and Cult Formation*. Berkeley: University of California Press.

Steensland, B., J. Z. Park, M. D. Regnerus, L. D. Robinson, W. B. Wilcox, and R. D. Woodberry. 2000. "The Measure of American Religion: Toward Improving the State of the Art." *Social Forces* 79 (1): 1–28.

Waite, L., and E. Lehrer. 2003. "The Benefits from Marriage and Religion in the United States: A Comparative Analysis." *Population and Development Review* 29 (2): 255–275.

Wilcox, W. B. 1998. "Conservative Protestant Childrearing: Authoritarian or Authoritative?" *American Sociological Review* 63 (6): 796–809.

———. 2004. *Soft Patriarchs, New Men: How Christianity Shapes Fathers and Husbands*. Chicago: University of Chicago Press.

11

▶ ▶ ▶ ▶ ▶ ▶ ▶ ▶ ▶ ▶ ▶ ▶ ◀ ◀ ◀ ◀ ◀ ◀ ◀ ◀ ◀ ◀ ◀ ◀

Religion, Family, and Women's Employment among Muslim and Christian Arab Americans

JEN'NAN GHAZAL READ

Religious influences on family and gender roles are at the center of numerous debates about the role of religion in contemporary American life (Bartkowski 2001; Gallagher 2003; Hardacre 1997; Sherkat 2000; Williams 1997). The accepted wisdom is that the tenets of major religious traditions restrict women's achievements in the public sphere by prioritizing their obligations to the home and family (for a review see Lehrer 1995). Recent studies on Judeo-Christian groups are beginning to challenge this view, finding that the relationships between family, religion, and women's economic activity are more complicated than previously believed (Becker and Hofmeister 2001; Gallagher 2003; Lehrer 1995, 1999; Sherkat 2000).

To a lesser but growing extent, research is also contesting homogeneous images that depict the Islamic faith as universally oppressive of U.S. women's achievements (Aswad 1994; Cainkar 1996; Read and Bartkowski 2000; Read 2002). Gender differentiation is a fundamental Islamic value, but similar to women affiliated with other religious traditions, there is considerable diversity in how strongly Muslim women adhere to these values. Some Muslim women are religiously devout, others are religiously moderate, and a sizable proportion are nonpracticing and secular, basically Muslim in name only, similar to a good number of U.S. Christians and Jews (McCloud 2003). These differences in religiosity are associated with disparate paths of integration in American society with respect to family behaviors and work patterns, with the most secular women having the fewest number of children and highest employment rates (Read 2003, 2004b). In other words, secular Muslim women look a lot more like secular Jewish and Christian women than they do devout Muslim women. Even among the more devout, U.S. Muslim women are more progressive than women in their countries of origin and more similar to devout Christian women, actively negotiating their gender identities and family expectations to meet the demands of daily life (Bartkowski and Read 2003).

Despite these similarities, most Americans believe that Islam is "very different" from their own religion (57 percent), that Islam encourages violence (46 percent), and that most Muslims are anti-American (42 percent) (Pew Research Center 2002, 2004). The oppression of women in Muslim societies in the Middle East often fuels these beliefs, but whether and how Islam influences women's lives in American society has received little empirical scrutiny. Accordingly, this chapter examines the influences of Muslim affiliation, degree of religiosity, and family structure on the employment of Arab American women, members of a small but growing ethnic population comprised of both Muslims and Christians. The analysis uses data from a national mail survey of Arab American women to examine the extent to which religious affiliation (Muslim versus Christian) and degree of religiosity inhibits women's labor force participation and whether the presence of children in the home mediates the relationships between religion and work.

Study Population and Rationale

Before proceeding with the literature review, it is important to clarify the terms "U.S. Muslim" and "Arab American," and explain why this chapter focuses on the latter group. U.S. Muslims represent the fastest growing religious population in the United States today (*World Almanac* 1998). Estimated at anywhere from three to seven million, they comprise several racial/ethnic groups, with African Americans (40 percent) being the single largest group (Carolan 1999). South Asians (30 percent) and Arabs (25 percent) make up the next two largest ethnic groups, followed by much a smaller number of Turks, Iranians, Africans, and white American converts. Arab Americans, on the other hand, are an ethnic group consisting of both Muslims and Christians. They trace their ancestries to eighteen Arabic-speaking countries[1] in North Africa and Western Asia, and the majority of the estimated three million Arab Americans are second- and third-generation descendants of Christian Arabs who emigrated from Greater Syria prior to World War I. Although most Arabs around the world are Muslim, Arabs in the United States are disproportionately Christian, reflecting distinct emigration patterns from the Middle East (Naff 1994; Read 2004b). Figure 11.1 illustrates the overlap in the Muslim and Arab American populations of the United States and highlights the population of interest for this study (solid circle).

Arab Americans are an ideal case for examining religious influences on gender and family roles because: (a) they are comprised of Muslims and Christians, offering a unique opportunity to assess empirically the effects of Muslim affiliation on women's behaviors, and (b) they are heterogeneous on a number of important factors that might mediate the effects of religion on women's achievements (e.g., generational status and social class). The data set for this study captures this heterogeneity, thereby overcoming a shortcoming in prior work on Arab Americans, namely that the studies lack variation in religious

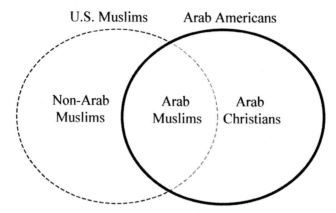

FIGURE 11.1 U.S. Muslim and Arab American populations.

affiliation, generational status, and socioeconomic position (e.g., Suleiman 1999). Without variation on these key characteristics, it has been difficult to determine whether women's achievements are restricted by Islamic religious beliefs, ties to traditional cultural values, lower levels of human capital, or a combination of these factors (for a review see Read 2004b).

Judeo-Christian Influences on Women's Employment

The impact of religion on women's allocation of time between the home and the public sphere is largely overlooked in research on the determinants of women's labor force activity (for a review see Lehrer 1999). Prior research on women's economic activity has focused on their human capital characteristics, family and household structure, race and industrial restructuring, and macroeconomic factors (Browne 2000; Cotter et al. 1998), with the influence of religious belief structures receiving less attention. Research on the family has also given less consideration to religious effects on women's paid employment than to other dimensions of family background. These oversights partly reflect the fact that most large, nationally representative data sets used in studies of female employment (e.g., U.S. Census) do not contain information on religion.

The few studies that do examine religious influences on women's labor force participation raise interesting questions about the mediating effects of family obligations on women's economic achievements (Hartman and Hartman 1996; Heaton and Cornwall 1989; Lehrer 1995; Sherkat 2000). In particular, these studies find that religious constraints on women's employment operate through their family roles. All major monotheistic religious traditions (Christianity, Judaism, and Islam) promote women's familial duties over their public sphere activity, and women who are married or who have young children present in the home are less likely to work than those without these family ties (Glass and

Jacobs 2005; Hartman and Hartman 1996; Hertel 1988). This is true for both Christian and Jewish denominations, although there are certainly denominational differences in how strictly these doctrines are interpreted (Hertel and Hughes 1987).

Moreover, there is considerable diversity within denominations in adherence to religious values, ranging from low to high religious commitment. Women with higher levels of commitment (i.e., more religiously devout) are more likely to eschew employment in favor of their domestic roles relative to those with lower levels of religiosity (Glass and Jacobs 2005). Recent attention to the life course perspective has also demonstrated that religious effects on women's labor force participation are not uniform over the life course (Lehrer 1999; Sherkat 2000). For example, Sherkat (2000) finds that conservative religious women are no less likely to work than nonconservative women once their children are older. In other words, religious beliefs about family roles are most salient when young children are in the home.

To date, the literature on these relationships has focused on America's more established Judeo-Christian populations, with less attention paid to religious influences on more recent immigrant groups. While there is a growing body of research on the role of religion in immigrant assimilation in U.S. society (Ebaugh and Chafetz 2000; Warner and Wittner 1998), very little is known about the effects of religion on immigrant women's labor force participation, especially in different phases of the life course. From existing studies, we know that religious traditions and institutions reinforce traditional gender expectations to varying extents for different immigrant groups, depending on their unique historical and situational circumstances. For some immigrant groups, religious traditions are secondary to the economic circumstances that necessitate women's labor force participation. Others shun women's labor force activity, regardless of economic situation, in favor of more traditional roles within the home (Haddad and Smith 1996). Again, degree of religiosity is an important determinant of immigrant women's opportunities in the public sphere, with the most religiously devout holding the most traditional views on gender roles (Read 2003).

Family and Religion among Arab Americans

Arab Americans present an interesting theoretical case for examining the relationships between the family, religion, and women's labor force participation for three reasons. First, they are an ethnic group comprised of both Muslims and Christians, which offers a rare opportunity to examine intraethnic, interreligious differences in women's behaviors and to compare the influences of religious affiliation and religiosity on women's achievements. As defined by the Census Bureau, Arab Americans are persons who trace their ancestries to eighteen Arabic-speaking countries in North Africa and Western Asia (see note

1 for a list of countries). They emigrated in two distinct waves from the Middle East over the past century, the first being predominantly Christians from Greater Syria (includes modern-day Lebanon, Syria, Palestine, and Israel) and the latter comprising mainly Muslims (Naff 1994). Their estimated size is three million, roughly equal to the Native American population (Zogby 1995).

The second reason is that stereotypes of Arab American women typically depict them as being oppressed by Islamic doctrines that proscribe their public sphere participation and marginalize them within the home. However, the impact of Muslim religious affiliation on women's economic achievements has received little empirical examination, especially in comparison with Christians. Existing evidence suggests that Muslim affiliation may be less important for women's employment than these stereotypes would suggest (Read 2002, 2004a). Third, the family is a central institution in Arab culture, yet few studies examine systematically its influence on Arab American assimilation (for reviews see Read 2003, 2004b). Most of what we currently know about the religion–family connection among Arab Americans stems from research on the Arab Muslim population, with much less known about Arab Christians (Haddad 1991; Sherif 1999). Nevertheless, we know that Islamic values have shaped many Arab cultural values for Muslim and Christian Arabs alike (Haddad 1994).

A fundamental Arab cultural value is rooted in the Islamic belief in distinct differences between men and women in terms of their social roles and responsibilities (Sherif 1999, 204). Muslim women are considered the cornerstone of the family and community and are prescribed accordingly to the home, with primary responsibility for socializing the children. The term "patriarchal connectivity," coined by Suad Joseph (1999), aptly describes the nature of relationships within Arab families, whereby women are socialized to view themselves in relation to the larger kinship structure that privileges male authority and dominance over their own achievements.

In theory, Muslim women's obligations to the family include modesty, premarital virginity, childbearing, and child rearing, and their family's honor is typically contingent on whether or not they fulfill these obligations. In reality, U.S. Muslim families actively negotiate these gender roles to fit the demands of Western life (Read and Bartkowski 2000). Like other immigrant groups, Muslim Arab Americans depart from traditional customs by allowing females to attend mosques and relaxing restrictions on male–female social interactions. Many U.S. Muslims allow their daughters to attend coeducational institutions, whereas separate schools are normative in many parts of the Middle East. Similarly, women frequently attend U.S. mosques, often intermingling with men during religious services, a practice that is rarely seen in the Middle East. In sum, Muslim affiliation does not necessarily signify an Arab's attachment to cultural traditions. Many Muslim Arab Americans distinguish between religious and ethnic identity, relegating patriarchal cultural practices to Arab ethnicity (Haddad and Smith 1996, 20).

Female labor force participation is among the most contentious issues facing Arab Muslim families because it is in direct conflict with women's familial obligations (Haddad and Smith 1996). However, qualitative studies indicate that Muslim Arab American views on women's employment are not monolithic and that women's participation in the public sphere varies by ethnic identity, religiosity, and social class (Cainkar 1996). Women living in families with stronger ties to ethnic values and customs are less likely to be employed and have less power in major family decisions than women living in families with weaker attachments to cultural traditions (Aswad 1994). In general, cultural bonds are strongest among the most recent Arab immigrant arrivals, many of who live in ethnic enclaves because of network ties (Cainkar 1996).

The influences of religiosity and social class on women's employment operate in the expected direction. Similar to other groups of U.S. women, Muslim Arab American women with stronger connections to religion usually have lower employment and higher fertility rates than women with weaker religious ties (cf. Hartman and Hartman 1996; Lehrer 1995). Educational attainment appears to have an independent effect on Arab American women's accomplishments. Even with similar levels of ethnic identity and religiosity, women with higher levels of education have higher work rates and earnings, greater personal autonomy, are more likely to share in major family decisions, and hold more egalitarian views on gender roles (Haddad and Smith 1996; Read 2004b).

Although there has been no systematic examination of the relationships between family, religion, and Arab American women's labor force activity to date, the existing literature allows me to posit the following three hypotheses: (a) Muslim affiliation will be less significant than degree of religiosity (i.e., strength of religious beliefs) for women's employment; (b) degree of religiosity will have a significant, negative impact on women's labor force participation; and (c) family characteristics (i.e., children) will moderate the impact of religiosity on women's employment.

Data and Methods

To test these hypotheses, I use data from a mail survey administered to a national sample of women with Arab surnames in the spring of 2000. Other national data sets classify Arab Americans with non-Hispanic whites, which contributes to the dearth of statistical data on this group and to the reliance on studies of localized Arab American communities (for exceptions see Zogby 1990, 1995). Although Arab ethnicity can be derived from the birth and ancestry questions on the long form of the U.S. Census, this resource is insufficient for this project because it contains no information on religious affiliation or religiosity.

The sampling frame for this study came from two sources: the membership roster of the Arab American Institute and a list of female registered voters assembled by Zogby International. The questionnaire was administered to a systematic, random sample of women drawn from these two frames, and a filter question was used to exclude non-Arab women. The question identifies the birthplace of the respondent, the respondent's mother and father, and the respondent's maternal and paternal grandparents. Since the majority of Arab American women are U.S. citizens and 88 percent are proficient in the English language (U.S. Bureau of the Census 2000), the questionnaire was administered in English. The final sample size was 501, with a response rate of 47.2 percent. The median age of women sampled is forty-five, and their geographic distribution is similar to that found in the 2000 census—32.4 percent are clustered in the East/Northeast (mainly in the New York and Washington DC areas), 35.3 percent are located in the Midwest (mainly in and around Detroit and Chicago), 25.6 percent live in the West (mainly in Los Angeles), and a minority (6.7 percent) live in the South (mainly Texas).

The sample for this study is limited to the 416 women who are between the working ages of eighteen and sixty-five and who are not retired, disabled,

TABLE 11.1

Means of Variables Used in the Analysis, Women Aged 18–64

	U.S. Census Data[a]		Read Survey Data
	White	Arab[b]	Arab
Employed in 1999	81.8%	66.6%	78.8%
Foreign-born	1.8	59.9	52.9
Education			
Less than high school	9.2	15.4	2.4
High school graduate	27.3	20.2	9.1
Some college	33.9	16.8	20.7
College degree	19.8	36.1	29.6
Advanced degree	9.8	11.5	38.2
Any children under six	16.5	26.2	13.7
Married	60.7	62.1[ns]	56.4
Age (mean years)	40.9	38.1	43.7

Note: Limited to comparisons between two census groups only.

a. Source is 2000 Census, 5 percent PUMS.

b. Means are significantly different from white means at $p < .05$ except where denoted by "ns."

or currently in school. Table 11.1 uses 2000 Census data to compare the sample to white women and Arab American women. As seen in Table 11.1, both groups of Arab women are more highly educated and more likely to be foreign-born than white women. Arab women in the current sample are older, more likely to be U.S.-born, more highly educated, have higher employment rates, and have fewer young children in the home compared to Arab women nationally (U.S. Bureau of the Census 2000). At the same time, the sample is more nationally representative than previous studies of this population, most of which have focused on Arab communities in Dearborn, Detroit, and Chicago (Abraham and Shryock 2000; Suleiman 1999). Arab Americans living in these locales tend to be disproportionately Muslims, newer immigrants, and have lower socioeconomic statuses than the population at large, which hinders attempts to disaggregate factors influencing their socioeconomic and cultural incorporation. The current sample is more heterogeneous with respect to nativity, social class, and significantly, religious affiliation (i.e., contains both Christians and Muslims), allowing for a more thorough examination of religious influences on women's labor force activity. The fact that the sample is skewed toward the more highly educated is beneficial for this study because the effects of religious beliefs on women's employment is less likely to be conflated with a lower-class emphasis on maintaining traditional gender roles (Aswad 1994; Read 2003).

The primary dependent variable for this study is labor force participation (1 = currently employed). I also examine married women's labor force decisions at two different stages in the life cycle: (a) after marriage and before children; and (b) when young children are present in the home. The independent variables include several measures of religion, family characteristics, and background factors known to effect women's employment. Three variables capture religious influences on women's employment: religious affiliation (1 = Muslim), religiosity over the life cycle (1 = high in childhood and adulthood), and belief in scriptural inerrancy (1 = strongly disagree to 5 = strongly agree). To address both Muslim and Christian respondents, I altered slightly the standard question on biblical inerrancy to read, "Do you agree or disagree that the holy book of your religion is the literal word of God?" I also created a religiosity index with the following five items: respondent's subjective religiosity (1 = not very religious to 4 = very religious), family's religiosity during the respondent's youth (1 = not very religious to 4 = very religious), frequency of attending religious services (1 = never to 7 = nearly every day), frequency of reading religious materials (1 = never to 7 = nearly everyday), and belief in scriptural inerrancy. The index ranges from 5 to 27, with an internal reliability coefficient of .765 (Cronbach's alpha). I recoded the index into three categories (low, medium, and high). The low category includes respondents who gave only low responses ("not very religious," "never attend services," etc.), the high category includes respondents who gave only high responses ("very religious," "attend nearly every day," etc.), and the medium category contains those who fall in between the low and high categories.

Four variables measure family structure: a dummy variable for marital status (1 = married), a continuous measure for number of children in the home, a dummy variable for any children under the age of five years, and a dummy variable for presence of other adult family in the home. Adult family can improve women's work opportunities by assisting them with their domestic responsibilities; conversely, adult family can add to women's household obligations and reduce their ability to work (Kahn and Whittington 1996). Household income is also a known determinant of women's labor supply, with financial constraints increasing the need for women's earnings and the availability of other household income decreasing it. Therefore, I include two dummy variables that identify women with low household income (less than $20,000 a year) and those with high household income (more than $50,000 a year) with those with moderate household income as the reference group ($20,000 to $50,000 a year).

Finally, this study includes several control variables that could reasonably affect Arab American women's labor force participation. Nativity, educational attainment, and labor market region are known determinants of U.S. women's labor supply (Stier and Tienda 1992), and are likewise important for Arab American women's employment (Read 2004a and 2004b). Accordingly, I consider these factors in the analysis. I also examined the effects of duration of U.S. residency in ancillary analyses but do not include it here because the vast majority of respondents have been in the United States for fifteen years or more: 88.5 percent of the 217 foreign-born respondents immigrated before the 1991 Gulf War. This partly reflects the sampling frame characteristics (i.e., more assimilated) and partly reflects the reality that emigration from the Middle East has slowed considerably over the past decade due to restrictive U.S. immigration policies. Finally, I include the respondent's age to account for potential generational effects on women's labor force activity. I use both a continuous measure (age in years) and a quadratic term that captures the nonlinear relationship between age and employment (i.e., the youngest and oldest women are least likely to be employed).[2]

Results

Table 11.2 highlights key comparisons among Muslim and Christian Arab American respondents. One-half of women sampled are Christian, 44.1 percent are Muslim, 1 percent report "other" religious affiliations, and 5 percent report no religious affiliation. Table 11.2 focuses on Muslim and Christian respondents, beginning with differences in their labor force activity. Overall, women sampled have high labor force participation rates, with nearly one-half (47.5 percent) of respondents employed full-time, one-third (31.5 percent) employed part-time, and only 21 percent out of the paid labor force. Their work rates vary by religious affiliation, with Muslim respondents nearly twice as likely to be out of the labor force (28.6 percent compared to 14.6 percent of the native-born) and

TABLE 11.2

Sample Characteristics, Women Aged 18–65

	Muslim (n = 182)	Christian (n = 207)
Labor force participation		
Not employed	28.6%	14.6%**
Employed part-time	34.1	30.6
Employed full-time	37.3	54.8
Religiosity over the life cycle		
Low in childhood and adulthood	9.9	5.3*
Decreased since childhood	9.3	9.2
Increased since childhood	14.3	7.7
High in childhood and adulthood	65.9	77.3
Belief in scriptural inerrancy		
"Holy book of my religion is literal word of God."		
Strongly disagree or disagree	6.1	27.5**
Neither agree nor disagree	11.7	30.9
Strongly agree or agree	82.1	41.7
Religiosity index		
Low	21.7	25.8*
Moderate	49.2	37.6
High	29.1	36.6
Married	75.1	63.1**
Presence of children in home	64.3	46.5
Presence of children less than five years old	17.6	9.7
Presence of adult family in home	17.5	15.5
Additional family income less than $20,000	19.5	36.7**
Additional family income $20,000 to $50,000	40.2	37.2
Additional family income more than $50,000	40.3	26.1
Foreign-born	69.2	49.1**
Less than bachelor's degree	32.9	35.3
South	8.7	16.5**
East	26.4	33.5
West	16.5	24.3
Midwest	48.4	25.7
Age (mean years)	41.2	45.6**

Note: Indicates significant differences at *p < .05; ** p < .01.

considerably less likely to be employed full-time, 37.3 percent compared to 54.8 percent of Christian respondents.

Table 11.2 also demonstrates that the sample's religious identity is strong, with two-thirds (65.9 percent) of Muslim and three-fourths (77.3 percent) of Christian respondents reporting high levels of religiosity over the life cycle. Muslim women are twice as likely to believe in scriptural inerrancy (82.1 percent compared to 41.7 percent), which may reflect the fact that belief in scriptural literalism is an elementary belief in Islam and not necessarily indicative of a conservative ideological stance. Muslim and Christian respondents also share similar scores on the five-item religiosity index, with three-fourths of each group having moderate to high levels. Christian respondents are more likely than Muslim women to report having the highest levels of religiosity (36.6 percent and 29.1 percent, respectively).

Looking at their family ties, Muslim women are more likely than Christians to be married (75.1 percent compared to 63.1 percent) and to have preschool children in the home (17.6 percent compared to 9.7 percent of Christian respondents). It is also worth noting that a relatively small proportion of the sample has children under the age of five years in the home, a finding that reflects their median age of forty-five. Muslim and Christian women are equally well educated, with nearly two-thirds of both groups holding a bachelor's degree or higher. The high educational attainments of these women contradict stereotypes of Arab women as backward and uneducated. Muslim women sampled are almost twice as likely as Christian respondents to live in affluent households (40.2 percent compared to 26.1 percent) and are considerably less likely to live in economically disadvantaged homes, 19.5 percent compared to 36.7 percent of Christian respondents. Consistent with known emigration patterns from the Middle East, Muslim respondents are more likely than Christians to be foreign-born, 69.2 percent and 49.1 percent, respectively.

Table 11.3 considers a central question of this study by examining whether religiosity has a direct relationship with women's work behaviors, or if it primarily affects family behaviors that are related to labor force participation. The cross tabulations in Table 11.3 examine the relationship between degree of religiosity and labor force activity, controlling for presence of children in the home. Muslim affiliation is not considered in this portion of the analysis due to sample size constraints. The religiosity index is recoded into three categories representing women with lower levels of religiosity (27.8 percent of the sample), those with more moderate levels of religiosity (40.8 percent), and women with higher levels of religiosity (31.4 percent).

The first section of Table 11.3 examines respondents with children present in the home, and finds a negative relationship between women's religiosity levels and degree of labor force commitment. Among women with children, highly religious respondents are more than three times as likely to remain in the home, compared to those with the lowest levels of religiosity (44.4 percent

TABLE 11.3

Percentage Distribution of Arab American Women's Labor Force Participation by Religiosity and Presence of Children

Religiosity index	Children in home			No children in home		
	Low	*Moderate*	*High*	*Low*	*Moderate*	*High*
Employment						
Not employed	13.5	25.0	44.4	9.8	12.2	16.4
Employed part-time	34.6	31.5	27.8	32.1	29.7	34.5
Employed full-time	51.9	43.5	27.8	57.0	58.1	49.1
	100%	100%	100%	100%	100%	100%
N =	52	92	72	61	74	55
	Gamma = -.263**			Gamma = -.128		

** p ≤ .01

compared to 13.5 percent). Likewise, women with the highest levels of religiosity are considerably less likely to work full-time (27.8 percent compared to 51.9 percent of women with the lowest religiosity levels). In contrast, for those respondents who have no children in the home, religiosity is relatively unimportant for their degree of labor force commitment. For example, looking only at those respondents without children, roughly half of those with low and high levels of religiosity are employed full-time (57.0 percent and 49.1 percent, respectively).

Table 11.3 also finds a relationship between presence of children and women's degree of labor force commitment, controlling for their religiosity levels. This relationship is strongest among respondents with high religiosity levels, where children significantly dampen women's labor activity. Nearly one-half (44.4 percent) of women with children present in the home are out of the labor force compared to 16.4 percent of women without children, and less than one-third (27.8 percent) of women with children work full-time, compared to 49.1 percent of women without those child-care responsibilities.

An important finding in Table 11.3 is that there is no relationship between women's religiosity levels and presence of children. Looking at the absolute numbers in the marginals, nearly one-half (46.0 percent) of women with low religiosity levels have children present in the home compared to 55.4 percent of those with moderate levels and 56.6 percent of those with high levels of religiosity. In other words, women with low levels of religiosity are just as likely as those with high levels to have children in the home. Overall, the findings in Table 11.3

suggest that presence of children in the home moderates the influence of religiosity on women's employment, which lends initial support to hypothesis (c): family characteristics (i.e., children) will moderate the impact of religiosity on women's employment.

Table 11.4 considers whether these relationships hold in the multivariate context, net of controls for other factors. The table presents a series of logistic regression models that examine the effects of women's religious and family ties on their labor force activity, controlling for nativity, educational attainment, labor market region, family income, and age. Model 1 examines the effects of Muslim affiliation, controlling for background factors; Model 2 includes the effects of nativity; Model 3 adds family variables; and Model 4 examines interaction effects between women's religiosity levels and the presence of children. Models 1 and 2 are primarily concerned with teasing out the effects of Muslim affiliation on women's employment, and Models 3 and 4 are examining the moderating influences of family factors.

In support of hypothesis (a)—Muslim affiliation will be less significant than degree of religiosity (i.e., strength of religious beliefs) for women's employment—Table 11.4 shows that Muslim affiliation per se has negligible effects on women's labor force participation. As I have demonstrated in prior work, Muslim respondents' weaker labor force attachments reflect their varying degrees of cultural assimilation—they are more likely to be foreign-born and newer immigrants, and correspondingly, they are slightly more traditional in their gender role attitudes, especially on issues concerning women's family responsibilities (Read 2002, 2003). Differences in acculturation, rather than Islam, per se, appear to account for variation in Muslim respondents' labor force activity. This result runs contrary to popular stereotypes that portray the Islamic religion as particularly oppressive of women's public sphere participation.

Table 11.4 also provides support for hypothesis (b), that high religiosity over the life cycle and belief in scriptural inerrancy are related to a lower likelihood of employment among these women, as are marriage and the presence of young children in the home (Model 3). Respondents who believe or strongly believe in scriptural literalism are considerably less likely to work compared to other women, and respondents reared in highly religious families who remain very religious in adulthood have much lower odds of labor force participation compared to all other women (those who have increased or decreased in religiosity since childhood and those with low religiosity in childhood and adulthood). The cumulative impact of conservative religious socialization and continued religious commitment is more significant for women's behaviors than is their degree of religiosity in any one phase of the life cycle (analysis not shown).

Model 4 tests one of the primary research questions by including an interaction term for number of children and high religiosity over the life cycle. The findings reveal that high levels of religiosity are most restrictive for

TABLE 11.4

Odds Ratios from Logistic Regression Models Predicting Arab American Women's Labor Force Participation, Aged 18–65 (n = 416)

	Model 1	Model 2	Model 3	Model 4
Predictor	Exp (B)	Exp (B)	Exp (B)	Exp (B)
Muslim affiliation (Christian/other)[a]	.488**	.567†	.733	.784
High religiosity over the life cycle	.641*	.608*	.528*	1.385
Belief in scriptural inerrancy	.684†	.732†	.752†	.684
Married			.371†	.365†
Number of children in home			.956	1.525
Any children less than five years old			.326**	.320**
Presence of adult family			2.143†	2.371†
Additional family income ($20,000 to $50,000)[a]				
Less than $20,000			3.266*	3.755**
More than $50,000			.240**	.248**
Foreign-born		.515*	.543*	.557†
Bachelor's degree +	2.380**	2.285**	2.525**	2.615**
East (South)[a]	3.063**	3.049**	2.933**	2.918**
West	2.012†	2.200†	1.924†	1.976†
Midwest	1.979†	1.968†	1.436	1.457
Age	.928*	.988*	.997*	.997*
Age^2	1.001*	1.001*	1.255*	1.270*
Number of children*high religiosity				.555**
Constant	2.483	1.397	-2.040	-3.105
-2 Log Likelihood	381.594	376.599	306.103	300.293

a. Denotes reference category.

† p ≤ .10   * p ≤ .05   ** p ≤ .01

women with children in the home, net of the effect of having young children in the home (under the age of five years). Similar to the results in Table 11.3, these findings indicate that children moderate the influences of religiosity on women's employment, supporting hypothesis (c). In analyses not shown here, I also included an interaction term for children under five years by high religiosity and found that the effect operated in the expected direction but was not significant due to small cell sizes—the sample is older (median age of forty-three) than the population at large, and only 13 percent have young children in the home. It is also worth noting that marriage has a restrictive effect on women's employment in both models, which follows known patterns among other groups of U.S. women. The background variables included as controls also operate in the expected direction: educational attainment and economic necessity increase the likelihood of employment, while additional family income and foreign birth decrease it.

In ancillary models (not shown), I considered the possibility that religiosity and family factors have different effects on Muslim and Christian women's employment by estimating separate models for each group. Although most factors operate the same for both groups, two differences are especially noteworthy. First, belief in scriptural inerrancy is restricting Christian women's employment (odds ratio of 0.34, p<.05), but not that of Muslim women (odds ratio of 0.83, not significant). Second, the presence of young children also appears more restrictive of Christian women's employment than Muslim women's, although these differences do not reach statistical significance because of the small sample sizes. This may indicate that Christian Arab women are more influenced by religious teachings on women's familial obligations than Muslim Arab women, or it may merely reflect a lack of variation in Muslim women's response to this question (i.e., 82.1 percent believe in scriptural inerrancy).

Although the data for this study are cross-sectional and cannot measure changes over the life course, they do contain retrospective questions on women's labor force decisions at different stages of the life cycle. Table 11.5 compares the labor force history of married women with high and low levels of religiosity at two stages in the life cycle: (a) after marriage and before children, and (b) after children are present in the home (n = 239). Here again, sample size restricts the ability to examine differences between Muslim and Christian respondents. Compared to women with low levels of religiosity, women with high levels are less likely to be in the labor force in either stage of the life cycle (26.7 percent compared to 21.3 percent). Conversely, women with low levels of religiosity are significantly more likely to be employed in both stages of the life course (47 percent compared to 18.6 percent). Consistent with family role explanations, highly religious women are more likely to exit the labor force once children are present in the home (40 percent compared to 26.8 percent of women with low levels of religiosity). Highly religious women are also more likely to enter the labor force after children are present in the home (14.7 percent compared to 4.9

TABLE 11.5

Percentage Distribution of Arab American Women's Labor Force
Participation by Degree of Religiosity and Life Course Position

	Low Religiosity	High Religiosity
Labor force history:		
Not employed before or after kids	21.3	26.7*
Entered labor force after kids	4.9	14.7**
Exited labor force after kids	26.8	40.0**
Employed before and after kids	47.0	18.6**
	n = 164	n = 75

* p ≤ .05 ** p ≤ .01

percent). This may reflect the low number of highly religious women in the labor force in the first place (i.e., there were more to enter because more stayed out of the labor force before children). It may also reflect unmeasured factors, such as economic necessity.

Discussion and Conclusions

Muslim affiliation is often seen as universally restrictive of women's achievements in the public sphere, but few studies have actually tested this thesis. This study begins to address this question by investigating the relationships between religion, family, and work among Arab American women at two stages of the life cycle. The primary question is whether religion has a direct relationship with women's work behaviors, or if it primarily operates through family behaviors that affect women's labor force decisions. Several noteworthy findings emerge from this research that provide further clarification of religious influences on contemporary gender roles.

First, Muslim affiliation is less important than degree of religiosity for determining women's labor force participation. Similar to research on other U.S. ethno-religious groups, belonging to a community of believers serves to reinforce lifestyles prescribed by that particular community (Ebaugh and Chafetz 2000). Since Islam and Christianity teach similar roles for women, this finding is not completely surprising but it does run contrary to popular perceptions of U.S. Muslim women. Second, although religiosity appears to be inversely related to women's labor force participation, the relationship only holds for women with children present in the home. Among women with no children, religiosity is unrelated to employment. Moreover, religiosity is not just operating through increased fertility; women with low and high levels of religiosity were equally likely to have children present in the home. In sum, the influence of religion on women's labor force decisions is most salient at specific phases of the life cycle (i.e., when children are present in the home). This suggests that future research must pay more attention to the precise mechanisms through which religion influences lifestyle decisions in contemporary American life and acknowledge that these mechanisms are fluid rather than static over the life course. Identifying such mechanisms could also demystify the experiences of newer, lesser known ethno-religious populations by highlighting factors they share in common with other more established groups.

This study is not without limitations. Because the data are cross-sectional rather than longitudinal, we can only examine women at different stages in the life cycle rather than follow them across their life course. The sample size further limits the examination to two phases of the life course (after marriage and before children and after children are present in the home). The findings would be enhanced greatly if we knew whether highly religious women reenter the labor force after their children are grown. Results from prior research suggest that this is indeed the case among conservative Christian women (Sherkat 2000). Sample size constraints also affected my ability to look at duration of U.S. residency (an important proxy for acculturation) and to test interactions between religiosity and the presence of young children, which is important given the strong main effect of having young children.

A larger sample of Arab American women would solve many of these limitations, and this is a solution that can be achieved with more refined measures of race/ethnicity in existing data collection efforts. Currently, Arabs, Iranians, and other Middle Easterners are categorized as "white" in most large national data sets, which not only obscures the experiences of these groups but also confounds the results for groups that we typically consider as falling into the "white" category (i.e., those with European ancestries). The same argument has been directed toward the (mis)classification of black immigrants with U.S.-born black Americans, which conceals the tremendous diversity that exists within this group by national origin (Read and Emerson 2005; Williams 1999). In the past, many of these groups have not warranted the same attention as Hispanic and Asian subgroups because of their smaller sizes. However, as we have seen since 9/11, population size is only one characteristic (albeit an important one) that contributes to the changing face of American society. The inclusion of two or three additional questions on place of birth, ancestry, and language could facilitate huge strides in our understanding of the diversity that exists within major U.S. racial/ethnic groups.

Finally, although the sample is more geographically diverse than previous studies on Arab American women, the ability to generalize findings remains limited, which is a common and often unavoidable problem in research on populations that are not identified in large national datasets. These limitations not withstanding, the data used in this study represent the most comprehensive and nationally representative information on Arab American women and have been used to examine a range of sociological issues such as identity politics (Marshall and Read 2003), cultural determinants of female employment (Read 2004a, 2004b), and religious influences of gender role attitudes (Read 2003).

In general, the results of this study provide a more nuanced understanding of the mechanisms (i.e., family behaviors) by which religion restricts women's labor force participation, but they do not necessarily challenge feminist critiques of religion as a patriarchal institution that legitimizes gender inequality through the maintenance of traditional gender roles within the home (for a review see Sherkat 2000). The primary goal of this study, however, was to broaden unidimensional conceptualizations of religion to examine its varying impact on women's behaviors at different phases in the life course, rather than contribute to a feminist discourse on patriarchy. The results suggest that future research on female labor force participation should pay further attention the interaction between family roles and religious belief systems. Religion may be restrictive of women's public sphere participation, but its effect may not be as universal as previously conceived.

NOTES

1. The Census Bureau defines Arab Americans as persons who trace their ancestries to Algeria, Egypt, Libya, Morocco, Sudan, Tunisia (North Africa), and to Bahrain, Iraq, Jordan, Kuwait, Lebanon, Oman, Palestine, Qatar, Saudi Arabia, Syria, United Arab Emirates, and Yemen (Western Asia).

2. I also examined age categories in analyses not shown here. They operated as expected but were not significant due to the small sample size.

REFERENCES

Abraham, N., and A. Shryock, eds. 2000. *Arab Detroit: From Margin to Mainstream.* Detroit: Wayne State University Press.

Aswad, B. 1994. "Attitudes of Immigrant Women and Men in the Dearborn Area toward Women's Employment and Welfare." In *Muslim Communities in North America*, ed. Y. Y. Haddad and J. I. Smith, 501–519. Albany: State University of New York Press.

Bartkowski, J. P. 2001. *Remaking the Godly Marriage: Gender Negotiation in Evangelical Families.* New Brunswick, NJ: Rutgers University Press.

Bartkowski, J. P., and J. G. Read. 2003. "Veiled Submission: Gender, Power, and Identity among Evangelical and Muslim Women in the U.S." *QualitativeSociology* 26: 71–92.

Becker, P. E., and H. Hofmeister. 2001. "Work, Family, and Religious Involvement for Men and Women." *Journal for the Scientific Study of Religion* 40:707–722.

Browne, I. 2000. "Opportunities Lost? Race, Industrial Restructuring, and Employment among Young Women Heading Households." *Social Forces* 78:907–929.

Cainkar, L. 1996. "Immigrant Palestinian Women Evaluate their Lives." In *Family and Gender among American Muslims: Issues Facing Middle Eastern Immigrants and their Descendants*, ed. B. C. Aswad and B. Bilge, 41–58. Philadelphia: Temple University Press.

Carolan, M. T. 1999. "Contemporary Muslim Women and the Family." In *Family Ethnicity: Strength in Diversity*, ed. H. P. McAdoo, 213–224. Thousand Oaks, CA: Sage Publications.

Cotter, D. A., J. DeFiore, J. M. Hermsen, B. M. Kowalewski, and R. Vanneman. 1998. "The Demand for Female Labor." *American Journal of Sociology* 103:1673–1699.

Ebaugh, H. R., and J. S. Chafetz. 2000. *Religion and the New Immigrants: Continuities and Adaptations in Immigrant Congregations.* New York: Altamira Press.

Gallagher, S. K. 2003. *Evangelical Identity and Gendered Family Life.* New Brunswick, NJ: Rutgers University Press.

Glass, J., and J. Jacobs. 2005. "Childhood Religious Conservatism and Adult Attainment among Black and White Women." *Social Forces* 84:555–579.

Haddad, Y. Y. 1991. "Introduction." In *The Muslims of America*, ed. Y. Y. Haddad, 3–10. New York: Oxford University Press.

———. 1994. "Maintaining the Faith of the Fathers: Dilemma of Religious Identity in the Christian and Muslim Arab-American Communities." In *The Development of Arab-American Identity*, ed. E. McCarus, 61–84. Ann Arbor: The University of Michigan Press.

Haddad, Y. Y., and J. I. Smith. 1996. "Islamic Values among American Muslims." In *Family and Gender among American Muslims: Issues Facing Middle Eastern Immigrants and their Descendants*, ed. B. C. Aswad and B. Bilge, 19–40. Philadelphia: Temple University Press.

Hardacre, H. 1997. "The Impact of Fundamentalisms on Women, the Family, and Interpersonal Relations." In *Fundamentalisms and Society: Reclaiming the Sciences, the Family, and Education*, ed. M. E. Marty and S. R. Appleby, 129–150. Chicago: University of Chicago Press.

Hartman, H., and M. Hartman. 1996. "More Jewish, Less Jewish: Implications for Education and Labor Force Characteristics." *Sociology of Religion* 57:175–193.

Heaton, T., and M. C. Cornwall. 1989. "Religious Group Variation in the Socioeconomic Status and Family Behavior of Women." *Journal for the Scientific Study of Religion* 28:283–299.

Hertel, B. R. 1988. "Gender, Religious Identity and Work Force Participation." *Journal for the Scientific Study of Religion* 27:574–592.

Hertel, B. R., and M. Hughes. 1987. "Religious Affiliation, Attendance, and Support for 'Pro-Family' Issues in the United States." *Social Forces* 65:858–882.

Joseph, S. 1999. "Introduction." In *Intimate Selving in Arab Families: Gender, Self, and Identity*, ed. S. Joseph, 1–13. New York: Syracuse University Press.

Kahn, J. R., and L. A. Whittington. 1996. "The Labor Supply of Latinas in the USA: Comparing Labor Force Participation, Wages, and Hours Worked with Anglo and Black Women." *Population Research and Policy Review* 15:45–73.

Lehrer, E. L. 1995. "The Effects of Religion on the Labor Supply of Married Women." *Social Science Research* 24:281–301.

———. 1999. "Married Women's Labor Supply Behavior in the 1990s: Differences by Life-Cycle Stage." *Social Science Quarterly* 80:574–590.

Marshall, S. E., and J. G. Read. 2003. "Identity Politics among Arab-American Women." *Social Science Quarterly* 84:875–891.

McCloud, A. B. 2003. "Islam in America: The Mosaic." In *Religion and Immigration: Christian, Jewish, and Muslim Experiences in the United States*, ed. Y. Y. Haddad, J. I. Smith, and J. L. Esposito, 159–174. New York: Altamira Press.

Naff, A. 1994. "The Early Arab Immigrant Experience." In *The Development of Arab-American Identity*, ed. E. McCarus, 23–35. Ann Arbor: The University of Michigan Press.

Pew Research Center. 2002. "Americans Struggle with Religion's Role at Home and Abroad." The Pew Forum on Religion and Public Life. Press release from telephone survey. Available at http://people-press.org/reports.

———. 2004. "Plurality Sees Islam as More Likely to Encourage Violence." The Pew Forum on Religion and Public Life. Press release from telephone survey. Available at http://pewforum.org/publications/surveys/islam.pdf.

Read, J. G. 2002. "Challenging Myths of Muslim Women: The Influence of Islam on Arab-American Women's Labor Force Participation." *Muslim World* 96:18–39.

———. 2003. "The Sources of Gender Role Attitudes among Christian and Muslim Arab-American Women." *Sociology of Religion* 64:207–222.

———. 2004a. "Coming to America: The Effects of Nativity and Culture on Arab-American Women's Employment." *International Migration Review* 38:52–77.

———. 2004b. *Culture, Class, and Work among Arab-American Women*. New York: LFB Scholarly Publishing.

Read, J. G., and M. O. Emerson. 2005. "Racial Context of Origin, Black Immigration, and the U.S. Black/White Health Disparity." *Social Forces* 84:183–201.

Read, J. G., and J. P. Bartkowski. 2000. "To Veil or Not to Veil? A Case Study of Identity Negotiation among Muslim Women Living in Austin, Texas." *Gender & Society* 4: 395–417.

Sherif, B. 1999. "Islamic Family Ideals and their Relevance to American Muslim Families." In *Family Ethnicity: Strength in Diversity*, ed. H. P. McAdoo, 203–212. Thousand Oaks, CA: Sage Publications.

Sherkat, D. E. 2000. "'That They Be Keepers of the Home': The Effect of Conservative Religion on Early and Late Transitions into Housewifery." *Review of Religious Research* 41:344–358.

Stier, H., and M. Tienda. 1992. "Family, Work, and Women: The Labor Supply of Hispanic Immigrant Wives." *International Migration Review* 26:1291–1313.

Suleiman, M. W., ed. 1999. *Arabs in America: Building a New Future*. Philadelphia: Temple University Press.

U.S. Bureau of the Census. 2000. *Census of Population and Housing. Public-Use Microdata Samples*. Washington, DC: U.S. Government Printing Office.

Warner, R. S., and J. G. Wittner, editors. 1998. *Gatherings in Diaspora: Religious Communities and the New Immigration*. Philadelphia: Temple University Press.

Williams, D. R. 1999. "The Monitoring of Racial/Ethnic Status in the USA: Data Quality Issues." *Ethnicity and Health* 4:121–137.

Williams, R. H., ed. 1997. *Culture Wars in American Politics: Critical Reviews of a Popular Myth*. New York: Aldine de Gruyter.

World Almanac. 1998. Mahwah, NJ: World Almanac Books.

Zogby, J. 1990. *Arab America Today: A Demographic Profile of Arab Americans*. Washington, DC: Arab American Institute.

———. 1995. *Arab American Institute/Zogby Group Poll. October 26–30*. Washington, DC: Arab American Institute.

PART TWO

Religion and Health Outcomes

12

Religion and Depressive Symptoms in Late Life

NEAL KRAUSE

The purpose of this chapter is to examine select issues in the relationship between religion and depressive symptoms among older adults. The discussion that follows addresses three main issues. First, data on the prevalence of depression and depressive symptomatology are examined. Following this, research on religion and depression is reviewed briefly. Finally, an effort is made to contribute to the literature on religion and depression by empirically evaluating a facet of religion that has received relatively little attention in this context: religious meaning.

The Prevalence of Depression in Late Life

Research consistently reveals that mental health problems in the United States are widespread. Evidence of this comes from two major nationwide surveys by Kessler and his associates. Data from the first survey (i.e., the National Comorbidity Survey) indicate that approximately 48 percent of the population has experienced a clinical form of mental disorder at some point in their lifetime (Kessler et al. 1994). This estimate was corroborated in a recent replication of this study. Once again, the data reveal that many (46.4 percent) have experienced clinically significant mental health problems at some point in their lives (Kessler et al. 2005). Among the most prevalent conditions are the mood disorders, which include major depression, dysthymia, and bipolar disorders. The data suggest that as many as 20.8 percent of the people in the United States have experienced a mood disorder at some point in their lifetime. It is especially important to note that the mood disorders tend to emerge fairly early in life, typically before age thirty or so (Kessler et al. 2005).

The data provided by Kessler and his associates deal solely with clinical psychiatric disorders that meet the diagnostic criteria in the DSM-IV (American Psychiatric Association 1994). In contrast, other researchers have worked with measures that assess subclinical or preclinical measures of symptomatology. Rather than producing a binary diagnosis (i.e., disorder is either present or disorder is absent), the indices used in these studies measure symptoms along a continuum. The Center for Epidemiologic Studies Depression Scale (CES-D) (Radloff 1977) is a good example of this latter approach.

Studies using measures like the CES-D Scale provide a somewhat different picture of the relationship between age and depressive symptoms than the one that emerges when clinical syndromes are examined. In particular, research by Newmann (1989) suggests there may be a nonlinear relationship whereby depressive symptoms are initially high early in life, decline through midlife, and then rise sharply around age sixty-five (see also Kessler et al. 1992; Mirowsky and Ross 1992). Support for these findings is provided by Gatz and Fiske (2003), who report that approximately half the cases of clinical depression that arise in late life have a late onset. This means that for many, depression appears for the first time around age sixty or so. It is also important to point out that suicide rates, a problem that is highly correlated with depression, are highest in late life as well (Manton, Blazer, and Woodbury 1987).

Taken together, the epidemiologic data reviewed here indicate that depression is a fairly prevalent mental health problem that may arise both early and late in life. To the extent that this is true, it is important to take steps to identify the factors that may be responsible for this bimodal onset pattern. A wide range of potential explanatory factors have been examined in secular settings, including stress (Krause 1986) and social support (Krause 2001). But it is especially important for the purpose of this chapter to note that a number of investigators have also turned to the potentially important influence of religion.

Religion and Depression

In their comprehensive review of the literature, Koenig, McCullough, and Larson (2001) report that over one hundred studies have been published on the relationship between religion and depression. It would be impossible to review this voluminous body of work here. Instead, three broad trends in the literature will be discussed. First, the data generally reveal that greater involvement in religion is associated with less depression. Second, because religion is a complex phenomenon that comprises many different dimensions or facets (Fetzer Institute/ National Institute on Aging Working Group 1999), a wide range of religious factors have been linked with depression. For example, research by Idler (1987) suggests that more frequent attendance at religious worship services is associated with lower levels of depression. In contrast, research by Kendler and his associates indicates that more frequent private prayer was inversely related to depressive symptoms (Kendler, Gardner, and Prescott 1997). Yet other studies provide evidence suggesting that religion may be associated with depression because it is an especially important resource during stressful times. More specifically, findings from Pargament's (1997) impressive research program reveal that a wide range of religious coping responses (e.g., turning to God for guidance during difficult times) are associated with fewer symptoms of depression.

Although most studies suggest that involvement in religion tends to lower the risk of experiencing depression or depressive symptoms, there are some notable exceptions. As research on religion continues to evolve, investigators are becoming increasingly aware that there are negative as well as positive facets of religion and instead of helping people avoid depression, religion may, at times, promote it. For example, research by Krause (2003a) suggests that some older people may have doubts about their faith and wrestle with basic teachings and principles of religion. Data from his nationwide survey indicate that greater doubt about religion is associated with more frequent symptoms of depression. Similarly, a study by Krause, Ellison, and Wulff (1998) suggests that interpersonal conflict may arise within the church, and when it does, people are more likely to experience depressed affect.

Although the findings from research on religion and depression have provided many valuable insights, it is incomplete because it doesn't provide a sufficient explanation for the bimodal pattern of depression over the life course. One way to approach this problem is to look to a dimension of religion that has often been overlooked in empirical research: religious meaning. There are two closely related reasons why religious meaning is an important construct to consider. First, as Baumeister (1991) convincingly argues, the need to have a meaningful life lies at the very core of human existence. In fact, he maintains that it is one of the primary motivating forces in life, and the search for meaning lies behind a good deal of human behavior. In addition, this construct is important because a number of investigators argue that one of the basic functions of religion is to help people find a sense of meaning in life. Evidence of this may be found, for example, in the classic work of Clark (1958, 419), who maintained that "religion more than any other human function satisfies the need for meaning in life."

But it may not be entirely clear why religious meaning may be useful for shedding light on the bimodal distribution of depression over the life course. In order to see why this may be so, it is important to reflect upon two issues. The first involves identifying key life transitions that occur during these developmental periods, whereas the second has to do with linking these life transitions to a crisis in meaning.

It is well known that a series of key developmental challenges and transitions arise during young adulthood that have implications for the rest of the life course. More specifically, a number of decisions must be made at this point about continuing education, getting married, having children, and starting a career. Childhood and adolescence are left far behind and young men and women are thrust headlong into the serious and demanding world of adult responsibilities. Not everyone is well prepared for these tasks. A different set of challenges face those entering late life. In this case, people must grapple with a series of transitions involving widowhood, retirement, the empty nest, and the health-related restriction of activities.

Considering these major transitions, it is easy to see how younger and older adults might lose their sense of direction as they are thrust into largely unfamiliar domains. One might argue that the developmental crises faced by younger and older adults are not unique, and that people face similar challenges throughout the life course. For example, a good deal has been written about the midlife crisis. However, recent evidence suggests that a midlife crisis is by no means common, and that most people fail to experience this type of difficulty (Wethington, Kessler, and Pixley 2004).

Given the major transitions and challenges that face younger and older adults, it is important to reflect on the needs they create and the role played by religion in meeting them. A closer examination of the developmental challenges discussed earlier reveals that they largely involve giving up old roles and assuming new ones. Stated more formally, they consist of role entrances and role exits. This suggests that there may be something about losing and gaining roles that is challenging, and that is capable of making some individuals depressed.

Some useful insights into this issue may be found by turning to the basic principles of identity theory (Stryker 2001). Identity theory rests on two core constructs: social roles and identities. Social roles are defined structurally as a position in a group. For example, an individual may be a father, a husband, and a provider. In contrast, identities refer to the kinds of information people emphasize when they think about themselves and when they present themselves to others. These identities are grounded in the roles people occupy. So, for example, a person might identify himself to others by acknowledging that, "I am a faculty member."

Associated with roles are clusters of norms and behavioral expectations that tell role occupants what to do and what to expect. As a result, these norms provide a sense of direction and purpose in life (Thoits 1991). They also provide the basis for evaluating the adequacy of role performance. Viewed more broadly, these norms and expectations are important because they are a major source of meaning in life. When people go through the major transitions discussed earlier, they leave a known and comfortable set of roles and norms for new ones, and they must learn new ways of acting, behaving, and evaluating what they do. At least initially, the norms and expectations in a new role may not be clear, and people may struggle with finding, implementing, and practicing them. The gap that arises during these transitions may create a vacuum in meaning. The essence of this dilemma for older people is captured succinctly by Rosow (1976), who refers to aging as a "roleless-role."

A central premise in this chapter is that religion plays a crucial role at precisely these junctures in the life course by meeting the need for meaning. In order to see why this may be the case, it is important to carefully consider what meaning is and what it entails.

Defining and Measuring Meaning in Life

Meaning is a very elusive construct. Perhaps the best way to get a handle on it is to review both verbal and operational definitions of meaning. Reker (1997, 710) defines meaning as "having a sense of direction, a sense of order, a reason for existence, a clear sense of personal identify and a greater social consciousness." This definition provides a good point of departure, but it is hard to get an intuitively pleasing sense of what meaning actually entails. It is for this reason that it is important to consider operational definitions as well. Krause (2002a) recently conducted a nationwide survey of religion among older people. One of the goals of this study was to flesh out the nature and content domain of religious meaning by conducting a series of qualitative studies. A brief six-item index of religious meaning was derived from this research program (Krause 2003b). (This scale is presented later in this Chapter in Table 12.1.) Three facets of religious meaning are contained in these indicators. The first is concerned with relying on religion to provide a sense of purpose in life and believing that life unfolds according to God's plan. The second has to do with a having a sense of direction in life. The third facet involves believing that religion infuses life with a sense of reason, order, and coherence. This is reflected in the items dealing with beliefs about understanding one's own self and others better.

How Religion Provides a Sense of Meaning in Life

If the primary goal of religion is to provide a sense of meaning in life, then it is important to reflect on how this happens. A central premise in this chapter is that a major conduit for the transmission of religious meaning may be found by turning to social relationships in the church. There are several reasons why this may be so. To begin with, a number of the classic social theorists maintained that social ties in the church form the very essence of religion itself. For example, Simmel ([1898] 1997, 108; emphasis in the original) argued, "The faith that has come to be regarded as the essence and substance of religion is first of all a relationship *between human beings.*" Similarly, Josiah Royce ([1911] 2001, 58), a close friend of William James and a leading philosopher of his day maintained that "our social experience is our principal source of religious insight. And the salvation that this insight brings to our knowledge is salvation through the fostering of human brotherhood."

If religion is a major source of meaning in life, and social relationships form the basis of religion, then it follows that social ties with religious others may be an important source of meaning in life. But, it is not entirely clear how religious others help people find a sense of meaning. The conceptual model depicted in Figure 12.1 was developed in an effort to take a modest first step toward providing some insight into this issue. The causal flow depicted in this model is relatively straightforward. It is proposed that people who attend church often tend to get more support from the people who worship there, and more support from significant others at church promotes a greater sense of meaning in life. Finally, people who have a sense of meaning will experience fewer symptoms of depression than individuals who have not found a sense of meaning in life.

This quick overview of the conceptual thrust of the model hardly does justice to the complexity of the issues involved here. Consequently, it may be useful to present the rationale behind this conceptual scheme in greater detail. There are two reasons why church attendance is contained in the model. First, it is perhaps the most widely used measure in studies of religion and health. As a result, it is important to show that other constructs, such as religious meaning, contribute to our understanding of depression above and beyond what can be attributed to church attendance. But the second and more important reason is that church attendance may play a role in promoting a sense of meaning in life. Attending church is obviously one of the most important ways of becoming involved in religion. If the primary goal of religion is to provide a sense of meaning in life, then people who attend church frequently should be more likely to find meaning than individuals who do not go to church as often. Unfortunately, church attendance is a very complex form of behavior that exposes an individual to a bewildering array of religious factors ranging from sermons and group prayers, to engaging in rituals like communion and singing hymns. Because each of these factors may

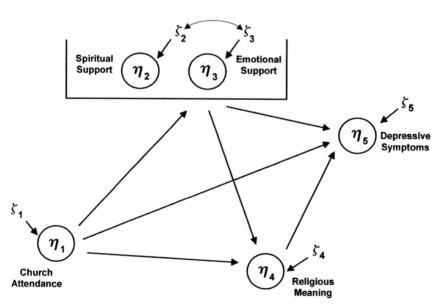

FIGURE 12.1 A conceptual model of church-based support, religious meaning, and depressive symptoms.

enhance a person's sense of meaning, relying solely on church attendance does not provide sufficient insight into precisely how religion promotes a sense of meaning in life.

Consistent with the rationale developed earlier, it is proposed that one of the primary ways that religion fosters meaning in life is through the influence of the people who worship in a congregation. But, this basic hypothesis is too simple and leaves too many questions unanswered. Exactly how do people in church promote a sense of meaning in life? As shown in the model depicted in Figure 12.1, this can happen in two ways that reflect the influence of different types of church-based social support.

Recently, Krause (2002b) devised a comprehensive battery of church-based social support measures. This work revealed that church-based social support is a complex multidimensional domain in its own right. It is, therefore, imperative that our thinking about church-based social support reflects this complexity. People in church may help each other in a number of ways. For example, they may exchange various forms of emotional support and tangible assistance. But these types of support may be found inside as well as outside the church. Consequently, in order to see if social ties in the church make a unique contribution to the development of meaning in life, it is important to bring another facet of church-based support to the foreground. Krause (2002b) refers to this as spiritual support. Spiritual support is assistance given by fellow church members that is specifically designed to deepen religious faith, and help the recipient adapt and apply the teachings of the faith in daily life. As the measures by Krause (2002b) reveal, individuals at church help each other find solutions to their problems in the Bible, they may help each other lead a better religious life, and they may help each other know God better. Viewed more broadly, spiritual support involves the oral transmission of fundamental religious tenets that serve as a strategic context for meaning-making in religious settings. This may be all good and well, but focusing solely on spiritual support may not go far enough.

As it stands, the theoretical rationale developed up to this point creates the impression that the only way in which meaning arises in religious settings is through the transmission and reinforcement of basic religious beliefs. But if this were true, then people who don't attend church would be unable to find meaning in life. Simple observation reveals this isn't the case. But more important than this, religious others live in both religious and secular worlds. As a result, their lives are a mix of both secular and sacred activities and functions. Consequently, fellow church members may help a study participant find meaning in both sacred and secular ways.

It was primarily for this reason that a measure of emotional support from fellow church members was also included in the model in Figure 12.1. Emotional support involves things like listening to others talk about their private problems and concerns, and letting others know they are loved and cared for. Helping others in this way may make them feel they are valued members of the group. Support for this is found in a recent nationwide survey by Krause and Wulff (2005). Their data reveal that emotional support from fellow church members makes people of all ages feel they belong in their congregation. Moreover, these data further reveal that belonging is associated, in turn, with better health. Although Krause and Wulff (2005) did not have a measure of meaning in their data, it seems reasonable to conclude that a feeling of belonging in a congregation is an important source of meaning in life.

By juxtaposing spiritual and emotional support in Figure 12.1, this model attempts to show how a sense of meaning arises from a combination of sacred and secular supportive behaviors. This appears to be the first time that church-based social support, meaning, and depressive symptoms have been examined empirically in the literature.

Evaluating the Model of Religious Meaning Empirically

Study Sample

The data used to estimate the model in Figure 12.1 come from a recent nationwide survey of older adults that was conducted by Krause (2002a). The study population was defined as all household residents who were either white or black, noninstitutionalized, English-speaking, and at least sixty-six years of age. Geographically, the study population was restricted to eligible persons residing in the coterminous United States (i.e., residents of Alaska and Hawaii were excluded). Finally, the study was restricted to people who were currently practicing Christians, individuals who were Christian in the past but no longer practice any religion, and people who were not affiliated with any faith at any point in their lifetime. Individuals who practice a religion other than Christianity (e.g., Jews or Muslims) were excluded because of the difficulty in devising a set of religion measures that would be suitable for people of all faiths.

The sampling frame consisted of all eligible persons contained in the Health Care Financing Administration (HCFA) Medicare Beneficiary Eligibility List (HCFA is now called the Centers for Medicare and Medicaid Services). Interviewing began in March 2001 and concluded in August 2001. All data collection was conducted by Harris Interactive in New York. A total of fifteen hundred interviews were completed. African Americans were over-sampled so that race differences in religion could be properly evaluated. The response rate for the study was 62 percent (see Krause 2002a for a more detailed discussion of the sampling procedures used in this study).

Although fifteen hundred older people participated in the study, some respondents were excluded from the estimation of the model in Figure 12.1. This model focuses on support received from people at church. However, people must first attend church in order to develop meaningful ties with the individuals who worship there. Consequently, when the study questionnaire was designed, the research team concluded that it did not make sense to ask about things like emotional support from church members if respondents never go to church or if they only attend religious services once or twice a year. Based on this rationale, the questions on church-based support were not administered to 374 study participants. As a result, these individuals were excluded from the analyses presented in the following.

After using listwise deletion to exclude cases containing item nonresponse, the sample used in the analysis of Figure 12.1 comprised 889 cases. Preliminary analysis revealed that the average age of the people in this sample was 73.9 years (standard deviation = 6.2 years). Approximately 40 percent were men, 50 percent were married at the time the interview took place, and 44 percent were older whites. The data also revealed that the study participants completed an average of 11.8 years of schooling (standard deviation = 3.4 years). These descriptive data, as well as the estimates that follow, are based on data that have been weighted.

Study Measures

Table 12.1 contains the indicators that were used to assess the constructs in the conceptual model. The procedures used to code these items are provided in the footnotes of this table. The main outcome measure in this model is depressive symptoms. This construct is measured with three indicators taken from the CES-D Scale (Radloff 1977). As shown in Table 12.1, the three items deal with the cognitive aspects of depression (e.g., feeling sad or blue). These items are coded so that a high score reflects more depressive symptomatology.

Church attendance is assessed with a standard measure that asks respondents how often they attend religious services. A high score on this indicator denotes more frequent church attendance.

The measures of emotional support and spiritual support are taken from the work of Krause (2002b). A high score on either scale represents older study participants who received relatively more emotional or spiritual support from their fellow church members.

Religious meaning is assessed with the six-item scale that was discussed earlier. A high score on these items denotes a greater sense of meaning in life through religion.

The relationships among church attendance, church-based social support, meaning, and depressive symptoms were evaluated after the effects of age, sex, marital status, education, and race were controlled statistically. Age is scored in a continuous format. In contrast, sex (1 = men, 0 = women), marital status (1 = married; 0 = otherwise), and race (1 = white; 0 = black) are coded in a binary format. Finally, education is a continuous measure that reflects the total number of years of completed schooling.

TABLE 12.1

Study Measures

1. Frequency of Church Attendance[a]

2. Emotional Support from Church Members[b]

   A. Other than your minister, pastor, or priest, how often does someone in your congregation let you know they love and care for you?

   B. How often does someone in your congregation talk with you about your private problems and concerns?

   C. How often does someone in your congregation express interest and concern in your well-being?

3. Spiritual Support from Church Members[b]

   A. Not counting Bible study groups, prayer groups, or church services, how often does someone in your congregation share their own religious experiences with you?

   B. Not counting Bible study groups, prayer groups, or church services, how often does someone in your congregation help you find solutions to your problems in the Bible?

   C. Not counting Bible study groups, prayer groups, or church services, how often does someone in your congregation help you to lead a better religious life?

4. Religious Meaning[c]

   A. God put me in this life for a purpose.

   B. God has a specific plan for my life.

   C. God has a reason for everything that happens to me.

   D. My faith gives me a sense of direction in my life.

   E. My faith helps me better understand myself.

   F. My faith helps me better understand other people.

5. Depressive Symptoms[d]

   A. I felt like I could not shake off the blues even with the help of my family and friends.

   B. I felt depressed.

   C. I felt sad.

---

a. This variable was scored in the following manner (coding in parentheses): Never (1), less than once a year (2), about once or twice a year (3), several times a year (4), about once a month (5), 2–3 times a month (6), nearly every week (7), every week (8), several times a week (9).

b. These variables were scored in the following manner: Never (1), once in a while (2), fairly often (3), very often (4).

c. These variables were scored in the following manner: Strongly disagree (1), disagree (2), agree (3), strongly agree (4).

d. These variables were scored in the following manner: Rarely or none of the time (1), some or a little of the time (2), occasionally or a moderate amount of the time (3), most or all of the time (4).

Results

Before turning to the substantive findings, it is important to briefly assess the fit of the model to the data and determine the basic psychometric properties of the study measures. The findings reveal that the fit of the model to the data was adequate. More specifically, the Normed Fit Index value of .904 is above the recommended cut point of .900 (Bentler and Bonett 1980). Similarly, Bollen's (1989) incremental fit index value of .919 as well as the Tucker–Lewis coefficient (Tucker and Lewis 1973) estimate of .919 are sufficiently close to the ideal target value of 1.0. Finally, the standardized root mean square residual estimate of .032 is below the recommended ceiling of .050 (Kelloway 1998).

The standardized factor loadings and standardized measurement error estimates for the indicators in the conceptual model are provided in Table 12.2. These coefficients are useful because they provide preliminary information on the psychometric properties of the measures. Although there are no firm guidelines in the literature, experience suggests that standardized factor loadings in excess of .400 indicate that measures have good reliability and validity. As shown in Table 12.2, the factor loadings range from .591 to .908, suggesting that the indicators have good psychometric properties.

Although the factor loadings and measurement error terms provide useful information about the reliability of each indicator, it would be helpful to know something about the reliability of the scales taken as a whole. Fortunately, it is possible to compute these estimates with a formula provided by Rock and his associates (Rock et al. 1977). Applying this formula to the data in Table 12.2 yields the following reliability estimates for the constructs contained in the conceptual model: spiritual support from fellow church members (.840), emotional support from church members (.800), religious meaning in life (.924), and depressive symptoms (.811).

Table 12.3 contains estimates of the substantive relationships among the constructs depicted in Figure 12.1. Several major results emerge from these data. First, the findings indicate that, compared to those who do not go to church often, older people who go to church frequently tend to receive more spiritual support (Beta = .336; $p < .001$) and more emotional support from the people who worship there (Beta = .377; $p < .001$).

The data further reveal that a sense of meaning in life is influenced by three factors: the frequency of church attendance (Beta = .138; $p < .001$), spiritual support (Beta = .222; $p < .001$), and emotional support from church members (Beta = .151; $p < .001$). Although the coefficient associated with spiritual support (Beta = .222; $p < .001$) appears to be larger than the estimate associated with emotional support (Beta = .151; $p < .001$), a subsequent test revealed that the difference in magnitude between these two estimates is not statistically significant. Viewed in a more general way, these data indicate that a sense of meaning in life is determined, at least in part, by support from fellow church members.

TABLE 12.2

Measurement Model Parameter Estimates (*N* = 889)

Construct	Factor Loadings[a]	Measurement Errors[b]
1. Frequency of Church Attendance	1.000	0.000
2. Emotional Support from Church Members		
A. Love and care for you[c]	.838	.298
B. Private problems and concerns	.591	.651
C. Interest and concern	.823	.322
3. Spiritual Support from Church Members		
A. Share religious experiences	.704	.504
B. Find solutions in the Bible	.845	.286
C. Lead a better religious life	.838	.298
4. Religious Meaning		
A. Life for a purpose	.821	.325
B. Specific plan for life	.796	.366
C. Reason for everything	.718	.484
D. Direction in life	.899	.193
E. Understand myself	.908	.176
F. Understand others	.856	.268
5. Depressive Symptoms		
A. Shake off blues	.722	.478
B. Felt depressed	.818	.332
C. Felt sad	.761	.421

a. Factor loadings are from the completely standardized solution. The first listed item in each latent construct was fixed at 1.0 in the unstandardized solution.

b. Measurement error estimates are from the completely standardized solution. All factor loadings and measurement error terms are significant at the .001 level.

c. Item content is paraphrased for the purpose of identification. See Table 12.1 for the complete text of each indicator.

Moreover, the analysis suggests that religious meaning arises from both overtly religious as well as more secular forms of assistance. This underscores the social origin of meaning in life. Taken together, the variables in the conceptual model explain just under 20 percent of the variance in religious meaning.

The data derived from estimating the model shown in Figure 12.1 also provide insight into the nature of the relationship between emotional and spiritual

TABLE 12.3

Church-Based Support, Religious Meaning, and Depressive Symptoms

Dependent Variables

Independent Variables	Church Attendance	Spiritual Support	Emotional Support	Religious Meaning	Depressive Symptoms
Age	.016[a]	-.204***	-.113***	.011	-.011
	(.004)[b]	(-.023)	(-.015)	(.001)	(-.001)
Sex	-.115***	-.037	-.115***	-.047	-.051
	(-.367)	(-.052)	(-.195)	(-.042)	(-.056)
Marital Status	.143***	.012	-.064	.014	-.085*
	(.445)	(.016)	(-.106)	(.013)	(-.090)
Education	.040	-.030	.019	.002	-.065
	(.018)	(-.006)	(.005)	(.001)	(-.010)
Race	-.019	-.212***	-.234***	-.089*	.068
	(-.060)	(-.292)	(-.392)	(-.080)	(.072)
Church Attendance		.336***	.377***	.138***	-.133***
		(.148)	(.201)	(.039)	(-.045)
Spiritual Support				.222***	.113
				(.144)	(.088)
Emotional Support				.151***	.051
				(.081)	(.033)
Religious Meaning					-.141***
					(-.169)

N = 889

a. Standardized factor loading

b. Metric (un-standardized) factor loading

* p < .05; ** p < .01; *** p < .001

support from fellow church members. These findings (not shown in Table 12.3) suggest that the correlation between these two forms of church-based support is statistically significant (.438; p < .001). However, when viewed another way, the data indicate only about 19 percent shared variance between the two dimensions of support. This is important because it suggests that emotional support and spiritual support from fellow church members represent phenomena that are conceptually distinct.

The data in Table 12.3 reveal that above and beyond the influence of church-based significant others, there are other facets of church attendance that appear to promote a sense of meaning in life (Beta = .138; p < .001). Nevertheless, in order to keep these findings in perspective, it is important to examine the data a bit more closely. Two findings are of interest in this regard. First, the data show that people who go to church often tend to get more support from the people who worship there. Second, the data further reveal that support from fellow church members, in turn, tends to help older people find a sense of meaning in life. This suggests that church attendance influences meaning indirectly through church-based social support. Therefore, in order to understand the role of church attendance more fully, it is important to examine its direct, indirect, and total effects on religious meaning. These estimates (not shown in Table 12.3) suggest that the indirect effect of church attendance on religious meaning (Beta = .132; p < .001) and the total effect of church attendance on meaning (Beta = .269; p < .001) are both statistically significant. Put another way, these coefficients are important because they reveal that fully 49 percent of the total effect of church attendance (.132/.269 = .49) operates indirectly through social relationships in the church. Consistent with the insights of the classic social theorists (e.g., Simmel [1898] 1997), these data suggest that one of the primary ways in which religion contributes to a sense of meaning in life arises from social ties that tend to flourish in the church.

One last finding in Table 12.3 is important. As the data show, a greater sense of meaning in life is, in turn, associated with fewer symptoms of depression (Beta = -.141; p < .001). Although the data that were derived from estimating the model in Figure 12.1 are helpful, it is important to view them in the wider context of the argument that was developed earlier. It was proposed that the onset of depression tends to emerge at two points in the life course (i.e., young and older adulthood). It was also suggested that this epidemiological pattern may reflect key developmental challenges that threaten a person's identity and, therefore, his or her sense of meaning in life. The church and the people who worship there were thought to help restore the sense of meaning that is eroded in young and older adulthood. The estimates derived from the model in Figure 12.1 shed light on some, but not all, of this process. In particular, the data show that religion, and especially church-based social support, help bolster and maintain a sense of meaning in life among older people, and that those who have a sense of meaning are less likely to experience symptoms of depression.

But the analyses are incomplete because they do not evaluate several other key aspects of the wider theoretical perspective. First, data were not available for younger adults. It would be intriguing to see if similar findings emerge in this age-group. In fact, a more complete test would involve comparing and contrasting young, middle-aged, and older adults. If the theoretical rationale developed earlier is accurate, religious meaning should play a larger role in determining the risk for depression in the younger and older, but not the middle-aged group.

Second, identity crises were invoked to explain the bimodal distribution of depression across the life course. Unfortunately, data were not available to see if younger and older adults do, in fact, experience this type of difficulty. A high priority for the future should be to examine this issue empirically.

Finally, the data presented here are cross-sectional. This makes it difficult to determine the temporal ordering among the constructs depicted in Figure 12.1. As a result, the causal ordering in this model was based on theoretical considerations alone. It would, however, be easy to reverse the specified order by arguing that older people who are depressed subsequently find little meaning in life. In fact, a case could be made for suggesting that a lack of meaning is little more than a symptom of depression. But this seems unlikely because the size of the relationship between meaning and depression (Beta = -.141) suggests that there is far from a one-to-one correspondence between these constructs. Even so, these thorny issues of causality must be more rigorously examined with data that have been gathered at more than two points in time.

Discussion and Conclusions

The overarching theme of this volume deals with religion, family, and health, yet little has been said about the family in this chapter. The reason for this is relatively straightforward. Most research on religion and the family focuses on issues involving adolescent sexuality, marriage and fertility, child rearing, and gender roles (Sherkat and Ellison 1999). In addition, and more importantly, none of the studies in this literature evaluate religious meaning empirically. Nevertheless, several studies are important because they provide an important point of departure for exploring religious meaning and well-being within the family. The empirical analyses presented in this chapter suggest that church-based social support is an important source of religious meaning, but the composition of these social networks has not been specified clearly. Because people frequently worship in church with members of their family, the church-based support measures presented here may be picking up assistance that is provided specifically by family members. The fact that religion strengthens family ties across the life course is fairly well documented in the literature. For example, research by King (2003) indicates that religious fathers are more deeply involved with their children and they report having higher quality relationships with their offspring. Similarly, King (1998) points out in a second study that greater involvement in religion among grandparents tends to promote stronger ties with their children and grandchildren (see also Myers 2004). Other studies suggest that the strong family relationships arising from deeper religious involvement tend to persist over the life course (Pearce 1998). Even though these studies have made a number of valuable contributions to the literature, they typically do not link closer family ties with either physical or mental health. And as a result, the reasons for these potentially important health-related benefits remain largely unexamined. If the findings presented in this chapter are valid, then close family ties arising from greater involvement in religion may provide mental health benefits because they help family members develop a deeper sense of religious meaning in life.

If this observation is correct, then it calls for a new way of conceptualizing and measuring church-based social support systems. Because family members worship together, it is important to devise more focused measures of church-based support that distinguish between support from family members who worship together, and assistance provided by people at church who are not family members. By approaching the measurement of church-based support systems in this way, it will be possible to determine the extent to which meaning and mental health is promoted by people at church who are also family members.

Unfortunately, trying to evaluate the amount of help provided by family members at church may not be as simple as it seems. Family members clearly assist each other both inside and outside of church. Although it is easy to make this distinction in theory, it is hard to see how the two can be distinguished empirically. Instead, it is likely that a sense of meaning in life arises from interaction with family members both inside and outside religious institutions. For example, a sense of meaning is likely to arise when a husband and wife pray together, read the Bible, and discuss religious issues at home. But a sense of meaning in life is also likely to arise when husbands and wives engage in precisely the same activities at church. In fact, activities such as studying the Bible in church with family members are likely to carry over and influence Bible study at home. As a result, it is hard to believe that study participants would be able to accurately differentiate between support from the family in each of these settings. Viewed more generally, this is another way of saying that social life really forms a seamless whole, and a price is paid by trying to differentiate between support provided inside and outside the church. Moreover, it is likely that family members do not contribute equally to the task of meaning-making. Instead, one might argue that a spouse is more likely to perform this important function than a child; and the role played by specific family members is likely to change across the life course. So, for example, parents may be a major influence on meaning-making for young adults, but this is not likely to be true for older people because their own parents have usually died.

Although the task of studying support from family and friends in the church is daunting, probing more deeply into this issue promises to provide valuable new theoretical insights. For example, as people enter late life, they are likely to lose a number of close family members, including their parents as well as their spouse. Moreover, offspring may move away, making regular interaction difficult. This raises the possibility that people who are not related to elders may rise to fill this void in family-based assistance. Since older people attend church frequently, unrelated church members may perform these important functions. The key issue, however, is whether support from those who are not kin is just as effective as support that was provided previously by family members.

These more specific issues aside, it is important not to lose sight of the wider themes in this chapter. Mental health problems are fairly prevalent across the life course. There is now convincing evidence that religion may play a role in helping people either avoid them, or deal more effectively with them when they arise. What we need now are better explanations for how the potentially beneficial effects of religion may arise. Carefully evaluating basic patterns in epidemiological data on mental disorders represents an important point of departure for finding the kind of answers we need. Hopefully, this approach, and the inductive reasoning coupled with it, provides a useful template for those who wish to probe more deeply into the important role played by religion.

NOTE

Support for the work presented in this chapter was provided by a grant from the National Institute on Aging (R01 AG014749).

REFERENCES

American Psychiatric Association. 1994. *Diagnostic and Statistical Manual of Mental Disorders: DMS-IV*. Washington, DC: American Psychiatric Association.

Baumeister, R. F. 1991. *Meanings of Life*. New York: Guilford.

Bentler, P. M., and D. G. Bonett. 1980. "Significance Tests and Goodness of Fit in Analysis of Covariance Structures." *Psychological Bulletin* 88:588–606.

Bollen, K. A. 1989. *Structural Equations with Latent Variables*. New York: Wiley.

Clark, W. H. 1958. *The Psychology of Religion*. New York: Macmillan.

Fetzer Institute/National Institute on Aging Working Group. 1999. *Multidimensional Measurement of Religiousness/Spirituality for Use in Health Research*. Kalamazoo, MI: Fetzer Institute.

Gatz, M., and A. Fiske. 2003. "Aging Women and Depression." *Professional Psychology: Research and Practice* 34:3–9.

Idler, E. L. 1987. "Religious Involvement and the Health of the Elderly: Some Hypotheses and an Initial Test." *Social Forces* 66:226–238.

Kelloway, E. K. 1998. *Using LISREL for Structural Equation Modeling: A Researcher's Guide*. Thousand Oaks, CA: Sage.

Kendler, K. S., C. O. Gardner, and C. A. Prescott. 1997. "Religion, Psychopathology, and Substance Use and Abuse: A Multimeasure, Genetic-Epidemiologic Study." *American Journal of Psychiatry* 154:322–329.

Kessler, R. C., P. Berglund, O. Demler, R. Jin, K. R. Merikangas, and E. E. Walters. 2005. "Lifetime Prevalence and Age-of-Onset Distributions of DSM-IV Disorders in the National Comorbidity Survey Replication." *Archives of General Psychiatry* 62:593–602.

Kessler, R. C., C. Foster, P. S. Webster, and J. S. House. 1992. "The Relationship between Age and Depressive Symptoms in Two National Surveys." *Psychology and Aging* 7:171–185.

Kessler, R. C., K. A. McGonagle, S. Zhao, C. B. Nelson, M. Hughes, S. Eshleman, H. U. Wittchen, and K. S. Kendler. 1994. "Lifetime and 12-Month Prevalence of DSM-III-R Psychiatric Disorders in the United States." *Archives of General Psychiatry* 51:8–19.

King, V. 1998. "Perceived Self-Efficacy and Grandparenting." *Journal of Gerontology: Social Sciences* 53B:S249–S257.

———. 2003. "The Influence of Religion on Fathers' Relationships with their Children." *Journal of Marriage and the Family* 65:382–395.

Koenig, H. G., M. E. McCullough, and D. B. Larson. 2001. *Handbook of Religion and Health.* New York: Oxford University Press.

Krause, N. 1986. "Social Support, Stress, and Well-Being among Older Adults." *Journal of Gerontology* 41:512–519.

———. 2001. "Social Support." In *Handbook of Aging and the Social Sciences,* 5th ed., ed. R. H. Binstock and L. K. George, 272–294. San Diego, CA: Academic Press.

———. 2002a. "Church-Based Social Support and Health: Exploring Variations by Race." *Journal of Gerontology: Social Sciences* 57B:S332–S347.

———. 2002b. "Exploring Race Differences in a Comprehensive Battery of Church-Based Social Support Measures." *Review of Religious Research* 44:126–149.

———. 2003a. "A Preliminary Assessment of Race Differences in the Relationship between Religious Doubt and Depressive Symptoms." *Review of Religious Research* 45:93–115.

———. 2003b. "Religious Meaning and Subjective Well-Being in Late Life." *Journal of Gerontology: Social Sciences* 58B:S160–S170.

Krause, N., C. G. Ellison, and K. M. Wulff. 1998. "Church-Based Emotional Support, Negative Interaction, and Psychological Well-Being: Findings from a National Sample of Presbyterians." *Journal for the Scientific Study of Religion* 37:725–741.

Krause, N., and K. M. Wulff. 2005. "Church-Based Social Ties, a Sense of Belonging in a Congregation, and Physical Health Status." *International Journal for the Psychology of Religion* 15:73–93.

Manton, K. G., D. G. Blazer, and M. A. Woodbury. 1987. "Suicide in Middle Age and Later Life: Sex and Race Specific Life Table and Cohort Analyses." *Journal of Gerontology* 42:219–227.

Mirowsky, J., and C. E. Ross. 1992. "Age and Depression." *Journal of Health and Social Behavior* 33:187–205.

Myers, S. M. 2004. "Religion and Intergenerational Assistance: Distinct Differences by Adult Children's Gender and Parent's Marital Status." *Sociological Quarterly* 45:67–89.

Newmann, J. P. 1989. "Aging and Depression." *Psychology and Aging* 4:150–165.

Pargament, K. I. 1997. *The Psychology of Religious Coping: Theory, Research, and Practice.* New York: Guilford.

Pearce, L. D. 1998. "The Impact of Family Religious Life on the Quality of Mother–Child Relations." *American Sociological Review* 63:810–828.

Radloff, L. S. 1977. "The CES-D Scale: A Self-Report Depression Scale for Research in General Populations." *Applied Psychological Measurement* 1:385–401.

Reker, G. G. 1997. "Personal Meaning, Optimism, and Choice: Existential Predictors of Depression in Community and Institutionalized Elderly." *Gerontologist* 37:709–716.

Rock, D. A., C. A. Werts, R. L. Linn, and K. G. Jöreskog. 1977. "A Maximum Likelihood Solution to Errors in Variables and Errors in Equations Models." *Journal of Multivariate Behavioral Research* 12:187–197.

Rosow, I. 1976. "Status and Role Change through the Life Span." In *Handbook of Aging and the Social Sciences,* ed. R. H. Binstock and E. Shanas, 457–482. New York: Van Nostrand Reinhold.

Royce, J. [1911] 2001. *The Sources of Religious Insight.* New York: Catholic University of America Press.

Sherkat, D. E., and C. G. Ellison. 1999. "Recent Developments and Current Controversies in the Sociology of Religion." *Annual Review of Sociology* 25:363–394.

Simmel, G. [1898] 1997. "A Contribution to the Sociology of Religion." In *Essays on Religion: Georg Simmel,* ed. H. J. Helle and L. Neider, 101–120. New Haven, CT: Yale University Press.

Stryker, S. 2001. "Traditional Symbolic Interactionism, Role Theory, and Structural Symbolic Interactionism: The Road to Identity Theory." In *Handbook of Sociological Theory*, ed. Jonathan H. Turner, 211–231. New York: Plenum.

Thoits, P. A. 1991. "Merging Identity Theory and Stress Research." *Social Psychology Quarterly* 54:101–112.

Tucker, L. R., and C. Lewis. 1973. "A Reliability Coefficient for Maximum Likelihood Factor Analysis." *Psychometrika* 38:1–10.

Wethington, E., R. C. Kessler, and J. E. Pixley. 2004. "Turning Points in Adulthood." In *How Healthy Are We? A National Study of Well-Being in Midlife*, ed. O. G. Brim, C. D. Ryff, and R. C. Kessler, 586–613. Chicago: University of Chicago Press.

13

Religion and Physical Health among U.S. Adults

MARC A. MUSICK AND MEREDITH G. F. WORTHEN

Recent studies have found that religious activities such as prayer and church attendance predict better self-rated health (Musick 1996; Koenig et al. 1997), mental health (Idler 1987; Ellison 1995; Idler and Kasl 1997a), life satisfaction and happiness (Ellison, Gay, and Glass 1989; Levin, Chatters, and Taylor 1995), and functional health (Idler and Kasl 1992; Idler and Kasl 1997b). However, this literature faces numerous limitations, including but not limited to an overreliance on cross-sectional data and narrow measures of religious activity and belief that are often dissimilar between data sets. Thus, although the theory in this area strongly suggests a beneficial effect of religion, the evidence remains insufficient for making a definitive statement on the issue.

Yet, the most methodologically sound studies, those examining service attendance and prospective mortality, are suggestive of such a positive link. For example, Strawbridge and colleagues (1997) showed that individuals who attend religious services most frequently had a significantly lower adjusted mortality rate over a twenty-eight-year follow-up (Strawbridge et al. 1997). Research teams headed by Musick (Musick, House, and Williams 2004) and others (Hummer et al. 1999; Kraut et al. 2004; Hill et al. 2005; Oman et al. 2002; Strawbridge, Cohen, and Shema 2000; Strawbridge et al. 2001) have shown similar beneficial effects for service attendance using data collected from different populations and with varying mortality follow-up periods.

In sum, findings on service attendance and mortality appear to be robust and fairly consistent across studies, indicating a likely beneficial effect of that activity on mortality in the general population. However, it is not as clear whether religion has a similar effect on other aspects of physical health, such as functional impairment, disease incidence, and self-rated health. Though studies in this area do exist, they are not as methodologically sound nor as consistent in their findings.

Thus, the purpose of this chapter it to focus attention on the nonmortality measures of physical health status and their relationship to various aspects of religious practice and belief. We begin by reviewing the literature in this area with special attention paid to studies published over the past few years. Next, we propose a series of theoretical models that might help us better understand any associations we might find between religion and physical health. Following this discussion, we use data from the Americans' Changing Lives data set to examine the effects of religious service attendance and other religious factors on functional impairment and self-rated health. We conclude with a discussion of our findings in the context of the larger religion and health literature and make suggestions for future research.

Literature Review

Since 2000, there has been an imbalance in religion in health studies: reviews of religion and health are numerous while new research is somewhat limited. This section provides a brief overview of those reviews and some of the newer original research in the area.

Reviews of Religion and Health since 2000

Reviews on religion and clinical practice (Chatters 2000; Flannelly, Flannelly, and Weaver 2002; O'Hara 2002) are few when compared to religion and health reviews (George, Ellison, and Larson 2002; Koenig, McCullough, and Larson 2001; Larson, Larson, and Koenig 2002; Miller and Thoresen 2003; Oman and Thoresen 2002, 2003; Powell, Shahabi, and Thoresen 2003; Seeman, Dubin, and Seeman 2003; Seybold and Hill 2001; Townsend et al. 2002). Numerous reviews on conceptualization and methodology of religion and health have also appeared (Hill et al. 2000; Hill and Pargament 2003; Sloan and Bagiella 2002; Thoresen and Harris 2002; Weaver, Flannelly, and Stone 2002). Other reviews focus on the connection between religion and mortality (Luskin 2000; McCullough et al. 2000). In general, these reviews point to the potentially beneficial effects of religion for health but also underscore the need for more intensive study in the area.

Religion and Physical Health

Physical health is often determined using physical functioning, chronic illness, and physical impairment. Some research provides evidence that religion improves health status (Kelley-Moore and Ferraro 2001; Koenig 2001). Specifically, Levin (2003) found that high levels of religiosity can actually decrease illness levels and promote individuals to heal faster with the aid of spiritual interventions. A study (Haley, Koenig, and Bruchett 2001) examining religion and physical functioning showed a connection between the two: individuals who engaged in prayer one time per week were less likely to be physically impaired. Meisenhelder and Chandler (2001) observed frequency of prayer and health of Presbyterian pastors and found that increases in prayer caused increases in vitality, general health, and mental health in their sample. Olphen and colleagues (2003) revealed that African American individuals with high involvement in religious activities were more likely to be in better general health than those who were not involved in religious activities.

Studies using health measures such as chronic illness have displayed similar findings. For example, Benjamins and her colleagues (2003) found that religious persons have lower chronic illness levels than similar nonreligious persons. Eng and colleagues (2002) focused on coronary health in relation to religion and reported that religious persons were more likely to be in better coronary health than the nonreligious. Similarly, a study of hypertension and religion (Krause et al. 2002) revealed that persons who experienced the death of a loved one but who also believed in an afterlife were less likely to have increased hypertension than those who did not believe in an afterlife. Steffen and colleagues (2001) found that those who engage in religious coping are likely to have lower levels of blood pressure when compared to those who do not engage in religious coping. Examining data from a sample of older adults, Benjamins (2004) revealed that those who attended church were more likely to be in better physical health and suffer fewer functional limitations than those who did not attend church. Finally, research has also focused on religious attendance and specific illness markers as indicative of physical health levels (King, Mainous III, and Pearson 2002; King et al. 2001). Specifically, King and colleagues (2002) examined diabetes and levels of CRP and found that diabetic persons who do not attend religious services regularly are more likely to have elevated levels of CRP than those diabetic persons who do attend religious services regularly. King and colleagues (2001) focused on cardiovascular inflammatory markers and discovered that people attended religious services regularly are less likely to have elevated levels of certain inflammatory markers when compared to those persons who do not attend religious services regularly.

Religion and Self-Rated Health

The connection between religion and self-rated health has not been well documented since 2000. Yet, self-rated health is an important predictor of mortality and deserves more attention in this literature. In one study examining religion and self-rated health, Shahabi and colleagues (2002) revealed that persons who perceive themselves as religious and spiritual had better self-rated health levels than those who did not perceive themselves as religious or spiritual. Another study used self-rated health and religion (Tanyi and Werner 2003) in a convenience sample of women on hemodialysis. The authors discovered that high spirituality levels are associated with higher levels of self-rated health. Krause, Ellison, and Marcum (2002) examined self-rated health, gender, and church-based emotional support and found that men are more likely to benefit from church-based emotional support than women.

Religion and Health Risk Factors

Some studies since 2000 have focused on the area of religion and health risk factors for specific illnesses. Studies of risk in developing cancers, specifically of the colon and breast, revealed that increased religious involvement leads to less risk of these types of cancers. Risks in developing cancer of the colon have been connected to limited emotional support and little religious involvement (Kinney et al. 2003). In this study, African Americans were affected more by the absence of emotional support and religious involvement and had higher risks of colon cancer than whites without emotional support and religious involvement. In addition, the risk of developing cancer of the breast has been connected to those persons who were not raised in a specific religion (Wrensch et al. 2003). Doster and colleagues (2002) found that cardiovascular risk is significantly associated with the absence of spirituality.

Religion in Clinical Practice

A final outlet of research on religion and health deals with religion in clinical practice. Some studies have examined the possible positive outcomes of introducing religion into clinical practice (Koenig 2000a, 2000b; Mueller, Plevak, and Rummans 2001). Koenig (2000a) suggested that physicians should inquire about the religion of their ill patients in order to supply a sense of comfort to their patients. Other studies have aimed more at understanding the healing mechanisms involved in religious practices (Gunderson 2000). Like Koenig (2000a), Gunderson (2000) recommended that physicians should introduce the use of religion in medical practice through discussion of religion with patients. Astrow, Puchalski, and Sulmasy (2001) examined religion in clinical practice in social, ethical, and practical considerations. They also proposed that physicians should find out the religious or spiritual preferences of their patients to perhaps allow religion and health to be melded together today as they once were in the past. Thus, the clinical research seems to advocate religion and health care to be connected through physician inquiry of patient religion.

An Overview of Religion–Health Theoretical Frameworks

This section discusses various model specifications thought to underlie the association between religion and health. Previous research (e.g., Musick, House, and Williams 2004) has examined various forms of these theoretical frameworks, but to our knowledge, no formal attempt has been made to summarize different forms of the theoretical specifications of the relationship. We acknowledge that the models presented are not fully representative of all types of models

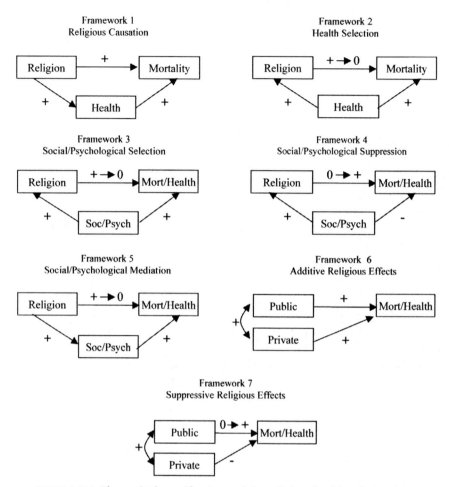

FIGURE 13.1 Theoretical specifications of the religion–health relationship.

in this area; however, those discussed tend to be the most commonly used in the literature and thus deserve the most attention.

Specifications of the Religion–Health Relationship with Focus Paid to Nonreligious Factors

FRAMEWORK 1: RELIGIOUS CAUSATION. As shown in Figure 13.1, the first model, religious causation, is the most simple. When using mortality or some other measure of physical health, such as self-rated health or functional impairment, this model predicts that religion will lead to both the mortality outcome and to any other measures of health that are included in the model. When predicting mortality (or self-rated health), the inclusion of health may reduce the effect of religion, but that will not necessarily be the case. Research that has shown a direct effect of religion on mortality net of other measures of health are examples of this model (e.g., Hummer et al. 1999; Musick, House, and Williams 2004).

FRAMEWORK 2: HEALTH SELECTION. This second model is the focus of much consternation and discussion in the religion and health literature. Some have argued that the underlying association between religion and health is due to the fact that poor health reduces levels of certain forms of religious practice, such as religious service attendance, and thus is responsible for the observed religion–health relationship. In terms of mortality, as shown in Figure 13.1, the model would predict that religion has beneficial effects on mortality, but once other measures of health are controlled, this effect is reduced or goes to zero. This model is complicated by the suggestion that while certain forms of religious practice, such as service attendance, should decline with poor health, other types, such as reading religious literature or watching religious programs, should increase. Nevertheless, the central idea behind this model is that health causes religion. Research meant to explore this issue has found mixed results. For example, Benjamins and her colleagues (2003) found that in a sample of older adults, higher numbers of chronic health conditions predicted lower levels of religious service attendance over a three-year follow-up period; however, those same conditions did not increase levels of religious media use, as had been predicted in the article. In other research on older adults, Idler and Kasl (1997b) similarly showed that higher levels of functional impairment are related to lower levels of service attendance over time. In short, although the evidence is not strong, it is possible that the health selection model has merit and should continue to be tested.

FRAMEWORK 3: SOCIAL/PSYCHOLOGICAL SELECTION. An abundance of research has shown that certain subpopulations in the United States, such as women, African Americans, and older adults, are more religious than their relevant counterparts (Levin, Taylor, and Chatters 1994). It might also be the case that certain psychological states, such as people seeking meaning or understanding in their lives, may also be drawn to religious practice. If these social and psychological factors do in fact lead to religion and also predict health, then it is possible that any association we observe between religion and health may be due to these underlying factors. The consequences of this model, as shown in Figure 13.1, are that any positive effects of religion on health decline or are reduced to zero once the factors are adjusted. It is important to note, however, that the factors must be positively related both to religion and health for this model to be appropriate.

FRAMEWORK 4: SOCIAL/PSYCHOLOGICAL SUPPRESSION. Like Framework 3, this model suggests that a set of factors predict both religion and health, but they do so in opposite ways. In Figure 13.1, we have diagrammed this relationship as one where the social/psychological variables lead to higher levels of religion but lower levels of health. This model is also appropriate when the third set of factors is negatively related to religion and positively related to health. As it happens, these factors appear to be much more common than those of use for the social/psychological selection model. For example, evidence shows that older adults and African Americans are both more religious and have worse health (Levin, Taylor, and Chatters 1994). Consequently, we should find that the effects of religion on health increase upon the inclusion of these factors, thus producing a suppression effect. This model is often implicitly tested in the literature on religion and health, though it is rarely discussed.

FRAMEWORK 5: SOCIAL/PSYCHOLOGICAL MEDIATION. In contrast to the prior two models, the mediation model has received a great deal of attention and discussion. Essentially, this model proposes that religion leads to certain social and psychological outcomes, such as self-esteem or social support, that in turn lead to better health. As noted by Musick and colleagues (2004), there are several sets of commonly tested factors within the mediation model: (a) avoidance of unhealthy behaviors; (b) availability of social support and the quality of social ties; (c) religious coping and meaning; (d) positive psychological states or activities, such as avoidance of anger and hostility; and (e) other prosocial activities that arise from religious activity, such as volunteering. This model predicts that once some or all of these factors are controlled, the effects of religious activity should decline or be reduced to zero. Musick and colleagues (2004) tested a variety of these mediators but found that the religious causation model still held even after their adjustment. This model is a valuable one and has produced a great deal of scholarship, though its utility appears mixed at this point. Nevertheless, researchers should continue testing the model but with an emphasis on better measurement of the mediators.

FRAMEWORK 6: ADDITIVE RELIGIOUS EFFECTS. As Idler and colleagues (2003) have noted, there are a variety of measures of religious activity including but not limited to service attendance, other forms of public religious activity, prayer, reading religious literature, and using religious media. Other measures of religion are religious affiliation, religious beliefs and the importance of religion, religious orientations (e.g., intrinsic versus extrinsic), and others. In short, to discuss the association between "religion" and health is overly simplistic given the complex ways that people live their religious lives. To better understand the association between religion and health, we must begin to think about the ways that different measures of religion predict health when they are simultaneously modeled. Framework 6 is the first, and most simple, way of considering the effects of a multifaceted measurement of religion on health. The framework suggests that although the different measures of religion are interrelated, they exert positive and independent effects on health. As its simplicity would suggest, this model receives little support in the literature. Rather, research finds that some religious variable, usually religious service attendance, carries the largest effect on health with the other measures of religion providing little to no independent effect on that outcome (e.g., Musick, House, and Williams 2004). Nevertheless, investigators should continue to test this model and avoid the temptation to combine measures of religion across types.

FRAMEWORK 7: SUPPRESSIVE RELIGIOUS EFFECTS. Another reason to avoid combining measures of religion is the suppressive religious effects model. This specification suggests that some aspects of religious activity or belief are actually detrimental to health even though they are positively associated with other forms of religious activity. The consequence of including these detrimental religious factors is a strengthening of the beneficial effects of other religious indicators on health. This model has been severely undertested yet shows great promise because it suggests that all previous studies that found little to no effect of religion on health, yet did not adjust for the *negative* aspects of religious activity and belief, may have been understating the beneficial effects of religion on health. Consequently, future research that intends to explore the effects of religion on health should seek out this third set of factors to better isolate the benefits of religion. Musick and his colleagues (2004) recently identified religious media use as one religious activity that might be detrimental for mortality outcomes. In an earlier article, Musick (2000) demonstrated that believing in the basic sinfulness of the world, a religious belief held by many conservative Protestants, was related to lower levels of well-being. In short, researchers have uncovered aspects of religious activity and belief that appear to be detrimental to health; investigators should continue searching for these damaging factors and attempt to include them in their own studies to better isolate the benefits of other religious activities and beliefs.

Plan of Analyses

The analyses in this chapter focus on two of the frameworks described earlier. First, we examine models that test the causal ordering of religious service attendance, other religious factors, and physical health status. Because we use survey data as the source of our analyses, we cannot test causation per se. However, we can construct structural equation models that are specified to test whether paths that flow from religion to health are more appropriate formulations than models that specify the path of causation flowing from health to religion. To conduct this analysis, we first use structural equation modeling to test the cross-sectional association between various measures of religion and three indicators of physical health. In the first model, we free the paths so that religion predicts health; in the second, we reverse the prediction so that health predicts religion. This cross-sectional analysis is limited in its utility; consequently, the second part of the structural equation modeling portion is to examine the interrelationship between religious service attendance and functional impairment over time. We include two models in this portion, one with a cross-lagged specification, and the other with a reciprocal effects specification. Based on both the cross-sectional and longitudinal analyses, we hope to address the question of the likely flow of causation between religion and health.

The second portion of the analyses focuses on self-rated health, an important but understudied indicator of physical health (Idler and Benyamini 1997). To study the effects of religion on self-rated health, we regress self-rated health measured in 1994 (T3) on self-rated health, religion, and other predictors measured in 1986 (T1). By using this longitudinal specification and ample measurement of physical health at the first wave, we can be fairly certain that any association we observe between religion and self-rated health is not due to underlying health status. However, it is possible that any effects we observe are due to sample selection across the waves of our study. As such, we include two forms of selection, mortality and being lost to follow-up, when estimating the effects of religion on self-rated health (e.g., Lantz et al. 2001).

Data, Measures, and Methods

Data

Data come from the Americans' Changing Lives study (House 1995). The data were collected by the Survey Research Center at the University of Michigan on a stratified, multistage, area probability sample of noninstitutionalized persons aged twenty-five and over and living in the coterminous United States. African Americans and persons aged sixty and over were over-sampled. Initial face-to-face interviews were completed by 3,617 respondents in 1986 (T1). Data were collected again in 1989 (T2) and 1994 (T3). The 1989 data collection procedure followed that of 1986, but the 1994 data was conducted via telephone. Table 13.1 reports levels of attrition due to mortality and other causes by the third wave. The data are weighted in all analyses, and cases with missing data were assigned mean values.

Measures

HEALTH AND ATTRITION OUTCOMES. Our measure of all-cause mortality was based on a 7.5-year follow-up period and was gathered through informant reports and through the National Death Index. For the purposes of this study, the mortality measure only takes into account whether or not a respondent died, and not the actual timing of death if it occurred. Respondents who did not respond to the third wave of data collection and who did not have a confirmed death were coded as cases lost to attrition. Some of these respondents could not be located after the first or second waves while others refused to respond to data collection attempts beyond the first wave.

The first measure of health status used as an outcome is functional impairment, measured at all three waves (from this point forward, the waves are referred to as T1, T2, and T3). This measure is an index coded such that the highest score (4) indicates confinement to a bed or chair all day and the lowest score (1) indicates no functional impairment. Second, we incorporate a standard measure of self-rated health (T1, T3). For the question, respondents were asked whether they would rate their health as (1) excellent, (2) very good, (3) good, (4) fair, or (5) poor. This measure was used to create a series of dichotomous variables representing very good, good, and fair/poor health, with excellent serving as the reference.

PREDICTORS. Our primary measure of religion is service attendance (T1, T2, T3), which ranges from never attend [1] to attend more than once a week [6]. Next, importance of beliefs (T1) indicates how important respondents' religious or spiritual beliefs are in their day-to-day lives. Responses range from not at all important [1] to very important [4]. Conservative Protestant (T1) is a dichotomous indicator that is coded [1], consistent with Roof and McKinney (1988), for respondents who report a religious affiliation with a conservative religious denomination and [0] otherwise. Our next measure, seek spiritual comfort, indicates how often respondents seek spiritual comfort and support when facing problems in their lives. Responses range from never [1] to almost always [5]. Finally, religious programs is an indicator of the frequency with which respondents watch or listen to religious programming and ranges from never [1] to more than once a week [6].

Several measures of chronic health conditions are used. The first, fatal conditions, is a sum of the number of the following potentially life-threatening conditions respondents experienced over the past year: lung disease, heart attack, diabetes, cancer, and stroke. The second, disabling conditions, is a sum of the following problematic conditions experienced by respondents in the previous year: arthritis, foot problems, broken bones, and urinary incontinence. Third, cognitive impairment, is a summed measure indicating the number of incorrect responses to a series of questions designed to test cognitive functioning. Examples of these indicators are knowing the current day and date, names of the current president and past president, and being able to count backward from twenty in intervals of three. The final indicator, sight problems, is a self-reported measure of how well respondents can see. Responses range from very well [1] to not at all well [5]. For all health measures, higher scores are indicative of worse functioning or health problems.

Body mass index (BMI) is measured by the ratio of weight for height, and higher scores indicate greater ratios; this is coded in categories. The first (overweight) of the two BMI-related variables is indicative of those who fall into the top 15 percent of the sex-specific BMI distribution, while the second (underweight) indicates those who are in the lowest 5 percent of the distribution. The reference category for both BMI variables is normal weight. Second, physical activity is a standardized mean index composed of three items: how often respondents (a) work in their garden or yard, (b) engage in active sports or exercise, and (c) take walks. Responses for each variable range from never [1] to often [4]. Third, hours of sleep is a self-reported measure of the hours of sleep respondents get in a typical night. Given the likelihood that hours of sleep will be most beneficial for those getting about eight hours a night, we also include a squared form of the variable to test for a nonlinear association. The sleep variable was centered before being squared to reduce the possibility of multicollinearity problems. Finally, smoking is a self-reported count of the average number of cigarettes respondents smoke in a day.

Our first measure of support, confidants, is a count of the number of people with whom respondents can share their feelings. Second, quality of social support is a standardized mean index composed of sets of items related to the receipt of social support and hassles from friends and family.

We include two psychosocial factors that should be related to religious factors, though only one is strictly religious in content. The first of these, fatalism ($\alpha = .77$), is a standardized mean index composed of four items: (a) "When bad things happen, we are not supposed to know why. We are just supposed to accept them"; (b) "People die when it is their time to die, and nothing can change that"; (c) "Everything that happens is a part of God's plan"; and (d) "If bad things happen, it is because they were meant to be." For each item, respondents were asked if they strongly disagreed [1], disagreed [2], agreed [3], or strongly agreed [4]. Our second measure, satisfaction from religion, is a dichotomous variable indicating whether respondents derive satisfaction from religion. More specifically, respondents were asked to name one or more of the most important sources of satisfaction in their lives. No categories were given; instead, respondents were allowed to cite sources in whatever manner they chose. Based on their answers, respondents were then coded into one of over forty-five categories of sources of satisfaction. Respondents were allowed to list up to five sources, though few respondents listed more than two. One source of support coded was church/religion, which included church activities, relationships with God, or private devotional activities. Our measure of satisfaction is a dichotomous variable coded [1] for all respondents who mentioned religion as a source of satisfaction and [0] otherwise.

Respondents were asked whether they had volunteered during the past year for each of five areas: (a) religious organizations, (b) educational organizations, (c) political groups or labor unions, (d) senior citizen groups, and (e) other organizations. Based on responses to these five questions we created three dichotomous variables. The first, volunteer-church only, is coded [1] for respondents who mentioned volunteering for religious organizations but no other organizations. The second, volunteer-church and secular, is coded [1] for respondents who mentioned volunteering for a religious organization and at least one secular area. The third variable, volunteer-secular only, is coded [1] for respondents who mentioned volunteering in at least one secular area but did not volunteer for a religious organization. For all variables, the reference category is composed of respondents who did not volunteer in the past year.

Our final set of predictors includes standard sociodemographic predictors. They include gender (female: 0 = male, 1 = female), race (black: 0 = nonblack, 1 = black), age (in years), marital status (married: 0 = not married, 1 = currently married), education (in years), and income of respondent and spouse (income: logged dollars).

Results

Table 13.1 presents means of all study variables along with their zero-order relationships to the religious variables. Religious activities, such as service attendance and seeking spiritual comfort, are fairly common. Likewise, respondents attach a great deal of importance to their religious beliefs: the mean for this item is between the two highest values on the response scale. About 29 percent of the sample reports an affiliation with a conservative Protestant denomination.

The correlation columns show that the religion variables are highly associated with one another. The most weakly related variable in this set is conservative Protestant; yet, even that variable is significantly associated with all the other religion variables. The religion variables are also associated with the psychosocial factors, both of which were included because of their theoretical ties to religion. Of the two psychosocial variables, the satisfaction from religion item shows more consistent associations with the religion variables, of which service attendance shows the strongest association.

At this zero-order level, various measures of religion appear to be associated with self-rated health at T1 and T3 and mortality. With the exception of religious programs, we find little association between religion and the other health measures, such as functional impairment and fatal conditions. Although only zero-order, these findings tend to support the idea that watching religious programming is in some way different than other types of religious activity. Of the remainder of the variables, service attendance shows the strongest and most consistent associations with health.

Our next step is to examine the association between various measures of religious activity and functional impairment. Recall that if we find an association, two frameworks could possibly inform this relationship: the health

TABLE 13.1

Descriptive Statistics and Zero-Order Associations of Study Variables[a]

	Mean			Correlations		
		Attend	Beliefs	Cons Prot	Comfort	Programs
Religious Factors						
Service attendance	3.31	—	—	—	—	—
Importance of beliefs	3.27	.53***	—	—	—	—
Cons. Protestant	.29	.18***	.22***	—	—	—
Seek spiritual comfort	3.25	.50***	.61***	.18***	—	—
Religious programs	2.92	.36***	.44***	.31***	.42***	—
Outcomes						
T1 Self-rated health	3.70	.08***	-.06**	-.05*	.01	-.10***
T3 Self-rated health	3.60	.06**	-.00	-.09***	-.00	-.11***
T3 Mortality	.10	-.08***	.05**	-.00	-.02	.10***
T3 Attrition	.15	-.02	.01	.01	-.00	.05**
T1 Functional impairment	1.27	-.05*	.01	-.01	.02	.12***
Sociodemographics						
Female	.53	-.04+	.11***	-.04+	.16***	-.07***
Black	.11	-.01	.04+	.21***	-.01	.17***
Age	47.11	.06**	.05**	-.08***	-.00	.13***
Married	.69	.10***	.01	.03+	-.02	-.05*
Education	12.37	.10***	-.14***	-.08***	.05*	-.19***
Income	9.98	.12***	-.13***	-.08***	.02	-.15***
Physical Health						
Fatal conditions	.18	-.04+	-.00	.00	.01	.09***
Disabling conditions	.84	-.01	.04*	-.00	.01	.10***
Cognitive impairment	.90	.04+	.05*	.04+	-.03	.07***
Sight problems	1.56	-.01	-.03	-.03	.02	.09***
Other Variables						
Overweight	.15	-.05*	.03	.03	-.03	.12***
Underweight	.05	-.04*	.01	.01	.03	-.03
Physical activity	-.00	.04*	-.04+	-.02	.05**	-.02

(continued)

Table 13.1. Descriptive Statistics and Zero-Order Associations of Study Variables[a] *(continued)*

	Mean	Attend	Beliefs	Cons Prot	Comfort	Programs
			Correlations			
Hours of sleep	7.34	-.02	.05*	.00	-.01	.03
Smoking	6.11	-.21***	.02	.05*	.02	.02
Confidants	2.32	.00	.03	-.03	.03	-.03
Quality of social support	-.00	.09***	.03	-.03	.03	-.03
Fatalism	-.00	.00	.17***	.03	.04+	.07***
Satisfaction from religion	.12	.25***	-.02	.10***	.09***	.14***
Volunteer-church only	.09	.25***	.00	.05*	.00	-.00
Volunteer-church and secular	.15	.30***	-.03	-.07**	.07***	.02
Volunteer-secular only	.21	-.14***	-.04+	-.01	.02	-.10***

a. All correlations with nonreligious variables are adjusted for the effects of the other religion variables. For example, correlations with service attendance are adjusted for importance of beliefs, seeking spiritual comfort, conservative Protestantism, and religious programs.

+ p < .10; * p < .05; ** p < .01; *** p < .001

selection framework, wherein poor health leads to low levels of religious activity, especially public religious activity, and the religious causation framework, which predicts that higher levels of religious activity lead to better health. We first test these dueling frameworks by estimating structural equation models specified to test the theoretical associations. In all of our structural equation models, we adjust for gender, race, age, and education, though those paths are not shown in the figures. The method of estimation is weighted least squares due to the inclusion of ordinal and dichotomous measures, variables that violate the assumptions of maximum likelihood estimation in this framework. We have been very conservative in freeing covariances between measurement errors and equation errors. However, we have done so where appropriate.

Figure 13.2 shows the health selection framework, that is, health leading to levels of religious practice. This model fits very well according to common measures of goodness of fit. The paths indicate that health is significantly related to service attendance such that those in worse health attend fewer services. However, health has no significant effect on any of the other religion variables. In Figure 13.3, we show the model specified as the religious causation framework. Here we see a pattern similar to that shown in Figure 13.2: higher levels of religious service attendance are associated with lower levels of poor health. Likewise, none of the other religious factors have an effect on poor health.

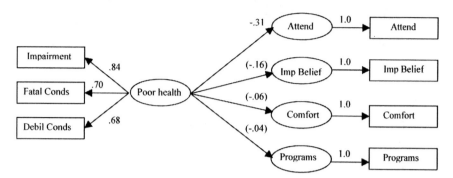

FIGURE 13.2 Health effects model (WLS structural equation modeling estimates; standardized solution).

Notes: Chi-square / d.f.: 98.86 / 21. Root mean square error of approximation: .032. Adjusted Goodness of fit index: .99. Coefficients in parentheses indicate a statistically insignificant path. The model is adjusted for gender, race, age, and education.

Two tentative conclusions can be reached based on these analyses. First, using cross-sectional data, it is difficult, if even possible, to determine the path of best causation between service attendance and physical health. Second, given the differential pattern of association between health and the religion factors, it is clearly not a good idea to combine religious factors when studying the association between religion and health. At least in these analyses, attendance is the primary factor linking religion and physical health; combining it with other measures of religion would likely dilute its effect or misrepresent the effects of other religion variables.

Given that both models fit the data equally well and that both show similar forms of the association between religion and physical health, it is still unclear if the health selection or religious causation model is most appropriate for these data. We also examined the interrelationships between service attendance and functional impairment over three waves of data. For these analyses, we have chosen to use only those two variables due to measurement issues for the other health and religion variables across the waves. To remain the most consistent across waves, the best scenario is to focus solely on those two variables. Note also that we adjust for gender, race, age, and education in these models, though those variables only predict attendance and functional impairment in the baseline wave. We have freed measurement error covariances between measures at successive waves but otherwise were very conservative in freeing measurement error parameters.

Figure 13.4 shows our first specification of the longitudinal religion–health model. This model incorporates cross-lagged effects; that is, variables in waves T2 and T3 are predicted by their own variables in the preceding waves along with the other variable in the preceding wave. In this fashion, we can estimate the effects of impairment and attendance on their opposites in successive waves

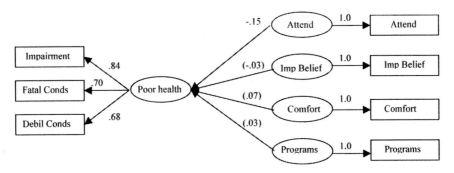

FIGURE 13.3 Religious effects model (WLS structural equation modeling estimates; standardized solution).

Notes: Chi-square / d.f.: 98.86 / 21. Root mean square error of approximation: .032. Adjusted Goodness of fit index: .99. Coefficients in parentheses indicate a statistically insignificant path. The model is adjusted for gender, race, age, and education.

controlling for the baseline effects of those variables. According to Figure 13.4, we find that T1 and T2 measures are very strong predictors of themselves in successive waves; however, the cross-lagged effects are much less strong. Indeed, of the four cross-lagged effects in the model, only the path between T1 service attendance and T2 functional impairment is significant. This path shows that higher levels of attendance at T1 are associated with lower levels of impairment at T2, net of levels of impairment at T1. Further, because T2 impairment is such a strong predictor of T3 impairment, the indirect effect of T1 attendance on T3 impairment is also negative and significant. In short, the religious causation framework receives support, but the health selection model does not.

In Figure 13.5, we test an alternative specification of the longitudinal model. In this case, we modeled the associations on the assumption that the associations we observe between religious activity and health are best modeled contemporaneously; that is, we allow impairment and attendance to predict one another in each of the second and third waves. To adequately test reciprocal effects models of this sort using structural equation models, one must include instrumental variables. In these models, we use the preceding equivalents of the impairment and attendance variables as the instrumental variables. Further, as was the case in the model in Figure 13.4, we adjust for the effects of gender, race, age and education at baseline, though the paths are not shown.

According to the reciprocal effects model, we find a story similar to that shown in the cross-lagged effects model. Here we find that attendance at T2 is a significant negative predictor of functional impairment at T2. In contrast, impairment has no effect on attendance at either T2 or T3. Also like the cross-lagged effects model, we find that T1 attendance has a significant negative association with T2 and T3 impairment through indirect effects. Not surprisingly, T2 attendance also has a significant negative indirect effect on T3 impairment.

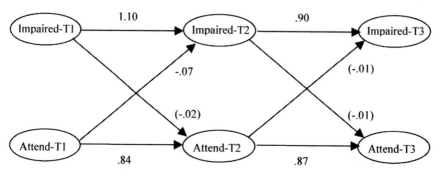

FIGURE 13.4 Cross-lagged effects model (WLS structural equation modeling estimates; standardized solution).

Notes: Chi-square / d.f.: 108.70 / 24. Root mean square error of approximation: .038. Adjusted Goodness of fit index: .99. Coefficients in parentheses indicate a statistically insignificant path. T1 impairment and attendance are adjusted for gender, race, age, and education.

Again, we find more support for the religious causation framework than the health selection framework.

The final step in our analyses was to examine the effects of all of the religion variables on an outcome composed of self-rated health, mortality, and attrition due to other factors. Results from these analyses are shown in Table 13.2. Because self-rated health is a five-category outcome variable, we employed multinomial logistic regression modeling for this outcome. Each column shown in Table 13.2 represents a single model broken down by different levels of the outcome. The first model serves as the baseline and only includes a control for baseline self-rated health. In this and all successive models, all predictors are measured at baseline.

According to this baseline model, religion has minor and somewhat inconsistent effects on the different levels of the outcome. For example, conservative Protestants are more likely to report lower levels of self-rated health and are somewhat more likely to have died or been lost by the third wave. In contrast, those who place more importance on their religious beliefs are less likely to report lower levels of self-rated health but are no more or less likely to have died or been lost over time. As Musick and colleagues (2004) and others (Hummer et al. 1999) have found, those who attend services more often are less likely to have died over the follow-up period. The other religion variable that stands out in this model is religious programs: those who watch or listen to more religious programs are more likely to report lower levels of self-rated health, are more likely to have died, and are more likely to have been lost over time.

However, as shown in Model 2, once sociodemographic variables such as race, age, education, and income are controlled, the effects of religious programs disappear. Table 13.1 helps in revealing the nature of this association: African Americans, older adults, and those with lower education are more likely to watch

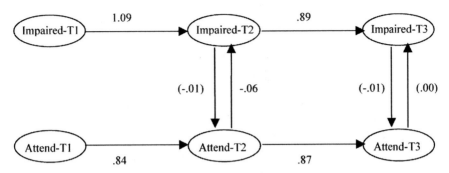

FIGURE 13.5 Reciprocal effects model (WLS structural equation modeling estimates; standardized solution).

Notes: Chi-square / d.f.: 109.47 / 24. Root mean square error of approximation: .038. Adjusted Goodness of fit index: .99. Coefficients in parentheses indicate a statistically insignificant path. T1 impairment and attendance are adjusted for gender, race, age, and education.

or listen to religious programs and are also more likely to have negative health outcomes. Consequently, it appears that for religious programming, the social selection framework is at work. Yet, the social selection framework does not appear to hold for any of the other religion factors given that their effects change little across the two models. Indeed, the only substantial change occurs for the effect of importance of beliefs on poor/fair self-rated health. In this instance, once the sociodemographics are controlled, the beneficial effect of importance of beliefs increases, indicating a suppression effect of the sociodemographic predictors. These findings again point to the need for researchers to be hesitant when deciding whether to combine different aspects of religious activity and belief into single predictors for use in regression models predicting health.

The remaining models in Table 13.2 test the health selection and social/ psychosocial frameworks. In Model 3, which contains adjustments for fatal conditions, disabling conditions, functional impairment, cognitive impairment, and sight problems, we find that even after all of these adjustments, the beneficial effects shown for religion in Model 2 remain. These findings alone cast serious doubt on the health selection framework; if that specification of the relationship were true in the population, we should have seen at least some movement in the effect of religion on the health and mortality outcomes. Yet, their inclusion did little to alter the effects of religion on T3 health, much less eradicate them altogether.

Model 4 tests the social and psychosocial mediation framework. Again, across all sets of mediators, the effects of religion remain consistent. We find that the beneficial effects of importance of belief on self-rated health and attrition remain, as does the effect of service attendance on mortality, though only marginally. Likewise, conservative Protestants remain more likely to report lower levels of self-rated health. In short, this model reveals that the social/

TABLE 13.2

**Estimated Net Effects of T1 Religious Practice, Belief, and
Affiliation on T3 Self-Rated Health, Mortality, and Attrition,
Stepped Models (Multinomial Logit Estimates)[a]**

	Model 1[b]	Model 2[c]	Model 3[d]	Model 4[e]
Poor/Fair SRH				
Service attendance	0.93	0.97	0.98	1.03
Importance of beliefs	0.82+	0.73**	0.75*	.73*
Cons. Protestant	1.70**	1.46*	1.46*	1.50*
Seek spiritual comfort	1.07	1.10	1.09	1.11
Religious programs	1.18***	1.09	1.07	1.08
Good SRH				
Service attendance	1.03	1.05	1.05	1.09+
Importance of beliefs	0.79*	0.75**	0.76**	.75**
Cons. Protestant	1.76***	1.72***	1.73***	1.79***
Seek spiritual comfort	1.00	1.00	1.00	1.02
Religious programs	1.08+	1.05	1.05	1.06
Very Good SRH				
Service attendance	1.03	1.04	1.04	1.06
Importance of beliefs	0.88	0.87	0.87	.86
Cons. Protestant	1.24	1.22	1.22	1.23
Seek spiritual comfort	1.01	1.02	1.03	1.04
Religious programs	1.07+	1.06	1.06	1.06
Mortality				
Service attendance	0.88*	0.86**	0.87*	.89+
Importance of beliefs	1.02	0.91	0.95	.89
Cons. Protestant	1.35+	1.45+	1.43+	1.28
Seek spiritual comfort	0.96	1.05	1.05	1.09
Religious programs	1.28***	1.05	1.03	1.04
Attrition				
Service attendance	0.95	1.01	1.01	1.05
Importance of beliefs	0.90	0.78*	0.79*	.74**
Cons. Protestant	1.49*	1.23	1.24	1.23

(continued)

Table 13.2. Estimated Net Effects of T1 Religious Practice, Belief, and Affiliation on T3 Self-Rated Health, Mortality, and Attrition, Stepped Models (Multinomial Logit Estimates)[a] *(continued)*

	Model 1[b]	Model 2[c]	Model 3[d]	Model 4[e]
Seek spiritual comfort	1.01	1.03	1.04	1.06
Religious programs	1.19***	1.06	1.05	1.07
x^2 / d.f.	1167 / 30	1886 / 60	2028 / 85	2133 / 115
R^2	.28	.41	.43	.45

a. Odds ratios are shown. The reference category for all outcomes is Excellent SRH.

b. Models 1–4 are adjusted for T1 self-rated health.

c. Models 2–4 are adjusted for T1 gender, age, race, education, income, and marital status.

d. Models 3–4 are adjusted for T1 functional impairment, fatal conditions, debilitating conditions, cognitive impairment, and sight problems.

e. Model 4 is adjusted for weight, physical activity, sleep patterns, smoking, confidants, quality of social support, fatalism, satisfaction from religion, and volunteering.

+ $p < .10$; * $p < .05$; ** $p < .01$; *** $p < .001$

psychosocial mediation model receives little support. Yet, it also indicates that the religion variables can and do have effects on health net of one another, a finding that is supportive of the additive religious effects framework.

Discussion and Conclusions

This chapter sought to specify and test a variety of frameworks related to the religion–health relationship using multiple waves of data, multiple health outcomes, multiple measures of religion, and a number of possible mediators. In general, we found support for some frameworks but not others. For example, using cross-sectional data, both the religious causation and health selection frameworks received some support; however, when using longitudinal data, only the religious causation framework was supported. The analyses yielded support for the social selection framework in that the effects of religious programming on health appear to be due to sociodemographic factors. We found little or no support for the other frameworks. For example, there was little evidence to suggest that the social and psychological mediators were in fact mediating any of the religious relationships with health. Of course, the religious relationships themselves were not strong, and without those relationships, there is little to mediate. On the other hand, a lack of relationships at the outset is useful for testing the social/psychological suppression framework, but that too found no support.

Where do we go from here? In general, based on our analyses and reading of the literature, we have several suggestions for future research in the field. First, more original research must examine the religion–health association using longitudinal data. Over the past few years, we have seen an abundance of reviews on the subject but little new empirical research. Moreover, although cross-sectional data can be useful, it does not help us disentangle issues of religious causation versus selection. To deal with these issues we must have longitudinal data that measures both religion and health at successive waves.

Second, given the multifaceted nature of religious experience, researchers must include multiple measures of religious activity and belief in their models. Unfortunately, to use these measures, they must be available, and too few large-scale epidemiological data sets are currently collecting high-quality data on religion. Yet, for the field to progress, researchers collecting data must make an effort to include measures of religion that go beyond simple indicators of frequency of prayer and service attendance. Idler and colleagues (2003) have created a multidimensional measurement strategy for religion that could easily be employed in large-scale epidemiological surveys. We should emphasize, however, that the literature shows the clearest links between religion and health are found using religious service attendance as a marker for religious activity. Given the lack of time and space available in large-scale surveys, it would not be surprising for researchers to be hesitant to include a dozen or more measures of religious activity and belief. However, given the strength of the findings for religious service attendance, at a minimum, any survey including measures of health and social factors should include a measure of service attendance.

Third, although little was said about it in this chapter, research should consider both the possible positive and negative effects of religion on health. Much of the research over the past few years has focused on the potential beneficial effects of religion on health but has ignored the potential negative ones. To consider the effects of religion in this way requires measurement of religious factors that could have these effects. As such, progress on this point must begin with more data collection on religious indicators.

Fourth, researchers should consider incorporating more biomarker data into their research. At present, most of the research on religion and physical health relies only on self-reported health problems or prospective mortality. This research may reveal that religion is related to these general health outcomes, but it cannot tell us what physiological mechanisms might underlie the associations. Again, more data on religion must be collected in the context of surveys that also contain biomarkers, such as blood pressure, cortisol levels, carotid artery atherosclerosis, and immune system functioning.

More could be said about what researchers should continue to pursue in the future. For example, more data and research is needed to examine religion and physical health outside of the United States and in non-Christian populations. Similarly, new ways of understanding religious and spiritual experience over the life course must be created and employed to understand the rich complexity of religious life. But, in general, to push the field forward researchers must continue to collect new data and think in new ways about how to measure and model religious experience.

REFERENCES

Astrow, A., C. M. Puchalski, and D. P. Sulmasy. 2001. "Religion, Spirituality, and Health Care: Social, Ethical, and Practical Considerations." *American Journal of Medicine* 110 (4): 283–287.

Benjamins, M. R. 2004. "Religion and Functional Health among the Elderly: Is There a Relationship and Is It Constant?" *Journal of Aging and Health* 16 (3): 355–374.

Benjamins, M. R., M. A. Musick, D. T. Gold, and L. K. George. 2003. "Age-Related Decline in Activity Level: The Relationship between Chronic Illness and Religious Activities." *Journal of Gerontology* 58B (6): S377–S385.

Chatters, L. M. 2000. "Religion and Health: Public Health Research and Practice." *Annual Review of Public Health* 21:335–367.

Doster, J. A., M. B. Harvey, C. A. Riley, A. J. Goven, and R. Moorefield. "Spirituality and Cardiovascular Risk." *Journal of Religion and Health* 41 (1): 69–79.

Ellison, C. G. 1995. "Race, Religious Involvement and Depressive Symptomatology in a Southeastern U.S. Community." *Social Science and Medicine* 40:1561–1572.

Ellison, C. G., D. A. Gay, and T. A. Glass. 1989. "Does Religious Commitment Contribute to Individual Life Satisfaction?" *Social Forces* 68:100–123.

Eng, P. M., E. B. Rimm, G. Fitzmaurice, and I. Kawachi. 2002. "Social Ties and Change in Social Ties in a Relation to Subsequent Total and Cause-Specific Mortality and Coronary Heart Disease Incidence in Men." *American Journal of Epidemiology* 155 (8): 700–709.

Flannelly, L. T., K. J. Flannelly, and A. J. Weaver. 2002. "Religious and Spiritual Variables in Three Major Oncology Nursing Journals: 1990–1999." *Oncology Nursing Forum* 29 (4): 649–685.

George, L. K., C. G. Ellison, and D. B. Larson. 2002. "Explaining the Relationships between Religious Involvement and Health." *Psychological Inquiry* 13 (2): 190–200.

Gunderson, G. R. 2000. "Backing onto Sacred Ground." *Public Health Reports* 115(2–3): 257–261.

Haley, K. C., H. G. Koenig, and B. M. Bruchett. 2001. "Relationship between Private Religious Activity and Physical Functioning in Older Adults." *Journal of Religion and Health* 40 (2): 305–312.

Hill, P., and K. Pargament. 2003. "Advances in the Conceptualization and Measurement of Religion and Spirituality." *American Psychologist* 58 (1): 64–74.

Hill, P., K. Pargament, R. Hood, Jr., M. McCullough, J. Swyers, D. Larson, and B. Zinnbauer. 2000. "Conceptualizing Religion and Spirituality: Points of Commonality, Points of Departure." *Journal for the Theory of Social Behavior* 30 (1): 51–77.

Hill, T. D., J. Angel, C. G. Ellison, and R. J. Angel. 2005. "Religious Attendance and Mortality: An 8-Year Follow-Up of Older Mexican Americans." *Journals of Gerontology Series B: Psychological Sciences and Social Sciences* 60B (2): S102–S109.

House, J. S. 1995. *Americans' Changing Lives: Waves I and II, 1986 and 1989.* Ann Arbor, MI: Interuniversity Consortium for Political and Social Research.

Hummer, R. A., R. G. Rogers, C. B. Nam, and C. G. Ellison. 1999. "Religious Involvement and U.S. Adult Mortality." *Demography* 36 (2): 273–285.

Idler, E. L. 1987. "Religious Involvement and the Health of the Elderly: Some Hypotheses and an Initial Test." *Social Forces* 66:226–238.

Idler, E. L., and Y. Benyamini. 1997. "Self-Rated Health and Mortality: A Review of Twenty-Seven Community Studies." *Journal of Health and Social Behavior* 38 (1): 21–37.

Idler, E. L., and S. V. Kasl. 1992. "Religion, Disability, Depression, and the Timing of Death." *American Journal of Sociology* 97:1052–1079.

———. 1997a. "Religion among Disabled and Nondisabled Persons I: Cross-Sectional Patterns in Health Practices, Social Activities, and Well-Being." *Journal of Gerontology: Social Sciences* 52:S294–S305.

———. 1997b. "Religion among Disabled and Nondisabled Persons II: Attendance at Religious Services as a Predictor of Course of Disability." *Journal of Gerontology: Social Sciences* 52:S306–S315.

Idler, E. L, M. A. Musick, C. G. Ellison, L. K. George, N. Krause, M. G. Ory, K. I. Pargament, L. H. Powell, L. G. Underwood, and D. R. Williams. 2003. "Measuring Multiple Dimensions of Religion and Spirituality for Health Research: Conceptual Background and Findings from the 1998 General Social Survey." *Research on Aging* 25 (4): 327–365.

Kelley-Moore, J. A., and K. F. Ferraro. 2001. "Functional Limitations and Religious Service Attendance in Later Life: Barrier and/or Benefit Mechanism?" *Journals of Gerontology Series B-Psychological Sciences and Social Sciences* 56 (6): S365–S373.

King, D. E., A. G. Mainous III, and W. S. Pearson. 2002. "C-Reactive Protein, Diabetes, and Attendance at Religious Services." *Diabetes Care* 25:1172–1176.

King, D. E., A. G. Mainous III, T. E. Steyer, and W. Pearson. 2001. "The Relationship between Attendance at Religious Services and Cardiovascular Inflammatory Markers." *International Journal of Psychiatry in Medicine* 31 (4): 415–425.

Kinney, A. Y., L. E. Bloor, W. N. Dudley, R. C. Millikan, E. Marshall, C. Martin, and R. S. Sandler. 2003. "Roles of Religious Involvement and Social Support in the Risk of Colon Cancer among Blacks and Whites." *American Journal of Epidemiology* 158 (11): 1097–1107.

Koenig, H. G. 2000a. "Religion, Spirituality, and Medicine: Application to Clinical Practice." *JAMA* 284 (13): 1708.

———. 2000b. "Should Doctors Prescribe Religion?" *Medical Economics* 77 (1): 145.

———. 2001. "Religion and Medicine IV: Religion, Physical Health, and Clinical Implications." *International Journal of Psychiatry in Medicine* 31 (3): 321–336.

Koenig, H. G., J. C. Hays, L. K. George, D. G. Blazer, D. Larson, and L. R. Landerman. 1997. "Modeling Cross-Sectional Relationships between Religion, Physical Health, Social Support, and Depressive Symptoms." *American Journal of Geriatric Psychiatry* 5:131–144.

Koenig, H. G., M. E. McCullough, and D. B. Larson. 2001. *Handbook of Religion and Health.* Oxford: Oxford University Press.

Krause, N., C. G. Ellison, J. P. Marcum. 2002. "The Effects of Church-Based Emotional Support on Health: Do They Vary by Gender?" *Sociology of Religion* 63 (1): 21–47.

Krause, N., J. Liang, B. A. Shaw, H. Sugisawa, H. Kim, and Y. Sugihara. 2002. "Religion, Death of a Loved One, and Hypertension among Older Adults in Japan." *Journals of Gerontology Series B-Psychological Sciences and Social Sciences* 57 (2): S96–S107.

Kraut, A., S. Melamed, D. Gofer, and P. Froom. 2004. "Association of Self-Reported Religiosity and Mortality in Industrial Employees: The CORDIS Study." *Social Science and Medicine* 58 (3): 595–603.

Lantz, P. M., J. W. Lynch, J. S. House, J. M. Lepkowksi, R. P. Mero, M. A. Musick, and D. R. Williams. 2001. "Socioeconomic Disparities in Health Change in a Longitudinal Study of U.S. Adults: The Role of Health-Risk Behaviors." *Social Science and Medicine* 53 (1): 29–40.

Larson, D., S. Larson, and H. G. Koenig. 2002. "Mortality and Religion/Spirituality: A Brief Review of Research." *Annals of Pharmacotherapy* 36 (6): 1090–1098.

Levin, J. S. 2003. "Spiritual Determinants of Health and Healing: An Epidemiologic Perspective on Salutogenic Mechanisms." *Alternative Therapies in Health and Medicine* 9 (6): 48–57.

Levin, J. S., L. M. Chatters, and R. J. Taylor. 1995. "Religious Effects on Health Status and Life Satisfaction among Black Americans." *Journal of Gerontology: Social Sciences* 50:S154–S163.

Levin, J. S., R. J. Taylor, and L. M. Chatters. 1994. "Race and Gender Differences in Religiosity among Older Adults: Findings from Four National Surveys." *Journal of Gerontology: Social Sciences* 49:S137–S145.

Luskin, F. 2000. "Review of the Effect of Spiritual and Religious Factors on Mortality and Morbidity with a Focus on Cardiovascular and Pulmonary Disease." *Journal of Cardiopulmonary Rehabilitation* 20:8–15.

McCullough, M. E., W. T. Hoyt, D. B. Larson, H. G. Koenig, and C. Thoresen. 2000. "Religious Involvement and Mortality: A Meta-Analytic Review." *Health Psychology* 19 (3): 211–222.

Meisenhelder, J. B., and E. N. Chandler. 2001. "Frequency of Prayer and Functional Health in Presbyterian Pastors." *Journal for the Scientific Study of Religion* 40 (2): 323–329.

Miller, W. R., and C. E. Thoresen. 2003. "Spirituality, Religion, and Health: an Emerging Research Field." *American Psychologist* 58 (1): 24–35.

Mueller, P. S., D. J. Plevak, and T. A. Rummans. 2001. "Religious Involvement, Spirituality, and Medicine: Implications for Clinical Practice." *Mayo Clinic Proceedings* 76 (12): 1225–1235.

Musick, M. A. 1996. "Religion and Subjective Health among Black and White Elders." *Journal of Health and Social Behavior* 37 (3): 221–237.

Musick, M. A. 2000. "Theodicy and Individual Well-Being among Black and White Americans." *Sociology of Religion* 61:267–287.

Musick, M. A., J. S. House, and D. R. Williams. 2004. "Attendance at Religious Services and Mortality in a National Sample." *Journal of Health and Social Behavior* 45 (2): 198–213.

O'Hara, D. P. 2002. "Is There a Role for Prayer and Spirituality in Health Care?" *Medical Clinics of North America* 86 (1): 33–46.

Olphen, J., A. Schulz, B. Isreal, L. Chatters, L. Klem, E. Parker, and D. Williams. 2003. "Religious Involvement, Social Support, and Health among African American Women on the East Side of Detroit." *Journal of General Internal Medicine* 18 (7): 549–557.

Oman, D., J. H. Kurata, W. J. Strawbridge, and R. D. Cohen. 2002. "Religious Attendance and Cause of Death over 31 Years." *International Journal of Psychiatry in Medicine* 32 (1): 69–89.

Oman, D., and C. E. Thoresen. 2002. "Does Religion Cause Health?: Differing Interpretations and Diverse Meanings." *Journal of Health Psychology* 7 (4): 365–380.

———. 2003. "Without Spirituality, Does Critical Health Psychology Risk Fostering Cultural Iatrogenesis?" *Journal of Health Psychology* 8 (2): 223–229.

Powell, L. H., L. Shahabi, and C. E. Thoresen. 2003. "Religion and Spirituality: Linkages to Physical Health." *American Psychologist* 58 (1): 36–52.

Roof, W. C., and W. McKinney. 1988. *American Mainline Religion: Its Changing Shape and Future.* New Brunswick, NJ: Rutgers University Press.

Seeman, T. E., L. F. Dubin, and M. Seeman. 2003. "Religiosity/Spirituality and Health." *American Psychologist* 58 (1): 53–63.

Seybold, K. S., and P. Hill. 2001. "The Role of Religion and Spirituality in Mental and Physical Health." *Current Directions in Psychological Science* 10 (1): 21–24.

Shahabi, L., L. H. Powell, M. A. Musick, K. I. Pargament, C. E. Thoresen, D. Williams, L. Underwood, and M. A. Ory. 2002. "Correlates of Self Perceptions of Spirituality in American Adults." *Annals of Behavioral Medicine* 24 (1): 59–68.

Sloan, R. P., and E. Bagiella. 2002. "Claims about Religious Involvement and Health Outcomes." *Annals of Behavioral Medicine* 24 (1): 14–21.

Steffen, P. R., A. L. Hinderliter, J. A. Blumethal, and A. Sherwood. 2001. "Religious Coping, Ethnicity, and Ambulatory Blood Pressure." *Psychosomatic Medicine* 63 (4): 523–530.

Strawbridge, W. J., R. D. Cohen, and S. J. Shema. 2000. "Comparative Strength of Association between Religious Attendance and Survival." *International Journal of Psychiatry in Medicine* 30 (4): 299–308.

Strawbridge, W. J., S. J. Shema, R. D. Cohen, and G. A. Kaplan. 1997. "Frequent Attendance at Religious Services and Morality over 28 Years." *American Journal of Public Health* 87:957–961.

———. 2001. "Religious Attendance Increases Survival by Improving and Maintaining Good Health Behaviors, Mental Health, and Social Relationships." *Annals of Behavioral Medicine* 23 (1): 68–74.

Tanyi, R. A., and J. S. Werner. 2003. "Adjustment, Spirituality, and Health in Women on Hemodialysis." *Clinical Nursing Research* 12 (3): 229–245.

Thoresen, C. E., and A. H. S. Harris. 2002. "Spirituality and Health: What's the Evidence and What's Needed?" *Annals of Behavioral Medicine* 24 (1): 3–13.

Townsend, M., V. Kladder, H. Ayele, and T. Mulligan. 2002. "Systematic Review of Clinical Trials Examining the Effects of Religion on Health." *Southern Medical Journal* 95 (12): 1429–1434.

Weaver, A. J., K. J. Flannelly, and H. W. Stone. 2002. "Research on Religion and Health: The Need for a Balanced and Constructive Critique." *Journal of Pastoral Care and Counseling* 56 (3): 213–219.

Wrensch M., T. Chew, G. Farren, J. Barlow, F. Belli, C. Clarke, C. A. Erdmann, M. Lee, M. Moghadassi, R. Peskin-Mentzer, C. P. Quesenberry, Jr., V. Souders-Mason, L. Spence, M. Suzuki, and M. Gould. 2003. "Risk Factors for Breast Cancer in a Population with High Incidence Rates." *Breast Cancer Research* 5 (4): R88–R102.

14

▶ ▶ ▶ ▶ ▶ ▶ ▶ ▶ ▶ ▶ ▶ ▶ ▶ ▶ ◀ ◀ ◀ ◀ ◀ ◀ ◀ ◀ ◀ ◀ ◀ ◀ ◀

Religious Involvement and Mortality Risk among Pre-Retirement Aged U.S. Adults

ROBERT A. HUMMER, MAUREEN R. BENJAMINS,
CHRISTOPHER G. ELLISON, AND RICHARD G. ROGERS

A growing body of research demonstrates that higher levels of religious involvement are associated with lower adult mortality risks in the United States. While a handful of clinically based and community-based studies have considered the impacts of private religiosity and strength and comfort received from religious faith on survival status among the elderly (e.g., Helm et al. 2000; Oxman, Freeman, and Manheimer 1995), the vast majority of sociological and epidemiological research in the area has focused on the most clearly social aspect of religious behavior: public religious attendance. The importance of public religious attendance for mortality risk was documented in a recent meta-analysis of the religion–mortality literature (McCullough et al. 2000), where nonattendance was found to be associated with about a 30 percent heightened mortality risk in follow-up studies compared to people who attend on a regular basis. Additionally, other recent in-depth reviews of the religion–health literature have confirmed this relationship (Hummer et al. 2004; Koenig, McCullough, and Larson 2001; Powell, Shahabi, and Thoresen 2003). Nevertheless, there remains substantial controversy in regard to this body of literature, in terms of both research approaches and the interpretation of findings (Bagiella, Hong, and Sloan 2005; Hummer 2005; Hummer et al. 2004; Koenig et al. 1999; Sloan, Bagiella, and Powell 1999; Sloan et al. 2000; Sloan and Bagiella 2002). Clearly, additional work is needed to sort out the overall strength of the association, the mechanisms by which it might work, and the subpopulations for whom religious involvement may or may not exert influences.

This chapter builds on our previous work by examining the relationship between religious attendance and mortality risk among pre-retirement individuals aged fifty-one to sixty-one at baseline in 1992 who are statistically followed for survival status for eight years. This age range is important because: (a) many studies of religious involvement and health and mortality outcomes to date have focused on the elderly, with much less attention on younger adults; (b) U.S. deaths in this age range are clearly premature and are largely preventable; and (c) one recent study in this area (Musick, House, and Williams 2004) found a much stronger relationship between religious attendance and mortality risk among younger adults (ages less than sixty) than among older adults (ages over sixty).

Here, we will not only estimate models of religious attendance and mortality risk among this cohort, but we also test whether or not the relationship between religious attendance and mortality risk differs among different sociodemographic subgroups of the population. We outline a brief rationale for examining such contingent relationships and test whether there are differences in the relationship between religious involvement and mortality risk across categories of sex, race, education, and marital status in this cohort.

Religious Involvement and Mortality Risk: Main Effects

Hummer and colleagues (1999) used nationally representative data on adults aged eighteen and above from the National Health Interview Survey linked to follow-up mortality data to show that lower levels of religious attendance at baseline were associated with higher adult mortality risk in a graded fashion over the ensuing eight years. While demographic factors, health selectivity, social ties, and health behavior were responsible for a portion of the differences, religious attendance maintained a moderately strong and graded relationship with mortality risk even in the most complete regression model. Nonattenders particularly stood out, exhibiting 50 percent higher risks of mortality in comparison to frequent (greater than one time per week) attenders, even after controls for a number of confounding and mediating factors. Musick and colleagues (2004) later included a wider range of religion variables than is typically the case in predicting adult mortality risks using a nationally representative sample of adults aged twenty-five and above from the Americans' Changing Lives Survey linked to follow-up mortality data. Their results showed that individuals who reported never attending at baseline also experienced a 50 percent increased risk of death in the six-year follow-up period compared to those who attended more frequently, net of the other religion variables and a range of demographic, socioeconomic, health, and behavioral characteristics. The Musick and colleagues study, however, did not exhibit a graded pattern by attendance: mortality risks were almost uniformly lower for those attending at least once a month compared to those who reported never attending.

A number of studies using data from specific communities have also shown a protective association between religious attendance and mortality risk. Strawbridge and colleagues (1997) found that frequent religious attendance was associated with lower all-cause mortality in a twenty-eight-year follow-up of respondents aged thirty to sixty-nine at baseline in the Alameda County

(California) Study data. In a later study using the same data, Oman and colleagues (2002) found lower mortality due to circulatory diseases, digestive diseases, respiratory diseases, and all causes combined for those attending services more frequently at baseline, even after adjusting for several individual chronic diseases and other health status indicators at baseline. Earlier, Oman and Reed (1998) used data from Marin County, California, to produce similar findings: individuals aged fifty-five and over who attended religious services at least weekly at baseline were 28 percent less likely to die over the follow-up period compared to individuals who reported never attending.

Koenig and colleagues (1999) analyzed a sample of community-dwelling individuals aged sixty-five and over in North Carolina and found a protective association between religious attendance and mortality risk; they found a 46 percent lower risk of death among those who attended once a week or more compared to those who attended less frequently. Using the same data, Dupre and colleagues (2006) also recently found strong protective effects of religious attendance for older adult mortality for both women and men and blacks and whites; such patterns were shown to have implications for the understanding of racial differences in mortality at older ages. Bagiella and colleagues (2005) recently pooled the North Carolina data with other three similar data sets from other areas of the United States and showed overall lower mortality among those who frequently attended religious services. This finding, however, was not uniform across the four sites. Indeed, somewhat weaker relationships between religious attendance and mortality risk were uncovered in two of the sites.

Religious Attendance and Mortality Risk: Subgroup Differences

Demographic Factors: Age, Gender, Race/Ethnicity, and Region

While most studies have consistently shown that religious attendance is associated with lower adult mortality risk, some (but clearly not all) of the evidence points toward stronger relative differences in the attendance–mortality relationship among younger adults, women, African Americans, and southerners. Rogers and colleagues (2000) revealed that while adults aged eighteen to sixty-four who never attended services had over twice the mortality risk compared to their frequently attending counterparts, adults sixty-five and over who never attended had just 24 percent higher mortality in the most complete model specified. Most recently, Musick and colleagues (2004) found that the overall relationship between religious attendance and mortality risk was much stronger among younger (less than age sixty) than older adults (sixty and over), a finding that was inconsistent with their hypothesis of stronger effects among the elderly. Indeed, a great deal of research in this area—particularly the community-based studies—have focused on the elderly in large part because of their overall higher levels of religious involvement compared to younger adults (Sherkat and Ellison 1999). But, two recent studies have now suggested that religious involvement may have its greatest impact, at least in a relative sense, among younger and middle-aged adults. While we cannot test age differences in the attendance–mortality relationship with the data set to be used here because it is limited to adults aged fifty-one to sixty-one at baseline, it is important to test this relationship among a subgroup of adults who are: (a) not the usual age-group of focus in the religion–mortality literature; and (b) clearly dying prematurely in the context of current U.S. life expectancy.

Indeed, behavioral factors such as cigarette smoking and physical activity have been shown to in part mediate the attendance–mortality relationship (Hummer et al. 1999; Musick, House, and Williams 2004; Strawbridge et al. 1997, 2001). That is, more actively religious individuals tend to exhibit more favorable distributions of healthy behavior, which are also related to lower adult mortality. Theoretical work has also discussed the strong potential for behavioral mechanisms—such as drug use, risky sexual behavior, and heavy alcohol use—in the attendance–mortality relationship (Ellison and Levin 1998; Jarvis and Northcott 1987). Such behavioral factors are clearly associated with lower premature adult mortality (Rogers, Hummer, and Nam 2000), but are not always available in the data sets used in this research. Thus, if religious involvement is indeed working through health behavior—at least in part—to affect adult mortality risks, there are important reasons to think that younger adults may be a population subgroup that may be prominently influenced.

Several previous community-level studies have found that the protective association between religious involvement and mortality risk is stronger among women than among men (Koenig et al. 1999; Strawbridge et al. 1997). This finding is consistent with extensive evidence that women are more religious by virtually any indicator than men (Sherkat and Ellison 1999). Researchers have speculated that the social activities and networks afforded by religious communities may be relatively more important for women than men (Strawbridge et al. 1997). Thus, the observed gender differences in the religion–mortality link may reflect the cumulative impact of women's greater religiosity and its impact on health over the life course. At the same time, however, other studies at the national level have found no statistical difference in the religion–mortality relationship between women and men (Hummer et al. 1999; Musick, House, and Williams 2004). In light of these discrepant findings, it is important to explore gender variations (if any) in the magnitude of the religion–mortality association among pre-retirement aged individuals.

Few studies have also examined race/ethnic differences in the religion–mortality relationship, although both Hummer and colleagues (1999) and Musick and colleagues (2004) reported no statistically significant differences in effects between blacks and whites in their nationally based studies. Hill and colleagues (2005) recently confirmed a strong relationship between religious attendance and lower mortality risk among older Hispanics living in the U.S. Southwest. Earlier, Ellison and colleagues (2000) examined African Americans and found very wide differences in follow-up mortality risk by religious attendance. Compared to African American adults who reported attending services more than once a week, those who reported never attending were more than twice as likely to die during the eight-year follow-up period, even net of a range of controls. The strong association between nonattendance and mortality risk was robust across all subgroups of this population, including both for women and men, although the strength of the relationship was found to be somewhat weaker among older (fifty-five and older) individuals. These results were generally consistent with an earlier, but smaller, study of religion and mortality among African Americans elders (Bryant and Rakowski 1992).

As with the female–male comparison, much research demonstrates that African Americans are more religious than whites in the United States. Not only are levels of attendance and church membership higher among African Americans (Taylor and Chatters 1991; Taylor 1993), but the institutional centrality of the Black Church is widely recognized (Lincoln and Mamiya 1990). Thus, it follows that those individuals who are not participating in this clearly important social institution may be at higher risk for mortality than their more religious counterparts. Nevertheless, such differential effects of religious involvement on mortality risk by race have not played out thus far among the studies that have tested this assertion, although it must be recognized that sample size limitations often presents an important obstacle.

Only one study to date has examined regional differences in the religion-mortality relationship. Among African Americans, the religion–mortality relationship was shown to be somewhat stronger among Southerners than among non-Southerners. Levels of religious attendance and membership have historically been, and continue to be, higher in the U.S. South than in other regions of the country (Sherkat and Ellison 1999). If there are distinct norms and benefits that accrue to individuals who are actively involved in religious communities, and this is the case especially in the South (not only in terms of level of religious involvement, but also in terms of the importance of religious involvement), then we might expect to find a stronger mortality difference between non-attenders and attenders in that region of the country.

Social Factors: Marital Status and Education

Even less work has examined the relationship between religious involvement and mortality risk among specific marital status and education subgroups of the U.S. population. At the same time, it is well recognized that there are substantial adult mortality differences by both marital status (Lillard and Waite 1995; Rogers 1995) and educational level (Elo and Preston 1996; Lauderdale 2001). Waite and Lehrer (2003) have drawn an important parallel between the literatures on religion–health and marriage–health, noting a number of generally positive associations between both religious involvement and marriage with health/mortality outcomes, and similar mechanisms by which they may work to influence the respective outcomes. Religious involvement in the United States is also strongly associated with marital status and stability (Booth et al. 1995; Call and Heaton 1997; Stolzenberg, Blair-Loy, and Waite 1995); that is, religious adults are more likely to be married and stay married than nonreligious adults. Further, Waite and Lehrer also point out that we know very little about the intersection of religion and marriage and how involvement and/or noninvolvement in both might be related to health outcomes. While there are no empirical antecedents to rely on in the religion–mortality literature, one possibility is that individuals who are neither married nor involved in a religious community may be at the highest risk of death because they are especially likely to exhibit poor health behavior and lack social integration and support—the common mechanisms that have they identified that link both religion and marriage to health and mortality outcomes (Waite and Lehrer 2003).

Unlike the relationship between marriage and religion, educational variations in religious involvement are less clear. Some studies have shown a rather weak but positive association between education and indicators of organizational religious participation (Roof and McKinney 1987; Ellison and Sherkat 1995). Others report a curvilinear association between education and attendance, with the lowest attendance found among the lowest and highest education groups. Education may also be inversely related to other dimensions of religious involvement, such as the strength of religious identity or salience, the frequency of private religious practices, and the endorsement of conservative theological tenets (Johnson 1997; Roof and McKinney 1987; Taylor and Chatters 1991). Thus, it may be that the meaning of religious involvement is generally less important in the lives of highly educated individuals in the United States and may have less of a health impact among individuals in such a structural position. At the same time, it may also be expected that those individuals who are both at low levels of education and who are not religiously involved may be at the highest risk of death in much the same way that this is expected among those individuals who are both unmarried and not religiously involved. That is, it may be precisely among more vulnerable (i.e., low educated, unmarried) individuals that religious involvement may have its potentially most important influences on mortality risk.

Data, Measures, and Methods

Data come from the first wave of the Health and Retirement Study (HRS). In addition, we include data from a follow-up file that links respondent data to the National Death Index (NDI) for the years 1992 to 1995 and from the HRS Tracker File that provides information on deaths occurring between 1996 and 2000 (for a thorough description of the data, see Health and Retirement Study Codebook 2004). The deaths reported in the HRS Tracker File for 1996 to 2000 are identified through spousal or other family member reports.

The HRS is a nationally representative panel study of noninstitutionalized adults designed to cover a broad range of issues pertinent to the United States' middle-aged population. The survey investigates the physical health, economic characteristics, and more of pre-retirement age adults (aged fifty-one to sixty-one in 1992) and their spouses. The multistage probability sampling design over-samples both blacks and Hispanics. In total, 12,654 interviews were successfully collected from 7,705 households during wave 1 of the HRS (Heeringa and Connor 1995). We include only those individuals born between 1931 and 1941, thus excluding the spouses of surveyed individuals outside of that age range. After exclusions, the analysis sample includes 9,423 cases; 834 of these individuals were identified as dying during the follow-up period.

Survival status, the outcome variable, is measured dichotomously to indicate whether or not the individual respondent survived or died during the follow-up. We also take into account the length of survival until death, or length of follow-up through the year 2000, with a duration variable (in years) that allows us to specify a proportional hazard model of mortality risk. The main predictor variable is religious attendance, which measures the respondent's frequency of attending religious services in the last year. As in our previous work, we consider this measure to reflect an individual's general level of involvement in a religious community and not necessarily a fully accurate accounting of their actual religious attendance at services (Ellison et al. 2000; Hummer et al. 1999). The self-reported attendance frequencies range from never to more than once a week and are categorized into three levels: no attendance, a low-to-moderate level of attendance (once or twice a year to two to three times a month), and a high level of attendance (once a week or more than once a week), which serves as the reference group in the regression analysis. We control for the religious denominational affiliation of individuals in this study, with mainline Protestants (the reference category) contrasted with Evangelical Protestants, Catholics, persons affiliated with other denominations, and unaffiliated persons. Because of substantial heterogeneity within these groupings and the limited number of deaths in the data set characterizing more refined denominational categories, mortality comparisons across these groups should be made with much caution.

Demographic control variables include gender (female is the reference category), race/ethnicity (a categorical variable indicating if the respondent is non-Hispanic white [reference category], non-Hispanic black, or other), region (Southerners, Westerners, and Northeast/Midwest [reference category]), and age at the time of the interview (a continuous variable measured in years, ranging from fifty-one to sixty-one). We include marital status as a categorical variable indicating if the respondent is married (reference), never married, widowed, or divorced/separated. Further, we measure education as a categorical variable indicating the number of years of school completed. Education is coded as high (thirteen years or more, which is the reference category), medium (twelve years), and low (less than twelve years).

Health status variables are also included to control for confounding in the relationship between attendance and mortality risk. Our first measure of health status is a scale that sums the reported activity limitations for each respondent. Limitations are determined by sixteen questions regarding activities of daily life (ADL) and higher scores represent a greater number of functional limitations. This scale includes activities that are highly relevant to religious attendance, such as the ability to walk one block, sit for two hours, and get up from a chair after sitting for long periods. Self-reported health at baseline is also controlled. This is a well-known five-category measure ranging from excellent to poor that has been strongly linked to mortality risk in many follow-up studies (e.g., Benjamins et al. 2004; Idler and Benyamini 1997). These two health status measures, which are both strongly related to subsequent mortality risks in our following models, should greatly diminish concerns over health selectivity in the attendance–mortality relationship. If anything, "overcontrolling" for baseline health may be an issue. Indeed, if religious involvement influences health across the life course, as some evidence points to (Koenig, McCullough, and Larson 2001), then controlling for baseline health indicators in studies of religion and mortality risk will yield conservative estimates of the religious attendance variable included in the models (Hummer et al. 2004).

Finally, we include health behavior measures—alcohol use, smoking, and exercise—in our models to help tap the mechanisms by which religious attendance might be associated with mortality risk. To assess alcohol use, we create categorical variables for respondents who typically drink less than two drinks a day, and more than three drinks per day, with nondrinkers serving as the reference category. For smoking, we include categorical variables for both current smokers and former smokers, with never smokers as the reference category. Physical exercise is measured by categorical variables comparing those who report no exercise or low levels of exercise (less than two times a week) to the reference group (two to three times a week or more).

To estimate risk of death over the follow-up period, we create a duration variable indicating length of follow-up, which ranges from zero to eight years, with those individuals surviving the entire period censored after eight follow-up years in 2000. We specify a series of proportional hazard regression models to estimate the association between religious attendance and mortality risk over the follow-up period (Cox 1972). We begin with a basic model of religious attendance and mortality risk, controlled only for demographic factors, and then progressively include the social factors (e.g., marital status and education), health selectivity controls, and behavioral mediators (Mirowsky 1999). We add interaction effects to test if the association between religious involvement and mortality risk varies by gender, race, region, marital status, and educational level in the context of the most complete regression model specified. Because the HRS is a multistage area probability design, we use STATA to correctly estimate variances by differentially weighting strata across sample clusters. Individual-level weights are included to adjust for unequal selection probabilities and differences in response rates, as well as for other sampling techniques (Heeringa and Connor 1995).

Results

Descriptive Results

Table 14.1 provides weighted descriptive statistics for the complete set of variables for both the sample as a whole and separately by religious attendance. While 35.3 percent of individuals reported attending services once a week or more, 28.1 percent reported never attending and 36.7 percent reporting attending less than once per week. Eight percent of the original sample died during the follow-up, with the highest mortality (11.1 percent) occurring among those persons who reported that they never attended religious services at baseline, and the lowest (6 percent) among those who reported that they attended one or more times a week at baseline. Along denominational lines, the two Protestant groups together comprise over 60 percent of the sample, with Catholics accounting for 28 percent. Nearly 6 percent of individuals claimed no denominational affiliation, almost all of whom report never attending services.

Looking at the other demographic and social characteristics, Table 14.1 shows that women, who make up 51.8 percent of the overall sample, comprise over 60 percent of the frequent attenders and just 42.3 percent of the never attenders. Similarly, blacks comprise 9.8 percent of the overall sample, but 12.2 percent of the frequent attenders and just 6.4 percent of the never attenders. More highly educated and married individuals are also somewhat more likely to be overrepresented among frequent attenders and are somewhat less represented among the never attenders, but the differences are not substantial. For example, individuals without a high school degree comprise 24.9 percent of the overall sample, but account for just 22.3 percent of frequent attenders while comprising 29.2 percent of the nonattenders.

The health and behavior variables also vary by religious attendance in predictable ways. For example, persons who rate their health as poor account for 7.4 percent of the overall sample, but 10.6 percent of those who report never attending services. Current smoking, heavy drinking, and no exercise are all much more highly concentrated among nonattenders than they are among frequent attenders. To understand how these demographic, social, health, and behavioral characteristics influence differences in mortality across levels of religious involvement, we now turn to the multivariate regression results.

Multivariate Results: Main Effects of Religious Attendance

Table 14.2 presents results from five multivariate Cox proportional hazard models that examine the association between the main effects of religious

TABLE 14.1

Weighted Percentage Distribution of Covariates for Full Sample and by Frequency of Religious Attendance, U.S. Adults Aged 51–61 in 1992

	All	*Religious Service Attendance* Once or more per week (35.3%)	Less than once per week (36.7%)	Never Attends (28.1%)
	%	%	%	%
% Died During Follow-Up	8.0	6.0	7.7	11.1
Age, in years (mean)	55.7	56.1	55.6	55.6
Sex				
Male	48.2	39.3	49.5	57.7
Female	51.8	60.7	50.5	42.3
Race/Ethnicity				
NH Black	9.8	12.2	10.0	6.4
NH White	81.7	77.3	81.0	88.9
Other	8.5	10.5	8.9	4.6
Region				
West	17.7	15.7	18.8	25.8
South	34.5	36.4	34.0	32.6
Northeast or Midwest	47.8	47.9	47.2	48.6
Religious Denomination				
Evangelical Protestant	19.8	21.2	19.6	18.2
Mainline Protestant	41.1	37.3	44.5	41.3
Catholic	28.0	36.6	28.3	16.7
No Denomination	5.5	0.0	0.1	19.3
Other	5.7	4.9	7.5	4.5
Marital Status				
Married	75.3	77.7	73.5	74.5
Divorced or Separated	14.4	11.2	15.8	16.4
Widowed	6.5	7.2	7.1	4.7
Never Married	3.9	4.0	3.6	4.3

(continued)

Table 14.1. Weighted Percentage Distribution of Covariates for Full Sample and by Frequency of Religious Attendance, U.S. Adults Aged 51–61 in 1992 *(continued)*

		Religious Service Attendance		
	All	Once or more per week (35.3%)	Less than once per week (36.7%)	Never Attends (28.1%)
	%	%	%	%
Education				
No High School Degree	24.9	22.3	24.0	29.2
High School Degree	36.8	39.4	34.7	36.3
Some College or More	38.4	38.4	41.3	34.5
ADL Score, mean	3.7	3.5	3.6	3.8
Self-Rated Health				
Poor	7.4	6.1	6.3	10.6
Fair	12.9	11.8	12.4	14.7
Good	26.7	26.3	28.0	22.5
Very Good	29.4	30.7	29.4	27.9
Excellent	23.6	25.1	24.0	21.3
Smoking Behavior				
Never Smoker	35.9	47.7	32.5	25.4
Current Smoker	26.8	15.4	29.7	37.2
Former Smoker	37.4	36.9	37.8	37.4
Drinking Behavior				
Nondrinker	36.4	48.1	29.1	31.2
Light (< 2 drinks/day)	58.2	50.4	65.7	58.4
Heavy (≥ 3 drinks/day)	5.3	1.5	5.2	10.4
Exercise				
No Exercise	9.5	7.9	7.7	13.7
Light (< 3 times/week)	37.5	37.0	39.7	35.3
Heavy (≥ 3 times/week)	53.0	55.1	52.6	51.0
Unweighted N	9,423	3,484	3,458	2,481

Source: Derived from the Health and Retirement Study (2004).

attendance and adult mortality risk. Model 1 shows that, net of basic demographic characteristics and religious denomination, middle-aged adults who never attend religious services experienced a significantly twofold higher risk of death over the follow-up period compared to their frequently attending counterparts. Individuals with infrequent religious attendance exhibit 33 percent higher mortality in comparison to frequent attenders. These patterns are consistent with previous literature that has found a graded association between religious attendance and adult mortality risk in the United States (Hummer et al. 1999).

Controlling for social factors in Model 2 results in an attenuation of the religious attendance association with mortality risk. Those who report never attending services at baseline now have a 90 percent higher risk of mortality than their frequently attending counterparts, while those who attend less than once a week have a 26 percent higher risk of mortality. These reductions suggests that there is some overlap between religious attendance, marital status, and education with mortality risk; however, all three show significant relationships with mortality risk in the expected direction net of one another. Model 3, which additionally controls for the scale of activities of daily living, results in a slightly weaker association between religious attendance and mortality risk. That is, never attending individuals now exhibit a 78 percent greater risk of mortality compared to frequently attending individuals, and the difference between infrequent and frequent attenders is now 22 percent, but still statistically significant. The addition of self-reported health in Model 4 further reduces the strength of the association between those who never attend and those who frequently attend. Nonattenders now have 64 percent higher risks of mortality than frequent attenders. Nevertheless, even net of these strong baseline health, social, and demographic controls, religious attendance still exhibits a graded and significant relationship with mortality risk, with nonattenders clearly standing out with the highest risk.

Notably, the activity limitation and self-reported health variables exhibit very strong relationships with mortality risk, as might be expected, and they add significant strength to the overall model as exhibited by the change in the log-likelihood at the bottom of the table. The reduction in the religious attendance and mortality risk association, once controlled for baseline health status, has been interpreted as the confounding influence of health (Hummer et al. 1999; Musick, House, and Williams 2004; Sloan and Bagiella 2002). Note, though, a second possibility as mentioned earlier: that controlling for baseline health status helps to eliminate any life course influences of religious involvement on health status up to the time of the survey. Thus, it is possible that the inclusion of such health variables "overcontrols" for the potential influence of health selection on the attendance–mortality relationship; it is impossible to fully sort out with these data. Thus, Model 4 of Table 14.2 is most likely a conservative estimate of the relationship between religious attendance and mortality risk among this cohort.

Model 5 demonstrates that the relationship between religious attendance and mortality risks is reduced again after the addition of health behaviors. Compared to frequently attending individuals, never attending individuals experience 34 percent higher mortality over the follow-up period, net of the complete set of demographic, social, health, and behavioral factors. The reduction of the nonattendance hazard ratio with the inclusion of health behaviors is consistent with conceptual frameworks and other recent findings that suggest that at least a portion of the religious attendance influence on mortality works through health behavior mechanisms (Ellison 1994; Ellison and Levin 1998; Jarvis and Northcott 1987; Levin 1994; Musick, House, and Williams 2004; Strawbridge et al. 1997). Notably, the difference between infrequent attenders and frequent attenders is no longer statistically significant in the context of this model, further suggesting that behavioral differences between religious attendance groups are clearly important in differentiating the baseline mortality risk across religious attendance categories. The next section of the chapter builds on the main associations demonstrated here, by looking specifically at the relationship between attendance and mortality risk across categories of gender, race, region, marital status, and education.

Multivariate Results: Interaction Effects

We also modeled the relationship between religious attendance and mortality risk across categories of gender, race, region, marital status, and education using multiplicative interaction terms. These models address the question of whether the association between religious attendance and mortality risk is stronger among one or more of these subpopulations as some, but clearly not all, recent work in the area has suggested. The findings we uncovered are simple: in no case did the relationship between religious attendance and mortality risk vary across levels of these demographic and social variables. That is, none of the multiplicative interaction terms for attendance by gender, attendance by race (black versus white), attendance by region, attendance by educational level, or attendance by marital status were statistically significant, nor did their addition improve the overall fit of Model 5 in Table 14.2. Only the religious attendance by marital status interaction terms, which hinted at a stronger association between attendance and mortality risk among unmarried persons compared to married persons, showed any indication of a differential pattern; again, though, none of the individual interaction effect coefficients achieved statistical significance at the .05 level. These interaction terms were further tested in the context of Model 4 in Table 14.2, which does not include the behavioral factors, and identical findings emerged. We are left with clear main effects of religious attendance on mortality risk that do not vary across demographic and social subgroups for this age-group of U.S. adults.

TABLE 14.2

Hazards Ratios Estimating the Relationship between Religious Attendance and Covariates on Subsequent Mortality Risk, U.S. Adults Aged 51–61 at Baseline: Main Effects Only

	Mortality Risk				
	Model 1 (H.R.)	Model 2 (H.R.)	Model 3 (H.R.)	Model 4 (H.R.)	Model 5 (H.R.)
Religious Attendance (> once per week)[a]					
Infrequent (< once per week)	1.33**	1.26**	1.22*	1.21*	1.07
Never attends	2.08***	1.90***	1.78***	1.64***	1.34**
Age, in years	1.10***	1.10***	1.09***	1.08***	1.08***
Sex (Female)					
Male	1.59***	1.82***	2.07***	1.92***	1.76***
Race/Ethnicity (NH White)					
NH Black	1.72***	1.44***	1.35***	1.22**	1.22*
Other	1.08	0.93	0.87	0.78	0.82
Region (Northeast or Midwest)					
West	0.88	0.91	0.90	0.91	0.91
South	1.07	1.06	1.04	0.99	0.96
Religious Denomination (Mainline Protestant)					
Evangelical Protestant	1.34***	1.24*	1.19	1.16	1.13
Catholic	1.15	1.15	1.13	1.14	1.09
No Denomination	0.84	0.84	0.89	0.87	0.88
Other	1.27	1.31	1.37	1.36	1.39
Marital Status (Married)					
Divorced or Separated		1.66***	1.44***	1.32**	1.18
Widowed		1.79***	1.65***	1.54***	1.42**
Never Married		0.92	0.85	0.81	0.85
Education (Some College or More)					
No High School Degree		1.60***	1.20	0.95	0.87
High School Degree		1.18	1.05	0.94	0.90

(continued)

Table 14.2. Hazards Ratios Estimating the Relationship between Religious Attendance and Covariates on Subsequent Mortality Risk, U.S. Adults Aged 51–61 at Baseline: Main Effects Only *(continued)*

	Mortality Risk				
	Model 1 (H.R.)	Model 2 (H.R.)	Model 3 (H.R.)	Model 4 (H.R.)	Model 5 (H.R.)
ADL Score			1.16***	1.06***	1.05***
Self-Rated Health (Excellent)					
Poor				5.37***	4.79***
Fair				3.68***	3.34***
Good				1.91***	1.79***
Very Good				1.28	1.26
Smoking Behavior (Never Smoked)					
Current Smoker					2.65***
Former Smoker					1.68***
Drinking Behavior (Nondrinker)					
Light (<2 drinks/day)					0.87*
Heavy (≥ 3 drinks/day)					0.93
Exercise (Heavy (≥ 3 times/week))					
No Exercise					1.37**
Light (< 3 times/week)					1.05
Log Pseudo-Likelihood	-6284.0	-6250.7	-6137.2	-6067.2	-6016.0
Unweighted N	9,423				

a. Reference categories in parentheses.

$*p < .05$, $**p < .01$, $***p < .001$

Discussion and Conclusions

This analysis offers more support for the overall association between higher levels of religious attendance and lower adult mortality in the United States (Ellison and Levin 1998; Hummer et al. 2004; Koenig, McCullough, and Larson 2001; McCullough et al. 2000; Powell, Shahabi, and Thoresen 2003), in this case among a group of individuals aged fifty-one to sixty-one at baseline and statistically followed for survival status for eight years. The clearest distinction was between nonattenders and frequent attenders; even after controlling for demographic, social, and health status confounding factors, nonattenders exhibited a 64 percent higher risk of mortality compared to frequent attenders. Thus, nonattenders (28 percent of this population) are the most important group to focus upon in further research. Are current nonattenders lifetime nonattenders? Were they once frequent attenders who are no longer attending? What other factors, besides health behavior, are mechanisms by which they experience higher mortality risks? In turn, there was a more modest mortality difference between infrequent attenders and frequent attenders, which stood at just over a 20 percent higher risk for moderate attenders prior to the inclusion of health behavior factors. The graded association between attendance and mortality risk, prior to the inclusion of health behaviors, supports earlier national-level work showing modestly higher mortality among less frequent attenders in comparison to frequent attenders (Hummer et al. 1999).

Both health controls (indicative of confounding) and health behaviors seem to be important mechanisms by which religious attendance is related to adult mortality risk. These findings are very similar to those in earlier, and different, national level data sets analyzed by Hummer and colleagues (1999) and Musick and colleagues (2004). We will need better longitudinal data on both religious involvement and health and behavioral change over time to more clearly sort out these mechanisms.

Our interaction results showed no statistically significant differences in the association between religious attendance and mortality risk among demographic and social subgroups of the population. While there was some hint of stronger attendance effects among unmarried persons (i.e., Waite and Lehrer 2003), even those coefficients did not achieve statistical significance. In part, of course, this is a consequence of fairly modest sample sizes. With 834 total deaths divided among three religious attendance groups, four marital status categories, and the combinations of religious attendance and marital status, standard errors become larger and statistical significance harder to attain. Nevertheless, at this point, there is little national-level evidence to suggest that the relationship between religious attendance varies across most demographic and social subgroups of the population. What is more convincing is that religious involvement is not just important for survival status among the elderly; relative differences are also sizable among the nonelderly (Musick, House, and Williams 2004; Rogers, Hummer, and Nam 2000).

Much work remains to be done in this area of study. Perhaps most important, the studies to date in this area have not been able to measure religious involvement in a life course fashion. Cross-sectional snapshots of religious involvement, while very useful, cannot tap variations in religious activities and beliefs that characterize individuals across the life course. Second, few studies in this area have been able to tap into the various dimensions of religion and religiosity that characterize individuals. The study by Musick and colleagues (2004) was most effective in this sense, but nonetheless, even that work was not able to fully tap into all of the religious variables that might be important for health and longevity. Third, there are a number of mechanisms by which religious involvement may be related to mortality risk that went untapped in the data set used here and in most related data sets. Religious individuals may have lower mortality risks because of reduced levels of stress, because of greater coping mechanisms, because of larger and more effective social supportive networks, and/or because of the strength and comfort they receive from their religion. For all of the items outlined earlier, new and more comprehensive data will be needed before these suggestions can be incorporated into new research. Finally, it remains the case that selectivity—into both religious involvement and into health/mortality outcomes—may be at least partially driving the relationship between religion and mortality (Hummer et al. 2004). Future studies should also attempt to better address the psychological, health, social, and biological selectivity that may be influencing both religious involvement and mortality risk among individuals. Doing so will involve more than just controlling for indicators of health at the time of the baseline survey, as was done in the present case.

NOTE

We gratefully acknowledge financial support from the National Institute on Aging (Grant #1 R01 AG18432) and from the National Science Foundation (Grants #SES-0243249 and #SES-0221093), and statistical advice from Marc Musick.

REFERENCES

Bagiella, E., V. Hong, and R. P. Sloan. 2005. "Religious Attendance as a Predictor of Survival in the EPESE Cohorts." *International Journal of Epidemiology* 34 (2): 444–451.

Benjamins, M. R., R. A. Hummer, I. E. Eberstein, and C. B. Nam. 2004. "Self-Reported Health and Adult Mortality Risk: An Analysis of Cause-Specific Mortality." *Social Science and Medicine* 59 (6): 1297–1306.

Booth, A., D. R. Johnson, A. Branaman, and A. Sica. 1995. "Belief and Behavior: Does Religion Matter in Today's Marriage?" *Journal of Marriage and the Family* 57:661–671.

Bryant, S., and W. Rakowski. 1992. "Predictors of Mortality among Elderly African Americans." *Research on Aging* 14:50–67.

Call, V. R., and T. B. Heaton. 1997. "Religious Influence on Marital Stability." *Journal for the Scientific Study of Religion* 36:382–392.

Cox, D. R. 1972. "Regression Models and Life Tables." *Journal of the Royal Statistical Society* 34:187–220.

Dupre, M. E., A. T. Franzese, and E. A. Parrado. 2006. "Religious Attendance and Mortality: Implications for the Black–White Mortality Crossover." *Demography* 43 (1): 141–164.

Ellison, C. 1994. "Religion, the Life Stress Paradigm, and the Study of Depression." In *Religion in Aging and Health: Theoretical Foundations and Methodological Frontiers*, ed. J. S. Levin, 78–124. Thousand Oaks, CA: Sage.

Ellison, C. G., R. A. Hummer, S. Cormier, and R. G. Rogers. 2000. "Religious Involvement and Mortality Risk among African American Adults." *Research on Aging* 22:630–667.

Ellison, C. G., and J. S. Levin. 1998. "The Religion–Health Connection: Evidence, Theory, and Future Directions." *Health, Education and Behavior* 25:700–720.

Ellison, C. G., and D. E. Sherkat. 1995. "The Semi-Involuntary Institution Revisited: Regional Variations in Church Participation among Black Americans." *Social Forces* 73:1415–1437.

Elo, I. T., and S. H. Preston. 1996. "Educational Differentials in Mortality: United States, 1979–1985." *Social Science and Medicine* 42:47–57.

Heeringa, S. G., and J. H. Connor. 1995. "Technical Description of the Health and Retirement Survey Sample Design." HRS/AHEAD Documentation Report DR-002.

Helm, H. M., J. C. Hays, E. P. Flint, H. G. Koenig, and D. G. Blazer. 2000. "Does Private Religious Activity Prolong Survival? A Six-Year Follow-up Study of 3,851 Older Adults." *Journal of Gerontology: Medical Sciences* 55A (7): M400–M405.

Hill, T. D., J. Angel, C. G. Ellison, and R. J. Angel. 2005. "Religious Attendance and Mortality: An 8-Year Follow-Up of Older Mexican Americans." *Journals of Gerontology Series B: Psychological Sciences and Social Sciences* 60B (2): S102–S109.

Health and Retirement Study Codebook. 2004. HRS/AHEAD Web site. http://www.umich.edu/~hrswww/ (accessed July 20, 2006).

Hummer, R. A. 2005. "Commentary: Understanding Religious Involvement and Mortality Risk in the United States: Comment on Bagiella, Hong, and Sloan." *International Journal of Epidemiology* 34(2): 452–453.

Hummer, R. A., C. G. Ellison, R. G. Rogers, B. E. Moulton, and R. R. Romero. 2004. "Religious Involvement and Adult Mortality in the United States: Review and Perspective." *Southern Medical Journal* 97 (12): 1223–1230.

Hummer, R. A., R. G. Rogers, C. B. Nam, and C. G. Ellison. 1999. "Religious Involvement and U.S. Adult Mortality." *Demography* 36 (2): 273–285.

Idler, E., and Y. Benyamini. 1997. "Self-Rated Health and Mortality: A Review of Twenty-Seven Community Studies." *Journal of Health and Social Behavior* 38:21–37.

Jarvis, G. K., and H. C. Northcott. 1987. "Religion and Differences in Morbidity and Mortality." *Social Science and Medicine* 25:813–824.

Johnson, D. 1997. "Formal Education versus Religious Belief: Soliciting New Evidence with Multinomial Logit Modeling." *Journal for the Scientific Study of Religion* 36:231–246.

Koenig, H. J., D. Hays, D. L. Larson, L. George, H. Cohen, M. McCullough, K. Meador, and D. Blazer. 1999. "Does Religious Attendance Prolong Survival? A Six-Year Follow-Up Study of 3,968 Older Adults." *Journal of Gerontology: Medical Sciences* 54A:M370–M376.

Koenig, H. G., M. E. McCullough, and D. B. Larson. 2001. *The Handbook of Religion and Health*. Oxford: Oxford University Press.

Lauderdale, D. S. 2001. "Education and Survival: Birth Cohort, Period, and Age Effects." *Demography* 38:551–562.

Levin, J. S. 1994. "Religion and Health: Is There an Association, Is It Valid, and Is It Causal?" *Social Science and Medicine* 38:1475–1482.

Lillard, L. A., and L. J. Waite. 1995. "Til Death Do Us Part: Marital Disruption and Mortality." *American Journal of Sociology* 100:1131–1156.

Lincoln, C. E., and L. Mamiya. 1990. *The Black Church in the African American Experience*. Durham, NC: Duke University Press.

McCullough, M., D. Larson, W. T. Hoyt, H. Koenig, and M. Milano. 2000. "Religious Involvement and Mortality: A Meta-Analytic Review." *Health Psychology* 19:211–222.

Mirowsky, J. 1999. "Analyzing Associations between Mental Health and Social Circumstances." In *Handbook of the Sociology of Mental Health*, ed. C. Aneshensel and J. Phelan, 105–123. New York: Kluwer Academic/Plenum Publishers.

Musick, M., J. S. House, and D. Williams. 2004. "Religion and Mortality in a National Sample." *Journal of Health and Social Behavior* 45 (2): 198–213.

Oman, D., J. H. Kurata, and W. J. Strawbridge. 2002. "Religious Attendance and Cause of Death Over 31 Years." *International Journal of Psychiatry in Medicine* 32:69–89.

Oman, D., and D. Reed. 1998. "Religion and Mortality among the Community-Dwelling Elderly." *American Journal of Public Health* 88:1469–1475.

Oxman, T., D. Freeman, and E. Manheimer. 1995. "Lack of Social Participation or Religious Strength and Comfort as Risk Factors for Death after Cardiac Surgery in the Elderly." *Psychosomatic Medicine* 57:5–15.

Powell, L. H., L. Shahabi, and C. E. Thoresen. 2003. "Religion and Spirituality: Linkages to Physical Health." *American Psychologist* (January): 36–52.

Rogers, R. G. 1995. "Marriage, Sex, and Mortality." *Journal of Marriage and the Family* 57:515–526.

Rogers, R. G., R. A. Hummer, and C. B. Nam. 2000. *Living and Dying in the USA: Behavioral, Health, and Social Differentials of Adult Mortality.* San Diego, CA: Academic Press.

Roof W., and W. McKinney. 1987. *American Mainline Religion.* New Brunswick, NJ: Rutgers University Press.

Sherkat, D. E., and C. G. Ellison. 1999. "Recent Developments and Current Controversies in the Sociology of Religion." *Annual Review of Sociology* 25:363–394.

Sloan, R. P., and E. Bagiella. 2002. "Claims about Religious Involvement and Health Outcomes." *Annals of Behavioral Medicine* 24:14–21.

Sloan, R. P., E. Bagiella, and T. Powell. 1999. "Viewpoint: Religion, Spirituality, and Medicine." *Lancet* 353:664–667.

Sloan, R. P., E. Bagiella, L. VandeCreek, M. Hover, C. Casalone, T. J. Hirsch, Y. Hasan, R. Kreger, and P. Poulos. 2000. "Should Physicians Prescribe Religious Activities?" *New England Journal of Medicine* 342:1913–1916.

Stolzenberg, R. M., M. Blair-Loy, and L. J. Waite. 1995. "Religious Participation over the Life Course: Age and Family Life Cycle Effects on Church Membership." *American Sociological Review* 60:84–103.

Strawbridge, W. J., R. D. Cohen, S. J. Shema, and G. J. Kaplan. 1997. "Frequent Attendance at Religious Services and Mortality Over 28 Years." *American Journal of Public Health* 87:957–961.

Strawbridge, W. J., S. J. Shema, R. D. Cohen, and G. J. Kaplan. 2001. "Religious Attendance Increases Survival by Improving and Maintaining Good Health Behaviors, Mental Health, and Social Relationships." *Annals of Behavioral Medicine* 23:68–74.

Taylor, R. J. 1993. "Religion and Religious Observances." In *Aging in Black America*, ed. J. Jackson, L. Chatters, and R. Taylor, 101–123. Newbury Park, CA: Sage.

Taylor, R. J., and L. Chatters. 1991. "Religious Life." In *Life in Black America*, ed. J. Jackson, 105–123. Newbury Park, CA: Sage.

Waite, L. J., and E. L. Lehrer. 2003. "The Benefits from Marriage and Religion in the United States: A Comparative Analysis." *Population and Development Review* 29:255–275.

15

Religious Attendance and Cause-Specific Mortality in the United States

RICHARD G. ROGERS, PATRICK M. KRUEGER,
AND ROBERT A. HUMMER

There is a growing literature about the relationship between religious involvement and overall mortality. As Flannelly and colleagues (2004, 1234) have noted, "the beneficial effects of church attendance on all-cause mortality rates is the most solidly established positive effect on religion and health."[1] But little research has examined the relationship between religious involvement and specific causes of death (for exceptions, see Hummer et al. 1999; Oman et al. 2002), even though cause-of-death analyses may provide insight into the mechanisms that lead to an association between religious involvement and mortality. Further, only limited research has examined these relationships by sex and for different age-groups, and much research on the association between religious attendance and mortality has been constrained by lack of national data, small sample sizes, few control variables, limited numbers of deaths, short follow-up periods, and lack of detail on specific causes of death (Sloan, Bagiella, and Powell 1999; Sloan et al. 2000). This chapter addresses these limitations by examining the relationship between religious involvement and overall and cause-specific mortality, using a large nationally representative prospective data set that includes a long follow-up period and that has identified a large number of deaths and includes controls for important confounding factors. Although some recent work has found gender differences in the religion–mortality relationship (Koenig et al. 1999; Strawbridge et al. 1997), other work has not (Hummer et al. 1999; Musick et al. 2004). The relationship between religious involvement and mortality may also operate differently for younger and older adults (Krause 2004; Musick, House, and Williams 2004). Therefore, we examine these relations for the adult population of the United States as a whole, as well as by specific age-groups and by gender.

Religious Involvement and Mortality Risk

Durkheim ([1897] 1951) first suggested, in a scientific sense, that religious involvement may reduce mortality by providing social integration within the family and the community, regulating health behavior, and mitigating the deleterious effects of daily stressors. Here we briefly review these three mechanisms and their implications for the religious involvement and mortality literature.

Social Integration

Participation in a religious community may provide individuals with social support and social ties that reduce adult mortality risks. Social integration is often associated with better health and lower mortality risks because it may provide people with the necessary social support at times of acute illness or chronically poor health, ties to others who have interests in caring for one's own health, and a meaningful orientation toward life that comes from being surrounded by significant others (Berkman and Glass 2000; House, Landis, and Umberson 1988). Compared to individuals who are not regularly involved in religious activities, those who are involved report more social ties and interactions, evaluate these ties more positively, have more friendship networks, and enjoy more social integration and social support in their community (Ellison and George 1994; Jarvis and Northcott 1987; Koenig 2004).

Various religious doctrines support marriage and the family, two key dimensions of social integration (Strawbridge et al. 1997). Compared to less religious individuals, those who are more religious are more likely to be married, and report greater marital stability and satisfaction (Koenig 2004). Spouses can provide advice on seeking medical care and can encourage each other to make and keep medical appointments, obtain prescriptions or treatment, and comply with medical regimens (Koenig 2004). Religious involvement may also strengthen family cohesiveness and intergenerational ties that can reduce stress and contribute to greater meaning in life (Flannelly, Ellison, and Strock 2004).

More religiously involved individuals have deeper and richer social networks than those who are less involved (Flannelly, Ellison, and Strock 2004), in part because many religious traditions advocate the importance of establishing and maintaining close personal connections, and in helping and caring for others (Krause 2004). Religious organizations often encourage social interaction, communication, and friendship by sponsoring social events such as dinner groups; organizing community excursions to plays, concerts, and sporting events; offering opportunities to sing in the choir, play musical instruments, or serve as an usher or greeter; and promoting educational programs (Musick, House, and Williams 2004). Congregation members may provide financial, emotional, and instrumental support for each other in the forms of loans, job-search networks, transportation, help with household chores, and health care advice (Taylor and Chatters 1986).

In addition to congregational members, church-based friends, and social networks, religious leaders may offer prayer and personal counseling; comfort friends, family, and loved ones during difficult times; and arrange social, emotional, instrumental, and spiritual support from congregational members or other community support services. When individuals experience a trauma, illness, or stressful event, they often turn to their priest, minister, or rabbi for advice and support. When someone loses a loved one through death, especially homicide, clergy can offer support and provide coping strategies (Thompson and Vardaman 1997).

The social integration provided by religious participation may impact some causes of death more than others. Increased levels of social integration may delay the onset of cardiovascular disease and aid in recovery from a stroke (Berkman and Glass 2000). Although some kinds of social contact clearly aid in the transmission of infectious diseases, some evidence suggests positive social contacts may improve immune functioning. Compared to those with few social contacts, HIV-positive men who have more social contacts may have a slower decline in immune function (Theorell et al. 1995); those who have more numerous social contacts may be less likely to develop a cold if they are exposed to the virus, and they may have fewer symptoms if they do get sick (Cohen et al. 1997). Finally, religious attendance may lead to lower risks of diabetes mortality, potentially because diabetics are more likely to maintain their care regimen if they have social support (Hummer et al. 1999).

Social Regulation of Behavior

Religious communities promote healthy behaviors and limit or proscribe unhealthy or risky behaviors through sacred teachings, moral messages from congregational leaders, social interactions, and congregational-based health awareness and intervention programs (Flannelly, Ellison, and Strock 2004; Hummer et al. 2004; Kumanyika and Charleston 1992). Compared to people who attend less regularly or not at all, those who attend religious services more often are less likely to smoke cigarettes, drink excessively, or use illegal drugs (Ironson et al. 2002; King, Mainous III, and Pearson 2002; Levin 1994a, 1994b), and are more likely to obtain regular health screenings and exercise regularly. Many religious organizations provide cancer education, screening, and counseling (Weaver and Flannelly 2004). Some churches have employed telephone counseling to encourage women to avail themselves of mammography screening (Duan et al. 2000). Compared to those who are more religiously involved, less involved individuals experience higher risks of invasive colon cancer and more advanced states of colon cancer, perhaps due to lower rates of screening (Kinney et al. 2003).

Churches may also initiate programs that aim to reduce high blood pressure, high cholesterol, diabetes, obesity, and inactivity. One major church-based weight-loss program combined group nutritional education, behavioral counseling, and support sessions; individual consultation with an on-site registered dietician; and exercise programs (Kumanyika and Charleston 1992). Religious leaders often extol the importance of maintaining respect for the body, which may explain why, compared to less religiously involved individuals, more religiously active individuals eat more balanced meals (McIntosh and Shiffett 1984) and are more likely to engage in physical activity to maintain or improve their health (Idler and Kasl 1997; Musick, House, and Williams 2004; Ott 1991).

Compared to individuals who attend religious services more frequently, those who attend less frequently are more likely to initiate smoking, exhibit higher smoking prevalence rates, and report fewer efforts to quit smoking (Whooley et al. 2002). Although most denominations do not explicitly prohibit cigarette smoking, some—Mormons for instance—do (Whooley et al. 2002). Instead, strong norms against smoking, coping strategies that reduce stress, and admonitions against risk-taking behaviors may contribute to low smoking rates among more religiously active individuals that, in turn, may contribute to low rates of cancer, especially lung cancer, respiratory disease, and heart disease (Rogers et al. 2005).

Some religious denominations allow drinking whereas others forbid alcohol consumption. Individuals are less likely to drink if they are affiliated with religious groups that have strong stances against drinking (Bock, Cochran, and Beeghley 1987), and among drinkers, more religious individuals are more likely to avoid heavy consumption (Gartner, Larson, and Allen 1991). The relationship between religious activity, drinking, and mortality is further complicated by the j-shaped relationship between alcohol consumption and mortality: mortality is slightly higher for nondrinkers, dips to its lowest level for light to moderate drinking, and is highest for heavy drinkers. Those who follow religious doctrines and abstain from drinking may avoid alcohol abuse but might miss some of the survival benefits of light alcohol consumption.

Compared to more religious individuals, those who are less involved in religious communities are more likely to be violent, carry and use weapons, and fight (Koenig, McCullough, and Larson 2001). And among those who engage in sexual intercourse, religiosity is associated with safer sex practices (Ironson et al. 2002). Higher propensities toward safe sex, light drinking or abstention, and nonviolence among more religiously involved individuals should result in lower risks of death from HIV/AIDS and cirrhosis of the liver, and from such external causes of death as suicide, homicide, and accidents.

Stress Reduction

Religious involvement may reduce stress and lower individuals' risks of death by providing them with a coherent worldview and greater meaning to life; a sense of belonging, comfort, and hope; feelings and thoughts of serenity and peace; positive coping strategies for bereavement and illness; better surgery outcomes, including improved recovery; lower blood pressure; and better immune function (Ellison 1994; Ironson et al. 2002; Kark et al. 1996; Krause 1998; Weaver and Flannelly 2004). Religious involvement may reduce stress by providing access to supportive clergy and congregational members who may offer emotional and spiritual support that help people to deal with feelings of anger, guilt, and hurt (Harrison et al. 2001; Weaver and Flannelly 2004). Religion can help individuals cope with chronic diseases including cancer, heart disease, diabetes, kidney disease, lung disease, and HIV/AIDS (Ironson et al. 2002; Koenig 2004; Olive 2004; Weaver and Flannelly 2004). Further, compared to individuals who reported that they received strength and comfort from religion, those who did not receive strength and comfort from religion were 3.25 times as likely to die within six months of open heart surgery, even net of age, participation in social groups, functional impairment, and prior surgical history (Oxman, Freedman, Jr., and Manheimer 1995). Those who are more religious also have greater overall well-being, less depression, less anxiety, lower rates of suicide, and greater feelings of efficacy (Harrison et al. 2001; Koenig 2004).

Religious involvement may help reduce biological measures of inflammation and stress. Prayer and religious rituals can contribute to the relaxation response—including lowered blood pressure, heart rate, breathing rate, and metabolic rate—which can lower the risk of hypertension (Krause 2004). Compared to less religiously involved individuals, those who are more involved are better able to control their blood pressure and exhibit lower levels of cortisol and advantageous levels of C-reactive protein (CRP), which improves their prognosis for heart disease, diabetes, and HIV/AIDS (King 2004; King, Mainous III, and Pearson 2002). Higher levels of CRP indicate increased stress, reduced immune function, and higher levels of depression and anxiety (King, Mainous III, and Pearson 2002). Indeed, among adults aged forty and older, diabetics who did not attended religious services were 1.9 times as likely to have elevated levels of CRP compared to diabetics who attended religious services, even after controlling for demographic factors, smoking, social support, body mass, and health status. Stress reduction should lower the risk of death from suicide and chronic diseases including cancer, heart disease, diabetes, kidney disease, lung disease, and HIV/AIDS.

Data and Methods

We use the 1987 National Health Interview Survey-Epidemiological Study (NHIS-ES), a nationally representative data set of 22,080 noninstitutionalized adults aged eighteen and older, with an array of demographic, socioeconomic, health status, social relationship, and health behavior variables (National Center for Health Statistics [NCHS] 1989). Our analysis of detailed causes of death is possible because the NCHS recently linked the NHIS-ES to deaths in the National Death Index (NDI) through the year 2002, via the Multiple Cause of Death (MCD) file (NCHS 2004b).

The survey records of individuals are probabilistically matched to deaths using a set of twelve identifying characteristics (including social security number, name, sex, race, date of birth, marital status, and state of birth and residence). The matching method—which has been tested extensively, applied to a number of different data sets, benchmarked with longitudinal data sets that were previously matched through active follow-up, and revised based on new information—includes such innovative techniques as matching the last name based on a soundalike system, and is considered quite accurate (see Patterson and Bilgrad 1986).

At the time of the interview, 1 percent of surveyed individuals did not provide enough information to be matched to subsequent mortality; these records are dropped from the analyses. Further, we excluded 7.8 percent of the remaining individuals who were missing data on religious attendance or other key variables. Our final analyses are based on 20,139 adults aged eighteen and above at the time of the survey. The NHIS-ES-MCD is particularly valuable because it ascertains vital status for individuals for up to sixteen years after the initial interview, includes ample numbers of deaths (3,934 decedents), and provides detailed cause-of-death classifications. Whereas previous studies could follow vital status for eight years (see, for example, Hummer et al. 1999), we can follow individuals for twice as long.

Self-reported religious attendance is the most theoretically relevant, empirically robust, and widely used measure of religious involvement in this literature (Flannelly, Ellison, and Strock 2004; Koenig, McCullough, and Larson 2001; McCullough et al. 2000; Musick, House, and Williams 2004). The NHIS-ES respondents were asked "How often do you go to church, temple, or other religious services?" and could report "never" or the number of times per week, month, or year they attended (Chyba and Washington 1993). We compared individuals who reported attending more than once per week (referent) to those who attended once per week, less than once per week, or never attend.

We control for demographic factors that likely influence both religious involvement and cause-specific mortality, including age in single years, sex (0 = female, 1 = male), race/ethnicity (0 = not non-Hispanic black, 1 = non-Hispanic black), and geographic region (0 = non-South, 1 = South). Socioeconomic factors include education and income. We use income equivalence, coded into $10,000 increments, to adjust family income by family size and age of family members, and to account for differences in consumption patterns among different sized families.[2] We code educational attainment categorically as zero to eleven years, twelve years, and thirteen or more years.

To assess social integration, we focus on marital status, social activities, and whether people have friends or relatives they can count on in times of need. We code marital status as currently (the referent), previously, or never married. We code participation in social activities dichotomously (0 = socially active, 1 = socially inactive). Finally, we assess integration as whether individuals can count on friends (0 = yes, 1 = no friends to count on) and relatives (0 = yes, 1 = no relatives to count on) in times of need.

We examine how religion might work through the regulation of health behaviors, such as cigarette smoking, alcohol consumption, and body mass. We code cigarette smoking as never smokers (those who have smoked fewer than one hundred cigarettes in their lifetime), former smokers (those who have smoked at least one hundred cigarettes in their lifetime but who no longer smoke), current light smokers (those who currently smoke less than a pack a day), and current heavy smokers (those who currently smoke one or more packs of cigarettes a day). Although body mass is not a health behavior per se, it reflects exercise, dietary, and smoking practices. We assess body mass with the body mass index (BMI), categorized as underweight (BMI < 18.5), normal weight (the referent, 18.5 < BMI < 25), overweight (25 < BMI < 30), obese class I (30 < BMI < 35), obese class II (35 < BMI < 40), and obese class III (BMI > 40). We code alcohol use into nondrinkers, light drinkers who usually drink one to three drinks of beer, wine, or liquor when they drink, and heavy drinkers who usually drink four or more drinks when they drink.

To control for the possibility of health selection—wherein less healthy individuals may be less able to attend religious services—we use three health status variables including activity limitations, self-reported health, and the number of days an individual was bedridden in the last year. Activity limitations (0 = not limited, 1 = limited) indicate whether individuals report any limitations in their daily activities. We code self-reported health status categorically as poor, fair, good, very good, and excellent (the referent). Finally, we control for the number of days individuals spent in bed, due to poor health, in the last year (0 = 30 or fewer, 1 = 31 or more).

A key feature of our research is its incorporation of detailed causes of death. We examine seven broad causes of death according to the Tenth Revision of the International Classification of Diseases (ICD): circulatory diseases (ICD-10 I00-I99), cancer (ICD-10 C00-D48), respiratory disease (ICD-10 J00-J98), diabetes (ICD-10 E10-E14), infectious diseases (ICD-10 A00-B99), external causes of death (ICD-10 U01-U03, V01-Y89), and a residual category (for similar coding, see Rogers, Hummer, and Nam 2000). Furthermore, we disaggregate circulatory diseases into ischemic heart disease (ICD-10 I20-I13), stroke (ICD-10 I60-I69), and all other circulatory diseases. It is important to separate lung cancer (ICD-10 C33-C34), which is primarily due to cigarette smoking, from other forms of cancer, many of which are less directly related to cigarette smoking. And we separate external causes into suicides (ICD-10 U03, X60-X84, Y87.0), suicides and homicides (ICD-10 U01-U02, X85-Y09, X87.1), and accidents (ICD-10 V01-X59, Y85-Y86). Although we can examine suicide separately, and suicide and homicide together, there are too few homicide deaths to examine separately. We combine causes of death as necessary, such as when disaggregating our sample by age and sex.

We use Cox proportional hazards models to examine whether individuals have survived or died of a specific cause, as well as the timing of death. We model the number of days until death or right censoring (i.e., the end of the follow-up period). For cause-specific analyses, those who die from other causes are censored at the time of death. Proportional hazard models are a valuable event history technique because they require no assumption about the form of the baseline hazard rate (Allison 1984). We correct all estimated coefficients and standard errors for weighting and sample design effects with STATA 8.0 software (StataCorp 2003), and incorporate the new NCHS adult sample person weights that adjust for the ineligible records (NCHS 2004b).

To consider the possibility that religious attendance can be related to mortality in both advantageous and detrimental ways, especially among specific causes of death, we employ two-tailed tests of significance. Although there is substantial evidence to support the salutary effects of religious attendance on overall mortality, some studies have suggested that religious attendance can contribute to higher levels of stress and risky behaviors (see, for instance, Pargament et al. 2001), which might manifest in specific causes of death.

We present our results through progressive model building: we begin with the basic demographic model and then progressively add controls for socioeconomic factors, social ties, health behaviors, and health status. This allows us to examine possible confounding and mediating pathways through which religious involvement may be related to mortality outcomes.

We control for the health and functional status of individuals at baseline to account for health selection, wherein less healthy individuals may be physically unable to maintain religious attendance. Because religious participation may have shaped the health and functional status at baseline, but might also be affected by health and functional status, controlling for health and functional status at the time of interview provides a stringent test of the relationship between religious involvement and mortality. Models that control for health and functional status may be conservatively biased and provide a lower bound for the relationship between religious attendance and mortality. Models that do not control for health and functional status will provide a less conservative portrait of the relationship between religious attendance and mortality.

Results

Table 15.1 displays means for our independent variables by religious attendance. Although similar proportions of males and females never attend religious services, a much greater proportion of females frequently attend religious services: among those who attend more than once per week, just 35 percent are male. Compared to whites and non-Southerners, relatively more blacks and Southerners frequently attend religious services. Those who more frequently attend religious services are more likely to be married than unmarried, to be more socially

TABLE 15.1

**Means of Model Covariates, by Religious Attendance,
U.S. Adults Aged 18 and Older, 1987**

		Frequency of Religious Attendance		
	Never	Less than once per week	Once per week	More than once per week
Demographic Variables				
Age	43.7	39.5	48.6	46.6
Sex (male = 1)	0.49	0.44	0.35	0.35
Race (non-Hispanic black = 1)	0.07	0.13	0.11	0.14
Region (South = 1)	0.30	0.34	0.33	0.50
Socioeconomic Status				
Income equivalence	1.87	2.04	1.94	1.74
Education				
0–11 years	0.28	0.17	0.22	0.24
12 years	0.38	0.38	0.38	0.38
13+ years	0.34	0.45	0.40	0.39
Social Ties				
Marital status				
Currently married	0.51	0.54	0.59	0.63
Previously married	0.27	0.21	0.26	0.22
Never married	0.22	0.25	0.15	0.15
Social activity (inactive = 1)	0.58	0.31	0.27	0.16
Friends to count on (none = 1)	0.18	0.10	0.13	0.10
Relatives to count on (none = 1)	0.14	0.08	0.08	0.08
Health Behaviors				
Cigarette smoking				
Current heavy	0.27	0.17	0.10	0.06
Current light	0.14	0.15	0.09	0.05
Former	0.22	0.20	0.23	0.25
Never	0.38	0.48	0.58	0.64
Body mass index				
Obese class III	0.01	0.01	0.01	0.01

(continued)

Table 15.1. Means of Model Covariates, by Religious Attendance, U.S. Adults Aged 18 and Older, 1987 *(continued)*

		Frequency of Religious Attendance		
	Never	*Less than once per week*	*Once per week*	*More than once per week*
Obese class II	0.02	0.02	0.02	0.03
Obese class I	0.08	0.08	0.09	0.10
Overweight	0.29	0.30	0.31	0.31
Normal weight	0.55	0.55	0.53	0.52
Underweight	0.05	0.04	0.04	0.03
Alcohol use				
Nondrinker	0.26	0.21	0.39	0.65
Light drinker	0.53	0.62	0.55	0.32
Heavy drinker	0.20	0.18	0.07	0.03
Health				
Activities (limited = 1)	0.21	0.13	0.17	0.19
Self-reported health				
Poor	0.05	0.02	0.03	0.03
Fair	0.11	0.07	0.09	0.10
Good	0.26	0.23	0.25	0.24
Very good	0.26	0.31	0.29	0.30
Excellent	0.33	0.37	0.34	0.33
Bed days (31 or more = 1)	0.04	0.03	0.03	0.04

Note: Full baseline sample, N = 20,139.

active, to have friends and relatives that they can count on, to abstain from drinking alcohol, and to have never smoked. For example, 41 percent of those who never attend religious services are current smokers, but only 11 percent of those who frequently attend religious services are current smokers.

Table 15.2 presents hazards ratios for religious attendance and overall mortality for all adults. Model 1 reveals a strong relationship between religious attendance and overall mortality: compared to individuals who attend religious services more than once a week, those who never attend experience 48 percent higher mortality over the follow-up period, controlling for demographic

TABLE 15.2

Hazards Ratios of Overall Mortality for Religious Attendance and Covariates, U.S. Adults Aged 18 and Older, 1987–2002

	Model 1	Model 2	Model 3	Model 4	Model 5	Model 6
Religious Attendance						
Never	1.48***	1.46***	1.34***	1.32***	1.24***	1.20***
Less than once per week	1.16	1.21**	1.15*	1.16**	1.12	1.10
Once per week	1.01	1.03	1.01	1.04	1.02	1.03
More than once per week	ref.	ref.	ref.	ref.	ref.	ref.
Demographic Variables						
Age	1.09***	1.08***	1.08***	1.09***	1.09***	1.08***
Sex (male=1)	1.52***	1.62***	1.68***	1.61***	1.65***	1.67***
Race (non-Hispanic black=1)	1.39***	1.22**	1.20**	1.22**	1.21**	1.110
Region (South=1)	0.72**	0.75*	0.76**	0.64**	0.65**	0.64***
Socioeconomic Status						
Income equivalence		0.86***	0.88***	0.88***	0.90***	0.94***
Education						
0–11 years		1.11***	1.09**	1.04	1.03	1.00
12 years		1.09***	1.09***	1.04	1.05*	1.06**
13+ years		ref.	ref.	ref.	ref.	ref.
Social Ties						
Marital status						
Currently married			ref.		ref.	ref.
Previously married			1.13***		1.10***	1.13***
Never married			1.23***		1.28***	1.33***
Social activity (inactive=1)			1.16***		1.10***	1.06**
Friends to count on (none=1)			1.02		1.03	1.01
Relatives to count on (none=1)			1.01		0.99	0.96*

(continued)

Table 15.2. Hazards Ratios of Overall Mortality for Religious Attendance and Covariates, U.S. Adults Aged 18 and Older, 1987–2002 *(continued)*

	Model 1	Model 2	Model 3	Model 4	Model 5	Model 6
Health Behaviors						
Cigarette smoking						
Current heavy				2.08***	2.07***	1.95***
Current light				1.59***	1.59***	1.50***
Former				1.26***	1.28***	1.23***
Never				ref.	ref.	ref.
Body mass index						
Obese class III				1.83***	1.82***	1.54***
Obese class II				1.57***	1.58***	1.36***
Obese class I				1.15***	1.17***	1.11**
Overweight				0.95	0.96	0.94
Normal weight				ref.	ref.	ref.
Underweight				1.36***	1.33***	1.24***
Alcohol use						
Nondrinker				1.30***	1.29***	1.21***
Heavy drinker				1.04	1.02	1.02
Light drinker				ref.	ref.	ref.
Health						
Activities (limited=1)						1.29***
Self-reported health						
Poor						2.06***
Fair						1.65***
Good						1.31***
Very good						1.14***
Excellent						ref.
Bed days (31 or more=1)						1.03
-2 Log-Likelihood	-18,210	-18,149	-18,132	-18,002	-17,990	-17,859

Note: Survivors N = 16,205; Decedents N = 3,934

* p < .10 ** p < .05 *** p < .01 (two-tailed tests)

variables (for similar results, see Musick, House, and Williams 2004). Controlling for socioeconomic factors (Model 2) slightly accentuates the relationship between religious attendance and mortality. Controlling for social ties (Model 3) dampens the relationship between religious participation and mortality, likely because religion reduces mortality risks by providing individuals with important forms of social integration. Controlling for health behaviors (Model 4) also dampens the relationship between religious attendance and mortality, perhaps because religious communities may regulate the behaviors of participants in ways that may promote healthy activities. Model 5 shows that social ties and health behaviors each uniquely impact the risk of death (compare log-likelihood ratios of Model 5 to Model 4 and to Model 3). Model 6 controls for health status to account for the possibility that less healthy individuals may be unable to attend religious services. Although this reduces the relationship between religious attendance and mortality, a significant relationship persists.

Table 15.3 shows cause-specific mortality differences by religious attendance. Tables 15.3 and 15.4 present models that control for the same covariates as the corresponding models in Table 15.2, but we present only the hazard ratios for religious attendance for reasons of space. Circulatory disease mortality, the leading cause of death in the United States, is associated with religious attendance. Model 1 shows that those who never attend religious services are 44 percent more likely to die from circulatory diseases over the follow-up period than those who attend services more than once a week. This effect is muted with controls for social ties (Model 3) and health behaviors (Model 4) separately, and drops from statistical significance once we control for both social ties and health behaviors (Model 5). The association between attendance at religious services and ischemic heart disease (the primary cause of circulatory diseases) is even stronger, and persists even after controlling for all other factors. Stroke mortality, however, shows a different pattern: after controlling for health behaviors, those who attend religious services less than once per week have lower risks of death than those who attend religious services more than once per week.

Mortality from all cancers and from non-lung cancers, respectively, show similar relationships with religious attendance as mortality from strokes; those who attend less than once per week have lower risks of death over the follow-up period than those who attend religious more than once per week. Lung cancer mortality exhibits a slightly different pattern. Model 1 shows a graded but nonsignificant relationship between religious attendance and lung cancer mortality over the follow-up period. This pattern disappears after adjusting for health behaviors.

Those who never attend religious services have 2.1 times the risk of respiratory disease mortality as those who attend services more than once per week (Model 1), a relationship that likely results from the social ties and behavioral regulation provided by religious communities (Models 3 though 5). Religious attendance is only significantly related to diabetes mortality when controlling for health behaviors, including obesity (Model 4), but disappears once we control for social ties (Model 5). Compared to those who attend religious services more than once per week, those who never attend have 2.6 times the risk of dying of infectious diseases over the follow-up period (Model 1); this relationship declines only modestly after controlling for socioeconomic status, social integration, behavioral regulation, and health status (Model 6).

Religious participation shows a graded but nonsignificant relationship with external causes of death; a similar pattern emerges when focusing on suicide or suicide and homicide jointly. But this pattern achieves statistical significance when examining accident mortality. Compared to those who attend religious services more than once per week, those who never attend have 2.4 times the risk of death from accidental causes over the follow-up period. This relationship drops from significance after controlling for health behaviors, perhaps because religious communities may prompt individuals to drink and smoke less, behaviors that are associated with risk-taking and drinking-related accidents. Finally, higher levels of religious attendance protect against the residual causes of death, even after controlling for socioeconomic, social ties, health behavior, and health status variables.

Sex- and Age-Specific Analyses

Table 15.4 presents hazard ratios for the relationships between religious attendance and overall mortality, separately by sex and age groups, and shows that the risks of overall mortality for religious attendance are remarkably similar by sex (for similar results, see Musick, House, Williams 2004). For all ages, the protective relationship between religious participation and mortality persists throughout all models. The hazards ratios of overall mortality for religious attendance are greatest among individuals aged forty-five to sixty-four, and somewhat lower among older and younger adults. Because of the small number of deaths among those aged eighteen to forty-four (N = 407), we do not present cause specific analyses for this age-group.

Table 15.5 shows the cause-specific analyses separately by sex and for ages forty-five to sixty-four and ages sixty-five and older. Within each subgroup, we present a baseline model (adjusting for demographic variables) and a full model (further adjusting for socioeconomic status, social ties, health behaviors, and baseline health). The coefficients for the full set of models are available elsewhere (Rogers, Krueger, and Hummer 2006). Among women, the baseline model shows that compared to those who attend religious services more than once per week, women who never attend have increased risks of death over the follow-up period from circulatory disease (including ischemic heart disease and other circulatory diseases), respiratory disease, infectious diseases, external causes, and residual causes. Adjusting for socioeconomic status, social ties, and health behaviors accounts for the relationship between religious attendance and the risk of death from external causes, respiratory disease, circulatory disease, and other circulatory diseases (full model)—indicating possible pathways that religious attendance might impact cause-specific mortality. Nevertheless, among women, the protective effect of high levels of religious attendance on ischemic

TABLE 15.3

Hazards Ratios of Cause Specific Mortality by Religious Attendance, U.S. Adults Aged 18 and Older, 1987–2002[a,b]

	Model 1	Model 2	Model 3	Model 4	Model 5	Model 6
Circulatory Disease (Deaths N = 1645)						
Never	1.44**	1.44**	1.33*	1.30*	1.24	1.21
Less than once per week	1.21	1.28	1.24	1.23	1.20	1.18
Once per week	0.99	1.01	1.00	1.03	1.01	1.04
Ischemic Heart Disease (Deaths N = 996)						
Never	1.47***	1.44***	1.36***	1.30**	1.28**	1.24*
Less than once per week	1.25	1.32*	1.28*	1.27	1.26	1.24
Once per week	0.96	0.97	0.96	0.99	0.99	1.02
Stroke (Deaths N = 245)						
Never	1.21	1.22	1.05	1.04	0.90	0.88
Less than once per week	0.90	0.95	0.89	0.86*	0.80***	0.77***
Once per week	0.98	1.01	0.97	0.97	0.93	0.93
Other Circulatory Disease (Deaths N = 404)						
Never	1.54*	1.57*	1.45	1.47*	1.37	1.34
Less than once per week	1.32	1.41	1.35	1.37	1.33	1.31
Once per week	1.08	1.13	1.11	1.15	1.13	1.17

Cancer (Deaths N=964)						
Never	1.05	1.04	1.02	0.90	0.90	0.88
Less than once per week	0.93	0.95	0.94	0.87*	0.87**	0.85**
Once per week	0.90	0.90	0.90	0.89	0.89	0.89
Lung Cancer (Deaths N = 256)[c]						
Never	1.89	1.77	1.65	0.93	0.91	0.92
Less than once per week	1.81	1.86	1.78	1.17	1.15	1.17
Once per week	1.33	1.33	1.30	1.10	1.09	1.12
Other Cancer (Deaths N = 708)						
Never	0.89	0.90	0.90	0.92	0.93	0.90
Less than once per week	0.76***	0.77***	0.77***	0.80***	0.80***	0.78***
Once per week	0.82	0.82	0.83	0.86	0.86	0.86
Respiratory Disease (Deaths N = 395)						
Never	2.12***	2.10***	1.74**	1.48**	1.32	1.24
Less than once per week	1.44	1.50	1.36	1.17	1.12	1.07
Once per week	1.01	1.03	0.97	0.92	0.89	0.91
Diabetes (Deaths N = 104)						
Never	1.64	1.54	1.15	1.71**	1.32	1.15
Less than once per week	0.94	1.00	0.87	1.10	0.96	0.89
Once per week	0.86	0.87	0.80	0.99	0.93	0.94

(continued)

Table 15.3. Hazards Ratios of Cause Specific Mortality by Religious Attendance, U.S. Adults Aged 18 and Older, 1987–2002[a,b] (continued)

	Model 1	Model 2	Model 3	Model 4	Model 5	Model 6
Infectious Diseases (Deaths N = 86)						
Never	2.63**	2.54**	1.90	2.81**	2.11**	2.15**
Less than once per week	1.39	1.45	1.29	1.67	1.47	1.48
Once per week	0.95	0.98	0.92	1.11	1.03	1.10
External Causes (Deaths N = 199)						
Never	2.36	2.30	2.31	2.13	2.21	2.19
Less than once per week	1.75	1.81	1.78	1.77	1.78	1.75
Once per week	1.58	1.61	1.59	1.59	1.59	1.59
Suicide (Deaths N = 33)						
Never	1.99	1.88	1.69	1.16	1.14	1.03
Less than once per week	1.50	1.32	1.22	0.94	0.94	0.86
Once per week	1.00	0.93	0.91	0.76	0.78	0.72
Suicide and Homicide (Deaths N = 50)						
Never	2.58	2.54	2.35	1.63	1.62	1.53
Less than once per week	2.12	2.03	1.92	1.46	1.47	1.41
Once per week	1.99	1.94	1.94	1.57	1.62	1.56

Accidents (Deaths N = 149)[d]

Never	2.37*	2.32*	2.40*	2.37	2.51	2.49
Less than once per week	1.73	1.85	1.86	1.98	2.02	1.98
Once per week	1.65	1.71	1.68	1.77	1.75	1.75

Residual Causes (Deaths N = 541)

Never	1.72***	1.67***	1.45***	1.76***	1.56***	1.49***
Less than once per week	1.15	1.19	1.11	1.26*	1.18*	1.14
Once per week	1.22	1.24*	1.18	1.30*	1.25*	1.27**

Note: N = 20,139

a. These models control for the same covariates as the corresponding models in Table 15.2.

b. In all models, those attending religious services more than once per week are the reference group.

c. In these data, all cancers of the respiratory or intrathoratic organs are specifically recorded as cancers of the trachea, bronchus, and lung.

d. Only 22 of the 135 accidents recorded in these data are specifically from motor vehicle accidents.

* p < .10 ** p < .05 *** p < .01 (two-tailed tests)

TABLE 15.4

Hazards Ratios of Overall Mortality for Religious Attendance, By Sex and Age, U.S. Adults Aged 18 and Older, 1987–2002[a,b]

	Model 1	Model 2	Model 3	Model 4	Model 5	Model 6
Females (Survivors N = 9,582; Dead N = 2,217)						
Never	1.51***	1.49***	1.37***	1.34***	1.27***	1.23***
Less than once per week	1.10	1.14	1.08	1.08	1.05	1.05
Once per week	0.97	0.98	0.96	0.98	0.97	1.00
Males (Survivors N = 6,623; Dead N = 1,717)						
Never	1.53***	1.52***	1.37***	1.36***	1.27***	1.20**
Less than once per week	1.26**	1.33***	1.25**	1.28**	1.22*	1.15
Once per week	1.11	1.15	1.12	1.14	1.11	1.09
Ages 18 to 44 (Survivors N = 11,171; Dead N = 407)						
Never	1.45***	1.36***	1.27***	1.18***	1.13**	1.11**
Less than once per week	1.04	1.06	1.02	0.98	0.96	0.96
Once per week	1.11	1.14	1.12	1.12	1.11	1.14
Ages 45 to 64 (Survivors N = 3,765; Dead N = 1,041)						
Never	1.73***	1.64***	1.52***	1.47***	1.43***	1.35***
Less than once per week	1.27***	1.35***	1.30***	1.31***	1.29***	1.21**
Once per week	0.97	1.00	0.99	1.02	1.02	1.00
Ages 65 and Older (Survivors N = 1,269; Dead N = 2,486)						
Never	1.44***	1.45***	1.31***	1.32***	1.23***	1.19***
Less than once per week	1.15	1.19	1.13	1.13	1.09	1.07
Once per week	1.01	1.03	1.00	1.02	1.00	1.02

a. These models control for the same covariates as the corresponding models in Table 15.2.

b. In all models, those attending religious services more than once per week are the reference group.

* $p < .10$ ** $p < .05$ *** $p < .01$ (two-tailed tests)

heart disease, infectious diseases, and residual causes of death remains significant in the full model.

Among women, increasing levels of religious attendance may not be beneficial for cancer mortality. Women who attend religious services less than once per week have between 19 percent and 28 percent lower risks of overall and other cancer mortality over the follow-up period, respectively, than women who attend services more than once per week (baseline model). These relationships persist after controlling for demographic, social ties, health behavior, and baseline health status variables (full model).

Among men, the baseline model reveals that compared to those who attend religious services more than once per week, men who attend less often have increased risks death over the follow-up period from circulatory disease (including ischemic heart disease), lung cancer, respiratory disease, external causes, and residual causes. The relationship between religious attendance and mortality from lung cancer, circulatory disease, and ischemic heart disease results from differences in socioeconomic status, social ties, and health behaviors among men (full model). Further, compared to men who attend services more than once per week, those who attend services less than once per week or weekly have lower risks of death from circulatory disease, ischemic heart disease, and stroke, after controlling for the social integration and behavioral variables (full model). Nevertheless, men who attend religious services once per week have increased risks of mortality from external and residual causes over the follow-up period than men who attend services more than once per week (full model). Among men, modest levels of religious participation may be associated with increased risks of death from some causes, but reduced risks of death from other causes.

The next set of models present the hazard ratios for the relationship between attendance at religious services and cause-specific mortality among adults aged forty-five to sixty-four at baseline. Compared to those who attend religious services more than once per week, those who never attend have increased risks of death from circulatory disease, ischemic heart disease, respiratory disease, and residual causes of death over the follow-up period (baseline model). Further, when examining other circulatory diseases, the hazard ratios for those who attend services less than once per week or once per week, are at the margins of significance (p = 0.118 for both hazard ratios), when compared to those who attend services more than once per week. Higher levels of social integration, healthier behaviors, and better baseline health among those who attend religious services helps to account for the relationships between religious attendance and mortality from respiratory disease, circulatory disease, and other circulatory diseases (full models). The hazard ratios for other circulatory diseases remain large and at the margins of statistical significance (hazard ratio = 2.90, p = .144 for those attending less than once per week, and hazard ratio = 2.87, p = .136 for those attending once per week, relative to those attending more than

TABLE 15.5
Hazards Ratios of Cause Specific Mortality for Religious Attendance, by Sex and Age, U.S. Adults, 1987–2002[a,b]

	Females		Males		Ages 45 to 64		Ages 65 and Older	
	Baseline Model	Full Model	Baseline Model	Full Model	Baseline Model	Full Model	Baseline Model	Full Model
Circulatory Disease	(Deaths N=955)		(Deaths N=690)		(Deaths N=359)		(Deaths N=1,193)	
Never	1.62**	1.39	1.22**	0.95	1.70***	1.20	1.45**	1.29
Less than once per week	1.24	1.25	1.10	0.98	1.37	1.25	1.23	1.23
Once per week	1.00	1.09	0.90	0.86***	0.97	1.00	1.02	1.08
Ischemic Heart Disease	(Deaths N=556)		(Deaths N=440)		(Deaths N=238)		(Deaths N=714)	
Never	1.54**	1.35*	1.31*	1.03	1.74***	1.22	1.43**	1.34*
Less than once per week	1.26	1.31	1.16**	1.05	1.28**	1.16**	1.29	1.36
Once per week	0.96	1.06	0.83	0.79**	0.78*	0.80	1.01	1.10
Stroke	(Deaths N=154)		(Deaths N=91)		(Deaths N=40)		(Deaths N=190)	
Never	1.25	0.92	1.15	0.81	0.91	0.72	1.12	0.78
Less than once per week	1.00	0.91	0.76	0.56**	0.53	0.49	0.88	0.69**
Once per week	1.06	1.04	0.81	0.71	0.50	0.54	0.98	0.87
Other Circulatory Disease	(Deaths N=245)		(Deaths N=159)		(Deaths N=81)		(Deaths N=289)	
Never	2.15**	1.92	0.98	0.75	2.71	1.81	1.75***	1.56*
Less than once per week	1.39	1.46	1.15	1.01	3.43	2.90	1.35	1.32
Once per week	1.07	1.20	1.18	1.13	3.07	2.87	1.05	1.15

	(Deaths N=530)		(Deaths N=434)		(Deaths N=358)		(Deaths N=498)	
Cancer								
Never	0.92	0.78	1.43	1.19	1.07	1.03	1.06	0.85
Less than once per week	0.81*	0.74**	1.24	1.15	1.04	1.09	0.92	0.78***
Once per week	0.81	0.81	1.19	1.17	0.84	0.91	0.94	0.89
	(Deaths N=110)		(Deaths N=146)		(Deaths N=111)		(Deaths N=120)	
Lung Cancer								
Never	1.44	0.51	2.51*	1.48	1.64	0.94	2.47*	0.92
Less than once per week	1.37	0.65	2.41	1.83	1.94	1.46	1.80	0.96
Once per week	1.30	0.91	1.51	1.34	1.23	1.17	1.47	1.03
	(Deaths N=420)		(Deaths N=288)		(Deaths N=247)		(Deaths N=378)	
Other Cancer								
Never	0.84	0.88	1.12	1.08	0.90	1.08	0.84	0.83
Less than once per week	0.72**	0.76**	0.91	0.89	0.77*	0.93	0.78	0.74**
Once per week	0.74	0.79	1.08	1.08	0.72**	0.83	0.86	0.87
	(Deaths N=216)		(Deaths N=179)		(Deaths N=100)		(Deaths N=271)	
Respiratory Disease								
Never	2.38***	1.34	1.85**	1.06	3.86**	2.02	1.94**	1.16
Less than once per week	1.67	1.13	1.23	0.94	2.09	1.30	1.50	1.11
Once per week	1.12	0.99	0.96	0.88	1.35	1.11	0.97	0.88
	(Deaths N=65)		(Deaths N=39)		(Deaths N=40)		(Deaths N=57)	
Diabetes								
Never	1.91	1.61	1.88	1.18	2.23	0.93	1.47	1.37
Less than once per week	0.49	0.67	2.05	1.50	1.66	0.96	0.67	0.74*
Once per week	0.85	1.21	0.86	0.83	1.62	1.22	0.59	0.75

(continued)

Table 15.5. Hazards Ratios of Cause Specific Mortality for Religious Attendance, by Sex and Age, U.S. Adults, 1987–2002[a,b] (continued)

	Females		Males		Ages 45 to 64		Ages 65 and Older	
	Baseline Model	Full Model	Baseline Model	Full Model	Baseline Model	Full Model	Baseline Model	Full Model
Infectious Diseases	(Deaths N=39)		(Deaths N=47)		(Deaths N=25)		(Deaths N=29)	
Never	3.98**	3.80**	1.76	1.22	2.50	1.97	1.68	3.04
Less than once per week	2.00	2.89*	1.04	0.98	1.22	1.75	0.65	1.18
Once per week	1.25	1.66	0.69	0.74	0.72	1.03	0.47	0.62
External Causes	(Deaths N=93)		(Deaths N=106)		(Deaths N=46)		(Deaths N=86)	
Never	2.21*	2.04	2.38	2.17	1.57	1.35	1.95*	2.06
Less than once per week	1.14	1.13	2.49*	2.36	0.83	0.77	0.97	1.03
Once per week	1.15	1.15	2.09**	2.10*	0.94	0.96	1.10	1.12
Residual Causes	(Deaths N=319)		(Deaths N=222)		(Deaths N=113)		(Deaths N=352)	
Never	1.62***	1.41***	2.24	1.78	4.33***	4.19***	1.64***	1.37***
Less than once per week	1.08	1.10	1.40	1.27	1.89**	2.18***	1.23	1.11
Once per week	1.03	1.10	1.78**	1.72**	1.37	1.58	1.34**	1.32**

Note: Women N = 11,799; Men N = 8,340; Ages 45 to 64 N = 4,806; Ages 65 and Older N = 3,755

a. In each subgroup, Model 1 controls for the same covariates as Table 15-2, Model 1, and Model 2 controls for the same covariates as Table 15.2, Model 6.

b. In all models, those attending religious services more than once per week are the reference group.

* p < .10 ** p < .05 *** p < .01 (two-tailed tests)

once per week), and those who attend religious services more than once per week have lower risks of mortality from ischemic heart disease and residual causes than those who attend less frequently, even after adjusting from the full set of covariates (full model).

The final set of models presents the hazard ratios for the relationship between attendance at religious services and cause-specific mortality among adults aged sixty-five and older at baseline. Compared to those who attend religious services more than once per week, those who never attend have increased risks of death from circulatory disease, ischemic heart disease, other circulatory disease, lung cancer, respiratory disease, external causes, and residual causes of death over the follow-up period (baseline model). Controls for socioeconomic status, social integration, and health behaviors account for the relationship between religious attendance and mortality from lung cancer, circulatory disease, respiratory disease, and external causes among older adults (full model). But increasing levels of religious involvement are associated with lower risks of mortality from ischemic heart disease and residual causes of death, even after controlling for socioeconomic, social integration, health behavior, and baseline health variables (full model). Among adults aged sixty-five and older, higher levels of religious attendance are not always associated with lower risks of mortality. After controlling for social ties and health behaviors, those who attend services less than once a week or weekly have lower risks of mortality from stroke, cancer, other cancers, and diabetes over the follow-up period than those who attend more than once per week.

Discussion and Conclusions

This chapter provides a rigorous and comprehensive assessment of the relationship between religious involvement and overall and cause-specific mortality among adults in the United States. We advance prior research by using a large nationally representative data set with a long follow-up period, examining overall and detailed causes of death by sex and for specific age-groups, controlling for a wide array of covariates, and making use of the ICD-10 codes for classifying causes of death. In general, our results show that more frequent attendance at religious services is associated with lower risks of overall mortality, and with lower risks of some specific causes of death, for men and women, and for individuals in various age groups.

We found little difference between men and women in the relationship between religious attendance and overall mortality, which is consistent with the findings of Musick and colleagues (2004). However, more differences emerged when focusing on cause-specific mortality. Both men and women who attended religious services less often had increased risks of death from ischemic heart disease, respiratory disease, external causes, and residual causes of death, compared to men and women who attended services more regularly (Table

15.5, baseline model). More frequent attendance protected women, but not men, against mortality from other circulatory diseases and infectious diseases, whereas more frequent attendance protected men, but not women, from lung cancer mortality (Table 15.5, baseline model). High lung cancer mortality among men is most likely due to the high cigarette consumption levels sustained by males for long periods of time.

The relationship between religious attendance and overall mortality appeared strongest among adults aged forty-five to sixty-four, and was somewhat weaker for older and younger adults. We only had enough deaths to examine specific causes among those aged forty-five to sixty-four and those aged sixty-five and older. More frequent religious attendance was associated with lower risks of death from causes including circulatory diseases, ischemic heart diseases, respiratory diseases, and residual causes, for both middle-aged and older adults (see Table 15.5, baseline model). But more frequent religious attendance protected older-aged, but not middle-aged adults, from other circulatory disease and lung cancer mortality (see baseline model). Because there is a long lag between cigarette smoking and lung cancer, and because most lung cancer deaths occur at older ages, it is reasonable to expect significant lung cancer mortality at the oldest ages (Rogers et al. 2005).

Higher levels of religious attendance are not always associated with lower risks of death. For both men and women, and among adults aged sixty-five and older, those who attend religious services less than once per week or weekly sometimes exhibit lower risks of death than those attending services more than once a week, from causes including ischemic heart diseases (males), strokes (males and older adults), other cancers (females and older adults), and diabetes (older adults). This may be because religious communities contribute to stress and risky behaviors in some instances (see Pargament et al. 2001), or because we possibly "overcontrol" for health, health behavior, and social factors. Nevertheless, this pattern manifests for other cancer deaths in the simplest models that pool all ages and both sexes (see Table 15.3, Model 1).

Certainly, there are enough unanswered questions about the relationship between religious involvement and mortality to warrant additional research, and to caution against hasty plans to fully and extensively incorporate religion into the health care setting or to give religious counseling and support to patients who do not want them. Further, some religious beliefs may conflict with medical treatment: Christian Scientists do not get immunized or take antibiotics and Jehovah's Witnesses do not accept blood products (Koenig 2004). Religious individuals may surrender control of their health to God and abandon an active role in their own health. And spiritual struggles—with anger; a sense of abandonment of, alienation from, or punishment by God; and social isolation, exclusion, and stigma from religious communities—can contribute to stress, depression, risky health behaviors, and negative coping strategies that can increase the risk of death (Ironson et al. 2002; Koenig 2004; Pargament et al.

2001, 2004). Future research must endeavor to clarify what mechanisms might drive the possible relationship between increasing religious involvement and death from some causes and for some specific groups.

We used the long mortality follow-up to take advantage of increased numbers of deaths and, along with the larger numbers of death, to examine more detailed causes of death. Our results confirm prior findings (see, for example, Musick, House, and Williams 2004), but produce more muted effects than Hummer and colleagues (1999). It is important to be mindful of status transitions over time: the longer the follow-up, the greater the chance that individuals will change their marital, smoking, or other statuses, or modify their religious participation.

It is important to remember that people may acquire religious beliefs and decide how active to be in their religious communities, without specifically thinking about their health. Although social policies may use religious organizations to effectively promote health (see, for example, the mentions of faith-based communities in the U.S. *Department of Health and Human Services Strategic Plan*, 2003), not all individuals will willingly participate in those initiatives. Further, those who are enticed into participation in religious communities may not receive the full health benefits experienced by those who have incorporated the social and spiritual dimensions of those communities into their daily lives. Nevertheless, those who do participate in religious communities may experience lower risks of overall and cause specific mortality.

NOTES

This chapter is based on work supported by the National Science Foundation under Grants No. 0243249, 0243189, and 0221093), the Agency for Healthcare Research and Quality (1R03 HS013996–01), and the Robert Wood Johnson Health and Society Scholars Program at the University of Pennsylvania. We thank the NCHS for assembling the data herein and for providing access to the data through their Research Data Center, Robert Krasowski (NCHS) for his expert advice and assistance in linking and analyzing the data sets, and Nancy Mann for editorial suggestions on an earlier draft. This chapter presents the perspectives of the authors and does not reflect the views of any organizations.

1. In many instances, we cite literature and follow convention by discussing church attendance. Nevertheless, our data measure attendance at religious services, which includes churches, synagogues, mosques, and other places of worship.

2. NHIS first asks respondents whether their family incomes are below $20,000 or $20,000 or above, and then follows up with a question about detailed family income. Because there are more missing values for the latter question, we exclude the small percentage of individuals who refuse to answer any question on family income, then impute values for those missing detailed family income by using regression to estimate income separately for those with family incomes in the two broad categories, based on a model that includes age, age-squared, marital status, employment status, education, and race. For those in the highest income category, we estimate a median value, based on the methodology developed by Parker and Fenwick (1983) and Wright (1976, 163), and applied by Krueger and colleagues (2004).

REFERENCES

Allison, P. 1984. *Event History Analysis: Regression for Longitudinal Event Data.* Beverly Hills: Sage.

Berkman, L. F., and T. Glass. 2000. "Social Integration, Social Networks, Social Support, and Health." In *Social Epidemiology*, ed. L. Berkman and I. Kawachi, 137–173. New York: Oxford University Press.

Bock, E. W., J. K. Cochran, and L. Beeghley. 1987. "Moral Messages: The Relative Influence of Denomination on the Religiosity-Alcohol Relationship." *Sociological Quarterly* 28 (1): 89–103.

Chyba, M. M., and L. R. Washington. 1993. "Questionnaires from the National Health Interview Survey, 1985–1989." *Vital and Health Statistics* 1 (31): 1–412.

Cohen, S., W. J. Doyle, D. P. Skoner, B. S. Rabin, and J. M. Gwaltney, Jr. 1997. "Social Ties and Susceptibility to the Common Cold." *Journal of the American Medical Association* 277 (24): 1940–1944.

Duan, N., S. A. Fox, K. P. Derose, and S. Carson. 2000. "Maintaining Mammography Adherence through Telephone Counseling in a Church Based Trail." *American Journal of Public Health* 90:1468–1471.

Durkheim, E. [1897] 1951. *Suicide: A Study in Sociology.* New York: Free Press.

Ellison, C. G. 1994. "Religion, the Life Stress Paradigm, and the Study of Depression." In *Religion in Aging and Health: Theoretical Foundations and Methodological Frontiers*, ed. J. S. Levin, 78–124. Thousand Oaks, CA: Sage Publications.

Ellison, C. G., and L. K. George. 1994. "Religious Involvement, Social Ties, and Social Support in a Southeastern Community." *Journal for the Scientific Study of Religion* 33:46–60.

Flannelly, K. J., C. G. Ellison, and A. L. Strock. 2004. "Methodologic Issues in Research on Religion and Health." *Southern Medical Journal* 97 (12): 1231–1241.

Gartner, J., D. B. Larson, and G. D. Allen. 1991. "Religious Commitment and Mental Health: A Review of the Empirical Literature." *Journal of Psychology and Theology* 19:6–25.

Harrison, M. O., H. G. Koenig, J. C. Hayes, A. G. Eme-Akwari, and K. I. Pargament. 2001. "The Epidemiology of Religious Coping: A Review of Recent Literature." *International Review of Psychiatry* 13:86–93.

House, J. S., K. R. Landis, and D. Umberson. 1988. "Social Relationships and Health." *Science* 241:540–545.

Hummer, R. A., C. G. Ellison, R. G. Rogers, B. E. Moulton, and R. R. Romero. 2004. "Religious Involvement and Adult Mortality in the United States: Review and Perspective." *Southern Medical Journal* 97 (12): 1223–1230.

Hummer, R. A., R. G. Rogers, C. B. Nam, and C. G. Ellison. 1999. "Religious Involvement and U.S. Adult Mortality." *Demography* 36 (2): 273–285.

Idler, E. L., and S. Kasl. 1997. "Religion among Disabled and Non-Disabled Persons II: Attendance at Religious Services as a Predictor of the Course of Disability." *Journals of Gerontology: Social Science* 52B:S306–S316.

Ironson, G., G. F. Solomon, E. G. Balbin, C. O'Cleirigh, A. George, M. Kumar, D. Larson, and T. E. Woods. 2002. "The Ironson–Woods Spirituality/Religiousness Index Is Associated with Long Survival, Health Behaviors, Less Distress, and Low Cortisol in People with HIV/AIDS." *Annals of Behavioral Medicine* 24 (1): 34–48.

Jarvis, G. K., and H. C. Northcott. 1987. "Religion and Differences in Morbidity and Mortality." *Social Science and Medicine* 25:813–824.

Kark, J. D., G. Shemi, Y. Friedlander, O. Martin, O. Manor, and S. H. Blondheim. 1996. "Does Religious Observance Promote Health? Mortality in Secular vs. Religious Kibbutzim in Israel." *American Journal of Public Health* 86:341–346.

King, D. E. 2004. "Publication in the Field of Spirituality, Religion, and Medicine: An Uphill Battle?" *Southern Medical Journal* 97 (12): 1150–1151.

King, D. E., A. G. Mainous, III, and W. S. Pearson. 2002. "C-Reactive Protein, Diabetes, and Attendance at Religious Services." *Diabetes Care* 25:1172–1176.

Kinney, A. Y., L. E. Bloor, W. N. Dudley, R. C. Millikan, E. Marshall, C. Martin, and R. S. Sandler. 2003. "Roles of Religious Involvement and Social Support in the Risk of Colon Cancer among Blacks and Whites." *American Journal of Epidemiology* 158 (11): 1097–1107.

Koenig, H. G. 2004. "Religion, Spirituality, and Medicine: Research Findings and Implications for Clinical Practice." *Southern Medical Journal* 97 (12): 1194–1200.

Koenig, H. G., J. C. Hays, D. B. Larson, L. K. George, H. J. Cohen, M. E. McCullough, K. G. Meador, and D. G. Blazer. 1999. "Does Religious Attendance Prolong Survival? A Six-Year Follow-Up Study of 3,968 Older Adults." *Journal of Gerontology* 54A:M370–M377.

Koenig, H. G., M. E. McCullough, and D. B. Larson. 2001. *Handbook of Religion and Health.* Oxford: Oxford University Press.

Krause, N. 1998. "Stressors in Highly Valued Roles, Religious Coping, and Mortality." *Psychology and Aging* 13:242–255.

———. 2004. "Religion, Aging, and Health: Exploring New Frontiers in Medical Care." *Southern Medical Journal* 97 (12): 1215–1222.

Krueger, P. M., R. G. Rogers, R. A. Hummer, and J. D. Boardman. 2004. "Body Mass, Smoking, and Overall and Cause-Specific Mortality among Older U.S. Adults." *Research on Aging* 26 (1): 82–107.

Kumanyika, S. K., and J. B. Charleston. 1992. "Lose Weight and Win: A Church-Based Weight Loss Program for Blood Pressure Control among Black Women." *Patient Education and Counseling* 19:19–32.

Levin, J. S. 1994a. "Investigating the Epidemiologic Effects of Religious Experience: Findings, Explanations, and Barriers." In *Religion in Aging and Health: Theoretical Foundations and Methodological Frontiers,* ed. J. S. Levin, 3–17. Thousand Oaks, CA: Sage Publications.

———. 1994b. "Religion and Health: Is There an Association, Is It Valid, and Is It Causal?" *Social Science and Medicine* 38:1475–1482.

McCullough, M. E., D. B. Larson, W. T. Hoyt, H. G. Koenig, and C. Thoresen. 2000. "Religious Involvement and Mortality: A Meta-Analytic Review." *Health Psychology* 19 (3): 211–222.

McIntosh, W. A., and P. A. Shifflett. 1984. "Dietary Behavior, Dietary Adequacy, and Religious Social Support: An Exploratory Study." *Review of Religious Research* 26:158–175.

Musick, M. A., J. S. House, and D. R. Williams. 2004. "Attendance at Religious Services and Mortality in a National Sample." *Journal of Health and Social Behavior* 45 (2): 198–213.

National Center for Health Statistics. 1989. *National Health Interview Survey, 1987: Cancer Risk Factor Supplement-Epidemiology Study. Data and Documentation.* Hyattsville, MD: Public Health Service.

———. 2004a. *Introduction to the 2004 National Health Interview Survey Linked Mortality File Release.* Hyattsville, MD: National Center for Health Statistics.

———. 2004b. *National Health Interview Survey-Multiple Cause of Death Public Use Data File: 1986–2000 Survey Years. Documentation and Codebook.* Hyattsville, MD: National Center for Health Statistics.

Olive, K. E. 2004. "Religion and Spirituality: Important Psychosocial Variables Frequently Ignored in Clinical Research." *Southern Medical Journal* 97 (12): 1152–1153.

Oman, D., J. H. Kurata, W. J. Strawbridge, and R. D. Cohen. 2002. "Religious Attendance and Cause of Death over 31 Years." *International Journal of Psychiatry in Medicine* 32:69–89.

Ott, P. W. 1991. "John Wesley on Health as Wholeness." *Journal of Religion and Health* 30:43–58.

Oxman, T. E., D. H. Freedman, Jr., and E. D. Manheimer. 1995. "Lack of Social Participation or Religious Strength and Comfort as Risk Factors after Cardiac Surgery in the Elderly." *Psychosomatic Medicine* 57:5–15.

Pargament, K. I., H. G. Koenig, N. Tarakeshwar, and J. Hahn. 2001. "Religious Struggle as a Predictor of Mortality among Medically Ill Elderly Patients: A 2-Year Longitudinal Study." *Archives of Internal Medicine* 161 (15): 1881–1885.

Pargament, K. I., S. McCarthy, P. Shah, G. Ano, N. Tarakeshwar, A. Wachholtz, N. Sirrine, E. Vasconcelles, N. Murray-Swank, A. Locher, and J. Duggan. 2004. "Religion and HIV: A Review of the Literature and Clinical Implications." *Southern Medical Journal* 97 (12): 1201–1209.

Parker, R. N., and R. Fenwick. 1983. "The Pareto Curve and Its Utility for Open-Ended Income Distributions in Survey Research." *Social Forces* 61 (3): 873–885.

Patterson, B. H., and R. Bilgrad. 1986. "Use of the National Death Index in Cancer Studies." *Journal of the National Cancer Institute* 77:877–881.

Rogers, R. G., R. A. Hummer, P. Krueger, and F. C. Pampel. 2005. "Mortality Attributable to Cigarette Smoking in the United States." *Population and Development Review* 31 (2): 259–292.

Rogers, R. G., R. A. Hummer, and C. B. Nam. 2000. *Living and Dying in the USA: Health, Behavioral, and Social Differentials of Adult Mortality.* San Diego, CA: Academic Press.

Rogers, R. G., P. M. Krueger, and R. A. Hummer. 2006. "Religious Attendance and U.S. Adult Cause-Specific Mortality." Working Paper #2006–06, Population Program, Institute of Behavioral Science, University of Colorado.

Sloan, R. P., E. Bagiella, and T. Powell. 1999. "Religion, Spirituality, and Medicine." *Lancet* 353:664–667.

Sloan, R. P., E. Bagiella, L. VandeCreek, and P. Poulos. 2000. "Should Physicians Prescribe Religious Activities?" *New England Journal of Medicine* 342:1913–1916.

StataCorp. 2003. *Stata Statistical Software: Release 8.0.* College Station, TX: Stata Corporation.

Strawbridge, W. J., R. D. Cohen, S. J. Shema, and G. A. Kaplan. 1997. "Frequent Attendance at Religious Services and Mortality Over 28 Years." *American Journal of Public Health* 87:957–961.

Taylor, R. J., and L. M. Chatters. 1986. "Church-Based Informal Support among Elderly Blacks." *Gerontologist* 26:637–642.

Theorell, T., V. Blomkvist, H. Jonsson, S. Schulman, E. Berntorp, and L. Stigendal. 1995. "Social Support and the Development of Immune Function in Human Immunodeficiency Virus Infection." *Psychosomatic Medicine* 57:32–36.

Thompson, M. P., and P. J. Vardaman. 1997. "The Role of Religion in Coping with the Loss of a Family Member to Homicide." *Journal for the Scientific Study of Religion* 36 (1): 44–51.

U.S. Department of Health and Human Services. 2003. *U.S. Department of Health and Human Services Strategic Plan.* Washington, DC: U.S. Department of Health and Human Services.

Weaver, A. J., and K. J. Flannelly. 2004. "The Role of Religion/Spirituality for Cancer Patients and Their Caregivers." *Southern Medical Journal* 97 (12): 1210–1214.

Whooley, M. A., A. L. Boyd, J. M. Gardin, and D. R. Williams. 2002. "Religious Involvement and Cigarette Smoking in Young Adults: The CARDIA Study." *Archives of Internal Medicine* 162:1604–1610.

Wright, E. O. 1976. "Class Structure and Income Inequality." PhD diss., University of California, Berkeley.

16

▶ ▶ ▶ ▶ ▶ ▶ ▶ ▶ ▶ ▶ ▶ ▶ ▶ ▶ ◀ ◀ ◀ ◀ ◀ ◀ ◀ ◀ ◀ ◀ ◀ ◀ ◀ ◀

Race, Religious Involvement, and Health

The Case of African Americans

CHRISTOPHER G. ELLISON, ROBERT A. HUMMER,
AMY M. BURDETTE, AND MAUREEN R. BENJAMINS

As the preceding chapters demonstrate, researchers from multiple disciplines have investigated the relationships between religion and health outcomes, including mental and physical health and mortality risk (Ellison and Levin 1998; Chatters 2000). Although this field has expanded rapidly over the past two decades, it remains in its early stages. Although the findings are not unanimous, and research on this topic continues to be controversial in some quarters (e.g., Sloan, Bagiella, and Powell 1999), mounting evidence links aspects of religious involvement with salutary health outcomes. Indeed, this is the conclusion rendered by the most extensive treatment of the field to date, *The Handbook of Religion and Health* (Koenig, McCullough, and Larson 2001), which offers a detailed summary, synthesis, and evaluation of approximately twelve hundred works (including eight hundred-plus empirical analyses) addressing aspects of this religion–health connection.

Despite the considerable theoretical and empirical advances in this area, until recently the vast majority of religion–health studies in the United States have focused on predominantly Euro-American (non-Hispanic white) samples, often giving short shrift to the potential for racial/ethnic variations in these relationships. This limitation has represented a significant oversight for at least two main reasons. First, racial/ethnic minority populations differ from non-Hispanic whites in patterns, levels, and types of religious involvement. On average, African Americans, in particular, tend to be more religious—by virtually any conventional indicator—than non-Hispanic whites from similar backgrounds. Moreover, a long tradition of work in sociology and allied fields underscores the distinctiveness of the Black Church and the religious experiences of African Americans. Second, racial/ethnic minorities—and African Americans in particular—confront significant disparities and challenges in the area of health

(Williams and Collins 1995; U.S. Department of Health and Human Services 2000). Although researchers and policymakers have explored the impact of economic marginality, discrimination, differential access to health care, residential contexts, and other factors that may give rise to racial/ethnic health inequalities, it is also important to understand the distribution and impact of potential protective factors, including religious involvement, within and between racial/ethnic subgroups.

This chapter begins with a very brief overview of major health and mortality disparities affecting African Americans, underscoring the importance of research on factors that influence health within this population. Next we identify key aspects of African American religious life that may be germane to health and well-being. Then we review the empirical evidence regarding links between religion and various health outcomes among African Americans, and where feasible, black–white differences in religion–health relationships. We also explore available data on several prominent explanations for religion–health relationships, including (a) health behaviors and lifestyles, (b) social integration and support, (c) psychological resources, and (d) coping styles and practices. The concluding section of this chapter identifies several of the most urgent directions for future research on the intersection of race, religion, and health.

African American Health and Mortality

The health and mortality profile of African Americans remains significantly disadvantaged compared to that of whites and most minority groups in the country. Despite tremendous improvements over the last one hundred years, life expectancy at birth for black males (68.9 years) remains over six years shorter than for white males (75.3 years), while the disadvantage for black females (75.9 years) compared to white females (80.4 years) is nearly five years (Arias 2007). These life expectancy figures reflect African American disadvantages in death rates starting at the first day of life and extending throughout the life span, with the possible exception of ages ninety and over, where blacks may have lower death rates than whites (Nam 1995).

Recent figures also show that death rates among blacks are especially high compared to whites during infancy and during early adulthood (Hummer, Benjamins, and Rogers 2004). Indeed, at age-group twenty to twenty-four, the non-Hispanic black mortality rate is 2.07 times higher than non-Hispanic whites; at age-group forty to forty-four, the reported disparity is 2.24 to 1. In contrast, the relative disparity shrinks to 1.68 at age-group sixty to sixty-four, 1.41 at age-group seventy to seventy-four, and 1.15 at age-group eighty to eighty-four, respectively (Hummer et al. 2004). These age patterns are reflective of especially wide black-to-white excesses in mortality due to homicide and infectious diseases at the younger ages (Rogers 1992). Earlier-age major onsets of heart disease and cancer mortality among middle-aged blacks relative to whites are also clearly important.

A considerable body of evidence also suggests that African Americans remain highly disadvantaged across most measures of physical health and disability compared to whites. For example, findings from several national-level surveys consistently show that blacks rate their own health less favorably than whites (Hummer et al. 2004; Smith and Kington 1997). This same pattern also holds across most observed indicators of health and function and the known presence of disease, such as diabetes, hypertension, heart conditions, and arthritis (Hayward et al. 2000; Smith and Kington 1997). Indeed, Hayward and Heron (1999, 88) conclude that, "the most disadvantaged group is blacks. Blacks live substantially fewer years than the other racial/ethnic groups, and they live a higher proportion of those years with a chronic health impairment."

The health and mortality disadvantages that African Americans experience have not only been at the forefront of public health and demographic research for many years, but they are also an important part of the national health agenda. In a prominent review of race, socioeconomic status, and health, Williams and Collins (1995, 380–381) wrote that "racial and socioeconomic inequality in health is arguably the single most important public health issue in the United States." This sentiment is echoed in official government health documents. Indeed, one of the two main goals of the Healthy People 2010 initiative (U.S. Department of Health and Human Services 2000) is to eliminate health disparities among Americans. Given that a number of the relative black–white health disparities in question currently remain as wide now as they were in 1990, the health disadvantages that African Americans face will remain a major concern for researchers and policymakers for at least the next decade.

Religion among African Americans

Religion has played a distinctive role in the collective and individual lives of African Americans. Throughout U.S. history, the Black Church has served as a symbolic center of African American life, as one of the only institutions operated and organized by and for African Americans. Religious organizations have served a range of functions, promoting individual and collective self-help, community leadership and economic development, racial socialization and political mobilization (Lincoln and Mamiya 1990). Not surprisingly, in one national survey, nearly 90 percent of African American adults held a positive view of the sociohistorical role of the Black Church and its contributions to African American life (Taylor, Thornton, and Chatters 1987), and in another study large majorities of older African Americans agreed that religion is important in sustaining black people in the face of racial injustice (Krause 2004b).

Throughout much of the twentieth century, African Americans have affiliated largely with Evangelical Protestant churches, especially the Baptist faith (Ellison and Sherkat 1990; Lincoln and Mamiya 1990). In recent decades, however, this dominance has eroded slowly, as more African Americans have joined other conservative Protestant groups (including various Pentecostal and Holiness churches such as COGIC), as well as nontraditional groups ranging from the Jehovah's Witnesses to the Nation of Islam (Ellison and Sherkat 1990; Sherkat 2002). Nevertheless, approximately half of African Americans continue to report Baptist ties, while only small percentages identify with Catholicism or other predominantly white faiths (Ellison and Sherkat 1990; Taylor, Chatters, and Levin 2004). The percentage of religiously unaffiliated African Americans is also climbing, particularly among younger persons, and among residents of urban and non-southern areas (Sherkat 2002).

Compared to whites from comparable backgrounds, African Americans consistently report higher levels of virtually every aspect of religious practice and belief that is measured in large-scale survey data. This includes the frequency of attendance at religious services and other types of congregational participation, as well as personal devotion (e.g., prayer, Bible reading, religious media consumption), subjective religious identity and religious salience, and orthodox beliefs (e.g., belief in biblical inerrancy, human sinfulness, etc.) (Taylor, Chatters, and Levin 2004; Krause and Chatters 2005). Within the African American population, most indicators of religiousness tend to be particularly high among women (versus men), older adults (versus younger persons), and Southern and rural residents (versus non-southerners and urbanites) (Taylor, Chatters, and Levin 2004). Social class variations in most types of religious practice (except for denominational affiliation patterns) appear to be muted among African Americans.

Observers have also noted several distinctive features of African American Christian theological understanding that may be germane to individual health and well-being (McRae, Carey, and Anderson-Scott 1998; Taylor, Chatters, and Levin 2004). First, God is often regarded as omnipotent and omniscient, and fundamentally beneficent (e.g., Cooper-Lewter and Mitchell 1986). Despite acknowledging the dual nature of God—as both just and merciful—in contrast with some other theological traditions (e.g., white fundamentalism), African American Christianity tends to emphasize God's care and love, as well as God's active participation in the lives of His creation. The God of many African American Christians is gracious and forgiving, a God of second chances. Themes of personal triumph and redemption, as well as collective liberation from oppression and injustice, are particularly prominent (Moyd 1979; Maynard-Reid 2000). African American beliefs highlight "survival theology," a perspective on faith that is practical and geared toward helping African Americans cope successfully with discrimination, marginality, and other problems encountered in daily life (Paris 1995; Krause 2004b). Indeed, African American Christianity has tended to center on close and ongoing personal relationships between individuals and God (or Jesus) (Washington 1994; Maynard-Reid 2000). As Mattis and Jagers (2001, 523) put it: "African American religiosity and worship traditions emphasize a profound sense of intimacy with the divine, and a horizontal extension of that intimacy into the human community." In practice, this is often manifested in close affective ties among coreligionists, and a strong sense of community among church members (Pargament et al. 1983; McRae, Carey, and Anderson-Scott 1998).

Religion, Health, and Mortality

The past decade has witnessed a number of studies linking religious variables with mental and physical health outcomes, including mortality. The following three subsections detail the findings and limitations of those studies, with particular attention to the small bodies of research on African Americans specifically, as well as comparisons of religion–health linkages across racial/ethnic populations.

Mortality

A growing body of research, now consisting of at least three dozen empirical analyses, demonstrates that religious involvement is a protective factor for all-cause and cause-specific mortality risk (see, e.g., Chapters 14 and 15 in this volume). This has been the conclusion of thematic and systematic reviews, and at least one formal meta-analysis (McCullough et al. 2000; Powell, Shahabi, and Thoresen 2003; Hummer et al. 2004). Although some studies have explored varied indicators of religiousness (e.g., religious coping, prayer), as well as religious affiliation, by far the most common measure of religious involvement is the frequency of self-reported attendance at religious services (Hummer et al. 2004). Despite the apparent strength of the research findings in this area, with few exceptions (e.g., Hill et al. 2005), investigations have used mostly non-Hispanic white and community samples, and very few studies of religion and mortality have focused specifically on African Americans. The first exception to this pattern of neglect was the work of Bryant and Rakowski (1992), who analyzed data on the African American subsample from the Longitudinal Study of Aging (LSOA). They documented salutary effects of religious attendance among African American elders, particularly women. A more recent study used data on all age groups used data on the African American subsample of the 1987 National Health Interview Survey Cancer Risk Factor Supplement (Ellison et al. 2000). Briefly, this study of African Americans revealed a strong protective effect of religious attendance on mortality risk, and specifically, evidence of a graded pattern of religious effects. Moreover, the effects of religious attendance on mortality risk differed significantly by gender, age, and region; these relationships were stronger for women, adults under age fifty-five, and southern residents, respectively. Thus, women and southerners benefit from religious attendance in two ways: (a) from higher levels, and (b) from stronger protective effects associated with each increment in attendance. By contrast, religious involvement had stronger effects for persons under fifty-five, who tend to be less religious than older adults. This pattern is consistent with the findings of Musick and colleagues (2004), and may reflect the general tendency for lifestyle factors to predict mortality strongly during middle age, whereas the effects of physical deterioration may swamp those of behavioral factors among older individuals.

A handful of published studies have conducted tests for race (i.e., black–white) differences in the relationships between religious involvement and mortality risk. In one study of elders (Koenig et al. 1999), and also in one study of U.S. adults of all ages (Hummer et al. 1999), no evidence of race differences was detected. One small-scale study of breast cancer survival reported a stronger effect of religious involvement among African American women as compared with whites, but on closer inspection this pattern was only marginally statistically significant (Van Ness, Kasl, and Jones 2003).

However, a more recent study by Dupre and colleagues (2006) offers a more nuanced perspective on this issue. Briefly, they used data on elders in a Southeastern U.S. community to examine the implications of religious attendance for the black–white mortality crossover, i.e., the tendency for African Americans to outlive their white counterparts once both reach very old age. Dupre and colleagues find evidence of both (a) protective effects of religious attendance (their lone religious indicator) on mortality risk and (b) a racial crossover in mortality for both men and women. Moreover, they add an important layer of complexity by modeling religious attendance in terms of differential frailty. With this innovation, they find that for women only, the effect of attendance is race- and age-dependent, modifying the age at crossover by ten years, but for men, the effect of attendance is unrelated to race and does not alter the crossover pattern. Dupre and associates conclude that having little or no religious involvement appears to prolong the mortality disadvantage faced by African Americans much later in the life course. Among women, however, frequent religious attendance offsets the higher mortality rates of African Americans generally found at younger ages, making the hazards for African Americans and whites nearly identical from age sixty-five to age eighty. These intriguing findings underscore the need for additional research on the race-, sex-, and age-contingent effects of various facets of religiousness and spirituality on mortality risk.

Physical Health

The research on mortality is one facet of a broader literature on religious variations in physical health. During the late 1980s, a series of published reviews identified several hundred empirical studies that (a) contained one or more religious indicators, (b) focused on one or more health outcomes, and (c) were published in the medical or epidemiologic literatures during the preceding century (Jarvis and Northcott 1987; Levin and Vanderpool 1987, 1989). More recently, Koenig and colleagues (2001) have identified an extensive body of studies on religion and health, including many analyses of associations between religious factors and physical health outcomes. This magisterial work reports at least some statistically findings linking measures of religious involvement to health indicators, or showing religious group differences in morbidity, have been found in studies of a wide range of diseases, including heart disease (numerous types), hypertension, stroke, cancer (numerous sites), gastrointestinal disease, immune function, and others, along with miscellaneous health indicators such as overall subjective or self-rated health, disability, and self-reported symptomatology. However, although such thematic reviews seem to provide impressive evidence (e.g., Luskin 2000), there are several problems with this work. First, as Musick and Worthen (Chapter 13, this volume) suggest, the literature contains surprisingly few original empirical data analyses. Second, numerous health outcomes have been the subject of only one or two isolated studies, resulting in an absence of cumulative, well-replicated findings. Third, Powell and colleagues (2003) have examined the available empirical findings via a probing "levels of analysis" approach, and have identified a number of methodological and other limitations of even the strongest studies (see also Sloan, Bagiella, and Powell 1999). Taking into account the number of studies, the quality of data, and the consistency of findings, Powell, Shahabi, and Thoresen (2003) conclude that evidence for a linkage between religion and physical health remains inconclusive.

Because relatively few studies in this literature have focused on minority samples, or have examined race differences in religious effects, the base of evidence on these issues is even thinner. Nevertheless, one relatively common outcome in the religion–health area is self-rated health, which has drawn the attention of researchers for several reasons: (a) it is correlated with other physical health indicators, including physician diagnoses; (b) it has been shown to predict mortality very strongly in follow-up studies, over and above the effects of other measures of health problems (e.g., Idler and Benyamini 1997); and (c) it is widely available in many epidemiologic, health, and social surveys. Perhaps two dozen studies over the years have reported religious variations in self-rated health, although most of these works are hindered by their reliance on cross-sectional data. Nevertheless, a few studies have focused specifically on African Americans, or have compared religious effects across black and white subgroups. In general, these studies have reported salutary associations between religious attendance—and sometimes other aspects of religious involvement—and the self-rated health of African Americans, but limited or null estimated net effects of religious involvement among whites (Ferraro and Koch 1994; St. George and McNamara 1984). However, Drevenstedt (1998) reported that these associations vary by race, gender, and age. In his study of adults under the age of sixty-five, the clearest evidence of positive multivariate associations between religious attendance and self-rated health emerge among non-Hispanic white men eighteen to thirty-nine and forty to sixty-five, non-Hispanic white women forty to sixty-five, and non-Hispanic black women aged eighteen to thirty-nine.

We are aware of only two longitudinal studies that have investigated this issue. Analyzing data on a sample of elders drawn in the southeastern U.S., Musick (1996) found that (a) religious attendance is positively associated with changes in self-rated health; (b) nonorganizational religiousness largely is unrelated with this outcome; and (c) conservative Protestant affiliation is linked with declines in self-rated health. However, no major race differences in these patterns surfaced in those data. However, in data from the Health and Retirement Survey, a large nationwide panel survey of middle-aged adults (see Hummer et al., Chapter 14 of this volume), Ellison and colleagues (2004) show that religious attendance has a modest positive effect on self-rated health among non-Hispanic whites but not among African Americans.

A second physical health outcome receiving occasional attention from religion–health researchers is hypertension (Levin and Vanderpool 1989), a health problem that afflicts African Americans at higher rates than non-Hispanic whites. Several studies suggest that religion and spirituality may have salutary effects on blood pressure and related cardiovascular conditions (e.g., Koenig et al. 1998; Luskin 2000), and that this pattern may be especially strong among African Americans. For example, in one early study conducted among 1,420 African Americans living in Washington County, Maryland, simply being affiliated with a religious congregation was associated with lower systolic and diastolic blood pressures (Livingston, Levine, and Moore 1991). More recently, Loustalot (2006) used data from the Jackson Heart Study, a large sample of southern African Americans, and found that frequency of religious attendance and personal prayer are associated with lower levels of systolic and diastolic blood pressure. In one clinical study comparing blacks and whites, Steffen and associates (2001) found that religious involvement—especially the experience of close personal relationships with God—is associated with lower blood pressure only among African Americans.

Mental Health and Psychological Well-Being

Contrary to the claims of a long tradition of psychological critics (e.g., Ellis 1962), careful reviews of the empirical research literature have documented a generally salutary relationship between aspects of religious involvement and a wide range of mental health outcomes (Koenig, McCullough, and Larson 2001). With regard to depression, one of the most common mental health outcomes investigated in these studies, a recent meta-analysis concluded that (a) multiple measures of religiousness (including organizational and nonorganizational behaviors, intrinsic religious orientation, God concept) exhibit robust inverse associations with measures of depression, and (b) these patterns are stronger among persons experiencing stressful life events or conditions, as compared with others (Smith, McCullough, and Poll 2003). Although most of this literature is based on mainly or exclusively on non-Hispanic white samples, a growing body of research focuses on the relationships between religious factors and negative mental health outcomes, such as distress and depression, among racial/ethnic minority groups, primarily African Americans.

These findings have been inconsistent; results from some community samples suggest a salutary role of religious involvement (e.g., Handal, Black-Lopez, and Moergen 1989; Brown, Ndubuisi, and Gary 1990), while others have yielded null or even negative findings (Brown et al. 1992). One analysis of panel data from a nationwide sample of African American adults has shown that the frequency of religious attendance is inversely associated with psychological distress over a three-year study period; this salutary effect is amplified at the highest levels of baseline attendance, i.e., for those persons who attend services several times per week. In addition, African Americans who receive a great deal of guidance from religion in their daily lives also report lower levels of distress compared with other respondents (Ellison, Musick, and Henderson 2008).

Although a number of studies have explored religious predictors of symptomatology, only a handful have examined religious effects on other mental health outcomes. One strand of this work focuses on the risk of major depressive episode or other specific clinical conditions (e.g., Koenig et al. 1998). For the most part, this literature is silent with regard to (a) African Americans or (b) race/ethnic differences in the effects of religiousness. In a rare exception, however, data from the panel NSBA revealed that religious guidance is inversely related to the risk of major depressive episode over a three-year study period, even with controls for stressors, self-esteem and mastery, lifetime history of depression, and demographic characteristics (Ellison and Flannelly 2009). Further, although other aspects of religious involvement in this study, including frequency of attendance, were not associated with major depression in a straightforward fashion, among the small number of high attenders there were zero (0) cases of major depression during the study period (Ellison and Flannelly 2009). A second strand of research has addressed possible religious influences on subjective well-being (e.g., life satisfaction). In marked contrast to the paucity of research on most other health-relevant outcomes, several investigators have focused on religion and subjective well-being among African American samples. They consistently report that multiple aspects of religious involvement are positively associated with life satisfaction, even with controls for health status and other potential confounding factors (Levin, Chatters, and Taylor 1995; Levin and Taylor 1998). At least one study of African Americans suggests that these religious effects are stronger among older persons and non-southerners, respectively, as compared with younger persons and southern residents (Ellison and Gay 1990).

As with the other health outcomes considered in this chapter, the literature contains only a handful of direct assessments of racial/ethnic variations in religious effects on mental health. One example of such a study used cross-sectional data on a sample of residents from a southeastern community sample, and reported that religious attendance is associated with fewer depressive symptoms among whites, but was unrelated to depression among African Americans. On the other hand, religious nonaffiliation was associated with higher depression for blacks, but not for whites (Ellison 1995). By contrast, among community-dwelling elders diagnosed with cancer residing in the same southeastern sampling area, religious activities reduced depressive symptoms mainly among African Americans, but much less so among whites (Musick et al. 1998). At least two studies have used data on nationwide samples to explore the intersection of race, religion, and life satisfaction, and both report that estimated religious effects appear stronger among African Americans, as compared with whites (St. George and McNamara 1984; Thomas and Holmes 1992).

Explanations for Religion–Health Relationships

Next we turn to a consideration of possible explanations of the religion–health relationships outlined earlier. Efforts to account for these associations remain in their early stages. Nevertheless, several theoretical discussions have centered on the role of religious involvement in (a) fostering positive health behaviors and healthy lifestyles, (b) promoting social and psychological resources, and (c) encouraging constructive coping styles and practices (Ellison and Levin 1998; George, Ellison, and Larson 2002). Taken together, these mechanisms are thought to contribute to health and well-being directly, and to enhance individual resilience in the face of stressful events and conditions. We draw on these ideas as a means of organizing recent literature on race, religion, and health.

Health Behaviors and Healthy Lifestyles

One common explanation for religious variations in morbidity and mortality lies with health behaviors and lifestyle factors. Briefly, religious groups often attempt to shape the behaviors of their adherents. In some instances (e.g., alcohol and substance use/abuse, sexual behavior, violence), there may be doctrinal bases for their moral guidelines. Religious influence may operate via a number of micro-level mechanisms, including: (a) communication of moral messages through formal channels (e.g., sermons, official statements); (b) guilt feelings due to internalization of religious values and norms; (c) threat of divine punishment; (d) embarrassment or social sanctions, e.g., ostracism, for violations of behavioral norms; (e) rewards of positive feedback and social esteem for conformity; (f) voluntary modification of behavior based on religious reference groups or role models; and others (Ellison and Levin 1998). But there is mounting evidence that religious attendance is linked with a broader array of health behaviors that are not directly linked with moral ideology, including diet and exercise, sleep, seat belt use, preventive health care utilization, and others (e.g., Benjamins and Brown 2004; Hill et al. 2006). These relationships may reflect a more general ethos of "moderation in all things," a belief in the instrumental value of physical vitality for members, the role of congregational information networks, or perhaps dispositional factors (e.g., risk aversion, planfulness). Some religious groups also sponsoring interventions or programs aimed at promoting positive health behaviors among members, e.g., weight loss, blood pressure control, and others (DeHaven et al. 2004; Campbell et al. 2007).

Although a growing literature focuses on religious variations in health behavior, only a modest body of work has explored the intersection of race, religion, and health behavior. One area receiving attention has been that of alcohol and tobacco use. Among African American adults, data from one community sample reveals inverse associations between religious involvement and (a) smoking among women of childbearing age (Ahmed et al. 1994) and (b) smoking and alcohol use among black men (Brown and Gary 1994). In data from a nationwide sample of older adults, Krause (2003c) finds that African Americans are more likely to abstain from alcohol in late life than their white counterparts, a pattern that appears due to (a) the greater tendency of older blacks to belong to fundamentalist churches and (b) the greater tendency of African American elders to derive a sense of meaning in life from religious faith.

Among adolescents, the evidence hints at a different pattern. For example, Wallace and colleagues (2003) found that highly religious white youth are more likely to avoid alcohol and marijuana than their African American counterparts. With regard to sexual behavior, studies of adolescents have tended to find weaker or negligible constraining effects of religion on the timing of coital debut and the number of sexual partners among African Americans, particularly males, as compared with whites (Whitehead, Wilcox, and Rostosky 2001; Rostosky, Regnerus, and Wright 2003). Among adults, the links between race, religion, and sexual behavior remain understudied. Although African Americans report higher rates of sexual infidelity in marriage than whites, and religious involvement is inversely related to infidelity (Burdette et al. 2007), we are aware of no evidence that the constraining effects of religion differ for blacks versus whites. However, at least one study shows that while African American males are more likely to commit acts of partner violence than whites, this is only the case among those who rarely or never attend religious services (Ellison et al. 2007b). Clearly a great deal of additional work is needed on the interplay of race, religion, and a broad array of health behaviors and lifestyle factors.

Social Integration and Social Support

In addition to their regulatory function, religious communities also have an important integrative role (Ellison and George 1994). In this connection, religious congregations may contribute to health and well-being through: (a) formal congregational programs, including health interventions; (b) clergy support, advice, counseling; (c) coreligionist network size, number and frequency of social contacts; (d) informal exchanges of tangible, socioemotional, informational, and spiritual support; (e) volunteering and provision of assistance to others; (f) perceived quality of support, anticipated support from others; and (g) religious influences on marital, family, and intergenerational support systems (Ellison and Levin 1998; Krause 2002, 2004a, and Chapter 12 of this volume).

Formal Support

As we noted earlier, the Black Church has traditionally served as a crucial source of assistance for African Americans dealing with the impact of discrimination, poverty, and social marginality (Lincoln and Mamiya 1990; Billingsley 1999). Formal support mechanisms, especially programs targeting specific groups in need, have been central to congregational life. African American churches often sponsor a wide array of programs for church members and others in the community, including family support programs, such as those to assist at-risk youths and working parents (Caldwell, Greene, and Billingsley 1992), and elders and shut-ins (Caldwell et al. 1995), as well as programs to aid the poor, promote civil rights and racial justice, community development, and other objectives (Barnes 2004). One area of interest has been health promotion, particularly the dissemination of health education and rudimentary health care via congregational interventions. Because African Americans, especially the poor, face barriers to accessing quality health care (especially preventive care), such initiatives have the potential to meet vital needs in an underserved population. To be sure, such programs are often effective in modifying health behaviors (DeHaven et al. 2004; Campbell et al. 2007). At the same time, studies indicate that health promotion efforts are more common in churches with ample resources (funds, staff, and members), well-educated clergy, and large numbers of other types of programs underway (Thomas et al. 1994; Trinitapoli, Ellison, and Boardman 2009). Further, although much of the published literature in this area involves case studies of African American congregational programs (e.g., Davis et al. 1994; Yanek et al. 2001), comparisons of black and white churches find little evidence that African American congregations offer more programs in the health arena (Trinitapoli, Ellison, and Boardman 2009) or other areas (e.g., Tsitsos 2003).

Clergy Support

Another potentially important source of aid and assistance is the clergy. Despite the rise of psychological and psychiatric care for family and mental health counseling, significant numbers of Americans continue to consult religious leaders. Indeed, the amount of time spent each week in counseling activities by Protestant clergy has increased since the 1950s. However, surprisingly few studies address the role of clergy in providing support, counseling, and other types of assistance. Consequently, we have limited information concerning (a) who seeks clergy aid, (b) what clergy do in various types of counseling, and the sources of variation in these practices, or (c) what effects clergy support has on mental or physical well-being (Weaver 1995). Nevertheless, several studies do suggest that pastors are particularly important sources of assistance for African Americans, because they are common in those communities, esteemed and trusted, and accessible to those with limited means (Neighbors, Musick, and Williams 1998; Ellison et al. 2006; Taylor et al. 2000). According to Neighbors and colleagues (1998), African Americans report consulting the clergy for a wide range of problems, but especially family and mental health issues. Clergy are often the last source of help even for blacks who initially sought assistance from other (often institutional) sources. Further, African Americans tend to express a high degree of satisfaction with the results of their clergy contacts. Among a nationwide sample of elderly adults, Krause (2002) reports that African Americans report receiving greater support from clergy members than their white counterparts. Further, on average, African American elders reap greater mental health benefits from talking with the clergy (Krause 2003a). Given (a) the prominence of clergy in African American communities, (b) the expansive role of pastors in the lives of church members and their families, and (c) the obstacles (financial and cultural) to the use of formal counseling services among African Americans, this is an area that warrants additional research in the future.

Informal Support

Turning to the topic of informal supportive exchanges, there is strong evidence that church-based support plays an important role for African Americans, especially elders. Investigators have found that church members provide a range of broad array of instrumental resources, i.e., goods and services, in the black community, and that this church-based assistance tends to complement, rather than replicate, the support elders receive from family members and associates outside the congregation (Taylor and Chatters 1986; Taylor, Chatters, and Levin 2004). Moreover, church members also constitute an important source of socioemotional support—i.e., companionship, confiding relationships, and encouragement—for their fellows (Walls and Zarit 1991; Taylor, Chatters, and Levin 2004). Krause (2002) finds that African American elders tend to report receiving and providing higher levels of several different types of church-based support, including tangible, socioemotional, and spiritual support, than older whites. In light of their embeddedness within these ongoing networks of supportive exchange, perhaps it is not surprising that older African Americans also report greater anticipated support, i.e., they express confidence that church members would help if and when aid is needed (Krause 2002). This latter finding is especially important because numerous studies over the years have revealed that anticipated support is more closely linked with health and well-being with actual provision or receipt of assistance.

Until recently, few studies actually explored the possible role of congregational support systems in explaining observed links between religious involvement and health outcomes among African Americans. Fortunately, several recent investigations address this long-standing gap in the literature. For example, in data on a nationwide sample of African American adults, much of the net effect of attendance on distress is mediated by congregational support (Jang and Johnson 2004; Ellison et al. 2007a). Although data comparing the effects of church-based support among whites and African Americans are scarce, recent work by Krause (2006) offers fresh insight on this issue among older adults. Briefly, based on a national longitudinal study of elders, he shows that: (a) emotional support from church members mitigates the harmful effects of financial strain on self-rated physical health; (b) support from secular network members fails to exert a similar effect; and (c) these stress-buffering effects of church-based emotional support surface only among older African Americans, and not among older whites. These findings underscore the potent, and unique, effects of African Americans' congregational support relationships. This is yet another area in which recent work illuminates new and important directions for further inquiry into the links between race, religion, and health outcomes.

Although it is quite appropriate for studies on religion and health—like Krause's (2006) study noted previously—to distinguish between religious support and support from secular sources (e.g., families), the links between religious and family support may be greater than has been recognized. This is the case because: (a) church and family members (e.g., extended kin) may overlap within some communities; (b) religious involvement may promote closer marital bonds and more harmonious contacts within families; and (c) religious values may shape norms regarding filial responsibility and obligation across generational lines, especially between parents and adult children. Further, African Americans as a group tend to exhibit both (a) high levels of religious involvement and (b) distinctive patterns of family life (e.g., low rates of marriage, high rates of divorce, cohabitation, and nonmarital childbearing), making the complex relations among religion, family, and health and well-being especially deserving of closer scrutiny. At least two studies provide useful information on these issues. First, in a nationwide sample of African American adults, multiple dimensions of religious involvement are positively associated with: (a) the number of family members with whom respondents were in regular contact; (b) the frequency of visits with nonresidential family members; and (c) the feelings of affective closeness toward family members (Ellison 1997). Comparative data from the National Survey of Families and Households reveals strong religious variations in elders' beliefs about (a) responsibilities of parents to assist adult children in need, and (b) responsibilities of adult children to help aging parents. Theological conservatism is more closely linked to these attitudes than affiliation or attendance, and the relationships between religious beliefs and filial norms were stronger for African Americans than non-Hispanic whites (Ellison, Xu, and Grayson 2007).

Psychological Resources

Critics have long contended that orthodox Christian beliefs in divine omnipotence and human sinfulness erode feelings of self-worth and personal mastery, breeding helplessness and hopelessness and robbing individuals of key psychological resources that can promote health and well-being (e.g., Ellis 1962). However, recent work calls these claims into question, on both theoretical and empirical grounds. First, the quality of fellowship often generated within religious congregations may build self-esteem and feelings of personal empowerment. For churchgoers, regular interaction with like-minded others from similar backgrounds may reinforce basic role identities, role expectations (e.g., definitions of a "good" parent, spouse, Christian), and role commitments. Individuals may gain affirmation that their values and emotions, and their responses to personal events and community affairs, are reasonable and appropriate (Ellison 1993). More generally, black churches may provide an interpersonal context in which members are evaluated by coreligionists—and hence come to evaluate themselves—on the basis of distinctive criteria that are not rooted in material, educational, or occupational attainments. These criteria may include: (a) their inherent uniqueness and worth as individuals, (b) their sociability and service to others, and (c) their spiritual qualities, such as wisdom and morality. Thus, regular interaction with coreligionists may give rise to positive reflected appraisals, long recognized as a crucial source of positive self-perceptions. Through congregational activism, individuals may gain opportunities to gain status and cultivate skills (e.g., leadership, mobilization); this may be especially valuable for persons who lack status or venues for skill building in other social roles.

Second, private devotional activities and personal spirituality may also enhance psychological resources. At least two theoretical approaches have been cited in support of this argument. On the one hand, individuals may construct personal relationships with a "divine other" in much the same way that they develop relationships with concrete social others (Pollner 1989). By identifying with figures portrayed in religious texts and media, individuals may come to define their own life circumstances in terms of a biblical figure's situation, and then begin to interpret their situations from the perspective of the "God-role" (i.e., what a divine other might expect in the way of human conduct). On the other hand, attachment theorists point to the importance of secure (i.e., warm and consistent)—as opposed to avoidant or anxious—attachment to God in fostering feelings of personal worth and self-confidence (Kirkpatrick 2004). Viewed from either vantage point, however, individuals may gain a sense of self-worth and control by developing a close personal relationship with a divine other who is believed to love and care for each person unconditionally. Individuals may interact with this divine other, or secure attachment figure, as needed for solace and guidance. They may also feel hopefulness, optimism, and a sense of control over their affairs by identifying with an omniscient, omnipotent God (e.g., "with God all things are possible"). Both organizational and nonorganizational religiousness—i.e., personal relationships with God, as well as close interpersonal bonds with coreligionists—may contribute to a sense of meaning among the faithful.

Several cross-sectional studies conducted among African Americans yield results that are consistent with these arguments. First, focusing exclusively on older adults, Krause and Van Tran (1989) report that organizational religious involvement (i.e., attendance at services, participation in other congregational activities) is positively associated with self-esteem, while nonorganizational religiousness (i.e., frequency of prayer, Bible reading, and religious media consumption) is linked with personal mastery. Among African American adults of all ages, Ellison (1993) shows that both organizational and nonorganizational religiousness are linked with self-esteem, while neither dimension of religious involvement is clearly associated with mastery. In addition, organizational religiousness buffers the deleterious effect of physical unattractiveness (as rated by in-person interviewers) on self-esteem, while nonorganizational religiousness mitigates the harmful effects of chronic illnesses on self-esteem. In a more recent study, Mattis and associates (2003) refine our understanding of the links between religiousness and optimism, highlighting the independent roles of organizational religious participation and the perceived quality of one's relationship with God as key explanatory variables.

Other recent studies have cast fresh light on race differences in links between religion and psychological resources, and their possible implications for health and well-being. For example, Krause (2003d) reports that African American elders are more prone to find meaning from religion than their white counterparts, and also that on average, the strength of the linkages among religious meaning, life satisfaction, self-esteem, and optimism are stronger for African Americans than for whites in late life. Additional work, also among older adults, explores race differences in the sense of God control and its effects on psychological well-being. Among a nationwide sample of older adults, Krause (2005) finds that African Americans are more inclined to believe that they are partners with God, collaborating with the divine in solving personal problems and navigating daily affairs. Moreover, these feelings of "God-mediated control" are more strongly predictive of life satisfaction, optimism, self-esteem, and death anxiety for African American elders as compared with older whites. In data on a large community sample of elders, Schieman and his associates (2005) find that "the sense of God control"—i.e., feelings that God is in control of one's affairs—is linked with higher self-esteem and mastery for older African Americans, but not for older whites. Further, links between divine control and feelings psychological distress are contingent upon race and SES; while salutary patterns surface for lower-SES African Americans, the effects seem to be deleterious among upper-SES whites (Schieman et al. 2006). This line of work adds an important layer of complexity to theory and research on perceived relationships with God and their potential implications for health and well-being.

Coping with Stress

Early research on coping with stress gave scant attention to the role of religion, assuming that this was a passive and maladaptive coping response. However, there is now mounting evidence that religious cognitions and practices are important for coping with undesirable or threatening events and conditions—including bereavement and serious health problems, chronic pain and physical disability, accidents, and other chronic and acute stressors—and that the consequences for health and well-being can be highly varied (Pargament 1997; Pargament, Koenig, and Perez 2000). Although most research on religious coping has employed samples comprising mainly or exclusively non-Hispanic whites, it appears that African Americans may be more inclined to use religious coping strategies than whites. Indeed, in one nationwide study of African American adults, approximately 75 percent of respondents reported turning to prayer or other spiritual practices when dealing with a broad array of personal problems, ranging from bereavement to financial strain and legal troubles (Ellison and Taylor 1996). Further, many African Americans find comfort and satisfaction via these coping responses, even in the absence of social support from fellow church members (e.g., Black 1999; Poindexter, Linsk, and Warner 1999).

In recent years researchers have made major strides in identifying specific types of religious coping practices that are associated with desirable (versus undesirable) health outcomes; key distinctions include positive versus negative coping, active or collaborative versus passive or deferring religious coping styles (Pargament 1997; Pargament, Koenig, and Perez 2000). Unfortunately, few studies using these constructs have included significant numbers of African Americans. In a rare exception to this overall pattern of neglect, Steffen and associates (2001) report that active/collaborative religious coping is inversely linked with ambulatory blood pressure among African Americans, but not whites, in a clinical study. In a study of African American adolescents, collaborative religious coping style was inversely linked with hopelessness, depression, and suicide attempts (Morlock et al. 2006). Although these early investigations seem promising, it is clear that more work is needed on race, religious coping styles, and mental and physical health outcomes.

An enduring theme in literature on African American religious life is its historic and contemporary role in bolstering individuals and communities in the face of injustice. Specifically, theologians and social scientists alike have emphasized the importance of religious institutions, practices, and values in shielding African Americans from the harsh effects of structural and interpersonal racism (e.g., Gilkes 1980; Lincoln and Mamiya 1990; Paris 1995). Until recently, however, there was little empirical evidence concerning this presumably beneficial relationship. In a small-scale study conducted among African American college students, Bowen-Reid and Harrell (2002) find that: (a) perceptions of racist experiences and racial stress are positively associated with negative mental health symptoms; (b) spirituality is inversely associated with these symptoms; and (c) spirituality tends to buffer the link between racist experiences and symptoms. In a more recent analysis of longitudinal data on a nationwide sample of African American adults, individuals who receive a high level of guidance from religion in daily life at baseline experience lower levels of distress following racist encounters than their less religious counterparts (Ellison, Musick, and Henderson 2008). Such findings bear out the conventional wisdom concerning the role of religious faith in countering the harmful psychic consequences of discrimination and other types of racial inequality. However, there is much more to learn about the mechanisms via which congregations and religious beliefs help to preserve the health and well-being of African Americans.

Negative Effects of Religion

Although much of the research on religion and health has highlighted salutary relationships, a small but growing literature also explores potential negative sequelae of certain facets of religiousness and spirituality (Exline 2002; Pargament 2002). Several authors refer to these as "spiritual struggles," of which there are at least three types: (a) interactional, reflecting troubled relationships with God (e.g., anger toward God, feelings of divine judgment or abandonment); (b) intrapsychic, involving chronic doubts or internal obstacles to faith; and (c) interpersonal, centering on negative interactions in religious settings (e.g., with church members or clergy). Within the past decade, researchers have documented important links between spiritual struggles and multiple health outcomes, even extending to mortality risk (Pargament et al. 2001). As is the case with so many specific issues in the religion–health literature, only a handful of these works focus on African Americans or race/ethnic differences in spiritual struggles and their consequences. For example, in one small-scale study of African American adults, the perception of a negative (i.e., judgmental, punishing) relationship with God is strongly predictive of dispositional pessimism (Mattis et al. 2003). In a nationwide sample of adults, Musick (2000) finds that: (a) conservative Christian notions of the ubiquity of human sin are inversely associated with life satisfaction; (b) these sin beliefs tend to exacerbate the deleterious effects of traumatic life events on well-being; (c) African Americans are more inclined to endorse these beliefs about sinfulness than whites; but (d) there are race differences in these associations, such that sin beliefs are less problematic for African Americans as compared with whites from similar backgrounds. Krause (2003b) reports that, on average, older blacks have fewer religious doubts than their white counterparts, and they are also more prone to forgive other people for transgressions. Taken together, these patterns are broadly consistent with the view that African American theology gives greater weight to themes of divine mercy and forgiveness than to images of God's judgment and punitiveness (Cooper-Lewter and Mitchell 1986; Paris 1995). The topic of spiritual struggles presents yet another area in which much closer attention to issues of race and race differences appears to be warranted.

One persistent concern about religion among some health researchers and health care providers is the potential for certain beliefs to breed complacency or fatalism. Specifically, critics worry that individuals who believe in a God who blesses and protects the faithful, and who intervenes in personal affairs to assist and heal them, may be: (a) less vigilant in monitoring their health status; (b) less inclined to avail themselves of preventive care; and (c) less willing to adhere vigorously to treatment regimens, as compared with other persons. However, defenders counter that such beliefs can have desirable consequences, promoting hopefulness and strength among persons dealing with adversity and health difficulties. These issues may be particularly germane to African Americans, among whom a rich qualitative literature documents the spiritualization of health beliefs (e.g., Abrums 2000). Indeed, based on analyses of in-depth interviews conducted among three-generational African American families, King and colleagues (2005) contend that religious faith constitutes an important element of a vibrant "health maintenance system." Holt and her associates (2003) have developed innovative strategies for measuring beliefs about spiritual locus of health control. They find that these beliefs are complex and multidimensional, and suggest that they can have both positive and negative implications for African American women's use of mammograms. Data collected in a southern U.S. city confirm that African Americans are more likely than whites to endorse religiously inspired fatalistic beliefs about health. However, such beliefs are associated only with some dietary behaviors but not others, and the strongest associations are with chronic illness (Franklin et al. 2007), raising the possibility that such beliefs are adaptive responses to—rather than causes of—health problems. Other work, however, seems to bear out the concerns of critics more directly. For example, after interviewing 682 women in the rural southeastern United States, Mitchell and associates (2002) find that belief in divine intervention can delay African American women from seeking medical care for breast lumps. In light of (a) high levels of African American religious involvement, (b) significant race disparities in morbidity and mortality, and (c) barriers to health care for minorities, the possible role of specific religious beliefs in discouraging positive health behaviors and use of preventive care or treatment clearly warrants closer investigation in the future.

Concluding Observations

Throughout this chapter, we have highlighted a number of themes at the intersection of race, religion, and health that warrant additional research. In this final section, we broaden this agenda by highlighting several overarching issues that have been neglected in the development of this literature.

First, despite the growing interest in race differences in the religion–health connection, it is important to investigate various sources of within-group heterogeneity among black Americans. Levels and types of religiousness or spirituality tend to vary by gender, age/cohort, place of residence (e.g., South versus non-South, urban versus rural), and perhaps socioeconomic status, and these factors may also condition the links between religious involvement and various health outcomes. In addition, the population of blacks in America includes significant numbers of non-native-born residents, including those who have migrated from Africa, the Caribbean, and elsewhere in the African Diaspora. Until recently there were no high-quality data with which to investigate this source of internal diversity; fortunately, the advent of the National Survey of American Life, which includes a large oversample of Caribbean blacks, should help to overcome this lacuna in the literature (Chatters et al. 2008; Taylor, Chatters, and Jackson 2007). On a related note, most previous studies—and hence, our review in this chapter—have concentrated on the implications of Christianity for African Americans' health and well-being. However, we also need more information on the role of non-Christian traditions, including various branches of Islam as well as spiritual practices of the African Diaspora (e.g., Yoruba religions, Santeria, etc.), which appear to be on the rise among blacks in certain areas of the United States.

A second major area for further work is the conceptualization and measurement of religiousness and spirituality. Early studies focused almost exclusively on religious behaviors (e.g., attendance and prayer), because (a) they are presumably easier to measure and involve less measurement error, and (b) they are nonsectarian behaviors that are common to most leading religious traditions. Efforts to explore the role of social support, coping, and other key explanatory factors often involved adding measures of these variables in a series of nested regression models (George, Ellison, and Larson 2002). Although this approach can gauge whether salutary religion–health relationships reflect higher levels of social support (or other explanatory variables) among more religious persons, studies of this kind were usually unable to determine (a) whether (or how much) of this support came from specifically religious sources (e.g., church members, clergy), or (b) whether any such religious support had distinctive health benefits (over and above those of support from secular sources). As we have noted at several points in this chapter, the best and most recent work now incorporates measures of religious functions, as well as (or instead of) religious behaviors (e.g., Pargament, Koenig, and Perez 2000; Krause 2002, 2003d). It will be important for researchers focused on African Americans or on race differences to continue in this direction.

In addition, some researchers have begun to explore the links between specific religious beliefs and practices, on the one hand, and health and well-being on the other. This could be a particularly productive direction for investigators examining religion and health among African Americans, or perhaps those pursuing comparison between blacks and whites. For example, recent work notes the salutary implications of specific God images, belief in (and specific images of) the afterlife, beliefs about human sinfulness and divine forgiveness, and a host of other religious cognitions that might influence health and well-being (e.g., Musick 2000; Flannelly et al. 2006). Moreover, a long tradition of work has underscored presumably distinctive features of African American worship styles, e.g., jubilant services that may involve shout-and-response preaching, enthusiastic singing, dancing and other physical movements, among other characteristics. It has been suggested that distinctive elements of African American theology and corporate worship may promote the management, articulation, and release of negative emotions (e.g., anger, guilt, grief), perhaps resulting in cathartic experiences that foster well-being (Gilkes 1980; Krause 2004b; Ellison, Musick, and Henderson 2008). Additional empirical examination of these ideas should be a high priority for future research.

Third, theory and research in the life stress paradigm typically explain group differences in levels of (or pathways to) health and well-being partly in terms of (a) differential exposure and (b) differential vulnerability to stressors. In turn, item (b) can reflect group differences in levels of social and psychological resources, or differences in the potency or effectiveness of these resources in coping and resilience. In addition to enjoying some distinctive resources, such as religious culture, African Americans may also face elevated exposure to certain stressors as a result of discrimination, barriers to prosperity and other race-related experiences. Examples of such stressful events and conditions might include the following: discrimination, economic exploitation, tokenism stress, work–family strain, neighborhood deterioration and its sequelae (e.g., criminal victimization, police harassment, substandard housing, noise pollution, etc.), and many others. A few studies have explored the role of religion in buffering the effects of discrimination on some health outcomes (e.g., Bowen-Reid and Harrell 2002; Ellison, Musick, and Henderson 2008); however, other race-related and race-specific stressors have received minimal attention in this context. This, too, suggests a fruitful direction for further inquiry.

Fourth, as we have noted throughout this chapter, there is a dearth of evidence concerning religious effects on a broad array of physical health outcomes. Thus, the field needs information about religious influences (or the lack thereof) on many, perhaps most specific chronic and acute conditions. It is important to distinguish here between two types of studies: (a) those oriented toward risk and prevention, which typically use representative samples of community-dwelling (and hence relatively healthy) populations; and (b) those focused on treatment or disease management trajectories, which are conducted in clinical settings and sample persons who suffer from a common condition or set of conditions at the baseline of the study. Although both types of studies are extremely important, they differ in their objectives, and often report seemingly divergent sets of findings concerning the roles of religiousness or spirituality. Moreover, while the field urgently needs more of both types of studies, it is remarkable how few studies of specific diseases (for exceptions, see Steffen et al. 2001; Kinney et al. 2003), especially in clinical context, have provided information on race and race differences in any observed effects of religiousness. Moreover, investigators are still exploring the links between religious engagement and possible physiological pathways to morbidity and mortality, such as allostatic load, or cumulative physiological dysregulation; few if any of these studies have given attention to race or race differences (e.g., Maselko et al. 2007). Conducting and publishing the results of such studies should be a particularly urgent priority for investigators.

In sum, although the field of religion and health has mushroomed over the past two decades, this growth has been uneven, and has left certain themes and topics neglected. One of these areas lies at the interface of race, religion, and health. In this chapter, we have reviewed the available evidence bearing on this area, centering our gaze on studies of within-group patterns among African Americans, and on studies that compare religious effects for African Americans and non-Hispanic whites. In doing so, we have identified a vast unexplored terrain that could shed valuable new light on the religion–health connection, and on the sources of, and potential remedies for, the alarming racial disparities in health outcomes that continue to plague American society. It is hoped that sufficient will and resources exist to promote the collection and rigorous analysis of needed data on these issues. The health status of future generations of African Americans may lie in the balance.

REFERENCES

Abrums, M. 2000. "'Jesus Will Fix It After Awhile': Meanings and Health." *Social Science and Medicine* 50:89–105.

Ahmed, F., D. R. Brown, L. E. Gary, and F. Saadatmand. 1994. "Religious Predictors of Cigarette Smoking: Findings from African American Women of Childbearing Age." *Behavioral Medicine* 20:34–43.

Arias, E. 2007. "United States Life Tables, 2003." *National Vital Statistics Reports* 54 (14): 1–40.

Barnes, S. L. 2004. "Priestly and Prophetic Influences on Black Church Social Services." *Social Problems* 51:202–221.

Benjamins, M. R., and C. Brown. 2004. "Religion and Preventive Health Care Utilization among the Elderly." *Social Science and Medicine* 58:109–118.

Billingsley, A. 1999. *Mighty Like a River: The Black Church and Social Reform.* New York: Oxford University Press.

Black, H. K. 1999. "Poverty and Prayer: Spiritual Narratives of Elderly African American Women." *Review of Religious Research* 40:359–374.

Bowen-Reid, T. L., and J. P. Harrell. 2002. "Racist Experiences and Health Outcomes: An Examination of Spirituality as a Buffer." *Journal of Black Psychology* 28:18–36.

Brown, D. R., and L. E. Gary. 1994. "Religious Involvement and Health Status among African-American Males." *Journal of the National Medical Association* 86:825–831.

Brown, D. R., L. E. Gary, A. Greene, and N. Milburn. 1992. "Patterns of Social Affiliation as Predictors of Depressive Symptoms among Urban Blacks." *Journal of Health and Social Behavior* 33:242–253.

Brown, D. R., S. C. Ndubuisi, and L. E. Gary. 1990. "Religiosity and Psychological Distress among Blacks." *Journal of Religion and Health* 29:55–68.

Bryant, S. M., and W. Rakowski. 1992. "Predictors of Mortality among Elderly African Americans." *Research on Aging* 14:50–67.

Burdette, A. M., C. G. Ellison, D. E. Sherkat, and K. R. Gore. 2007. "Are There Religious Variations in Marital Infidelity?" *Journal of Family Issues* 28:1553–1581.

Caldwell, C. H., L. M. Chatters, A. Billingsley, and R. J. Taylor. 1995. "Church-Based Support Programs for Elderly Black Adults: Congregational and Clergy Characteristics." In *Aging, Spirituality and Religion: A Handbook*, ed. M. A. Kimble, S. H. McFadden, J. W. Ellor, and J. J. Seeber, 306–324. Minneapolis, MN: Augsburg Fortress.

Caldwell, C. H., A. D. Greene, and A. Billingsley. 1992. "The Black Church as a Family Support System: Instrumental and Expressive Functions." *National Journal of Sociology* 6:421–440.

Campbell, M. K., M. A. Hudson, K. Resnicow, N. Blakeney, A. Paxton, and M. Baskin. 2007. "Church-Based Health Promotion Interventions: Evidence and Lessons Learned." *Annual Review of Public Health* 28:213–234.

Chatters, L. M. 2000. "Religion and Health: Public Health Research and Practice." *Annual Review of Public Health* 21:335–367.

Chatters, L. M., R. J. Taylor, K. D. Lincoln, and J. S. Jackson. 2008. "Religious Coping among African Americans, Caribbean Blacks, and Non-Hispanic Whites." *Journal of Community Psychology* 36:371–386.

Cooper-Lewter, N. C., and H. H. Mitchell. 1986. *Soul Theology: The Heart of American Black Culture*. San Francisco: Harper and Row.

Davis, D. T., A. Bustamante, P. Brown, G. Wolde-Tsadik, E. W. Savage, X. Cheng, and L. Howland. 1994. "The Urban Church and Cancer Control: A Source of Social Influence." *Public Health Reports* 109 (4): 500–506.

DeHaven, M., I. Hunter, L. Wilder, J. Walton, and J. Berry. 2004. "Health Programs in Faith-Based Organizations: Are They Effective?" *American Journal of Public Health* 94:1030–1036.

Drevenstedt, G. L. 1998. "Race and Ethnic Differences in the Effects of Religious Attendance on Subjective Health." *Review of Religious Research* 39:245–263.

Dupre, M. E., A. T. Franzese, and E. A. Parrado. 2006. "Religious Attendance and Mortality: Implications for the Black-White Mortality Crossover." *Demography* 43:141–164.

Ellis, A. 1962. *Reason and Emotion in Psychotherapy*. Secaucus, NJ: Lyle Stuart.

Ellison, C. G. 1993. "Religious Involvement and Self-Perception among Black Americans." *Social Forces* 71:1027–1055.

———. 1995. "Race, Religious Involvement, and Depressive Symptomatology in a Southeastern U.S. Community." *Social Science and Medicine* 40:1561–1572.

———. 1997. "Religious Involvement and the Subjective Quality of Family Life among African Americans." In *Family Life in Black America*, ed. R. J. Taylor, J. S. Jackson, and L. M. Chatters, 117–131. Thousand Oaks, CA: Sage.

Ellison, C. G., J. D. Boardman, and R. A. Hummer. 2004. "Race/Ethnicity, Religious Involvement, and Self-Rated Health: Findings from the Health and Retirement Study." Unpublished manuscript, University of Texas at Austin and University of Colorado at Boulder.

Ellison, C. G., and K. J. Flannelly. 2009. "Religious Involvement and Risk of Major Depression in a Prospective Nationwide Study of African American Adults." *Journal of Nervous and Mental Disease* 197(8): 568–573.

Ellison, C. G., and D. A. Gay. 1990. "Region, Religious Commitment, and Life Satisfaction among Black Americans." *Sociological Quarterly* 31:123–147.

Ellison, C. G., and L. K. George. 1994. "Religious Involvement, Social Ties, and Social Support in a Southeastern Community." *Journal for the Scientific Study of Religion* 33:46–61.

Ellison, C. G., R. A. Hummer, S. Cormier, and R. G. Rogers. 2000. "Religious Involvement and Mortality Risk among African American Adults." *Research on Aging* 22:630–667.

Ellison, C. G., and J. S. Levin. 1998. "The Religion–Health Connection: Evidence, Theory, and Future Directions." *Health Education and Behavior* 25:700–720.

Ellison, C. G., M. A. Musick, and A. K. Henderson. 2008. "Balm in Gilead: Racism, Religious Involvement, and Psychological Distress among African American Adults." *Journal for the Scientific Study of Religion* 47: 291–309.

Ellison, C. G., M. A. Musick, J. S. Levin, R. J. Taylor, and L. M. Chatters. 2007a. "The Effects of Religious Attendance, Guidance, and Support on Psychological Distress among African American Adults: Longitudinal Findings from the National Survey of Black Americans." Manuscript under review.

Ellison, C. G., and D. E. Sherkat. 1990. "Patterns of Religious Mobility among Black Americans." *Sociological Quarterly* 31:551–568.

Ellison, C. G., and R. J. Taylor. 1996. "Turning to Prayer: Social and Situational Antecedents of Religious Coping among African Americans." *Review of Religious Research* 38:111–131.

Ellison, C. G., J. A. Trinatapoli, K. L. Anderson, and B. Johnson. 2007b. "Race/Ethnicity, Religious Involvement, and Domestic Violence." *Violence Against Women* 13:1094–1112.

Ellison, C. G., M. L. Vaaler, K. J. Flannelly, and A. J. Weaver. 2006. "Clergy as a Source of Mental Health Assistance: What Americans Believe." *Review of Religious Research* 48:190–211.

Ellison, C. G., X. Xu, and C. D. Grayson. 2007. "Religion, Race/Ethnicity, and Norms of Filial Responsibility among U.S. Elders." Manuscript under review.

Exline, J. J. 2002. "Stumbling Blocks on the Religious Road: Fractured Relationships, Nagging Vices, and the Inner Struggle to Believe." *Psychological Inquiry* 13:182–189.

Ferraro, K. F., and J. Koch. 1994. "Religion and Health among Black and White Adults: Examining Social Support and Consolation." *Journal for the Scientific Study of Religion* 33:362–375.

Flannelly, K. J., H. G. Koenig, C. G. Ellison, K. C. Galek, and N. Krause. 2006. "Belief in Life after Death and Mental Health: Findings from a National Survey." *Journal of Nervous and Mental Disease* 194 (7): 524–529.

Franklin, M. D., D. G. Schlundt, L. H. McClellan, T. Kinebrew, J. Sheats, R. Belue, A. Brown, D. Smikes, K. Patel, and M. Hargreaves. 2007. "Religious Fatalism and its Association with Health Behaviors and Outcomes." *American Journal of Health Behavior* 31:563–572.

George, L. K., C. G. Ellison, and D. B. Larson. 2002. "Explaining the Relationships between Religious Involvement and Health." *Psychological Inquiry* 13:190–200.

Gilkes, C. T. 1980. "The Black Church as a Therapeutic Community: Suggested Areas for Research into the Black Religious Experience." *Journal of the Interdenominational Theological Center* 8:29–44.

Handal, P., W. Black-Lopez, and S. Moergen. 1989. "Preliminary Investigation of the Relationship between Religion and Psychological Distress in Black Women." *Psychological Reports* 65:971–975.

Hayward, M. D., E. M. Crimmins, T. P. Miles, and Y. Yang. 2000. "The Significance of Socioeconomic Status in Explaining the Racial Gap in Chronic Health Conditions." *American Sociological Review* 65:910–930.

Hayward, M. D., and M. Heron. 1999. "Racial Inequality in Active Life among Adult Americans." *Demography* 36 (1): 77–92.

Hill, T. D., J. L. Angel, C. G. Ellison, and R. J. Angel. 2005. "Religious Attendance and Mortality: An 8-Year Follow-Up of Older Mexican Americans." *Journal of Gerontology: Social Sciences* 60B:S102–S109.

Hill, T. D., A. M. Burdette, C. G. Ellison, and M. A. Musick. 2006. "Religious Attendance and the Health Behaviors of Texas Adults." *Preventive Medicine* 42:309–312.

Holt, C. L., E. M. Clark, M. W. Kreuter, and D. M. Rubio. 2003. "Spiritual Health Locus of Control and Breast Cancer Beliefs among Urban African American Women." *Health Psychology* 22:294–299.

Hummer, R. A., M. R. Benjamins, and R. G. Rogers. 2004. "Race/Ethnic Disparities in Health and Mortality among the Elderly: A Documentation and Examination of Social Factors." In *Racial and Ethnic Differentials in Health in Late Life*, ed. N. Anderson, R. Bulatao, and B. Cohen, 53–94. Washington, DC: National Research Council.

Hummer, R. A., C. G. Ellison, R. G. Rogers, B. E. Moulton, and R. R. Romero. 2004. "Religious Involvement and Adult Mortality in the United States: Review and Perspective." *Southern Medical Journal* 97:1223–1230.

Hummer, R. A., R. G. Rogers, C. B. Nam, and C. G. Ellison. 1999. "Religious Involvement and U.S. Adult Mortality." *Demography* 36:273–285.

Idler, E. L., and Y. Benyamini. 1997. "Self-Rated Health and Mortality: A Review of Twenty-Seven Community Studies." *Journal of Health and Social Behavior* 38:21–37.

Jang, S. J., and B. R. Johnson. 2004. "Explaining Religious Effects on Distress among African Americans." *Journal for the Scientific Study of Religion* 43:239–260.

Jarvis, G., and H. Northcott. 1987. "Religion and Differences in Morbidity and Mortality." *Social Science and Medicine* 25:813–824.

King, S. V., E. O. Burgess, M. Akinyela, M. Counts-Spriggs, and N. Parker. 2005. "Your Body is God's Temple: The Spiritualization of Health Beliefs in Multigenerational African American Families." *Research on Aging* 27(4): 420–446.

Kinney, A. Y., L. E. Bloor, W. N. Dudley, R. C. Millikan, E. Marshall, C. Martin, and R. S. Sandler. 2003. "The Roles of Religious Involvement and Social Support in the Risk of Colon Cancer among Blacks and Whites." *American Journal of Epidemiology* 158: 1097–1107.

Kirkpatrick, L. A. 2004. *Attachment, Evolution, and the Psychology of Religion*. New York: Guilford Press.

Koenig, H. G., J. C. Hays, D. B. Larson, L. K. George, H. J. Cohen, M. E. McCullough, K. G. Meador, and D. G. Blazer. 1999. "Does Religious Attendance Prolong Survival? A Six-Year Follow-Up Study of 3,968 Older Adults." *Journal of Gerontology: Medical Sciences* 54A:M370–M377.

Koenig, H. G., L. K. George, H. J. Cohen, J. Hays, D. B. Larson, and D. G. Blazer. 1998. "The Relationship between Religious Activities and Blood Pressure in Older Adults." *International Journal of Psychiatry in Medicine* 28:189–213.

Koenig, H. G., M. McCullough, and D. B. Larson. 2001. *The Handbook of Religion and Health*. New York: Oxford University Press.

Krause, N. 2002. "Church-Based Social Support and Health in Old Age: Exploring Variations by Race." *Journal of Gerontology: Social Sciences* 57 (6): S332–S347.

———. 2003a. "Exploring Race Differences in the Relationship between Social Interaction with the Clergy and Feelings of Self-Worth in Late Life." *Sociology of Religion* 64:183–205.

———. 2003b. "A Preliminary Assessment of Race Differences in the Relationship between Religious Doubt and Depressive Symptoms." *Review of Religious Research* 45:93–115.

———. 2003c. "Race, Religion, and Abstinence from Alcohol in Late Life." *Journal of Aging and Health* 15:508–533.

———. 2003d. "Religious Meaning and Subjective Well-Being in Late Life." *Journal of Gerontology: Social Sciences* 58B:S160–S170.

———. 2004a. "Assessing the Relationships among Prayer Expectancies, Race, and Self-Esteem in Late Life." *Journal for the Scientific Study of Religion* 43:395–408.

———. 2004b. "Common Facets of Religion, Unique Facets of Religion, and Life Satisfaction among Older African Americans." *Journal of Gerontology: Social Sciences* 59B:S109–S117.

———. 2005. "God-Mediated Control and Psychological Well-Being in Late Life." *Research on Aging* 27:136–164.

————. 2006. "Exploring the Stress-Buffering Effects of Church-Based and Secular Social Support on Self-Rated Health in Late Life." *Journal of Gerontology: Social Sciences* 61B:S35–S43.

Krause, N., and L. M. Chatters. 2005. "Exploring Race Differences in a Multidimensional Battery of Prayer Measures." *Sociology of Religion* 66:23–44.

Krause, N., and T. Van Tran. 1989. "Stress and Religious Involvement among Older Blacks. *Journal of Gerontology: Social Sciences* 44:S4–S13.

Levin, J. S., L. M. Chatters, and R. J. Taylor. 1995. "Religious Effects on Health Status and Life Satisfaction among Black Americans." *Journal of Gerontology: Social Sciences* 50B:S154–S163.

Levin, J. S., and R. J. Taylor. 1998. "Panel Analysis of Religious Involvement and Well-Being in African Americans: Contemporaneous vs. Longitudinal Effects." *Journal for the Scientific Study of Religion* 37:695–709.

Levin, J. S., and H. Y. Vanderpool. 1987. "Is Frequent Religious Attendance Really Conducive to Better Health? Toward an Epidemiology of Religion." *Social Science and Medicine* 24:589–600.

————. 1989. "Is Religion Therapeutically Significant for Hypertension?" *Social Science and Medicine* 29:69–78.

Lincoln, C. E., and L. H. Mamiya. 1990. *The Black Church in the African American Experience.* Durham, NC: Duke University Press.

Livingston, I., D. Levine, and R. Moore. 1991. "Social Integration and Black Intraracial Variation in Blood Pressure." *Ethnicity and Disease* 1:135–149.

Loustalot, F. 2006. "Race, Religion, and Blood Pressure." PhD diss., School of Nursing, University of Mississippi Medical Center.

Luskin, F. 2000. "Review of the Effect of Spiritual and Religious Factors on Mortality and Morbidity with a Focus on Cardiovascular and Pulmonary Disease." *Journal of Cardiopulmonary Rehabilitation* 20:8–15.

Maselko, J., L. Kubzansky, I. Kawachi, T. Seeman, and L. Berkman. 2007. "Religious Service Attendance and Allostatic Load among High-Functioning Elderly." *Psychosomatic Medicine* 69:464–472.

Mattis, J. S., D. L. Fontenot, C. A. Hatcher-Kay, N. A. Grayman, and R. L. Beale. 2003. "Religiosity, Optimism, and Pessimism among African Americans." *Journal of Black Psychology* 30:187–207.

Mattis, J. S., and R. Jagers. 2001. "A Relational Framework for the Study of Religiosity and Spirituality in the Lives of African Americans." *Journal of Community Psychology* 29:519–539.

Maynard-Reid, P. U. 2000. *Diverse Worship: African American, Caribbean, and Hispanic Perspectives.* Downers Grove, IL: Intervarsity Press.

McCullough, M., D. B. Larson, W. Hoyt, H. G. Koenig, and C. E. Thoresen. 2000. "Religious Involvement and Mortality: A Meta-Analytic Review." *Health Psychology* 19:211–222.

McRae, M. B., P. M. Carey, and R. Anderson-Scott. 1998. "Black Churches as Therapeutic Systems: A Group Process Perspective." *Health Education and Behavior* 25:778–789.

Mitchell, J., D. R. Lannin, H. F. Matthews, and M. S. Swanson. 2002. "Religious Beliefs and Breast Cancer Screening." *Journal of Women's Health* 11:907–915.

Morlock, S. D., R. Puri, S. Matlin, and C. Barksdale. 2006. "Relationship between Religious Coping and Suicidal Behaviors among African American Adolescents." *Journal of Black Psychology* 32:366–389.

Moyd, O. 1979. *Redemption in Black Theology.* Valley Forge, PA: Judson Press.

Musick, M. A. 1996. "Religion and Subjective Health among Black and White Elders." *Journal of Health and Social Behavior* 37:221–237.

———. 2000. "Theodicy and Life Satisfaction among Black and White Americans." *Sociology of Religion* 61:267–287.

Musick, M. A., J. S. House, and D. R. Williams. 2004. "Religion and Mortality in a National Sample." *Journal of Health and Social Behavior* 45 (2): 198–213.

Musick, M. A., H. G. Koenig, J. Hays, and H. J. Cohen 1998. "Religious Activity and Depression among Community-Dwelling Elderly Persons with Cancer: The Moderating Effect of Race." *Journal of Gerontology: Social Sciences* 53B:S218–S227.

Nam, C. B. 1995. "Another Look at Mortality Crossovers." *Social Biology* 42 (1–2): 133–142.

Neighbors, H. W., M. A. Musick, and D. R. Williams. 1998. "The African American Minister as a Source of Help for Serious Personal Crises: Bridge or Barrier to Mental Health Care?" *Health Education and Behavior* 25:759–777.

Pargament, K. I. 1997. *The Psychology of Religion and Coping: Theory, Research, and Practice.* New York: Guilford.

———. 2002. "The Bitter and the Sweet: Assessing the Costs and Benefits of Religion." *Psychological Inquiry* 13:168–181.

Pargament, K. I., H. G. Koenig, and L. Perez. 2000. "The Many Methods of Religious Coping: Development and Initial Validation of the RCOPE." *Journal of Clinical Psychology* 56:519–543.

Pargament, K. I., H. G. Koenig, N. Tarakeshwar, and J. Hahn. 2001. "Religious Struggle as a Predictor of Mortality among Medically Ill Elderly Patients: A 2-Year Longitudinal Study." *Archives of Internal Medicine* 161:1881–1885.

Pargament, K. I., W. Silverman, S. Johnson, R. Echemendia, and S. Snyder. 1983. "The Psychosocial Climate of Religious Congregations." *American Journal of Community Psychology* 11:351–383.

Paris, P. J. 1995. *The Spirituality of African Peoples.* Minneapolis, MN: Fortress Press.

Poindexter, C., N. Linsk, and R. S. Warner. 1999. "'He Listens . . . and Never Gossips': Spiritual Coping without Church Support among Older, Predominantly African American Caregivers of Persons with HIV." *Review of Religious Research* 40:230–243.

Pollner, M. L. 1989. "Divine Relations, Social Relations, and Well-Being." *Journal of Health and Social Behavior* 30:92–104.

Powell, L. H., L. Shahabi, C. E. Thoresen. 2003. "Religion and Spirituality: Linkages to Physical Health." *American Psychologist* 58:36–52.

Rogers, R. G. 1992. "Living and Dying in the USA: Sociodemographic Determinants of Death among Blacks and Whites." *Demography* 29(2): 287–304.

Rostosky, S. S., M. D. Regnerus, and M. L. C. Wright. 2003. "Coital Debut: The Role of Religiosity and Sex Attitudes in the Add Health Survey." *Journal of Sex Research* 40:356–367.

Schieman, S., T. Pudrovska, and M. A. Milkie. 2005. "The Sense of Divine Control and the Self-Concept: A Study of Race Differences in Late Life." *Research on Aging* 27:165–196.

Schieman, S., T. Pudrovska, L. I. Pearlin, and C. G. Ellison. 2006. "The Sense of Divine Control and Psychological Distress: Variations across Race and Class." *Journal for the Scientific Study of Religion* 45:529–549.

Sherkat, D. E. 2002. "African American Religious Affiliation in the Late 20th Century: Cohort Variations and Patterns of Switching, 1973–1998." *Journal for the Scientific Study of Religion* 41:485–493.

Sloan, R., E. Bagiella, and T. Powell. 1999. "Religion, Spirituality, and Medicine." *Lancet* 353:664–667.

Smith, J. P., and R. S. Kington. 1997. "Race, Socioeconomic Status, and Health in Late Life." In *Racial and Ethnic Differences in the Health of Older Americans*, ed. L. G. Martin and B. J. Soldo, 105–162. Washington, DC: National Academy Press.

Smith, T. B., M. E. McCullough, and J. Poll. 2003. "Religiousness and Depression: Evidence for a Main Effect and the Moderating Influence of Stressful Life Events." *Psychological Bulletin* 129:614–636.

St. George, A., and P. H. McNamara. 1984. "Religion, Race, and Psychological Well-Being." *Journal for the Scientific Study of Religion* 23:351–363.

Steffen, P. R., A. L. Hinderliter, J. A. Blumenthal, and A. Sherwood. 2001. "Religious Coping, Ethnicity, and Ambulatory Blood Pressure." *Psychosomatic Medicine* 63:523–530.

Taylor, R. J., and L. M. Chatters. 1986. "Patterns of Informal Support to Elderly Black Adults: Family, Friends, and Church Members." *Social Work* 31:432–438.

Taylor, R. J., L. M. Chatters, and J. S. Jackson. 2007. "Religious and Spiritual Involvement among Older African Americans, Caribbean Blacks, and Non-Hispanic Whites." *Journal of Gerontology: Social Sciences* 62B:S238–S250.

Taylor, R. J., L. M. Chatters, and J. S. Levin. 2004. *Religion in the Lives of African Americans: Social, Psychological, and Health Perspectives.* Thousand Oaks, CA: Sage.

Taylor, R. J., C. G. Ellison, L. M. Chatters, J. S. Levin, and K. D. Lincoln. 2000. "Mental Health Services within Faith Communities: The Role of Clergy in Black Churches." *Social Work* 45:73–87.

Taylor, R. J., M. C. Thornton, and L. M. Chatters. 1987. "Black Americans' Perceptions of the Sociohistorical Role of the Church." *Journal of Black Studies* 18:123–138.

Thomas, M. D., and B. Holmes. 1992. "Determinants of Satisfaction for Blacks and Whites." *Sociological Quarterly* 33:459–472.

Thomas, S., S. Crouse Quinn, A. Billingsley, and C. H. Caldwell. 1994. "The Characteristics of Northern Black Churches with Community Health Outreach Programs." *American Journal of Public Health* 84:575–579.

Trinitapoli, J., C. G. Ellison, and J. D. Boardman. 2009. "U.S. Religious Congregations and the Sponsorship of Health-Related Programs." *Social Science and Medicine* 68: 2231–2239.

Tsitsos, W. 2003. "Race Differences in Congregational Social Service Activity." *Journal for the Scientific Study of Religion* 42:205–215.

U.S. Department of Health and Human Services. 2000. *Healthy People 2010.* 2nd ed. Washington, DC: U.S. GPO.

Van Ness, P. H. S. V. Kasl, and B. A. Jones. 2003. "Religion, Race, and Breast Cancer Survival." *International Journal of Psychiatry in Medicine* 33:357–375.

Wallace, J. M., Jr., T. N. Brown, J. G. Bachman, and T. A. LaVeist. 2003. "The Influence of Race and Religion on Abstinence from Alcohol, Cigarettes, and Marijuana." *Journal of Studies on Alcohol* 64:843–848.

Walls, C., and S. Zarit. 1991. "Informal Support from Black Churches and the Well-Being of Elderly Blacks." *Gerontologist* 31:490–495.

Washington, J. M. 1994. *Conversations with God: Two Centuries of Prayers by African Americans.* New York: Harper.

Weaver, A. J. 1995. "Has There Been a Failure to Prepare and Support Parish-Based Clergy in Their Role as Front-line Community Mental Health Workers? A Review." *Journal of Pastoral Care* 49:129–149.

Whitehead, B. D., B. L. Wilcox, and S. S. Rostosky. 2001. *Keeping the Faith: The Role of Religion and Faith Communities in Preventing Teen Pregnancy.* Washington, DC: National Campaign to Prevent Teen Pregnancy.

Williams, D. R., and C. Collins. 1995. "U.S. Socioeconomic and Racial Differences in Health: Patterns and Explanations." *Annual Review of Sociology* 21:349–386.

Yanek, L. R., D. M. Becker, T. F. Moy, J. Gittelsohn, and D. M. Koffman. 2001. "Project Joy: Faith-Based Cardiovascular Health Promotion for African American Women." *Public Health Reports* 116:S61–S68.

17

Jewish Identity and
Self-Reported Health

ISAAC W. EBERSTEIN AND KATHLEEN M. HEYMAN

One of the central questions of this volume is the extent to which religious involvement is beneficial for health and mortality. We consider this question within the American Jewish population. We look to understand how differences among Jews in a set of distinctively Jewish behaviors as well as in stronger or weaker subjective Jewish identification, factors that mark group membership per se, might be associated with self-reported health. Specifically, we examine: (a) the extent to which indicators of "Jewish identity," conceptualized in terms of ritual observance and subjective identification, are associated with self-reported health; (b) the extent to which this relationship is maintained net of basic demographic controls and objective health limitations; and (c) the extent to which other factors considered important for the expression of Jewish identity may help provide insight into the mechanisms of this association.

Background

Consistent with research demonstrating denominational and religiosity differences in health and mortality (Hummer et al. 2004, 1999; Koenig, McCullough, and Larson 2001; Musick, House, and Williams 2004), Jews in the United States and internationally have been determined to have distinctive patterns of mortality and illness/disease (Koenig, McCullough, and Larson 2001). For instance, Goldstein (1996) observed a survival advantage of 3.3 years of life expectancy at birth among Jewish males in Rhode Island and a 0.5 year disadvantage among Jewish females, with the female disadvantage due in particular to higher Jewish mortality at the older ages. As another example, Shkolnikov and colleagues (2004) found a Jewish mortality advantage among males in Moscow, due primarily to lower mortality from heart and cerebrovascular diseases, accidents, violence, smoking-related cancers, and stomach cancers. Jewish women in this study exhibited slightly lower overall mortality than non-Jewish women, with some advantage in deaths from heart and cerebrovascular diseases but higher mortality from breast cancer and other cancers. Finally, comparing adult mortality in a matched sample of religious and secular kibbutzim (collective settlements) in Israel over a sixteen-year period, higher mortality rates were found among residents of the secular kibbutzim for all major causes of death (Kark et al. 1996).

Multiple causal mechanisms are hypothesized to underlie these relationships (Hummer et al. 2004; Koenig, McCullough, and Larson 2001). Better health and mortality are typically considered a result of the distinctive behavioral prescriptions and proscriptions associated with particular religious observance, along with benefits that seem to be more broadly characteristic of greater religious involvement per se (e.g., psychic benefits and social support). Further, in the particular case of Jews (compared to non-Jews), there are other characteristics of the population, such as higher education, that are associated with ethnicity and that may be a factor in more advantageous mortality. For instance, the relative Jewish survival advantage in Russia was attributed to a combination of behavioral, biogenetic, and social support differences between the Jewish and non-Jewish populations (Shkolnikov et al. 2004, 324–325). Higher Jewish education was found in particular to account for the entire female mortality differential but only half of the male differential. Similarly, unable to explain their observed differentials with controls for conventional risk factors, Kark and colleagues (1996) attributed the protective effect of residing in a religious community to a combination of behaviors that follow from being religiously observant (e.g., eating more fish in a kosher diet) and greater stress reduction from social support and religious participation.

In this regard, American Jews are a diverse lot, ranging from fundamentalist Ultra-Orthodox (*haredi*) to so-called Modern Orthodox, Conservative, Reform, and the "Just Jewish" (Grossman 2005). Indeed, the latter group may be nonreligious (even antireligious) and/or with perhaps distant Jewish ancestry or only perceived ethnic ties or affinity (Sklare 1971, 26–33). There are wide variations among Jews in the extent of traditional religious observance and in subjective Jewish identification (e.g., Amyot and Sigelman 1996; Dashefsky, Lazerwitz, and Tabory 2003; Horowitz 2002; Linzer 1998; Rebhun 2004b; Zenner 1985). These within-group differences in Jewish identity have been studied in terms of ethnic assimilation and pluralism, as well as in the more specific contexts of Jewish continuity, transformation, and denominationalism within American society (e.g., Cohen 1988; Goldscheider 1986, 2003; Gurock 1998; Lazerwitz et al. 1998; Liebman 2001; Linzer 1998; Lipset and Raab 1995; Rebhun 2004a; Waxman 2001).

The guiding question for the present study concerns the health implications of varying levels of traditional religious observance and subjective group identification among American Jews. We first highlight issues pertinent to Jewish identity in this context and then provide an overview of subjective health.

Jewish Identity

Jews in America are an ethnic group, a cultural group with a core in the traditions of Judaism. The group can be viewed to emphasize ethnicity and/or religion, and the concept of Jewish identity is central (e.g., Goldstein 1992; Kaufman 2005; Kivisto and Nefzger 1993; Linzer 1998; Sklare 1971). We consider Jewish identity in terms of two dimensions, subjective identification and traditional religious behavior, general constructs that would seem to apply to ethnic and religious groups more broadly and that have important and well-recognized meaning within the particular context of American Jews. This approach is in many ways a simplification of this extensive literature and, although appropriate for the specific question of our research, it is necessary to acknowledge the existence of nuances and distinctions between these concepts that we may gloss over (Dashefsky, Lazerwitz, and Tabory 2003; Herman 1977).

The changing geographic, demographic, and social characteristics of the American Jewish population have been closely associated with patterns of Jewish identity. Geographic factors are important because the possibilities of Jewish life are different outside areas with large Jewish concentrations (e.g., Heilman 2002; Horowitz 1999). There has been substantial migration from the Northeast, where American Jews have traditionally been concentrated, to the South and West (Goldstein and Goldstein 1996). Jewish identity varies by denominational preference, with the Orthodox having much greater adherence to traditional rituals than the Conservative, Reform, or "Just Jewish" (Lazerwitz et al. 1998). Finally, Jewish identity varies according to a range of demographic characteristics, including immigrant generation, education, marital status, and religion of spouse/partner (Goldstein 1992; Gurock 1998; Hartman and Hartman 1996; Heilman 1982; Kivisto and Nefzger 1993; Legge 1997; Medding et al. 1992; Rebhun 1995; Wilder 1996). Most research has dealt mainly with ritual observance, and it is not clear that differentials in subjective identification are parallel (but see, e.g., Amyot and Sigelman 1996).

Self-Reported Health

We use as our indicator of health the individual's subjective general evaluation of their health. Self-reported health is a common measure of individual health in social, demographic, and other health-oriented literatures. This subjective rating correlates cross-sectionally with a variety of diseases, functional status and mental health, health care use, and also predicts mortality prospectively (Benjamins et al. 2004; Liang et al. 2005). Most studies find that self-reported health remains an independent predictor of subsequent health outcomes, net of other more objective measures of self-reported and physician-observed health status, behavioral and psychosocial risk factors, and environmental factors (Benyamini and Idler 1999; Franks, Gold, and Fiscella 2003; Goldman, Glei, and Chang 2004; Idler, Russell, and Davis 2000; Jenkinson and McGee 1998). As such, self-reported health is a simple but valid proxy measure for overall health status (Ferraro and Farmer 1999).

A growing body of research has examined the explanatory power of religious activity for self-reported health, where findings suggest a general positive association (Broyles and Drenovsky 1992; Daaleman, Perera, and Studenski 2004; Drevenstedt 1998; Ferraro and Albrecht-Jensen 1991; Frankel and Hewitt 1994; Hyyppa and Maki 2001; Levin and Markides 1986; Levin and Vanderpool 1987; McCullough and Laurenceau 2005; Spreitzer and Snyder 1974; St. George and McNamara 1984; Veenstra 2000; Witter et al. 1985). Most of these studies utilize cross-sectional data that focus on sex, age (especially elders), and racial/ethnic differences. For example, Levin and Markides (1986) report a positive association between religious service attendance and self-reported health among Mexican American Catholic women aged sixty-five through eighty years. Another study found a zero-order association between attendance and self-rated health among white men and women aged forty to sixty-five years (Drevenstedt 1998). These positive associations were relatively independent of many measures of socioeconomic status, health behavior, physical functioning, social support, and psychosocial factors (Broyles and Drenovsky 1992; Daaleman, Perera, and Studenski 2004; Drevenstedt 1998; McCullough and Laurenceau 2005).

Contrary to the preceding, several researchers urge caution due to the inadequacy of cross-sectional data (Matthews et al. 1998; Musick 1996; Musick et al. 2000). Levin and Vanderpool (1987) posit that the relationship between attendance and health may be partly spurious, such that both measures may be predicted by functional status. Cross-sectional data on older adults living in the Northeastern United States produced no association between religious attendance and self-rated health (Idler and Benyamini 1997). Musick (1996) found similar results with an elder population in North Carolina when functional status was added as a control. Acknowledging these important concerns, it remains the case that religion seems to play some as yet undetermined role in individuals' self-reports of their health status (see Hummer et al. 2004, 1227 for a more complete review of confounders).

We extend the current literature by considering whether "identity" differences among Jews may be related with self-rated health. To our knowledge, there are no comparable studies within any single religio-ethnic group.

Hypotheses

Overall, we expect health patterns to vary with the ethnic and religious characteristics of the individual. To the extent that Jewish religiosity is beneficial for health, we expect that more ritually observant Jews will have better health. To the extent that subjective group identification is beneficial for health, we expect those who identify more strongly as Jews to have better health. In view of research demonstrating that public religious participation is more important for health than is private religiosity (Hummer et al. 2004), we expect Jewish religious behavior to be more important than subjective identification. Finally, research suggests that the extent of subjective Jewish identification and degree of religious observance, although conceptually distinct, are also interrelated (e.g., Kivisto and Nefzger 1993; Rebhun 2004b). Thus, we expect that each will have smaller health benefits net of the other. Although limited by cross-sectional data, our examination of within-group variation in subjective health among a diverse population of American Jews is a new and important test that adds an interesting theoretical twist to extant research in this area.

Data and Methods

Data are taken from the National Jewish Population Survey (NJPS), 2000–2001 (United Jewish Communities 2003a). This survey was funded by Jewish organizations to guide communal planning, particularly in response to concerns over population decline and assimilation trends that had been observed in analyses of earlier data sets (United Jewish Communities 2003b).[1]

The NJPS was collected via random digit dialing across strata emphasizing the top forty metropolitan areas in the country. All adults were screened in cooperating households, with households classified as Jewish or Persons of Jewish Background (PJB) based on the presence of these individuals. A randomly selected Jewish adult was used as a household informant. The survey obtained a response rate of 28.2 percent, although because of problems in moving from screening to complete interviews, some segments of the population have a lower effective rate (United Jewish Communities 2003c).

The NJPS identified Jewish adults based on responses to four questions asked in sequence: Jewish religion (includes "Jewish" in combination with other religions), Jewish mother or father, "raised Jewish," and "consider self Jewish." A "yes" answer to any of these four questions was taken to indicate a Jewish individual, with two exceptions. If the respondent answered "no" to "self" but "yes" to any of the first three questions, then the respondent was considered a PJB rather than a currently Jewish adult. Similarly, if the respondent answered "yes" to self but "no" to all of the first three questions, they were not considered Jewish or PJB (United Jewish Communities 2003c, 48–50). The result of these decision rules was to exclude the most assimilated persons of Jewish origin from the data set entirely. Further, PJB were not asked many of the "Jewish" behavior questions (e.g., observance of religious rituals), based on the a priori assumption that these would not be applicable. The consequence of these decisions is to limit the data available for the present analysis to exclude PJB as well as those of more distant Jewish ancestry or affinity (Kadushin, Phillips, and Saxe 2005; Klaff and Mott 2005; United Jewish Communities 2003c, 26–41).

The NJPS is highly controversial because of this and other assumptions, methodological strategies, and problems in implementation, compounded by the high nonresponse (see Kadushin, Phillips, and Saxe 2005; Kosmin 2005).

Nonetheless, these data arguably provide the most comprehensive and up-to-date picture of the U.S. Jewish population (Klaff and Mott 2005). Although the NJPS may have important shortcomings when estimating population character-istics (DellaPergola 2005), the data are very useful for estimating relationships among these characteristics (Klaff and Mott 2005).

Our dependent variable is self-reported health, measured by the respon-dent's answer to the question: "Would you say your health, in general, is excel-lent, good, fair, or poor?" (United Jewish Communities 2003c). This question form is typical of research in this area, although the precise wording and number of response categories may vary (cf. Baron-Epel et al. 2005; Liang et al. 2005).

The primary independent variable is Jewish identity. There are numerous approaches for measuring Jewish identity in its various conceptualizations (e.g., Amyot and Sigelman 1996; Dashefsky, Lazerwitz, and Tabory 2003; Goldstein and Goldstein 1996; Kivisto and Nefzger 1993; Rebhun 2004b). We emphasize two related dimensions of this larger concept, subjective identification and traditional religious behavior. Denominational preference is considered sepa-rately as an important factor per se and also as a basis for validating the other measurement operations. We use three indicators of subjective identification available from the NJPS (sense of belonging, how I see myself [reversed], and importance of being Jewish). These items are converted to a five-point scale (i.e., highest identification equals highest score) and averaged, with the result-ing index internally consistent at an alpha of .64.

The measure of traditional religious behavior includes nine items that represent ritual performance and its close correlates, including synagogue membership and attendance, along with specific religious rituals of lighting Sab-bath candles, attending Seder on Passover, lighting Hanukkah candles, keeping kosher at home, fasting on Yom Kippur, not handling money on the Sabbath, and keeping kosher outside of home. Items are converted to 1 for "yes" and summed, leading to a measure with good internal consistency (alpha = .84).

Jewish denominational preference is not always straightforward, with responses according to fixed markers of institutional boundaries (Lazerwitz et al. 1998). This concept is measured by combining responses to the question: "Thinking about Jewish religious denominations, do you consider yourself to be . . . ," followed by a fixed list of five responses (Orthodox, Conservative, Reform, Reconstructionist, or Just Jewish) and a residual category of "Something else," coupled with a lengthy series of possible specifications (United Jewish Com-munities 2003c). There were forty-six distinct response patterns in the data on this item, which we coded into four groups of the three largest Jewish religious movements of Orthodox, Conservative, and Reform (including Reconstruction-ist), along with a separate category of "Other." The range of denominational constructions is impressive, with substantial diversity in each group. It is par-ticularly instructive that "Other" includes some who identify in nonspecific religious terms (Just Jewish, No Jewish Denomination), in non-religious and even antireligious terms (Secular, Humanistic, Non-practicing Jew, Agnostic, Atheist, No Religion), and in terms of non-Jewish faith traditions (Messianic, Catholic, Baptist, Pentecostal). Some of these respondents would not be considered Jewish based strictly on religious grounds (e.g., Zenner 1985, 124–128), but it is nonetheless arguably appropriate to include them from a sociological or ethnic point of view (cf. Sklare 1971, 26–33).

The analysis includes a range of additional variables. Noteworthy is an objective indicator of health conditions, based on respondents' answers to a question "Do you currently have any kind of physical, mental, or other health condition that limits employment, education, or daily activities, and has lasted for at least six months?" If necessary, the question was specified by adding "Daily activities include walking, climbing stairs, dressing, eating and carrying" (United Jewish Communities 2003c). Prior research suggests it is important to control for objective health conditions when considering the possible link between aspects of Jewish identity and our dependent variable of self-reported (perceived) health (Hummer et al. 1999; Musick, House, and Williams 2004). Remaining independent variables include region, immigrant generation, religion of spouse/partner (Jewish, not Jewish, no spouse/partner), age, and education.

We analyze the relationships between the two measures of Jewish identification and self-reported health. The analysis uses STATA version 9.1 (Statacorp 2005) to estimate ordered logit models (Long and Cheng 2004). All statistical analyses are weighted to represent the population characteristics without inflating sample size, and significance tests are based on robust standard errors corrected for the complex sample design of the survey (Kadushin, Phillips, and Saxe 2005, 10–12).

Results

Percentage distributions of variables are presented in Table 17.1. Relatively few of the NJPS respondents consider their health to be poor (4.9 percent), and a slightly higher percentage reports objective health limitations that have lasted six months or more (7.4 percent). More report themselves to be in "excellent" (41.3 percent) or "good" (40.5 percent) health. This is comparable to findings in other general population studies (cf. Benjamins et al. 2004).

Approximately 15 percent of the respondents are immigrants, and a somewhat larger percentage is three or more generations removed from the immigrant experience (20.5 percent fourth generation or more). One indicator of the degree of marital assimilation is that some 42 percent of married or cohabiting respondents in the sample are in interfaith couples. Although a plurality lives in the Northeast (39.2 percent), nearly one-half reside in the South and West, in approximately equal numbers. Finally, the data indicate the high education levels of the Jewish population, where fully 50 percent of adults ages eighteen

TABLE 17.1

Percentage Distributions of Variables in the Analysis

	%	N^a
Self-Reported Health		
Excellent	41.3	2151
Good	40.5	2049
Fair	13.3	667
Poor	4.9	247
Health Condition		
Yes	7.4	498
No	92.6	4650
Immigrant Generation		
First	14.8	749
Second	25.8	1445
Third	38.8	2043
Fourth	20.5	767
Marital Status		
Married to Jew	34.7	1703
Married to Non-Jew	25.2	1069
Unmarried	40.1	2359
Education		
0–11	4.9	196
12	19.6	869
13–15	24.3	1149
16	29.4	1611
17+	21.8	1274
Sex		
Male	46.5	2281
Female	53.5	2867
Age		
18–24	12.5	492
25–44	32.5	1647

(continued)

Table 17.1. Percentage Distributions of Variables in the Analysis (*continued*)

	%	N^a
45–64	33.0	1779
65–84	20.2	1069
85+	1.7	118
Region		
Northeast	39.2	2631
Midwest	12.5	445
South	24.6	1111
West	23.7	953

a. Percentage distributions are weighted. Sample sizes are unweighted. Total sample size = 5,148. Missing values are not shown in the table.

and over have completed college, in comparison with about 26 percent of the U.S. white population (U.S. Bureau of the Census 2000).

Table 17.2 contains information on the two measures of Jewish identity, along with the specific items that comprise each index. Considering subjective identification, most respondents have very positive reports. Over half strongly agree that they have a strong sense of belonging to the Jewish people, half indicate that being Jewish is a factor in how they see themselves, and half say that being Jewish is very important in their life. When these items are combined and averaged, the median response is 4 on a scale of 1 to 5, with a mean of 3.82, suggesting a pattern of high subjective identity. This is reinforced by other distributional measures not shown in the table; for instance, the eightieth percentile is 5, the highest possible score.

In contrast, scores on the measure of traditional religious behavior are clustered toward the low end. While over two-fifths (43.3 percent) of the respondents report that someone in their household is currently a member of a synagogue, only about one-fifth attends services monthly or more. Similarly, roughly one-fifth always light candles on the Sabbath and about the same percentage keeps kosher at home. Passover and Hanukkah observances are more widespread, with a majority attending Seder (57.3 percent) and about half lighting Hanukkah candles most or all nights (48.0 percent). A majority (56.7 percent) fast some or all day on Yom Kippur. The questions on keeping kosher outside the

Measures of Jewish Identity

	%	N^a
17–2A. Subjective Jewish Identification. ($\alpha = .64$)[b]		
I have a strong sense of belonging to the Jewish people.		
Strongly agree	57.1	2,505
Somewhat agree	28.2	1,275
Neither A/D	1.1	46
Somewhat Disagree	8.9	399
Strongly Disagree	4.6	220
Overall, the fact that I am a Jew has very little to do with how I see myself.[c]		
Strongly agree	25.8	1,142
Somewhat agree	21.9	978
Neither A/D	2.1	94
Somewhat Disagree	20.7	909
Strongly Disagree	29.5	1,247
How important is being Jewish in your life?		
Very	49.9	2,138
Somewhat	35.2	1,598
Not very	10.1	481
Not at all	4.8	229
17–2B. Jewish Ritual Behavior. ($\alpha = .83$)[d]		
Synagogue member in household (yes = 1; otherwise = 0)		
Current Member	43.3	1,778
Nonmember	56.7	2,691
Synagogue attendance frequency past year (monthly or more)		
Never	50.0	2,103
Occasionally (<1 per month)	30.7	1,809
Monthly or more	19.3	1,051
Frequency of lighting Sabbath candles (usually or always)		
Always (every week)	19.3	773
Usually	7.3	316
Sometimes	25.9	1,108
Never	47.5	2,257

(continued)

Table 17.2. Measures of Jewish Identity *(continued)*

	%	N[a]
Held/Attended Seder last Passover (yes)		
Yes	57.3	3,425
No	42.7	1,674
Number of nights lit candles last Hanukkah (most or all nights)		
All eight nights	40.7	2,357
Most nights	7.3	455
Some nights	14.3	819
None of the nights	37.7	1,488
Keep kosher in your home (yes)		
Yes	20.4	881
No	77.1	3,477
Other responses	2.5	105
Fast during last Yom Kippur (part or all of the day)		
All day	44.3	1,934
Part of the day	12.4	584
Did not fast	38.9	1,725
Could not (health, age, etc.)	4.4	202
Refrain from handling money on Sabbath (yes)[e]		
Yes	25.6	610
No	74.4	1,706
Keep kosher outside home (yes)[e]		
Yes	58.8	537
No	33.7	294
Other	7.5	43

a. Percentages are weighted. Sample sizes are unweighted. Total sample size = 5,148. Missing values are not shown in the table.

b. Statistics for Identification: mean = 3.82; standard deviation = 1.01; median = 4; minimum = 1; maximum = 5.

c. Reversed in creating the index.

d. Statistics for Ritual Observance: mean = 3.38; standard deviation = 2.55; median = 3; minimum = 0; maximum = 9.

e. Among respondents who light Sabbath candles at least sometimes or who keep kosher at home.

home and handling money on the Sabbath were only asked of a subsample who reported keeping kosher at home or lighting Sabbath candles at least sometimes (United Jewish Communities 2003c), so the percentages in the table are not directly comparable to the other items. Among persons who observe these rituals, almost 60 percent keep kosher outside their home and about one-quarter do not handle money on the Sabbath. When combined into the overall index of ritual behavior, the NJPS sample reports affirmatively on only a third of the nine items (mean = 3.38; median = 3), with relatively few at the highest end of ritual observance (eightieth percentile = 6).

Denominational preference is associated with subjective identification and ritual behavior. Mean values on these measures are presented by current denominational preference in Table 17.3. As expected, the Orthodox are highest on both, followed in turn by Conservative, Reform, and Other. All denominational differences are significant. Subjective identification does not vary as strongly by denomination as does behavior. Traditional religious observance is at its maximum among the Orthodox (where the median is the highest score possible on the index [not shown in the table]). The percentage distribution of denomination is shown in the last column of the table. Reform is the largest denomination, at 34 percent, followed closely by Other (31.3 percent). Conservative is preferred by about a quarter (25.5 percent) and Orthodox by fewer than one-tenth (9.1 percent).

TABLE 17.3

Mean Values of Jewish Identity by Denomination

	Identification[a]	Ritual[b]	%	N[c]
Orthodox[d]	4.49	7.45	9.1	422
Conservative	4.14	4.20	25.5	1,121
Reform	3.88	3.04	34.0	1,504
Other	3.29	1.83	31.3	1,437
F	261.43***	992.31***		
df_1, df_2	3, 4322	3, 4353		

a. All interdenominational comparisons are statistically significant.

b. All interdenominational comparisons are statistically significant.

c. Percentages are weighted. Sample sizes are unweighted. Total sample size = 5,148. Missing values are excluded from the analysis.

d. For information on the denominational categories, see the text.

Table 17.4 reports hypothesis tests in the form of odds ratios from ordered logit regressions of self-reported health on subjective identification and ritual observance, overall and after controlling for the other variables.[2] The marital status variable is coded as married or unmarried, since marriage and cohabitation are associated with better reported health irrespective of the religion of spouse or partner. The evidence in the table is consistent with all of the hypotheses. First, both Jewish identification and religious behavior are positively associated with self-reported health. Second, after adjusting for the other variables, it is apparent that this relationship is indirect for identification but that a positive net association remains for ritual behavior. This suggests that ritual behavior mediates the relationship between subjective identification and health, and this implies ritual observance is the more important of the two

TABLE 17.4

Odds Ratios from Ordered Logit Regressions of Self-Reported Health on Independent Variables

	Unadjusted	Multivariate			
	(1)	(2)	(3)	(4)	(5)
Subjective Identification	1.08**	1.01		0.97	0.97
Ritual Behavior	1.08***		1.05**	1.08***	1.06**
Religious Affiliation (Cons)					
Orthodox	1.00	0.85	0.72**	0.71**	0.75*
Reform	1.06	0.86	0.92	0.96	0.93
Other	0.73***	0.67***	0.77**	0.76**	0.77**
Generation 1 (2,3,4)	0.52***	0.48***	0.48***	0.57***	0.50***
Married (unmarried)	1.28***	1.22**	1.20**	1.41***	1.21**
Age (years)	0.97***	0.97***	0.97***	0.96***	0.97***
Education (years)	1.35***	1.29***	1.28***	1.31***	1.30***
Male (Female)	1.16**	0.98	1.04	1.01	1.01
North (Remainder of U.S.)	1.07	0.86*	0.82**	0.87*	0.83**
Health Conditions (No)	0.09***	0.08***	0.08***		0.08***
Observations		4131	4164	4046	4046
F		70.81	73.14	42.92	63.61
Df		4124	4157	4039	4039

* p < .10; ** p < .05; *** p < .01

for health. This finding is also consistent with the last hypothesis, that the net relationships of both aspects of Jewish identity would be smaller than before controls. Importantly, although the presence of health limitations is associated with both lower religious observance and worse self-reported health (data not shown), controlling for this variable does not erase the links between Jewish ritual behavior and better health.

One intriguing finding in Table 17.4 concerns the pattern of denominational differences in self-reported health. Unadjusted comparisons show no differences among Orthodox, Conservative, and Reform, but significantly worse health among persons with other preferences. After adjusting for the independent variables and, in particular, the two measures of Jewish identity, the Orthodox are similarly seen to have worse self-reported health. This suggests that the health advantages of religion may not be bound up in more or less fundamentalist faith traditions per se, but in specific religious behavior and subjective identification that may be related to denomination but still cut across these traditions.

Discussion and Conclusions

We find that the more "distinctively Jewish" Jews, expressed in terms of subjective identification and traditional religious behavior, report better health, overall and after controls for important potential confounders, including the presence of health limitations that might serve to constrain public religious participation. This finding is consistent with the larger literature on the potential health benefits or buffering effects of religious participation (e.g., Hummer et al. 2004; Koenig, McCullough, and Larson 2001), and our work comprises an important extension of extant research by examining variability in this association within this non-Christian religious and ethnic group. Indeed, ours is the first study we know of to examine differences in self-reported health among Jews. As such, it is an important complement to the existing research examining mortality patterns between Jews and non-Jews (Goldstein 1996; Kark et al. 1996; Shkolnikov et al. 2004). There is a larger body of work on religious differences in health and disease that has included Jews (Koenig, McCullough, and Larson 2001), but this research has not typically considered within-group variation in these patterns.

The observed linkages between subjective identification, traditional religious behavior, and self-reported health among Jews would seem to have important implications for our understanding of the possible mechanisms through which religion might be associated with health advantage. For instance, we consider the American Jewish community in religio-ethnic terms. Some of the respondents in our sample do not express Judaism as their religious preference; their ties to the Jewish community are solely "ethnic." One question is whether the extent of community solidarity or the strength of ethnic ties, expressed in nonreligious terms of positive identity or distinctively ethnic behavior, would likewise be associated with advantaged health among, say, blacks, Hispanics, or other minorities. If the underlying mechanisms for a religion and health relationship involve social support or analogous processes, it might be expected that ethnic identity would operate in the same way among these groups as our measures of Jewish identity have among Jews. If parallel findings are uncovered when within-group health patterns are examined relative to measures of ethnic pride/identification stated in other than religious terms, this would seem to indicate less of a role for distinctively religious mechanisms (e.g., stress reduction from prayer/meditation or behavioral prescriptions/proscriptions that create a "moderate" lifestyle). Of course, this would not negate the existence of religious differences in health among minority groups or the possibility of differences across groups (e.g., Musick's work among elderly blacks and whites [1996]), but it would extend our understanding of the underlying mechanisms to include analogous social processes. Our exploration of the mechanisms of this association is constrained by the limitation of our sample to Jews.

In addition, we are unable to explore in greater detail the role of distinctively religious mechanisms in the observed relationship. We have not examined direct measures of religious practice such as prayer or meditation. Similarly, although we have included adherence to the Jewish dietary laws in the measure of traditional observance, we have not considered if there are specific nutritional or dietary mechanisms that might be associated with better health. The benefits of such detailed investigation are attenuated in the present case due to the cross-sectional nature of the sample and the consequent inability to prospectively examine these relationships fully controlling for health selectivity at baseline. Nonetheless, these possibilities are intriguing and suggest avenues for the future.

Finally, it is important consider whether another methodological limitation might have a role in these findings. As discussed earlier, the NJPS sample design excludes the most assimilated persons of Jewish origin (Kadushin, Phillips, and Saxe 2005; Klaff and Mott 2005; United Jewish Communities 2003c, 26–41). However, rather than a confounding bias, it would seem that the effect of this limitation would be to constrain the variation on the independent variables of subjective identification and Jewish ritual observance and, thereby, to attenuate the magnitude of the relationships we observed. That we find significant associations even within this more narrowly delimited group would seem to make the findings more important.

New longitudinal data sets are necessary for the prospective study of the health implications of religion and religious practice. These should include detailed information on both public and private religious practices of a sufficient number of persons from a range of faith traditions as well as from nonreligious ethnic backgrounds. Although these data requirements are substantial, the potential importance of the general hypothesis that religion is beneficial for health would seem to warrant the effort and expense. Perhaps by adding these kinds of questions to ongoing studies, data can be collected that would move this literature toward a more definitive examination of the possible implications of religion for health in general as well as among American Jews.

NOTES

We are grateful to Sidney Goldstein and Alice Goldstein for very helpful comments on an earlier draft.

1. Complete information on the NJPS 2000–2001 and earlier population studies is available at www.jewishdatabank.org and United Jewish Communities (www.ujc.org/njps).

2. Analysis indicates violation of the assumption of parallel regressions (chi-squared = 66, p <.001), particularly for sex, marital status, age, generation, and health conditions. Inspection of the cumulative logit models for self-reported health across these variables indicates no substantive differences in the coefficients for health conditions (chi-squared = 8.32, p <.05), age (chi-squared = 8.41, p <.05), and generation (chi-squared = 8.82, p <.05), depending on response categories. Men are more likely to report fair than poor health (chi-squared = 12.41, p <.01), and married respondents are more likely to report excellent health than good, fair, or poor (chi-squared = 8.10, p <.05). Even with these violations, we retain the ordered logit specification in the interest of parsimony since these variables are controls rather than the variables of interest in the hypothesis tests.

REFERENCES

Amyot, R. P., and L. Sigelman. 1996. "Jews without Judaism? Assimilation and Jewish Identity in the United States." *Social Science Quarterly* 77 (1): 177–189.

Baron-Epel, O., G. Kaplan, A. Haviv-Messika, J. Tarabeia, M. S. Green, and D. Nitzan Kaluski. 2005. "Self-Reported Health as a Cultural Health Determinant in Arab and Jewish Israelis: MABAT—National Health and Nutrition Survey 1999–2001." *Social Science and Medicine* 61 (6): 1256–1266.

Benjamins, M. R., R. A. Hummer, I. W. Eberstein, and C. B. Nam. 2004. "Self-Reported Health and Adult Mortality Risk: An Analysis of Cause-Specific Mortality." *Social Science and Medicine* 59 (6): 1297–1306.

Benyamini, Y., and E. Idler. 1999. "Community Studies Reporting Association between Self-Rated Health and Mortality: Additional Studies, 1995 to 1998." *Research on Aging* 21 (3): 392–401.

Broyles, P. A., and C. K. Drenovsky. 1992. "Religious Attendance and the Subjective Health of the Elderly." *Review of Religious Research* 34:152–160.

Cohen, S. M. 1988. *American Assimilation or Jewish Revival?* Bloomington: Indiana University Press.

Daaleman, T. P., S. Perera, and S. A. Studenski. 2004. "Religion, Spirituality, and Health Status in Geriatric Outpatients." *Annals of Family Medicine* 2 (1): 49–53.

Dashefsky, A., B. Lazerwitz, and E. Tabory. 2003. "A Journey of the 'Straight Way' or the 'Roundabout Path': Jewish Identity in the United States and Israel." In *Handbook of the Sociology of Religion*, ed. M. Dillon, 240–260. Cambridge: Cambridge University Press.

DellaPergola, S. 2005. "Was it the Demography? A Reassessment of U.S. Jewish Population Estimates, 1945–2001." *Contemporary Jewry* 25:85–131.

Drevenstedt, G. T. 1998. "Race and Ethnic Differences in the Effects of Religious Attendance on Subjective Health." *Review of Religious Research* 39:245–263.

Ferraro, K. F., and C. M. Albrecht-Jensen. 1991. "Does Religion Influence Adult Health?" *Journal for the Scientific Study of Religion* 30 (2): 193–202.

Ferraro, K. F., and M. M. Farmer. 1999. "Utility of Health Data from Social Surveys: Is There a Gold Standard for Measuring Morbidity?" *American Sociological Review* 38:38–54.

Frankel, B. G., and W. E. Hewitt. 1994. "Religion and Well-Being among Canadian University Students: The Role of Faith Groups on Campus." *Journal for the Scientific Study of Religion* 33 (1): 62–73.

Franks, P., M. R. Gold, and K. Fiscella. 2003. "Sociodemographics, Self-Rated Health, and Mortality in the United States." *Social Science and Medicine* 56 (12): 2505–2514.

Goldman, N., D. A. Glei, and M.-C. Chang. 2004. "The Role of Clinical Risk Factors in Understanding Self-Rated Health." *Annals of Epidemiology* 14 (1): 49–57.

Goldscheider, C. 1986. *Jewish Continuity and Change: Emerging Patterns in America*. Bloomington: Indiana University Press.

———. 2003. "Are American Jews Vanishing Again?" *Contexts* 2 (1): 18–24.

Goldstein, S. 1992. "Profile of American Jewry: Insights from the 1990 National Jewish Population Survey." *American Jewish Yearbook* 92:77–173.

———. 1996. "Changes in Jewish Mortality and Survival, 1963–1987." *Social Biology* 43 (1–2): 72–97.

Goldstein, S., and A. Goldstein. 1996. *Jews on the Move: Implications for Jewish Identity*. Albany, NY: SUNY Press.

Grossman, L. 2005. "Jewish Religious Denominations." In *The Cambridge Companion to American Judaism*, ed. D. E. Kaplan, 81–100. New York: Cambridge University Press.

Gurock, J. 1998. "America's Challenge to Jewish Identity: A Historical Perspective on Voluntarism and Assimilation." In *A Portrait of the American Jewish Community*, ed. N. Linzer, D. J. Schnall, and J. A. Chanes, 13–27. Westport, CN: Praeger.

Hartman, H., and M. Hartman. 1996. "More Jewish, Less Jewish: Implications for Education and Labor Force Characteristics." *Sociology of Religion* 57 (2): 175–193.

Heilman, S. 2002. "The Importance of Residence: Goldscheider's Contribution to Explaining Orthodoxy's Vitality." *Contemporary Jewry* 23:220–236.

Heilman, S. C. 1982. "The Sociology of American Jewry: The Last Ten Years." *Annual Review of Sociology* 8:135–160.

Herman, S. N. 1977. *Jewish Identity: A Social Psychological Perspective*. Beverly Hills, CA: Sage.

Horowitz, B. 1999. "Jewishness in New York: Exception or the Rule?" In *National Variations in Jewish Identity*, ed. S. M. Cohen and G. Horencyzk, 223–240. Albany, NY: SUNY Press.

———. 2002. "Reframing the Study of Contemporary American Jewish Identity." *Contemporary Jewry* 23:14–34.

Hummer, R. A., C. G. Ellison, R. G. Rogers, B. E. Moulton, and R. R. Romero. 2004. "Religious Involvement and Adult Mortality in the United States: Review and Perspective." *Southern Medical Journal* 97 (12): 1223–1230.

Hummer, R. A., R. G. Rogers, C. B. Nam, and C. G. Ellison. 1999. "Religious Involvement and U.S. Adult Mortality." *Demography* 36 (2): 273–285.

Hyyppa, M., and J. Maki. 2001. "Individual-Level Relationships between Social Capital and Self-Rated Health in a Bilingual Community." *Preventive Medicine* 32 (2): 148.

Idler, E., and Y. Benyamini. 1997. "Self-Rated Health and Mortality: A Review of Twenty-Seven Community Studies." *Journal of Health and Social Behavior* 38:21–37.

Idler, E., L. Russell, and D. Davis. 2000. "Survival, Functional Limitations, and Self-Rated Health in the NHANES I Epidemiologic Follow-up Study, 1992." *American Journal of Epidemiology* 152 (9): 874–883.

Jenkinson, C., and H. M. McGee. 1998. *Health Status Measurement: A Brief but Critical Intro-duction*. Oxon, UK: Radcliffe Medical Press.

Kadushin, C., B. T. Phillips, and L. Saxe. 2005. "National Jewish Population Survey 2000–01: A Guide for the Perplexed." *Contemporary Jewry* 25:1–31.

Kark, J. D., G. Shemi, Y. Friedlander, M. Oz, M. Orly, and S. H. Blondheim. 1996. "Does Religious Observance Promote Health? Mortality in Secular versus Religious Kibbutzim in Israel." *American Journal of Public Health* 86 (3): 341–347.

Kaufman, D. 2005. "The Place of Judaism in American Jewish Identity." In *Cambridge Companion to American Judaism*, ed. D. Kaplan, 169–186. Cambridge: Cambridge University Press.

Kivisto, P., and B. Nefzger. 1993. "Symbolic Ethnicity and American Jews: The Relationship of Ethnic Identity to Behavior and Group Affiliation." *Social Science Journal* 30 (1): 1–12.

Klaff, V., and F. Mott. 2005. "NJPS 2000/01: A Vehicle for Exploring Social Structure and Social Dynamics in the Jewish Population." *Contemporary Jewry* 25:226–256.

Koenig, H., M. McCullough, and D. B. Larson. 2001. *Handbook of Religion and Health*. New York: Oxford University Press.

Kosmin, B. 2005. "The Need for a Systematic Comparative Approach to National Population Surveys of Jews." *Contemporary Jewry* 25:33–49.

Lazerwitz, B., J., A. Winter, A. Dashefsky, and E. Tabory. 1998. *Jewish Choices: American Jewish Denominationalism*. Albany, NY: SUNY Press.

Legge, J. S., Jr. 1997. "The Religious Erosion—Assimilation Hypothesis: The Case of U.S. Jewish Immigrants." *Social Science Quarterly* 78 (2): 472–486.

Levin, J. S., and K. S. Markides. 1986. "Religious Attendance and Subjective Health." *Journal for the Scientific Study of Religion* 25 (1): 31–40.

Levin, J. S., and H. Y. Vanderpool. 1987. "Is Frequent Religious Attendance Really Conducive to Better Health?: Toward an Epidemiology of Religion." *Social Science and Medicine* 24 (7): 589–600.

Liang, J., B. A. Shaw, N. Krause, J. M. Bennett, E. Kobayashi, T. Fukaya, and Y. Sugihara. 2005. "How Does Self-Assessed Health Change With Age? A Study of Older Adults in Japan." *Journal of Gerontology B: Psychological Sciences and Social Sciences* 60 (4): S224–232.

Liebman, C. S. 2001. "Some Research Proposals for the Study of American Jews." *Contemporary Jewry* 22:99–119.

Linzer, N. 1998. "The Changing Nature of Jewish Identity." In *A Portrait of the American Jewish Community*, ed. N. Linzer, D.J. Schnall, and J. Chanes, 1–12. Westport, CN: Praeger.

Lipset, S. M., and E. Raab. 1995. *Jews and the New American Scene*. Cambridge, MA: Harvard University Press.

Long, J. S., and S. Cheng. 2004. "Regression Models for Categorical Outcomes." In *Handbook of Data Analysis*, ed. M. Hardy and A. Bryman, 259–284. Thousand Oaks, CA: Sage.

Matthews, D. A., M. E. McCullough, D. B. Larson, H.G. Koenig, J. P. Swyers, and M. G. Milano. 1998. "Religious Commitment and Health Status: A Review of the Research and Implications for Family Medicine." *Archives of Family Medicine* 7 (2): 118–124.

McCullough, M. E., and J. P. Laurenceau. 2005. "Religiousness and the Trajectory of Self-Rated Health across Adulthood." *Personality and Social Psychology Bulletin* 31 (4): 560–573.

Medding, P. Y., G. A. Tobin, S. B. Fishman, and M. Rimor. 1992. "Jewish Identity in Conversionary and Mixed Marriages." *American Jewish Yearbook* 1992:3–76.

Musick, M. A. 1996. "Religion and Subjective Health among Black and White Elders." *Journal of Health and Social Behavior* 37 (3): 221–237.

Musick, M. A., J. S. House, and D. R. Williams. 2004. "Attendance at Religious Services and Mortality in a National Sample." *Journal of Health and Social Behavior* 16:198–213.

Musick, M. A., J. W. K. Traphagan, H. G. Koenig, and D. B. Larson. 2000. "Spirituality in Physical Health and Aging." *Journal of Adult Development* 7 (2): 73–86.

Rebhun, U. 1995. "Geographic Mobility and Religioethnic Identification: Three Jewish Communities in the United States." *Journal for the Scientific Study of Religion* 34 (4): 485–498.

———. 2004a. "Jewish Identification in Contemporary America: Gans' Symbolic Ethnicity and Religiosity Revisited." *Social Compass* 51 (3): 349–366.

———. 2004b. "Jewish Identity in America: Structural Analyses of Attitudes and Behaviors." *Review of Religious Research* 46 (1): 43–63.

Shkolnikov, V. M., E. M. Andreev, J. Anson, and F. Mesle. 2004. "The Peculiar Pattern of Mortality of Jews in Moscow, 1993–95." *Population Studies* 58 (3): 311–329.

Sklare, M. 1971. *America's Jews*. New York: Random House.

Spreitzer, E., and E. E. Snyder. 1974. "Correlates of Life Satisfaction among the Aged." *Journals of Gerontology* 29 (4): 454–458.

St. George, A., and P. H. McNamara. 1984. "Religion, Race, and Psychological Well-Being." *Journal for the Scientific Study of Religion* 23:351–363.

Statacorp. 2005. *Stata Statistical Software: Release 9.1.* College Station, TX: Stata Corporation.

United Jewish Communities. 2003a. *National Jewish Population Survey, 2000–01 [MRDF].* Storrs, CT: North American Jewish Data Bank.

———. 2003b. *The National Jewish Population Survey, 2000–01: Strength, Challenge, and Diversity in the American Jewish Population.* New York: United Jewish Communities.

———. 2003c. *National Jewish Population Survey/National Survey of Religion and Ethnicity 2000–01: Study Documentation.* New York: United Jewish Communities.

U.S. Bureau of the Census. 2000. "Educational Attainment." In *Current Population Survey.* www.bls.census.gov/cps/cpsmain.htm.

Veenstra, G. 2000. "Social Capital, SES and Health: An Individual-Level Analysis." *Social Science and Medicine* 50 (5): 619–627.

Waxman, C. 2001. *Jewish Baby Boomers: A Communal Perspective.* Albany, NY: SUNY Press.

Wilder, E. 1996. "Socioeconomic Attainment and Expressions of Jewish Identification, 1970 and 1990." *Journal for the Scientific Study of Religion* 35 (2): 109–127.

Witter, R. A., W. A. Stock, M. A. Okun, and M. J. Haring. 1985. "Religion and Subjective Well-Being in Adulthood: A Quantitative Synthesis." *Review of Religious Research* 26 (1): 332–342.

Zenner, W. P. 1985. "Jewishness in America: Ascription and Choice." *Ethnic and Racial Studies* 8 (1): 117–133.

18

Religion, Sexually Risky Behavior, and Reproductive Health

The Mormon Case

TIM B. HEATON

Scholars have long recognized that religion and the family are mutually rein-forcing institutions (D'Antonio and Aldous 1983). There are numerous reasons for this close linkage (Houseknecht and Pankhurst 2000; Dollahite, Marks, and Goodman 2004). Moreover, each of these institutions can have beneficial health consequences. In this chapter, I explore the possibility that religious con-straints on sexual behavior may reduce the risk of certain reproductive health problems, focusing on members of The Church of Jesus Christ of Latter-day Saints (the LDS Church). More specifically, I examine the relationship between LDS membership, sexually risky behaviors, and sexually transmitted infections (STIs), unwanted pregnancies, and abortion. I focus on members of the LDS Church (Mormons) because of this church's unique beliefs about marriage and the corresponding teaching that sex should be restricted to marital partners. Emphasis on nonmarital chastity, however, is not unique to Mormons. Thus, the analysis will include comparisons with other major religious groups in the United States.

The Sexual Revolution and Its Consequences

The sex revolution beginning in the 1960s entailed substantial change in a vari-ety of attitudes and behaviors including increasing acceptance of and engage-ment in premarital sex and higher nonmarital fertility and cohabitation. Most people now have sex with several partners over the course of a lifetime (Kost and Forrest 1992; Billy et al. 1993; Santelli et al. 1998; Robinson et al. 1991). Sexual intimacy, childbearing, and marriage have become less connected (Popenoe 1993; Heaton 1993). Marriage is no longer seen as the best resolution of non-marital pregnancy (Ku et al. 1998). These changes increasingly exposed teens to the risk of unwanted pregnancy and STIs (Finer, Darrroch, and Singh 1999;

Warren et al. 1998). The introduction and spread of HIV added a serious threat to reproductive health (Newcomer and Baldwin 1992).

Because of the possible consequences for adolescents and children born to teens and unmarried couples, changes in adolescent sexual behavior have motivated discussion of appropriate policy (Miller and Moore 1990). Several efforts have been undertaken to promote behavior that will reduce the changes of negative health outcomes associated with the sexual revolution. These include the promotion of contraceptive use, especially condoms, and sex education. Research indicates that these efforts have had some impact, but have not eliminated negative consequences. Contraceptive use has increased substantially since the early 1970s, and condom use has become particularly popular among the never married population (Piccinino and Mosher 1998). Even though nonmarital sex decreased, condom use increased, and abortion rates declined in the late 1980s and early 1990s, significant proportions of adults still engage in sexually risky behaviors, thus putting them at risk of STIs (Sonenstein et al. 1998; Anderson et al. 1999; Henshaw 1998).

Formal education about AIDS and birth control are associated with modest but statistically significant decreases in sexually risky behaviors (Ku, Sonenstein, and Pleck 1992). Research indicates that parent–teen communication also influences adolescent sexual attitudes and behaviors (Holtzman and Rubinson 1995; Luster and Small 1994). Parent–teen communication is not closely related to demographic variables, but depends more on relationships and attitudes toward sexual behavior (Raffaelli, Bogenschneider, and Flood 1998). In contrast to efforts aimed at education and promotion of contraceptive use, others believe that promotion of sexual abstinence is a more effective solution to the problems of unwanted pregnancy and STIs. Although it is common sense that those who do not have sex will not get pregnant or contract an STI, effective implementation of abstinence-based programs is more problematic. A recent review (Bennett and Assefi 2005) concludes that even though school-based abstinence and abstinence-plus programs can alter some adolescent behaviors, the long-term impact on sexual behavior may be modest at best. Even thought benefits of such school-based programs remain in question, the approach raises important questions about the social contexts that discourage adolescent sexual involvement.

Religion and the LDS Context

Religious institutions and beliefs can play an important role in formation of sexual attitudes and behaviors. The Judeo-Christian tradition restricts sexual activity to married heterosexual couples (DeLamater 1981). Religious attendance and religiousness are negatively associated with premarital sexual permissiveness among college students (Haerich 1992). Religion is also a primary source of teenage attitudes toward abortion (Stone and Waszak 1992). But various Christian churches have responded to the sex revolution in different ways.

Disapproval of premarital sex has not declined among conservative Protestants who attend church regularly, but there is a substantial decline in disapproval among Catholics and mainline Protestants (Petersen and Donnenwerth 1997). Premarital sex is less likely among members of "Institutional Sects" (e.g., Pentecostals, Mormons, and Jehovah's Witnesses) than among other religious groups (Beck, Cole, and Hammond 1991). Some scholars speculate that the reason for these differences is not so much the theological teachings as it is the level of commitment in these groups.

Cochran and Beeghley (1991) argue that affiliation alone is an inadequate indicator of religious experience. Religious groups not only promulgate beliefs, they also provide reference groups that reinforce religious teachings and practices. To be correctly specified, models of religious influence should include measures of participation in the group. Indeed, they find that the relationship between measures of religiosity and attitudes toward sexual behavior varies across religious groups. Consistent with the reference group perspective, Jensen, Newell, and Holman (1990) find that the lowest rates of nonmarital sexual activity occur among those with high levels of church attendance and low levels of sexual permissiveness.

Research suggests that families are an important context for reinforcing religious beliefs. Thornton and Camburn (1987) find that parents' religious affiliation and commitment influence adolescent attitudes and sexual behavior. Sexual behavior can be viewed as part of a courtship and mating process (Thornton 1990; Miller and Moore 1990). This process is shaped by parental attitudes (Jaccard, Dittus, and Gordon 1996), marital status of parents, family processes (Miller, Forehand, and Kotchick 1999; Rodgers 1999), and by older siblings (Rodgers, Rowe, and Harris 1992). To the degree that religious ideologies shape family attitudes, processes, and structure, these ideologies will be reinforced within the family context.

The LDS Church is an interesting context for the examination of sexual behavior. Founded in upstate New York in 1830, the LDS Church was a radical departure from predominant religious norms. Conflict with surrounding communities led to a series of migrations, culminating in settlement in the Great Basin in 1847. Isolated in the mid-1880s, Mormonism thrived while maintaining distinctive practices such as polygamy and integration of church and state. Advances in transportation and communication, and efforts to obtain statehood, ended the period of relative isolation. A series of accommodations, including elimination of polygamy, communitarian economics, and close ties between church and state, reduced differences between Mormons and the rest of U.S. society, but important differences remain. Research comparing Mormons with the U.S. population indicates that Mormons have higher rates of church attendance, lower crime rates, higher levels of mental and physical health, and tend to be politically conservative (Heaton, Bahr, and Jacobson 2004). Prominent family behaviors include above average rates of marriage, remarriage, and childbearing. Mormon mothers are less likely to report unwanted pregnancies, more likely to report they breastfeed, and more likely to be married when their children were born. Mormon women are as likely to use birth control as are women nationally, and adolescent attitudes toward contraceptive use are similar to national trends in most respects (Heaton, Bahr, and Jacobson 2004).

The LDS position on sexual behavior derives from a unique theology of the family. LDS theology holds that couples who marry in LDS temples and who remain faithful to religious covenants will remain married in heaven (Holman and Harding 1996). Research from a variety of different studies document lower rates of premarital sex among Mormons. Comparisons of college students in Denmark, the U.S. Midwest, and Utah show that significant differences persisted through the onset of the sexual revolution (Christensen 1982). Moreover, the relationship between religiosity and abstinence from premarital sex among Mormons is observed in different geographic areas, regardless of the concentration of adherents (Top and Chadwick 1998). A review of research on LDS families concluded that abstinence before marriage is one of the major distinctive markers of Mormon behavior (Heaton 1987). Analysis of more recent surveys indicate that this difference has persisted (Holman and Harding 1996; Heaton, Bahr, and Jacobson 2004) into the 1980s and 1990s. Mormon attitudes also reflect LDS teachings. They are less likely to say that premarital sex, cohabitation, and marital infidelity are acceptable (Holman and Harding 1996).

McQuillan (2004, 49–50) argues that three conditions must be present for religion to exert an influence on fertility:

> First, the religion in question must articulate behavioral norms that have linkages to fertility outcomes. Second, a religious group must possess the means to communicate its teachings to its members and to enforce compliance. Finally, religious groups are more likely to influence the demographic choices of their followers when members feel a strong sense of attachment to the religious community.

Similar conditions could be postulated in order for religion to influence sexual behavior. The LDS Church teaches a strict moral code that specifies that sexual intercourse should only occur between married partners. This code is reinforced by a doctrine that marital relationships can persist after death, if couples adhere to certain standards of belief and behavior (Holman and Harding 1996). Although other major religious groups such as Catholicism also teach the importance of chastity and fidelity, the LDS doctrine linking conformity with prospects of continued marital relationships after death is unique.

Several mechanisms have been institutionalized to reinforce the norm of premarital abstinence. From adolescence, LDS members are taught the importance of the moral code. Local leaders are instructed to interview youth on a regular basis and encourage obedience. Couples are not allowed to be married in LDS temples unless they are in compliance with the "law of chastity."

Students who attend LDS universities must agree to this code of conduct. Finally, infidelity may result in excommunication from the Church. In combination, these rules and procedures constantly remind members of the importance of sexual morality.

The LDS Church is considered to be a high-demand religion. Not only do they have restrictions on sexual behavior, but they also prohibit the use of tobacco and alcohol. Attendance rates are comparatively high, as is participation of adherents in the functioning of congregations, which are staffed entirely by local volunteers. In conjunction, these characteristics create a strong sense of attachment to the religious community.

In short, Mormons have mechanisms in place that would reduce the likelihood of engagement in a variety of sexually risky behaviors such as premarital sex, cohabitation, having a large number of sexual partners, and unprotected sex. It is also possible, however, that sexually restrictive subgroups do not adequately prepare adolescents against risk when sexual activity begins. Thus, Mormons may have less information about human reproduction, STIs, and contraception. This lack of knowledge could place them at greater risk of infection and unwanted pregnancy.

In order to explore the linkages between religion, sexually risky behavior, and negative health outcomes, I evaluate a model with religious affiliation and frequency of attendance as independent variables. Sexually risky behaviors including premarital sex, number of sex partners, cohabitation, unprotected sex, and sex education are treated as intervening variables. The outcomes of interest are having been treated for STIs (syphilis, gonorrhea, chlamydia, and genital warts), having been tested for HIV other than when donating blood, wantedness of first pregnancy, and ever having an abortion. Family background characteristics including parental education, race, age, and parental marital history are also taken into account. The 1995 National Survey of Family Growth (NSFG) is used to evaluate these relationships.

Summary Model

Existing research suggests a model in which religions emphasizing premarital chastity have lower rates of risky behaviors such as premarital sex, unprotected sex, cohabitation, and higher numbers of sexual partners. But the discouragement of nonmarital sex may also reduce communication between parents and children about sexual reproduction and health if these topics are seen as taboo. Lower rates of incidence of risky behaviors will, in turn, be associated with reduced risk of negative health outcomes including STIs, unwanted pregnancy, and abortion. Moreover, the role of religious affiliation should be more evident among active participants. But the role of religion may be confounded by other demographic determinants of sexual activity such as family structure, socioeconomic status, and race. There are important ethnic and gender differences in the timing of first intercourse (Upchurch et al. 1998). Black adolescents report younger age at first sexual intercourse and a larger number of partners (Warren et al. 1998). Family structure is also related to timing of first sexual intercourse and premarital childbearing (Miller and Moore 1990; Albrecht and Teachman 2003; South 1999). Family formation also varies by type of residence (Snyder, Brown, and Condo 2004; Heaton, Lichter, and Amoateng 1989). These potential confounding factors will be taken into account.

Data and Methods

Analysis is based on the 1995 NSFG. The NSFG interviewed over ten thousand women aged fifteen to forty-four. Questions focus on many aspects of sexual behavior. These data were selected because of the relatively large number of Mormons (n = 246) and because variables of interest are included in the survey. Information about the NSFG can be found at http://www.cdc.gov/nchs/nsfg.htm.

Health outcomes of interest include ever having an abortion (coded 1 for yes and 0 for no), status of the first pregnancy (coded 0 for no pregnancy, 1 for wanted at the time pregnancy occurred, and 2 for unwanted or mistimed pregnancy), ever having been treated for an STI (coded 1 if respondent has been treated for syphilis, gonorrhea, chlamydia, or genital warts and 0 otherwise), and ever having been tested for HIV outside of a blood donation (coded 0 if no test was reported or if the test was solely part of a blood donation and 1 for all other tests).

Results

Descriptive Results

Table 18.1 reports religious group differences in background characteristics. Mormons have several characteristics that could reduce the risk of negative health outcomes. Compared with other groups, they are more likely to live in nonmetropolitan areas, have low minority group membership, are less exposed to parental marital disruption, and have more educated mothers. Although they are more concentrated in Western states, they are not concentrated on the West Coast (state of residence is not included in the data).

There are other major demographic differences among religious groups that could account for sexual behavior. For example, Jews are more concentrated in urbanized areas of the Northeast, while Baptists and fundamentalists are more likely to live in the South and in nonmetropolitan areas. Catholics have the highest percentage of Hispanics, while Baptists and fundamentalists have large black populations. Like Mormons, Jews have lower exposure to marital disruption of parents. Catholics and fundamentalists come from homes with comparatively low maternal education. Mothers of Baptists had their first child by age twenty on average, while Jewish mothers were the oldest on average when they had their first child.

TABLE 18.1

Demographic Characteristics of Religious Denominational Groups

Religion	(n)	Suburb	Non metro-politan	North Central	South	West	Hispanic	Black	Other Race	Parents Divorced	Parents married at birth	Mother's education (mean)	Mean Age of mother at 1st birth
None	610	45.4%	17.4%	24.1%	23.4%	36.7%	8.5%	15.7%	6.2%	12.5%	81.6%	11.98	20.99
Catholic	3386	52.0%	12.6%	21.8%	22.9%	27.9%	32.5%	2.2%	2.5%	9.6%	91.2%	10.95	21.87
Jewish	119	63.9%	2.5%	16.8%	16.8%	22.7%	4.0%	1.7%	0.0%	7.6%	97.5%	13.21	24.58
Baptist	2461	35.4%	23.5%	21.2%	60.1%	9.1%	1.8%	53.6%	1.1%	11.3%	79.5%	11.32	19.98
Mainline Protestant	1797	49.4%	26.0%	34.0%	29.1%	19.8%	2.2%	12.0%	1.9%	10.4%	93.9%	12.68	22.40
Other Christian	523	49.9%	21.2%	28.3%	20.7%	29.3%	7.3%	11.1%	4.4%	11.5%	91.2%	12.26	22.17
Fundamentalist	527	38.1%	22.2%	22.0%	41.9%	20.1%	13.1%	35.7%	1.9%	13.1%	83.3%	10.79	20.07
Mormon	233	42.5%	33.1%	12.9%	25.8%	58.8%	4.7%	1.7%	4.3%	7.3%	95.7%	12.42	21.64
Other	256	48.1%	14.5%	21.5%	23.4%	34.8%	5.9%	9.8%	36.3%	6.6%	89.1%	11.53	21.70
Total	9912	46.0%	19.4%	24.1%	34.2%	22.8%	13.9%	21.4%	3.2%	10.5%	87.9%	11.55	21.39

Table 18.2 demonstrates substantial differences in health outcomes for different religious groups. Jews and those with no religious preference are most likely to report having an abortion with over a fourth reporting in the affirmative. There is little variation among most Christian groups where about a fifth of the women have had an abortion. Mormon rates are substantially below average, with only 13.4 percent reporting an abortion.

Status of the first pregnancy also differs by religion, partially because some groups are less likely to have experienced a pregnancy. Among those who have had a pregnancy, the ratio varies substantially from a high of nearly two unwanted pregnancies for every wanted pregnancy among those with no religious preference, to a low of eight unwanted pregnancies to every ten wanted pregnancies for Jews and Mormons.

Nearly 15 percent of those with no religious preference report being treated for an STI. For most groups, the percentage is closer to 10. Mormons are noticeably below all other groups with 4.5 percent reporting such treatment. Correspondingly, Mormons are also less likely to report being tested for HIV outside of a blood donation.

Our model hypothesizes that religious differences in the health outcomes reported in Table 18.2 are mediated by sexually risky behaviors. Religious differences in these risky behaviors are reported in Table 18.3. There are clear differences in the percentages of women who have had premarital sex, ranging from the midfifties for Mormons and the "other" category to over 80 percent for Jews, Baptists, mainline Protestants, and those with no religious preference. Some of the groups with low rates of premarital sex also have comparatively low percentages for those that did not use contraception at first intercourse, such as Mormons and the "other" category. In contrast, some groups have high rates of premarital sex, but tend to use contraception. For example, Jews are among the most likely to have premarital sex but have the lowest rate of unprotected first intercourse.

Cohabitation also varies across religious groups. The two groups that were lowest on premarital sex also have the lowest percentages that have ever cohabited (Mormons and the "other" category). Likewise, groups with high rates of premarital sex such as Jews and those with no religious preference have the highest rates of cohabitation, with values over 50 percent. A similar pattern is evident for average number of sex partners, where Mormons are at the low end at 3.1 and those with no religious preference are at the high end with over eight partners, on average.

Although groups such as Mormons may reduce the risk of sexually risky behaviors by strong emphasis on chastity, youth in these groups may be unprepared for sex when it happens. To explore this possibility, an index of sex information from parents is included. Catholics and those in the "other" category are least likely to have had their parents provide sex education—only about half have received information from their parents. At the other end of the spectrum, just over three-fourths of Jews have received information from their parents.

TABLE 18.2

Sex-Related Health Risks by Adolescent Religion

| Religion | (n) | % had abortion | Pregnancy status | | | | % treated for STI | % HIV Test w/out blood donation |
			none	wanted	unwanted	ratio unwanted to wanted		
None	683	25.8	34.5	22.9	42.6	1.86	14.1	39.7
Catholic	3633	20.6	28.0	37.2	34.8	0.94	10.1	36.4
Jewish	126	26.2	38.9	34.1	27	0.79	10.5	42.1
Baptist	2744	20.3	23.8	29.4	46.8	1.59	10.8	42.0
Mainline Protestant	1880	21.2	30.0	34.6	35.4	1.02	11.7	33.4
Other Christian	548	21.5	35.7	29.6	34.6	1.17	12	33.8
Fundamentalist	578	18.9	26.3	35.2	38.5	1.09	8.5	36.2
LDS	246	13.4	34.0	36.0	30.0	0.83	4.5	24.7
All other	272	18.8	37.2	31.4	31.4	1.00	8.2	33.6
x^2		23.4		199.4			27.7	64.6
d.f.		8		16			8	8
p		<0.003		<.001			<0.001	<.001

TABLE 18.3

Risky Behavior by Adolescent Religion

Religion	% reporting				Average # of nonmarital sex partners
	Premarital sex	Unprotected 1st sex	Cohabitation	Sex education from parents	
None	83.1	41.3	50.6	60.9	8.1
Catholic	76.8	42.9	42.1	51.3	5.0
Jewish	81.0	25.4	50.0	76.2	7.9
Baptist	84.1	42.3	42.6	60.1	7.7
Mainline Protestant	83.9	34.5	44.8	62.6	6.2
Other Christian	77.3	35.3	40.4	64.3	5.4
Fundamentalist	72.0	45.1	40.2	55.4	5.1
LDS	59.1	36.7	33.6	60.3	3.1
All other	56.8	37.0	30.0	46.8	4.4
x^2	251.2	65.8	54.4	132.8	F = 4.25
d.f.	8	8	8	8	8
p	<.001	<.001	<.001	<.001	<.001

Multivariate Results

The next step in the analysis is to examine religious group effects on health outcomes controlling for risky behavior. Table 18.4 presents results of logistic regression equations for each health indicator. The first of each set of models includes only religious affiliation. The coefficients for this model simply duplicate the information in Table 18.2, but in the context of logistic regression coefficients. The "no religion" category is the comparison group. The second model of each pair includes religious affiliation and each of the demographic characteristics reported in Table 18.1. The difference in coefficients for religion between Model 1 and Model 2 is the portion of the religious effect attributable to demographic composition of religious groups. The third model adds sexually risky behaviors.

Demographic composition generally does not account for religious group differences in abortion or STIs. Some effects are attenuated by including demographic controls. For example, low abortion among Catholics and mainline Protestants is partially due to such differences. But coefficients for abortion among Baptists and fundamentalists are actually a little larger with controls included. For other groups, the controls do not make a big difference in

TABLE 18.4

Religious Group Differences (Logistic Regression Coefficients) in Reproductive Health, Adjusting for Background Characteristics and Risky Behaviors

Religion	Abortion			Unwanted pregnancy			STI			HIV Test		
	1	2	3	1	2	3	1	2	3	1	2	3
Catholic	-.316*	-.156	-.120	-.324*	-.174	-.188	-.410*	-.160	-.094	-.166	-.078	-.048
Jewish	.005	.101	.029	-.668*	-.335	-.401	-.415	-.319	-.498	.070	.291	.243
Baptist	-.320*	-.407*	-.357*	.125	-.083	.032	-.379*	-.380	-.265	.055	-.160	-.104
Mainline Protestant	-.272	-.082	-.063	-.304*	-.131	-.151	.271*	-.161	-.111	-.289*	-.133	-.129
Other Christian	-.259	-.146	.027	-.322*	-.200	-.085	-.308	-.217	-.018	-.356*	-.239	-.179
Fundamentalist	-.389*	-.417*	-.247	-.137	-.273*	.072	-.642*	.575*	-.372	-.148	-.266*	-.158
Mormon	-.936*	-.830*	-.475	-.618*	-.500*	.085	-1.244*	-1.258*	-.928*	-.733*	-.620*	-.350
Other (no religion implicit)	-.338	-.259	.164	-.422	-.275	.065	-.661*	-.391	.004	-.307*	-.218	.056
Wald	23.8	33.9	20.7	103.7*	14.6	13.6	25.6	25.1	13.5	58.3	22.8	9.9
p	.003	<.001	.008	<.001	n.s.	n.s.	<.001	<.001	n.s.	.001	.004	n.s.

Note: Model 1 only includes religious groups, Model 2 adds control variables, and Model 3 adds risky behaviors.

abortion. Indeed, the Wald statistic for religion is actually larger in the model with demographic controls. Likewise, most of the religious group differences in STIs are not explained by demographic controls. The coefficient indicating low rates of STIs among Catholics becomes small with controls added, and the coefficient for "other" is reduced by nearly half, but other coefficients do not change a great deal. The Wald statistic for religious differences in STIs remains virtually unchanged when controls are added.

In contrast to abortion and STIs, much of the religious group difference in unwanted pregnancy can be accounted for by demographic differences. Once controls are added, only the coefficients for fundamentalists and Mormons remain statistically significant. Moreover, the Wald statistic for religion drops from 103.7 to a statistically insignificant 14.6 when controls are added.

Results for HIV are mixed. The coefficients for mainline Protestants become much smaller and nonsignificant. A few coefficients increase in magnitude, and many are not greatly altered. The Wald statistic for the HIV model is reduced by more than half when controls are added.

There is substantial support for the hypothesis that religious group differences in health risks are due to differences in risky behaviors. Most of the religious group coefficients become smaller in the abortion model when risky behaviors are included and the Wald statistic is noticeably reduced. Lower rates of risky behavior account for a substantial share of the lower abortion rates among fundamentalists and Mormons.

Risky behaviors do not have large an impact on many religious group coefficients in the models for unwanted pregnancy, but Mormons and fundamentalists are the exception. In each of these groups, the coefficients become small and nonsignificant.

Several religious group differences in STIs and HIV are reduced by inclusion of controls for risky behaviors, and the Wald statistics for religious group effects become nonsignificant for both outcomes. As with other outcomes, coefficients for Mormons and fundamentalists are particularly affected by controlling for the risky behaviors.

In short, demographic composition and sexually risky behaviors account for much of the religious group differences in unwanted pregnancy, STIs, and being tested for HIV. Only the Mormon coefficient in the STI model remains statistically significant when these two sets of variables are taken into account. Demographic composition and sexually risky behaviors make less difference in the abortion model.

Religious Attendance

Reference group theory implies that frequency of church attendance will reduce the likelihood of risky behaviors and negative health outcomes noted earlier. This hypothesis is tested in Table 18.5. There is strong and consistent support for the first hypothesis. People who attended church more often as

TABLE 18.5

Risky Behaviors and Sex-Related Health Risks by Religious Attendance

			Attendance				
	Never	*<1 month*	*1–3 month*	*1 week*	*>1 week*	*P-level*	*Multivariate p-level*
# of partners	8.3	7.5	5.8	5.4	5.5	<.001	<.001
% premarital sex	86.2	83.5	82.1	79.1	70.8	<.001	<.001
% unprotected sex	43.8	39.4	41.6	40.3	38.3	<.01	<.001
% cohabit	55.1	46.6	42.4	40.1	37.7	<.001	n.s.
% sex education	56.7	61.2	59.9	56.4	56.2	<.001	n.s.
% had abortion	25.6	26.2	19.8	20.1	16.7	<.001	n.s.
% unwanted birth	42.9	39.3	39.1	37.5	36.4	<.001	n.s.
% STI	14.8	13.6	10.1	9.3	9.4	<.001	n.s.
% HIV test	40.8	37.8	36.8	36.3	36.4	<.05	n.s.

adolescents are less likely to engage in each of the risky behaviors, and are also less likely to report each of the health outcomes, except being tested for HIV. Results are particularly strong for premarital sex and number of sex partners. When attendance is included in a multivariate model with demographic variables included, its relationship to risky behaviors remains significant. When attendance, demographic variables, and risky sex behaviors are included in a model to predict negative health outcomes, attendance is no longer significant. Much of the relationship between attendance and health risks is mediated by risky behavior. By implication, youth who attend services more often are less likely to have negative health outcomes because they are less likely to engage in risky behavior.

Discussion and Conclusions

Religious teachings about sexuality and family life are an integral aspect of religious worldviews. In the United States, changing patterns of family formation have challenged traditional beliefs at the same time that reproductive technology and spread of sexually transmitted diseases have changed the health risks associated with sexual behavior. Although a majority of adolescents in the U.S. state that religious faith is an important part of their lives, these adolescents do not necessarily hold to traditional beliefs of the groups to which they belong (Smith and Denton 2005). Thus, it is reasonable to expect some connection between adolescent religion and sexual behavior, but not to expect that adolescents would always adhere to strict standards of sexual conduct. This analysis demonstrates substantial religious group differences in both sexually risky behaviors and reproductive health outcomes associated with those behaviors.

A modest portion of the religious group difference can be explained by religious group difference in demographic characteristics, including place of residence, race, and family background. Even after taking demographic characteristics into account, there is still substantial religious group variation in sexually risky behaviors and sex-related health risks.

Conservative groups such as Baptists, fundamentalists, and Mormons have been most resistant to the sexual revolution. Mormons represent a clear case of a group that takes a strong doctrinal position against nonmarital sex and reinforces this teaching through a variety of mechanisms. The norm of premarital chastity is articulated in religious activities and parents are also encouraged to reinforce these norms. Mormon adolescents are among the least likely to engage in sexually risky behaviors and are less likely to experience negative health outcomes. The results indicate that the ideological and social context within which Mormon youth are raised is a significant but not overpowering influence on their sexual conduct.

Religious group differences in sexually risky behaviors and exposure to sex-related health problems are large enough to merit careful consideration by policymakers. Although direct intervention in the religious lives of its citizens violates notions of separation of church and state in the United States, efforts to promote responsible sexual behavior among adolescents could benefit from a more complete understanding of contexts that influence adolescent behavior. This study has merely demonstrated that religion is one context that matters. More detailed data and analysis would be required to specify what it is about religion that makes a difference.

Caution must be used in interpreting results. Even when large national samples are representative of the nation's population, small geographically concentrated groups such as Mormons may be either over- or under-sampled, depending on where sample clusters are chosen. Reports of sexual behavior may be influenced by a variety of factors including social acceptability, individual embarrassment, and definitions of what sex entails. This study has only captured some of the relevant risky behaviors and health outcomes that may be important. Finally, results are based on a onetime survey. Some have argued that the relationship between religion and sexual behavior is bidirectional, but at least one recent study contradicts this view (Hardy and Raffaelli 2003). Although we have attempted to capture time sequencing by using religious behavior in adolescence, changes in sexual behavior may alter interpretation of religious experience such that results from cross-sectional surveys are incomplete.

REFERENCES

Albrecht, C., and J. D. Teachman. 2003. "Childhood Living Arrangements and the Risk of Premarital Intercourse." *Journal of Family Issues* 24:867–894.

Anderson, J. E., R. Wilson, L. Doll, T. S. Hones, and P. Barker. 1999. "Condom Use and HIV Risk Behaviors among U.S. Adults: Data from a National Survey." *Family Planning Perspectives* 31:24–28.

Beck, S. H., B. S. Cole, and J. A. Hammond. 1991. "Religious Heritage and Premarital Sex: Evidence from a National Sample of Young Adults." *Journal for the Scientific Study of Religion* 30:173–180.

Bennett, S. E., and N. P. Assefi. 2005. "School-Based Teenage Pregnancy Prevention Programs: A Systematic Review of Randomized Controlled Trials." *Journal of Adolescent Health* 36:72–81.

Billy, J. O., K. Tanfer, W. R. Grady, and D. H. Klepinger. 1993. "The Sexual Behavior of Men in the United States." *Family Planning Perspectives* 25:52–60.

Christensen, H. T. 1982. "The Persistence of Chastity: A Built-In Resistance within Mormon Culture to Secular Trends." *Sunstone* 7:6–14.

Cochran, J. K., and L. Beeghley. 1991. "The Influence of Religion on Attitudes toward Nonmarital Sexuality: A Preliminary Assessment of Reference Group Theory." *Journal for the Scientific Study of Religion* 30:45–62.

D'Antonio, W. V., and J. Aldous. 1983. *Families and Religions: Conflict and Change in Modern Society*. Beverly Hills: Sage Publications.

DeLamater, J. 1981. "The Social Control of Sexuality." *Annual Review of Sociology* 7:263–290.

Dollahite, D. C., L. D. Marks, and M. A. Goodman. 2004. "Families and Religious Beliefs, Practices, and Communities." In *Handbook of Contemporary Families*, ed. M. Comeman and L. H. Ganong, 411–431. Thousand Oaks, CA: Sage Publications.

Finer, L. B., J. E. Darroch, and S. Singh. 1999. "Sexual Partnership Patterns as a Behavior Risk Factor for Sexually Transmitted Diseases." *Family Planning Perspectives* 31:228–236.

Haerich, P. 1992. "Premarital Sexual Permissiveness and Religious Investigation: A Preliminary Investigation." *Journal for the Scientific Study of Religion* 31:361–365.

Hardy, S. A., and M. Raffaelli. 2003. "Adolescent Religiosity and Sexuality: An Investigation of Reciprocal Influences." *Journal of Adolescence* 26:731–739.

Heaton, T. B. 1987. "Four Characteristics of the Mormon Family." *Dialogue* 20:101–114.

———. 1993. "Family Decline and Disassociation: Changing Family Demographics since the 1950s." *Family Perspective* 27 (2): 127–146.

Heaton, T. B., S. Bahr, and C. K. Jacobson. 2004. *Health, Wealth and Social Life of Mormons*. Lewiston, NY: The Edwin Mellen Press.

Heaton, T. B., D. T. Lichter, and A. Y. Amoateng. 1989. "The Timing of Family Formation: Rural–Urban Differentials in First Intercourse, Childbirth, and Marriage." *Rural Sociology* 54 (1): 1–16.

Henshaw, S. K. 1998. "Abortion Incidence and Services in the United States, 1995–1996." *Family Planning Perspectives* 30:263–270 and 287.

Holman, T. B., and J. R. Harding. 1996. "The Teaching of Nonmarital Sexual Abstinence and Members Sexual Attitudes and Behaviors: The Case of Latter-Day Saints." *Review of Religious Research* 38:51–60.

Holtzman, D., and R. Rubinson. 1995. "Parent and Peer Communication Effects on AIDS Related Behavior among U.S. High School Students." *Family Planning Perspectives* 27 (6): 235–240.

Houseknecht, S. K., and J. G. Pankhurst. 2000. *Family, Religion, and Social Change in Diverse Societies*. New York: Oxford University Press.

Jaccard, J., P. J. Dittus, and V. V. Gordon. 1996. "Maternal Correlates of Adolescent Sexual and Contraceptive Behavior." *Family Planning Perspectives* 28:159–167.

Jensen, L., R. J. Newell, and T. Holman. 1990. "Sexual Behavior, Church Attendance, and Permissive Beliefs among Unmarried Young Men and Women." *Journal for the Scientific Study of Religion* 29:113–117.

Kost, K., and J. D. Forrest. 1992. "American Women's Sexual Behavior and Exposure to Risk of Sexually Transmitted Diseases." *Family Planning Perspectives* 24:244–254.

Ku, L. C., F. L. Sonenstein, L. D. Lindberg, C. H. Bradner, S. Boggess, and J. H. Pleck. 1998. "Understanding Changes in Sexual Activity among Young Metropolitan Men: 1979–1995." *Family Planning Perspectives* 30:256–262.

Ku, L. C., F. L. Sonenstein, and J. H. Pleck. 1992. "The Association of AIDS Education and Sex Education with Sexual Behavior and Condom Use among Teenage Men." *Family Planning Perspectives* 24:100–106.

Luster, T., and S. A. Small. 1994. "Factors Associated with Sexual Risk-Taking Behavior among Adolescents." *Journal of Marriage and the Family* 56 (3): 622–632.

Miller, B. C., and K. A. Moore. 1990. "Adolescent Sexual Behavior, Pregnancy, and Parenting: Research through the 1980s." *Journal of Marriage and the Family* 52:1025–1044.

Miller, K. S., R. Forehand, and B. A. Kotchick. 1999. "Adolescent Sexual Behavior in Two Ethnic Minority Samples: The Role of Family Variables." *Journal of Marriage and the Family* 61:85–98.

McQuillan, K. 2004. "When Does Religion Influence Fertility?" *Population and Development Review* 30 (1): 25–56.

Newcomer, S., and W. Baldwin. 1992. "Demographics of Adolescent Sexual Behavior, Contraception, Pregnancy, and STDs." *Journal of School Health* 62:265–270.

Petersen, L. R., and G. V. Donnenwerth. 1997. "Secularization and the Influence of Religion on Beliefs about Premarital Sex." *Social Forces* 75:1071–1089.

Piccinino, L. J., and W. D. Mosher. 1998. "Trends in Contraceptive Use in the United States: 1982–1995." *Family Planning Perspectives* 30:4–10 and 46.

Popenoe, D. 1993. "American Family Decline, 1960–1990." *Journal of Marriage and the Family* 55:527–555.

Raffaelli, M., K. Bogenschneider, and M. F. Flood. 1998. "Parent–Teen Communication about Sexual Topics." *Journal of Family Issues* 19:315–333.

Robinson, I., K. Ziss, B. Ganza, and S. Katz. 1991. "Twenty Years of the Sexual Revolution, 1965–1985: An Update." *Journal of Marriage and the Family* 53:216–220.

Rodgers, J. L., D. C. Rowe, and D. F. Harris. 1992. "Sibling Differences in Adolescent Sexual Behavior: Inferring Process Models from Family Composition Patterns." *Journal of Marriage and the Family* 54:142–152.

Rodgers, K. B. 1999. "Parenting Processes Related to Sexual Risk-Taking Behaviors of Adolescent Males and Females." *Journal of Marriage and the Family* 61:99–109.

Santelli, J. S., N. D. Brener, R. Lowery, A. Bhatt, and L. S. Zabin. 1998. "Multiple Sexual Partners among U.S. Adolescents and Young Adults." *Family Planning Perspectives* 30:271–275.

Smith, C., with M. L. Denton. 2005. *Soul Searching: The Religious and Spiritual Lives of American Teenagers.* Oxford: Oxford University Press.

Snyder, A. R., S. L. Brown, and E. P. Condo. 2004. "Residential Differences in Family Formation: The Significance of Cohabitation." *Rural Sociology* 69 (2): 235–260.

Sonenstein, F. L., L. C. Ku, L. D. Lindberg, C. Turner, and J. Pleck. 1998. "Changes in Sexual Behavior and Condom Use among Teenaged Males: 1988 to 1995." *American Journal of Public Health* 88:956–959.

South, S. J. 1999. "Historical Changes and Life Course Variation in the Determinants of Premarital Childbearing." *Journal of Marriage and the Family* 61:752–763.

Stone, R., and C. Waszak. 1992. "Adolescent Knowledge and Attitudes about Abortion." *Family Planning Perspectives* 24:52–57.

Thornton, A. 1990. "The Courtship Process and Adolescent Sexuality." *Journal of Family Issues* 11:239–273.

Thornton, A., and D. Camburn 1987. "The Influence of the Family on Premarital Sexual Attitudes and Behavior." *Demography* 24:323–341.

Top, B., and B. Chadwick. 1998. *Rearing Righteous Youth of Zion: Great News, Good News, Not-so-good News.* Salt Lake City, UT: Bookcraft.

Upchurch, D. M., L. Levy-Storms, C. A. Sucoff, and C. S. Aneshensel. 1998. "Gender and Ethnic Differences in the Timing of First Sexual Intercourse." *Family Planning Perspectives* 30:121–127.

Warren, C. W., J. S. Santelli, S. A. Everett, L. Kann, J. L. Collins, C. Cassell, L. Morris, and L. J. Kolbe. 1998. "Sexual Behavior among U.S. High School Students, 1990–1995." *Family Planning Perspectives* 30:170–172 and 200.

19

Religion and the New Immigrants

Impact on Health Behaviors and Access to Health Care

HELEN ROSE EBAUGH

The new immigrants, those who have arrived since the radical change in U.S. immigrant laws in 1965, have introduced diversity of all kinds into American society. They come from more varied countries than earlier waves of immigrants; are more racially and ethnically diverse; speak more varied languages and dialects; and, related to the focus of this chapter, have introduced Americans to forms of religion that were unfamiliar prior to their arrival. In addition to bringing with them forms of religion little known in this country, they have helped to introduce new expressions of Christianity to Americans. Because of their large numbers and increasing involvement in public life, the new immigrants are impacting virtually every institution in contemporary society. Health care is no exception and, as health care policymakers have come to realize, the demographic attributes and cultural values of this growing population influence budgets as well as service delivery in many parts of the nation.

This chapter is organized as follows. I first provide an overview of immigration flows to the United States over the past one hundred years in order to place contemporary immigration figures within a broader context. I next address the issue of how changes in immigration flows have impacted the religious landscape in the United States. Thirdly, I discuss some of the functions that immigrant religious institutions provide for their members, over and above their obvious purpose of providing worship opportunities. Finally, I conclude by suggesting ways in which religious patterns among the new immigrants are impacting their health status.

Immigration Trends in the United States, 1900–2004

Slightly more than one million immigrants arrive in the United States each year. About seven hundred thousand are legal permanent residents; another three hundred thousand or so arrive as undocumented immigrants (Bean and Stevens

2003). Indeed, the United States is currently experiencing the largest wave of immigration in history, surpassing the decades of the late nineteenth and early twentieth centuries, which often have been referred to as "peaks" in U.S. immigration history (Fix and Passel 1994; Bean and Stevens 2003). The first large in-migration wave began in the 1840s and peaked in the 1880s, a decade during which slightly more than five million immigrants arrived in the United States. The majority came from northern and western Europe as a result of revolutions, famine, and economic dislocations in their home countries.

The next major immigration wave peaked in the first decade of the twentieth century, when nine million immigrants entered the country (Fix and Passel 1994). This wave consisted mainly of large numbers of Italians, Poles, and Eastern European Jews. In the 1920s the United States Congress passed restrictive legislation that, together with the Great Depression, brought an abrupt halt to this massive immigration wave. During the 1930s, only a half million immigrants entered during the entire decade, and only twice that many during the 1940s. After World War II, immigration began to build again and it has increased steadily since. During the 1990s, about ten million immigrants entered the United States, the highest number in America's history. In 2001 and 2002, the latest years for which we have complete statistics, over one million new immigrants came to the United States annually (U.S. Immigration and Naturalization Service 2001a, 2002a; U.S. Immigration and Naturalization Service 2001b, 2002b). Directly (through the arrival of new residents) and indirectly (through immigrant childbearing) immigrants now account for almost 60 percent of annual population growth in the United States, making it the major force producing population change (Bean, Swicegood, and Berg 2000).

Along with the aforementioned trends in the absolute number of immigrants, we must also take into account changes in the percentage of foreign-born relative to native-born Americans. The 1990 census, for example, counted 19.7 million foreign-born persons in the United States, 34 percent more than in 1980 (U.S. Bureau of the Census 1992). By 2000, almost 20 percent of all births in the United States occurred to foreign-born mothers (Ventura, Curtin, and Mathews 2000). Yet, while the number of foreign-born persons in the United States is at an all-time high, the percentage of the American population that is foreign-born (8 percent in 1990) is much lower than it was throughout the 1870–1920 period, when close to 15 percent of the population was foreign-born (Fix and Passel 1994).

Perhaps the most dramatic fact about shifts in immigrant flows over the past one hundred years relates not to overall numbers of immigrants but to shifting patterns in their nations of origin, the result of the 1965 legislative changes. In the 1950s, Europe accounted for two-thirds of legal immigrants while by the 1990s only 13 percent came from that continent. The increase in Asian immigrants has been the most dramatic, up from 6 percent in the 1950s to 31 percent in the 1990s. Latin America's share of legal immigrants increased from

17 percent to 36 percent in the same time span (U.S. Bureau of the Census 2000). Within the last four decades, the new immigrants transformed the foreign-born population in the United States. In 1960, about 75 percent of all foreign-born residents were European. In 2000 only 15 percent were from Europe, 26 percent originated in Asia, and 51 percent came from Latin America (U.S. Bureau of the Census 2000). In addition, while the top ten sending countries accounted for 65 percent of legal immigrants in 1960, they only provided 52 percent in 1990, and the number of countries sending at least one hundred thousand foreign-born residents increased from twenty in 1970, to 27 in 1980, to forty-one in 1990 (Fix and Passel 1994).

Settlement patterns of the new immigrants have also shifted over the past decades. Traditionally, inner cities, with their public transportation, job opportunities, and lower cost housing, have drawn the majority of immigrants. Increasingly, new immigrants are settling in suburbs (Alba et al. 1999, 2000). In addition to settling permanently within the major gateway cities, such as New York, Los Angeles, Miami, and Houston, cities throughout the Midwest and Northeast are becoming the destinations of increasing numbers of immigrants.

New Immigrant Religious Institutions

In addition to racial and ethnic diversity, the new immigrants are also enhancing religious diversity in the United States. The vast majority of new immigrants are Christian, both because of the fact that disproportionately more Christians emigrate and due to conversion upon immigration to the United States. For example, in a study of Koreans in Chicago, Hurh and Kim (1990) found that while South Korea is only 25 percent Christian, 52 percent were affiliated with Christian churches before emigrating and half of the remainder join Christian churches after arriving in the United States. Yang (1999, 2000) shows that, while Christians are a small minority in China, the number of Chinese Protestant churches, most of them nondenominational, jumped from sixty-six in 1952 to eight hundred by 2002.

Even though significant numbers of new immigrants are Christian, they are altering American Christianity by the introduction of varied languages, customs, and independent churches. Warner and Wittner (1998) estimate that there are about thirty-five hundred Catholic parishes where Mass is celebrated in Spanish and seven thousand Hispanic/Latino Protestant congregations nationwide, most of them Pentecostal and/or evangelical. One out of five Asian Americans are Catholic, including two-thirds of Filipino Americans and 20 percent of Vietnamese Americans (Lien and Carnes 2004). The one million Korean Americans are gathered into over three thousand ethnic churches, many of them aligned with a new denomination, the Korean Presbyterian Church in America (Warner 2001). The Christianity espoused by new immigrants tends to be heavily evangelical and/or fundamentalist in character. Lien and Carnes (2004) estimate that approximately 25 percent of Asian Americans are evangelical Catholics and Protestants. Most Chinese Christian churches are organizationally independent and evangelical in doctrine. Those that do affiliate with American denominations tend to favor those that are theologically conservative, with the majority (150 churches) affiliating with the Southern Baptist Convention (Yang 2002).

In addition to the "new face" of Christianity projected by immigrants from all over the world, a small but growing share of America's religious mosaic is made up of non-Judeo-Christian religions. In 1973–1980, the General Social Survey (GSS) indicated that they accounted for 0.8 percent of the American adult population. This grew to 1.3 percent in 1981–1990 and 2.6 percent in 1990–2000 (Sherkat and Ellison 1999; Davis et al. 2001). The American Religious Identity Surveys (ARIS) project similar figures, with the non-Judeo-Christian religions at 1.5 percent in 1990 and 2.4 percent in 2001 (Kosmin and Lachman 1993; Kosmin, Mayer, and Keysar 2001). Approximately one-half of the adherents to other religions are Buddhist (1.5 million people and 1,656 temples), Hindu (approximately 1 million people and 629 temples), and Muslim (under two million people and 1,209 mosques) (Smith 2002). The remaining nontraditional religions vary across a wide mix of faiths, each with small numbers of adherents. In the GSS in 1991–2000, for example, other Eastern religions (e.g., Jainism, Sikhism, and Taoism), Native American religions, pagans and witches/Wiccans, and those with "personal" religions each number about 0.1 percent each (Smith 2002).

While the numbers of non-Judeo-Christian adherents and places of worship have been growing in the United States since 1965, it is important to keep these numbers in perspective. First, the vast majority of new immigrants are Judeo-Christian, even though they are introducing culturally variant forms of religious expression. Secondly, non-Judeo-Christian immigrants number less than 3 percent of the population, with the 1998–2000 GSS estimating 2.7 percent in the "other" category and the 2001 ARIS survey reporting "other religions" at 2.1 percent. While their numbers are still small, both numerically and as a percentage, nontraditional religions are gaining visibility, with temples, mosques, gudwaras, shrines, and other places of worship springing up in neighborhoods across America.

Vocabulary is a major challenge when considering the varieties of new immigrant religious institutions and the myriad terms they use to indicate their places of worship (e.g., temples, mosques, gudwaras, churches, storefronts, shrines, home gatherings). While some groups, such as the Hindus, are uncomfortable with the term "congregation" because of its historically Christian connotation, I opt to use that term in the broader sociological sense to indicate groupings of people who gather together for religious purposes and who create an ongoing structure to worship, share a religious tradition, interact as a group, and attempt to raise their children with specific religious beliefs, customs, rituals, and values (for comparable usage, see Warner and Wittner 1998).

Functions of Immigrant Congregations

Field researchers who study newly arriving immigrants document the fact that one of the first things they do upon arrival is to seek out an ethnic religious institution where they know fellow nationals gather (Kwon 2000; Hagan and Ebaugh 2003; Kurien 1998). In addition to wanting the comfort of worshipping in a familiar religion, with rituals, architecture, and language that they understand, ethnic congregations also serve many other functions for these "strangers in a new land." These include ethnic reproduction, enhancement of social status, skills of civic incorporation, and the provision of social services. In this section, I discuss ways in which immigrant congregations fulfill each of these needs.

Ethnic Reproduction

A major reason new immigrants seek out and join ethnic congregations is to enjoy the company and sociability of those who share their ethnic and/or national origins background. They want to develop social networks with others like themselves while they struggle to adapt to their new circumstances (Rutledge 1985; Haddad and Lummis 1987; Williams 1988; Kwon, Ebaugh, and Hagan 1997; Warner and Wittner 1998; Ebaugh and Chafetz 2000). Simultaneously, they seek to maintain their old-country identity and to pass to their children a sense of who they are in terms of cultural values and practices. Immigrant congregations provide the physical and social spaces where those who share the same traditions, customs, and languages can reproduce their native culture for themselves and pass them on to their children.

With their emphasis upon tradition, music, storytelling, ritual, and repetitive liturgies, religious institutions are well suited to reinforcing cultural identity and passing it on to future generations. Key elements in the ways that ethnic reproduction is achieved in immigrant congregations are: the use of vernacular languages; physical reproductions of religious rituals; incorporation of ethnic rituals and holidays into religious ceremonies; domestic religious practices; and congregationally based social activities.

While language usage is a contested arena in most immigrant congregations, especially those that are multiethnic and/or multilingual, the use of an old-country language provides a comfort zone for immigrants and is public affirmation of ethnic commitment. For example, in the Vietnamese Buddhist Temple we studied in Houston (Ebaugh and Chafetz 2000), many people would spend their entire Sunday at the temple. Several interviewees said they were willing to work in American places of business and speak English six days a week, but on their day off (i.e., Sunday) they wanted to worship their own deity in their old-country ways, speak their own language, visit with their own people, and eat Vietnamese food.

The use of native vernaculars enables clergy to better instruct the laity in their religious beliefs and practices, permits immigrants to understand the religious services, and creates a sense of comfort for newcomers. In turn, familiarity and comfort contribute to institutional commitment by members, and often to religious conversion of fellow language-speakers, as was the case for many Argentine Catholics who came to Houston but failed to find an Argentine ethnic Catholic church in the city. Many of them converted to Evangelical Protestantism when they began to attend an Argentine Assembly of God Church where Argentine Spanish was the common language (Cook 2000, 2002).

In addition to the use of native language, another major way that congregations reproduce ethnicity is by recreating physical aspects of home country religious structures, such as temples, pagodas, golden domes, icons, steeples, statues, and the use of native construction materials. Many immigrant groups, such as Chinese, Vietnamese, and Cambodian Buddhists, Indian Hindus, and Eastern Orthodox communities, go to great effort and expense to import building materials, architects, and artisans to recreate the distinctive physical structures common in their home country. For example, several years ago members of a South Indian Hindu temple brought dozens of artisans to Houston to carve images in the great white marble pillars of the main temple. During the dedication ceremony, twelve Hindu priests from India were present to bless the temple in traditional Hindu fashion (Jacob and Thakur 2000). Likewise, a Taiwanese temple in Houston reflects traditional Buddhist temples in the home country by the use of native materials and designs imported from Taiwan (Yang 2000). When these visual images are combined with the smells of incense and traditional ethnic food, sounds of native music, the feel of sacred objects and oils, and the sound of vernacular languages, immigrant congregations flood the senses with physical reminders of the home country. By attending these immigrant congregational settings in the United States, offspring of first-generation immigrants are socialized into beliefs, values, and practices that constitute the religion and broader culture brought from the home country.

Immigrant congregations also make their members feel more "at home" in their religious settings by incorporating ethnic rituals and holidays into formal religious ceremonies, which also serves to reinforce ethnic/religious identity in the second generation. For example, ancestral altars, ash houses (traditional Buddhists customs that accompany the forty-nine days of mourning for a deceased person), communal meals with ethnic food, and celebrating national holidays such as Chinese and Vietnamese New Year, recreate a sense of home country ties. In fact, on one occasion, by means of a visual monitor and satellite hookup, Buddhists in Houston celebrated Chinese New Year simultaneously with a fellow Buddhist temple in Taiwan. Each could view the celebrations of the other via cyberspace (Yang 2000). Likewise, Id al-Fitr, the Islamic feast of fast-breaking during Ramadan, is shared by Muslims worldwide and creates a sense of religious identity with fellow Muslims. Diverse images of the Virgin Mary among Hispanic immigrants stem from their home country devotions (Díaz-Stevens 1993; Flores 1994; Wellmeier 1998; Sullivan 2000).

To focus solely upon formal religious services within immigrant congregations overlooks a significant portion of their religious worship and practices, since many groups center a substantial part of their religious observances on domestic rituals practiced at home altars or shrines. For most Eastern religious groups, home shrines involve images of ancestors and routine rituals that demonstrate respect for them. The Zoroastrians customarily display an oil-burning lamp or candle on their home altars, as well as scented incense and prayer beads, reminiscent of practices in their homeland of India or Pakistan (Rustomji 2000). Often life cycle events, such as infant blessings, engagements, weddings, and remembrances of the dead are enacted before these home edifices (Brown 1991; Wellmeier 1998; Huynh 2000). These domestic religious customs function to reproduce traditional ethnic-religious practices and identity for family members.

Finally, most immigrant congregations serve as social activity centers for members. Unlike religious institutions in the home countries, places of worship in the United States provide much more than simply religious spaces for communal prayer and ritual (Warner and Wittner 1998; Ebaugh and Chafetz 2000). Rather, they develop community centers that house such activities as meals, festivals, holiday celebrations, fundraisers, language and citizenship classes, cultural lectures, political rallies, and youth activities. One function of such activities is to maintain social ties among members and to pass on both religious and ethnic culture to the next generation.

Enhancement of Social Status

Downward social mobility often occurs, especially for men, among a number of immigrant groups. This phenomenon has been documented, for example, in the case of males from Kerala, India, who frequently migrated after their wives found employment as nurses in the United States and later sponsored the immigration of their husbands and families. Frequently, the jobs these men obtained were of lower status and income than those held by their wives, due to the necessity of retraining and credentialing in new trades and professions (George 1998). Likewise, Kwon (1997) documents a similar process for Korean men.

Religious institutions often provide positions within their structure to compensate these men for lost social status. In the Orthodox Christian Church that George (1998) describes, attended by Kerala immigrants, only men were allowed to serve in administrative positions. Because leadership roles in the church are reserved for socially and economically prominent members of the community, lay leadership is associated with high social status. For the immigrant male members suffering from a loss of status professionally, the church becomes a space to exercise leadership, which is considered high social status within the community.

A similar process occurs among Korean Christians (Kwon 1997, 2000). Korean Christian churches typically have an elaborate organizational structure with numerous departments such as music, publication, Korean language classes, finance, physical facilities, etc., almost always headed by a male member of the church. These churches also utilize the "cell group ministry," whereby church members are divided into smaller groups based either on residential geographical proximity or some social characteristic (e.g., age or profession). Each cell group meets regularly for informal services and discussion at members' homes, on a rotating basis. Cell groups also serve as the basis of an informal social service provision network as cell members get to know and care for one another. Leadership of a cell group carries high social status and is usually held by a male in the group. The many and varied official positions open to lay members in the Korean Christian Church are perceived as positions of social power and status that compensate for the immigrants' lack of power and status within the larger American society. Among members of the church, a statement like "his father is an elder of the church" creates the same respect as a statement like "his father is a judge" would among native-born Americans (Kwon 1997).

Wellmeier (1998) describes the status afforded the Catholic men from Santa Eulalia, Guatemala, who migrated to central Los Angeles and meet weekly to pray together, to conduct marimba performances, and plan the annual Fiesta of Santa Eulalia. The marimba, to many Maya people, embodies the soul of their culture and is regarded as semisacred. While playing the marimba by a woman is not formally forbidden, "no self-respecting father would allow his daughter to be involved in an activity that is frequently associated with drinking" (Wellmeier 1998, 111). The Mayan men who play, however, are highly regarded among their immigrant countrymen. As in the cases of the Kerala Orthodox Christian men and those of the Korean Christian Church, the marimba players in the Mayan Catholic church garnered the respect and status that they lacked in the broader American society.

Immigrant congregations also provide opportunities for increased social status for women, albeit under very different circumstances than for men (Ebaugh and Chafetz 1999). The combination of a congregational structure and community center model, part of the structural adaptations that such congregations make in the United States, results in the creation of a large number of formal lay roles within religious institutions, ranging from authoritative council/board positions to Sunday School teachers to committee, fellowship, cell, and ministry leaders. The assumption of such roles is status enhancing for their incumbents. As immigrant men, who often first occupy such roles, find employment and are pressured by time constraints, women frequently move into them.

Over time, most immigrant women, and especially their American-born or raised daughters, expand their resources through better education than was typically available for them in the old country. Additionally, their labor force participation is frequently required to help support families in their new setting. As women respond to the increased demand for their participation by becoming more involved in religious congregations, and as they accrue more resources, they become increasingly likely to seek yet further status-enhancing opportunities within their congregations. Thus, the "demand" factor of congregational needs and the "supply" factor of resource-enriched women's desire to participate more fully produce at least token representations of women within the congregational decision-making structure as well as more involvement in other congregational roles. In addition, when first- and second-generation women are employed, and especially when they are well educated, they often begin to question culturally and religiously rooted restrictions on the lay, and even religious, organizational roles to which they are permitted access. As they begin to occupy more and more formal roles within their congregation, they also frequently begin to question why they do not have access to all positions available to men in the congregation.

Gaining Skills of Civic Incorporation

Religious institutions have a special role to play in the socialization of members in the skills and attitudes necessary for civic engagement (Verba, Schlozman, and Brady 1995). These include training and experience in public speaking, organizing meetings and campaigns, letter writing, holding leadership positions, and participation in community events. Congregations also encourage their members to volunteer for community service and to be aware of political issues in their neighborhoods.

Congregational settings are also frequently the site for voting precinct activities, citizenship and language classes, and a venue for politicians who want to debate issues and solicit votes. Especially within lower class ethnic neighborhoods, local religious establishments often serve as community gathering places for political candidates and their advocates.

The process of acquiring civic skills is not necessarily isomorphic with the notion of "civic incorporation," a term that indicates identification with and participation in the public life of American society. The degree to which immigrant congregations enhance civic incorporation is a debatable and empirical issue. Some research indicates that religious congregations facilitate assimilation of immigrants into American society (Feher 1998; Kurien 1998; Yang 2000), while other studies show that ethnic religious institutions function as cultural and religious enclaves that provide a refuge for cultural and linguistic reproduction (Hepner 1998; Huynh 2000).

Provision of Social Services

In earlier waves of immigration to the United States, both Protestant and Catholic churches organized to meet material needs that arose in the process of immigrants' relocation and settlement. As Dolan (1985) documents, Catholic parishes in the nineteenth and early twentieth centuries became the centers around which neighborhood charitable societies were organized. Mutual benefit services were organized in ethnic parishes, especially among German immigrants, to provide financial assistance to members who were sick and/or disabled. Among the immigrant congregations that responded to a telephone survey of all such institutions we could locate in Houston (N = 332), Catholic churches offer far more formal social services than other immigrant congregations. Nearly two-thirds of Catholic churches run some sort of food pantry and half have a St. Vincent de Paul Society, the traditional parish organization designed to assist poor members. Regardless of religion, the Asian and Middle Eastern congregations included in the survey rarely provide formal social services, with only 19 of the 115 included in the survey doing so (Ebaugh and Chafetz 2000). Among the thirteen congregations included in our fieldwork of new immigrant congregations in Houston, we found that over half offer few, if any, social service programs for their members or their neighborhoods. The two that do offer an extensive array of such services are large, multiethnic, originally Anglo Christian congregations. There are two reasons why half of the immigrant congregations offer few, if any, formally organized social services: (a) most of their members arrive in Houston with high levels of human capital and jobs already lined up and therefore do not need such services; and (b) both religious leaders and most members define formal social service delivery as outside the scope of the religious institutions. Zoroastrian, Hindu, Vietnamese and Chinese Buddhist, Greek Orthodox, and Muslim interviewees described the majority of their congregations' members as having no need for material assistance. The Chinese have many local ethnically specific agencies and businesses available for aid. Most members of the Hindu and Buddhist temples define social service provision as inappropriate for their religious institutions.

Nevertheless, immigrants have an array of needs to meet, even if these do not include jobs, financial assistance, or other tangible aid. Information and emotional support are ubiquitous needs, regardless of the level of human capital the immigrants bring with them. These needs, along with the more material ones, are in fact met substantially within their congregations, but their primary mechanism is through the informal social networks they find in their congregations.

Immigrant congregations play a central role in providing the social space where fellow ethnics can meet one another, share information, and form networks for mutual support and assistance. Clergy are well placed to identify people in need, and to connect them with other congregants who can offer assistance. The fact that congregations have a religious norm that both encourages the needy to seek help in religious institutions and a sense of obligation to assist those in need fosters the formation of informal social service provision.

Creating a community center, or activities building, in tandem with a worship center, although alien to many religions abroad, is a common pattern among new immigrant congregations in the United States. Only two of our thirteen immigrant congregations in Houston neither have one nor have immediate plan to build one. Twelve of the thirteen congregations offer secular classes, most frequently native language and culture classes for children, as well as English-as-second-language, GED, and/or citizenship classes for adults, in these centers. Six of the congregations had recreational facilities. They also serve as a place for social gatherings, including a place to share native food after worship services, a common custom in many immigrant congregations. In addition, many of these community centers provide space for local health providers to educate the congregation in regard to health issues, to immunize children, to provide screening services for diabetes, heart problems, pregnancy, and respiratory illnesses. It is quite common to see a mobile health van on congregational property or an adopt-a-nurse program in the community center. While immigrants may be hesitant to visit a hospital or health clinic, many of them display trust in health care programs that are incorporated into their religious settings.

Implications for Health

There are a number of ways in which the changing immigrant landscape in the United States is impacting health care. In this concluding section, I consider several ways in which new immigrant religions may impacts health, including: (a) religious attitudes and behaviors of immigrants that affect health practices; (b) the use of immigrant congregations to disseminate health knowledge and encourage healthy practices; and (c) the use of congregations as physical sites for health care delivery.

In their extensive review of existing studies relating immigrant status and health, Kandula, Kersey, and Lurie (2004) state that the health status and needs of immigrants are poorly documented (see also Abraido-Lanza et al. 1999; Singh and Siahpush 2001). However, a cursory analysis of the 127 referenced studies indicates almost no inclusion of the role that religion and religious institutions play in facilitating immigrant health and their access to health care resources. Yet, recent studies (e.g., Zhou and Bankston 1998; Harker 2001; Menjivar 2002) suggest a number of ways in which religion may impact the health and health behavior of the new immigrants.

While not extensively documented across immigrant groups, an increasing number of studies acknowledge the fact that religious beliefs, attitudes, and practices impact the health of immigrants. In her analysis of health and psychological well-being of immigrant youth, Harker (2001) suggests that religious beliefs and support systems are mediating factors that explain the fact that first-generation immigrant youth score significantly better on health measures than second- and third-generation youth. Zhou and Bankston (1998), in their research on Vietnamese youth in the United States, present data that shows a positive correlation between religious participation, both in Catholic and Buddhist communities, and indicators of health and well-being. In addition, they describe churches and temples as social service organizations that operate a wide range of programs for youth, including health and counseling services. Menjivar (2002) describes the role that religious congregations play both in praying for Latino women who do not feel well and in providing social networks for information on obtaining medical help.

In their textbook for medical practitioners, Huff and Kline (1999) outline a number of immigrant religious beliefs that must be taken into account in promoting health in multicultural populations. For example, belief in the power of the "evil eye" among Mexican immigrants can prevent their acceptance of modern medicines to cure a child until a traditional healer removes the curse. In some religious systems, illness is seen as punishment for "bad" behavior and hence adherents do not want to admit illness. Cultural/religious norms regarding male–female interactions can also affect the way female patients disclose intimate physical symptoms to male physicians or the reluctance of male patients to submit to physical examinations by a female physician (Huff and Kline 1999). Often, immigrants who depend on nontraditional, spiritual sources of healing may be reluctant to tell health care providers about their use of spiritual healers and religious rituals (Ngo-Metzger et al. 2003).

Immigrant congregations are in an especially good position to inform and legitimate for their members the health and social services available in the community. In our Houston study, we found that health care providers routinely disseminate health information, both preventative knowledge and the information about the availability of health care services, by means of bulletin board announcements, leaflets left in the churches and temples, and announcements made by clergy. Health care workers in a number of cities (e.g., Houston, New York, Miami) have used these congregational gathering places to provide both information and care to targeted immigrant populations. For example, in Houston a mobile health unit from a local hospital offers free vaccinations for children and diabetes testing for adults at several immigrant congregations, including a Hindu temple and several Christian churches where they know there are large Hispanic populations. By soliciting the assistance of clergy at these sites, immigrants are encouraged to take advantage of the services. Often immigrants will visit a mobile van on congregational property but refuse to negotiate the bureaucratic setup of hospitals and doctors' offices.

Health care for undocumented immigrants is an especially difficult issue. In most states, subsidized care is limited to emergency assistance; preventative care visits, as well as pre- and postnatal visits, are precluded. In the case of disadvantaged immigrants who cannot afford private insurance, their medical conditions are frequently acute and require extensive and expensive care before they are seen by professional personnel. Increasingly, immigrant congregations are beginning to work with medical facilities to provide health information, vaccinations, screenings, and, in some cases, basic care through clinics associated with the congregation or through the use of mobile health units. Often, undocumented immigrants feel more comfortable and safe with receiving medical services provided in congregational settings because of assurances that they will not be reported to federal immigration authorities. In fact, many congregations and faith-based organizations in Houston have agreements with the federal government that undocumented immigrants will not be apprehended on or near congregational property (Ebaugh and Chafetz 2000).

In summary, the rapidly changing demographic and religious context of the United States, in large part due to recent immigration flows, has numerous implications for our nation's health and health care system. Yet, relatively little systematic research has been conducted on the impact of the new immigrants on our health care system, or the role that religious congregations might play in immigrant-related health and health care. Indeed, there are few documented studies of ways in which religion affects health practices and the utilization of health care services among immigrant populations. Specifically helpful in constructing effective health care policy would be comparative studies of health behavior, health outcomes, and health care across ethnic and religious groups, with particular focus given to the immigrant subpopulations of these groups. As health policy researchers analyze current trends in American society that impact our health care system, it is crucial that they cease to ignore the presence of an increasingly diverse immigrant population, one with diverse religious backgrounds and congregations.

REFERENCES

Abraido-Lanza, A. F., B. P. Dohrenwend, D. S. NgMak, and J. B. Turner. 1999. "The Latino Mortality Paradox: A Test of the 'Salmon Bias' and Healthy Migrant Hypotheses." *American Journal of Public Health* 89:1543–1548.

Alba, R. D., J. R. Logan, B. J. Stults, G. Marzan, and W. Zhang. 1999. "Immigrant Groups in the Suburbs: A Reexamination of Suburbanization and Spatial Assimilation." *American Sociological Review* 64:446–460.

———. 2000. "The Changing Neighborhood Contexts of the Immigrant Metropolis." *Social Forces* 79:587–621.

Bean, F. D., and G. Stevens. 2003. *America's Newcomers and the Dynamics of Diversity*. New York: Russell Sage Foundation.

Bean, F. D., C. G. Swicegood, and R. Berg. 2000. "Mexican-Origin Fertility: New Patterns and Interpretations." *Social Science Quarterly* 81 (1): 404–420.

Brown, K. M. 1991. *Mama Lola: A Vodou Priestess in Brooklyn*. Berkeley: University of California Press.

Cook, D. 2000. "Iglesia Cristiana Evangelica: Arriving in the Pipeline." In *Religion and the New Immigrants: Continuities and Adaptations in Immigrant Congregations*, ed. H. R. Ebaugh and J. S. Chafetz, 171–192. Walnut Creek, CA: AltaMira Press.

———. 2002. "Forty Years of Religion across Borders: Twilight of a Transnational Field?" In *Religion across Borders: Transnational Immigrant Networks*, ed. H. R. Ebaugh and J. S. Chafetz, 51–92. Walnut Creek, CA: Alta Mira Press.

Davis, J. A., T. W. Smith, and P. V. Marsden. 2001. *General Social Surveys, 1972–2000: Cumulative Codebook*. Chicago: NORC.

Díaz-Stevens, A. M. 1993. "The Saving Grace: The Matriarchal Core of Latino Catholicism." *Latino Studies Journal* (September): 60–78.

Dolan, J. P. 1985. *The American Catholic Experience*. Garden City, NY: Image Books.

Ebaugh, H. R., and J. S. Chafetz. 1999. "Agents for Cultural Reproduction and Structural Change: The Ironic Role of Women in Immigrant Religious Institutions." *Social Forces* 78:585–612.

———. 2000. "Introduction." In *Religion and the New Immigrants: Continuities and Adaptations in Immigrant Congregations*, ed. H. R. Ebaugh and J. S. Chafetz, 1–13. Walnut Creek, CA: Alta Mira Press.

Feher, S. 1998. "From the Rivers of Babylon to the Valleys of Los Angeles: The Exodus and Adaptation of Iranian Jews." In *Gatherings in Diaspora: Religious Communities and the New Immigration*, ed. R. S. Warner and J. G. Wittner, 71–94. Philadelphia: Temple University Press.

Fix, M., and J. S. Passel. 1994. *Immigration and Immigrants: Setting the Record Straight*. Washington, DC: The Urban Institute.

Flores, R. R. 1994. "Para el Niño Dios: Sociability and Commemorative Sentiment in Popular Religious Practice." In *An Enduring Flame*, ed. Anthony M. Stevens-Arroyo and Ana Maria Díaz-Stevens, 171–189. New York: Bildner Center for Western Hemispheric Studies.

George, S. 1998. "Caroling with the Keralities: The Negotiation of Gendered Space in an Indian Immigrant Church." In *Gatherings in Diaspora: Religious Communities and the New Immigration*, edited by R. S. Warner and J. G. Wittner, 265–294. Philadelphia: Temple University Press.

Haddad, Y. Y., and A. T. Lummis. 1987. *Islamic Values in the United States: A Comparative Study*. New York: Oxford University Press.

Hagan, J., and H. R. Ebaugh. 2003. "Calling Upon the Sacred: Migrants' Use of Religion in the Migration Process." *Social Forces* 37:1145–1162.

Harker, K. 2001. "Immigrant Generation, Assimilation and Adolescent Psychological Well-Being." *Social Forces* 78:969–1004.

Hepner, R. L. 1998. "The House That Rasta Built: Church-Building among New York Rastafari." In *Gatherings in Diaspora: Religious Communities and the New Immigration*, edited by R. S. Warner and J. G. Wittner, 197–234. Philadelphia: Temple University Press.

Huff, R. M., and M. V. Kline, eds. 1999. *Promoting Health in Multicultural Populations: A Handbook for Practitioners*. Thousand Oaks, CA: Sage.

Hurh, W. M., and K. C. Kim 1990. "Religious Participation of Korean Immigrants in the United States." *Journal for the Scientific Study of Religion* 29:19–34.

Huynh, T. 2000. "Center for Vietnamese Buddhism: Recreating Home." In *Religion and the New Immigrants: Continuities and Adaptations in Immigrant Congregations*, ed. H. R. Ebaugh and J. S. Chafetz, 45–66. Walnut Hill, CA: AltaMira Press.

Jacob, S., and P. Thakur. 2000. "Jyothi Temple: One Religion, Many Practices." In *Religion and the New Immigrants: Continuities and Adaptations in Immigrant Congregations*, ed. H. R. Ebaugh and J. S. Chafetz, 229–242. Walnut Creek, CA: AltaMira Press.

Kandula, N. R., M. Kersey, and N. Lurie. 2004. "Assuring the Health of Immigrants: What the Leading Health Indicators Tell Us." *Annual Review of Public Health* 25:357–376.

Kosmin, B. A., and S. P. Lachman. 1993. *One Nation Under God: Religion in Contemporary American Society*. New York: Harmony Books.

Kosmin, B. A., E. Mayer, and A. Keysar. 2001. *American Religious Identification Survey*. New York: University of New York.

Kurien, P. 1998. "Becoming American by Becoming Hindu: Indian Americans Take Their Place at the Multi-Cultural Table." In *Gatherings in Diaspora: Religious Communities and the New Immigration*, ed. R. S. Warner and J. G. Wittner, 37–70. Philadelphia: Temple University Press.

Kwon, V. H. 1997. *Entrepreneurship and Religion: Korean Immigrants in Houston, Texas*. New York and London: Garland Publishing, Inc.

——. 2000. "Houston Korean Ethnic Church: An Ethnic Enclave." In *Religion and the New Immigrants: Continuities and Adaptations in Immigrant Congregations*, ed. H. R. Ebaugh and J. S. Chafetz, 109–124. Walnut Creek, CA: AltaMira Press.

Kwon, V. H., H. R. Ebaugh, and J. Hagan.1997. "The Structure and Function of Cell Group Ministry in a Korean Christian Church." *Journal for the Scientific Study of Religion* 36:247–256.

Lien, P., and T. Carnes. 2004. "The Religious Demography of Asian American Boundary Crossing." In *Asian American Religions: The Making and Remaking of Borders and Boundaries*, ed. T. Carnes and F. Yang, 38–51. New York: New York University Press.

Menjivar, C. 2002. "The Ties That Heal: Guatemalan Immigrant Women's Networks and Medical Treatment." *International Migration Review* 36:437–466.

Ngo-Metzger, Q., M. P. Massagli, B. R. Clarridge, M. Manocchia, R. B. Davis, L. I. Lezzoni, and R. Phillips. 2003. "Linguistic and Cultural Barriers to Care." *Journal of General Internal Medicine* 18:44–50.

Rustomji, Y. 2000. "The Zoroastrian Center: An Ancient Faith in Diaspora." In *Religion and the New Immigrants: Continuities and Adaptations in Immigrant Congregations*, ed. H. R. Ebaugh and J. S. Chafetz, 243–254. Walnut Creek, CA: AltaMira Press.

Rutledge, P. J. 1985. *The Role of Religion in Ethnic Self-Identity: A Vietnamese Community*. Lanham, MD: University Press of America.

Sherkat, D. E., and C. G. Ellison.1999. "Recent Developments and Current Controversies in the Sociology of Religion." *Annual Reviews in Sociology* 25:363–384.

Singh, G. K., and M. Siahpush. 2001. "All-Cause and Cause-Specific Mortality of Immigrants and Native Born in the United States." *American Journal of Public Health* 91:392–399.

Smith, T. W. 2002. "Religious Diversity in America: The Emergence of Muslims, Buddhists, Hindus, and Others." *Journal for the Scientific Study of Religion* 41 (3): 577–586.

Sullivan, K. 2000. "St. Mary's Catholic Church: Celebrating Domestic Religion." In *Religion and the New Immigrants: Continuities and Adaptations in Immigrant Congregations*, ed. H. R. Ebaugh and J. S. Chafetz, 255–290. Walnut Creek, CA: AltaMira Press.

U.S. Bureau of the Census. 1992. *Census of the Population: General Social and Economic Characteristics, PC (1)-C23.1*. Washington, DC: U.S. Government Printing Office.

——. 2000. *Statistical Abstract of the United States*. Washington, DC: U.S. Government Printing Office.

U.S. Immigration and Naturalization Service. 2001a. *INS Annual Report*. Washington, DC: U.S. Government Printing Office.

——. 2001b. *Statistical Yearbook of the Immigration and Naturalization Service*. Washington, DC: U.S. Government Printing Office.

——. 2002a. *INS Annual Report*. Washington, DC: U.S. Government Printing Office.

——. 2002b. *Statistical Yearbook of the Immigration and Naturalization Service*. Washington, DC: U.S. Government Printing Office.

Ventura, S. J., S. C. Curtin, and T. J. Mathews. 2000. "Variations in Teenage Birth Rates, 1991–98: National and State Trends." *National Vital Statistics Reports* 48 (6): 1–13.

Verba, S., K. L. Schlozman, and H. E. Brady. 1995. *Voice and Equality: Civic Voluntarism in American Politics*. Cambridge, MA: Harvard University Press.

Warner, R. S. 2001. "The Korean Immigrant Church as Case and Model." In *Korean Americans and Their Religions: Pilgrims and Missionaries from a Different Shore*, ed. H. Kwan, K. C. Kim, and R. S. Warner, 25–52. University Park: Pennsylvania State University Press.

Warner, R. S., and J. G. Wittner, eds. 1998. *Gatherings in Diaspora: Religious Communities and the New Immigration*. Philadelphia: Temple University Press.

Wellmeier, N. J. 1998. "Santa Eulalia's People in Exile: Maya Religion, Culture and Identity in Los Angeles." In *Gatherings in Diaspora: Religious Communities and the New Immigration*, ed. R. S. Warner and J. G. Wittner, 97–122. Philadelphia: Temple University Press.

Williams, R. B. 1988. *Religions of Immigrants from India and Pakistan: New Threads in the American Tapestry*. New York: Cambridge University Press.

Yang, F. 1999. *Chinese Christians in America: Conversion, Assimilation, and Adhesive Identities*. University Park: Pennsylvania State University Press.

———. 2000. "The Hsi-Nan Chinese Buddhist Temple: Seeking to Americanize." In *Religion and the New Immigrants: Continuities and Adaptations in Immigrant Congregations*, ed. H. R. Ebaugh and J. S. Chafetz, 89–108. Walnut Creek, CA: AltaMira Press.

———. 2002. "Religious Diversity among The Chinese in America." In *Religions in Asian America: Building Faith Communities*, ed. P. G. Min and J. H. Kim, 71–98. Walnut Creek, CA: AltaMira Press.

Zhou, M., and C. L. Bankston, III. 1998. *Growing Up American: How Vietnamese Children Adapt to Life in the United States*. New York: Russell Sage Foundation.

PART THREE

Looking Ahead

20

▶▶ ▶▶ ▶▶ ▶▶ ▶▶ ▶▶ ▶▶ ▶▶ ▶▶ ◀ ◀ ◀ ◀ ◀ ◀ ◀ ◀ ◀ ◀ ◀ ◀ ◀

The Religious Demography
of the United States

Dynamics of Affiliation, Participation, and Belief

DARREN E. SHERKAT

Religion is one of the cornerstone social institutions in American Society, profoundly impacting family relations, politics, health, and culture. Until recently, however, little systematic data were available that would enable a systematic demographic portrait of American religion. The data gap looms large because of U.S. religious diversity by denomination, race, generation, and life cycle. Further, U.S. Census data on religious affiliation and participation have not been collected for more than half a century, and the sporadic collection efforts of the past were ill suited for the construction of a demographic profile of American religion. Over the course of the twentieth century, scholarship on U.S. religious demography has been invigorated by the accumulation of cross-sectional surveys that enable cautious inferences about the dynamics of affiliation, participation, and some aspects of religious belief, and by increased attention to religious factors by demographers (Stolzenberg, Blair-Loy, and Waite 1995; Hout, Greeley, and Wilde 2001).

Using data from the 1973–2002 General Social Surveys (GSS), I examine the religious market share of major religious groupings, and how this is impacted by religious switching, intermarriage, fertility, and immigration. I also explore generational and religious affiliation differences in these demographic processes, and differences in age structure and socioeconomic status. Additionally, I investigate the impact of immigration on denominational distributions—a much neglected source of religious vitality in the United States.

American Religious Demography: Retrospect and Prospect

U.S. Census data on American religious bodies were collected for nearly a century, with somewhat varying degrees of comprehensiveness of coverage. Data collection efforts began in the 1850 Census, and continued until an abortive effort in 1946 (Finke and Stark 1992). These Census collections used data from churches to assess the distribution of religious congregations by denomination (including non-Christian bodies), their membership, the age structure of congregations, and some indication of the numbers of congregational leaders. Finke and Stark (1992) provided a comprehensive historical assessment of American religious demography based on these data (see also Land, Deane, and Blau 1991), and projected their congregational findings backwards using a census of American churches from 1776 (Finke and Stark 1992). Finke and Stark's (1992) analysis revealed that the United States was an irreligious nation at its founding, with a small proportion of Americans holding an affiliation in any faith, and small oligopolies of religious firms providing the only spiritual services in most places. Indeed, fewer women were members of churches than were having nonmarital sex (Finke and Stark 1992, 22). Finke and Stark (1992) demonstrate the effectiveness of Methodist and Baptist sectarian groups in converting and retaining the masses of people who were unwelcome in the "mainline" denominations (the Episcopalians, Presbyterians, and Congregationalists).

Over time, religious denominations often change the religious products they generate, and these shifts in cultural production alter the appeal of religious denominations to demographic constituencies. Since religious firms are run by educated elites, denominations tend to produce religious goods that increasingly appeal to elite constituencies (Stark and Bainbridge 1985, 1987). Unlike in other cultural markets, elite demand does not trickle down into mass appeal. The cycle of intradenominational change in religious production is well documented and referred to as the church-sect cycle (Stark and Bainbridge 1985, 1987; Finke and Stark 1992). The cycle begins with religious groups altering their theologies to provide a more worldly religion, and this spurs schisms and defection among members who prefer more otherworldly theologies. The effects of this internal secularization are quite dramatic for some denominations, such as the Methodists in the twentieth-century United States (Finke and Stark 1992; Sherkat 2001a).

Immigrants have profoundly influenced American religious demography, and Catholicism has continued to benefit from waves of immigrants (Finke and Stark 1992). For immigrants, religious groups help to provide an institutional basis for transitions to the destination country, enabling the continuity of language and generating a community of coethnics capable of providing tangible and social support (Ebaugh and Chafetz 2000; Yang and Ebaugh 2001; Bankston and Zhou 1997; Zhou and Bankston 1996). Lutherans, the Dutch Reformed, various Orthodox bodies, and the Catholic Church are all historically immigrant religious institutions. Because of its size, diversity, and organizational strength, the Catholic Church has long been a major player in the religious market of the United States, in spite of some strong opposition from Protestant movements.

Still, there is limited research on the demography of religious affiliation and participation in the United States. Only a few studies have ventured beyond the exploration of Catholic–Protestant differences when addressing fertility differentials by religion, differences in rates of intermarriage, recruitment of new immigrants to religious affiliations, the age structure of denominations, ethnic and racial distributions of affiliations, or rates of participation. In the 1970s, many demographers expected that religious factors would decline in importance for predicting marriage, divorce, fertility, child rearing, and migration patterns. This expectation seemed to be supported by research showing declining Catholic–Protestant differences in fertility (Westoff and Jones 1979) and child rearing values (Alwin 1986). Yet, empirical studies over the past three decades have continued to find religious differences in a number of demographic, family, and health outcomes. Such findings have helped lead to efforts to increase the quality of "standard" questions about religious affiliation and behavior asked in demographic and social surveys. By 1972, the GSS implemented a near-full compliment of denominational groupings; and, in 1973, the GSS added indicators of religion when a respondent was about age sixteen and spouse's religious affiliation. Together with the standard indicator of church attendance, and other demographic information available in the GSS, this resource became a gold mine for demographers and sociologists of religion.

The accumulation of three decades of GSS and other major national studies have enabled demographers to elaborate the distribution of religious affiliations (Kluegel 1980; Roof and McKinney 1987; Sherkat 2001a); describe the religious variations of African Americans (Ellison and Sherkat 1990; Sherkat 2001a); explore relationships between religion, immigration, and ethnicity (Cadge and Ecklund 2006; Hamilton and Form 2003; Jasso et al. 2003); document the association between religious factors and mortality (Ellison et al. 2000; Hummer et al. 1999); navigate the relationships between religion and marriage, family, and fertility (Pearce 2002; Pearce and Axinn 1998; Thornton, Axinn, and Hill 1992); and examine the impact of religious factors on migration (Myers 2000). Yet, we still lack large-scale longitudinal data that would enable a more complete and accurate assessment of religious change across the life course and across multiple birth cohorts. Indeed, very few longitudinal studies have collected data on religion, and the data collected are generally quite scant—often only including a simple measure of affiliation, church attendance, or membership in a church organization.

Following the collapse of the U.S. Census of Religious Bodies, a cooperative group of religious researchers have made efforts to collect similar data on congregations by county. These data are often referred to as the Glenmary Data, named for the Glenmary Research Center, which motivated the collection. Early collection efforts included information from fifty-three of the largest denominations in the United States, while the latest 2000 data contain county-level data from 149 Christian groups, along with information from Jewish, Islamic, and six other non-Christian faiths (www.thearda.com/archive/ChMember.asp). While these aggregate accountings from a small proportion of the more than two thousand religious groups in the United States are far from comprehensive (as I comment on further later), they do provide important information on groups that affiliate the vast majority of Americans. And, these data have been used to engage important sociological and demographic questions about religious effects (e.g., Pescosolido and Georgianna 1989; Ellison, Burr, and McCall 1997).

Assessing Religious Dynamics

Religious change is a result of shifting religious affiliations, rates of participation, and belief. Religious dynamics occur over the life course and in response to a variety of life course events such as migration, marriage, child rearing, aging, and widowhood. Examinations of religious dynamics are limited in cross-sectional studies like the GSS. Age is systematically related to religious switching, with switching rates increasing early in the life course then decreasing later in life (Roof 1989; Sherkat 1991). Further, young people will often lapse in religious participation and affiliation, and return switching is common (Wilson and Sherkat 1994). Child rearing often spurs recommitment to religion, and lowers the likelihood of disaffiliation (Sherkat and Wilson 1995; Sandomirsky and Wilson 1990; Stolzenberg, Blair-Loy, and Waite 1995; Myers 1996; Sherkat 1991, 1998). In contrast, both religious intermarriage and geographic mobility have been linked with religious change. Those who intermarry are more likely to switch religious faiths, and children of heterogamous marriages are more likely to change affiliations (Sandomirsky and Wilson 1990; Sherkat 1991; Musick and Wilson 1995). Many life course events impact religious participation, including intermarriage, geographic mobility, and childrearing (Myers 1996; Stolzenberg, Blair-Loy, and Waite 1995).

Classifying Religious Groups

The classification of denominations is well established, based on theological orientations and ethnic configurations (Roof and McKinney 1987; Kluegel 1980; Ellison and Sherkat 1990; Sherkat 2001a). Generally, classifications of religious affiliation attempt to separate conservative or fundamentalist religious affiliations from more moderate or liberal religious groups (Smith 1990). Most of the debate in terms of classification is focused on Protestant groups, since there is substantial diversity across them. Groups with similar names also can have quite different theological orientations, such as the ultraliberal United Church of Christ and the fundamentalist Churches of Christ. Liberal Protestant groups include Presbyterians, Episcopalians, and the United Church of Christ; smaller groups like the Quakers and Unitarians are also generally placed in the liberal Protestant category. Moderate Protestants are denominations like the United Methodists, Reformed, Brethren, Lutherans (except for Wisconsin and Missouri Synod Lutherans, who are classified as conservative), and Disciples of Christ. Conservative groups include Baptists (except American Baptists, who are moderate), Assembly of God, Pentecostal, Holiness, Churches of Christ, Nazarene, and a host of other small denominations. Conservative groups are typically called "sects" because of their tension with broader society (Finke and Stark 1992). Beyond these groups, American religion contains a variety of other religious traditions, some spawned from Christianity (e.g., Catholics, Orthodox Christians, Mormons, and Jehovah's Witnesses), and others from distinct religious traditions (e.g., Jews, Buddhists, Hindus, Muslims, and others).

Scholars examining differences across religious groups must be attentive to differences across the entire set of denominational affiliations, across cohorts, and most importantly, across racial/ethnic groups. Recent attempts to improve on classification schemes often confuse affiliation, identities, and participation; they also fail to address variation in the African American market (e.g., Steensland et al. 2000). Given the distribution of respondents, demographers must be thorough, yet realistic, about classification. In the cumulative GSS, we are able to make some inferences about relatively small groups like Mormons. And, given their distinctiveness, researchers should separate Mormons from other conservative religious groups when using large samples, if at all possible. If large samples are available, investigators should also separate Baptists from other sectarian groups, Episcopalians from other liberal Protestant groups, and Lutherans from other Moderate Protestant denominations. Diversity among non-Christian groups is often a problem for empirical researchers (Sherkat 1999). Few studies will have enough respondents to meaningfully examine differences between Hindus, Muslims, Jews, or Buddhists—although some useful data sets have recently been developed (see, e.g., Chapters 11, 17, and 18 in this volume).

Among African Americans, Baptists and to a lesser extent Methodists have dominated the religious marketplace. These two groups comprise the "Black Mainline" commonly examined in research on the religious dynamics of African Americans (Sherkat and Ellison 1991; Ellison and Sherkat 1990; Hunt and Hunt 1999; Sherkat 2001a, 2002). For African Americans, being a Baptist places one at the center of African American life, and African American Baptist groups are known for civic activism and social liberalism—in contrast to white Baptists. As among whites, African American sectarian groups are growing, particularly the Church of God in Christ and various Pentecostal and Holiness groups (Ellison and Sherkat 1990; Sherkat 2002). African American Catholics are a distinct group on several demographic factors (Hunt 1998). African American members of traditionally white Protestant denominations may be analyzed together (Ellison and Sherkat 1990; Sherkat 2001a). Several studies have examined Islamic religious expressions among African Americans (Frazier 1964; Glenn 1964; Glenn and Gotard 1977; Lincoln 1974), but Islamic groups remain a very small proportion (0.3 percent in the 2000–2004 GSS) of the African American population. Also, among African Americans, there are insufficient numbers of Mormons and Jews to analyze effectively using available data.

The Religious Affiliation of White Americans across Cohorts

Table 20.1 presents the distribution of white GSS respondents across denominational groupings in seven U.S. birth cohorts of adults aged eighteen and over.

TABLE 20.1
Current and Origin Religious Affiliation by Birth Cohort: White Americans in the 1973–2002 GSS

	1883–1919 Cohort	1920–1929 Cohort	1930–1939 Cohort	1940–1949 Cohort	1950–1959 Cohort	1960–1969 Cohort	1970–1984 Cohort
Liberal Protestant	9.6%	8.8%	7.5%	6.5%	5.7%	3.7%	3.2%
At Age 16	8.4%	7.7%	7.9%	7.8%	7.2%	4.6%	4.5%
Episcopalian	3.6%	3.4%	2.9%	2.8%	2.0%	2.3%	1.3%
At Age 16	2.8%	2.9%	2.6%	2.5%	2.4%	2.5%	1.6%
Moderate Protestant	17.2%	14.4%	13.1%	10.7%	9.9%	8.8%	7.2%
At Age 16	20.9%	17.3%	15.3%	13.9%	11.9%	10.5%	9.6%
Lutheran	10.7%	9.4%	8.8%	8.0%	7.9%	7.2%	5.1%
At Age 16	11.1%	9.7%	8.9%	8.3%	8.6%	7.6%	5.9%
Baptist	14.9%	16.3%	17.3%	15.4%	13.9%	15.2%	15.4%
At Age 16	16.3%	17.6%	18.5%	18.0%	16.2%	17.3	16.7%
Sect	8.0%	7.0%	8.0%	7.8%	7.5%	7.2%	6.1%

At Age 16	6.9%	6.1%	6.4%	6.7%	7.0%	6.8%	6.2%
Mormon	1.6%	1.9%	1.8%	1.6%	1.4%	1.4%	.8%
At Age 16	1.6%	1.7%	1.3%	1.2%	1.0%	1.1%	.8%
Other Protestant	4.9%	5.3%	5.0%	4.6%	4.1%	3.8%	3.4%
At Age 16	4.3%	3.0%	2.6%	2.2%	2.1%	2.5%	2.5%
Catholic	28.7%	29.4%	29.0%	28.3%	27.5%	27.5%	24.0%
At Age 16	34.1%	36.0%	35.4%	31.9%	29.3%	27.4%	24.3%
Jewish	2.1%	1.7%	2.4%	2.7%	2.4%	2.8%	3.3%
At Age 16	2.4%	1.7%	2.5%	2.8%	2.5%	2.9%	3.4%
Other Religion	3.4%	3.0%	2.6%	2.1%	1.2%	1.0%	.9%
At Age 16	2.0%	1.8%	1.2%	1.1%	.9%	1.2%	.9%
None	20.9%	14.2%	12.4%	9.6%	5.8%	4.1%	3.6%
At Age 16	10.2%	7.0%	4.4%	3.6%	3.9%	2.9%	2.4%
N	1,421	4,115	6,951	5,819	3,973	4,032	5,173

Assessing religious dynamics can be productively accomplished by comparing the origin distributions of the earliest cohorts with the destination distribution of the more recent cohorts. Because younger respondents have not had time to switch religious affiliations, rates of mobility in the youngest group tend to be lower.

The demographic portrait is clear: liberal and Moderate Protestant religious groups are losing market share. While 8.4 percent of the oldest cohort (born between 1883 and 1919) grew up in a liberal Protestant denomination, and even more switched to these groups, fewer than 4 percent of the youngest two cohorts hold these affiliations. The slide is less dramatic for Episcopalians, but even more pronounced for the Moderate Protestant religious groups, which held nearly 21 percent of the origin affiliations of the oldest cohort, but less than 9 percent of the youngest two cohorts. Lutherans have also lost market share, though less dramatically. And, while Jews once comprised 3.4 percent of affiliates, they garner only about 2 percent in the youngest two cohorts.

In contrast, Baptists and sectarian groups are relatively stable, while Mormons have gained market share. Catholics have also made dramatic gains, notably evident in increasing proportions of origin affiliates among younger cohorts. This suggests an infusion of members due to high fertility and/or high immigration levels. Table 20.1 also shows that while around 24 percent of the oldest cohort grew up Catholic, approximately 35 percent of the youngest three cohorts grew up Catholic, and 29 percent held a Catholic affiliation at the time of interview. Nonaffiliation has also become increasingly prevalent across cohorts (Glenn 1987; Hout and Fischer 2002). While only 3.6 percent of the oldest cohorts claimed no religious affiliation, that figure balloons to 21 percent in the youngest cohort. Many of the youngest cohort will likely return to claiming a religious affiliation later in the life course (Wilson and Sherkat 1994).

African Americans' Religious Affiliations across Cohorts

GSS analyses presented in Table 20.2 show that among African Americans, Baptist and Methodist affiliations are in decline, while conservative sects are gaining members. Only 3.4 percent of the eldest African Americans held a sectarian affiliation when growing up, while 16 percent of the 1960–1969 birth cohort are members of sectarian religious groups. Membership in traditionally white mainline churches is not changing across cohorts of African Americans—remaining small but stable. Other non-Christian groups have gone from being virtually unobserved among the oldest cohorts, to accounting for 3–5 percent of affiliates in the youngest three cohorts. Growth among "other Protestant" groups (typically interdenominational and nondenominational churches) is also substantial across cohorts. Growth in this nondenominational grouping may be a function of niche dynamics, with more educated, highly religious, and younger mainliners leaving the Baptists and Methodists for nondenominational churches (Sherkat 2001a, 2002). Younger generations of African Americans are also more likely

TABLE 20.2

African American Religious Distributions across Birth Cohorts: 1973–2002 GSS

	1883–1919 Cohort	1920–1929 Cohort	1930–1939 Cohort	1940–1949 Cohort	1950–1959 Cohort	1960–1969 Cohort	1970–1984 Cohort
White Mainline Protestant	2.9%	5.1%	2.9%	3.7%	2.9%	3.2%	2.5%
At Age 16	4.1%	3.8%	3.8%	4.6%	3.4%	3.9%	3.3%
Methodist	19.8%	14.9%	14.3%	10.9%	9.9%	6.8%	6.8%
At Age 16	25.3%	16.7%	16.8%	13.9%	11.1%	8.8%	8.7%
Baptist	58.9%	57.6%	54.3%	50.8%	49.6%	45.0%	39.9%
At Age 16	63.4%	67.5%	64.2%	61.2%	58.7%	52.7%	46.0%
Sect	10.5%	11.9%	11.7%	12.2%	13.1%	16.1%	11.9%
At Age 16	3.4%	5.2%	5.9%	5.3%	9.4%	11.7%	11.2%
Other Protestant	1.5%	.9%	2.0%	2.8%	2.6%	3.3%	5.4%
At Age 16	.7%	1.2%	.3%	1.0%	1.2%	1.2%	2.5%
Catholic	3.8%	6.6%	8.5%	9.8%	9.4%	11.2%	10.1%
At Age 16	2.6%	5.6%	7.1%	11.1%	12.1%	13.4%	13.8%
Other Religion	.7%	1.3%	1.5%	2.5%	4.5%	3.3%	4.7%
At Age 16	0	0	.3%	.4%	2.0%	2.0%	2.9%
None	1.9%	1.7%	4.9%	7.4%	8.0%	11.2%	18.7%
At Age 16	.5%	.2%	1.6%	2.6%	2.1%	6.3%	11.6%
N	683	545	615	894	1,202	753	278

to affiliate with the Catholic Church. This is likely fueled by immigration from African and Caribbean nations. Finally, the distribution of African American nonaffiliates has dramatically increased, to nearly equal that of whites among the youngest birth cohort.

Retention Rates and Gains and Losses from Switching

Table 20.3 uses data from white GSS respondents to summarize retention of members across cohorts, and the proportion of the original market share gained or lost because of religious switching. If large proportions of members leave one affiliation and join another, a denomination will have to heavily recruit to replace them or else they will lose market share. Groups with ethnic and quasi-ethnic characteristics (e.g., Jews, Lutherans, Baptists) have higher retention rates than do others; however, these groups also find it hard to recruit members. Table 20.3 also shows that the largest proportional losses from switching are for the Moderate Protestant denominations, but liberal Protestants and Episcopalians have also lost sizable proportions in the youngest cohort. Notably, in the oldest cohort, both liberal Protestants and Episcopalians gained members from switching. This reversed for liberal Protestants in the 1930–1949 cohort, while Episcopalians continued to gain from switching in this cohort. Baptists are losing members from switching, despite their high retention rates. Notably, Catholics have increasing losses from switching across the cohorts, and particularly in the youngest cohort. Continued increases in Catholic marginal proportions are certainly a reflection of the impact of immigration.

Table 20.3 also shows that Mormons, sectarian groups, and the non-denominational churches are gaining members from switching exchanges. Gains for the "other Protestants" are dramatic because of the small baseline proportions. Other religions are also charting strong gains from switching in the two younger cohorts. Finally, nonaffiliation is an increasingly popular choice, and may be becoming a more stable religious option as reflected in its increasing "retention" rate.

Patterns of Switching and Intermarriage across Denominations

Recent studies have shown that religious commonalities structure both religious switching and intermarriage. When people choose to switch religious denominations, they tend to move to a denomination similar to the one from which they came. Studies find high rates of exchange between Episcopalian and liberal Protestants, between Moderate Protestants and liberal Protestants, and between Baptists and other sectarian groups (Sherkat 2001b, 2002). In contrast, switching between Catholics and conservative sects is particularly rare. Similar findings are found for intermarriage, with people tending to marry a spouse from a similar denominational group if they marry outside of their faith (Sherkat

2004). Intermarriage has been shown to have a negative impact on fertility (Lehrer 1998, 1996) and to influence the religious ties of children—making religious switching more likely (Nelsen 1990; Sherkat 1991).

Table 20.4 examines denominational differences in age, intermarriage rates, and fertility across cohorts. In the younger cohorts, liberal and Moderate Protestant groups, Lutherans, and sectarian groups have significantly higher rates of intermarriage than the cohort average. In contrast, Baptists, Mormons, and Catholics have significantly lower intermarriage rates compared to the cohort average. For Lutherans, Moderate Protestants, Episcopalians, Catholics, Jews, and liberal Protestants, rates of intermarriage appear to be increasing substantially across cohorts. Intermarriage rates are stable for sectarians and Baptists. The increase in intermarriage is dramatic among Jews. Only 17 percent of the eldest cohort married a non-Jew, while 53 percent of married Jews in the 1950–1964 birth cohort are married to non-Jews. Because of its impact on fertility and religious switching, high rates of intermarriage could dramatically impact the proportion of Jews over the course of the twenty-first century.

Fertility and Age Structure

Together with intermarriage, fertility has a substantial impact on the religious demography of the United States. Table 20.4 presents GSS data revealing that fertility is significantly lower among liberal Protestants, Episcopalians, and Jews, particularly in the younger cohorts. Moderate Protestants also have lower than average fertility in the eldest cohort. In contrast, Baptists, member of sectarian groups, and Mormons chart higher than average levels of fertility in every cohort. Fertility among Mormons is remarkably high, with the average Mormon having over 3.5 children in the two oldest cohorts (where fertility is completed for most respondents). In the middle cohort, Catholics have higher than average fertility. Given the dominance of parental influences on religious affiliations and beliefs, these fertility differences will loom large in determining the future demographic portrait of the United States. For example, while Jews and Mormons have roughly equivalent proportions of affiliates in contemporary surveys, Mormons have double the level of fertility in the two younger cohorts. Together with their exceptionally high rates of member retention, we should expect to see substantially more Mormons than Jews in the coming decades (Stark 1996).

The average members of several denominations and religious groups are quite old, and this is potentially a serious problem that could lead to congregational and denominational decline. Age structure can have a profound impact on the niche position of a religious group, since homophyly drives people into denominations with members similar in age, education, and income to their own (Sherkat 1991, 2001a; Toth 1999; Popielarz and McPherson 1995; McPherson and Rotolo 1996). Table 20.4 shows that liberal Protestants, Episcopalians, Moderate Protestants, Lutherans, and Jews are significantly older than the average

TABLE 20.3

Retention and Switching Dynamics across Birth
Cohorts: White Americans in the GSS

	1883–1929 Cohort	1930–1949 Cohort	1950–1969 Cohort
Liberal Protestant			
Retention	63.6%	53.5%	57.7%
% Gain/Loss from Switching	12.2%	-10.5%	-19.6%
Episcopalian			
Retention	67.2%	58.4%	64.7%
% Gain/Loss from Switching	25.4%	15.6%	-12.4%
Moderate Protestant			
Retention	60.5%	56.0%	64.0%
% Gain/Loss from Switching	-17.8%	-19.6%	-16.0%
Lutheran			
Retention	74.2%	68.8%	71.3%
% Gain/Loss from Switching	-2.5%	-4.1%	-7.9%
Baptist			
Retention	70.5%	66.4%	71.1%
% Gain/Loss from Switching	-7.0%	-11.5%	-12.6%
Sect			
Retention	60.3%	60.3%	65.7%
% Gain/Loss from Switching	17.6%	15.4%	16.4%
Mormon			
Retention	85.1%	92.9%	91.3%
% Gain/Loss from Switching	11.5%	28.3%	21.1%
Other Protestant			
Retention	48.2%	52.6%	58.8%
% Gain/Loss from Switching	45.9%	104.8%	86.4%
Catholic			
Retention	88.1%	80.5%	76.4%
% Gain/Loss from Switching	-1.0%	-9.0%	-17.8%

(continued)

Table 20.3. Retention and Switching Dynamics across Birth Cohorts:
White Americans in the GSS *(continued)*

	1883–1929 Cohort	*1930–1949* Cohort	*1950–1969* Cohort
Jewish			
Retention	92.0%	82.5%	81.1%
% Gain/Loss from Switching	-3.8%	-5.7%	-5.3%
Other Religion			
Retention	56.0%	65.7%	67.5%
% Gain/Loss from Switching	-12.3%	68.6%	97.3%
None			
Retention	29.8%	33.0%	57.7%
% Gain/Loss from Switching	45.4%	117.7%	146.9%
N	9,054	9,662	10,912

GSS respondent. These groups have relatively low fertility, and suffer losses from switching in younger cohorts. Religious nonaffiliates are significantly younger than other respondents, in part because of life course factors that may eventually lead them back into expressing an affiliation. Interestingly, members of other non-Christian religious groups are also significantly younger than the average GSS respondent—which could indicate a potential for growth among non-Christian religious groups.

Immigration and Religious Affiliation

In the late 1990s, a number of scholars began investigating the emerging immigrant congregations in ethnic communities and beyond (Ebaugh and Chafetz 2000; Yang and Ebaugh 2001; Bankston and Zhou 1997; Zhou and Bankston 1996). In spite of the importance of immigration for numerous social and economic outcomes, few quantitative studies have examined the impact of immigration on the religious demography of the United States.

Table 20.5 reveals that in each birth cohort, immigrants to the United States are largely Catholic. Roughly 45 percent of immigrants from the two cohorts born before 1950 are Catholic. This declines slightly to 42 percent among the cohort born between 1950 and 1969. The Catholic Church has remained an immigrant religion throughout the twentieth century, and now into the twenty-first. While

TABLE 20.4

Age, Intermarriage, and Fertility across Religious Groups and Birth Cohorts: White Americans in the GSS

	Average Age Total / 1998–2002	1883–1929 Cohort	1930–1949 Cohort	1950–1969 Cohort
Liberal Protestant	50.5* / 52.1*			
% Intermarried		70.2%*	80.0%*	82.5%*
Number of Children		2.27*	2.19*	1.03
Episcopalian	49.5*/ 54.2*			
% Intermarried		76.3%*	88.5%*	88.9%*
Number of Children		2.38	2.08*	.81*
Moderate Protestant	49.4* / 51.3*			
% Intermarried		60.1%*	64.8%*	72.8%*
Number of Children		2.40*	2.35	1.09
Lutheran	47.9* / 50.2*			
% Intermarried		54.4%	67.8%*	74.7%*
Number of Children		2.59	2.27	1.14
Baptist	45.2 / 46.8			
% Intermarried		45.2%*	48.6%*	49.3%*
Number of Children		2.85*	2.46*	1.27*
Sect	45.3 / 46.8			
% Intermarried		68.2%*	66.8%*	66.7%*
Number of Children		2.95*	2.58*	1.42*
Mormon	42.0* / 46.3			
% Intermarried		33.3%*	56.0%	30.2%*
Number of Children		3.55*	3.59*	1.63*
Other Protestant	43.9 / 43.3*			
% Intermarried		76.6%*	68.5%	74.0%*
Number of Children		2.44	2.27	1.28*
Catholic	43.7* / 45.0			
% Intermarried		33.7%*	37.0%*	43.5%*
Number of Children		2.67	2.52*	1.13

(continued)

Table 20.4. Age, Intermarriage, and Fertility across Religious Groups and Birth Cohorts: White Americans in the GSS (*continued*)

	Average Age Total / 1998–2002	1883–1929 Cohort	1930–1949 Cohort	1950–1969 Cohort
Jewish	48.6* / 50.5*			
% Intermarried		17.0%*	22.0%*	53.3%
Number of Children		2.01*	1.87*	.76*
Other Religion	39.0* / 38.7*			
% Intermarried		63.6%	48.3%	46.4%
Number of Children		2.12*	1.57*	.97
None	37.9* / 39.3*			
% Intermarried		84.7%*	83.1%*	75.1%
Number of Children		2.32*	1.73*	.88
Total	45.1 / 46.0			
% Intermarried		51.1%	54.6%	57.8%
Number of Children		2.58	2.35	1.13

*Difference from cohort mean is significant at the .05 alpha level, two tailed.

there has been much discussion of Latin American Protestantism (Hunt 1999), GSS data show that immigration continues to fuel Catholic growth.

Table 20.5 also shows that earlier cohorts of immigrants, particularly second-generation immigrants, may have used conversion to liberal Protestant and mainline denominations as a way to assimilate to American culture (Form 2000). While 7.4 percent of the eldest immigrants affiliated with liberal Protestant groups, and 6 percent of first-generation immigrants joined the Episcopal Church, these percentages decline considerably in later cohorts. Liberal and Moderate Protestant groups are particularly common affiliations for second-generation immigrants of mixed immigrant/native stock in the eldest generation. Perhaps this is a function of nation of origin differences across cohorts. Indeed, immigration exclusion acts determined that a large percentage of older immigrants were from Europe, and this made it more likely that they would hold affiliations in Lutheran, Catholic, Reformed, Anglican, and Presbyterian churches. Immigrants from younger cohorts are increasingly affiliated with sects and with Baptist congregations. Immigrants are also more likely to claim a non-denominational Protestant affiliation across generations, and the proportion of immigrants with no religious affiliation is higher in the later two birth cohorts.

TABLE 20.5

Percentage of First- and Second-Generation Immigrants by Religious Group and Birth Cohort in the United States

	Immigrant	Second Generation, Both Parents	Second Generation, One Parent
Liberal Protestant 1883–1929	7.4%	4.5%	10.0%
1930–1949 Cohort	3.5%	4.2%	5.7%
1950–1969 Cohort	2.9%	1.4%	4.6%
Episcopalian 1883–1929	6.2%	2.7%	3.2%
1930–1949 Cohort	3.8%	1.7%	2.8%
1950–1969 Cohort	1.9%	1.4%	3.4%
Moderate Protestant 1883–1929	5.0%	4.9%	10.5%
1930–1949 Cohort	3.5%	3.1%	6.6%
1950–1969 Cohort	3.8%	2.4%	3.9%
Lutheran 1883–1929	9.7%	12.4%	15.3%
1930–1949 Cohort	5.3%	5.9%	5.7%
1950–1969 Cohort	2.2%	2.4%	5.5%
Baptist 1883–1929	2.9%	1.5%	5.4%
1930–1949 Cohort	4.2%	3.1%	6.6%
1950–1969 Cohort	6.3%	2.7%	6.0%
Sect 1883–1929	3.5%	2.4%	3.7%
1930–1949 Cohort	6.0%	3.8%	4.6%
1950–1969 Cohort	7.1%	5.5%	4.8%
Mormon 1883–1929	1.0%	.1%	1.4%
1930–1949 Cohort	.3%	.7%	1.1%
1950–1969 Cohort	1.2%	1.0%	1.4%
Other Protestant 1883–1929	1.0%	1.6%	3.4%
1930–1949 Cohort	2.8%	3.8%	4.1%
1950–1969 Cohort	4.7%	3.4%	7.8%
Catholic 1883–1929	44.6%	53.9%	36.7%
1930–1949 Cohort	45.1%	47.9%	44.1%
1950–1969 Cohort	41.9%	52.9%	37.5%

(continued)

Table 20.5. Percentage of First- and Second-Generation Immigrants by Religious Group and Birth Cohort in the United States *(continued)*

	Immigrant	Second Generation, Both Parents	Second Generation, One Parent
Jewish 1883–1929	9.7%	9.4%	4.9%
1930–1949 Cohort	3.6%	11.9%	5.2%
1950–1969 Cohort	1.8%	5.2%	3.9%
Other Religion 1883–1929	3.5%	2.9%	1.1%
1930–1949 Cohort	10.4%	4.9%	3.4%
1950–1969 Cohort	13.2%	6.2%	3.2%
None 1883–1929	5.4%	3.8%	4.5%
1930–1949 Cohort	11.5%	8.7%	10.1%
1950–1969 Cohort	12.9%	15.5%	17.8%
N	484 (5.3%)	1,080 (11.9%)	649 (7.2%)
N	714 (7.4%)	286 (3.0%)	562 (5.8%)
N	1,119 (10.3%)	291 (2.7%)	562 (5.2%)

Table 20.5 further reveals that the percentage of immigrants who are Jewish has also declined considerably in the younger cohorts. Nearly 10 percent of immigrants in the pre-1930 cohort were Jewish, while fewer than 2 percent of immigrants in the 1950–1969 birth cohort are Jews. The declining percentage of Jews among immigrants is offset by an increase in the percentage affiliated with other non-Christian traditions. In the oldest cohort, only 3.5 percent claimed a non-Jewish, non-Christian affiliation, while in the youngest cohort, 13 percent claim such ties. We should, however, be cautious of this total given the diverse set of often-Christian groups in the GSS category for "other religions" (Sherkat 1999). Importantly, Table 20.5 also shows that the proportion of first-generation immigrants increases dramatically across cohorts; while immigrants comprised around 5 percent of the eldest cohort, they accounted for 10 percent of the 1950–1969 birth cohort.

Socioeconomic Sources of Denominationalism

Religious groups are stratified by socioeconomic status, and this influences both the trajectory of religious groups as well as the socioeconomic fortunes of members. Research has shown that otherworldly sectarian religious groups often preach an anti-intellectual message that hinders postsecondary academic

TABLE 20.6

Income and Education across Religious Groups and Birth Cohorts: White Americans in the GSS

	1883–1929 Cohort	*1930–1949* Cohort	*1950–1969* Cohort
Liberal Protestant			
Income Z-score	.11*	.55*	.26*
Years of Education	12.7*	14.3*	14.3*
Episcopalian			
Income Z-score	.26*	.54*	.29*
Years of Education	13.4*	14.8*	14.8*
Moderate Protestant			
Income Z-score	-.19	.35	.11
Years of Education	11.6*	13.1	13.7*
Lutheran			
Income Z-score	-.16	.34	.18*
Years of Education	11.0	13.2	13.6*
Baptist			
Income Z-score	-.41*	.18*	-.02*
Years of Education	10.1*	12.0*	12.6*
Sect			
Income Z-score	-.56*	.06*	-.11*
Years of Education	9.6*	11.8*	12.5*
Mormon			
Income Z-score	-.15	.24	.01
Years of Education	12.1*	13.4	13.9*
Other Protestant			
Income Z-score	-.20	.29	.12
Years of Education	11.1	13.3	13.4
Catholic			
Income Z-score	-.09	.36	.17*
Years of Education	10.9	13.0	13.4

(continued)

Table 20.6. Income and Education across Religious Groups and Birth Cohorts: White Americans in the GSS *(continued)*

	1883–1929 Cohort	1930–1949 Cohort	1950–1969 Cohort
Jewish			
Income Z-score	.43*	.78*	.44*
Years of Education	13.1*	15.8*	15.8*
Other Religion			
Income Z-score	-.04	.27	-.00
Years of Education	11.6	14.6*	14.2*
None			
Income Z-score	.01*	.32	-.00
Years of Education	12.1*	14.1*	13.5
Total			
Income Z-score	-.15	.32	.10
Years of Education	11.2	13.1	13.4

*Difference from cohort mean is significant at the .05 alpha level, two tailed.

achievement and employment options (particularly for women), as well as wealth attainment (Darnell and Sherkat 1997; Keister 2003; Sherkat and Darnell 1999; Sherkat 2001b). Configurations of social status will help determine the future composition of denominations, since people will be attracted to denominations with socioeconomic attributes similar to their own (McPherson and Rotolo 1996; Popielarz and McPherson 1995).

Table 20.6 presents cohort and denominational differences in income and educational attainment. Because the GSS changes the metric of the income measure periodically, income is indicated by a standardized Z score (mean = 0, standard deviation = 1). In every cohort, liberal Protestants and Episcopalians have significantly higher incomes and educational attainment. Moderate Protestants are significantly above average in educational attainment in the oldest and youngest cohorts, and Lutherans from the youngest cohort have more education and income than the cohort average.

Table 20.6 also shows that members of sectarian groups and Baptists have significantly lower educational attainment and income in every cohort. Both Baptists and sectarians have about one year less education than the average member of their cohorts—and they lag about two years behind liberal Protestants and Episcopalians. The gap was somewhat larger in the eldest cohort, when the average sectarian and Baptist attained only ten years of education, while liberal Protestants and Episcopalians averaged about thirteen years.

Jewish educational and income advantages are clearly evident in Table 20.6. Jews chart the highest average incomes in every cohort, and are only exceeded by Episcopalians in the eldest cohort on educational attainment. Jewish educational attainment is three years higher than sectarians or Baptists. In the last two cohorts, the educational attainment of other non-Christian groups is also significantly above average; however, these other religious groups have not been able to translate human capital advantages into earnings advantages.

Table 20.6 also reveals that Mormons have higher than average educational attainment in the eldest and youngest cohorts. The Mormon emphasis on educational attainment is a long-standing part of their mission and distinguishes them from less educated sectarians. Catholics chart average educational attainment and income across the two older cohorts, and they have higher than average income in the youngest cohort. Unlike sectarians and Baptists, nondenominational affiliates have average levels of income and educational attainment. Nondenominational sectarian churches may fill a market niche for those with somewhat higher education and income who still want otherworldly religion (Sherkat 2002).

The Demography of Belief and Participation

Without belief, religion is no different from other social clubs. In the United States, the primary indicator of Christian religious beliefs is a profession of faith in the Bible as the inerrant word of God. While this profession may mean many different things, it is a significant marker that has a profound effect on family relations, child rearing practices, political values and commitments, gender role orientations, educational attainment, and income attainment. Further, while many contend that Biblical inerrancy is unorthodox among liberal and Moderate Protestants, this privileges the current interpretation of elites in those denominations and ignores the fact that fundamentalism and inerrancy were the official denominational positions of these groups well into the twentieth century (Finke and Stark 1992).

Looking across cohorts in Table 20.7, support for Biblical inerrancy has clearly waned. Even among sectarians and Baptists, there are declining percentages of members who adhere to inerrancy. Still, even in the youngest cohort, more than one-half of Baptists and 60 percent of sectarians believe the Bible is the actual word of their gods. In every cohort, sectarians and Baptists are significantly more likely to support Biblical inerrancy, while liberal Protestants, Catholics, and Episcopalians are significantly less enamored with literalist interpretations of scripture. For Catholics, inerrancy has long been viewed as a rejection of dogma and Papal authority. Mormons are no more likely than other

Americans to adhere to Biblical inerrancy. In the youngest cohort, the nondenominational "other Protestants" hold significantly stronger inerrant positions on scriptures than average, which, together with their high church attendance rates, suggests that they are the next wave of sectarian denominations. Predictably, Jews largely reject Biblical inerrancy, as it connotes adherence to Christianity. In contrast, "other religions" do not differ from the mean, probably because about one-third of these respondents are Christians, and many are fundamentalists (Sherkat 1999).

Beyond belief, there must be action to provide resources for religious groups, and ensure continuity of belief through the socialization of members. Denominations with low rates of participation will have fewer human capital resources to generate benefits for members, and smaller infusions of actual resources for collective action. When members do not regularly participate, costs of defection are lower and this can drive religious switching (Sherkat and Wilson 1995). Table 20.7 shows that there is a decline in church attendance across cohorts in every denomination. Part of this is likely a function of changing life course patterns, and the age of interview in the youngest two cohorts. GSS data are not ideal for assessing the life cycle sources of change. Church attendance probably has declined somewhat, generally because high rates in the 1960s and 1970s were a function of overconsumption, spurred by normative constraints and few alternative social options (Ellison and Sherkat 1995; Sherkat and Ellison 1999; Sherkat 1998).

Table 20.7 also shows that in the eldest cohort, liberal Protestants, Episcopalians, and Moderate Protestants are significantly below average in church attendance. Liberal and moderate groups do not differ from average in later cohorts (though they are significantly less active when compared to sectarians, Baptists, and Mormons). Baptists, sectarians, and Catholics have significantly higher rates of church participation—and all three groups are significantly above the mean in all three cohorts. Mormons also have high rates of church attendance, and are significantly above average in the younger two cohorts. Notably, participation increases across cohorts for the "other Protestants," reflecting affiliation with groups that are sectarian in orientation.

Jews have low rates of participation in every cohort, though there are no substantial declines in participation across cohorts. Members of "other religions" have average rates of participation. Predictably, the unaffiliated do not attend services very often.

Problems of Contemporary Approaches

Survey designs are inherently limited, particularly given the considerable diversity of American religions. Indeed, the religious and ethnic diversity of the United States makes it very difficult to assess patterns of change and association. A complex and changing set of religious groups are distributed unevenly across

TABLE 20.7

Bible Beliefs and Church Attendance across Denominations
and Birth Cohort: White Americans in the GSS

	1883–1929 Cohort	1930–1949 Cohort	1950–1969 Cohort
Liberal Protestant			
Biblical Inerrancy	.26*	.17*	.18*
Church Attendance	4.0*	3.7	3.6
Episcopalian			
Biblical Inerrancy	.21*	.10*	.16*
Church Attendance	3.6*	3.7	3.3
Moderate Protestant			
Biblical Inerrancy	.39	.24	.23
Church Attendance	4.0*	3.6	3.3
Lutheran			
Biblical Inerrancy	.40	.29	.27
Church Attendance	4.3	4.1	3.6*
Baptist			
Biblical Inerrancy	.69*	.55*	.50*
Church Attendance	4.6*	4.1*	3.8*
Sect			
Biblical Inerrancy	.72*	.65*	.61*
Church Attendance	5.4*	5.2*	4.9*
Mormon			
Biblical Inerrancy	.28	.26	.29
Church Attendance	4.7	5.1*	5.3*
Other Protestant			
Biblical Inerrancy	.30	.31	.37*
Church Attendance	2.9*	3.1	3.6
Catholic			
Biblical Inerrancy	.30*	.19*	.16*
Church Attendance	5.2*	4.6*	3.9*

(continued)

Table 20.7. Bible Beliefs and Church Attendance across Denominations and Birth Cohort: White Americans in the GSS *(continued)*

	1883–1929 Cohort	1930–1949 Cohort	1950–1969 Cohort
Jewish			
Biblical Inerrancy	.08*	.09*	.06*
Church Attendance	2.8*	2.7*	2.5*
Other Religion			
Biblical Inerrancy	.26	.22	.23
Church Attendance	3.9	3.0*	3.2
None			
Biblical Inerrancy	.08*	.06*	.09*
Church Attendance	.6*	.71*	.8*
Total			
Biblical Inerrancy	.40	.29	.26
Church Attendance	4.3	3.9	3.4

*Difference from cohort mean is significant at the .05 alpha level, two tailed.

ethnic and regional lines, with literally thousands of religious groups operating at any give time (Melton 1991). Sample surveys have difficulty dealing with minority religious groups, since their likelihood of selection is low. In 2002, for example, the GSS interviewed 2,765 people and identified forty-eight Jews (1.7 percent) and thirteen Muslims (0.5 percent). This is a problem for establishing statistical inferences about subpopulations, even when minority groups account for millions of U.S. residents. The GSS sampling frame is also limited to English-speaking households, and institutionalized populations are excluded.

Repeated cross-sectional studies are problematic for attempting to separate age, period, and cohort (APC) effects. Some scholars have argued that there are substantial cohort effects on religious participation (Chaves 1989), while others have claimed that life course processes are more influential (Hout and Greeley 1990). Technical solutions to the APC problem may be hampered because of shifts in the GSS sampling design and units. Because of the extreme religious diversity in the United States, shifts in the sampling methods or sampling units can have a dramatic impact on inferences. In the GSS, changes in sampling design and sampling units has caused considerable volatility in the proportions of certain religious groupings, particularly Mormons, Jews, and those with no religious affiliation. Between 1973 and 1978, the GSS found that no more than one-half of 1 percent of respondents grew up Mormon. Between 1978 and 1980, after a restructuring of the sampling design, the GSS found more than twice the proportion of Mormons, at 1.1 percent. From 1983 to 1991, the GSS identified Mormons as comprising between 1.3 percent and 2.3 percent of U.S. adults. After 1993, the GSS identified no more than 0.9 percent Mormon (in 1994) and as few as 0.4 percent Mormon (in 1998). Notably, the erratic trend in percent Mormon is juxtaposed with a contrasting distribution of nonaffiliates (that is, the fewer Mormons, the more nonaffiliates, and vice versa). Indeed, the zero-order correlation between percent Mormon and percent no-religious affiliation across years of the GSS after 1983 is -.847. Thus, caution is warranted when making inferences about trends in religion based on repeated cross-sections like the GSS.

Discussion and Conclusions

U.S. scholars have increasingly viewed religion from a demographic perspective characterized by increased attention to life course events, fertility, mortality, migration, and the power of numbers (Hout, Greeley, and Wilde 2001; Stolzenberg, Blair-Loy, and Waite 1995; Myers 1996; Sherkat 1991, 1998). In earlier periods, sociologists considered religion to be largely outside the purview of normal sociological processes, and they tended to explain religious dynamics with reference to grand theories. The demographic perspective is advantaged by learning from and contributing to empirical sociological research, while providing a more flexible framework for explaining religious dynamics. Lacking a census, the demography of American religion requires high-quality survey research with large sample sizes and complete sets of questions that enable an elucidation of the incredible diversity of the religious marketplace of the United States. The GSS was an enormous leap forward in our progress toward a systematic social accounting of American social values and social diversity. This chapter has examined the demography of American religion, paying particular attention to the empirical distribution of denominations, dynamics of affiliation, and demographic issues like immigration, fertility, intermarriage, and socioeconomic status.

The continued development of the demographic model is threatened by cuts in data collection, lower response rates in recent surveys, systematic nonresponse in contemporary surveys (Sherkat 2005), and continued opposition to the reinstitution of Census questions about religion. Recent developments in the GSS core and modular composition have rendered it increasingly less useful for the demography of religion. Only religious affiliation and participation are now included in the core component of the GSS (which is asked to all respondents), and this hurts the prospects for the more complete understanding of the demography of U.S. religion. Worse still was the elimination of the question about spouse's religious affiliation after the 1994 GSS. Other studies have helped fill a number of the open gaps by incorporating questions about religion, but even high-quality longitudinal efforts like the National Survey of Adolescent Health are too small and focused to hope to generate estimates of important population parameters like the percentage Hindu or Muslim, or the educational gap between Seventh-Day Adventists and Baptists. Indeed, no current longitudinal data set in the United States has sufficient numbers of African Americans to investigate religious diversity among this important population subgroup. Assessing the importance of immigration for potentially reshaping American religion will also require large samples.

Another looming problem for religious demographers is the declining response rate now characterizing major data collection efforts. The GSS regularly garnered over 80 percent of prospective respondents throughout the 1970s and 1980s; however, in the last three editions, the response rate has been about 70 percent. Worse yet, there is evidence that certain types of conservative Christians are more likely to refuse to participate (Sherkat 2005). Given the contemporary political climate, it is also likely that non-Christians (perhaps especially Muslims) will be less forthcoming with information for survey researchers. Over time, these data issues will substantially hamper our efforts to construct a demographic portrait of American religion.

REFERENCES

Alwin, D. 1986. "Religion and Parental Child-Rearing Orientations: Evidence of a Catholic Protestant Convergence." *American Journal of Sociology* 92:412–430.

Bankston, C. L., and M. Zhou. 1997. "The Social Adjustment of Vietnamese American Adolescents: Evidence for a Segmented-Assimilation Approach." *Social Science Quarterly* 78:508–523.

Cadge, W., and E. H. Ecklund. 2006. "Religious Service Attendance among Immigrants: Evidence from the New Immigrant Survey-Pilot." *American Behavioral Scientist* 49 (11): 1574–1595.

Chaves, M. 1989. "Secularization and Religious Revival: Evidence from U.S. Church Attendance Rates, 1972–1986." *Journal for the Scientific Study of Religion* 28:464–477.

Darnell, A., and D. E. Sherkat. 1997. "The Impact of Fundamentalism on Educational Attainment." *American Sociological Review* 62:306–315.

Ebaugh, H. R., and J. S. Chafetz. 2000. *Religion and the New Immigrants: Continuities and Adaptations in Immigrant Congregations.* Walnut Creek, CA: AltaMira.

Ellison, C. G., J. A. Burr, and P. McCall. 1997. "Religious Homogeneity and Metropolitan Suicide Rates." *Social Forces* 76:273–299.

Ellison, C. G., R. A. Hummer, Cormier, S., and Rogers, R. G. 2000. "Religious Involvement and Mortality Risk among African American Adults." *Research on Aging* 22:630–667.

Ellison, C. G., and D. E. Sherkat. 1990. "Patterns of Religious Mobility among Black Americans." *Sociological Quarterly* 4:551–568.

————. 1995. "The Semi-Involuntary Institution Revisited: Regional Variations in Church Participation among Black Americans." *Social Forces* 73:1415–1437.

Finke, R., and R. Stark. 1992. *The Churching of America, 1776–1990: Winners and Losers in Our Religious Economy.* New Brunswick, NJ: Rutgers University Press.

Form, W. 2000. "Italian Protestants: Religion, Ethnicity, and Assimilation." *Journal for the Scientific Study of Religion* 39:307–320.

Frazier, E. F. 1964. *The Negro Church in America.* New York: Random House.

Glenn, N. 1964. "Negro Religion and Negro Status in the United States." In *Religion, Culture, and Society*, ed. L. Schneider, 623–639. New York: John Wiley and Sons.

——. 1987. "The Trend in 'No Religion' Respondents to U.S. National Surveys, Late 1950s to Early 1980s." *Public Opinion Quarterly* 51:293–314.

Glenn, N., and E. Gotard. 1977. "The Religion of Blacks in the United States: Some Recent Trends and Current Characteristics." *American Journal of Sociology* 83:443–451.

Hamilton, R. F., and W. H. Form. 2003. "Categorical Usages and Complex Realities: Race, Ethnicity and Religion in the United States." *Social Forces* 81:693–714.

Hout, M., and C. S. Fischer. 2002. "Why More Americans Have No Religious Preference: Politics and Generations." *American Sociological Review* 67 (2): 165–190.

Hout, M., and A. Greeley. 1990. "The Cohort Doesn't Hold: Comment on Chaves (1989)." *Journal for the Scientific Study of Religion* 29:519–524.

Hout, M., A. Greeley, and M. J. Wilde. 2001. "The Demographic Imperative in Religious Change in the United States." *American Journal of Sociology* 107:468–500.

Hummer, R. A., R. G. Rogers, C. B. Nam, and C. G. Ellison. 1999. "Religious Involvement and U.S. Adult Mortality." *Demography* 36:273–285.

Hunt, L. L. 1998. "Religious Affiliation among Blacks in the United States: Black Catholic Status Advantages Revisited." *Social Science Quarterly* 79:170–192.

——. 1999. "Hispanic Protestantism in the United States: Trends by Decade and Generation." *Social Forces* 77 (4): 1601–1623.

Hunt, L. L., and M. O. Hunt. 1999. "Regional Patterns of African American Church Attendance: Revisiting the Semi-Involuntary Thesis." *Social Forces* 78 (2): 779–791.

Jasso, G., D. S. Massey, M. R. Rosenzweig, and J. P. Smith. 2003. "Exploring the Religious Preference of Recent Immigrants to the United States: Evidence from the New Immigrant Pilot Survey." In *Religion and Immigration*, ed. Y. Y. Haddad and J. L. Esposito, 217–253. Walnut Creek, CA: AltaMira Press.

Keister, L. A. 2003. "Religion and Wealth: The Role of Religious Affiliation and Participation in Early Adult Asset Accumulation." *Social Forces* 82:175–207.

Kluegel, J. R. 1980. "Denominational Mobility: Current Patterns and Recent Trends." *Journal for the Scientific Study of Religion* 19:26–39.

Land, K. C., G. Deane, and J. R. Blau. 1991. "Religious Pluralism and Church Membership: A Spatial Diffusion Model." *American Sociological Review* 56 (2): 237–249.

Lehrer, E. L. 1996. "Religion as a Determinant of Marital Fertility." *Journal of Population Economics* 9:173–196.

——. 1998. "Religious Intermarriage in the United States: Determinants and Trends." *Social Science Research* 27:245–263.

Lincoln, C. E. 1974. *The Black Church since Frazier*. New York: Schocken.

McPherson, J. M., and T. Rotolo. 1996. "Testing a Dynamic Model of Social Composition: Diversity and Change in Voluntary Groups." *American Sociological Review* 61:179–202.

Melton, G. 1991. *The Encyclopedia of American Religions*. 3rd ed. Tarrytown, NY: Triumph Books.

Musick, M., and J. Wilson. 1995. "Religious Switching for Marriage Reasons." *Sociology of Religion* 56:257–270.

Myers, S. M. 1996. "An Interactive Model of Religiosity Inheritance: The Importance of Family Context." *American Sociological Review* 61:858–866.

——. 2000. "The Impact of Religious Involvement on Mobility." *Social Forces* 79 (2): 755–783.

Nelsen, H. M. 1990. "The Religious Identification of Children of Interfaith Marriages." *Review of Religious Research* 32:122–134.

Pearce, L. D. 2002. "The Influence of Early Life Course Religious Exposure on Young Adults' Dispositions toward Childbearing." *Journal for the Scientific Study of Religion* 41 (2): 325–340.

Pearce, L. D., and W. G. Axinn. 1998. "The Impact of Family Religious Life on the Quality of Mother-Child Relations." *American Sociological Review* 63:810–828.

Pescosolido, B. A., and S. Georgianna. 1989. "Durkheim, Suicide, and Religion: Toward a Network Theory of Suicide." *American Sociological Review* 54:33–48.

Popielarz, P. A., and J. M. McPherson. 1995. "On the Edge or in Between: Niche Position, Niche Overlap, and the Duration of Voluntary Association Memberships." *American Journal of Sociology* 101:698–720.

Roof, W. C. 1989. "Multiple Religious Switching: A Research Note." *Journal for the Scientific Study of Religion* 28:530–535.

Roof, W. C., and W. McKinney. 1987. *American Mainline Religion: Its Changing Shape and Future.* New Brunswick, NJ: Rutgers University Press.

Sandomirsky, S., and J. Wilson. 1990. "Processes of Disaffiliation: Religious Mobility among Men and Women." *Social Forces* 68:1211–1229.

Sherkat, D. E. 1991. "Leaving the Faith: Testing Theories of Religious Switching Using Survival Models." *Social Science Research* 20:171–187.

———. 1998. "Counterculture or Continuity? Examining Competing Influences on Baby Boomers' Religious Orientations and Participation." *Social Forces* 76:1087–1115.

———. 1999. "Tracking the Other: Dynamics and Composition of 'Other' Religions in the General Social Survey 1973–1996." *Journal for the Scientific Study of Religion* 38:551–560.

———. 2001a. "Investigating the Sect-Church-Sect Cycle: Cohort Specific Attendance Differences across African American Denominations." *Journal for the Scientific Study of Religion* 40:221–233.

———. 2001b. "Tracking the Restructuring of American Religion: Religious Affiliation and Patterns of Mobility 1973–1998." *Social Forces* 79:1459–1492.

———. 2002. "African American Religious Affiliation in the Late 20th Century: Trends, Cohort Variations, and Patterns of Switching 1973–1998." *Journal for the Scientific Study of Religion* 41:485–494.

———. 2004. "Religious Intermarriage in the United States: Trends, Patterns, Predictors." *Social Science Research* 33:606–626.

———. 2005. "Explaining the Moral Voter Gap between Surveys and Voting." Paper presented at the annual meeting of the Association for the Sociology of Religion, Philadelphia, PA.

Sherkat, D. E., and A. Darnell. 1999. "The Effect of Parents' Fundamentalism on Children's Educational Attainment: Examining Differences by Gender and Children's Fundamentalism." *Journal for the Scientific Study of Religion* 38:23–35.

Sherkat, D. E., and C. G. Ellison. 1991. "The Politics of Black Religious Change: Disaffiliation from Black Mainline Denominations." *Social Forces* 70:431–454.

———. 1999. "Recent Developments and Current Controversies in the Sociology of Religion." *Annual Review of Sociology* 25:363–394.

Sherkat, D. E., and J. Wilson. 1995. "Preferences, Constraints, and Choices in Religious Markets: An Examination of Religious Switching and Apostasy." *Social Forces* 73:993–1026.

Smith, T. 1990. "Classifying Protestant Denominations." *Review of Religious Research* 31:225–246.

Stark, R. 1996. "So Far, So Good: A Brief Assessment of Mormon Membership Projections." *Review of Religious Research* 38:18–27.

Stark, R., and W. S. Bainbridge. 1985. *The Future of Religion: Secularization, Revival, and Cult Formation*. Berkeley: University of California Press.

———. 1987. *A Theory of Religion*. New Brunswick, NJ: Rutgers University Press.

Steensland, B., J. Z. Park, M. D. Regnerus, L. D. Robinson, W. B. Wilcox, and R. D. Woodberry. 2000. "The Measure of American Religion: Toward Improving the State of the Art." *Social Forces* 79:291–318

Stolzenberg, R. M., M. Blair-Loy, and L. J. Waite. 1995. "Religious Participation over the Early Life Course: Age and Family Life Cycle Effects on Church Membership." *American Sociological Review* 60:84–103.

Thornton, A., W. G. Axinn, and D. H. Hill. 1992. "Reciprocal Effects of Religiosity, Cohabitation, and Marriage." *American Journal of Sociology* 98:628–651.

Toth, J. F., Jr. 1999. "Power and Paradox in an African American Congregation." *Review of Religious Research* 40:213–229.

Westoff, C., and E. F. Jones. 1979. "The End of Catholic Fertility." *Demography* 16:209–217.

Wilson, J., and D. E. Sherkat. 1994. "Returning to the Fold." *Journal for the Scientific Study of Religion* 33:148–161.

Yang, F., and H. R. Ebaugh. 2001. "Religion and Ethnicity among New Immigrants: The Impact of Majority/Minority Status in Home and Host Countries." *Journal for the Scientific Study of Religion* 40 (3): 367–378.

Zhou, M., and C. L. Bankston. 1996. "Social Capital and the Adaptation of the Second Generation: The Case of Vietnamese Youth in New Orleans." In *The New Second Generation*, ed. A. Portes, 197–220. New York: Russell Sage Foundation.

21

Future Directions in Population-Based Research on Religion, Family Life, and Health in the United States

CHRISTOPHER G. ELLISON AND ROBERT A. HUMMER

The aim of this volume was to bring together a number of leading sociologists and social demographers to investigate whether and how religion continues to shape family life, socioeconomic attainment, and health in the contemporary United States. Given the careful theoretical and empirical consideration of these issues throughout these chapters, the overall conclusion is straightforward: religion matters for our understanding of a broad set of demographic outcomes, and this general verdict seems unlikely to change anytime in the near future. The contributors to this volume have demonstrated clear evidence of religious variations in a host of important domains of life experience. These include key aspects of family life, such as adolescent sexuality, the timing of first marriage, and selection of marital partners, childbearing and child rearing, intergenerational relations, and women's roles. Religious factors also influence socioeconomic trajectories, including educational attainment and wealth accumulation. And finally, religious involvement has important implications for mental health, physical health, and mortality risk among U.S. adults.

Although each of these chapters augments previous related research literature, advancing our understanding of the complex links between religion and demographic outcomes, the individual chapters also raise many additional questions for future investigation. Thus, we close out the volume by briefly focusing on the future, outlining several key themes that should guide the further development of this area of study. Four areas stand out as particularly important: (a) the need for refinements in the conceptualization and measurement of religion in research on these issues; (b) the need for closer attention to subgroup variations in the relationships between religion and major outcomes of interest, such as family life and health; (c) the need for more careful and rigorous approaches to the issue of causality in research on religion and population outcomes; and (d) the ongoing need for high-quality data at the population level to allow for continued investigation of the topics raised in this volume. In the remainder of this final chapter, we consider each of these themes in greater detail.

Conceptualizing and Measuring Religion

One challenging issue facing researchers concerns how best to conceptualize and measure religious involvement. For social and behavioral scientists who specialize in religion, this is a perennial topic of contention. For decades, investigators have recognized that religion is a multidimensional phenomenon, and that there exist a plethora of strategies for measuring specific facets of religiousness (Hill and Hood 1999), but they have disagreed over (a) how many dimensions are worth measuring, and (b) which of these dimensions are relevant for research in any given area (Idler et al. 2003). Many studies linking religion with demographic outcomes, including those in this volume, rely on large-scale secondary databases, with high-quality samples of the U.S. population or specific segments thereof. Because these data collection efforts were not designed specifically for research on religion, they typically contain only a few, very rudimentary items tapping this domain. The most common of the survey items on major national surveys focus on: (a) religious affiliation or identity (usually gauged in terms of denominational preference or affiliation); (b) the frequency of attendance at religious services; and (c) self-rated religiousness (e.g., how religious are you?) or religious salience (e.g., how important is religion in your life?). Although such items are somewhat useful in distinguishing individual-level variations in organizational or subjective religiousness, they are crude devices for mapping such complex, variegated terrain. Moreover, they are generally not the specific aspects of religion that are specified by theoretical work as germane to family life, socioeconomic attainment, health, or other outcomes of interest to population scholars. In general, they cannot help to answer the "why" question; in other words, they cannot clarify the specific pathways, mechanisms, or processes via which religion may influence these outcomes (George, Ellison, and Larson 2002). For these reasons, reliance on generic religious measures is likely to yield low-ball estimates of the overall role of religion in these areas. Further, there is also a pernicious catch-22 situation here. On the one hand, if research using such measures turns up evidence of religious effects, then subsequent studies are likely to replicate or recycle the same limited array of measures, which may impede progress in the field. On the other hand, if studies using these measures reveal weak or negligible religious effects, then investigators may dismiss the significance of religion prematurely.

Fortunately, recent developments in multiple disciplines offer fresh approaches to this difficult issue. Researchers are increasingly inclined to distinguish between behavioral versus functional, or distal versus proximal, dimensions and measures of religiousness (Ellison and Levin 1998; Mahoney et al. 1999; Pargament 1997). Thus, in addition to the generic indicators discussed earlier (e.g., frequency of religious attendance), numerous investigators also focus on measures that tap specific, theoretically grounded facets of religion that are thought to influence family or health outcomes. These more specific measures often gauge particular functions that religion plays in the lives of individuals, rather than behaviors, and they are closer to the specific outcomes of interest. They may help to explain how and why religious affiliation or practice shapes outcomes of interest. In the religion–health field, for example, researchers have produced a rich body of theoretical and empirical work on styles of religious coping, illuminating the diverse ways in which individuals draw upon faith resources in dealing with chronic strains or traumatic events (Pargament 1997; Pargament, Koenig, and Perez 2000). Researchers have also designed sophisticated measures of the multiple dimensions of congregational social ties and support processes (Krause 2008). These efforts have been accelerated by several organized efforts, including a working group in the late 1990s cosponsored by the Fetzer Institute and the National Institute on Aging (Idler et al. 2003), as well as major funding initiatives underwritten by private entities such as the John Templeton Foundation, as well as the dynamic research programs of individual investigators. A growing body of evidence indicates that each of these functional or proximal indicators: (a) is a stronger predictor of outcomes of interest than behavioral or distal religious measures; and (b) helps to explain the associations between those generic measures and mental and physical health outcomes. Additional work in the religion–health area has focused on character strengths or virtues that are often (but not exclusively) linked with religion (Peterson and Seligman 2004). Specific examples of this trend include work on forgiveness, meaning and purpose, hopefulness, gratitude, and others (e.g., Krause 2006; Krause and Ellison 2003). Although few studies have probed the links between specific religious beliefs and health outcomes, recent research has begun to address this gap in the literature (e.g., Flannelly et al. 2007, 2008). To be sure, these lines of inquiry remain in their early stages, but the findings to date are intriguing and potentially important.

Progress in conceptualizing and measuring relevant aspects of religiousness has proceeded more slowly in the religion–family area. Nevertheless, there are clear signs of progress in this domain as well. Of particular note is the concept of sanctification, defined by Pargament and Mahoney (2005, 182) as "the process through which seemingly secular aspects of life are perceived as having spiritual character and significance." They go on to distinguish between theistic forms of sanctification, in which an object may be perceived as a manifestation of God (e.g., as reflecting God's involvement in one's life), and nontheistic variants of this process, via which objects are invested with qualities that are associated with the divine (e.g., transcendental meaning, ultimate purpose, moral purity). Sanctification offers one potentially valuable conceptual tool for understanding how religious meaning comes to infuse intimate relationships, which has been a major gap in religion–family research. Thus, investigators explicitly treat sanctification as a proximal religious construct that mediates, or helps to explain, the widely observed links between generic forms of religiousness and marital or relationship quality. In one provocative, but small-scale, study of married couples, marital sanctification was positively associated with marital happiness and satisfaction, more constructive problem-solving and conflict resolution practices (i.e., more use of negotiation and collaboration, less use of stalemate and withdrawal), and fewer arguments among partners (Mahoney et al. 1999). Although the sanctification concept is only now beginning to surface in studies using large-scale probability samples, the findings to date confirm the robust promise of this approach. Specifically, sanctification has been linked with multiple indicators of marital quality, a pattern that is stronger among (a) racial minorities, (b) couples facing financial strain and high overall stress, and (c) partners with potentially problematic attachment styles (Ellison, Burdette, and Wilcox forthcoming; Ellison et al. 2009b). Clearly, additional work is needed on this and other potential pathways linking religious involvement with specific facets of family life.

In addition to clarifying the role of behavioral versus functional, or distal versus proximal, measures of religiousness, researchers must deal with another challenging issue: the need to maintain a balanced evaluation of the role of religion (Pargament 2002). This has become a particularly contentious theme in the religion–health area, in which skeptics have alleged "pro-religious" bias on the part of some investigators (e.g., Sloan 2006). Although the weight of the empirical evidence indicates that religious involvement is often related to desirable outcomes in the areas of health, family, and other domains, some researchers have also reported null or even negative religious influences. In recent years, religion–health investigators have pursued work on several types of "spiritual struggle" (Pargament et al. 2005). Specific examples of this include: (a) divine struggle or troubled relationships with God, which often surface in the context of coping with stressors; (b) interpersonal struggle or negative interactions within religious settings; and (c) intrapsychic struggle or chronic religious doubts. Studies have linked each of these facets of struggle with negative mental and/or physical health outcomes (Exline 2002; Pargament 2002; Pargament et al. 2005). The evidence of salutary religious effects notwithstanding, it is also important for investigators to continue examining facets of religiousness that have potentially deleterious implications for individuals.

Future research on the topics discussed in this volume must also take into account shifts in the religious environment. Many of the theories and measures in this area have been geared, explicitly or implicitly, toward Judeo-Christian faith traditions that have historically dominated the U.S. cultural and religious landscape. Although the U.S. population continues to exhibit comparatively high levels of religious affiliation, practice, and belief (Finke 2005; Sherkat and Ellison 1999), investigators should be attentive to several important changes and trends in this area. First, while Christianity remains the leading religion among the American public, a growing percentage (roughly 15 percent) of U.S. adults now report "no religion," a pattern that some observers attribute to both generational change and antipathy toward the political role of religious conservatives (Hout and Fischer 2002). This pattern is part of a broader trend toward religious individualism that began to take hold among members of the "baby boomer" generation. Even many persons who report preference for, or affiliation with, a mainstream faith community may also (a) reject key doctrinal and social teachings of their chosen religion, and (b) pursue personal spirituality that can encompass specific beliefs and practices from non-Christian, New Age, or other modes of thought or practice, along with those of their stated religious tradition (Roof 2000). To some extent, these developments are not entirely new; alternative spiritual teachings have long flourished in the United States. However, one recent development that has elicited considerable scholarly attention is the apparent growth in the percentage of persons who describe themselves as "spiritual, but not religious" (Zhai et al. 2008). Although the conceptualization and measurement of spirituality remain mired in controversy (Koenig 2008; Zinnbauer, Pargament, and Scott 1999), the implications of such emergent identities for family life, health, and other population processes and outcomes clearly warrant closer investigation.

Moreover, the presence and visibility of non-Christian world religions in the United States has increased significantly, due to post-1965 immigration from Asia, Africa, and the Middle East (Cadge and Ecklund 2007). To be sure, survey-based estimates of Muslims, Buddhists, Hindus, and other non-Western traditions are modest (Smith 2002; Wuthnow 2005), and until recently adherents have been disproportionately concentrated in major metropolitan areas, although there are signs of change, growth, and dispersion. These relatively new forms of religious pluralism in the United States are likely to require fresh thinking about links between religion and family, health, and other domains, as well as innovative measurement approaches. And these challenges will quickly multiply as research on these topics moves to non-U.S. and non-Western societal contexts. To date, investigators have studied facets of the religion–health connection in settings as divergent as Israel (Anson and Anson 2000), Japan (Krause et al. 2002; Roemer 2007), China (Zhang 2008), and many others. This line of comparative inquiry remains in its infancy, but studies in this vein suggest that religion may influence health and mortality in complex and diverse ways in societies around the world. At the same time, focused critiques have demonstrated that approaches for conceptualizing and measuring religion and religiousness developed in Western settings may be misleading or inappropriate when applied to diverse other contexts (Traphagan 2005). New measurement approaches currently in development hold considerable potential to advance our understanding of these issues among non-Judeo-Christian groups (e.g., Tarakeshwar, Pargament, and Mahoney 2003).

Finally, our understanding of the issues explored in this volume could benefit from a multilevel approach to religion. Briefly, religious involvement is often theorized and analyzed exclusively as an individual-level variable, much like age, education, or other attributes measured via survey data. Clearly, this strategy has paid major dividends, as the contributions to this volume have demonstrated. However, it may also be useful to consider religious influences at supraindividual levels of analysis. Several recent works report on the influence of congregational characteristics and support processes on health outcomes and health behaviors. The possible role of family-level religious dynamics for health has been widely neglected by researchers. However, one hint of the possibilities comes in a reexamination of marital status differentials in alcohol use; that study reveals that tendencies for married persons to refrain from drinking—especially at high levels—is confined almost entirely to conservative Protestants and sectarians in same-faith couples (Ellison, Barrett, and Moulton 2008). The role of religious homogamy and dissonance in shaping other facets of mental and physical health remains to be explored. Fortunately, a longer tradition of work examines family-level religion on marital and family outcomes. While same-faith marital and intergenerational relationships tend to fare well in general, certain patterns of mixed-faith marriage are associated with elevated rates of conflict and divorce (Curtis and Ellison 2002; Lehrer and Chiswick 1993; Vaaler, Ellison, and Powers 2009), and religious dissonance between parents and adolescents is also linked with poorer relationship quality (Pearce and Axinn 1998; Stokes and Regnerus 2009) and elevated risk of adolescent delinquency (Pearce and Haynie 2004). At the community level, a long tradition of ecological work dating to Durkheim's *Suicide* ([1897] 1951) has linked the religious composition of areal units with rates of mortality and other social pathologies (Blanchard et al. 2008; Ellison, Burr, and McCall 1997), but it remains unclear whether community-level religious composition (a) influences individual- or family-level outcomes directly, or (b) moderates the effects of religion or religiousness at other levels on such outcomes. Given the increasing availability of multilevel data and the now widespread use of hierarchical linear modeling (HLM) and allied techniques, studies investigating the interplay of religious influences at varying analytical levels should be a priority for future research.

Subgroup Variations

Despite the growing interest in the implications of religious involvement for family, health, stratification, and other demographic outcomes, we lack a sound understanding of possible subgroup variations in these relationships. To be sure, a long tradition of research has consistently shown that aspects of religious affiliation, practice, and belief differ by gender, age/cohort, race and ethnicity, family structure, socioeconomic status (SES), and other important dimensions of social location. For example, women tend to be more religious—by virtually every conventional indicator—than men at all stages of the life course in the United States and most other Western societies (Sherkat and Ellison 1999). The reasons for this observed gender difference remain in dispute; although some observers continue to account for this pattern via differential socialization, ongoing research hints that biological (e.g., genetic) factors may also play a role (Bradshaw and Ellison 2009).

It has long been recognized that race and ethnicity may influence not only denominational loyalties, but also other facets of religious involvement. In addition to African Americans, who are much more religious on average than their non-Hispanic white counterparts (Ellison et al., Chapter Sixteen in this volume), some segments of the Latino/a population in the United States exhibit comparatively high levels of religious commitment (Stevens-Arroyo and Diaz-Stevens 1998).

There are also robust age differences in religiousness. By most measures, older adults tend to be more religious than their younger counterparts, a pattern that may reflect the complex interplay of social, developmental, and cohort processes. Conventional religiousness also tends to vary by family status; married persons, especially those with children, are typically more religiously active than their divorced, separated, or never married counterparts. Finally, contrary to patterns observed in many other societies, U.S. data reveal only modest and uneven associations between most religious indicators and SES. Indeed, there is a slight positive link between household income and measures of organizational religious participation, such as attendance at religious services. Moreover, despite widespread popular wisdom that educational attainment and religiousness are inversely correlated, recent research among younger adults convincingly rebuts such claims, particularly with regard to church membership and attendance (Uecker, Regnerus, and Vaaler 2007). On the other hand, lower-SES persons, e.g., those with less education and verbal ability, are especially likely to engage in private devotional activities, such as frequent prayer, and to embrace conservative theological doctrines, such as belief in the inerrancy of the Bible. According to most indicators, among U.S. adults, levels of religiousness tend to be greater in rural areas and in the South and lower Midwest, and particularly low throughout much of the Pacific Northwest.

Although such patterning in levels and types of religiousness is well documented, surprisingly few studies have explored whether the effects of religious involvement on demographic outcomes vary according to these or other social parameters. For example, do links between religion and health, family, or attainment differ by gender? Despite intermittent interest in this question, the evidence to date is decidedly mixed. To be sure, several studies have reported gender differences in the associations between religion and family practices such as domestic violence (Ellison, Bartkowski, and Anderson 1999) and reports of couples' arguments (Curtis and Ellison 2002), and others have concentrated specifically on religious effects on women's education and labor force participation and other demographic outcomes (Glass and Jacobs 2005; Lehrer , Chapter Eleven in this volume). In the area of religion–health research, however, research on gender-specific patterns of religious effects has turned up only inconsistent findings. Early works noted apparent gender differences in links between religion and mental health among the elderly (e.g., Idler 1987), but such results have surfaced only occasionally in subsequent research. Other studies have reported that while women receive higher levels of church-based emotional support, men actually derive proportionally greater health benefits from this support (Krause, Ellison, and Marcum 2002). A more consistent set of findings regarding gender differences emerges in the literature on religion and mortality risk, specifically among older adults. At least two high-quality community studies indicate that religious attendance is more strongly predictive of longevity among older women as compared with men, even when a host of potentially confounding factors is taken into account (Koenig et al. 1999; Strawbridge et al. 1997). These results dovetail with findings from a more recent study of high-functioning elderly, in which religious attendance was linked with lower allostatic load—the cumulative wear and tear on various physiological systems, as measured via biological markers—but only among older women (Maselko et al. 2007, discussed further later). Although such results may reveal distinctive elements of religious practice and experience among women in late life, e.g., as a special source of meaning or social support, it is also possible that these and other findings reflect the cumulative salutary effects of gender differences in religiousness. In other words, the health effects of the "gender gap" in religiousness, which appears at virtually every point in the life course, may impact mortality risk only in late life.

The links between religion and demographic outcomes may also be contingent on race and ethnicity. However, the growing research literature on religion, family, and health has not kept pace with rapid changes in the composition of the U.S. population. Over the past three decades, immigration to the United States has reached levels that parallel those of the early twentieth century. In contrast to earlier periods, however, the vast majority (85 percent or more) of these recent immigrants have come from Latin America and Asia, rather than from Europe (Guzman and McConnell 2002; Martin and Midgley 2003). Due to comparatively high rates of (im)migration and fertility, Hispanics have recently surpassed African Americans in number, thus becoming the single largest minority population in the United States. Immigration has also led to sharp increases in the Asian American population, which has contributed to increasing religious pluralism in the United States, although it is important to remember that significant numbers of these Asian Americans are (or become) Christians. As we noted earlier, investigators have become more engaged with the issue of race and ethnic variations in religion and health. This trend is seen most clearly in the growing body of work on African Americans (see Ellison et al., this volume). To date, however, few studies have explored possible race differences in the relationships between religion and family or religion and attainment processes. In one exception to this general pattern of neglect, Glass and Nath (2006) showed that the effects of religious conservatism (gauged in terms of denominational affiliation and belief in biblical inerrancy) on labor market behavior following family transitions differs for African American women as compared with whites. For example, among white women conservative affiliation predicted decreased labor force involvement following marriage or childbirth, while for African American women conservative affiliation was associated with an increase in working following childbirth. Another recent study shows that marital sanctification is particularly important for relationship quality among African Americans, as compared with non-Hispanic whites (Ellison, Burdette, and Wilcox forthcoming).

Nevertheless, the scarcity of empirical work on these and related topics is particularly unfortunate in light of distinctiveness of African American religious institutions, practices, and beliefs, and the persistence of substantial racial inequalities in aspects of marriage and family life as well as socioeconomic attainment. Additional work is clearly needed to address this important gap. However, the near absence of research on demographic correlates or sequelae of religion among Latino/a Americans or Asian Americans is especially dramatic. A handful of studies have linked religion with health among Hispanic elders, revealing protective effects of religious attendance on the trajectory of cognitive decline and the risk of mortality (Hill et al. 2005, 2006). Research on working-age Mexican-origin adults in California reveals that subjective religiousness also appears to be protective vis-à-vis depressive symptoms, especially for women (Ellison et al. 2009a). However, few if any studies explore the religion–health connection among Hispanic nationality groups other than Mexican Americans. Moreover, there is little systematic information on the impact of religion on family, attainment, or other demographic outcomes. Only recently have social scientists begun to investigate the possible implications of the rise of Latino Protestantism (which is mainly evangelical in orientation) in the political arena; work in this domain reveals strong associations with Latino opinion on social and family issues such as abortion (Ellison, Echevarria-Cruz, and Smith 2005), but it remains unclear whether religion actually influences family processes and outcomes. Unfortunately, the scarcity of population-based religion research on Hispanics and Asian Americans stem partly from the dearth of adequate data to explore these issues.

In addition to these major research gaps involving gender and race/ethnic variations, surprisingly few studies have investigated how religious influences on family or health may vary across levels of SES, e.g., education, income and wealth, and occupational attainment. Perspectives directly traceable to the classical theories of Marx and Weber suggest that religion may: (a) provide cognitive, social, or material resources that compensate for the deficits otherwise experienced by low-SES groups; or (b) serve to validate, legitimize, and augment the lifestyles of more privileged elements (Schieman, Ngyuen, and Elliott 2003). Yet the implications of these competing compensatory versus amplification logics have not been fully explored in the research literature. Indeed, few studies have systematically examined SES variations in the role of religion in family processes or outcomes, although several recent works identify salutary effects of religious involvement on relationship quality among samples of low-income, urban, disproportionately minority families (Lichter and Carmalt 2009; Wilcox and Wolfinger 2008). This line of investigation is somewhat more developed in the health area. For example, there is mounting evidence that facets of religious involvement—e.g., belief, private devotion—are more closely related to psychological well-being among persons with lower levels of formal education (Ellison 1991; Krause 1995). More recently, Schieman and colleagues (2006) have reported that the links between one specific aspect of religiousness—the sense of divine control or presence in one's life—and psychological distress among older adults is contingent upon the combination of SES and race. For example, divine control is inversely associated with distress among low-SES African Americans, but it bears a modest positive association with distress for upper-SES white elders. Another set of studies examines the role of religious involvement in buffering the deleterious impact of material deprivation on health and well-being. Among older adults, it appears that certain aspects of religiousness do indeed mitigate the harmful effects of chronic financial strain, neighborhood deterioration, and other indicators of scarcity. One relevant line of work focuses on the link between subjective SES, a topic of mounting interest among researchers, and psychological distress in a general population sample of U.S. adults. Findings from this study indicate that belief in an afterlife is particularly beneficial for those persons who feel their financial well-being has declined over the preceding five years (Ellison, Burdette, and Hill 2009). As these and other examples suggest, the weight of the evidence to date seems to support a compensatory perspective on religion's role in shaping mental health outcomes. However, few if any studies have focused on SES variations in the effects of religious involvement on physical health or mortality risk. This should be an important area for systematic investigation in the future.

There are other important sources of potential subgroup variation as well. Given the evidence of age and cohort variations in religiousness, it will be useful to clarify whether religion–family or religion–health relationships differ across the life span, and/or by generation. A few researchers have begun to pursue this avenue, with intriguing results. In the family area, for example, Myers (2006) has analyzed data from a unique three-generational study, and has reported that religious (denominational) homogamy is a robust predictor of marital satisfaction among the oldest generation but declines sharply to insignificance across subsequent generations. This trend may imply a diminishing link between the institutions of religion and marriage, or it may reflect the waning salience of

denominational labels (perhaps accompanied by the rising importance of religious beliefs or commitment) among younger cohorts of Americans. Although
religion–health research has developed most rapidly in the multidisciplinary
field of social gerontology and aging studies (Idler et al. 2003; Krause 2008),
the evidence concerning age variations in these relationships is surprisingly
limited. At least one study has shown stronger protective effects of religious
attendance on mortality risk among middle-aged adults, as compared with
their older counterparts (Musick, House, and Williams 2004). This pattern is
consistent with findings concerning other behavioral and lifestyle factors, the
impacts of which are most evident in predicting early or premature mortality,
prior to the widespread onset of disability and disease within the overall population. In the area of mental health, scattered evidence reveals age differences
in the links between specific facets of religiousness and psychological distress
(e.g., Krause et al. 1999). In particular, both the incidence of religious doubting
and the extent of its pernicious effects appear to decline across age categories,
a finding that now has been replicated and extended by several other studies.
This coherent body of findings is broadly compatible with several prominent
perspectives in cognitive psychology. These welcome contributions to the literature notwithstanding, important questions remain concerning: (a) whether
age-graded religious effects result mainly from aging, cohort-specific socialization experiences, or other factors; (b) whether these patterns extend to other
mental and physical health outcomes; and (c) whether similar age and cohort
influences emerge among diverse racial and ethnic subgroups.

Finally, in light of the common association of religious involvement with
social integration and support, it could be worthwhile to explore whether
religious involvement—especially attendance at services or other indicators
of congregational involvement—yield greater psychological or physical health
benefits for persons who are unpartnered, or who lack friends, relatives, or
other nonreligious sources of social ties. This substitution hypothesis would be
compatible with a long tradition of theory in the sociology of religion, in which
religious communities are characterized in terms as "family surrogates." Despite
the obvious appeal and clear intellectual value of this line of investigation, it is
difficult to find any studies that address it squarely. Resolving this issue could
clarify a number of issues in religion–health research, and could also be useful
in designing various types of outreach and intervention efforts aimed at enhancing health and longevity, particularly among older adults. Given our earlier discussion of multilevel theory and measurement of religion, it would be helpful
for researchers to explore variations in effects of religious involvement across
regions of the United States and types of communities. A better understanding
of the role of religious institutions, practices, and beliefs in shaping demographic outcomes across areas with very different cultural influences, religious
concentrations, and opportunities for secular social integration could pay major
dividends for investigators in this area.

The Issue of Causality

The contributions to this volume illustrate a growing body of research document-ing relationships between multiple dimensions of religion and demographic outcomes. Despite the increasing sophistication of such studies, not everyone is convinced that these associations reflect causal effects of religious engagement. Several important issues and concerns have emerged in this area over recent years. First, some observers contend that only studies based on experimental design can adequately demonstrate causal relationships. Because this would require random assignment of individuals into categories of religious affiliation, practice, and other dimensions, experimental studies are obviously not feasible. Thus, researchers employ observational studies, using statistical analyses of secondary data on representative samples drawn from broader populations in order to infer causal effects of religion on families, health, and other outcomes. In the eyes of some critics, even the best of these observational studies are insuf-ficient to sustain claims of causality (e.g., Sloan 2006). However, this standard would also discount research on a host of other issues for which experimental studies would be impossible, such as the health effects of education, long-term poverty, heavy cigarette smoking, and many others for which human subjects' guidelines for the protection of human subjects and other restrictions preclude random assignment into experimental "treatment" conditions.

At a minimum, establishing causal relationships requires longitudinal data, ideally collected at more than two observation points. Adequate control variables to rule out confounding influences in the religion–family and reli-gion–health areas must be included in statistical models. These include basic sociodemographic variables (e.g., age, gender, race/ethnicity, socioeconomic status), and in studies of religious influences on health and mortality, it is cru-cial to incorporate sufficient measures of baseline physical health conditions that could affect both religiousness (especially attendance) and the outcomes of interest. Even more challenging, however, are unmeasured variables and selection processes that may affect these relationships. For example, some have suggested that personality or dispositional factors (e.g., sensation-seeking, con-scientiousness) may incline individuals to avoid or embrace religion, and may also influence their relationship stability, health behaviors, or other factors. If this is indeed the case, then observed religion–family or religion–health rela-tionships may be overestimated in conventional statistical models. Economists have led the way in raising questions about causality in social science research. Moreover, for the many occasions in which direct measures of potentially confounding variables are unavailable, they have advanced various modeling techniques designed to address these threats to inference (Currie 2005; Duncan 2008; Moffitt 2005). Such approaches would include: (a) matching estimators (e.g., propensity scores or nearest neighbor estimators); (b) fixed-effects mod-els; and (c) instrumental variable models, among others. Despite their potential advantages, each of these approaches has important limitations (Currie 2005; Duncan 2008; Lillard and Price 2007). Economists commonly employ these and other techniques in their work, including some studies involving religion (e.g., Altonji, Elder, and Taber 2005; Gruber 2005). However, few sociologists or other demographers have used such econometric approaches to investigate the effects of religion on family life, health, or other outcomes considered in this volume (for an exception, see Keister 2003).

Our ability to infer casual relationships involving religion is also complicated by possible response biases in the reporting of religious involvement as well as family and health outcomes. Briefly, several studies have indicated that individual survey respondents tend to overstate the frequency with which they actually attend religious services, resulting in overestimates of aggregate attendance patterns in the United States, and perhaps elsewhere as well (Hadaway, Marler, and Chaves 1993). This is an important issue given the number of population-based studies that rely on self-reported religious attendance as a key (and perhaps the sole) indicator of religious involvement. Investigators initially attributed apparent overreporting to social desirability bias, suggesting that individuals exaggerated their attendance to create a more favorable impression in the eyes of interviewers. Subsequent research suggests that some persons may report attending services more often than they actually do, as an expression of overall religiousness (i.e., not interpreting the survey item on attendance literally) (Hadaway, Marler, and Chaves 1998). It has also become clear that self-reports of attendance are affected by the mode of survey administration (e.g., face-to-face interviews, computer-assisted interviews, telephone interviews, pencil-and-paper tests), and that aggregate estimates can also be influenced by sampling strategies, survey timing (e.g., on holidays or during summer vacation), external conditions such as weather, and other factors (Presser and Stinson 1998; Woodberry 1998).

Yet despite these issues, attendance is consistently linked with a wide array of desirable family, socioeconomic, and health outcomes, including reduced mortality risk, even when other aspects of religiousness are considered simultaneously (Hummer et al. 2004; Musick, House, and Williams 2004). Nevertheless, a number of issues remain unresolved, including: (a) the reasons for apparent overreporting; (b) which types of individuals (in terms of religious background, social location, demographic characteristics, and personality orientations) are most prone to exaggerate their attendance at services; (c) whether differential reporting also affects other religious measures; and (d) whether any reporting biases affect studies of religious influences on family, socioeconomic attainment, and health. In a useful contribution to the discussions on these issues, Regnerus and colleagues have explored links between religious involvement and sensitive behaviors (e.g., sexual activities) among adolescents and young adults, attempting to control for tendencies to give socially desirable responses, as well as various dispositional factors (e.g., planfulness). They find little evidence that such factors bias estimates of religious effects in this area (Regnerus and Smith 2005; Regnerus and Uecker 2007). It will also be important for future researchers to use more sophisticated tools for tapping social desirability bias, such as Paulhus's (1991) Balanced Inventory of Desirable Responses, which gauges tendencies toward both impression management (fooling others) and self-deception (fooling oneself).

Another key issue that should command attention from researchers interested in religion, families, and health is the potential role of genetic factors. Although this area has a checkered past in the social and behavioral sciences, investigators in multiple disciplines are now keenly interested in moving past the "nature–nurture debate" to explore the interplay of genetic and environmental influences on human behavior. Indeed, a burgeoning literature reports genetic influences—some modest, others dramatic—on a vast array of processes and outcomes, including many of the family, health, and stratification outcomes that are the focus of this volume (e.g., Kendler and Prescott 2006; Nielsen 2006; Reiss et al. 2000). A growing body of work using data on twin siblings reveals that aspects of religiousness are at least partly heritable, although the extent of potential genetic influence varies across specific religious dimensions and age or life cycle stage. For example, among adults at midlife, the genetic component of individual-level variations in religious attendance patterns appears to be roughly 25 percent, while nearly 70 percent of variation in subjective religious experience may be due to heritability (Bradshaw and Ellison 2008). By contrast, the evidence of genetic influence on religiousness among adolescents and young adults is much more limited (Eaves et al. 2008). In addition to heritability of outcomes and religiousness, a voluminous literature documents the role of genetic factors for a host of their covariates, underscoring the need for studies that take potential genetic influences and confounding relationships into account. There are several distinct modes of interplay between genetic and environmental factors, including: (a) passive, active, and evocative variants of gene–environment correlation; and (b) gene–environment interaction (Reiss et al. 2000; Scarr and McCartney 1983; Shanahan and Hofer 2005). For example, individuals may inherit dispositions toward religiousness and family or health outcomes, parents may provide environments that give expression to these genetic tendencies, and individuals may select niches or environments based on those genetically-predisposed motivations. Any or all of these processes may give rise to high correlations among genetic and environmental influences, creating challenges for those seeking to disentangle their relative effects. Moreover, religious influences may moderate the effects of genetic influences on various family or health outcomes, perhaps suppressing or delaying the expression of genetic predispositions in these domains. Work on these and related possibilities has only just begun, but early findings are promising and provocative, and the careful consideration of gene–environment interplay is necessary in order to clarify the causal role of religion.

A final point pertains mainly to the mushrooming body of work on relationships between religion and health, including mortality risk. In order to specify the place of religion in the chain of causality, it will integrate physiological mechanisms into the current explanatory frameworks. To be sure, this area remains in its early stages (Brown 2002), and to date some of the most compelling findings involve specialized practices such as Transcendental Meditation (TM) (Seeman, Fagan Dubin, and Seeman 2003). Nevertheless, several recent developments offer promising hints of what is to come in this exciting area. First, our understanding of religion and mental health, particularly anxiety and tranquility (e.g., Ellison, Burdette, and Hill 2009), may benefit from recent experimental findings linking the degree of religious conviction with reduced activity in the anterior cingulate cortex among individuals under stressful conditions. This is the region of the brain that is involved in the experience of anxiety and helps to modify behavior (Inzlicht et al. 2009). This work is one example of a broader line of study that reveals important relationships between religious beliefs and practices and specific areas of brain functioning, an area with implications for correlations between individual-level variations in religiousness and a host of cognitions and behaviors (McNamara 2006). Another important strand or work links religion with the concept of allostatic load, or the overall wear and tear on one's body caused by cumulative exposure to environmental stressors. Briefly, this thinking is premised on the idea that daily living requires the body to react to a wide range of stressors. Repeated or chronic demands can overtax physiological systems, compromising the body's ability to react successfully to stresses while maintaining system parameters within normal operating ranges. This physiological dysregulation can be gauged by a number of biological markers, tapping cardiovascular activity, metabolic processes, and the functioning of sympathetic nervous system and hypothalamic-pituitary-adrenal axis, and others. A recent study of high-functioning elderly linked religious attendance with substantially reduced allostatic load among older women but not their male counterparts (Maselko et al. 2007). Although these are starting points, and there is much work to be done, such innovative directions hold great promise in helping to explain the observed effects of religious involvement on health and mortality risk.

The Quest for High-Quality Data

A recurrent theme throughout this concluding chapter has been the scarcity of adequate data with which to pursue the questions engaged in this volume. The study of population processes in general depends heavily on advances in the quantity and quality of data, and perhaps nowhere is this more important than in the study of neglected topics like the role of religion in shaping family, health, socioeconomic, and other outcomes. To be sure, the inclusion of rudimentary religion items in major nationwide surveys has been crucial for the kinds of analyses presented in the preceding chapters. As we stressed earlier, however, there are important limits to the insights that such investigations provide. Although these analyses clearly establish that religion is a "marker" of differences that are correlated with many types of demographic outcomes, continued reliance on such limited measures constrains our ability to understand the processes that underlie these associations. For continued advancement of this scientific agenda, a number of developments are essential.

To move the field forward, an adequate array of religious measures must be included in large-scale data collection efforts in the areas of family, health, socioeconomic attainment, and others. At a minimum, it is necessary to incorporate measures of religious affiliation (e.g., open-ended items with sufficient detail to permit a range of post hoc classification schemes), organizational and nonorganizational practices (e.g., religious attendance and prayer), and subjective religiousness (e.g., religious and spiritual identity, degree of guidance from religion). But ideally, these measures will be only a starting point. Beyond these rather generic measures, which may be useful for analyzing a broad array of outcomes, it will be desirable for major studies to include additional religious measures that are keyed to the specific domains under investigation by sound theory and/ or prior empirical evidence. In practice, this is likely to mean that data collection efforts focused on health and aging may incorporate very different sets of religious items than those focused on family life, and so on. If such special modules cannot be asked of all respondents for reasons of cost or logistical difficulty, then the use of randomized, split-ballot designs may be worth considering.

At least three distinct approaches have been employed in efforts to enhance the availability of suitable measures for use in population-based studies. Each of these approaches derives support from partnerships of public agencies and private sources. One model involves assembling a team of leading social and behavioral scientists to reach broad consensus over how best to conceptualize and measure religiousness for research in a given domain. This model was used during the late 1990s, in a partnership between the National Institute on Aging (NIA) and the Fetzer Institute, which resulted in the development of a brief instrument for the investigation of religiousness and spirituality (Idler et al. 2003). With additional funding from Fetzer, these items were subsequently incorporated into the NORC General Social Survey, and they were disseminated widely to individual researchers in health and aging via Fetzer and the NIA, and have been used in numerous studies—clinical as well as population based—since the late 1990s.

A second model for the development of religious measurement is offered by a major study of older adults directed by Krause (2002, 2008), and funded by the NIA. In contrast to the "top-down" approach exemplified by the Fetzer–NIA working group, Krause pursued a "bottom-up" model. Briefly, he began by convening a number of focus groups (of varying composition) to elicit input from elders on the role of religion and spirituality in their lives. He then developed an extensive battery of items tapping issues raised in the focus groups and convened a group of experts in this area to refine and condense these items. Next, he conducted cognitive interviews with a purposive sample of older adults, to clarify issues of interpretation and meaning in these items. As a final step, Krause developed the Religion Aging and Health (RAH) survey, an ongoing nationwide panel survey consisting of equal subsamples of African American and non-Hispanic white elders. A subsequent project extends this approach to the study of older Hispanics, with support from the John Templeton Foundation.

Yet a third model attempts to incorporate batteries of religious measures into ongoing, large-scale data collection efforts funded by the National Institutes of Health and other federal agencies. In the most coordinated effort to date, the Templeton Foundation provided seed money to support a team of social scientists, who identified promising candidate surveys (in the United States and elsewhere) that could benefit from the addition of religious measures. Based on the initial findings of this group, individual investigators have pursued additional public and private funding to support the incorporation of batteries of religious measures into major nationwide surveys. One important outgrowth of this initiative is a module of items on the dynamics of religious behavior and generosity in the 2011 Panel Study of Income Dynamics. It will be extremely valuable if efforts in other domains, such as family life, can follow one or more of these models. Further, because researchers who collect data using federal funds are required to make those data publicly available, such initiatives can be accessed and analyzed by the broader community of social and health scientists, which can yield further insights beyond the findings initially reported by the primary investigators.

Although careful consideration of religious measurement is essential, other data issues are also vitally important. As we noted earlier, our understanding of racial and ethnic diversity in the links between religion and demographic outcomes has been hampered by a lack of adequate data on certain minority populations, especially the internally diverse and rapidly expanding Latino/a and Asian American populations. Moreover, recent high-quality data collection efforts focused on these groups have omitted any serious attention to religiousness or spirituality. It is crucial for future projects to address this pattern of neglect. Moreover, future population-based surveys in health, family, and other areas will need to include sample sizes that are large enough and diverse enough to permit close investigation of variations in religious effects by race/ethnicity, nativity, gender, age, SES, and other key parameters. Oversampling of particular racial and ethnic subgroups may be necessary in many instances to permit researchers to generate reliable estimates regarding religious effects for the increasingly diverse U.S. population.

Conclusion: Continued Momentum in Population-Based Research on Religion

This volume makes it abundantly clear that population-based, empirical research on the connections between religion and demographic and socioeconomic outcomes is alive and well. We began the volume by describing the United States as continuing to be a religious nation. While we also pointed out that there are both changes in the level of individuals who choose "no religion" on surveys and changes in the diversity of religious denomination membership among U.S. individuals, it continues to be the case that religion remains a vibrant and important part of American social life. Moreover, it is also clear from this volume, as well as related studies, that there are important impacts of religion on the health and well-being, family life, and socioeconomic attainment levels of U.S. individuals. While such impacts may differ to some degree by gender, race and ethnicity, age, SES, and perhaps other dimensions (e.g., by region, by urban–rural geography, and more), work in this area is pressing forward with improved data sets, innovative research designs, and high-quality statistical methodologies that are sensitive to issues of causality.

We close here by noting substantial forward momentum in this area of research. Just in the last few months, two major new research volumes have appeared that examine religion and wealth/poverty outcomes (Keister 2009) and religion and economic outcomes (Lehrer 2009), respectively. Just a few years ago, Lehrer (2004) developed a conceptual economic framework for understanding relationships between religion and demographic outcomes, and Waite and Lehrer (2003) spelled out intriguing parallels between religion and marriage in terms of their relationships to demographic outcomes in the United States. Similarly, the religion–health area continues to be characterized by exciting new theoretical and empirical work (e.g., Krause 2008). Thus, while there is much yet to be learned, sociologists, economists, demographers, and epidemiologists are already contributing in exciting ways to an area of research that is ripe for further development, particularly given the evolving character of religious behavior and beliefs in the United States and a rapidly diversifying population.

REFERENCES

Altonji, J., T. Elder, and C. Taber. 2005. "Selection on Observed and Unobserved Variables: Assessing the Effectiveness of Catholic Schools." *Journal of Political Economy* 113:151–184.

Anson, J., and O. Anson. 2000. "Thank God It's Friday: The Weekly Cycle of Mortality in Israel." *Population Research and Policy Review* 19:143–154.

Blanchard, T. C., J. P. Bartkowski, T. L. Matthews, and K. R. Kerley. 2008. "Faith, Morality, and Mortality: The Ecological Impact of Religion on Population Health." *Social Forces* 86:1591–1620

Bradshaw, M., and C. G. Ellison. 2008. "Do Genetic Factors Influence Religious Life? Findings from a Behavior Genetic Analysis of Twin Siblings." *Journal for the Scientific Study of Religion* 47:529–544.

———. 2009. "The Nature–Nurture Debate is Over and Both Sides Lost! Implications Understanding Gender Differences in Religiosity." *Journal for the Scientific Study of Religion*48: 241–251.

Brown, W. S. 2002. "PNI and Western Religious Traditions." In *The Link between Religion and Health*, ed. H. G. Koenig and H. J. Cohen, 262–274. New York: Oxford University Press.

Cadge, W., and E. H. Ecklund. 2007. "Immigration and Religion." *Annual Review of Sociology* 33:359–379.

Currie, J. 2005. "When Do We Know What We Think We Know? Determining Causality." In *Work, Family, Health, and Well-Being*, ed. S. Bianchi and L. Casper, 275–292. Mahwah, NJ: Lawrence Erlbaum Associates.

Curtis, K. T., and C. G. Ellison. 2002. "Religious Heterogamy and Marital Conflict: Findings from the National Survey of Families and Households." *Journal of Family Issues* 23:551–576.

Duncan, G. J. 2008. "When to Promote, and When to Avoid, a Population Perspective." *Demography* 45 (4): 763–784.

Durkheim, E. [1897] 1951. *Suicide*, translated by G. Simpson. New York: Free Press.

Eaves, L. J., P. K. Hatemi, E. C. Prom-Womley, and L. Murrelle. 2008. "Social and Genetic Influences on Adolescent Religious Attitudes and Practices." *Social Forces* 86:1621–1646.

Ellison, C. G. 1991. "Religious Involvement and Subjective Well-Being." *Journal of Health and Social Behavior* 32:80–99.

Ellison, C. G., J. B. Barrett, and B. E. Moulton. 2008. "Gender, Marital Status, and Alcohol Behavior: The Neglected Role of Religion." *Journal for the Scientific Study of Religion* 47:660–677.

Ellison, C. G., J. P. Bartkowski, and K. L. Anderson. 1999. "Are There Religious Variations in Domestic Violence?" *Journal of Family Issues* 20: 87–113.

Ellison, C. G., A. M. Burdette, and T. D. Hill. 2009. "Blessed Assurance: Religion, Anxiety, and Tranquility among U.S. Adults." *Social Science Research* 38: 656–667.

Ellison, C. G., A. M. Burdette, and W. B. Wilcox. Forthcoming. "The Couple That Prays Together: Religious Involvement, Race/Ethnicity, and Relationship Quality among Working-Age Couples." *Journal of Marriage and Family*.

Ellison, C. G., J. A. Burr, and P. L. McCall. 1997. "Religious Homogeneity and Metropolitan Suicide Rates." *Social Forces* 76:273–299.

Ellison, C. G., S. Echevarria-Cruz, and B. Smith. 2005. "Religion and Abortion Attitudes among U.S. Hispanics: Findings from the 1990 Latino National Political Survey." *Social Science Quarterly* 86:192–208.

Ellison, C. G., B. K. Finch, D. N. Ryan, and J. J. Salinas. 2009a. "Religious Involvement and Depressive Symptoms among Mexican-Origin Adults in California." *Journal of Community Psychology* 37:171–193.

Ellison, C. G., A. K. Henderson, K. E. Harkrider, and N. D. Glenn. 2009b. "Marital Sanctification and Marital Quality: Exploring Variations by Stress Levels and Attachment Styles." Manuscript under review.

Ellison, C. G., and J. S. Levin. 1998. "The Religion–Health Connection: Evidence, Theory, and Future Directions." *Health Education and Behavior* 25:700–720.

Exline, J. J. 2002. "Stumbling Blocks on the Religious Road: Fractured Relationships, Nagging Vices, and the Inner Struggle to Believe." *Psychological Inquiry* 13:182–189.

Finke, R. 2005. "Church Membership in America: Trends and Explanations." In *Handbook of Religion and Social Institutions*, ed. H. R. Ebaugh, 335–352. New York: Springer.

Flannelly, K. J., C. G. Ellison, H. G. Koenig, and K. Galek. 2008. "Beliefs about Life-after-Death, Psychiatric Symptomatology, and Cognitive Theories of Psychopathology." *Journal of Psychology and Theology* 36:94–103.

Flannelly, K. J., H. G. Koenig, K. Galek, and C. G. Ellison. 2007. "Beliefs, Mental Health, and Evolutionary Threat Assessment Systems in the Brain." *Journal of Nervous and Mental Disease* 195 (12): 996–1003.

George, L. K., C. G. Ellison, and D. B. Larson. 2002. "Explaining Relationships between Religious Involvement and Health." *Psychological Inquiry* 13:190–200.

Glass, J., and J. Jacobs . 2005. "Childhood Religious Conservatism and Adult Attainment among Black and White Women." *Social Forces* 83: 555–579.

Glass, J., and L. E. Nath. 2006. "Religious Conservatism and Women's Market Behavior Following Marriage and Childbirth." *Journal of Marriage and Family* 68:611–629.

Gruber, J. 2005. "Religious Market Structure, Religious Participation, and Outcomes: Is Religion Good for You?" NBER Working Paper no. 11377.

Guzman, B., and E. D. McConnell. 2002. "The Hispanic Population: 1990–2000 Growth and Change." *Population Research and Policy Review* 21: 109–128.

Hadaway, C. K., P. L. Marler, and M. Chaves. 1993. "What the Polls Don't Show: A Closer Look at U.S. Church Attendance." *American Sociological Review* 58:741–752.

———. 1998. "Over-Reporting Church Attendance in America: Evidence that Demands the Same Verdict." *American Sociological Review* 63:122–130.

Hill, T. D., J. L. Angel, C. G. Ellison, and R. J. Angel. 2005. "Religious Attendance and Mortality: An Eight-year Follow-Up Study of Older Mexican Americans." *Journal of Gerontology: Social Sciences* 60B:S102–S109.

Hill, T. D., A. M. Burdette, J. L. Angel, and R. J. Angel. 2006. "Religious Attendance and Cognitive Functioning among Older Mexican Americans." *Journal of Gerontology: Psychological Sciences* 61B:P3–P9.

Hill, P. C., and R. W. Hood, Jr. (eds). 1999. *Measures of Religiosity*. Birmingham, AL: Religious Education Press.

Hout, M., and C. S. Fischer. 2002. "Why More Americans Have No Religious Preference: Politics and Generations." *American Sociological Review* 67:165–190.

Hummer, R. A., C. G. Ellison, R. G. Rogers, B. E. Moulton, and R. R. Romero. 2004. "Religious Involvement and Adult Mortality in the United States: Review and Perspective." *Southern Medical Journal* 97:1223–1230.

Idler, E. L. 1987. "Religious Involvement and the Health of the Elderly: Some Hypotheses and an Initial Test." *Social Forces* 66:226–238.

Idler, E. L., M. A. Musick, C. G. Ellison, L. K. George, N. M. Krause, M. Ory, K. I. Pargament, L. H. Powell, L. G. Underwood, and D. R. Williams. 2003. "Measuring Multiple Dimensions of Religiousness and Spirituality for Health Research: Conceptual Background and Findings from the 1998 General Social Survey." *Research on Aging* 25:327–366.

Inzlicht, M., I. McGregor, J. B. Hirsh, and K. Nash. 2009. "Neural Markers of Religious Conviction." *Psychological Science* 20: 385–392.

Keister, L. A. 2003. "Religion and Wealth: The Role of Religious Affiliation and Participation in Early Adult Asset Accumulation." *Social Forces* 82: 175–207.

———. 2009. *Faith and Money: How Religious Belief Contributes to Wealth and Poverty*. New York: Cambridge University Press.

Kendler, K. S., and C. A. Prescott. 2006. *Genes, Environment, and Psychopathology*. New York: Guilford.

Koenig, H. G. 2008. "Concerns about Measuring 'Spirituality' in Research." *Journal of Nervous and Mental Disease* 196 (5): 349–355.

Koenig, H. G., J. C. Hays, D. B. Larson, L. K. George, H. J. Cohen, M. E. McCullough, K. G. Meador, and D. G. Blazer. 1999. "Does Religious Attendance Prolong Survival? A Six-Year Follow-Up Study of 3,968 Older Adults." *Journal of Gerontology: Medical Sciences* 54A:M370–M377.

Krause, N. 1995. "Religiosity and Self-Esteem among Older Adults." *Journal of Gerontology: Psychological Sciences* 50B:P236–P246.

———. 2002. "A Comprehensive Strategy for Developing Closed-Ended Survey Items for Use in Studies of Older Adults." *Journal of Gerontology: Social Sciences* 57(B): S263-S274.

———. 2006. "Gratitude toward God, Stress, and Health in Late Life." *Research on Aging* 28:163–183.

———. 2008. *Aging in the Church: How Social Relationships Affect Health.* West Conshohocken, PA: Templeton Foundation Press.

Krause, N., and C. G. Ellison. 2003. "Forgiveness by God, Forgiveness of Others, and Psychological Well-Being in Late Life." *Journal for the Scientific Study of Religion* 42:77–93.

Krause, N., C. G. Ellison, and J. P. Marcum. 2002. "The Effects of Church-Based Emotional Support on Health: Do They Vary by Gender?" *Sociology of Religion* 63:23–47.

Krause, N., B. Ingersoll-Dayton, C. G. Ellison, and K. Wulff. 1999. "Aging, Religious Doubt, and Psychological Well-Being." *Gerontologist* 39:525–533.

Krause, N., J. Liang, B. A. Shaw, H. Sugisawa, H.-K. Kim, and Y. Sugihara. 2002. "Religion, Death of a Loved One, and Hypertension among Older Adults in Japan." *Journal of Gerontology: Social Sciences* 57B:S96–S107.

Lehrer, E. L. 2004. "Religion as a Determinant of Economic and Demographic Behavior in the United States." *Population and Development Review* 30 (4): 707–726.

———. 2009. *Religion, Economics, and Demography: The Effects of Religion on Education, Work, and the Family.* New York: Routledge.

Lehrer, E. L., and C. U. Chiswick. 1993. "Religion as a Determinant of Marital Stability." *Demography* 30: 385–404.

Lichter, D., and J. Carmalt. 2009. "Religion and Marital Quality among Low-income Couples." *Social Science Research* 38: 168–187.

Lillard, D. R., and J. Price. 2007. "The Impact of Religion on Youth in Disadvantaged Families." Paper presented at conference on The Impact of Religion and Faith-Based Organizations on the Lives of Low-Income Families, sponsored by the National Poverty Center, Washington, DC, June.

Mahoney, A., K. Pargament, T. Jewell, A. B. Swank, E. Scott, E. Emery, and M. Rye. 1999. "Marriage in the Spiritual Realm: The Role of Proximal and Distal Religious Constructs in Marital Functioning." *Journal of Family Psychology* 13:321–338.

Martin, P., and E. Midgley. 2003. "Immigration: Shaping and Reshaping America." *Population Bulletin* 58(2): 1–58.

Maselko, J., L. Kubzansky, I. Kawachi, T. Seeman, and L. Berkman. 2007. "Religious Engagement and Allostatic Load among High Functioning Elderly." *Psychosomatic Medicine* 69:464–472.

McNamara, P., ed. 2006. *Where God and Science Meet.* 3 vols. New York: Praeger.

Moffitt, R. 2005. "Remarks on the Analysis of Causal Relationships in Population Research." *Demography* 42:91–108.

Musick, M. A., J. S. House, and D. R. Williams 2004. "Attendance at Religious Services and Mortality in a National Sample." *Journal of Health and Social Behavior* 45:198–213.

Myers, S. M. 2006. "Religious Homogamy and Marital Quality: Historical and Generational Patterns, 1980–1997." *Journal of Marriage and Family* 68:292–304.

Nielsen, F. 2006. "Achievement and Ascription in Educational Attainment: Genetic and Environmental Influences on Adolescent Schooling." *Social Forces* 85:193–216.

Pargament, K. I. 1997. *The Psychology of Religion and Coping.* New York: Guilford.

———. 2002. "The Bitter and the Sweet: An Evaluation of the Costs and Benefits of Religiousness." *Psychological Inquiry* 13:168–181.

Pargament, K. I., H. G. Koenig, and L. Perez. 2000. "The Many Methods of Religious Coping: Development and Validation of the RCOPE." *Journal of Clinical Psychology* 56:519–543.

Pargament, K. I., and A. Mahoney. 2005. "Sacred Matters: Sanctification as a Vital Topic for the Psychology of Religion." *International Journal for the Psychology of Religion* 15:179–198.

Pargament, K. I., N. Murray-Swank, G. M. Magyar, and G. G. Ano. 2005. "Spiritual Struggle: A Phenomenon of Interest to Psychology and Religion." In *Judeo-Christian Perspectives on Psychology: Human Nature, Motivation, and Change*, ed. W. R. Miller and H. D. Delaney, 245–268. Washington, DC: American Psychological Association.

Paulhus, D. L. 1991. "Measurement and Control of Response Bias." In *Measures of Personality and Social Psychological Attitudes*, vol. 1, ed. J. P. Robinson, P. R. Shaver, and L. S. Wrightsman, 17–60. San Diego: Academic.

Pearce, L. D., and W. G. Axinn. 1998. "The Impact of Family Religious Life on the Quality of Parent-Child Relationships." *American Sociological Review* 63:810–828.

Pearce, L. D., and D. L. Haynie. 2004. "Intergenerational Religious Dynamics and Adolescent Delinquency." *Social Forces* 82:1553–1572.

Peterson, C. P., and M. E. P. Seligman. 2004. *Character Strengths and Virtues: A Classification and Handbook.* New York: American Psychological Association and Oxford University Press.

Presser, S., and L. Stinson 1998. "Data Collection Mode and Social Desirability Bias in Self-Reported Religious Attendance." *American Sociological Review* 63:137–145.

Regnerus, M. D., and C. S. Smith. 2005. "Selection Effects in Studies of Religious Influence." *Review of Religious Research* 47:23–50.

Regnerus, M. D., and J. E. Uecker. 2007. "Religious Influences on Sensitive Self-Reported Behaviors: The Product of Social Desirability, Deceit, or Embarrassment?" *Sociology of Religion* 68:145–164.

Reiss, D., J. M. Neiderhiser, E. M. Hetherington, and R. Plomin. 2000. *The Relationship Code.* Cambridge, MA: Harvard University Press.

Roemer, M. K. 2007. "Ritual Participation and Social Support in a Major Japanese Festival." *Journal for the Scientific Study of Religion* 46:185–200.

Roof, W. C. 2000. *Spiritual Marketplace.* Princeton, NJ: Princeton University Press.

Scarr, S., and K. McCartney. 1983. "How People Make Their Own Environments: A Theory of Genotype and Environment Effects." *Child Development* 54:424–435.

Schieman, S., K. Nguyen, and D. Elliott. 2003. "Religiosity, Socioeconomic Status, and the Sense of Mastery." *Social Psychology Quarterly* 66:202–221.

Schieman, S. H., T. Pudrovska, L. I. Pearlin, and C. G. Ellison. 2006. "The Sense of Divine Control and Psychological Distress: Variations across Race and Socioeconomic Status." *Journal for the Scientific Study of Religion* 45:529–549.

Seeman, T. E., L. Fagan Dubin, and M. Seeman. 2003. "Religiosity/Spirituality and Health: A Critical Review of the Evidence for Biological Pathways." *American Psychologist* 58:53–63.

Shanahan, M. J., and S. M. Hofer. 2005. "Social Context in Gene-Environment Interaction: Retrospect and Prospect." *Journal of Gerontology: Social Sciences* 60B:S65–S76.

Sherkat, D. E., and C. G. Ellison. 1999. "Recent Developments and Current Controversies in the Sociology of Religion." *Annual Review of Sociology* 25:363–394.

Sloan R. P. 2006. *Blind Faith: The Unholy Alliance of Religion and Medicine.* New York: St. Martin's Press.

Smith, T. W. 2002. "Religious Diversity in America: The Emergence of Muslims, Buddhists, Hindus, and Others." *Journal for the Scientific Study of Religion* 41:577–585.

Stevens-Arroyo, A., and A. Diaz-Stevens. 1998. *The Emmaus Paradigm: Recognizing the Latino Resurgence in Religion.* Boulder, CO: Westview Press.

Stokes, C. E., and M. D. Regnerus. 2009. "When Faith Divides Family: Religious Discord and Adolescent Reports of Parent–Child Relations." *Social Science Research* 38:155–167.

Strawbridge, W. J., R. D. Cohen, S. J. Shema, and G. A. Kaplan. 1997. "Frequent Attendance at Religious Services and Mortality over 28 Years." *American Journal of Public Health* 87: 957–961.

Tarakeshwar, N., K. I. Pargament, and A. Mahoney. 2003. "Measures of Hindu Pathways: Development and Preliminary Evidence of Reliability and Validity." *Cultural Diversity and Ethnic Minority Psychology* 9:316–332.

Traphagan, J. W. 2005. "Multidimensional Measurement of Religiousness/Spirituality for Health Research in Cross-Cultural Perspective." *Research on Aging* 27:387–419.

Uecker, J. E., M. D. Regnerus, and M. L. Vaaler. 2007. "Losing My Religion: The Social Sources of Religious Decline in Early Adulthood." *Social Forces* 85:1667–1692.

Vaaler, M. L., C. G. Ellison, and D. A. Powers. 2009. "Religious Influences on the Risk of Marital Dissolution." *Journal of Marriage and the Family* 71:917–934.

Waite, L. J., and E. L. Lehrer. 2003. "The Benefits from Marriage and Religion in the United States: A Comparative Analysis." *Population and Development Review* 29 (2): 255–276.

Wilcox, W. B., and N. H. Wolfinger. 2008. "Living and Loving Decent: Religion and Relationship Quality among Urban Parents." *Social Science Research* 37:828–843.

Woodberry, R. D. 1998. "Comment: When Surveys Lie and People Tell the Truth: How Surveys Oversample Church Attenders." *American Sociological Review* 63:119–122.

Wuthnow, R. 2005. *America and the Challenges of Religious Diversity.* Princeton, NJ: Princeton University Press.

Zhai, J. E., C. G. Ellison, C. E. Stokes, and N. D. Glenn. 2008. "'Spiritual but Not Religious': The Influence of Parental Divorce on the Religious and Spiritual Identities of Young Adults." *Review of Religious Research* 49:359–374.

Zhang, W. 2008. "Religious Participation and Mortality Risk among the Oldest Old in China." *Journal of Gerontology: Social Sciences* 63B:S293–S297.

Zinnbauer, B. J., K. I. Pargament, and A. B. Scott. 1999. "The Emerging Meanings of Religiousness and Spirituality: Problems and Prospects." *Journal of Personality* 67:889–919.

CONTRIBUTORS

DUANE F. ALWIN is McCourtney Professor of Sociology and Demography, and Director of the Center on Population Health and Aging at Pennsylvania State University.

JOHN P. BARTKOWSKI is Professor of Sociology at the University of Texas at San Antonio.

MAUREEN R. BENJAMINS is Senior Epidemiologist at Mt. Sinai Urban Health Institute, Chicago.

AMY M. BURDETTE is Assistant Professor of Sociology, Anthropology, and Social Work at Mississippi State University.

HELEN ROSE EBAUGH is Professor of Sociology at the University of Houston.

ISAAC W. EBERSTEIN is Charles Meade Grigg Professor of Sociology, and Director of the Center for Demography and Population Health at Florida State University.

CHRISTOPHER G. ELLISON is Elsie and Stanley E. Adams, Sr. Centennial Professor in Liberal Arts in the Department of Sociology, and Faculty Research Associate in the Population Research Center at the University of Texas at Austin.

JACOB L. FELSON is Instructor in the Department of Sociology at William Patterson University.

TIM B. HEATON is Professor in the Department of Sociology and Family Studies Center at Brigham Young University.

KATHLEEN M. HEYMAN is an Associate Service Fellow in the Division of Health Interview Statistics at the National Center for Health Statistics.

ROBERT A. HUMMER is Professor and Chairperson in the Department of Sociology, and Faculty Research Associate in the Population Research Center at the University of Texas at Austin.

LISA A. KEISTER is Professor of Sociology, and Faculty Affiliate of the Asian Pacific Studies Institute and the Center for the Study of Race, Ethnicity, and Gender in the Social Sciences at Duke University.

VALARIE KING is Associate Professor of Sociology, Demography, and Human Development and Family Studies at Pennsylvania State University.

NEAL KRAUSE is Professor of Health Education and Health Behavior, and Senior Research Scientist in the Institute of Gerontology at the University of Michigan, Ann Arbor.

PATRICK M. KRUEGER is Assistant Professor in the Department of Sociology and in the Department of Health and Behavioral Sciences at the University of Colorado-Denver and Faculty Research Associate in the Population Program at the University of Colorado at Boulder.

EVELYN LEHRER is Professor and Director of Undergraduate Studies in the Department of Economics at the University of Illinois at Chicago.

ALISA C. LEWIN is Lecturer in the Department of Sociology and Anthropology at the University of Haifa, Israel.

MARC A. MUSICK is Associate Professor of Sociology, and Associate Dean in the College of Liberal Arts at the University of Texas at Austin.

LISA D. PEARCE is Associate Professor of Sociology, and Faculty Fellow in the Carolina Population Center at the University of North Carolina at Chapel Hill.

JEN'NAN GHAZAL READ is Associate Professor of Sociology, and Director of Postdoctoral Research in Global Health at Duke University.

MARK D. REGNERUS is Associate Professor of Sociology, and Faculty Research Associate in the Population Research Center at the University of Texas at Austin.

RICHARD G. ROGERS is Professor and Chairperson in the Department of Sociology, and Faculty Research Associate of the Population Program in the Institute for Behavioral Sciences at the University of Colorado, Boulder.

DARREN E. SHERKAT is Professor of Sociology at Southern Illinois University.

TERESA A. SULLIVAN is Provost and Executive Vice President for Academic Affairs, and Professor of Sociology at the University of Michigan, Ann Arbor.

LINDA J. WAITE is Lucy Flower Professor in Urban Sociology, Codirector of the Alfred P. Sloan Center on Parents, Children and Work, and Codirector of the MD/PhD Program in Medicine, the Social Sciences, and Aging at the University of Chicago. She is also Director of the Center on Aging at the National Opinion Research Center.

MEREDITH G. F. WORTHEN is an Assistant Professor in the Department of Sociology at the University of Oklahoma.

XIAOHE XU is Professor of Sociology in the Department of Sociology at the University of Texas at San Antonio.

INDEX

Page ranges in **bold** refer to authored essays in this volume.